Microsoft

W9-BNT-764

Microsoft Visual C#
Step by Step, 8th Edition

JOHN SHARP

PUBLISHED BY
Microsoft Press
A Division of Microsoft Corporation
One Microsoft Way
Redmond, Washington 98052-6399

Library of Congress Control Number: 2015940217
ISBN: 978-1-5093-0104-1

Printed and bound in the United States of America.

2   16

Microsoft Press books are available through booksellers and distributors worldwide. If you need support related to this book, email Microsoft Press Support at mspinput@microsoft.com. Please tell us what you think of this book at http://aka.ms/tellpress.

Acquisitions and Developmental Editor: Devon Musgrave
Project Editor: John Pierce
Editorial Production: Rob Nance and John Pierce
Technical Reviewer: Marc Young
Copyeditor: John Pierce
Indexer: Christina Yeager, Emerald Editorial Services
Cover: Twist Creative • Seattle and Joel Panchot

Contents at a glance

Contents

Chapter 3   Writing methods and applying scope   59

Chapter 4   Using decision statements   87

Chapter 9   Creating value types with enumerations and structures   201

Chapter 10   Using arrays   221

Chapter 14 Using garbage collection and resource management 305

PART III   DEFINING EXTENSIBLE TYPES WITH C#

Chapter 15 Implementing properties to access fields   329

Chapter 18 Using collections   399

Chapter 19 Enumerating collections   423

Chapter 20 Decoupling application logic and handling events   439

Chapter 21 Querying in-memory data by using query expressions   469

Chapter 22 Operator overloading   **493**

PART IV   **BUILDING UNIVERSAL WINDOWS PLATFORM APPLICA-
TIONS WITH C#**

Chapter 23 Improving throughput by using tasks   **517**

Chapter 24 Improving response time by performing asynchronous operations   559

Chapter 25 Implementing the user interface for a Universal Windows Platform app   601

Chapter 26 Displaying and searching for data in a Universal Windows Platform app · 651

Chapter 27 Accessing a remote database from a Universal Windows Platform app · 697

Introduction

Microsoft Visual C# is a powerful but simple language aimed primarily at developers who create applications built on the Microsoft .NET Framework. Visual C# inherits many of the best features of C++ and Microsoft Visual Basic, but few of the inconsistencies and anachronisms, which results in a cleaner and more logical language. C# 1.0 made its public debut in 2001. With the advent of C# 2.0 with Visual Studio 2005, several important new features were added to the language, including generics, iterators, and anonymous methods. C# 3.0, which was released with Visual Studio 2008, added extension methods, lambda expressions, and most famously of all, the Language-Integrated Query facility, or LINQ. C# 4.0, was released in 2010 and provided further enhancements that improved its interoperability with other languages and technologies. These features included support for named and optional arguments and the *dynamic* type, which indicates that the language runtime should implement late binding for an object. An important addition to the .NET Framework, and released concurrently with C# 4.0, were the classes and types that constitute the Task Parallel Library (TPL). Using the TPL, you can build highly scalable applications that can take full advantage of multicore processors. C# 5.0 added native support for asynchronous task-based processing through the *async* method modifier and the *await* operator. C# 6.0 is an incremental upgrade with features that are intended to make life simpler for developers. These features include items such as string interpolation (you need never use *String.Format* again!), enhancements to the ways in which properties are implemented, expression-bodied methods, and others. They are all described in this book.

Another important event for Microsoft is the launch of Windows 10. This new version of Windows combines the best (and most loved) aspects of previous versions of the operating system and supports highly interactive applications that can share data and collaborate as well as connect to services running in the cloud. The key notion in Windows 10 is Universal Windows Platform (UWP) apps—applications designed to run on any Windows 10 device, whether a fully fledged desktop system, a laptop, a tablet, a smartphone, or even an IoT (Internet of Things) device with limited resources. Once you have mastered the core features of C#, gaining the skills to build applications that can run on all these platforms is important.

Voice activation is another feature that has come to the fore, and Windows 10 includes Cortana, your personal voice-activated digital assistant. You can integrate your own apps with Cortana to allow them to participate in data searches and other operations. Despite the complexity normally associated with natural-language speech analysis, it is surprisingly easy to enable your apps to respond to Cortana's requests, and I cover this in Chapter 26. Additionally, the cloud has become such an important element in the architecture of many systems, ranging from large-scale enterprise applications to mobile apps running on users smartphones, that I decided to focus on this aspect of development in the final chapter of the book.

The development environment provided by Visual Studio 2015 makes these features easy to use, and the many new wizards and enhancements included in the latest version of Visual Studio can greatly improve your productivity as a developer. I hope you have as much fun working through this book as I had writing it!

Who should read this book

This book assumes that you are a developer who wants to learn the fundamentals of programming with C# by using Visual Studio 2015 and the .NET Framework version 4.6. By the time you complete this book, you will have a thorough understanding of C# and will have used it to build responsive and scalable applications that can run on the Windows 10 operating system.

Who should not read this book

This book is aimed at developers new to C# but not completely new to programming. As such, it concentrates primarily on the C# language. This book is not intended to provide detailed coverage of the multitude of technologies available for building enterprise-level applications for Windows, such as ADO.NET, ASP.NET, Windows Communication Foundation, or Windows Workflow Foundation. If you require more information on any of these items, you might consider reading some of the other titles available from Microsoft Press.

Organization of this book

This book is divided into four sections:

- Part I, "Introducing Microsoft Visual C# and Microsoft Visual Studio 2015," provides an introduction to the core syntax of the C# language and the Visual Studio programming environment.

- Part II, "Understanding the C# object model," goes into detail on how to create and manage new types in C# and how to manage the resources referenced by these types.

- Part III, "Defining extensible types with C#," includes extended coverage of the elements that C# provides for building types that you can reuse across multiple applications.

- Part IV, "Building Universal Windows Platform applications with C#," describes the universal Windows 10 programming model and how you can use C# to build interactive applications for this new model.

Finding your best starting point in this book

This book is designed to help you build skills in a number of essential areas. You can use this book if you are new to programming or if you are switching from another programming language such as C, C++, Java, or Visual Basic. Use the following table to find your best starting point.

If you are	Follow these steps
New to object-oriented programming	1. Install the practice files as described in the upcoming section, "Code samples."
	2. Work through the chapters in Parts I, II, and III sequentially.
	3. Complete Part IV as your level of experience and interest dictates.
Familiar with procedural programming languages such as C but new to C#	1. Install the practice files as described in the upcoming section, "Code samples."
	2. Skim the first five chapters to get an overview of C# and Visual Studio 2015, and then concentrate on Chapters 6 through 22.
	3. Complete Part IV as your level of experience and interest dictates.
Migrating from an object-oriented language such as C++ or Java	1. Install the practice files as described in the upcoming section, "Code samples."
	2. Skim the first seven chapters to get an overview of C# and Visual Studio 2015, and then concentrate on Chapters 8 through 22.
	3. For information about building Universal Windows Platform applications, read Part IV.

If you are	Follow these steps
Switching from Visual Basic to C#	1. Install the practice files as described in the upcoming section, "Code samples."
	2. Work through the chapters in Parts I, II, and III sequentially.
	3. For information about building Universal Windows Platform applications, read Part IV.
	4. Read the Quick Reference sections at the end of the chapters for information about specific C# and Visual Studio 2015 constructs.
Referencing the book after working through the exercises	1. Use the index or the table of contents to find information about particular subjects.
	2. Read the Quick Reference sections at the end of each chapter to find a brief review of the syntax and techniques presented in the chapter.

Most of the book's chapters include hands-on samples that let you try out the concepts you just learned. No matter which sections you choose to focus on, be sure to download and install the sample applications on your system.

Conventions and features in this book

This book presents information by using conventions designed to make the information readable and easy to follow.

- Each exercise consists of a series of tasks, presented as numbered steps (1, 2, and so on) listing each action you must take to complete the exercise.

- Boxed elements with labels such as "Note" provide additional information or alternative methods for completing a step successfully.

- Text that you type (apart from code blocks) appears in bold.

- A plus sign (+) between two key names means that you must press those keys at the same time. For example, "Press Alt+Tab" means that you hold down the Alt key while you press the Tab key.

System requirements

You will need the following hardware and software to complete the practice exercises in this book:

- Windows 10 Professional (or above) edition.

- Visual Studio Community 2015 edition, Visual Studio Professional 2015 edition, or Visual Studio Enterprise 2015 edition.

 Important You must install the Universal Windows App Development Tools and the Windows 10 SDK with Visual Studio 2015. Without them, the practice excercises will not work.

- Computer that has a 1.6 GHz or faster processor (2 GHz recommended).

- 1 GB (32-bit) or 2 GB (64-bit) RAM (add 512 MB if running in a virtual machine).

- 10 GB of available hard disk space.

- 5400 RPM hard-disk drive.

- DirectX 9–capable video card running at 1024 × 768 or higher resolution display.

- DVD-ROM drive (if installing Visual Studio from a DVD).

- Internet connection to download software or chapter examples.

Depending on your Windows configuration, you might require local Administrator rights to install or configure Visual Studio 2015.

You also need to enable developer mode on your computer to be able to create and run UWP apps. For details on how to do this, see "Enable Your Device for Development," at *https://msdn.microsoft.com/library/windows/apps/dn706236.aspx*.

Code samples

Most of the chapters in this book include exercises with which you can interactively try out new material learned in the main text. You can download all the sample projects, in both their preexercise and postexercise formats, from the following page:

http://aka.ms/sharp8e/companioncontent

> **Note** In addition to the code samples, your system should have Visual Studio 2015 installed. If available, install the latest service packs for Windows and Visual Studio.

Installing the code samples

Follow these steps to install the code samples on your computer so that you can use them with the exercises in this book.

1. Unzip the CSharpSBS.zip file that you downloaded from the book's website, extracting the files into your Documents folder.

2. If prompted, review the end-user license agreement. If you accept the terms, select the Accept option, and then click Next.

> **Note** If the license agreement doesn't appear, you can access it from the same webpage from which you downloaded the CSharpSBS.zip file.

Using the code samples

Each chapter in this book explains when and how to use any code samples for that chapter. When it's time to use a code sample, the book will list the instructions for how to open the files.

> **Important** Many of the code samples have dependencies on NuGet packages that are not included with the code. These packages are downloaded automatically the first time you build a project. As a result, if you open a project and examine the code before doing a build, Visual Studio may report a large number of errors for unresolved references. Building the project will cause these references to be resolved, and the errors should disappear.

For those of you who like to know all the details, here's a list of the sample Visual Studio 2015 projects and solutions, grouped by the folders where you can find them. In many cases, the exercises provide starter files and completed versions of the same projects that you can use as a reference. The completed projects for each chapter are stored in folders with the suffix "- Complete".

Project/Solution	Description
Chapter 1	
TextHello	This project gets you started. It steps through the creation of a simple program that displays a text-based greeting.
Hello	This project opens a window that prompts the user for his or her name and then displays a greeting.
Chapter 2	
PrimitiveDataTypes	This project demonstrates how to declare variables by using each of the primitive types, how to assign values to these variables, and how to display their values in a window.
MathsOperators	This program introduces the arithmetic operators (+ − * / %).
Chapter 3	
Methods	In this project, you'll reexamine the code in the MathsOperators project and investigate how it uses methods to structure the code.
DailyRate	This project walks you through writing your own methods, running the methods, and stepping through the method calls by using the Visual Studio 2015 debugger.
DailyRate Using Optional Parameters	This project shows you how to define a method that takes optional parameters and call the method by using named arguments.
Chapter 4	
Selection	This project shows you how to use a cascading *if* statement to implement complex logic, such as comparing the equivalence of two dates.
SwitchStatement	This simple program uses a *switch* statement to convert characters into their XML representations.
Chapter 5	
WhileStatement	This project demonstrates a *while* statement that reads the contents of a source file one line at a time and displays each line in a text box on a form.
DoStatement	This project uses a *do* statement to convert a decimal number to its octal representation.

Project/Solution	Description
Chapter 6	
MathsOperators	This project revisits the MathsOperators project from Chapter 2 and shows how various unhandled exceptions can make the program fail. The *try* and *catch* keywords then make the application more robust so that it no longer fails.
Chapter 7	
Classes	This project covers the basics of defining your own classes, complete with public constructors, methods, and private fields. It also shows how to create class instances by using the *new* keyword and how to define static methods and fields.
Chapter 8	
Parameters	This program investigates the difference between value parameters and reference parameters. It demonstrates how to use the *ref* and *out* keywords.
Chapter 9	
StructsAndEnums	This project defines a *struct* type to represent a calendar date.
Chapter 10	
Cards	This project shows how to use arrays to model hands of cards in a card game.
Chapter 11	
ParamsArray	This project demonstrates how to use the *params* keyword to create a single method that can accept any number of *int* arguments.
Chapter 12	
Vehicles	This project creates a simple hierarchy of vehicle classes by using inheritance. It also demonstrates how to define a virtual method.
ExtensionMethod	This project shows how to create an extension method for the *int* type, providing a method that converts an integer value from base 10 to a different number base.
Chapter 13	
Drawing	This project implements part of a graphical drawing package. The project uses interfaces to define the methods that drawing shapes expose and implement.
Drawing Using Interfaces	This project acts as a starting point for extending the Drawing project to factor common functionality for shape objects into abstract classes.

Project/Solution	Description
Chapter 14	
GarbageCollectionDemo	This project shows how to implement exception-safe disposal of resources by using the Dispose pattern.
Chapter 15	
Drawing Using Properties	This project extends the application in the Drawing project developed in Chapter 13 to encapsulate data in a class by using properties.
AutomaticProperties	This project shows how to create automatic properties for a class and use them to initialize instances of the class.
Chapter 16	
Indexers	This project uses two indexers: one to look up a person's phone number when given a name and the other to look up a person's name when given a phone number.
Chapter 17	
BinaryTree	This solution shows you how to use generics to build a type-safe structure that can contain elements of any type.
BuildTree	This project demonstrates how to use generics to implement a type-safe method that can take parameters of any type.
Chapter 18	
Cards	This project updates the code from Chapter 10 to show how to use collections to model hands of cards in a card game.
Chapter 19	
BinaryTree	This project shows you how to implement the generic *IEnumerator<T>* interface to create an enumerator for the generic *Tree* class.
IteratorBinaryTree	This solution uses an iterator to generate an enumerator for the generic *Tree* class.
Chapter 20	
Delegates	This project shows how to decouple a method from the application logic that invokes it by using a delegate. The project is then extended to show how to use an event to alert an object to a significant occurrence, and how to catch an event and perform any processing required
Chapter 21	
QueryBinaryTree	This project shows how to use LINQ queries to retrieve data from a binary tree object.

Project/Solution	Description
Chapter 22	
ComplexNumbers	This project defines a new type that models complex numbers and implements common operators for this type.
Chapter 23	
GraphDemo	This project generates and displays a complex graph on a UWP form. It uses a single thread to perform the calculations.
Parallel GraphDemo	This version of the GraphDemo project uses the *Parallel* class to abstract out the process of creating and managing tasks.
GraphDemo With Cancellation	This project shows how to implement cancellation to halt tasks in a controlled manner before they have completed.
ParallelLoop	This application provides an example showing when you should not use the *Parallel* class to create and run tasks.
Chapter 24	
GraphDemo	This is a version of the GraphDemo project from Chapter 23 that uses the *async* keyword and the *await* operator to perform the calculations that generate the graph data asynchronously.
PLINQ	This project shows some examples of using PLINQ to query data by using parallel tasks.
CalculatePI	This project uses a statistical sampling algorithm to calculate an approximation for pi. It uses parallel tasks.
Chapter 25	
Customers	This project implements a scalable user interface that can adapt to different device layouts and form factors. The user interface applies XAML styling to change the fonts and background image displayed by the application.
Chapter 26	
DataBinding	This is a version of the Customers project that uses data binding to display customer information retrieved from a data source in the user interface. It also shows how to implement the *INotifyPropertyChanged* interface so that the user interface can update customer information and send these changes back to the data source.
ViewModel	This version of the Customers project separates the user interface from the logic that accesses the data source by implementing the Model-View-ViewModel pattern.
Cortana	This project integrates the Customers app with Cortana. A user can issue voice commands to search for customers by name.

Project/Solution	Description
Chapter 27	
Web Service	This solution includes a web application that provides an ASP.NET Web API web service that the Customers application uses to retrieve customer data from a SQL Server database. The web service uses an entity model created with the Entity Framework to access the database.

Acknowledgments

Despite the fact that my name is on the cover, authoring a book such as this is far from a one-man project. I'd like to thank the following people who have provided unstinting support and assistance throughout this exercise.

First, Devon Musgrave at Microsoft Press, who awoke me from my interedition slumber. (I was actually quite busy writing material for Microsoft Patterns & Practices but managed to take a sabbatical to work on this edition of the book.) He prodded, cajoled, and generally made sure I was aware of the imminent arrival of Windows 10 and Visual Studio 2015, drew up the contract, and made sure that I signed it in blood, with agreed delivery dates!

Next, Jason Lee, my former underling and now immediate boss at Content Master (it's a somewhat complicated story, but he seems to have found some interesting photographic negatives I left lying carelessly around). He took on much of the initial donkey work generating new screen shots and making sure that the code for the first 20 or so chapters was updated (and corrected) for this edition. If there are any errors, I would like to point the finger at him, but of course any issues and mistakes are entirely my responsibility for missing them during review.

I also need to thank Marc Young, who had the rather tedious task of examining my code to make sure it stood a decent chance of compiling and running. His advice was extremely useful.

Of course, like many programmers, I might understand the technology, but my prose is not always as fluent or clear as it could be. I would like to show my gratitude to John Pierce for correcting my grammar, fixing my speling, and generally making my material much easier to understand.

Finally, I must thank my long-suffering wife, Diana, who thought I was going slowly mad (maybe I was) when I started uttering peculiar phrases at my laptop to try to coax Cortana into understanding my application code. She thought I was continually on the phone to Orlando Gee (one of the sample customers used in the exercises toward the end of the book) because I kept repeating his name quite loudly. Sadly, because of my accent, Cortana kept thinking I was asking for Orlando T, Orlando Key, or even Orlando Quay, so I subsequently changed the example to refer to Brian Johnson instead. At one point I overheard a conversation Diana was having with our decorator, Jason (who was painting our hallway at the time), about whether he would be able to convert one of the bedrooms into a padded cell, such was her concern with my state of mind! Still, that is now all water under the bridge, or "water under the breach" if you are Cortana trying to recognize my hybrid Gloucestershire/Kentish mode of speech.

And finally, finally, my daughter Francesca would be frightfully upset if I didn't mention her. Although she still lives at home, she is all grown up and now works for a software development company in Cam, Gloucestershire (they didn't offer me any freebies, so I am not going to mention their name).

Errata and book support

We've made every effort to ensure the accuracy of this book and its companion content. Any errors that have been reported since this book was published are listed on our Microsoft Press site at:

http://aka.ms/sharp8e/errata

If you find an error that is not already listed, you can report it to us through the same page.

If you need additional support, email Microsoft Press Book Support at *mspinput@ microsoft.com*.

Please note that product support for Microsoft software is not offered through the addresses above.

We want to hear from you

At Microsoft Press, your satisfaction is our top priority, and your feedback is our most valuable asset. Please tell us what you think of this book at:

http://aka.ms/tellpress

The survey is short, and we read every one of your comments and ideas. Thanks in advance for your input!

Stay in touch

Let's keep the conversation going! We're on Twitter: *http://twitter.com/MicrosoftPress*

Introducing Microsoft Visual C# and Microsoft Visual Studio 2015

This introductory part of the book covers the essentials of the C# language and shows you how to get started building applications with Visual Studio 2015.

In Part I, you'll learn how to create new projects in Visual Studio and how to declare variables, use operators to create values, call methods, and write many of the statements you need when implementing C# programs. You'll also learn how to handle exceptions and how to use the Visual Studio debugger to step through your code and spot problems that might prevent your applications from working correctly.

CHAPTER 1

Welcome to C#

After completing this chapter, you will be able to:

- Use the Microsoft Visual Studio 2015 programming environment.

- Create a C# console application.

- Explain the purpose of namespaces.

- Create a simple graphical C# application.

This chapter provides an introduction to Visual Studio 2015, the programming environment and tool-set designed to help you build applications for Microsoft Windows. Visual Studio 2015 is the ideal tool for writing C# code, and it provides many features that you will learn about as you progress through this book. In this chapter, you will use Visual Studio 2015 to build some simple C# applications and get started on the path to building highly functional solutions for Windows.

Beginning programming with the Visual Studio 2015 environment

Visual Studio 2015 is a tool-rich programming environment containing the functionality that you need to create large or small C# projects running on Windows. You can even construct projects that seamlessly combine modules written in different programming languages, such as C++, Visual Basic, and F#. In the first exercise, you will open the Visual Studio 2015 programming environment and learn how to create a console application.

> **Note** A console application is an application that runs in a Command Prompt window instead of providing a graphical user interface (GUI).

Create a console application in Visual Studio 2015

1. On the Windows taskbar, click Start, type **Visual Studio 2015**, and then press Enter.

   Visual Studio 2015 starts and displays the Start page, similar to the following. (Your Start page might be different, depending on the edition of Visual Studio 2015 you are using.)

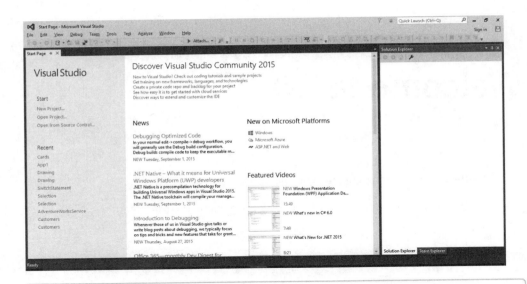

Note If this is the first time you have run Visual Studio 2015, you might see a dialog box prompting you to choose your default development environment settings. Visual Studio 2015 can tailor itself according to your preferred development language. The default selections for the various dialog boxes and tools in the integrated development environment (IDE) are set for the language you choose. From the Development Settings list, select Visual C# and then click the Start Visual Studio button. After a short delay, the Visual Studio 2015 IDE appears.

2. On the File menu, point to New, and then click Project.

The New Project dialog box opens. This dialog box lists the templates that you can use as a starting point for building an application. The dialog box categorizes templates according to the programming language you are using and the type of application.

3. In the left pane, expand the Installed node (if it is not already expanded), expand Templates, and then click Visual C#. In the middle pane, verify that the combo box at the top of the pane displays .NET Framework 4.6, and then click Console Application.

4. In the Location box, type **C:\Users*YourName*\Documents\Microsoft Press\VCSBS\ Chapter 1**. Replace the text *YourName* in this path with your Windows user name.

> **Note** To avoid repetition and save space, throughout the rest of this book I will refer to the path C:\Users*YourName*\Documents simply as your Documents folder.

> **Tip** If the folder you specify does not exist, Visual Studio 2015 creates it for you.

5. In the Name box, type **TestHello** (type over the existing name, ConsoleApplication1).

6. Ensure that the Create Directory For Solution check box is selected and that the Add To Source Control check box is clear, and then click OK.

Visual Studio creates the project by using the Console Application template. If you see the following dialog box asking about the source code control mechanism to use, you forgot to clear the Add To Source Control check box. In this case, simply click Cancel, and the project will be created without using source control.

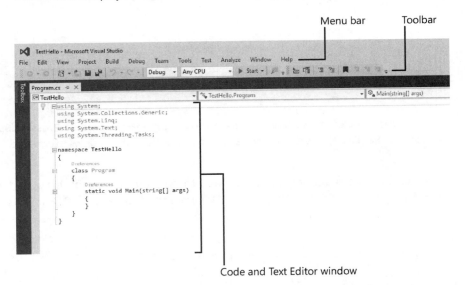

Choose Source Control

Choose a source control system for the new project:

- ⦿ Team Foundation Version Control
  Team Foundation Version Control uses a single centralized server repository to track and version files. Local changes are always checked in to the central server where other developers can get the latest changes.

- ○ Git
  Git is a distributed version control system that uses a local repository to track and version files. Changes are shared with other developers by pushing and pulling changes through a remote, shared repository.

- ☐ Use the selected system when creating new projects in the future

[OK] [Cancel]

Visual Studio displays the starter code for the project, like this:

Menu bar   Toolbar

Code and Text Editor window

The menu bar at the top of the screen provides access to the features you'll use in the programming environment. You can use the keyboard or mouse to access the menus and commands, exactly as you can in all Windows-based programs. The toolbar is located beneath the menu bar. It provides button shortcuts to run the most frequently used commands.

The Code and Text Editor window, occupying the main part of the screen, displays the contents of source files. In a multifile project, when you edit more than one file, each source file has its own tab labeled with the name of the source file. You can click the tab to bring the named source file to the foreground in the Code and Text Editor window.

The Solution Explorer pane appears on the right side of the IDE, adjacent to the Code and Text Editor window:

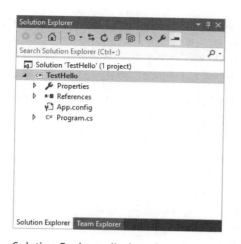

Solution Explorer displays the names of the files associated with the project, among other items. You can also double-click a file name in Solution Explorer to bring that source file to the foreground in the Code and Text Editor window.

Before writing any code, examine the files listed in Solution Explorer, which Visual Studio 2015 has created as part of your project:

- **Solution 'TestHello'**   This is the top-level solution file. Each application contains a single solution file. A solution can contain one or more projects, and Visual Studio 2015 creates the solution file to help organize these projects. If you use File Explorer to look at your Documents\Microsoft Press\VCSBS\Chapter 1\TestHello folder, you'll see that the actual name of this file is TestHello.sln.

- **TestHello**   This is the C# project file. Each project file references one or more files containing the source code and other artifacts for the project, such as graphics images. You must write all the source code in a single project in the same programming language. In File Explorer, this file is actually called TestHello.csproj, and it is stored in the \Microsoft Press\VCSBS\Chapter 1\TestHello\TestHello folder in your Documents folder.

- **Properties**   This is a folder in the TestHello project. If you expand it (click the arrow next to Properties), you will see that it contains a file called AssemblyInfo.cs. AssemblyInfo.cs is a special file that you can use to add attributes to a program, such as the name of the author, the date the program was written, and so on. You can specify additional attributes to modify the way in which the program runs. Explaining how to use these attributes is beyond the scope of this book.

- **References**   This folder contains references to libraries of compiled code that your application can use. When your C# code is compiled, it is converted into a library and given a unique name. In the Microsoft .NET Framework, these libraries are called *assemblies*. Developers use assemblies to package useful functionality that they have written so that they can distribute it to other developers who might want to use these features in their own applications. If you expand the References folder, you will see the default set of references that Visual Studio 2015 adds to your project. These assemblies provide access to many of the commonly used features of the .NET Framework and are provided by Microsoft with Visual Studio 2015. You will learn about many of these assemblies as you progress through the exercises in this book.

- **App.config**   This is the application configuration file. It is optional, and it might not always be present. You can specify settings that your application uses at run time to modify its behavior, such as the version of the .NET Framework to use to run the application. You will learn more about this file in later chapters of this book.

- **Program.cs**   This is a C# source file, and it is displayed in the Code and Text Editor window when the project is first created. You will write your code for the console application in this file. It also contains some code that Visual Studio 2015 provides automatically, which you will examine shortly.

Writing your first program

The Program.cs file defines a class called *Program* that contains a method called *Main*. In C#, all executable code must be defined within a method, and all methods must belong to a class or a struct. You will learn more about classes in Chapter 7, "Creating and managing classes and objects," and you will learn about structs in Chapter 9, "Creating value types with enumerations and structures."

The *Main* method designates the program's entry point. This method should be defined in the manner specified in the *Program* class as a static method; otherwise, the .NET Framework might not recognize it as the starting point for your application when you run it. (You will look at methods in detail in Chapter 3, "Writing methods and applying scope," and Chapter 7 provides more information on static methods.)

> **Important** C# is a case-sensitive language. You must spell *Main* with an uppercase *M*.

In the following exercises, you write the code to display the message "Hello World!" to the console window, build and run your Hello World console application, and learn how namespaces are used to partition code elements.

Write the code by using Microsoft IntelliSense

1. In the Code and Text Editor window displaying the *Program.cs* file, place the cursor in the *Main* method, immediately after the opening curly brace ({), and then press Enter to create a new line.

2. On the new line, type the word **Console**; this is the name of another class provided by the assemblies referenced by your application. It provides methods for displaying messages in the console window and reading input from the keyboard.

As you type the letter **C** at the start of the word *Console*, an IntelliSense list appears.

This list contains all of the C# keywords and data types that are valid in this context. You can either continue typing or scroll through the list and double-click the Console item with the mouse. Alternatively, after you have typed **Cons**, the IntelliSense list automatically homes in on the Console item, and you can press the Tab or Enter key to select it.

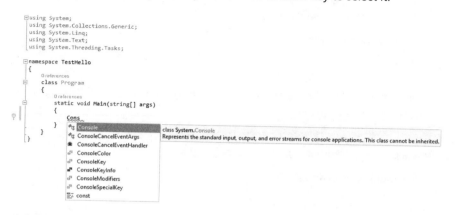

Main should look like this:

```
static void Main(string[] args)
{
    Console
}
```

> **Note** *Console* is a built-in class.

3. Type a period immediately following *Console*.

   Another IntelliSense list appears, displaying the methods, properties, and fields of the *Console* class.

4. Scroll down through the list, select *WriteLine*, and then press Enter. Alternatively, you can continue typing the characters **W, r, i, t, e, L** until *WriteLine* is selected, and then press Enter.

   The IntelliSense list closes, and the word *WriteLine* is added to the source file. *Main* should now look like this:

```
static void Main(string[] args)
{
    Console.WriteLine
}
```

5. Type an opening parenthesis, (. Another IntelliSense tip appears.

This tip displays the parameters that the *WriteLine* method can take. In fact, *WriteLine* is an *overloaded method*, meaning that the *Console* class contains more than one method named *WriteLine*—it actually provides 19 different versions of this method. You can use each version of the *WriteLine* method to output different types of data. (Chapter 3 describes overloaded methods in more detail.) *Main* should now look like this:

```
static void Main(string[] args)
{
    Console.WriteLine(
}
```

Tip You can click the up and down arrows in the tip to scroll through the different overloads of *WriteLine*.

6. Type a closing parenthesis,), followed by a semicolon, ;.

    Main should now look like this:

    ```
    static void Main(string[] args)
    {
        Console.WriteLine();
    }
    ```

7. Move the cursor and type the string **"Hello World!"**, including the quotation marks, between the left and right parentheses following the *WriteLine* method.

    Main should now look like this:

    ```
    static void Main(string[] args)
    {
        Console.WriteLine("Hello World!");
    }
    ```

Tip Get into the habit of typing matched character pairs, such as parentheses— (and)—and curly brackets—{ and }—before filling in their contents. It's easy to forget the closing character if you wait until after you've entered the contents.

IntelliSense icons

When you type a period after the name of a class, IntelliSense displays the name of every member of that class. To the left of each member name is an icon that depicts the type of member. Common icons and their types include the following:

Icon	Meaning
	Method (discussed in Chapter 3)
	Property (discussed in Chapter 15, "Implementing properties to access fields")
	Class (discussed in Chapter 7)
	Struct (discussed in Chapter 9)
	Enum (discussed in Chapter 9)
	Extension method (discussed in Chapter 12, "Working with Inheritance")
	Interface (discussed in Chapter 13, "Creating interfaces and defining abstract classes")
	Delegate (discussed in Chapter 17, "Introducing generics")
	Event (discussed in Chapter 17)
{ }	Namespace (discussed in the next section of this chapter)

You will also see other IntelliSense icons appear as you type code in different contexts.

You will frequently see lines of code containing two forward slashes (//) followed by ordinary text. These are comments, which are ignored by the compiler but are very useful for developers because they help document what a program is actually doing. Take, for instance, the following example:

```
Console.ReadLine(); // Wait for the user to press the Enter key
```

The compiler skips all text from the two slashes to the end of the line. You can also add multiline comments that start with a forward slash followed by an asterisk (/*). The compiler skips everything until it finds an asterisk followed by a forward slash sequence (*/), which could be many lines lower down. You are actively encouraged to document your code with as many meaningful comments as necessary.

Build and run the console application

1. On the Build menu, click Build Solution.

   This action compiles the C# code, resulting in a program that you can run. The Output window appears below the Code and Text Editor window.

> **Tip** If the Output window does not appear, click Output on the View menu to display it.

In the Output window, you should see messages similar to the following, indicating how the program is being compiled:

```
1>------ Build started: Project: TestHello, Configuration: Debug Any CPU ------
1>  TestHello -> C:\Users\John\Documents\Microsoft Press\Visual CSharp Step By Step\
Chapter
1\TestHello\TestHello\bin\Debug\TestHello.exe
========== Build: 1 succeeded, 0 failed, 0 up-to-date, 0 skipped ==========
```

If you have made any mistakes, they will be reported in the Error List window. The following image shows what happens if you forget to type the closing quotation marks after the text Hello World in the *WriteLine* statement. Notice that a single mistake can sometimes cause multiple compiler errors.

> **Tip** To go directly to the line that caused the error, you can double-click an item in the Error List window. You should also notice that Visual Studio displays a wavy red line under any lines of code that will not compile when you enter them.

If you have followed the previous instructions carefully, there should be no errors or warnings, and the program should build successfully.

> **Tip** There is no need to save the file explicitly before building because the Build Solution command automatically saves it.
>
> An asterisk after the file name in the tab above the Code and Text Editor window indicates that the file has been changed since it was last saved.

2. On the Debug menu, click Start Without Debugging.

   A command window opens and the program runs. The message "Hello World!" appears. The program now waits for you to press any key, as shown in the following graphic:

> **Note** The prompt "Press any key to continue" is generated by Visual Studio; you did not write any code to do this. If you run the program by using the Start Debugging command on the Debug menu, the application runs, but the command window closes immediately without waiting for you to press a key.

3. Ensure that the command window displaying the program's output has the focus (meaning that it's the window that's currently active), and then press Enter.

   The command window closes, and you return to the Visual Studio 2015 programming environment.

4. In Solution Explorer, click the *TestHello* project (not the solution), and then, on the Solution Explorer toolbar, click the Show All Files button. Be aware that you might need to click the double-arrow button on the right edge of the Solution Explorer toolbar to make this button appear.

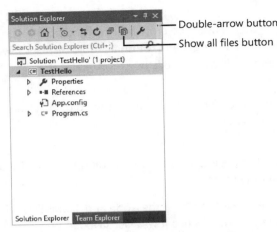

Double-arrow button

Show all files button

Entries named *bin* and *obj* appear above the *Program.cs* file. These entries correspond directly to folders named bin and obj in the project folder (Microsoft Press\VCSBS\Chapter 1\TestHello\TestHello). Visual Studio creates these folders when you build your application; they contain the executable version of the program together with some other files used to build and debug the application.

5. In Solution Explorer, expand the *bin* entry.

Another folder named Debug appears.

> **Note** You might also see a folder named Release.

6. In Solution Explorer, expand the Debug folder.

Several more items appear, including a file named *TestHello.exe*. This is the compiled program, which is the file that runs when you click Start Without Debugging on the Debug menu. The other files contain information that is used by Visual Studio 2015 if you run your program in debug mode (when you click Start Debugging on the Debug menu).

Using namespaces

The example you have seen so far is a very small program. However, small programs can soon grow into much bigger programs. As a program grows, two issues arise. First, it is harder to understand and maintain big programs than it is to understand and maintain smaller ones. Second, more code usually means more classes, with more methods, requiring you to keep track of more names. As the number of names increases, so does the likelihood of the project build failing because two or more names clash; for example, you might try to create two classes with the same name. The situation becomes more complicated when a program references assemblies written by other developers who have also used a variety of names.

In the past, programmers tried to solve the name-clashing problem by prefixing names with some sort of qualifier (or set of qualifiers). This is not a good solution because it's not scalable; names become longer, and you spend less time writing software and more time typing (there is a difference), and reading and rereading incomprehensibly long names.

Namespaces help solve this problem by creating a container for items such as classes. Two classes with the same name will not be confused with each other if they live in different namespaces. You can create a class named *Greeting* inside the namespace named *TestHello* by using the *namespace* keyword like this:

```
namespace TestHello
{
    class Greeting
    {
        ...
    }
}
```

You can then refer to the *Greeting* class as *TestHello.Greeting* in your programs. If another developer also creates a *Greeting* class in a different namespace, such as *NewNamespace*, and you install the assembly that contains this class on your computer, your programs will still work as expected because they are using your *TestHello.Greeting* class. If you want to refer to the other developer's *Greeting* class, you must specify it as *NewNamespace.Greeting*.

It is good practice to define all your classes in namespaces, and the Visual Studio 2015 environment follows this recommendation by using the name of your project as the top-level namespace. The .NET Framework class library also adheres to this recommendation; every class in the .NET Framework lives within a namespace. For example, the *Console* class lives within the *System* namespace. This means that its full name is actually *System.Console*.

Of course, if you had to write the full name of a class every time you used it, the situation would be no better than prefixing qualifiers or even just naming the class with some globally unique name such as *SystemConsole*. Fortunately, you can solve this problem with a *using* directive in your programs. If you return to the *TestHello* program in Visual Studio 2015 and look at the file *Program.cs* in the Code and Text Editor window, you will notice the following lines at the top of the file:

```
using System;
using System.Collections.Generic;
using System.Linq;
using System.Text;
using System.Threading.Tasks;
```

These lines are *using* directives. A *using* directive brings a namespace into scope. In subsequent code in the same file, you no longer need to explicitly qualify objects with the namespace to which they belong. The five namespaces shown contain classes that are used so often that Visual Studio 2015 automatically adds these *using* directives every time you create a new project. You can add more *using* directives to the top of a source file if you need to reference other namespaces.

The following exercise demonstrates the concept of namespaces in more depth.

Try longhand names

1. In the Code and Text Editor window displaying the *Program.cs* file, comment out the first *using* directive at the top of the file, like this:

    ```
    //using System;
    ```

2. On the Build menu, click Build Solution.

    The build fails, and the Error List window displays the following error message:

    ```
    The name 'Console' does not exist in the current context.
    ```

3. In the Error List window, double-click the error message.

    The identifier that caused the error is highlighted in the *Program.cs* source file with a red squiggle.

4. In the Code and Text Editor window, edit the *Main* method to use the fully qualified name *System.Console*.

    Main should look like this:

    ```
    static void Main(string[] args)
    {
        System.Console.WriteLine("Hello World!");
    }
    ```

> **Note** When you type the period after *System*, IntelliSense displays the names of all the items in the *System* namespace.

5. On the Build menu, click Build Solution.

    The project should build successfully this time. If it doesn't, ensure that *Main* is exactly as it appears in the preceding code, and then try building again.

6. Run the application to be sure that it still works by clicking Start Without Debugging on the Debug menu.

7. When the program runs and displays "Hello World!" in the console window, press Enter to return to Visual Studio 2015.

Namespaces and assemblies

A *using* directive simply brings the items in a namespace into scope and frees you from having to fully qualify the names of classes in your code. Classes are compiled into *assemblies*.

An assembly is a file that usually has the .dll file name extension, although strictly speaking, executable programs with the .exe file name extension are also assemblies.

An assembly can contain many classes. The classes that the .NET Framework class library includes, such as *System.Console*, are provided in assemblies that are installed on your computer together with Visual Studio. You will find that the .NET Framework class library contains thousands of classes. If they were all held in the same assembly, the assembly would be huge and difficult to maintain. (If Microsoft were to update a single method in a single class, it would have to distribute the entire class library to all developers!)

For this reason, the .NET Framework class library is split into a number of assemblies, partitioned by the functional area to which the classes they contain relate. For example, a "core" assembly (actually called *mscorlib.dll*) contains all the common classes, such as *System.Console*, and other assemblies contain classes for manipulating databases, accessing web services, building GUIs, and so on. If you want to make use of a class in an assembly, you must add a reference to that assembly to your project. You can then add *using* directives to your code that bring the items in namespaces in that assembly into scope.

You should note that there is not necessarily a 1:1 equivalence between an assembly and a namespace: A single assembly can contain classes defined in many namespaces, and a single namespace can span multiple assemblies. For example, the classes and items in the *System* namespace are actually implemented by several assemblies, including *mscorlib.dll, System.dll,* and *System.Core.dll,* among others. This all sounds very confusing at first, but you will soon get used to it.

When you use Visual Studio to create an application, the template you select automatically includes references to the appropriate assemblies. For example, in Solution Explorer for the TestHello project, expand the References folder. You will see that a console application automatically contains references to assemblies called *Microsoft.CSharp, System, System.Core, System.Data, System.Data.DataSetExtensions, System.Net.Http, System.Xml,* and *System.Xml.Linq*. You might be surprised to see that *mscorlib.dll* is not included in this list. The reason for this is that all .NET Framework applications must use this assembly because it contains fundamental runtime functionality. The References folder lists only the optional assemblies; you can add or remove assemblies from this folder as necessary.

To add references for additional assemblies to a project, right-click the References folder and then click Add Reference—you will perform this task in later exercises. You can remove an assembly by right-clicking the assembly in the References folder and then clicking Remove.

Creating a graphical application

So far, you have used Visual Studio 2015 to create and run a basic console application. The Visual Studio 2015 programming environment also contains everything you need to create graphical applications for Windows 10. These templates are referred to as Universal Windows Platform (UWP) apps because they enable you to create apps that function on any device that runs Windows, such as desktop computers, tablets, and phones. You can design the user interface (UI) of a Windows application interactively. Visual Studio 2015 then generates the program statements to implement the user interface you've designed.

Visual Studio 2015 provides you with two views of a graphical application: the *design view* and the *code view*. You use the Code and Text Editor window to modify and maintain the code and program logic for a graphical application, and you use the Design View window to lay out your UI. You can switch between the two views whenever you want.

In the following set of exercises, you'll learn how to create a graphical application by using Visual Studio 2015. This program displays a simple form containing a text box where you can enter your name and a button that when clicked displays a personalized greeting in a message box.

If you want more information about the specifics of writing UWP apps, the final few chapters in Part IV of this book provide more detail and guidance.

Create a graphical application in Visual Studio 2015

1. Start Visual Studio 2015 if it is not already running.

2. On the File menu, point to New, and then click Project.

   The New Project dialog box opens.

3. In the left pane, expand the Installed node (if it is not already expanded), expand Templates, expand Visual C#, expand Windows, and then click Universal.

4. In the middle pane, click the Blank App (Windows Universal) icon.

   > **Note** XAML stands for Extensible Application Markup Language, which is the language that Universal Windows Platform applications use to define the layout for the GUI of an application. You will learn more about XAML as you progress through the exercises in this book.

5. Ensure that the Location field refers to the \Microsoft Press\VCSBS\Chapter 1 folder in your Documents folder.

6. In the Name box, type **Hello**.

7. Ensure that the Create Directory For Solution check box is selected, and then click OK.

   If this is the first time that you have created a UWP application, you might be prompted to enable developer mode for Windows 10. Depending on your device and your version of Windows 10, you may or may not be able to enable developer mode through the user interface. For more guidance on enabling developer mode, see "Enable your device for development" at *https://msdn.microsoft.com/library/windows/apps/xaml/dn706236.aspx*.

Developer Mode

Enable Developer Mode for Windows 10

You need to enable Developer Mode on your device to develop this style of app for Windows 10. This lets you install and test the app on this computer before Microsoft tests and certifies it.

To enable Developer Mode on your device, go to Settings > For Developers and select Developer Mode.

This device is not currently in developer mode.

OK

> **Note** This dialog box might appear when you create a new UWP application or the first time you attempt to run a UWP application from Visual Studio.

8. After the app has been created, look in the Solution Explorer pane.

    Don't be fooled by the name of the application template—although it is called Blank App, this template actually provides a number of files and contains some code. For example, if you expand the MainPage.xaml folder, you will find a C# file named MainPage.xaml.cs. This file is where you add the code that runs when the UI defined by the MainPage.xaml file is displayed.

9. In Solution Explorer, double-click MainPage.xaml.

    This file contains the layout of the UI. The Design View window shows two representations of this file:

At the top is a graphical view depicting the screen of, by default, a 5-inch phone. The lower pane contains a description of the contents of this screen using XAML. XAML is an XML-like language used by UWP applications to define the layout of a form and its contents. If you have knowledge of XML, XAML should look familiar.

In the next exercise, you will use the Design View window to lay out the UI for the application, and you will examine the XAML code that this layout generates.

Tip Close the Output and Error List windows to provide more space for displaying the Design View window.

Note Before going further, it is worth explaining some terminology. In traditional Windows applications, the UI consists of one or more *windows*, but in a Universal Windows Platform app the corresponding items are referred to as *pages*. For the sake of clarity, I will simply refer to both items by using the blanket term *form*. However, I will continue to use the word *window* to refer to items in the Visual Studio 2015 IDE, such as the Design View window.

In the following exercises, you will use the Design View window to add three controls to the form displayed by your application. You will also examine some of the C# code automatically generated by Visual Studio 2015 to implement these controls.

Create the user interface

1. Click the Toolbox tab that appears to the left of the form in the Design View window.

   The Toolbox appears and displays the various components and controls that you can place on a form.

2. Expand the Common XAML Controls section.

   This section displays a list of controls that most graphical applications use.

   Tip The All XAML Controls section displays a more extensive list of controls.

3. In the Common XAML Controls section, click TextBlock, and then drag the *TextBlock* control onto the form displayed in the Design View window.

   Tip Be sure that you select the *TextBlock* control and not the *TextBox* control. If you accidentally place the wrong control on a form, you can easily remove it by clicking the item on the form and then pressing Delete.

A *TextBlock* control is added to the form (you will move it to its correct location in a moment), and the Toolbox disappears from view.

> **Tip** If you want the Toolbox to remain visible but not hide any part of the form, at the right end of the Toolbox title bar, click the Auto Hide button (it looks like a pin). The Toolbox is docked on the left side of the Visual Studio 2015 window, and the Design View window shrinks to accommodate it. (You might lose a lot of space if you have a low-resolution screen.) Clicking the Auto Hide button once more causes the Toolbox to disappear again.

4. The *TextBlock* control on the form is probably not exactly where you want it. You can click and drag the controls you have added to a form to reposition them. Using this technique, move the *TextBlock* control so that it is positioned toward the upper-left corner of the form. (The exact placement is not critical for this application.) Notice that you might need to click away from the control and then click it again before you are able to move it in the Design View window.

The XAML description of the form in the lower pane now includes the *TextBlock* control, together with properties such as its location on the form, governed by the *Margin* property, the default text displayed by this control in the *Text* property, the alignment of text displayed by this control as specified by the *HorizontalAlignment* and *VerticalAlignment* properties, and whether text should wrap if it exceeds the width of the control.

Your XAML code for the *TextBlock* will look similar to this (your values for the *Margin* property might be slightly different, depending on where you positioned the *TextBlock* control on the form):

```
<TextBlock x:Name="textBlock" HorizontalAlignment="Left" Margin="10,10,0,0"
TextWrapping="Wrap"
Text="TextBlock" VerticalAlignment="Top"/>
```

The XAML pane and the Design View window have a two-way relationship with each other. You can edit the values in the XAML pane, and the changes will be reflected in the Design View window. For example, you can change the location of the *TextBlock* control by modifying the values in the *Margin* property.

5. On the View menu, click Properties Window.

If it was not already displayed, the Properties window appears at the lower right of the screen, under the Solution Explorer pane. You can specify the properties of controls by using the XAML pane under the Design View window, but the Properties window provides a more convenient way for you to modify the properties for items on a form, as well as other items in a project.

The Properties window is context sensitive in that it displays the properties for the currently selected item. If you click the form displayed in the Design View window (outside the

TextBlock control), you can see that the Properties window displays the properties for a *Grid* element. If you look at the XAML pane, you should see that the *TextBlock* control is contained within a *Grid* element. All forms contain a *Grid* element that controls the layout of displayed items; for example, you can define tabular layouts by adding rows and columns to the *Grid*.

6. In the Design View window, click the *TextBlock* control. The Properties window displays the properties for the *TextBlock* control again.

7. In the Properties window, expand the *Text* property. Change the *FontSize* property to **20 pt** and then press Enter. This property is located next to the drop-down list box containing the name of the font, which will show Segoe UI:

FontSize property

> **Note** The suffix *pt* indicates that the font size is measured in points, where 1 point is equal to 1/72 of an inch.

8. In the XAML pane below the Design View window, examine the text that defines the *TextBlock* control. If you scroll to the end of the line, you should see the text FontSize="26.667". This is an approximate conversion of the font size from points to pixels (3 points is assumed to be roughly 4 pixels, although a precise conversion would depend on your screen size and resolution). Any changes that you make using the Properties window are automatically reflected in the XAML definitions, and vice versa.

   Type over the value of the *FontSize* attribute in the XAML pane and change it to **24**. The font size of the text for the *TextBlock* control in the Design View window and the Properties window changes.

9. In the Properties window, examine the other properties of the *TextBlock* control. Feel free to experiment by changing them to see their effects.

   Notice that as you change the values of properties, these properties are added to the definition of the *TextBlock* control in the XAML pane. Each control that you add to a form has a default set of property values, and these values are not displayed in the XAML pane unless you change them.

10. Change the value of the *Text* property of the *TextBlock* control from TextBlock to **Please enter your name**. You can do this either by editing the *Text* element in the XAML pane or by changing the value in the Properties window (this property is located in the Common section in the Properties window).

Notice that the text displayed in the *TextBlock* control in the Design View window changes.

11. Click the form in the Design View window, and then display the Toolbox again.

12. In the Toolbox, click and drag the *TextBox* control onto the form. Move the *TextBox* control so that it is directly below the *TextBlock* control.

> **Tip** When you drag a control on a form, alignment indicators appear automatically when the control becomes aligned vertically or horizontally with other controls. This gives you a quick visual cue to ensure that controls are lined up neatly.

13. In the Design View window, place the mouse over the right edge of the *TextBox* control. The mouse pointer should change to a double-headed arrow, indicating that you can resize the control. Drag the right edge of the *TextBox* control until it is aligned with the right edge of the *TextBlock* control above; a guide should appear when the two edges are correctly aligned.

14. While the *TextBox* control is selected, at the top of the Properties window, change the value of the *Name* property from textBox to **userName**, as illustrated here:

> **Note** You will learn more about naming conventions for controls and variables in Chapter 2, "Working with variables, operators, and expressions."

15. Display the Toolbox again, and then click and drag a *Button* control onto the form. Place the *Button* control to the right of the *TextBox* control on the form so that the bottom of the button is aligned horizontally with the bottom of the text box.

16. Using the Properties window, change the *Name* property of the *Button* control to **ok** and change the *Content* property (in the Common section) from Button to **OK**, and then press Enter. Verify that the caption of the *Button* control on the form changes to display the text *OK*.

The form should now look similar to the following figure:

> **Note** The drop-down menu in the upper-left corner of the Design View window enables you to view how your form will render on different screen sizes and resolutions. In this example, the default view of a 5-inch phone with a 1920 x 1080 resolution is selected. To the right of the drop-down menu, two buttons enable you to switch between portrait view and landscape view. The projects used in subsequent chapters will use a 13.3-inch Desktop view as the design surface, but you can keep the 5-inch phone form factor for this exericse.

17. On the Build menu, click Build Solution, and then verify that the project builds successfully.

18. Ensure that the Debug Target drop-down list is set to Local Machine as shown below. (It might default to Device and attempt to connect to a Windows phone device, and the build will probably fail). Then, on the Debug menu, click Start Debugging.

The application should run and display your form. The form looks like this:

📋 **Note** When you run a Universal Windows Platform app in Debug mode, two pairs of numbers appear in the upper-left corner of the form. These numbers track the frame rate, and developers can use this information to determine when an application starts to become less responsive than it should be (possibly an indication of performance issues). These numbers appear only when an application runs in Debug mode. A full description of what these numbers mean is beyond the scope of this book, so you can ignore them for now.

In the text box, you can overtype the existing text with your name, and then click OK, but nothing happens yet. You need to add some code to indicate what should happen when the user clicks the OK button, which is what you will do next.

19. Return to Visual Studio 2015. On the Debug menu, click Stop Debugging.

You have managed to create a graphical application without writing a single line of C# code. It does not do much yet (you will have to write some code soon), but Visual Studio 2015 actually generates a lot of code for you that handles routine tasks that all graphical applications must perform, such as starting up and displaying a window. Before adding your own code to the application, it helps to have an understanding of what Visual Studio has produced for you. The following section describes these automatically generated artifacts.

Examining the Universal Windows Platform app

In Solution Explorer, expand the MainPage.xaml node. The file MainPage.xaml.cs appears; double-click this file. The following code for the form is displayed in the Code and Text Editor window:

```
using System;
using System.Collections.Generic;
using System.IO;
using System.Linq;
using System.Runtime.InteropServices.WindowsRuntime;
using Windows.Foundation;
using Windows.Foundation.Collections;
using Windows.UI.Xaml;
using Windows.UI.Xaml.Controls;
using Windows.UI.Xaml.Controls.Primitives;
using Windows.UI.Xaml.Data;
using Windows.UI.Xaml.Input;
using Windows.UI.Xaml.Media;
using Windows.UI.Xaml.Navigation;

// The Blank Page item template is documented at http://go.microsoft.com/fwlink/?LinkId=402352&
clcid=0x409

namespace Hello
{
    /// <summary>
    /// An empty page that can be used on its own or navigated to within a Frame.
    /// </summary>
    public sealed partial class MainPage : Page
    {
        public MainPage()
        {
            this.InitializeComponent();
        }
    }
}
```

In addition to a good number of *using* directives bringing into scope some namespaces that most UWP apps use, the file contains the definition of a class called *MainPage* but not much else. There is a little bit of code for the *MainPage* class known as a *constructor* that calls a method named *Initialize-*

Component. A constructor is a special method with the same name as the class. It runs when an instance of the class is created and can contain code to initialize the instance. You will learn about constructors in Chapter 7.

The class actually contains a lot more code than the few lines shown in the MainPage.xaml.cs file, but much of it is generated automatically based on the XAML description of the form and is hidden from you. This hidden code performs operations such as creating and displaying the form and creating and positioning the various controls on the form.

> **Tip** You can also display the C# code file for a page in a UWP app by clicking Code on the View menu when the Design View window is displayed.

At this point, you might be wondering where the *Main* method is and how the form gets displayed when the application runs. Remember that in a console application *Main* defines the point at which the program starts. A graphical application is slightly different.

In Solution Explorer, you should notice another source file called App.xaml. If you expand the node for this file, you will see another file called App.xaml.cs. In a UWP app, the App.xaml file provides the entry point at which the application starts running. If you double-click App.xaml.cs in Solution Explorer, you should see some code that looks similar to this:

```csharp
using System;
using System.Collections.Generic;
using System.IO;
using System.Linq;
using System.Runtime.InteropServices.WindowsRuntime;
using Windows.ApplicationModel;
using Windows.ApplicationModel.Activation;
using Windows.Foundation;
using Windows.Foundation.Collections;
using Windows.UI.Xaml;
using Windows.UI.Xaml.Controls;
using Windows.UI.Xaml.Controls.Primitives;
using Windows.UI.Xaml.Data;
using Windows.UI.Xaml.Input;
using Windows.UI.Xaml.Media;
using Windows.UI.Xaml.Navigation;

// The Blank Application template is documented at http://go.microsoft.com/fwlink/?LinkId=40234
7&clcid=0x409

namespace Hello
{
    /// <summary>
    /// Provides application-specific behavior to supplement the default Application class.
    /// </summary>
    sealed partial class App : Application
    {
        /// <summary>
        /// Allows tracking page views, exceptions and other telemetry through the Microsoft
Application Insights service.
```

```
        /// </summary>
        public static Microsoft.ApplicationInsights.TelemetryClient TelemetryClient;

        /// <summary>
        /// Initializes the singleton application object.  This is the first line of authored
code
        /// executed, and as such is the logical equivalent of main() or WinMain().
        /// </summary>
        public App()
        {
                Microsoft.ApplicationInsights.WindowsAppInitializer.InitialzeAsync(
                Microsoft.ApplicationInsights.WindowsCollectors.Metadata |
                Microsoft.ApplicationInsights.WindowsCollectors.Session);
            this.InitializeComponent();
            this.Suspending += OnSuspending;
        }

        /// <summary>
        /// Invoked when the application is launched normally by the end user.  Other entry
points
        /// will be used such as when the application is launched to open a specific file.
        /// </summary>
        /// <param name="e">Details about the launch request and process.</param>
        protected override void OnLaunched(LaunchActivatedEventArgs e)
        {

#if DEBUG
            if (System.Diagnostics.Debugger.IsAttached)
            {
                this.DebugSettings.EnableFrameRateCounter = true;
            }
#endif

            Frame rootFrame = Window.Current.Content as Frame;

            // Do not repeat app initialization when the Window already has content,
            // just ensure that the window is active
            if (rootFrame == null)
            {
                // Create a Frame to act as the navigation context and navigate to the first
page

                rootFrame = new Frame();

                rootFrame.NavigationFailed += OnNavigationFailed;

                if (e.PreviousExecutionState == ApplicationExecutionState.Terminated)
                {
                    //TODO: Load state from previously suspended application
                }

                // Place the frame in the current Window
                Window.Current.Content = rootFrame;
            }
            if (rootFrame.Content == null)
            {
```

```
                    // When the navigation stack isn't restored navigate to the first page,
                    // configuring the new page by passing required information as a navigation
                    // parameter
                    rootFrame.Navigate(typeof(MainPage), e.Arguments);
                }
                // Ensure the current window is active
                Window.Current.Activate();
            }


            /// <summary>
            /// Invoked when Navigation to a certain page fails
            /// </summary>
            /// <param name="sender">The Frame which failed navigation</param>
            /// <param name="e">Details about the navigation failure</param>
            void OnNavigationFailed(object sender, NavigationFailedEventArgs e)
            {
                throw new Exception("Failed to load Page " + e.SourcePageType.FullName);
            }


            /// <summary>
            /// Invoked when application execution is being suspended.  Application state is saved
            /// without knowing whether the application will be terminated or resumed with the
contents
            /// of memory still intact.
            /// </summary>
            /// <param name="sender">The source of the suspend request.</param>
            /// <param name="e">Details about the suspend request.</param>
            private void OnSuspending(object sender, SuspendingEventArgs e)
            {
                var deferral = e.SuspendingOperation.GetDeferral();
                //TODO: Save application state and stop any background activity
                deferral.Complete();
            }
        }
    }
```

Much of this code consists of comments (the lines beginning "///") and other statements that you don't need to understand just yet, but the key elements are located in the *OnLaunched* method, high-lighted in bold. This method runs when the application starts, and the code in this method causes the application to create a new *Frame* object, display the MainPage form in this frame, and then activate it. It is not necessary at this stage to fully comprehend how this code works or the syntax of any of these statements, but it's helpful that you simply appreciate that this is how the application displays the form when it starts running.

Adding code to the graphical application

Now that you know a little bit about the structure of a graphical application, the time has come to write some code to make your application actually do something.

Write the code for the OK button

1. In the Design View window, open the MainPage.xaml file (double-click MainPage.xaml in Solution Explorer).

2. Still in the Design View window, click the OK button on the form to select it.

3. In the Properties window, click the Event Handlers button for the selected element.

   This button displays an icon that looks like a bolt of lightning, as demonstrated here:

The Properties window displays a list of event names for the *Button* control. An event indicates a significant action that usually requires a response, and you can write your own code to perform this response.

4. In the box adjacent to the *Click* event, type **okClick**, and then press Enter.

   The MainPage.xaml.cs file appears in the Code and Text Editor window, and a new method named *okClick* is added to the *MainPage* class. The method looks like this:

```
private void okClick(object sender, RoutedEventArgs e)
{

}
```

   Do not worry too much about the syntax of this code just yet—you will learn all about methods in Chapter 3.

5. Add the following *using* directive shown in bold to the list at the top of the file (the ellipsis character [...] indicates statements that have been omitted for brevity):

```
using System;
...
using Windows.UI.Xaml.Navigation;
using Windows.UI.Popups;
```

6. Add the following code shown in bold to the *okClick* method:

```csharp
private void okClick(object sender, RoutedEventArgs e)
{
    MessageDialog msg = new MessageDialog("Hello " + userName.Text);
    msg.ShowAsync();
}
```

This code will run when the user clicks the OK button. Again, do not worry too much about the syntax, just be sure that you copy the code exactly as shown; you will find out what these statements mean in the next few chapters. The key things to understand are that the first statement creates a *MessageDialog* object with the message "Hello *<YourName>*", where *<YourName>* is the name that you type into the *TextBox* on the form. The second statement displays the *MessageDialog*, causing it to appear on the screen. The *MessageDialog* class is defined in the *Windows.UI.Popups* namespace, which is why you added it in step 5.

> **Note** You might notice that Visual Studio 2015 adds a wavy green line under the last line of code you typed. If you hover over this line of code, Visual Studio displays a warning that states "Because this call is not awaited, execution of the current method continues before the call is completed. Consider applying the 'await' operator to the result of the call." Essentially, this warning means that you are not taking full advantage of the asynchronous functionality that the .NET Framework provides. You can safely ignore this warning.

7. Click the MainPage.xaml tab above the Code and Text Editor window to display the form in the Design View window again.

8. In the lower pane displaying the XAML description of the form, examine the *Button* element, but be careful not to change anything. Notice that it now contains an attribute named *Click* that refers to the *okClick* method.

```xaml
<Button x:Name="ok" ... Click="okClick" />
```

9. On the Debug menu, click Start Debugging.

10. When the form appears, in the text box, type your name over the existing text, and then click OK.

A message dialog box appears displaying the following greeting:

11. Click Close in the message box.

12. Return to Visual Studio 2015 and then, on the Debug menu, click Stop Debugging.

Summary

In this chapter, you saw how to use Visual Studio 2015 to create, build, and run applications. You created a console application that displays its output in a console window, and you created a Universal Windows Platform application with a simple GUI.

- If you want to continue to the next chapter, keep Visual Studio 2015 running and turn to Chapter 2.

- If you want to exit Visual Studio 2015 now, on the File menu, click Exit. If you see a Save dialog box, click Yes to save the project.

Quick Reference

To	Do this
Create a new console application using Visual Studio 2015	On the File menu, point to New, and then click Project to open the New Project dialog box. In the left pane, expand Installed, expand Templates, and then click Visual C#. In the middle pane, click Console Application. In the Location box, specify a directory for the project files. Type a name for the project, and then click OK.
Create a new blank Universal Windows Platform app using Visual Studio 2015	On the File menu, point to New, and then click Project to open the New Project dialog box. In the left pane, expand Installed, expand Templates, expand Visual C#, expand Windows, and then click Universal. In the middle pane, click Blank App (Windows Universal). In the Location box, specify a directory for the project files. Type a name for the project, and then click OK.
Build the application	On the Build menu, click Build Solution.
Run the application in Debug mode	On the Debug menu, click Start Debugging.
Run the application without debugging	On the Debug menu, click Start Without Debugging.

CHAPTER 2

Working with variables, operators, and expressions

After completing this chapter, you will be able to:

■ Understand statements, identifiers, and keywords.

■ Use variables to store information.

■ Work with primitive data types.

■ Use arithmetic operators such as the plus sign (+) and the minus sign (–).

■ Increment and decrement variables.

Chapter 1, "Welcome to C#," presents how to use the Microsoft Visual Studio 2015 programming environment to build and run a console program and a graphical application. This chapter introduces you to the elements of Microsoft Visual C# syntax and semantics, including statements, keywords, and identifiers. You'll study the primitive types that are built in to the C# language and the characteristics of the values that each type holds. You'll also see how to declare and use local variables (variables that exist only in a method or other small section of code), learn about the arithmetic operators that C# provides, find out how to use operators to manipulate values, and learn how to control expressions containing two or more operators.

Understanding statements

A *statement* is a command that performs an action, such as calculating a value and storing the result or displaying a message to a user. You combine statements to create methods. You'll learn more about methods in Chapter 3, "Writing methods and applying scope," but for now, think of a method as a named sequence of statements. *Main*, which was introduced in the previous chapter, is an example of a method.

Statements in C# follow a well-defined set of rules describing their format and construction. These rules are collectively known as *syntax*. (In contrast, the specification of what statements *do* is collectively known as *semantics*.) One of the simplest and most important C# syntax rules states that you must terminate all statements with a semicolon. For example, Chapter 1 demonstrates that without the terminating semicolon, the following statement won't compile:

```
Console.WriteLine("Hello, World!");
```

> **Tip** C# is a "free format" language, which means that white space, such as a space character or a new line, is not significant except as a separator. In other words, you are free to lay out your statements in any style you choose. However, you should adopt a simple, consistent layout style to make your programs easier to read and understand.

The trick to programming well in any language is to learn the syntax and semantics of the language and then use the language in a natural and idiomatic way. This approach makes your programs easier to maintain. As you progress through this book, you'll see examples of the most important C# statements.

Using identifiers

Identifiers are the names that you use to identify the elements in your programs, such as namespaces, classes, methods, and variables. (You will learn about variables shortly.) In C#, you must adhere to the following syntax rules when choosing identifiers:

- You can use only letters (uppercase and lowercase), digits, and underscore characters.

- An identifier must start with a letter or an underscore.

For example, *result*, *_score*, *footballTeam*, and *plan9* are all valid identifiers, whereas *result%*, *footballTeam$*, and *9plan* are not.

> **Important** C# is a case-sensitive language: *footballTeam* and *FootballTeam* are two different identifiers.

Identifying keywords

The C# language reserves 77 identifiers for its own use, and you cannot reuse these identifiers for your own purposes. These identifiers are called *keywords*, and each has a particular meaning. Examples of keywords are *class*, *namespace*, and *using*. You'll learn the meaning of most of the C# keywords as you proceed through this book. The following is the list of keywords:

abstract	do	in	protected	true
as	double	int	public	try
base	else	interface	readonly	typeof
bool	enum	internal	ref	uint
break	event	is	return	ulong
byte	explicit	lock	sbyte	unchecked
case	extern	long	sealed	unsafe
catch	false	namespace	short	ushort
char	finally	new	sizeof	using
checked	fixed	null	stackalloc	virtual
class	float	object	static	void
const	for	operator	string	volatile
continue	foreach	out	struct	while
decimal	goto	override	switch	
default	if	params	this	
delegate	implicit	private	throw	

> **Tip** In the Visual Studio 2015 Code and Text Editor window, keywords are colored blue when you type them.

C# also uses the following identifiers. These identifiers are not reserved by C#, which means that you can use these names as identifiers for your own methods, variables, and classes, but you should avoid doing so if at all possible.

add	get	remove
alias	global	select
ascending	group	set
async	into	value
await	join	var
descending	let	where
dynamic	orderby	yield
from	partial	

Using variables

A *variable* is a storage location that holds a value. You can think of a variable as a box in the computer's memory that holds temporary information. You must give each variable in a program an unambiguous name that uniquely identifies it in the context in which it is used. You use a variable's name to refer to the value it holds. For example, if you want to store the value of the cost of an item in a store, you might create a variable simply called *cost* and store the item's cost in this variable. Later on, if you refer to the *cost* variable, the value retrieved will be the item's cost that you stored there earlier.

Naming variables

You should adopt a naming convention for variables that helps you avoid confusion concerning the variables you have defined. This is especially important if you are part of a project team with several developers working on different parts of an application; a consistent naming convention helps to avoid confusion and can reduce the scope for bugs. The following list contains some general recommendations:

- Don't start an identifier with an underscore. Although this is legal in C#, it can limit the interoperability of your code with applications built by using other languages, such as Microsoft Visual Basic.

- Don't create identifiers that differ only by case. For example, do not create one variable named *myVariable* and another named *MyVariable* for use at the same time because it is too easy to confuse one with the other. Also, defining identifiers that differ only by case can limit the ability to reuse classes in applications developed with other languages that are not case sensitive, such as Visual Basic.

- Start the name with a lowercase letter.

- In a multiword identifier, start the second and each subsequent word with an uppercase letter. (This is called *camelCase notation*.)

- Don't use Hungarian notation. (If you are a Microsoft Visual C++ developer, you are probably familiar with Hungarian notation. If you don't know what Hungarian notation is, don't worry about it!)

For example, *score*, *footballTeam*, *_score*, and *FootballTeam* are all valid variable names, but only the first two are recommended.

Declaring variables

Variables hold values. C# has many different types of values that it can store and process—integers, floating-point numbers, and strings of characters, to name three. When you declare a variable, you must specify the type of data it will hold.

You declare the type and name of a variable in a declaration statement. For example, the statement that follows declares that the variable named *age* holds *int* (integer) values. As always, you must terminate the statement with a semicolon.

```
int age;
```

The variable type *int* is the name of one of the *primitive* C# types, *integer*, which is a whole number. (You'll learn about several primitive data types later in this chapter.)

Note If you are a Visual Basic programmer, you should note that C# does not allow implicit variable declarations. You must explicitly declare all variables before you use them.

After you've declared your variable, you can assign it a value. The statement that follows assigns *age* the value 42. Again, note that the semicolon is required.

```
age = 42;
```

The equal sign (=) is the *assignment* operator, which assigns the value on its right to the variable on its left. After this assignment, you can use the *age* variable in your code to refer to the value it holds. The next statement writes the value of the *age* variable (42) to the console:

```
Console.WriteLine(age);
```

Tip If you leave the mouse pointer over a variable in the Visual Studio 2015 Code and Text Editor window, a ScreenTip indicates the type of the variable.

Working with primitive data types

C# has a number of built-in types called *primitive data types*. The following table lists the most commonly used primitive data types in C# and the range of values that you can store in each.

Data type	Description	Size (bits)	Range	Sample usage
int	Whole numbers (integers)	32	-2^{31} through $2^{31}-1$	`int count;` `count = 42;`
long	Whole numbers (bigger range)	64	-2^{63} through $2^{63}-1$	`long wait;` `wait = 42L;`
float	Floating-point numbers	32	-3.4×10^{-38} through 3.4×10^{38}	`float away;` `away = 0.42F;`
double	Double-precision (more accurate) float-ing-point numbers	64	$\pm 5.0 \times 10^{-324}$ through $\pm 1.7 \times 10^{308}$	`double trouble;` `trouble = 0.42;`
decimal	Monetary values	128	28 significant figures	`decimal coin;` `coin = 0.42M;`

string	Sequence of char-acters	16 bits per character	Not applicable	`string vest`
				`vest = "forty`
				`two";`

char	Single character	16	0 through $2^{16}-1$	`char grill;` `grill = 'x';`
bool	Boolean	8	True or false	`bool teeth;` `teeth = false;`

Unassigned local variables

When you declare a variable, it contains a random value until you assign a value to it. This behavior was a rich source of bugs in C and C++ programs that created a variable and accidentally used it as a source of information before giving it a value. C# does not allow you to use an unassigned variable. You must assign a value to a variable before you can use it; otherwise, your program will not compile. This requirement is called the *definite assignment rule*. For example, the following state-ments generate the compile-time error message "Use of unassigned local variable 'age'" because the *Console.WriteLine* statement attempts to display the value of an uninitialized variable:

```
int age;
Console.WriteLine(age); // compile-time error
```

Displaying primitive data type values

In the following exercise, you use a C# program named PrimitiveDataTypes to demonstrate how several primitive data types work.

Display primitive data type values

1. Start Visual Studio 2015 if it is not already running.

2. On the File menu, point to Open, and then click Project/Solution.

   The Open Project dialog box appears.

3. Move to the \Microsoft Press\VCSBS\Chapter 2\PrimitiveDataTypes folder in your Documents folder.

4. Select the PrimitiveDataTypes solution file, and then click Open.

   The solution loads, and Solution Explorer displays the PrimitiveDataTypes project.

> **Note** Solution file names have the .sln suffix, such as PrimitiveDataTypes.sln. A solution can contain one or more projects. Visual C# project files have the .csproj suffix. If you open a project rather than a solution, Visual Studio 2015 automatically creates a new solution file for it. This situation can be confusing if you are not aware of this feature because it can result in you accidentally generating multiple solutions for the same project.

5. On the Debug menu, click Start Debugging.

   You might see some warnings in Visual Studio. You can safely ignore them. (You will correct them in the next exercise.)

6. In the Choose A Data Type list, click *string*.

   The value "forty two" appears in the Sample Value box.

7. Again, in the Choose A Data Type list, click the *int* type.

The value "to do" appears in the Sample Value box, indicating that the statements to display an *int* value still need to be written.

8. Click each data type in the list. Confirm that the code for the *double* and *bool* types is not yet implemented.

9. Return to Visual Studio 2015 and then, on the Debug menu, click Stop Debugging.

You can also close the window to stop debugging.

Use primitive data types in code

1. In Solution Explorer, expand the PrimitiveDataTypes project (if it is not already expanded), and then double-click MainPage.xaml.

The form for the application appears in the Design View window.

> **Hint** If your screen is not big enough to display the entire form, you can zoom in and out in the Design View window by using Ctrl+Alt+= and Ctrl+Alt+- or by selecting the size from the Zoom drop-down list in the lower-left corner of the Design View window.

2. In the XAML pane, scroll down to locate the markup for the *ListBox* control. This control displays the list of data types in the left part of the form, and it looks like this (some of the properties have been removed from this text):

```
<ListBox x:Name="type" ... SelectionChanged="typeSelectionChanged">
  <ListBoxItem>int</ListBoxItem>
  <ListBoxItem>long</ListBoxItem>
  <ListBoxItem>float</ListBoxItem>
  <ListBoxItem>double</ListBoxItem>
  <ListBoxItem>decimal</ListBoxItem>
  <ListBoxItem>string</ListBoxItem>
  <ListBoxItem>char</ListBoxItem>
  <ListBoxItem>bool</ListBoxItem>
</ListBox>
```

The *ListBox* control displays each data type as a separate *ListBoxItem*. When the application is running, if a user clicks an item in the list, the *SelectionChanged* event occurs (this is a little bit like the *Click* event that occurs when the user clicks a button, which is demonstrated in Chapter 1). You can see that in this case, the *ListBox* invokes the *typeSelectionChanged* method. This method is defined in the MainPage.xaml.cs file.

3. On the View menu, click Code.

The Code and Text Editor window opens, displaying the MainPage.xaml.cs file.

Note Remember that you can also use Solution Explorer to access the code. Click the arrow to the left of the MainPage.xaml file to expand the node, and then double-click MainPage.xaml.cs.

4. In the Code and Text Editor window, find the *typeSelectionChanged* method.

Tip To locate an item in your project, on the Edit menu, point to Find And Replace, and then click Quick Find. A menu opens in the upper-right corner of the Code and Text Editor window. In the text box on this shortcut menu, type the name of the item you're looking for, and then click Find Next (the right-arrow symbol next to the text box):

Find menu   Find Next button

```
MainPage.xaml.cs ⊟ × MainPage.xaml
C# PrimitiveDataTypes                          ▼ ⚙ PrimitiveDataTypes.MainPage              ▼ ⚙ typeSelectionChanged(object sender, SelectionCh ▼
using System;                                                              ▼  typeSelectionChanged             → ▼ ×
using System.Collections.Generic;
using System.IO;                                                            Aa Abl .* Current Document          ▼
using System.Linq;
using System.Runtime.InteropServices.WindowsRuntime;
using Windows.Foundation;
using Windows.Foundation.Collections;
using Windows.UI.Xaml;
using Windows.UI.Xaml.Controls;
using Windows.UI.Xaml.Controls.Primitives;
using Windows.UI.Xaml.Data;
using Windows.UI.Xaml.Input;
using Windows.UI.Xaml.Media;
using Windows.UI.Xaml.Navigation;

// The Blank Page item template is documented at http://go.microsoft.com/fwlink/?LinkId=402352&clcid=0x409

namespace PrimitiveDataTypes
{
    /// <summary>
    /// An empty page that can be used on its own or navigated to within a Frame.
    /// </summary>
    4 references
    public sealed partial class MainPage : Page
    {
        0 references
        public MainPage()
        {
            this.InitializeComponent();
        }

        1 reference
        private void typeSelectionChanged(object sender, SelectionChangedEventArgs e)
        {
            ListBoxItem selectedType = (type.SelectedItem as ListBoxItem);
            switch (selectedType.Content.ToString())
            {
                case "int":
```
100 % ▼

By default, the search is not case sensitive. If you want to perform a case-sensitive search, click the Match Case button (Aa) below the text to search for.

Instead of using the Edit menu, you can also press Ctrl+F to display the Quick Find dialog box. Similarly, you can press Ctrl+H to display the Quick Replace dialog box.

As an alternative to using the Quick Find functionality, you can also locate the methods in a class by using the class members drop-down list box above the Code and Text Editor window, on the right.

The class members drop-down list box displays all the methods in the class, together with the variables and other items that the class contains. (You will learn more about these items in later chapters.) In the drop-down list, click the *typeSelectionChanged* method, and the cursor will move directly to the *typeSelectionChanged* method in the class.

If you have programmed using another language, you can probably guess how the *typeSelectionChanged* method works; if not, Chapter 4, "Using decision statements," makes this code clear. At present, all you need to understand is that when the user clicks an item in the *ListBox* control, the details of the item are passed to this method, which then uses this information to determine what happens next. For example, if the user clicks the *float* value, this method calls another method named *showFloatValue*.

5. Scroll down through the code and find the *showFloatValue* method, which looks like this:

```
private void showFloatValue()
{
  float floatVar;
  floatVar = 0.42F;
  value.Text = floatVar.ToString();
}
```

The body of this method contains three statements. The first statement declares a variable named *floatVar* of type *float*.

The second statement assigns *floatVar* the value 0.42F.

> **Important** The *F* is a type suffix specifying that 0.42 should be treated as a *float* value. If you forget the *F*, the value 0.42 is treated as a *double* and your program will not compile, because you cannot assign a value of one type to a variable of a different type without writing additional code—C# is very strict in this respect.

The third statement displays the value of this variable in the value text box on the form. This statement requires your attention. As is illustrated in Chapter 1, the way you display an item in a text box is to set its *Text* property (you did this by using XAML in Chapter 1). You can also perform this task programmatically, which is what is going on here. Notice that you access the property of an object by using the same dot notation that you saw for running a method. (Remember *Console.WriteLine* from Chapter 1?) Also, the data that you put in the *Text* property must be a string and not a number. If you try to assign a number to the *Text* property, your program will not compile. Fortunately, the .NET Framework provides some help in the form of the *ToString* method.

Every data type in the .NET Framework has a *ToString* method. The purpose of *ToString* is to convert an object to its string representation. The *showFloatValue* method uses the *ToString* method of the *float* variable *floatVar* object to generate a string version of the value of this variable. You can then safely assign this string to the *Text* property of the value text box. When you create your own data types and classes, you can define your own implementation of the *ToString* method to specify how your class should be represented as a string. You learn more about creating your own classes in Chapter 7, "Creating and managing classes and objects."

6. In the Code and Text Editor window, locate the *showIntValue* method:

```
private void showIntValue()
{
    value.Text = "to do";
}
```

The *showIntValue* method is called when you click the *int* type in the list box.

7. At the start of the *showIntValue* method, on a new line after the opening brace, type the following two statements shown in bold:

```
private void showIntValue()
{
    int intVar;
    intVar = 42;
    value.Text = "to do";
}
```

The first statement creates a variable called *intVar* that can hold an *int* value. The second statement assigns the value 42 to this variable.

8. In the original statement in this method, change the string *"to do"* to *intVar.ToString()*;

The method should now look exactly like this:

```
private void showIntValue()
{
    int intVar;
    intVar = 42;
    value.Text = intVar.ToString();
}
```

9. On the Debug menu, click Start Debugging.

   The form appears again.

10. In the Choose A Data Type list, select the *int* type. Confirm that the value 42 is displayed in the Sample Value text box.

11. Return to Visual Studio and then, on the Debug menu, click Stop Debugging.

12. In the Code and Text Editor window, find the *showDoubleValue* method.

13. Edit the *showDoubleValue* method exactly as shown in bold type in the following code:

```
private void showDoubleValue()
{
    double doubleVar;
    doubleVar = 0.42;
    value.Text = doubleVar.ToString();
}
```

   This code is similar to the *showIntValue* method, except that it creates a variable called *doubleVar* that holds double values and is assigned the value 0.42.

14. In the Code and Text Editor window, locate the *showBoolValue* method.

15. Edit the *showBoolValue* method exactly as follows:

```
private void showBoolValue()
{
    bool boolVar;
    boolVar = false;
    value.Text = boolVar.ToString();
}
```

   Again, this code is similar to the previous examples, except that *boolVar* can only hold a Boolean value, *true* or *false*. In this case, the value assigned is *false*.

16. On the Debug menu, click Start Debugging.

17. In the Choose A Data Type list, select the *float*, *double*, and *bool* types. In each case, verify that the correct value is displayed in the Sample Value text box.

18. Return to Visual Studio and then, on the Debug menu, click Stop Debugging.

Using arithmetic operators

C# supports the regular arithmetic operations you learned in your childhood: the plus sign (+) for addition, the minus sign (−) for subtraction, the asterisk (*) for multiplication, and the forward slash (/) for division. The symbols +, −, *, and / are called *operators* because they "operate" on values to create new values. In the following example, the variable *moneyPaidToConsultant* ends up holding the product of 750 (the daily rate) and 20 (the number of days the consultant was employed):

```
long moneyPaidToConsultant;
moneyPaidToConsultant = 750 * 20;
```

> **Note** The values on which an operator performs its function are called *operands*. In the expression 750 * 20, the * is the operator, and 750 and 20 are the operands.

Operators and types

Not all operators are applicable to all data types. The operators that you can use on a value depend on the value's type. For example, you can use all the arithmetic operators on values of type *char, int, long, float, double,* or *decimal.* However, with the exception of the plus operator (+), you can't use the arithmetic operators on values of type *string,* and you cannot use any of them with values of type *bool.* So, the following statement is not allowed because the *string* type does not support the minus operator (subtracting one string from another is meaningless):

```
// compile-time error
Console.WriteLine("Gillingham" - "Forest Green Rovers");
```

However, you can use the + operator to concatenate string values. You need to be careful because this can have unexpected results. For example, the following statement writes "431" (not "44") to the console:

```
Console.WriteLine("43" + "1");
```

> **Tip** The .NET Framework provides a method called *Int32.Parse* that you can use to convert a string value to an integer if you need to perform arithmetic computations on values held as strings.

String interpolation

A new feature in the latest version of C# is string interpolation, which renders many uses of the + operator obsolete for concatenating strings.

A common use of string concatenation is to generate string values that include variable values. You saw an example of this in the exercises in Chapter 1 that created a graphical application. In the *okClick* method you added the following line of code:

MessageDialog msg = new MessageDialog("Hello " + userName.Text);

String interpolation lets you use the following syntax instead:

MessageDialog msg = new MessageDialog($"Hello {userName.Text}");

The $ symbol at the start of the string indicates that it is an interpolated string and that any expressions between the { and } characters should be evaluated and the result substituted in their place. Without the leading $ symbol, the string {username.Text} would be treated literally.

String interpolation is more efficient than using the + operator. (String concatenation using the + operator can be memory hungry by virtue of the way in which strings are handled by the .NET Framework.) String interpolation is also arguably more readable and less error prone.

You should also be aware that the type of the result of an arithmetic operation depends on the type of the operands used. For example, the value of the expression 5.0/2.0 is 2.5; the type of both operands is *double*, so the type of the result is also *double*. (In C#, literal numbers with decimal points are always *double*, not *float*, to maintain as much accuracy as possible.) However, the value of the expression 5/2 is 2. In this case, the type of both operands is *int*, so the type of the result is also *int*. C# always rounds toward zero in circumstances like this. The situation gets a little more complicated if you mix the types of the operands. For example, the expression 5/2.0 consists of an *int* and a *double*. The C# compiler detects the mismatch and generates code that converts the *int* into a *double* before performing the operation. The result of the operation is therefore a *double* (2.5). However, although this works, it is considered poor practice to mix types in this way.

C# also supports one less-familiar arithmetic operator: the *remainder*, or *modulus*, operator, which is represented by the percent sign (%). The result of x % y is the remainder after dividing the value x by the value y. So, for example, 9 % 2 is 1 because 9 divided by 2 is 4, remainder 1.

Note If you are familiar with C or C++, you know that you can't use the remainder operator on *float* or *double* values in these languages. However, C# relaxes this rule. The remainder operator is valid with all numeric types, and the result is not necessarily an integer. For example, the result of the expression 7.0 % 2.4 is 2.2.

Numeric types and infinite values

There are one or two other features of numbers in C# about which you should be aware. For example, the result of dividing any number by zero is infinity, which is outside the range of the *int, long*, and *decimal* types; consequently, evaluating an expression such as 5/0 results in an error. However, the *double* and *float* types actually have a special value that can represent infinity, and the value of the expression 5.0/0.0 is *Infinity*. The one exception to this rule is the value of the expression 0.0/0.0. Usually, if you divide zero by anything, the result is zero, but if you divide anything by zero the result is infinity. The expression 0.0/0.0 results in a paradox—the value must be zero and infinity at the same time. C# has another special value for this situation called *NaN*, which stands for "not a number." So if you evaluate 0.0/0.0, the result is *NaN*.

NaN and *Infinity* propagate through expressions. If you evaluate 10 + *NaN*, the result is *NaN*, and if you evaluate 10 + *Infinity*, the result is *Infinity*. The value of the expression *Infinity* * 0 is *NaN*.

Examining arithmetic operators

The following exercise demonstrates how to use the arithmetic operators on *int* values.

Run the MathsOperators project

1. Start Visual Studio 2015 if it is not already running.

2. Open the MathsOperators project, located in the \Microsoft Press\VCSBS\Chapter 2\MathsOperators folder in your Documents folder.

3. On the Debug menu, click Start Debugging.

   The following form appears:

```
MathsOperators                                          —  □  ×
 008   000
            Left Operand                        Right Operand

    ┌──────────────────┐      ◉ + Addition        ┌──────────────────┐
    │                  │      ○ - Subtraction     │                  │
    └──────────────────┘      ○ * Multiplication  └──────────────────┘
                              ○ / Division
                              ○ % Remainder

        ┌──────────────┐
        │  Calculate   │
        └──────────────┘

        Expression:

          Result:
```

4. In the Left Operand box, type **54**.

5. In the Right Operand box, type **13**.

   You can now apply any of the operators to the values in the text boxes.

6. Click the – Subtraction option, and then click Calculate.

   The text in the Expression box changes to 54 – 13, but the value 0 appears in the Result box; this is clearly wrong.

7. Click the / Division option, and then click Calculate.

   The text in the Expression box changes to 54/13, and again the value 0 appears in the Result box.

8. Click the % Remainder button, and then click Calculate.

   The text in the Expression box changes to 54 % 13, but, once again, the value 0 appears in the Result text box. Test other combinations of numbers and operators; you will find that they all currently yield the value 0.

> **Note** If you type a noninteger value into either of the operand boxes, the application detects an error and displays the message "Input string was not in a correct format." You will learn more about how to catch and handle errors and exceptions in Chapter 6, "Managing errors and exceptions."

9. When you have finished, return to Visual Studio and then, on the Debug menu, click Stop Debugging.

As you might have guessed, none of the calculations is currently implemented by the MathsOperators application. In the next exercise, you will correct this.

Perform calculations in the MathsOperators application

1. Display the MainPage.xaml form in the Design View window. (In Solution Explorer, in the MathsOperators project, double-click the file MainPage.xaml.)

2. On the View menu, point to Other Windows, and then click Document Outline.

   The Document Outline window appears, showing the names and types of the controls on the form. The Document Outline window provides a simple way to locate and select controls on a complex form. The controls are arranged in a hierarchy, starting with the *Page* that constitutes the form. As mentioned in Chapter 1, a Universal Windows Platform (UWP) app page contains a *Grid* control, and the other controls are placed within this *Grid*. If you expand the Grid node in the Document Outline window, the other controls appear, starting with another *Grid* (the outer *Grid* acts as a frame, and the inner *Grid* contains the controls that you see on the form). If you expand the inner *Grid*, you can see each of the controls on the form.

   If you click any of these controls, the corresponding element is highlighted in the Design View window. Similarly, if you select a control in the Design View window, the corresponding control is selected in the Document Outline window. (To see this in action, pin the Document Outline window in place by deselecting the Auto Hide button in the upper-right corner of the Document Outline window.)

3. On the form, click the two *TextBox* controls in which the user types numbers. In the Document Outline window, verify that they are named *lhsOperand* and *rhsOperand*.

   When the form runs, the *Text* property of each of these controls holds the values that the user enters.

4. Toward the bottom of the form, verify that the *TextBlock* control used to display the expression being evaluated is named *expression* and that the *TextBlock* control used to display the result of the calculation is named *result*.

5. Close the Document Outline window.

6. On the View menu, click Code to display the code for the MainPage.xaml.cs file in the Code and Text Editor window.

7. In the Code and Text Editor window, locate the *addValues* method. It looks like this:

```
private void addValues()
{
    int lhs = int.Parse(lhsOperand.Text);
    int rhs = int.Parse(rhsOperand.Text);
    int outcome = 0;
    // TODO: Add rhs to lhs and store the result in outcome
    expression.Text = $"{lhsOperand.Text} + {rhsOperand.Text}";
    result.Text = outcome.ToString();
}
```

The first statement in this method declares an *int* variable called *lhs* and initializes it with the integer corresponding to the value typed by the user in the lhsOperand box. Remember that the *Text* property of a *TextBox* control contains a string, but *lhs* is an *int*, so you must convert this string to an integer before you can assign it to *lhs*. The *int* data type provides the *int.Parse* method, which does precisely this.

The second statement declares an *int* variable called *rhs* and initializes it to the value in the rhsOperand box after converting it to an *int*.

The third statement declares an *int* variable called *outcome*.

A comment stating that you need to add *rhs* to *lhs* and store the result in *outcome* follows. This is the missing bit of code that you need to implement, which you will do in the next step.

The fifth statement uses string interpolation to construct a string that indicates the calculation being performed and assigns the result to the *expression.Text* property. This causes the string to appear in the Expression box on the form.

The final statement displays the result of the calculation by assigning it to the *Text* property of the Result box. Remember that the *Text* property is a string, and the result of the calculation is an *int*, so you must convert the *int* to a string before assigning it to the *Text* property. Recall that this is what the *ToString* method of the *int* type does.

8. Below the comment in the middle of the *addValues* method, add the following statement (shown below in bold):

```
private void addValues()
{
    int lhs = int.Parse(lhsOperand.Text);
    int rhs = int.Parse(rhsOperand.Text);
    int outcome = 0;
```

```
    // TODO: Add rhs to lhs and store the result in outcome
    outcome = lhs + rhs;
    expression.Text = $"{lhsOperand.Text} + {rhsOperand.Text}";
    result.Text = outcome.ToString();
}
```

This statement evaluates the expression *lhs + rhs* and stores the result in *outcome*.

9. Examine the *subtractValues* method. You should see that it follows a similar pattern. Here you need to add the statement to calculate the result of subtracting *rhs* from *lhs* and store it in *outcome*. Add the following statement (in bold) to this method:

```
private void subtractValues()
{
    int lhs = int.Parse(lhsOperand.Text);
    int rhs = int.Parse(rhsOperand.Text);
    int outcome = 0;
    // TODO: Subtract rhs from lhs and store the result in outcome
    outcome = lhs - rhs;
    expression.Text = $"{lhsOperand.Text} - {rhsOperand.Text}";
    result.Text = outcome.ToString();
}
```

10. Examine the *multiplyValues*, *divideValues*, and *remainderValues* methods. Again, they are all missing the crucial statement that performs the specified calculation. Add the appropriate statements to these methods (shown in bold).

```
private void multiplyValues()
{
    int lhs = int.Parse(lhsOperand.Text);
    int rhs = int.Parse(rhsOperand.Text);
    int outcome = 0;
    // TODO: Multiply lhs by rhs and store the result in outcome
    outcome = lhs * rhs;
    expression.Text = $"{lhsOperand.Text} * {rhsOperand.Text}";
    result.Text = outcome.ToString();
}

private void divideValues()
{
    int lhs = int.Parse(lhsOperand.Text);
    int rhs = int.Parse(rhsOperand.Text);
    int outcome = 0;
    // TODO: Divide lhs by rhs and store the result in outcome
    outcome = lhs / rhs;
    expression.Text = $"{lhsOperand.Text} / {rhsOperand.Text}";
    result.Text = outcome.ToString();
}

private void remainderValues()
{
    int lhs = int.Parse(lhsOperand.Text);
    int rhs = int.Parse(rhsOperand.Text);
    int outcome = 0;
    // TODO: Work out the remainder after dividing lhs by rhs and store the result in
```

```
outcome
    outcome = lhs % rhs;
    expression.Text = $"{lhsOperand.Text} % {rhsOperand.Text}";
    result.Text = outcome.ToString();
}
```

Test the MathsOperators application

1. On the Debug menu, click Start Debugging to build and run the application.

2. Type **54** in the Left Operand box, type **13** in the Right Operand box, click the + Addition option, and then click Calculate.

    The value 67 should appear in the Result box.

3. Click the − Subtraction option, and then click Calculate. Verify that the result is now 41.

4. Click the * Multiplication option, and then click Calculate. Verify that the result is now 702.

5. Click the / Division option, and then click Calculate. Verify that the result is now 4.

    In real life, 54/13 is 4.153846 recurring, but this is not real life—this is C# performing integer division. When you divide one integer by another integer, the answer you get back is an integer, as explained earlier.

6. Click the % Remainder option, and then click Calculate. Verify that the result is now 2.

    When dealing with integers, the remainder after dividing 54 by 13 is 2; (54 − ((54/13) * 13)) is 2. This is because the calculation rounds down to an integer at each stage. (My high school math teacher would be horrified to be told that (54/13) * 13 does not equal 54!)

7. Return to Visual Studio and stop debugging.

Controlling precedence

Precedence governs the order in which an expression's operators are evaluated. Consider the following expression, which uses the + and * operators:

```
2 + 3 * 4
```

This expression is potentially ambiguous: do you perform the addition first or the multiplication? The order of the operations matters because it changes the result:

- If you perform the addition first, followed by the multiplication, the result of the addition (2 + 3) forms the left operand of the * operator, and the result of the whole expression is 5 * 4, which is 20.

- If you perform the multiplication first, followed by the addition, the result of the multiplication (3 * 4) forms the right operand of the + operator, and the result of the whole expression is 2 + 12, which is 14.

In C#, the multiplicative operators (*, /, and %) have precedence over the additive operators (+ and –), so in expressions such as 2 + 3 * 4, the multiplication is performed first, followed by the addition. The answer to 2 + 3 * 4 is therefore 14.

You can use parentheses to override precedence and force operands to bind to operators in a different way. For example, in the following expression, the parentheses force the 2 and the 3 to bind to the + operator (making 5), and the result of this addition forms the left operand of the * operator to produce the value 20:

```
(2 + 3) * 4
```

> **Note** The term *parentheses* or *round brackets* refers to (). The term *braces* or *curly brackets* refers to { }. The term *square brackets* refers to [ ].

Using associativity to evaluate expressions

Operator precedence is only half the story. What happens when an expression contains different operators that have the same precedence? This is where *associativity* becomes important. Associativity is the direction (left or right) in which the operands of an operator are evaluated. Consider the following expression that uses the / and * operators:

```
4 / 2 * 6
```

At first glance, this expression is potentially ambiguous. Do you perform the division first or the multiplication? The precedence of both operators is the same (they are both multiplicative), but the order in which the operators in the expression are applied is important because you can get two different results:

- If you perform the division first, the result of the division (4/2) forms the left operand of the * operator, and the result of the whole expression is (4/2) * 6, or 12.

- If you perform the multiplication first, the result of the multiplication (2 * 6) forms the right operand of the / operator, and the result of the whole expression is 4/(2 * 6), or 4/12.

In this case, the associativity of the operators determines how the expression is evaluated. The * and / operators are both left associative, which means that the operands are evaluated from left to right. In this case, 4/2 will be evaluated before multiplying by 6, giving the result 12.

Associativity and the assignment operator

In C#, the equal sign (=) is an operator. All operators return a value based on their operands. The assignment operator = is no different. It takes two operands: the operand on the right side is evaluated and then stored in the operand on the left side. The value of the assignment operator is the value that was assigned to the left operand. For example, in the following assignment statement, the value returned by the assignment operator is 10, which is also the value assigned to the variable *myInt*:

```
int myInt;
myInt = 10; // value of assignment expression is 10
```

At this point, you might be thinking that this is all very nice and esoteric, but so what? Well, because the assignment operator returns a value, you can use this same value with another occurrence of the assignment statement, like this:

```
int myInt;
int myInt2;
myInt2 = myInt = 10;
```

The value assigned to the variable *myInt2* is the value that was assigned to *myInt*. The assignment statement assigns the same value to both variables. This technique is useful if you want to initialize several variables to the same value. It makes it very clear to anyone reading your code that all the variables must have the same value:

```
myInt5 = myInt4 = myInt3 = myInt2 = myInt = 10;
```

From this discussion, you can probably deduce that the assignment operator associates from right to left. The rightmost assignment occurs first, and the value assigned propagates through the variables from right to left. If any of the variables previously had a value, it is overwritten by the value being assigned.

You should treat this construct with caution, however. One frequent mistake that new C# programmers make is to try to combine this use of the assignment operator with variable declarations. For example, you might expect the following code to create and initialize three variables with the same value (10):

```
int myInt, myInt2, myInt3 = 10;
```

This is legal C# code (because it compiles). What it does is declare the variables *myInt*, *myInt2*, and *myInt3* and initialize *myInt3* with the value 10. However, it does not initialize *myInt* or *myInt2*. If you try to use *myInt* or *myInt2* in an expression such as

```
myInt3 = myInt / myInt2;
```

the compiler generates the following errors:

```
Use of unassigned local variable 'myInt'
Use of unassigned local variable 'myInt2'
```

Incrementing and decrementing variables

If you want to add 1 to a variable, you can use the + operator, as demonstrated here:

```
count = count + 1;
```

However, adding 1 to a variable is so common that C# provides its own operator just for this purpose: the ++ operator. To increment the variable *count* by 1, you can write the following statement:

```
count++;
```

Similarly, C# provides the -- operator that you can use to subtract 1 from a variable, like this:

```
count--;
```

The ++ and -- operators are *unary* operators, meaning that they take only a single operand. They share the same precedence and are both left associative.

Prefix and postfix

The increment (++) and decrement (--) operators are unusual in that you can place them either before or after the variable. Placing the operator symbol before the variable is called the *prefix form* of the operator, and using the operator symbol after the variable is called the *postfix form*. Here are examples:

```
count++; // postfix increment
++count; // prefix increment
count--; // postfix decrement
--count; // prefix decrement
```

Whether you use the prefix or postfix form of the ++ or -- operator makes no difference to the variable being incremented or decremented. For example, if you write *count++*, the value of *count* increases by 1, and if you write *++count*, the value of *count* also increases by 1. Knowing this, you're probably wondering why there are two ways to write the same thing. To understand the answer, you must remember that ++ and -- are operators and that all operators are used to evaluate an expression that has a value. The value returned by *count++* is the value of *count* before the increment takes place, whereas the value returned by *++count* is the value of *count* after the increment takes place. Here is an example:

```
int x;
x = 42;
Console.WriteLine(x++); // x is now 43, 42 written out
x = 42;
Console.WriteLine(++x); // x is now 43, 43 written out
```

The way to remember which operand does what is to look at the order of the elements (the operand and the operator) in a prefix or postfix expression. In the expression *x++*, the variable *x* occurs first, so its value is used as the value of the expression before *x* is incremented. In the expression *++x*, the operator occurs first, so its operation is performed before the value of *x* is evaluated as the result.

These operators are most commonly used in *while* and *do* statements, which are presented in Chapter 5, "Using compound assignment and iteration statements." If you are using the increment and decrement operators in isolation, stick to the postfix form and be consistent.

Declaring implicitly typed local variables

Earlier in this chapter, you saw that you declare a variable by specifying a data type and an identifier, like this:

```
int myInt;
```

It was also mentioned that you should assign a value to a variable before you attempt to use it. You can declare and initialize a variable in the same statement, such as illustrated in the following:

```
int myInt = 99;
```

Or, you can even do it like this, assuming that *myOtherInt* is an initialized integer variable:

```
int myInt = myOtherInt * 99;
```

Now, remember that the value you assign to a variable must be of the same type as the variable. For example, you can assign an *int* value only to an *int* variable. The C# compiler can quickly work out the type of an expression used to initialize a variable and indicate whether it does not match the type of the variable. You can also ask the C# compiler to infer the type of a variable from an expression and use this type when declaring the variable by using the *var* keyword in place of the type, as demonstrated here:

```
var myVariable = 99;
var myOtherVariable = "Hello";
```

The variables *myVariable* and *myOtherVariable* are referred to as *implicitly typed* variables. The *var* keyword causes the compiler to deduce the type of the variables from the types of the expressions used to initialize them. In these examples, *myVariable* is an *int*, and *myOtherVariable* is a *string*. However, it is important for you to understand that this is a convenience for declaring variables only, and that after a variable has been declared you can assign only values of the inferred type to it—you cannot assign *float*, *double*, or *string* values to *myVariable* at a later point in your program, for example. You should also understand that you can use the *var* keyword only when you supply an expression to initialize a variable. The following declaration is illegal and causes a compilation error:

```
var yetAnotherVariable; // Error - compiler cannot infer type
```

Important If you have programmed with Visual Basic in the past, you might be familiar with the *Variant* type, which you can use to store any type of value in a variable. I emphasize here and now that you should forget everything you ever learned when programming with Visual Basic about *Variant* variables. Although the keywords look similar, *var* and *Variant* mean totally different things. When you declare a variable in C# by using the *var* keyword, the type of values that you assign to the variable *cannot change* from that used to initialize the variable.

If you are a purist, you are probably gritting your teeth at this point and wondering why on earth the designers of a neat language such as C# should allow a feature such as *var* to creep in. After all, it sounds like an excuse for extreme laziness on the part of programmers and can make it more difficult to understand what a program is doing or track down bugs (and it can even easily introduce new bugs into your code). However, trust me that *var* has a very valid place in C#, as you will see when you work through many of the following chapters. However, for the time being, we will stick to using explicitly typed variables except for when implicit typing becomes a necessity.

Summary

In this chapter, you saw how to create and use variables and learned about some of the common data types available for variables in C#. You also learned about identifiers. In addition, you used a number of operators to build expressions, and you learned how the precedence and associativity of operators determine how expressions are evaluated.

- If you want to continue to the next chapter, keep Visual Studio 2015 running and turn to Chapter 3.

- If you want to exit Visual Studio 2015 now, on the File menu, click Exit. If you see a Save dialog box, click Yes and save the project.

Quick Reference

To	Do this
Declare a variable	Write the name of the data type, followed by the name of the variable, followed by a semicolon. For example: `int outcome;`
Declare a variable and give it an initial value	Write the name of the data type, followed by the name of the variable, followed by the assignment operator and the initial value. Finish with a semicolon. For example: `int outcome = 99;`
Change the value of a variable	Write the name of the variable on the left, followed by the assignment operator, followed by the expression calculating the new value, followed by a semicolon. For example: `outcome = 42;`

Generate a string representation of the value in a variable	Call the *ToString* method of the variable. For example:
	
	`int intVar = 42;`
	`string stringVar = intVar.ToString();`

Convert a string to an int	Call the *System.Int32.Parse* method. For example:
	
	`string stringVar = "42";`
	`int intVar = System.Int32.Parse(stringVar);`

Override the precedence of an operator	Use parentheses in the expression to force the order of evaluation. For example: `(3 + 4) * 5`
Assign the same value to several variables	Use an assignment statement that lists all the variables. For example: `myInt4 = myInt3 = myInt2 = myInt = 10;`
Increment or decrement a variable	Use the ++ or -- operator. For example: `count++;`

CHAPTER 3

Writing methods and applying scope

After completing this chapter, you will be able to:

- Declare and call methods.

- Pass information to a method.

- Return information from a method.

- Define local and class scope.

- Use the integrated debugger to step into and out of methods as they run.

In Chapter 2, "Working with variables, operators, and expressions," you learned how to declare variables, how to create expressions using operators, and how precedence and associativity control the way in which expressions containing multiple operators are evaluated. In this chapter, you'll learn about methods. You'll see how to declare and call methods, how to use arguments and parameters to pass information to a method, and how to return information from a method by using a return statement. You'll also see how to step into and out of methods by using the Microsoft Visual Studio 2015 integrated debugger. This information is useful when you need to trace the execution of your methods if they do not work quite as you expect. Finally, you'll learn how to declare methods that take optional parameters and how to invoke methods by using named arguments.

Creating methods

A *method* is a named sequence of statements. If you have previously programmed by using a language such as C, C++, or Microsoft Visual Basic, you will see that a method is similar to a function or a subroutine. A method has a name and a body. The method name should be a meaningful identifier that indicates the overall purpose of the method (*calculateIncomeTax*, for example). The method body contains the actual statements to be run when the method is called. Additionally, methods can be given some data for processing and can return information, which is usually the result of the processing. Methods are a fundamental and powerful mechanism.

Declaring a method

The syntax for declaring a C# method is as follows:

```
returnType methodName ( parameterList )
{
    // method body statements go here
}
```

The following is a description of the elements that make up a declaration:

- The *returnType* is the name of a type and specifies the kind of information the method returns as a result of its processing. This can be any type, such as *int* or *string*. If you're writing a method that does not return a value, you must use the keyword *void* in place of the return type.

- The *methodName* is the name used to call the method. Method names follow the same identifier rules as variable names. For example, *addValues* is a valid method name, whereas *add$Values* is not. For now, you should follow the camelCase convention for method names; for example, *displayCustomer*.

- The *parameterList* is optional and describes the types and names of the information that you can pass into the method for it to process. You write the parameters between opening and closing parentheses, ( ), as though you're declaring variables, with the name of the type followed by the name of the parameter. If the method you're writing has two or more parameters, you must separate them with commas.

- The method body statements are the lines of code that are run when the method is called. They are enclosed between opening and closing braces, { }.

> **Important** If you program in C, C++, and Visual Basic, you should note that C# does not support global methods. You must write all your methods inside a class; otherwise, your code will not compile.

Here's the definition of a method called *addValues* that returns an *int* result and has two *int* parameters, *leftHandSide* and *rightHandSide*:

```
int addValues(int leftHandSide, int rightHandSide)
{
    // ...
    // method body statements go here
    // ...
}
```

> **Note** You must explicitly specify the types of any parameters and the return type of a method. You cannot use the *var* keyword.

Here's the definition of a method called *showResult* that does not return a value and has a single *int* parameter, called *answer*:

```
void showResult(int answer)
{
    // ...
}
```

Notice the use of the keyword *void* to indicate that the method does not return anything.

> **Important** If you're familiar with Visual Basic, notice that C# does not use different keywords to distinguish between a method that returns a value (a function) and a method that does not return a value (a procedure or subroutine). You must always specify either a return type or *void*.

Returning data from a method

If you want a method to return information (that is, its return type is not *void*), you must include a *return* statement at the end of the processing in the method body. A *return* statement consists of the keyword *return* followed by an expression that specifies the returned value and a semicolon. The type of the expression must be the same as the type specified by the method declaration. For example, if a method returns an *int*, the *return* statement must return an *int*; otherwise, your program will not compile. Here is an example of a method with a *return* statement:

```
int addValues(int leftHandSide, int rightHandSide)
{
    // ...
    return leftHandSide + rightHandSide;
}
```

The *return* statement is usually positioned at the end of the method because it causes the method to finish, and control returns to the statement that called the method, as described later in this chapter. Any statements that occur after the *return* statement are not executed (although the compiler warns you about this problem if you place statements after the *return* statement).

If you don't want your method to return information (that is, its return type is *void*), you can use a variation of the *return* statement to cause an immediate exit from the method. You write the keyword *return* and follow it immediately by a semicolon. For example:

```
void showResult(int answer)
{
    // display the answer
    Console.WriteLine($"The answer is {answer}");
    return;
}
```

If your method does not return anything, you can also omit the *return* statement because the method finishes automatically when execution arrives at the closing brace at the end of the method. Although this practice is common, it is not always considered good style.

Using expression-bodied methods

Some methods can be very simple, performing a single task or returning the results of a calculation without involving any additional logic. C# supports a simplified form for methods that comprise a single expression. These methods can still take parameters and return values, and they operate in the same way as the methods that you have seen so far. The following code examples show simplified versions of the *addValues* and *showResult* methods written as expression-bodied methods:

```
int addValues(int leftHandSide, int rightHandSide) => leftHandSide + rightHandSide;

void showResult(int answer) => Console.WriteLine($"The answer is {answer}");
```

The main differences are the use of the => operator to reference the expression that forms the body of the method and the absence of a *return* statement. The value of the expression is used as the return value; if the expression does not return a value, then the method is void.

There is actually no difference in functionality between using an ordinary method and an expression-bodied method—an expression-bodied method is merely a syntactic convenience. However, you will see examples later in the book where expression-bodied methods can clarify a program by removing lots of extraneous { and } characters, making the code easier to read.

In the following exercise, you will examine another version of the MathsOperators project from Chapter 2. This version has been improved by the careful use of some small methods. Dividing code in this way helps to make it easier to understand and more maintainable.

Examine method definitions

1. Start Visual Studio 2015 if it is not already running.

2. Open the Methods project, which is in the \Microsoft Press\VCSBS\Chapter 3\Methods folder in your Documents folder.

3. On the Debug menu, click Start Debugging.

4. Visual Studio 2015 builds and runs the application. It should look the same as the application from Chapter 2. Refamiliarize yourself with the application and how it works and then return to Visual Studio. On the Debug menu, click Stop Debugging.

5. Display the code for MainPage.xaml.cs in the Code and Text Editor window (in Solution Explorer, expand the MainPage.xaml file and then double-click MainPage.xaml.cs).

6. In the Code and Text Editor window, locate the *addValues* method, which looks like this:

    ```
    private int addValues(int leftHandSide, int rightHandSide)
    ```

```
        {
            expression.Text = $"{leftHandSide} + {rightHandSide}";
            return leftHandSide + rightHandSide;
        }
```

> **Note** For the moment, don't worry about the *private* keyword at the start of the definition of this method; you will learn what this keyword means in Chapter 7, "Creating and managing classes and objects."

The *addValues* method contains two statements. The first statement displays the calculation being performed in the *expression* box on the form.

The second statement uses the *int* version of the + operator to add the values of the *leftHandSide* and *rightHandSide int* variables, and then returns the result of this operation. Remember that adding two *int* values together creates another *int* value, so the return type of the *addValues* method is *int*.

If you look at the methods *subtractValues, multiplyValues, divideValues,* and *remainderValues,* you will see that they follow a similar pattern.

7. In the Code and Text Editor window, locate the *showResult* method, which looks like this:

```
private void showResult(int answer) => result.Text = answer.ToString();
```

This is an expression-bodied method that displays a string representation of the *answer* parameter in the *result* box. It does not return a value, so the type of this method is *void*.

> **Tip** There is no minimum length for a method. If a method helps to avoid repetition and makes your program easier to understand, the method is useful regardless of how small it is.
>
> There is also no maximum length for a method, but usually you want to keep your method code small enough to get the job done. If your method is more than one screen in length, consider breaking it into smaller methods for readability.

Calling methods

Methods exist to be called! You call a method by name to ask it to perform its task. If the method requires information (as specified by its parameters), you must supply the information requested. If the method returns information (as specified by its return type), you should arrange to capture this information somehow.

Specifying the method call syntax

The syntax of a C# method call is as follows:

```
result = methodName ( argumentList )
```

The following is a description of the elements that make up a method call:

- The *methodName* must exactly match the name of the method you're calling. Remember, C# is a case-sensitive language.

- The *result* = clause is optional. If specified, the variable identified by *result* contains the value returned by the method. If the method is *void* (that is, it does not return a value), you must omit the *result* = clause of the statement. If you don't specify the *result* = clause and the method does return a value, the method runs but the return value is discarded.

- The *argumentList* supplies the information that the method accepts. You must supply an argument for each parameter, and the value of each argument must be compatible with the type of its corresponding parameter. If the method you're calling has two or more parameters, you must separate the arguments with commas.

> **Important** You must include the parentheses in every method call, even when calling a method that has no arguments.

To clarify these points, take a look at the *addValues* method again:

```
int addValues(int leftHandSide, int rightHandSide)
{
    // ...
}
```

The *addValues* method has two *int* parameters, so you must call it with two comma-separated *int* arguments, such as this:

```
addValues(39, 3);      // okay
```

You can also replace the literal values 39 and 3 with the names of *int* variables. The values in those variables are then passed to the method as its arguments, like this:

```
int arg1 = 99;
int arg2 = 1;
addValues(arg1, arg2);
```

If you try to call *addValues* in some other way, you will probably not succeed for the reasons described in the following examples:

```
addValues;             // compile-time error, no parentheses
addValues();           // compile-time error, not enough arguments
addValues(39);         // compile-time error, not enough arguments
addValues("39", "3");  // compile-time error, wrong types for arguments
```

The *addValues* method returns an *int* value. You can use this *int* value wherever an *int* value can be used. Consider these examples:

```
int result = addValues(39, 3);      // on right-hand side of an assignment
showResult(addValues(39, 3));       // as argument to another method call
```

The following exercise continues with the Methods application. This time, you will examine some method calls.

Examine method calls

1. Return to the Methods project. (This project is already open in Visual Studio 2015 if you're continuing from the previous exercise. If you are not, open it from the \Microsoft Press\ VCSBS\Chapter 3\Methods folder in your Documents folder.)

2. Display the code for MainPage.xaml.cs in the Code and Text Editor window.

3. Locate the *calculateClick* method, and look at the first two statements of this method after the *try* statement and opening brace. (You will learn about *try* statements in Chapter 6, "Managing errors and exceptions.")

    These statements look like this:

    ```
    int leftHandSide = System.Int32.Parse(lhsOperand.Text);
    int rightHandSide = System.Int32.Parse(rhsOperand.Text);
    ```

    These two statements declare two *int* variables, called *leftHandSide* and *rightHandSide*. Notice the way in which the variables are initialized. In both cases, the *Parse* method of the *System.Int32* struct is called. (*System* is a namespace, and *Int32* is the name of the struct in this namespace. You will learn about structs in Chapter 9, "Creating value types with enumerations and structures.") You have seen this method before—it takes a single *string* parameter and converts it to an *int* value. These two lines of code take what the user has typed into the *lhsOperand* and *rhsOperand* text box controls on the form and converts it to *int* values.

4. Look at the fourth statement in the *calculateClick* method (after the *if* statement and another opening brace):

    ```
    calculatedValue = addValues(leftHandSide, rightHandSide);
    ```

    This statement calls the *addValues* method, passing the values of the *leftHandSide* and *rightHandSide* variables as its arguments. The value returned by the *addValues* method is stored in the *calculatedValue* variable.

5. Look at the next statement:

    ```
    showResult(calculatedValue);
    ```

    This statement calls the *showResult* method, passing the value in the *calculatedValue* variable as its argument. The *showResult* method does not return a value.

6. In the Code and Text Editor window, find the *showResult* method you looked at earlier.

    The only statement of this method is this:

```
result.Text = answer.ToString();
```

Notice that the *ToString* method call uses parentheses even though there are no arguments.

> **Tip** You can call methods belonging to other objects by prefixing the method with the name of the object. In the preceding example, the expression *answer.ToString()* calls the method named *ToString* belonging to the object called *answer*.

Applying scope

You create variables to hold values. You can create variables at various points in your applications. For example, the *calculateClick* method in the Methods project creates an *int* variable called *calculatedValue* and assigns it an initial value of zero, like this:

```
private void calculateClick(object sender, RoutedEventArgs e)
{
    int calculatedValue = 0;
    ...
}
```

This variable comes into existence at the point where it is defined, and subsequent statements in the *calculateClick* method can then use this variable. This is an important point: a variable can be used only after it has been created. When the method has finished, this variable disappears and cannot be used elsewhere.

When a variable can be accessed at a particular location in a program, the variable is said to be in *scope* at that location. The *calculatedValue* variable has method scope; it can be accessed throughout the *calculateClick* method but not outside that method. You can also define variables with different scope; for example, you can define a variable outside a method but within a class, and this variable can be accessed by any method within that class. Such a variable is said to have *class scope*.

To put it another way, the scope of a variable is simply the region of the program in which that variable is usable. Scope applies to methods as well as variables. The scope of an identifier (of a variable or method) is linked to the location of the declaration that introduces the identifier in the program, as you will learn next.

Defining local scope

The opening and closing braces that form the body of a method define the scope of the method. Any variables you declare inside the body of a method are scoped to that method; they disappear when the method ends and can be accessed only by code running in that method. These variables are called *local variables* because they are local to the method in which they are declared; they are not in scope in any other method.

The scope of local variables means that you cannot use them to share information between methods. Consider this example:

```
class Example
{
    void firstMethod()
    {
        int myVar;
        ...
    }
    void anotherMethod()
    {
        myVar = 42; // error - variable not in scope
        ...
    }
}
```

This code fails to compile because *anotherMethod* is trying to use the variable *myVar*, which is not in scope. The variable *myVar* is available only to statements in *firstMethod* that occur after the line of code that declares *myVar*.

Defining class scope

The opening and closing braces that form the body of a class define the scope of that class. Any variables you declare within the body of a class (but not within a method) are scoped to that class. The proper C# term for a variable defined by a class is *field*. As mentioned earlier, in contrast with local variables, you can use fields to share information between methods. Here is an example:

```
class Example
{
    void firstMethod()
    {
        myField = 42; // ok
        ...
    }
    void anotherMethod()
    {
        myField++; // ok
        ...
    }

    int myField = 0;
}
```

The variable *myField* is defined in the class but outside the methods *firstMethod* and *anotherMethod*. Therefore, *myField* has class scope and is available for use by all methods in that class.

There is one other point to notice about this example. In a method, you must declare a variable before you can use it. Fields are a little different. A method can use a field before the statement that defines the field—the compiler sorts out the details for you.

Overloading methods

If two identifiers have the same name and are declared in the same scope, they are said to be *overloaded*. Often an overloaded identifier is a bug that is trapped as a compile-time error. For example, if you declare two local variables with the same name in the same method, the compiler reports an error. Similarly, if you declare two fields with the same name in the same class, or two identical methods in the same class, you also get a compile-time error. This fact might seem hardly worth mentioning given that everything so far has turned out to be a compile-time error. However, there is a way that you can overload an identifier for a method that is both useful and important.

Consider the *WriteLine* method of the *Console* class. You have already used this method for writing a string to the screen. However, when you type *WriteLine* in the Code and Text Editor window when writing C# code, notice that Microsoft IntelliSense gives you 19 different options! Each version of the *WriteLine* method takes a different set of parameters; one version takes no parameters and simply outputs a blank line, another version takes a *bool* parameter and outputs a string representation of its value (*True* or *False*), yet another implementation takes a *decimal* parameter and outputs it as a string, and so on. At compile time, the compiler looks at the types of the arguments you are passing in and then arranges for your application to call the version of the method that has a matching set of parameters. Here is an example:

```
static void Main()
{
    Console.WriteLine("The answer is ");
    Console.WriteLine(42);
}
```

Overloading is primarily useful when you need to perform the same operation on different data types or varying groups of information. You can overload a method when the different implementations have different sets of parameters—that is, when they have the same name but a different number of parameters or when the types of the parameters differ. When you call a method, you supply a comma-separated list of arguments, and the number and type of the arguments are used by the compiler to select one of the overloaded methods. However, keep in mind that although you can overload the parameters of a method, you can't overload the return type of a method. In other words, you can't declare two methods with the same name that differ only in their return type. (The compiler is clever, but not that clever.)

Writing methods

In the following exercises, you'll create a method that calculates how much a consultant would charge for a given number of consultancy days at a fixed daily rate. You will start by developing the logic for the application and then use the Generate Method Stub Wizard to help you write the methods that are used by this logic. Next, you'll run these methods in a console application to get a feel for the program. Finally, you'll use the Visual Studio 2015 debugger to step into and out of the method calls as they run.

Develop the logic for the application

1. Using Visual Studio 2015, open the DailyRate project, which is in the \Microsoft Press\VCSBS\ Chapter 3\DailyRate folder in your Documents folder.

2. In Solution Explorer, in the DailyRate project, double-click the file Program.cs to display the code for the program in the Code and Text Editor window.

   This program is simply a test harness for you to try out your code. When the application starts running, it calls the *run* method. You add to the *run* method the code that you want to try. (The way in which the method is called requires an understanding of classes, which you look at in Chapter 7.)

3. Add the following statements shown in bold to the body of the *run* method, between the opening and closing braces:

```
void run()
{
    double dailyRate = readDouble("Enter your daily rate: ");
    int noOfDays = readInt("Enter the number of days: ");
    writeFee(calculateFee(dailyRate, noOfDays));
}
```

   The block of code you have just added to the *run* method calls the *readDouble* method (which you will write shortly) to ask the user for the daily rate for the consultant. The next statement calls the *readInt* method (which you will also write) to obtain the number of days. Finally, the *writeFee* method (to be written) is called to display the results on the screen. Notice that the value passed to *writeFee* is the value returned by the *calculateFee* method (the last one you will need to write), which takes the daily rate and the number of days and calculates the total fee payable.

> **Note** You have not yet written the *readDouble, readInt, writeFee*, and *calculateFee* methods, so IntelliSense does not display these methods when you type this code. Do not try to build the application yet—it will fail.

Write the methods by using the Generate Method Stub Wizard

1. In the Code and Text Editor window, in the *run* method, right-click the *readDouble* method call.

   A shortcut menu appears that contains useful commands for generating and editing code, as shown here:

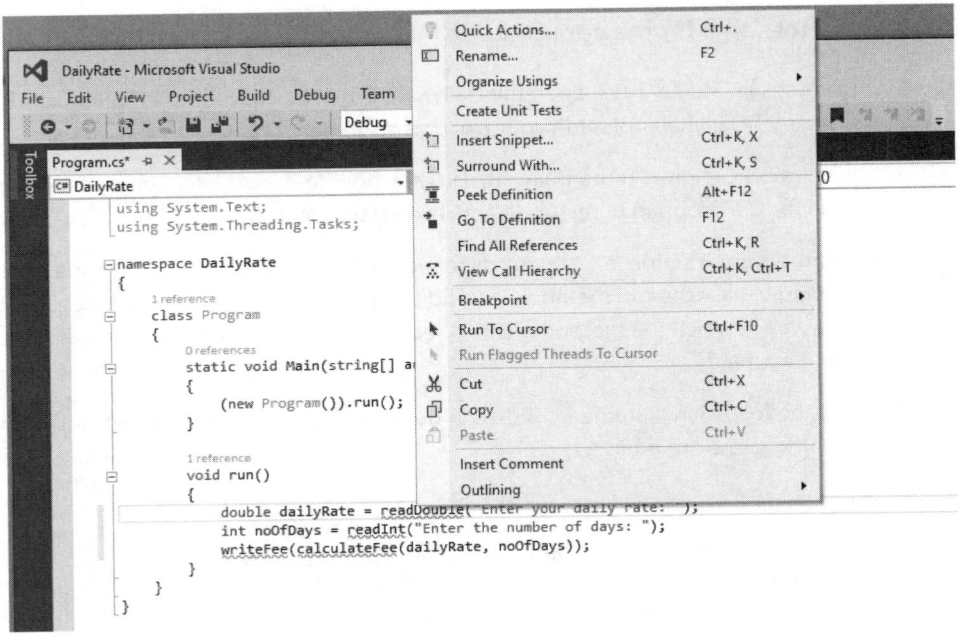

2. On the shortcut menu, click Quick Actions.

Visual Studio verifies that the *readDouble* method does not exist and displays a wizard that enables you to generate a stub for this method. Visual Studio examines the call to the *readDouble* method, ascertains the type of its parameters and return value, and suggests a default implementation, as shown in the following image:

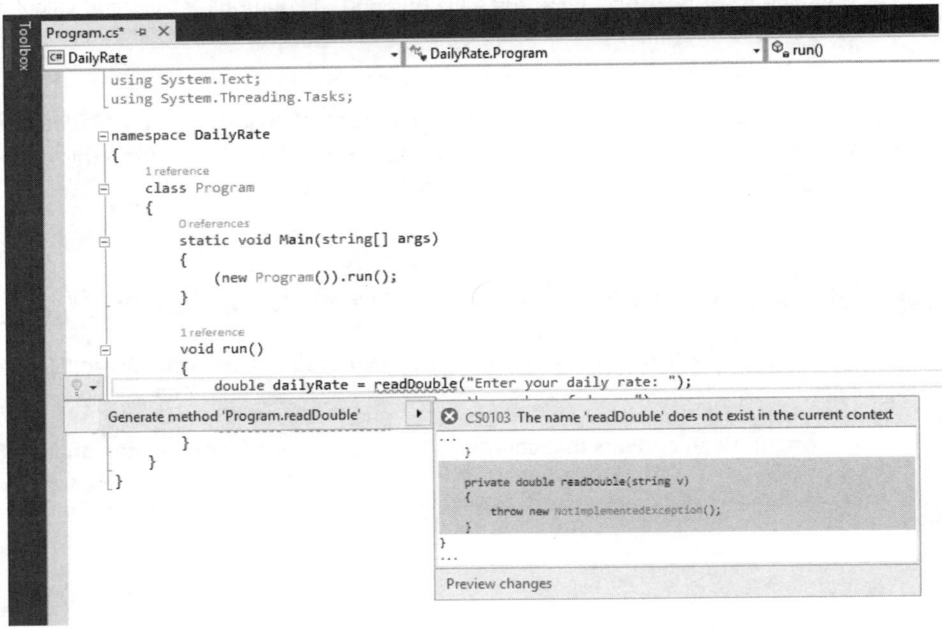

3. Click Generate Method 'Program.readDouble'. Visual Studio adds the following method to your code:

```
private double readDouble(string v)
{
    throw new NotImplementedException();
}
```

The new method is created with the *private* qualifier, which is described in Chapter 7. The body of the method currently just throws a *NotImplementedException* exception. (Exceptions are described in Chapter 6.) You replace the body with your own code in the next step.

4. Delete the *throw new NotImplementedException();* statement from the *readDouble* method and replace it with the following lines of code shown in bold:

```
private double readDouble(string v)
{
    Console.Write(v);
    string line = Console.ReadLine();
    return double.Parse(line);
}
```

This block of code displays the string in variable *v* to the screen. This variable is the string parameter passed in when the method is called; it contains the message prompting the user to type in the daily rate.

> **Note** The *Console.Write* method is similar to the *Console.WriteLine* statement that you have used in earlier exercises, except that it does not output a newline character after the message.

The user types a value, which is read into a *string* using the *ReadLine* method and converted to a *double* using the *double.Parse* method. The result is passed back as the return value of the method call.

> **Note** The *ReadLine* method is the companion method to *WriteLine*; it reads user input from the keyboard, finishing when the user presses the Enter key. The text typed by the user is passed back as the return value. The text is returned as a string value.

5. In the *run* method, right-click the call to the *readInt* method, click Quick Actions, and then click Generate Method 'Program.readInt'.

The *readInt* method is generated like this:

```
private int readInt(string v)
{
    throw new NotImplementedException();
}
```

6. Replace the *throw new NotImplementedException();* statement in the body of the *readInt* method with the following code shown in bold:

```
private int readInt(string v)
{
    Console.Write(v);
    string line = Console.ReadLine();
    return int.Parse(line);
}
```

This block of code is similar to the code for the *readDouble* method. The only difference is that the method returns an *int* value, so the *string* typed by the user is converted to a number using the *int.Parse* method.

7. Right-click the call to the *calculateFee* method in the *run* method, click Quick Actions, and then click Generate Method 'Program.calculateFee'.

The *calculateFee* method is generated like this:

```
private object calculateFee(double dailyRate, int noOfDays)
{
    throw new NotImplementedException();
}
```

Notice in this case that Visual Studio uses the names of the arguments passed in to generate names for the parameters. (You can, of course, change the parameter names if they are not suitable.) What is more intriguing is the type returned by the method, which is *object*. Visual Studio is unable to determine exactly which type of value should be returned by the method from the context in which it is called. The *object* type just means a "thing," and you should change it to the type you require when you add the code to the method. Chapter 7 covers the *object* type in greater detail.

8. Change the definition of the *calculateFee* method so that it returns a *double*, as shown in bold type here:

```
private double calculateFee(double dailyRate, int noOfDays)
{
    throw new NotImplementedException();
}
```

9. Replace the body of the *calculateFee* method and change it to an expression-bodied method with the following expression shown in bold. This statement calculates the fee payable by multiplying the two parameters together:

```
private double calculateFee(double dailyRate, int noOfDays) => dailyRate * noOfDays;
```

10. Right-click the call to the *writeFee* method in the *run* method, click Quick Actions, and then click Generate Method 'Program.writeFee'.

Notice that Visual Studio uses the definition of the *writeFee* method to work out that its parameter should be a *double*. Also, the method call does not use a return value, so the type of the method is *void*:

```
private void writeFee(double v)
{
    ...
}
```

> **Tip** If you feel sufficiently comfortable with the syntax, you can also write methods by typing them directly into the Code and Text Editor window. You do not always have to use the Generate menu option.

11. Replace the code in the body of the *writeFee* method with the following statement, which calculates the fee and adds a 10 percent commission before displaying the result. Again, notice that this is now an expression-bodied method:

```
private void writeFee(double v) => Console.WriteLine($"The consultant's fee is: {v *
1.1}");
```

12. On the Build menu, click Build Solution.

Refactoring code

A very useful feature of Visual Studio 2015 is the ability to refactor code.

Occasionally, you will find yourself writing the same (or similar) code in more than one place in an application. When this occurs, highlight and right-click the block of code you have just typed, click Quick Actions, and then click Extract Method. The selected code is moved to a new method named *NewMethod*. The Extract Method Wizard is also able to determine whether the method should take any parameters and return a value. After the method has been generated, you should change its name (by overtyping) to something meaningful and also change the statement that has been generated to call this method with the new name.

Test the program

1. On the Debug menu, click Start Without Debugging.

Visual Studio 2015 builds the program and then runs it. A console window appears.

2. At the Enter Your Daily Rate prompt, type **525**, and then press Enter.

3. At the Enter The Number of Days prompt, type **17**, and then press Enter.

The program writes the following message to the console window:

```
The consultant's fee is: 9817.5
```

4. Press the Enter key to close the application and return to Visual Studio 2015.

In the next exercise, you'll use the Visual Studio 2015 debugger to run your program in slow motion. You'll see when each method is called (which is referred to as *stepping into the method*) and then see how each *return* statement transfers control back to the caller (also known as *stepping out of the method*). While you are stepping into and out of methods, you can use the tools on the Debug toolbar. However, the same commands are also available on the Debug menu when an application is running in debug mode.

Step through the methods by using the Visual Studio 2015 debugger

1. In the Code and Text Editor window, find the *run* method.

2. Move the cursor to the first statement in the *run* method:

   ```
   double dailyRate = readDouble("Enter your daily rate: ");
   ```

3. Right-click anywhere on this line, and then click Run To Cursor.

   The program starts, runs until it reaches the first statement in the *run* method, and then pauses. A yellow arrow in the left margin of the Code and Text Editor window indicates the current statement, and the statement itself is highlighted with a yellow background.

```
Program.cs  ⊟ ✕
C# DailyRate                                              ▾  ⚛ DailyRate.Program

    ⊟namespace DailyRate
     {
         1 reference
     ⊟   class Program
         {
             0 references
     ⊟       static void Main(string[] args)
             {
                 (new Program()).run();
             }

             1 reference
     ⊟       void run()
             {
  ⇨            double dailyRate = readDouble("Enter your daily rate: ");
                 int noOfDays = readInt("Enter the number of days: ");
                 writeFee(calculateFee(dailyRate, noOfDays));
             }

             1 reference
     ⊟       private void writeFee(double v)
             {
                 Console.WriteLine($"The consultant's fee is: {v * 1.1}");
             }
         }
100 %  ▾
```

4. On the View menu, point to Toolbars, and then ensure that the Debug toolbar is selected.

   If it was not already visible, the Debug toolbar opens. It might appear docked with the other toolbars. If you cannot see the toolbar, try using the Toolbars command on the View menu to hide it, and look to see which buttons disappear. Then display the toolbar again. The Debug toolbar looks like this:

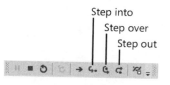

5. On the Debug toolbar, click the Step Into button. (This is the sixth button from the left on the Debug toolbar.)

This action causes the debugger to step into the method being called. The yellow cursor jumps to the opening brace at the start of the *readDouble* method.

6. Click Step Into again to advance the cursor to the first statement:

```
Console.Write(v);
```

 Tip You can also press F11 rather than repeatedly clicking Step Into on the Debug toolbar.

7. On the Debug toolbar, click Step Over. (This is the seventh button from the left.)

This action causes the method to execute the next statement without debugging it (stepping into it). This action is useful primarily if the statement calls a method but you don't want to step through every statement in that method. The yellow cursor moves to the second statement of the method, and the program displays the Enter Your Daily Rate prompt in a console window before returning to Visual Studio 2015. (The console window might be hidden behind Visual Studio.)

 Tip You can also press F10 rather than clicking Step Over on the Debug toolbar.

8. On the Debug toolbar, click Step Over again.

This time, the yellow cursor disappears, and the console window gets the focus because the program is executing the *Console.ReadLine* method and is waiting for you to type something.

9. Type **525** in the console window, and then press Enter.

Control returns to Visual Studio 2015. The yellow cursor appears on the third line of the method.

10. Hover the mouse over the reference to the *line* variable on either the second or third line of the method. (It doesn't matter which.)

A ScreenTip appears, displaying the current value of the *line* variable ("525"). You can use this feature to ensure that a variable has been set to an expected value while you step through methods.

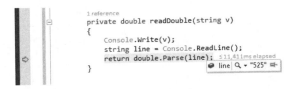

```csharp
1 reference
private double readDouble(string v)
{
    Console.Write(v);
    string line = Console.ReadLine();
    return double.Parse(line);
}
```

11. On the Debug toolbar, click Step Out. (This is the eighth button from the left.)

    This action causes the current method to continue to run uninterrupted to its end. The *readDouble* method finishes, and the yellow cursor is placed back at the first statement of the *run* method. This statement has now finished running.

    💡 **Tip** You can also press Shift+F11 instead of clicking Step Out on the Debug toolbar.

12. On the Debug toolbar, click Step Into.

    The yellow cursor moves to the second statement in the *run* method:

    ```csharp
    int noOfDays = readInt("Enter the number of days: ");
    ```

13. On the Debug toolbar, click Step Over.

    This time, you have chosen to run the method without stepping through it. The console window appears again, prompting you for the number of days.

14. In the console window, type **17**, and then press Enter.

    Control returns to Visual Studio 2015 (you might need to bring Visual Studio to the foreground). The yellow cursor moves to the third statement of the *run* method:

    ```csharp
    writeFee(calculateFee(dailyRate, noOfDays));
    ```

15. On the Debug toolbar, click Step Into.

    The yellow cursor jumps to the expression that defines the body of the *calculateFee* method. This method is called first, before *writeFee*, because the value returned by this method is used as the parameter to *writeFee*.

16. On the Debug toolbar, click Step Out.

    The *calculateFee* method call completes, and the yellow cursor jumps back to the third statement of the *run* method.

17. On the Debug toolbar, click Step Into.

This time, the yellow cursor jumps to the statement that defines the body of the *writeFee* method.

18. Place the mouse over the *v* parameter in the method definition.

   The value of *v*, 8925, is displayed in a ScreenTip.

19. On the Debug toolbar, click Step Out.

   The message "The consultant's fee is: 9817.5" is displayed in the console window. (You might need to bring the console window to the foreground to display it if it is hidden behind Visual Studio 2015.) The yellow cursor returns to the third statement in the *run* method.

20. On the toolbar, click Continue to cause the program to continue running without stopping at each statement.

> **Tip** If the Continue button is not visible, click the Add Or Remove Buttons drop-down menu that appears at the end of the Debug toolbar, and then select Continue. The Continue button should now appear. Alternatively, you can press F5 to continue running the application without debugging.

The application completes and finishes running. Notice that the Debug toolbar disappears when the application finishes—by default, the toolbar is displayed only when you are running an application in debug mode.

Using optional parameters and named arguments

You have seen that by defining overloaded methods, you can implement different versions of a method that take different parameters. When you build an application that uses overloaded methods, the compiler determines which specific instances of each method it should use to satisfy each method call. This is a common feature of many object-oriented languages, not just C#.

However, developers can use other languages and technologies for building Windows applications and components that do not follow these rules. A key feature of C# and other languages designed for the .NET Framework is the ability to interoperate with applications and components written with other technologies. One of the principal technologies that underpins many Windows applications and services running outside the .NET Framework is the Component Object Model (COM). In fact, the common language runtime (CLR) used by the .NET Framework is also heavily dependent on COM, as is the Windows Runtime of Windows 10. COM does not support overloaded methods; instead, it uses methods that can take optional parameters. To make it easier to incorporate COM libraries and components into a C# solution, C# also supports optional parameters.

Optional parameters are also useful in other situations. They provide a compact and simple solution when it is not possible to use overloading because the types of the parameters do not vary sufficiently to enable the compiler to distinguish between implementations. For example, consider the following method:

```
public void DoWorkWithData(int intData, float floatData, int moreIntData)
{
    ...
}
```

The *DoWorkWithData* method takes three parameters: two *int*s and a *float*. Now suppose that you want to provide an implementation of *DoWorkWithData* that takes only two parameters: *intData* and *floatData*. You can overload the method like this:

```
public void DoWorkWithData(int intData, float floatData)
{
    ...
}
```

If you write a statement that calls the *DoWorkWithData* method, you can provide either two or three parameters of the appropriate types, and the compiler uses the type information to determine which overload to call:

```
int arg1 = 99;
float arg2 = 100.0F;
int arg3 = 101;

DoWorkWithData(arg1, arg2, arg3); // Call overload with three parameters
DoWorkWithData(arg1, arg2);       // Call overload with two parameters
```

However, suppose that you want to implement two additional versions of *DoWorkWithData* that take only the first parameter and the third parameter. You might be tempted to try this:

```
public void DoWorkWithData(int intData)
{
    ...
}

public void DoWorkWithData(int moreIntData)
{
    ...
}
```

The issue here is that to the compiler, these two overloads appear identical. Your code will fail to compile and will instead generate the error "Type '*typename*' already defines a member called 'DoWorkWithData' with the same parameter types." To understand why this is so, think what would happen if this code were legal. Consider the following statements:

```
int arg1 = 99;
int arg3 = 101;

DoWorkWithData(arg1);
DoWorkWithData(arg3);
```

Which overload or overloads would the calls to *DoWorkWithData* invoke? Using optional parameters and named arguments can help to solve this problem.

Defining optional parameters

You specify that a parameter is optional when you define a method by providing a default value for the parameter. You indicate a default value by using the assignment operator. In the *optMethod* method shown next, the *first* parameter is mandatory because it does not specify a default value, but the *second* and *third* parameters are optional:

```
void optMethod(int first, double second = 0.0, string third = "Hello")
{
    ...
}
```

You must specify all mandatory parameters before any optional parameters.

You can call a method that takes optional parameters in the same way that you call any other method: you specify the method name and provide any necessary arguments. The difference with methods that take optional parameters is that you can omit the corresponding arguments, and the method will use the default value when it runs. In the example that follows, the first call to the *optMethod* method provides values for all three parameters. The second call specifies only two arguments, and these values are applied to the *first* and *second* parameters. The *third* parameter receives the default value of "Hello" when the method runs.

```
optMethod(99, 123.45, "World"); // Arguments provided for all three parameters
optMethod(100, 54.321);         // Arguments provided for first two parameters only
```

Passing named arguments

By default, C# uses the position of each argument in a method call to determine which parameter the argument applies to. Hence, the second example of the *OptMethod* method shown in the previous section passes the two arguments to the *first* and *second* parameters in the method because this is the order in which they occur in the method declaration. With C#, you can also specify parameters by name. This feature lets you pass the arguments in a different sequence. To pass an argument as a named parameter, you specify the name of the parameter, followed by a colon and the value to use. The following examples perform the same function as those shown in the previous section, except that the parameters are specified by name:

```
optMethod(first : 99, second : 123.45, third : "World");
optMethod(first : 100, second : 54.321);
```

Named arguments give you the ability to pass arguments in any order. You can rewrite the code that calls the *optMethod* method such as shown here:

```
optMethod(third : "World", second : 123.45, first : 99);
optMethod(second : 54.321, first : 100);
```

This feature also makes it possible for you to omit arguments. For example, you can call the *optMethod* method and specify values for the *first* and *third* parameters only and use the default value for the *second* parameter, like this:

```
optMethod(first : 99, third : "World");
```

Additionally, you can mix positional and named arguments. However, if you use this technique, you must specify all the positional arguments before the first named argument.

```
optMethod(99, third : "World");  // First argument is positional
```

Resolving ambiguities with optional parameters and named arguments

Using optional parameters and named arguments can result in some possible ambiguities in your code. You need to understand how the compiler resolves these ambiguities; otherwise, you might find your applications behaving in unexpected ways. Suppose that you define the *optMethod* method as an overloaded method, as shown in the following example:

```
void optMethod(int first, double second = 0.0, string third = "Hello")
{
    . . .
}

void optMethod(int first, double second = 1.0, string third = "Goodbye", int fourth = 100 )
{
    . . .
}
```

This is perfectly legal C# code that follows the rules for overloaded methods. The compiler can distinguish between the methods because they have different parameter lists. However, as demonstrated in the following example, a problem can arise if you attempt to call the *optMethod* method and omit some of the arguments corresponding to one or more of the optional parameters:

```
optMethod(1, 2.5, "World");
```

Again, this is perfectly legal code, but which version of the *optMethod* method does it run? The answer is the version that most closely matches the method call, so the code invokes the method that takes three parameters and not the version that takes four. That makes good sense, so consider this one:

```
optMethod(1, fourth : 101);
```

In this code, the call to *optMethod* omits arguments for the *second* and *third* parameters, but it specifies the *fourth* parameter by name. Only one version of *optMethod* matches this call, so this is not a problem. This next example will get you thinking, though:

```
optMethod(1, 2.5);
```

This time, neither version of the *optMethod* method exactly matches the list of arguments provided. Both versions of the *optMethod* method have optional parameters for the second, third, and fourth arguments. So, does this statement call the version of *optMethod* that takes three parameters and use the default value for the *third* parameter, or does it call the version of *optMethod* that takes four parameters and use the default value for the *third* and *fourth* parameters? The answer is that it does neither. This is an unresolvable ambiguity, and the compiler does not let you compile the application. The same situation arises with the same result if you try to call the *optMethod* method as shown in any of the following statements:

```
optMethod(1, third : "World");
optMethod(1);
optMethod(second : 2.5, first : 1);
```

In the final exercise in this chapter, you will practice implementing methods that take optional parameters and calling them by using named arguments. You will also test common examples of how the C# compiler resolves method calls that involve optional parameters and named arguments.

Define and call a method that takes optional parameters

1. Using Visual Studio 2015, open the DailyRate project, which is in the \Microsoft Press\VCSBS\ Chapter 3\DailyRate Using Optional Parameters folder in your Documents folder.

2. In Solution Explorer, in the DailyRate project, double-click the file Program.cs to display the code for the program in the Code and Text Editor window.

    This version of the application is empty apart from the *Main* method and the skeleton version of the *run* method.

3. In the *Program* class, after the *run* method, add the *calculateFee* method below the *run* method. This is the same version of the method that you implemented in the previous set of exercises, except that it takes two optional parameters with default values. The method also prints a message indicating the version of the *calculateFee* method that was called. (You will add overloaded implementations of this method in the following steps.)

    ```
    private double calculateFee(double dailyRate = 500.0, int noOfDays = 1)
    {
        Console.WriteLine("calculateFee using two optional parameters");
        return dailyRate * noOfDays;
    }
    ```

4. Add another implementation of the *calculateFee* method to the *Program* class, as shown in the code below. This version takes one optional parameter, called *dailyRate*, of type *double*. The body of the method calculates and returns the fee for a single day only.

    ```
    private double calculateFee(double dailyRate = 500.0)
    {
        Console.WriteLine("calculateFee using one optional parameter");

        int defaultNoOfDays = 1;
    ```

```
        return dailyRate * defaultNoOfDays;
    }
```

5. Add a third implementation of the *calculateFee* method to the *Program* class. This version takes no parameters and uses hardcoded values for the daily rate and number of days.

```
private double calculateFee()
{
    Console.WriteLine("calculateFee using hardcoded values");
    double defaultDailyRate = 400.0;
    int defaultNoOfDays = 1;
    return defaultDailyRate * defaultNoOfDays;
}
```

6. In the *run* method, add the following statements in bold that call *calculateFee* and display the results:

```
public void run()
{
    double fee = calculateFee();
    Console.WriteLine($"Fee is {fee}");
}
```

> **Tip** You can quickly view the definition of a method from the statement that invokes it. To do so, right-click the method call and then click Peek Definition. The following image shows the Peek Definition window for the *calculateFee* method.

> This feature is extremely useful if your code is split across multiple files, or even if it is in the same file but the file is very long.

7. On the Debug menu, click Start Without Debugging to build and run the program.

The program runs in a console window and displays the following messages:

```
calculateFee using hardcoded values
Fee is 400
```

The *run* method called the version of *calculateFee* that takes no parameters rather than either of the implementations that take optional parameters because that version most closely matches the method call.

Press any key to close the console window and return to Visual Studio.

8. In the *run* method, modify the statement that calls *calculateFee* to match the code shown in bold here:

```
public void run()
{
    double fee = calculateFee(650.0);
    Console.WriteLine($"Fee is {fee}");
}
```

9. On the Debug menu, click Start Without Debugging to build and run the program.

The program displays the following messages:

```
calculateFee using one optional parameter
Fee is 650
```

This time, the *run* method called the version of *calculateFee* that takes one optional parameter. As before, this is the version that most closely matches the method call.

Press any key to close the console window and return to Visual Studio.

10. In the *run* method, modify the statement that calls *calculateFee* again:

```
public void run()
{
    double fee = calculateFee(500.0, 3);
    Console.WriteLine($"Fee is {fee}");
}
```

11. On the Debug menu, click Start Without Debugging to build and run the program.

The program displays the following messages:

```
calculateFee using two optional parameters
Fee is 1500
```

As you might expect from the previous two cases, the *run* method called the version of *calculateFee* that takes two optional parameters.

Press any key to close the console window and return to Visual Studio.

12. In the *run* method, modify the statement that calls *calculateFee* and specify the *dailyRate* parameter by name:

```
public void run()
{
    double fee = calculateFee(dailyRate : 375.0);
    Console.WriteLine($"Fee is {fee}");
}
```

13. On the Debug menu, click Start Without Debugging to build and run the program.

The program displays the following messages:

```
calculateFee using one optional parameter
Fee is 375
```

As earlier, the *run* method calls the version of *calculateFee* that takes one optional parameter. Changing the code to use a named argument does not change the way in which the compiler resolves the method call in this example.

Press any key to close the console window and return to Visual Studio.

14. In the *run* method, modify the statement that calls *calculateFee* and specify the *noOfDays* parameter by name.

```
public void run()
{
    double fee = calculateFee(noOfDays : 4);
    Console.WriteLine($"Fee is {fee}");
}
```

15. On the Debug menu, click Start Without Debugging to build and run the program.

The program displays the following messages:

```
calculateFee using two optional parameters
Fee is 2000
```

This time, the *run* method called the version of *calculateFee* that takes two optional parameters. The method call has omitted the first parameter (*dailyRate*) and specified the second parameter by name. The version of the *calculateFee* method that takes two optional parameters is the only one that matches the call.

Press any key to close the console window and return to Visual Studio.

16. Modify the implementation of the *calculateFee* method that takes two optional parameters. Change the name of the first parameter to *theDailyRate* and update the *return* statement to match that shown in bold in the following code:

```
private double calculateFee(double theDailyRate = 500.0, int noOfDays = 1)
{
    Console.WriteLine("calculateFee using two optional parameters");
    return theDailyRate * noOfDays;
}
```

17. In the *run* method, modify the statement that calls *calculateFee* and specify the *theDailyRate* parameter by name.

```
public void run()
{
    double fee = calculateFee(theDailyRate : 375.0);
    Console.WriteLine("Fee is {fee}");
}
```

18. On the Debug menu, click Start Without Debugging to build and run the program.

The program displays the following messages:

```
calculateFee using two optional parameters
Fee is 375
```

The previous time that you specified the fee but not the daily rate (step 12), the *run* method called the version of *calculateFee* that takes one optional parameter. This time, the *run* method called the version of *calculateFee* that takes two optional parameters. In this case, using a named argument has changed the way in which the compiler resolves the method call. If you specify a named argument, the compiler compares the argument name to the names of the parameters specified in the method declarations and selects the method that has a parameter with a matching name. If you had specified the argument as aDailyRate: 375.0 in the call to the *calculateFee* method, the program would have failed to compile because no version of the method has a parameter that matches this name.

Press any key to close the console window and return to Visual Studio.

Summary

In this chapter, you learned how to define methods to implement a named block of code. You saw how to pass parameters into methods and how to return data from methods. You also saw how to call a method, pass arguments, and obtain a return value. You learned how to define overloaded methods with different parameter lists, and you saw how the scope of a variable determines where it can be accessed. Then, you used the Visual Studio 2015 debugger to step through code as it runs. Finally, you learned how to write methods that take optional parameters and how to call methods by using named parameters.

- If you want to continue to the next chapter, keep Visual Studio 2015 running and turn to Chapter 4, "Using decision statements."

- If you want to exit Visual Studio 2015 now, on the File menu, click Exit. If you see a Save dialog box, click Yes and save the project.

Quick reference

To	Do this

Declare a method	Write the method within a class. Specify the method name, parameter list, and return type, followed by the body of the method between braces. For example:
	
	`int addValues(int leftHandSide, int rightHandSide)`
	`{`
	` ... `
	`}`

Return a value from within a method	Write a *return* statement within the method. For example: `return leftHandSide + rightHandSide;`
Return from a method before the end of the method	Write a *return* statement within the method. For example: `return;`

Define an expression-bodied method	Use the => sequence followed by the expression that defines the body of the method and a closing semicolon. For example:
	
	`double calculateFee(double dailyRate, int noOfDays)`
	`   => dailyRate * noOfDays;`

Call a method	Write the name of the method followed by any arguments between parentheses. For example: `addValues(39, 3);`
Use the Generate Method Stub Wizard	Right-click a call to the method, and then click Generate Method Stub.
Display the Debug toolbar	On the View menu, point to Toolbars, and then click Debug.
Step into a method	On the Debug toolbar, click Step Into. or On the Debug menu, click Step Into.
Step out of a method	On the Debug toolbar, click Step Out. or On the Debug menu, click Step Out.

Specify an optional parameter to a method	Provide a default value for the parameter in the method declaration. For example:
	
	`void optMethod(int first, double second = 0.0,`
	`              string third = "Hello")`
	`{`
	` ... `
	`}`

Pass a method argument as a named parameter	Specify the name of the parameter in the method call. For example: `optMethod(first : 100, third : "World");`

CHAPTER 4

Using decision statements

After completing this chapter, you will be able to:

- Declare Boolean variables.

- Use Boolean operators to create expressions whose outcome is either true or false.

- Write *if* statements to make decisions based on the result of a Boolean expression.

- Write *switch* statements to make more complex decisions.

Chapter 3, "Writing methods and applying scope," shows how to group related statements into methods. It also demonstrates how to use parameters to pass information to a method and how to use *return* statements to pass information out of a method. Dividing a program into a set of discrete methods, each designed to perform a specific task or calculation, is a necessary design strategy. Many programs need to solve large and complex problems. Breaking up a program into methods helps you to understand these problems and focus on how to solve them, one piece at a time.

The methods in Chapter 3 are very straightforward, with each statement executing sequentially after the previous statement completes. However, to solve many real-world problems, you also need to be able to write code that selectively performs different actions and that takes different paths through a method depending on the circumstances. In this chapter, you'll learn how to accomplish this task.

Declaring Boolean variables

In the world of C# programming (unlike in the real world), everything is black or white, right or wrong, true or false. For example, if you create an integer variable called *x*, assign the value 99 to it, and then ask whether *x* contains the value 99, the answer is definitely true. If you ask if *x* is less than 10, the answer is definitely false. These are examples of *Boolean expressions*. A Boolean expression always evaluates to true or false.

Visual C# provides a data type called *bool*. A *bool* variable can hold one of two values: *true* or *false*. For example, the following three statements declare a *bool* variable called *areYouReady*, assign *true* to that variable, and then write its value to the console:

```
bool areYouReady;
areYouReady = true;
Console.WriteLine(areYouReady); // writes True to the console
```

Using Boolean operators

A Boolean operator is an operator that performs a calculation whose result is either true or false. C# has several very useful Boolean operators, the simplest of which is the *NOT* operator, represented by the exclamation point (!). The *!* operator negates a Boolean value, yielding the opposite of that value. In the preceding example, if the value of the variable *areYouReady* is true, the value of the expression *!areYouReady* is false.

Understanding equality and relational operators

Two Boolean operators that you will frequently use are equality (==) and inequality (!=). These are binary operators with which you can determine whether one value is the same as another value of the same type, yielding a Boolean result. The following table summarizes how these operators work, using an *int* variable called *age* as an example.

Operator	Meaning	Example	Outcome if age is 42
==	Equal to	age == 100	false
!=	Not equal to	age != 0	true

Don't confuse the *equality* operator == with the *assignment* operator =. The expression *x==y* compares *x* with *y* and has the value *true* if the values are the same. The expression *x=y* assigns the value of *y* to *x* and returns the value of *y* as its result.

Closely related to == and != are the *relational* operators. You use these operators to find out whether a value is less than or greater than another value of the same type. The following table shows how to use these operators.

Operator	Meaning	Example	Outcome if age is 42
<	Less than	age < 21	false
<=	Less than or equal to	age <= 18	false
>	Greater than	age > 16	true
>=	Greater than or equal to	age >= 30	true

Understanding conditional logical operators

C# also provides two other binary Boolean operators: the logical AND operator, which is represented by the && symbol, and the logical OR operator, which is represented by the || symbol. Collectively, these are known as the *conditional logical operators*. Their purpose is to combine two Boolean expressions or values into a single Boolean result. These operators are similar to the equality and relational operators in that the value of the expressions in which they appear is either true or false, but they differ in that the values on which they operate must also be either true or false.

The outcome of the && operator is *true* if and only if both of the Boolean expressions it's evaluating are *true*. For example, the following statement assigns the value *true* to *validPercentage* if and only if the value of *percent* is greater than or equal to 0 and the value of *percent* is less than or equal to 100:

```
bool validPercentage;
validPercentage = (percent >= 0) && (percent <= 100);
```

> **Tip** A common beginner's error is to try to combine the two tests by naming the *percent* variable only once, like this:
>
> ```
> percent >= 0 && <= 100 // this statement will not compile
> ```
>
> Using parentheses helps to avoid this type of mistake and also clarifies the purpose of the expression. For example, compare
>
> ```
> validPercentage = percent >= 0 && percent <= 100
> ```
>
> and
>
> ```
> validPercentage = (percent >= 0) && (percent <= 100)
> ```
>
> Both expressions return the same value because the precedence of the && operator is less than that of >= and <=. However, the second expression conveys its purpose in a more readable manner.

The outcome of the || operator is *true* if either of the Boolean expressions it evaluates is *true*. You use the || operator to determine whether any one of a combination of Boolean expressions is *true*. For example, the following statement assigns the value *true* to *invalidPercentage* if the value of *percent* is less than 0 or the value of *percent* is greater than 100:

```
bool invalidPercentage;
invalidPercentage = (percent < 0) || (percent > 100);
```

Short circuiting

The && and || operators both exhibit a feature called *short circuiting*. Sometimes, it is not necessary to evaluate both operands when ascertaining the result of a conditional logical expression. For example, if the left operand of the && operator evaluates to *false*, the result of the entire expression must be *false*, regardless of the value of the right operand. Similarly, if the value of the left operand of the || operator evaluates to *true*, the result of the entire expression must be *true*, irrespective of the value of the right operand. In these cases, the && and || operators bypass the evaluation of the right operand. Here are some examples:

```
(percent >= 0) && (percent <= 100)
```

In this expression, if the value of *percent* is less than 0, the Boolean expression on the left side of && evaluates to *false*. This value means that the result of the entire expression must be *false*, and the Boolean expression to the right of the && operator is not evaluated.

```
(percent < 0) || (percent > 100)
```

In this expression, if the value of *percent* is less than 0, the Boolean expression on the left side of || evaluates to *true*. This value means that the result of the entire expression must be *true,* and the Boolean expression to the right of the || operator is not evaluated.

If you carefully design expressions that use the conditional logical operators, you can boost the performance of your code by avoiding unnecessary work. Place simple Boolean expressions that can be evaluated easily on the left side of a conditional logical operator, and put more complex expressions on the right side. In many cases, you will find that the program does not need to evaluate the more complex expressions.

Summarizing operator precedence and associativity

The following table summarizes the precedence and associativity of all the operators you have learned about so far. Operators in the same category have the same precedence. The operators in categories higher up in the table take precedence over operators in categories lower down.

Category	Operators	Description	Associativity
Primary	()	Precedence override	Left
	++	Post-increment	
	--	Post-decrement	

Category	Operators	Description	Associativity
Unary	!	Logical NOT	Left
	+	Returns the value of the operand unchanged	
	–	Returns the value of the operand negated	
	++	Pre-increment	
	––	Pre-decrement	
Multiplicative	*	Multiply	Left
	/	Divide	
	%	Division remainder (modulus)	
Additive	+	Addition	Left
	–	Subtraction	
Relational	<	Less than	Left
	<=	Less than or equal to	
	>	Greater than	
	>=	Greater than or equal to	
Equality	==	Equal to	Left
	!=	Not equal to	
Conditional AND	&&	Conditional AND	Left
Conditional OR	||	Conditional OR	Left
Assignment	=	Assigns the right-hand operand to the left and returns the value that was assigned	Right

Notice that the && operator and the || operator have a different precedence: && is higher than ||.

Using *if* statements to make decisions

In a method, when you want to choose between executing two different statements depending on the result of a Boolean expression, you can use an *if* statement.

Understanding *if* statement syntax

The syntax of an *if* statement is as follows (*if* and *else* are C# keywords):

```
if ( booleanExpression )
    statement-1;
else
    statement-2;
```

If *booleanExpression* evaluates to *true*, *statement-1* runs; otherwise, *statement-2* runs. The *else* keyword and the subsequent *statement-2* are optional. If there is no *else* clause and the *booleanExpression* is *false*, execution continues with whatever code follows the *if* statement. Also, notice that the Boolean expression must be enclosed in parentheses; otherwise, the code will not compile.

For example, here's an *if* statement that increments a variable representing the second hand of a stopwatch. (Minutes are ignored for now.) If the value of the *seconds* variable is 59, it is reset to 0; otherwise, it is incremented by using the ++ operator:

```
int seconds;
...
if (seconds == 59)
    seconds = 0;
else
    seconds++;
```

Boolean expressions only, please!

The expression in an *if* statement must be enclosed in parentheses. Additionally, the expression must be a Boolean expression. In some other languages—notably C and C++—you can write an integer expression, and the compiler will silently convert the integer value to *true* (nonzero) or *false* (0). C# does not support this behavior, and the compiler reports an error if you write such an expression.

If you accidentally specify the assignment operator (=) instead of the equality test operator (==) in an *if* statement, the C# compiler recognizes your mistake and refuses to compile your code, such as in the following example:

```
int seconds;
...
if (seconds = 59)  // compile-time error
...
if (seconds == 59) // ok
```

Accidental assignments were another common source of bugs in C and C++ programs, which would silently convert the value assigned (59) to a Boolean expression (with anything nonzero considered to be true), with the result being that the code following the *if* statement would be performed every time.

Incidentally, you can use a Boolean variable as the expression for an *if* statement, although it must still be enclosed in parentheses, as shown in this example:

```
bool inWord;
...
if (inWord == true) // ok, but not commonly used
...
if (inWord)            // more common and considered better style
```

Using blocks to group statements

Notice that the syntax of the *if* statement shown earlier specifies a single statement after the *if (booleanExpression)* and a single statement after the *else* keyword. Sometimes, you'll want to perform more than one statement when a Boolean expression is true. You could group the statements inside a new method and then call the new method, but a simpler solution is to group the statements inside a *block*. A block is simply a sequence of statements grouped between an opening brace and a closing brace.

In the following example, two statements that reset the *seconds* variable to 0 and increment the *minutes* variable are grouped inside a block, and the entire block executes if the value of *seconds* is equal to 59:

```
int seconds = 0;
int minutes = 0;
...
if (seconds == 59)
{
    seconds = 0;
    minutes++;
}
else
{
    seconds++;
}
```

> **Important** If you omit the braces, the C# compiler associates only the first statement (*seconds = 0;*) with the *if* statement. The subsequent statement (*minutes++;*) will not be recognized by the compiler as part of the *if* statement when the program is compiled. Furthermore, when the compiler reaches the *else* keyword, it will not associate it with the previous *if* statement; instead, it will report a syntax error. Therefore, it is good practice to always define the statements for each branch of an *if* statement within a block, even if a block consists of only a single statement. It might save you some grief later if you want to add additional code.

A block also starts a new scope. You can define variables inside a block, but they will disappear at the end of the block. The following code fragment illustrates this point:

```
if (...)
{
    int myVar = 0;
    ... // myVar can be used here
} // myVar disappears here
else
{
    // myVar cannot be used here
    ...
}
// myVar cannot be used here
```

Cascading *if* statements

You can nest *if* statements inside other *if* statements. In this way, you can chain together a sequence of Boolean expressions, which are tested one after the other until one of them evaluates to *true*. In the following example, if the value of *day* is 0, the first test evaluates to *true* and *dayName* is assigned the string *"Sunday"*. If the value of *day* is not 0, the first test fails and control passes to the *else* clause, which runs the second *if* statement and compares the value of *day* with 1. The second *if* statement executes only if the first test is *false*. Similarly, the third *if* statement executes only if the first and second tests are *false*.

```
if (day == 0)
{
    dayName = "Sunday";
}
else if (day == 1)
{
    dayName = "Monday";
}
else if (day == 2)
{
    dayName = "Tuesday";
}
else if (day == 3)
{
    dayName = "Wednesday";
}
else if (day == 4)
{
    dayName = "Thursday";
}
else if (day == 5)
{
    dayName = "Friday";
}
else if (day == 6)
{
    dayName = "Saturday";
}
else
{
    dayName = "unknown";
}
```

In the following exercise, you'll write a method that uses a cascading *if* statement to compare two dates.

Write *if* statements

1. Start Microsoft Visual Studio 2015 if it is not already running.

2. Open the Selection project, which is located in the \Microsoft Press\VCSBS\Chapter 4\ Selection folder in your Documents folder.

3. On the Debug menu, click Start Debugging.

Visual Studio 2015 builds and runs the application. The form displays two *DatePicker* controls, called *firstDate* and *secondDate*. Both controls display the current date.

4. Click Compare.

The following text appears in the text box in the lower half of the window:

```
firstDate == secondDate : False
firstDate != secondDate : True
firstDate <  secondDate : False
firstDate <= secondDate : False
firstDate >  secondDate : True
firstDate >= secondDate : True
```

The Boolean expression, *firstDate == secondDate*, should be *true* because both *firstDate* and *secondDate* are set to the current date. In fact, only the less-than operator and the greater-than-or-equal-to operator seem to be working correctly. The following image shows the application running.

5. Return to Visual Studio 2015. On the Debug menu, click Stop Debugging.

6. Display the code for the MainPage.xaml.cs file in the Code and Text Editor window.

7. Locate the *compareClick* method, which should look like this:

```
private void compareClick(object sender, RoutedEventArgs e)
{
    int diff = dateCompare(firstDate.Date.LocalDateTime, secondDate.Date.LocalDateTime);
    info.Text = "";
    show("firstDate == secondDate", diff == 0);
    show("firstDate != secondDate", diff != 0);
    show("firstDate < secondDate", diff < 0);
    show("firstDate <= secondDate", diff <= 0);
    show("firstDate > secondDate", diff > 0);
    show("firstDate >= secondDate", diff >= 0);
}
```

This method runs whenever the user clicks the Compare button on the form. The expressions *firstDate.Date.LocalDateTime* and *secondDate.Date.LocalDateTime* hold *DateTime* values; they represent the dates displayed in the *firstDate* and *secondDate* controls on the form elsewhere in the application. The *DateTime* data type is just another data type, like *int* or *float*, except that it contains subelements with which you can access the individual pieces of a date, such as the year, month, or day.

The *compareClick* method passes the two *DateTime* values to the *dateCompare* method. The purpose of this method is to compare dates and return the *int* value 0 if they are the same, −1 if the first date is less than the second, and +1 if the first date is greater than the second. A date is considered greater than another date if it comes after it chronologically. You will examine the *dateCompare* method in the next step.

The *show* method displays the results of the comparison in the *info* text box control in the lower half of the form.

8. Locate the *dateCompare* method, which should look like this:

```
private int dateCompare(DateTime leftHandSide, DateTime rightHandSide)
{
    // TO DO
    return 42;
}
```

This method currently returns the same value whenever it is called—rather than 0, −1, or +1— regardless of the values of its parameters. This explains why the application is not working as expected. You need to implement the logic in this method to compare two dates correctly.

9. Remove the *// TO DO* comment and the *return* statement from the *dateCompare* method.

10. Add the following statements shown in bold to the body of the *dateCompare* method:

```
private int dateCompare(DateTime leftHandSide, DateTime rightHandSide)
{
    int result = 0;

    if (leftHandSide.Year < rightHandSide.Year)
    {
        result = -1;
    }
    else if (leftHandSide.Year > rightHandSide.Year)
```

```
            {
                result = 1;
            }
        }
```

Note Don't try to build the application yet. The *dateCompare* method is not complete and the build will fail.

If the expression *leftHandSide.Year < rightHandSide.Year* is *true*, the date in *leftHandSide* must be earlier than the date in *rightHandSide*, so the program sets the *result* variable to *-1*. Otherwise, if the expression *leftHandSide.Year > rightHandSide.Year* is *true*, the date in *leftHandSide* must be later than the date in *rightHandSide*, and the program sets the *result* variable to *1*.

If the expression *leftHandSide.Year < rightHandSide.Year* is *false* and the expression *leftHandSide.Year > rightHandSide.Year* is also *false*, the *Year* property of both dates must be the same, so the program needs to compare the months in each date.

11. Add the following statements shown in bold to the body of the *dateCompare* method. Type them after the code you entered in the preceding step:

```
private int dateCompare(DateTime leftHandSide, DateTime rightHandSide)
{
    ...
    else if (leftHandSide.Month < rightHandSide.Month)
    {
        result = -1;
    }
    else if (leftHandSide.Month > rightHandSide.Month)
    {
        result = 1;
    }
}
```

These statements compare months following a logic similar to that used to compare years in the preceding step.

If the expression *leftHandSide.Month < rightHandSide.Month* is *false* and the expression *leftHandSide.Month > rightHandSide.Month* is also *false*, the *Month* property of both dates must be the same, so the program finally needs to compare the days in each date.

12. Add the following statements to the body of the *dateCompare* method after the code you entered in the preceding two steps:

```
private int dateCompare(DateTime leftHandSide, DateTime rightHandSide)
{
    ...
    else if (leftHandSide.Day < rightHandSide.Day)
    {
        result = -1;
    }
```

```
    else if (leftHandSide.Day > rightHandSide.Day)
    {
        result = 1;
    }
    else
    {
        result = 0;
    }

    return result;
}
```

You should recognize the pattern in this logic by now.

If *leftHandSide.Day* < *rightHandSide.Day* and *leftHandSide.Day* > *rightHandSide.Day* both are *false*, the value in the *Day* properties in both variables must be the same. The *Month* values and the *Year* values must also be identical, respectively, for the program logic to have reached this point, so the two dates must be the same, and the program sets the value of *result* to *0*.

The final statement returns the value stored in the *result* variable.

13. On the Debug menu, click Start Debugging.

The application is rebuilt and runs.

14. Click Compare.

The following text appears in the text box:

```
firstDate == secondDate : True
firstDate != secondDate : False
firstDate <  secondDate: False
firstDate <= secondDate: True
firstDate >  secondDate: False
firstDate >= secondDate: True
```

These are the correct results for identical dates.

15. Use the *DatePicker* controls to select a later date for the second date and then click Compare.

The following text appears in the text box:

```
firstDate == secondDate: False
firstDate != secondDate: True
firstDate <  secondDate: True
firstDate <= secondDate: True
firstDate >  secondDate: False
firstDate >= secondDate: False
```

Again, these are the correct results when the first date is earlier than the second date.

16. Test some other dates, and verify that the results are as you would expect. Return to Visual Studio 2015 and stop debugging when you have finished.

Comparing dates in real-world applications

Now that you have seen how to use a rather long and complicated series of *if* and *else* statements, I should mention that this is not the technique you would employ to compare dates in a real-world application. If you look at the *dateCompare* method from the preceding exercise, you will see that the two parameters, *leftHandSide* and *rightHandSide*, are *DateTime* values. The logic you have written compares only the date part of these parameters, but they also contain a time element that you have not considered (or displayed). For two *DateTime* values to be considered equal, they should have not only the same date but also the same time. Comparing dates and times is such a common operation that the *DateTime* type actually has a built-in method called *Compare* for doing just that: it takes two *DateTime* arguments and compares them, returning a value indicating whether the first argument is less than the second, in which case the result will be negative; whether the first argument is greater than the second, in which case the result will be positive; or whether both arguments represent the same date and time, in which case the result will be 0.

Using *switch* statements

Sometimes when you write a cascading *if* statement, each of the *if* statements look similar because they all evaluate an identical expression. The only difference is that each *if* compares the result of the expression with a different value. For example, consider the following block of code that uses an *if* statement to examine the value in the *day* variable and work out which day of the week it is:

```
if (day == 0)
{
    dayName = "Sunday";
}
else if (day == 1)
{
    dayName = "Monday";
}
else if (day == 2)
{
    dayName = "Tuesday";
}
else if (day == 3)
{
    ...
}
else
{
    dayName = "Unknown";
}
```

Often in these situations, you can rewrite the cascading *if* statement as a *switch* statement to make your program more efficient and more readable.

Understanding *switch* statement syntax

The syntax of a *switch* statement is as follows (*switch, case,* and *default* are keywords):

```
switch ( controllingExpression )
{
    case constantExpression :
        statements
        break;
    case constantExpression :
        statements
        break;

    ...
    default :
        statements
        break;
}
```

The *controllingExpression*, which must be enclosed in parentheses, is evaluated once. Control then jumps to the block of code identified by the *constantExpression* whose value is equal to the result of the *controllingExpression*. (The *constantExpression* identifier is also called a *case label.*) Execution runs as far as the *break* statement, at which point the *switch* statement finishes and the program continues at the first statement that follows the closing brace of the *switch* statement. If none of the *constantExpression* values is equal to the value of the *controllingExpression*, the statements below the optional *default* label run.

> **Note** Each *constantExpression* value must be unique so that the *controllingExpression* will match only one of them. If the value of the *controllingExpression* does not match any *constantExpression* value and there is no *default* label, program execution continues with the first statement that follows the closing brace of the *switch* statement.

So, you can rewrite the previous cascading *if* statement as the following *switch* statement:

```
switch (day)
{
    case 0 :
        dayName = "Sunday";
        break;
    case 1 :
        dayName = "Monday";
        break;
    case 2 :
        dayName = "Tuesday";
        break;
    ...
    default :
        dayName = "Unknown";
        break;
}
```

Following the *switch* statement rules

The *switch* statement is very useful, but unfortunately, you can't always use it when you might like to. Any *switch* statement you write must adhere to the following rules:

- You can use *switch* only on certain data types, such as *int*, *char*, or *string*. With any other types (including *float* and *double*), you must use an *if* statement.

- The *case* labels must be constant expressions, such as 42 if the *switch* data type is an *int*, '4' if the *switch* data type is a *char*, or "42" if the *switch* data type is a *string*. If you need to calculate your *case* label values at run time, you must use an *if* statement.

- The *case* labels must be unique expressions. In other words, two *case* labels cannot have the same value.

- You can specify that you want to run the same statements for more than one value by providing a list of *case* labels and no intervening statements, in which case the code for the final label in the list is executed for all cases in that list. However, if a label has one or more associated statements, execution cannot fall through to subsequent labels; in this case, the compiler generates an error. The following code fragment illustrates these points:

```
switch (trumps)
{
    case Hearts :
    case Diamonds :        // Fall-through allowed - no code between labels
        color = "Red";     // Code executed for Hearts and Diamonds
        break;
    case Clubs :
        color = "Black";
    case Spades :          // Error - code between labels
        color = "Black";
        break;
}
```

> **Note** The *break* statement is the most common way to stop fall-through, but you can also use a *return* statement to exit from the method containing the *switch* statement or a *throw* statement to generate an exception and abort the *switch* statement. The *throw* statement is described in Chapter 6, "Managing errors and exceptions."

switch fall-through rules

Because you cannot accidentally fall through from one *case* label to the next if there is any intervening code, you can freely rearrange the sections of a *switch* statement without affecting its meaning (including the *default* label, which by convention is usually—but does not have to be—placed as the last label).

C and C++ programmers should note that the *break* statement is mandatory for every case in a *switch* statement (even the default case). This requirement is a good thing—it is common in C or C++ programs to forget the *break* statement, allowing execution to fall through to the next label and leading to bugs that are difficult to spot.

If you really want to, you can mimic C/C++ fall-through in C# by using a *goto* statement to go to the following *case* or *default* label. Using *goto* in general is not recommended, though, and this book does not show you how to do it.

In the following exercise, you will complete a program that reads the characters of a string and maps each character to its XML representation. For example, the left angle bracket character (<) has a special meaning in XML (it's used to form elements). If you have data that contains this character, it must be translated into the text entity *<* so that an XML processor knows that it is data and not part of an XML instruction. Similar rules apply to the right angle bracket (>), ampersand (&), single quotation mark ('), and double quotation mark (") characters. You will write a *switch* statement that tests the value of the character and traps the special XML characters as *case* labels.

Write *switch* statements

1. Start Visual Studio 2015 if it is not already running.

2. Open the SwitchStatement project, which is located in the \Microsoft Press\VCSBS\Chapter 4\SwitchStatement folder in your Documents folder.

3. On the Debug menu, click Start Debugging.

   Visual Studio 2015 builds and runs the application. The application displays a form containing two text boxes separated by a Copy button.

4. Type the following sample text into the upper text box:

   inRange = (lo <= number) && (hi >= number);

5. Click Copy.

   The statement is copied verbatim into the lower text box, and no translation of the <, &, or > characters occurs, as shown in the following screen shot.

SwitchStatement

inRange = (lo <= number) && (hi >= number);

Copy

inRange = (lo <= number) && (hi >= number);

6. Return to Visual Studio 2015 and stop debugging.

7. Display the code for MainPage.xaml.cs in the Code and Text Editor window and locate the *copyOne* method.

The *copyOne* method copies the character specified as its input parameter to the end of the text displayed in the lower text box. At the moment, *copyOne* contains a *switch* statement with a single *default* action. In the following few steps, you will modify this *switch* statement to convert characters that are significant in XML to their XML mapping. For example, the < character will be converted to the string *<*.

8. Add the following statements shown in bold to the *switch* statement after the opening brace for the statement and directly before the *default* label:

```
switch (current)
{
    case '<' :
        target.Text += "&lt;";
        break;
    default:
        target.Text += current;
        break;
}
```

If the current character being copied is a left angle bracket (<), the preceding code appends the string "<" to the text being output in its place.

9. Add the following statements to the *switch* statement after the *break* statement you have just added and above the *default* label:

```
case '>' :
    target.Text += "&gt;";
    break;
case '&' :
    target.Text += "&amp;";
    break;
case '\"' :
    target.Text += "&#34;";
    break;
case '\'' :
    target.Text += "&#39;";
    break;
```

Note The single quotation mark (') and double quotation mark (") have a special meaning in C#—they are used to delimit character and string constants. The backslash (\) in the final two *case* labels is an escape character that causes the C# compiler to treat these characters as literals rather than as delimiters.

10. On the Debug menu, click Start Debugging.

11. Type the following text into the upper text box:

    inRange = (lo <= number) && (hi >= number);

12. Click Copy.

    The statement is copied into the lower text box. This time, each character undergoes the XML mapping implemented in the *switch* statement. The target text box displays the following text:

    inRange = (lo <= number) && (hi >= number);

13. Experiment with other strings, and verify that all special characters (<, >, &, " , and ') are handled correctly.

14. Return to Visual Studio and stop debugging.

Summary

In this chapter, you learned about Boolean expressions and variables. You saw how to use Boolean expressions with the *if* and *switch* statements to make decisions in your programs, and you combined Boolean expressions by using the Boolean operators.

- If you want to continue to the next chapter, keep Visual Studio 2015 running and turn to Chapter 5, "Using compound assignment and iteration statements."

- If you want to exit Visual Studio 2015 now, on the File menu, click Exit. If you see a Save dialog box, click Yes and save the project.

Quick reference

To	Do this	Example
Determine whether two values are equivalent	Use the == operator or the != operator.	`answer == 42`
Compare the value of two expressions	Use the <, <=, >, or >= operator.	`age >= 21`
Declare a Boolean variable	Use the *bool* keyword as the type of the variable.	`bool inRange;`
Create a Boolean expression that is true only if two conditions are both true	Use the && operator.	`inRange = (lo <= number)` `        && (number <= hi);`
Create a Boolean expression that is true if either of two conditions is true	Use the || operator.	`outOfRange = (number < lo)` `        || (hi < number);`
Run a statement if a condition is true	Use an *if* statement.	`if (inRange)` `    process();`

Run more than one statement if a condition is true	Use an *if* statement and a block.	`if (seconds == 59)`
		`{`
		`    seconds = 0;`
		`    minutes++;`
		`}`

Associate different statements with different values of a controlling expression	Use a *switch* statement.	`switch (current)`
		`{`
		`    case 0:`
		`        ...`
		`        break;`
		`    case 1:`
		`        ...`
		`        break;`
		`    default :`
		`        ...`
		`        break;`
		`}`

CHAPTER 5

Using compound assignment and iteration statements

After completing this chapter, you will be able to:

- Update the value of a variable by using compound assignment operators.

- Write *while, for*, and *do* iteration statements.

- Step through a *do* statement and watch as the values of variables change.

Chapter 4, "Using decision statements," demonstrates how to use the *if* and *switch* constructs to run statements selectively. In this chapter, you'll see how to use a variety of iteration (or *looping*) statements to run one or more statements repeatedly.

When you write iteration statements, you usually need to control the number of iterations that you perform. You can achieve this by using a variable, updating its value as each iteration is performed, and stopping the process when the variable reaches a particular value. To help simplify this process, you'll start by learning about the special assignment operators that you should use to update the value of a variable in these circumstances.

Using compound assignment operators

You've already seen how to use arithmetic operators to create new values. For example, the following statement uses the plus operator (+) to display to the console a value that is 42 greater than the variable *answer*:

```
Console.WriteLine(answer + 42);
```

You've also seen how to use assignment statements to change the value of a variable. The following statement uses the assignment operator (=) to change the value of *answer* to 42:

```
answer = 42;
```

If you want to add 42 to the value of a variable, you can combine the assignment operator and the plus operator. For example, the following statement adds 42 to *answer*. After this statement runs, the value of *answer* is 42 more than it was before:

```
answer = answer + 42;
```

Although this statement works, you'll probably never see an experienced programmer write code like this. Adding a value to a variable is so common that C# provides a way for you to perform this task in a shorthand manner by using the operator +=. To add 42 to *answer*, you can write the following statement:

```
answer += 42;
```

You can use this notation to combine any arithmetic operator with the assignment operator, as the following table shows. These operators are collectively known as the *compound assignment operators*.

Don't write this	Write this
variable = variable * number;	variable *= number;
variable = variable / number;	variable /= number;
variable = variable % number;	variable %= number;
variable = variable + number;	variable += number;
variable = variable - number;	variable -= number;

> **Tip** The compound assignment operators share the same precedence and right associativity as the simple assignment operator (=).

The += operator also works on strings; it appends one string to the end of another. For example, the following code displays "Hello John" on the console:

```
string name = "John";
string greeting = "Hello ";
greeting += name;
Console.WriteLine(greeting);
```

You cannot use any of the other compound assignment operators on strings.

> **Tip** Use the increment (++) and decrement (--) operators instead of a compound assignment operator when incrementing or decrementing a variable by 1. For example, replace
>
> ```
> count += 1;
> ```
>
> with
>
> ```
> count++;
> ```

Writing *while* statements

You use a *while* statement to run a statement repeatedly for as long as some condition is true. The syntax of a *while* statement is as follows:

```
while ( booleanExpression )
    statement
```

The Boolean expression (which must be enclosed in parentheses) is evaluated, and if it is true, the statement runs and then the Boolean expression is evaluated again. If the expression is still true, the statement is repeated, and then the Boolean expression is evaluated yet again. This process continues until the Boolean expression evaluates to false, at which point the *while* statement exits. Execution then continues with the first statement that follows the *while* statement. A *while* statement shares the following syntactic similarities with an *if* statement (in fact, the syntax is identical except for the keyword):

- The expression must be a Boolean expression.

- The Boolean expression must be written within parentheses.

- If the Boolean expression evaluates to false when first evaluated, the statement does not run.

- If you want to perform two or more statements under the control of a *while* statement, you must use braces to group those statements in a block.

Here's a *while* statement that writes the values 0 through 9 to the console. Note that as soon as the variable *i* reaches the value 10, the *while* statement finishes and the code in the statement block does not run:

```
int i = 0;
while (i < 10)
{
    Console.WriteLine(i);
    i++;
}
```

All *while* statements should terminate at some point. A common beginner's mistake is to forget to include a statement to cause the Boolean expression eventually to evaluate to false and terminate the loop, which results in a program that runs forever. In the example, the statement *i++;* performs this role.

Note The variable *i* in the *while* loop controls the number of iterations that the loop performs. This is a common idiom, and the variable that performs this role is sometimes called the *sentinel* variable. You can also create nested loops (one loop inside another), and in these cases it is common to extend this naming pattern to use the letters *j*, *k*, and even *l* as the names of the sentinel variables used to control the iterations in these loops.

Tip As with *if* statements, it is recommended that you always use a block with a *while* statement, even if the block contains only a single statement. This way, if you decide to add more statements to the body of the *while* construct later, it is clear that you should add them to the block. If you don't do this, only the first statement that immediately follows the Boolean expression in the *while* construct will be executed as part of the loop, resulting in difficult-to-spot bugs such as this:

```
int i = 0;
while (i < 10)
    Console.WriteLine(i);
    i++;
```

This code iterates forever, displaying an infinite number of zeros, because only the *Console.WriteLine* statement—and not the *i++;* statement—is executed as part of the *while* construct.

In the following exercise, you will write a *while* loop to iterate through the contents of a text file one line at a time and write each line to a text box in a form.

Write a *while* statement

1. Using Microsoft Visual Studio 2015, open the WhileStatement project, which is located in the \Microsoft Press\VCSBS\Chapter 5 \WhileStatement folder in your Documents folder.

2. On the Debug menu, click Start Debugging.

   Visual Studio 2015 builds and runs the application. The application is a simple text file viewer that you can use to select a text file and display its contents.

3. Click Open File.

   The Open file picker appears and displays the files in the Documents folder, as shown in the following screen shot (the list of files and folders might be different on your computer).

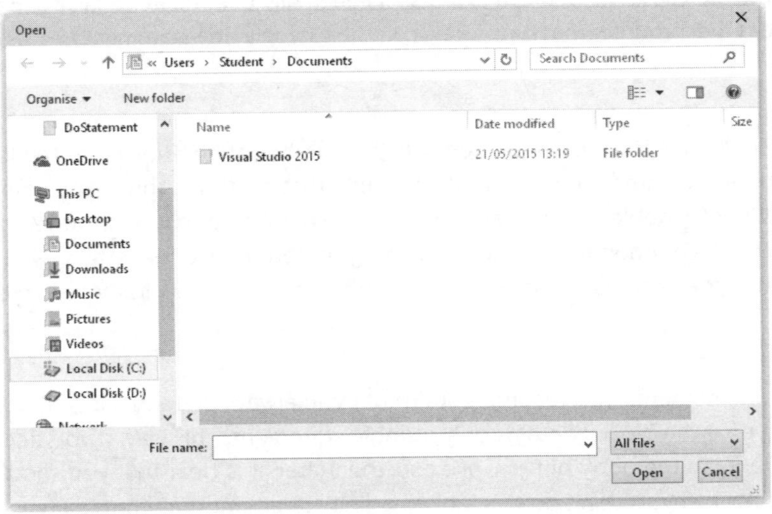

You can use this dialog to move to a folder and select a file to display.

4. Move to the \Microsoft Press\VCSBS\Chapter 5\WhileStatement\WhileStatement folder in your Documents folder.

5. Select the file MainPage.xaml.cs, and then click Open.

   The name of the file, MainPage.xaml.cs, appears in the text box at the top of the form, but the contents of the file do not appear in the large text box. This is because you have not yet implemented the code that reads the contents of the file and displays it. You will add this functionality in the following steps.

6. Return to Visual Studio 2015 and stop debugging.

7. Display the code for the file MainPage.xaml.cs in the Code and Text Editor window, and locate the *openFileClick* method.

   This method runs when the user clicks the Open button to select a file in the Open dialog box. It is not necessary for you to understand the exact details of how this method works at this point—simply accept the fact that this method prompts the user for a file (using a *FileOpenPicker* or *OpenFileDialog* window) and opens the selected file for reading.

   The final two statements in the *openFileClick* method are important, however. They look like this:

```
TextReader reader = new StreamReader(inputStream.AsStreamForRead());
displayData(reader);
```

   The first statement declares a *TextReader* variable called *reader*. *TextReader* is a class provided by the Microsoft.NET Framework that you can use for reading streams of characters from sources such as files. It is located in the *System.IO* namespace. This statement makes the data in the file specified by the user in the *FileOpenPicker* available to the *TextReader* object, which can then be used to read the data from the file. The final statement calls a method named *displayData*, passing *reader* as a parameter to this method. The *displayData* method reads the data by using the *reader* object and displays it to the screen (or it will do so once you have written the code to accomplish this).

8. Examine the *displayData* method. It currently looks like this:

```
private void displayData(TextReader reader)
{
    // TODO: add while loop here

}
```

   You can see that, other than the comment, this method is currently empty. This is where you need to add the code to fetch and display the data.

9. Replace the *// TODO: add while loop here* comment with the following statement:

```
source.Text = "";
```

The *source* variable refers to the large text box on the form. Setting its *Text* property to the empty string ("") clears any text that is currently displayed in this text box.

10. Add the following statement after the previous line that you added to the *displayData* method:

```
string line = reader.ReadLine();
```

This statement declares a *string* variable called *line* and calls the *reader.ReadLine* method to read the first line from the file into this variable. This method returns either the next line of text from the file or a special value called *null* when there are no more lines to read.

11. Add the following statements to the *displayData* method, after the code you have just entered:

```
while (line != null)
{
    source.Text += line + '\n';
    line = reader.ReadLine();
}
```

This is a *while* loop that iterates through the file one line at a time until there are no more lines available.

The Boolean expression at the start of the *while* loop examines the value in the *line* variable. If it is not *null*, the body of the loop displays the current line of text by appending it to the *Text* property of the *source* text box, together with a newline character ('\n'—the *ReadLine* method of the *TextReader* object strips out the newline characters as it reads each line, so the code needs to add it back in again). The *while* loop then reads in the next line of text before performing the next iteration. The *while* loop finishes when there is no more text to read in the file and the *ReadLine* method returns a *null* value.

12. Type the following statement after the closing brace at the end of the *while* loop:

```
reader.Dispose();
```

This statement releases the resources associated with the file and closes it. This is good practice because it makes it possible for other applications to use the file and also frees up any memory and other resources used to access the file.

13. On the Debug menu, click Start Debugging.

14. When the form appears, click Open File.

15. In the Open file picker or Open dialog box, move to the \Microsoft Press\VCSBS\Chapter 5\ WhileStatement\WhileStatement folder in your Documents folder, select the file MainPage .xaml.cs, and then click Open.

Note Don't try to open a file that does not contain text. If you attempt to open an executable program or a graphics file, for example, the application will simply display a text representation of the binary information in this file. If the file is large, it might hang the application, requiring you to forcibly terminate it.

This time, the contents of the selected file appear in the text box—you should recognize the code that you have been editing. The following image shows the application running:

```
WhileStatement
000    002

                   Open File            eStatement\WhileStatement\MainPage.xaml.cs


             private void displayData(TextReader reader)
             {
                 source.Text = "";
                 string line = reader.ReadLine();
                 while (line != null)
                 {
                     source.Text += line + '\n';
                     line = reader.ReadLine();
                 }
                 reader.Dispose();
             }
         }
     }
```

16. Scroll through the text in the text box and find the *displayData* method. Verify that this method contains the code you just added.

17. Return to Visual Studio and stop debugging.

Writing *for* statements

In C#, most *while* statements have the following general structure:

```
initialization
while (Boolean expression)
{
    statement
    update control variable
}
```

The *for* statement in C# provides a more formal version of this kind of construct by combining the initialization, Boolean expression, and code that updates the control variable. You'll find the *for* statement useful because in a *for* statement, it is much harder to accidentally leave out the code that initializes or updates the control variable, so you are less likely to write code that loops forever. Here is the syntax of a *for* statement:

```
for (initialization; Boolean expression; update control variable)
    statement
```

The statement that forms the body of the *for* construct can be a single line of code or a code block enclosed in braces.

You can rephrase the *while* loop shown earlier that displays the integers from 0 through 9 as the following *for* loop:

```
for (int i = 0; i < 10; i++)
{
    Console.WriteLine(i);
}
```

The initialization occurs just once, at the very beginning of the loop. Then, if the Boolean expression evaluates to *true*, the statement runs. The control variable update occurs, and then the Boolean expression is reevaluated. If the condition is still true, the statement is executed again, the control variable is updated, the Boolean expression is evaluated again, and so on.

Notice that the initialization occurs only once, that the statement in the body of the loop always executes before the update occurs, and that the update occurs before the Boolean expression reevaluates.

> **Tip** As with the *while* statement, it is considered good practice to always use a code block even if the body of the *for* loop contains just a single statement. If you add additional statements to the body of the *for* loop later, this approach will help to ensure that your code is always executed as part of each iteration.

You can omit any of the three parts of a *for* statement. If you omit the Boolean expression, it defaults to *true*, so the following *for* statement runs forever:

```
for (int i = 0; ;i++)
{
    Console.WriteLine("somebody stop me!");
}
```

If you omit the initialization and update parts, you have a strangely spelled *while* loop:

```
int i = 0;
for (; i < 10; )
{
    Console.WriteLine(i);
    i++;
}
```

> **Note** The initialization, Boolean expression, and update control variable parts of a *for* statement must always be separated by semicolons, even when they are omitted.

You can also provide multiple initializations and multiple updates in a *for* loop. (You can have only one Boolean expression, though.) To achieve this, separate the various initializations and updates with commas, as shown in the following example:

```
for (int i = 0, j = 10; i <= j; i++, j--)
{
    ...
}
```

As a final example, here is the *while* loop from the preceding exercise recast as a *for* loop:

```
for (string line = reader.ReadLine(); line != null; line = reader.ReadLine())
{
    source.Text += line + '\n';
}
```

Understanding *for* statement scope

You might have noticed that you can declare a variable in the initialization part of a *for* statement. That variable is scoped to the body of the *for* statement and disappears when the *for* statement finishes. This rule has two important consequences. First, you cannot use that variable after the *for* statement has ended because it's no longer in scope. Here's an example:

```
for (int i = 0; i < 10; i++)
{
    ...
}
Console.WriteLine(i); // compile-time error
```

Second, you can write two or more *for* statements that reuse the same variable name because each variable is in a different scope, as shown in the following code:

```
for (int i = 0; i < 10; i++)
{
    ...
}
for (int i = 0; i < 20; i += 2) // okay
{
    ...
}
```

Writing *do* statements

Both the *while* and *for* statements test their Boolean expression at the beginning of the loop. This means that if the expression evaluates to *false* on the first test, the body of the loop does not run—not even once. The *do* statement is different: its Boolean expression is evaluated after each iteration, so the body always executes at least once.

The syntax of the *do* statement is as follows (don't forget the final semicolon):

```
do
    statement
while (booleanExpression);
```

You must use a *statement* block if the body of the loop contains more than one statement (the compiler will report a syntax error if you don't). Here's a version of the example that writes the values 0 through 9 to the console, this time constructed by using a *do* statement:

```
int i = 0;
do
{
    Console.WriteLine(i);
    i++;
}
while (i < 10);
```

The *break* and *continue* statements

In Chapter 4, you saw how to use the *break* statement to jump out of a *switch* statement. You can also use a *break* statement to jump out of the body of an iteration statement. When you break out of a loop, the loop exits immediately and execution continues at the first statement that follows the loop. Neither the update nor the continuation condition of the loop is rerun.

In contrast, the *continue* statement causes the program to perform the next iteration of the loop immediately (after reevaluating the Boolean expression). Here's another version of the example that writes the values 0 through 9 to the console, this time using *break* and *continue* statements:

```
int i = 0;
while (true)
{
    Console.WriteLine(i);
    i++;
    if (i < 10)
        continue;
    else
        break;
}
```

This code is absolutely ghastly. Many programming guidelines recommend using *continue* cautiously or not at all because it is often associated with hard-to-understand code. The behavior of *continue* is also quite subtle. For example, if you execute a *continue* statement from within a *for* statement, the update part runs before performing the next iteration of the loop.

In the following exercise, you will write a *do* statement to convert a positive decimal whole number to its string representation in octal notation. The program is based on the following algorithm, which is based on a well-known mathematical procedure:

```
store the decimal number in the variable dec
do the following
    divide dec by 8 and store the remainder
    set dec to the quotient from the previous step
while dec is not equal to zero
combine the values stored for the remainder for each calculation in reverse order
```

For example, suppose that you want to convert the decimal number 999 to octal. You perform the following steps:

1. Divide 999 by 8. The quotient is 124 and the remainder is 7.

2. Divide 124 by 8. The quotient is 15 and the remainder is 4.

3. Divide 15 by 8. The quotient is 1 and the remainder is 7.

4. Divide 1 by 8. The quotient is 0 and the remainder is 1.

5. Combine the values calculated for the remainder at each step in reverse order. The result is 1747. This is the octal representation of the decimal value 999.

Write a *do* statement

1. Using Visual Studio 2015, open the DoStatement project, which is located in the \Microsoft Press\VCSBS\Chapter 5\DoStatement folder in your Documents folder.

2. Display the MainPage.xaml form in the Design View window.

   The form contains a text box called *number* in which the user can enter a decimal number. When the user clicks the Show Steps button, the octal representation of the number entered is generated. The text box to the right, called *steps*, shows the results of each stage of the calculation.

3. Display the code for MainPage.xaml.cs in the Code and Text Editor window and locate the *showStepsClick* method.

   This method runs when the user clicks the Show Steps button on the form. Currently it is empty.

4. Add the following statements shown in bold to the *showStepsClick* method:

```
private void showStepsClick(object sender, RoutedEventArgs e)
{
    int amount = int.Parse(number.Text);
    steps.Text = "";
    string current = "";
}
```

   The first statement converts the string value in the *Text* property of the *number* text box into an *int* by using the *Parse* method of the *int* type and stores it in a local variable called *amount*.

   The second statement clears the text displayed in the lower text box by setting its *Text* property to the empty string.

   The third statement declares a *string* variable called *current* and initializes it to the empty string. You will use this string to store the digits generated at each iteration of the loop that is used to convert the decimal number to its octal representation.

5. Add the following *do* statement (shown in bold) to the *showStepsClick* method:

```
private void showStepsClick(object sender, RoutedEventArgs e)
{
    int amount = int.Parse(number.Text);
    steps.Text = "";
    string current = "";

    do
    {
        int nextDigit = amount % 8;
        amount /= 8;
        int digitCode = '0' + nextDigit;
        char digit = Convert.ToChar(digitCode);
        current = digit + current;
        steps.Text += current + "\n";
    }
    while (amount != 0);
}
```

   The algorithm used here repeatedly performs integer arithmetic to divide the *amount* variable by 8 and determine the remainder. The remainder after each successive division constitutes the next digit in the string being built. Eventually, when *amount* is reduced to 0, the loop finishes. Notice that the body must run at least once. This behavior is exactly what is required because even the number 0 has one octal digit.

Look more closely at the code; you will see that the first statement executed by the *do* loop is this:

```
int nextDigit = amount % 8;
```

This statement declares an *int* variable called *nextDigit* and initializes it to the remainder after dividing the value in *amount* by 8. This will be a number somewhere between 0 and 7.

The next statement in the *do* loop is

```
amount /= 8;
```

This is a compound assignment statement and is equivalent to writing *amount = amount / 8;*. If the value of *amount* is 999, the value of *amount* after this statement runs is 124.

The next statement is this:

```
int digitCode = '0' + nextDigit;
```

This statement requires a little explanation. Characters have a unique code according to the character set used by the operating system. In the character sets frequently used by the Windows operating system, the code for character "0" has integer value 48. The code for character "1" is 49, the code for character "2" is 50, and so on, up to the code for character "9," which has integer value 57. With C#, you can treat a character as an integer and perform arithmetic on it, but when you do so, C# uses the character's code as the value. So the expression *'0' + nextDigit* actually results in a value somewhere between 48 and 55 (remember that *nextDigit* will be between 0 and 7), corresponding to the code for the equivalent octal digit.

The fourth statement in the *do* loop is

```
char digit = Convert.ToChar(digitCode);
```

This statement declares a *char* variable called *digit* and initializes it to the result of the *Convert.ToChar(digitCode)* method call. The *Convert.ToChar* method takes an integer holding a character code and returns the corresponding character. So, for example, if *digitCode* has the value 54, *Convert.ToChar(digitCode)* returns the character '6'.

To summarize, the first four statements in the *do* loop have determined the character representing the least-significant (rightmost) octal digit corresponding to the number the user typed in. The next task is to prepend this digit to the string to be output, like this:

```
current = digit + current;
```

The next statement in the *do* loop is this:

```
steps.Text += current + "\n";
```

This statement adds to the *steps* text box the string containing the digits produced so far for the octal representation of the number. It also appends a newline character so that each stage of the conversion appears on a separate line in the text box.

Finally, the condition in the *while* clause at the end of the loop is evaluated:

```
while (amount != 0);
```

Because the value of *amount* is not yet 0, the loop performs another iteration.

In the final exercise of this chapter, you will use the Visual Studio 2015 debugger to step through the previous *do* statement to help you understand how it works.

Step through the *do* statement

1. In the Code and Text Editor window displaying the MainPage.xaml.cs file, move the cursor to the first statement of the *showStepsClick* method:

```
int amount = int.Parse(number.Text);
```

2. Right-click anywhere in the first statement, and then click Run To Cursor.

3. When the form appears, type **999** in the number text box on the left, and then click Show Steps.

   The program stops, and you are placed in Visual Studio 2015 debug mode. A yellow arrow in the left margin of the Code and Text Editor window and yellow highlighting on the code indicates the current statement.

4. Display the Debug toolbar if it is not visible. (On the View menu, point to Toolbars, and then click Debug.)

> **Note** The commands on the Debug toolbar are also available on the Debug menu displayed on the menu bar.

5. On the Debug toolbar, click the drop-down arrow, point to Add Or Remove Buttons, and then select Windows, as shown in the following image:

This action adds the Breakpoints Window button to the toolbar.

6. On the Debug toolbar, click the arrow that appears next to the Breakpoints Window button, and then click Locals.

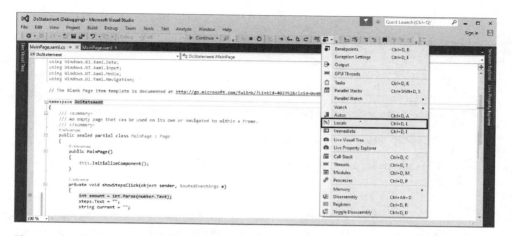

The Locals window appears (if it wasn't already open). This window displays the name, value, and type of the local variables in the current method, including the *amount* local variable. Notice that the value of *amount* is currently 0:

7. On the Debug toolbar, click the Step Into button.

The debugger runs the following statement:

```
int amount = int.Parse(number.Text);
```

The value of *amount* in the Locals window changes to 999, and the yellow arrow moves to the next statement.

8. Click Step Into again.

   The debugger runs this statement:

   ```
   steps.Text = "";
   ```

   This statement does not affect the Locals window because *steps* is a control on the form and not a local variable. The yellow arrow moves to the next statement.

9. Click Step Into.

   The debugger runs the statement shown here:

   ```
   string current = "";
   ```

   The yellow arrow moves to the opening brace at the start of the *do* loop. The *do* loop contains three local variables of its own: *nextDigit*, *digitCode*, and *digit*. Notice that these local variables appear in the Locals window, and the value of all three variables is initially set to 0.

10. Click Step Into.

    The yellow arrow moves to the first statement within the *do* loop.

11. Click Step Into.

    The debugger runs the following statement:

    ```
    int nextDigit = amount % 8;
    ```

    The value of *nextDigit* in the Locals window changes to 7. This is the remainder after dividing 999 by 8.

12. Click Step Into.

    The debugger runs this statement:

    ```
    amount /= 8;
    ```

    The value of *amount* changes to 124 in the Locals window.

13. Click Step Into.

    The debugger runs this statement:

    ```
    int digitCode = '0' + nextDigit;
    ```

    The value of *digitCode* in the Locals window changes to 55. This is the character code of the character "7" (48 + 7).

14. Click Step Into.

The debugger continues to this statement:

```
char digit = Convert.ToChar(digitCode);
```

The value of *digit* changes to "7" in the Locals window. The Locals window shows *char* values using both the underlying numeric value (in this case, 55) and also the character representation ("7").

Note that in the Locals window, the value of the *current* variable is still "".

15. Click Step Into.

The debugger runs the following statement:

```
current = current + digit;
```

The value of *current* changes to "7" in the Locals window.

16. Click Step Into.

The debugger runs the statement shown here:

```
steps.Text += current + "\n";"
```

This statement displays the text "7" in the *steps* text box, followed by a newline character to cause subsequent output to be displayed on the next line in the text box. (The form is currently hidden behind Visual Studio, so you won't be able to see it.) The cursor moves to the closing brace at the end of the *do* loop.

17. Click Step Into.

The yellow arrow moves to the *while* statement to evaluate whether the *do* loop has completed or whether it should continue for another iteration.

18. Click Step Into.

The debugger runs this statement:

```
while (amount != 0);
```

The value of *amount* is 124, the expression *124 != 0* evaluates to *true*, so the *do* loop performs another iteration. The yellow arrow jumps back to the opening brace at the start of the *do* loop.

19. Click Step Into.

The yellow arrow moves to the first statement within the *do* loop again.

20. Repeatedly click Step Into to step through the next three iterations of the *do* loop and watch how the values of the variables change in the Locals window.

21. At the end of the fourth iteration of the loop, the value of *amount* is 0 and the value of *current* is "1747". The yellow arrow is on the *while* condition at the end of the *do* loop:

```
while (amount != 0);
```

Because the value of *amount* is now 0, the expression *amount != 0* evaluates to *false*, and the *do* loop should terminate.

22. Click Step Into.

The debugger runs the following statement:

```
while (amount != 0);
```

As predicted, the *do* loop finishes, and the yellow arrow moves to the closing brace at the end of the *showStepsClick* method.

23. On the Debug menu, click Continue.

The form appears, displaying the four steps used to create the octal representation of 999: 7, 47, 747, and 1747.

24. Return to Visual Studio 2015. On the Debug menu, click Stop Debugging.

Summary

In this chapter, you learned how to use the compound assignment operators to update numeric variables and append one string to another. You saw how to use *while*, *for*, and *do* statements to execute code repeatedly while some Boolean condition is *true*.

- If you want to continue to the next chapter, keep Visual Studio 2015 running and turn to Chapter 6, "Managing errors and exceptions."

- If you want to exit Visual Studio 2015 now, on the File menu, click Exit. If you see a Save dialog box, click Yes and save the project.

Quick reference

To	Do this
Add an amount to a variable	Use the compound addition operator. For example: `variable += amount;`
Subtract an amount from a variable	Use the compound subtraction operator. For example: `variable -= amount;`

Run one or more statements zero or more times while a condition is true	Use a *while* statement. For example:
	<pre>int i = 0;
	while (i < 10)
	{
	    Console.WriteLine(i);
	    i++;
	}</pre>
	Alternatively, use a *for* statement. For example:
	<pre>for (int i = 0; i < 10; i++)
	{
	    Console.WriteLine(i);
	}</pre>

Repeatedly execute statements one or more times	Use a *do* statement. For example:
	<pre>int i = 0;
	do
	{
	    Console.WriteLine(i);
	    i++;
	}
	while (i < 10);</pre>

CHAPTER 6

Managing errors and exceptions

After completing this chapter, you will be able to:

- Handle exceptions by using the *try*, *catch*, and *finally* statements.

- Control integer overflow by using the *checked* and *unchecked* keywords.

- Raise exceptions from your own methods by using the *throw* keyword.

- Ensure that code always runs, even after an exception has occurred, by using a *finally* block.

You have now seen the core C# statements that you need to know to perform common tasks such as writing methods, declaring variables, using operators to create values, writing *if* and *switch* statements to run code selectively, and writing *while*, *for*, and *do* statements to run code repeatedly. However, the previous chapters haven't considered the possibility (or probability) that things can go wrong.

It is very difficult to ensure that a piece of code always works as expected. Failures can occur for a large number of reasons, many of which are beyond your control as a programmer. Any applications that you write must be capable of detecting failures and handling them in a graceful manner, either by taking the appropriate corrective actions or, if that is not possible, by reporting the reasons for the failure in the clearest possible way to the user. In this final chapter of Part I, you'll learn how C# uses exceptions to signal that an error has occurred and how to use the *try*, *catch*, and *finally* statements to catch and handle the errors that these exceptions represent.

By the end of this chapter, you'll have a solid foundation in all the fundamental elements of C#, and you will build on this foundation in Part II.

Coping with errors

It's a fact of life that bad things sometimes happen. Tires are punctured, batteries run down, screwdrivers are never where you left them, and users of your applications behave in unpredictable ways. In the world of computers, hard disks become corrupt, other applications running on the same computer as your program run amok and use up all the available memory, wireless network connections disappear at the most awkward moment, and even natural phenomena such as a nearby lightning strike can have an impact if it causes a power outage or network failure. Errors can occur at almost any stage when a program runs, and many errors might not actually be the fault of your own application, so how do you detect them and attempt to recover?

Over the years, a number of mechanisms have evolved. A typical approach adopted by older systems such as UNIX involved arranging for the operating system to set a special global variable whenever a method failed. Then, after each call to a method, you checked the global variable to see whether the method succeeded. C# and most other modern object-oriented languages don't handle errors in this manner; it's just too painful. Instead, they use *exceptions*. If you want to write robust C# programs, you need to know about exceptions.

Trying code and catching exceptions

Errors can happen at any time, and using traditional techniques to manually add error-detecting code around every statement is cumbersome, time-consuming, and error prone in its own right. You can also lose sight of the main flow of an application if each statement requires contorted error-handling logic to manage each possible error that can occur at every stage. Fortunately, C# makes it easy to separate the error-handling code from the code that implements the primary logic of a program by using exceptions and exception handlers. To write exception-aware programs, you need to do two things:

- Write your code within a *try* block (*try* is a C# keyword). When the code runs, it attempts to execute all the statements in the *try* block, and if none of the statements generates an exception, they all run, one after the other, to completion. However, if an error condition occurs, execution jumps out of the *try* block and into another piece of code designed to catch and handle the exception—a *catch* handler.

- Write one or more *catch* handlers (*catch* is another C# keyword) immediately after the *try* block to handle any possible error conditions. A *catch* handler is intended to capture and handle a specific type of exception, and you can have multiple *catch* handlers after a *try* block, each one designed to trap and process a specific exception. This enables you to provide different handlers for the different errors that could arise in the *try* block. If any one of the statements within the *try* block causes an error, the runtime throws an exception. The runtime then examines the *catch* handlers after the *try* block and transfers control directly to the first matching handler.

Here's an example of a *try* block that contains code that attempts to convert strings that a user has typed in some text boxes on a form to integer values. The code then calls a method to calculate a value and writes the result to another text box. Converting a string to an integer requires that the string contain a valid set of digits and not some arbitrary sequence of characters. If the string contains invalid characters, the *int.Parse* method throws a *FormatException*, and execution transfers to the corresponding *catch* handler. When the *catch* handler finishes, the program continues with the first statement that follows the handler. Note that if there is no handler that corresponds to the exception, the exception is said to be unhandled (this situation will be described shortly).

```
try
{
    int leftHandSide = int.Parse(lhsOperand.Text);
    int rightHandSide = int.Parse(rhsOperand.Text);
```

```
        int answer = doCalculation(leftHandSide, rightHandSide);
        result.Text = answer.ToString();
    }
    catch (FormatException fEx)
    {
        // Handle the exception
        ...
    }
```

A *catch* handler employs syntax similar to that used by a method parameter to specify the exception to be caught. In the preceding example, when a *FormatException* is thrown, the *fEx* variable is populated with an object containing the details of the exception.

The *FormatException* type has a number of properties that you can examine to determine the exact cause of the exception. Many of these properties are common to all exceptions. For example, the *Message* property contains a text description of the error that caused the exception. You can use this information when handling the exception, perhaps recording the details in a log file or displaying a meaningful message to the user and then asking the user to try again.

Unhandled exceptions

What happens if a *try* block throws an exception and there is no corresponding *catch* handler? In the previous example, it is possible that the *lhsOperand* text box could contain the string representation of a valid integer but the integer it represents is outside the range of valid integers supported by C# (for example, "2147483648"). In this case, the *int.Parse* statement would throw an *OverflowException*, which will not be caught by the *FormatException catch* handler. If this occurs and the *try* block is part of a method, the method immediately exits and execution returns to the calling method. If the calling method uses a *try* block, the runtime attempts to locate a matching *catch* handler for this *try* block and execute it. If the calling method does not use a *try* block or there is no matching *catch* handler, the calling method immediately exits and execution returns to its caller, where the process is repeated. If a matching *catch* handler is eventually found, the handler runs and execution continues with the first statement that follows the *catch* handler in the catching method.

> ⚠️ **Important** Notice that after catching an exception, execution continues in the method containing the *catch* block that caught the exception. If the exception occurred in a method other than the one containing the *catch* handler, control does *not* return to the method that caused the exception.

If, after cascading back through the list of calling methods, the runtime is unable to find a matching *catch* handler, the program will terminate with an unhandled exception.

You can easily examine exceptions generated by your application. If you are running the application in Microsoft Visual Studio 2015 in debug mode (that is, on the Debug menu you selected Start Debugging to run the application) and an exception occurs, a dialog box similar to the one shown in the following image appears and the application pauses, helping you to determine the cause of the exception:

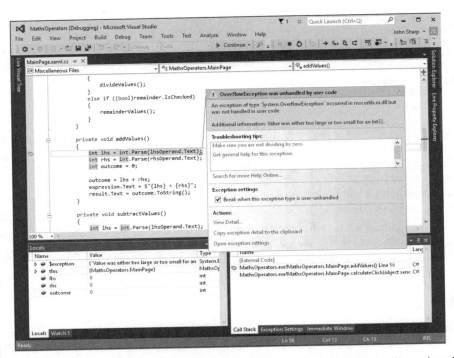

The application stops at the statement that caused the exception, and you drop into the debugger. You can examine the values of variables, you can change the values of variables, and you can step through your code from the point at which the exception occurred by using the Debug toolbar and the various debug windows.

Using multiple catch handlers

The previous discussion highlighted how different errors throw different kinds of exceptions to represent different kinds of failures. To cope with these situations, you can supply multiple *catch* handlers, one after the other, such as in the following:

```
try
{
    int leftHandSide = int.Parse(lhsOperand.Text);
    int rightHandSide = int.Parse(rhsOperand.Text);
    int answer = doCalculation(leftHandSide, rightHandSide);
    result.Text = answer.ToString();
}
catch (FormatException fEx)
{
    //...
}
catch (OverflowException oEx)
{
    //...
}
```

If the code in the *try* block throws a *FormatException* exception, the statements in the *catch* block for the *FormatException* exception run. If the code throws an *OverflowException* exception, the *catch* block for the *OverflowException* exception runs.

> **Note** If the code in the *FormatException catch* block generates an *OverflowException* exception, it does not cause the adjacent *OverflowException catch* block to run. Instead, the exception propagates to the method that invoked this code, as described earlier in this section.

Catching multiple exceptions

The exception-catching mechanism provided by C# and the Microsoft .NET Framework is quite comprehensive. The .NET Framework defines many types of exceptions, and any programs you write can throw most of them. It is highly unlikely that you will want to write *catch* handlers for every possible exception that your code can throw—remember that your application must be able to handle exceptions that you might not have even considered when you wrote it! So, how do you ensure that your programs catch and handle all possible exceptions?

The answer to this question lies in the way the different exceptions are related to one another. Exceptions are organized into families called *inheritance hierarchies*. (You will learn about inheritance in Chapter 12, "Working with inheritance.") *FormatException* and *OverflowException* both belong to a family called *SystemException*, as do a number of other exceptions. *SystemException* is itself a member of a wider family simply called *Exception*, and this is the great-granddaddy of all exceptions. If you catch *Exception*, the handler traps every possible exception that can occur.

> **Note** The *Exception* family includes a wide variety of exceptions, many of which are intended for use by various parts of the .NET Framework. Some of these exceptions are somewhat esoteric, but it is still useful to understand how to catch them.

The next example shows how to catch all possible exceptions:

```
try
{
    int leftHandSide = int.Parse(lhsOperand.Text);
    int rightHandSide = int.Parse(rhsOperand.Text);
    int answer = doCalculation(leftHandSide, rightHandSide);
    result.Text = answer.ToString();
}
catch (Exception ex) // this is a general catch handler
{
    //...
}
```

Note If you want to catch *Exception*, you can actually omit its name from the *catch* handler because it is the default exception:

```
catch
{
    // ...
}
```

However, this is not recommended. The exception object passed in to the *catch* handler can contain useful information concerning the exception, which is not easily accessible when using this version of the *catch* construct.

There is one final question you should be asking at this point: What happens if the same exception matches multiple *catch* handlers at the end of a *try* block? If you catch *FormatException* and *Exception* in two different handlers, which one will run? (Or will both execute?)

When an exception occurs, the runtime uses the first handler it finds that matches the exception and the others are ignored. This means that if you place a handler for *Exception* before a handler for *FormatException*, the *FormatException* handler will never run. Therefore, you should place more specific *catch* handlers above a general *catch* handler after a *try* block. If none of the specific *catch* handlers matches the exception, the general *catch* handler will.

Exception filters

Exception filters are a new feature of C# that affect the way in which exceptions are matched against catch handlers. An exception filter enables you to specify additional conditions under which the catch handler is used. These conditions take the form of a Boolean expression prefixed by the *when* keyword. The following example illustrates the syntax:

```
catch (Exception ex) when (ex.GetType() != typeof(System.OutOfMemoryException))
{
    // Handle all previously uncaught exceptions except OutOfMemoryException
}
```

This example catches all exceptions (the *Exception* type), but the filter specifies that if the type of the exception is an out-of-memory exception, then this handler should be ignored. (The *GetType* method returns the type of the variable specified as the argument.) This provides a neat way to handle all exceptions except out-of-memory exceptions. If an out-of-memory exception occurs, the runtime will continue looking for another exception handler to use, and if it fails to find one, then the exception will be treated as an unhandled exception.

In the following exercises, you will see what happens when an application throws an unhandled exception, and then you will write a *try* block and catch and handle an exception.

Observe how the application reports unhandled exceptions

1. Start Visual Studio 2015 if it is not already running.

2. Open the MathsOperators solution, which is located in the \Microsoft Press\VCSBS\Chapter 6\ MathsOperators folder in your Documents folder.

   This is a version of the program in Chapter 2, "Working with variables, operators, and expressions," that demonstrates the different arithmetic operators.

3. On the Debug menu, click Start Without Debugging.

> **Note** For this exercise, ensure that you actually run the application without debugging.

The form appears. You are now going to enter some text in the Left Operand box that will cause an exception. This operation will demonstrate the lack of robustness in the current version of the program.

4. In the Left Operand box, type **John**, and in the Right Operand box, type **2**. Click the + Addition button, and then click Calculate.

   This input triggers Windows default exception handling: the application simply terminates, and you are returned to the desktop!

Now that you have seen how the application behaves when an unhandled exception occurs, the next step is to make the application more robust by handling invalid input and preventing unhandled exceptions from arising.

Write a *try/catch* statement block

1. Return to Visual Studio 2015.

2. On the Debug menu, click Start Debugging.

3. When the form appears, in the Left Operand box, type **John**, and in the Right Operand box, type **2**. Click the + Addition button, and then click Calculate.

   This input should cause the same exception that occurred in the previous exercise, except that now you are running in debug mode, so Visual Studio traps the exception and reports it.

   Visual Studio displays your code and highlights the statement that caused the exception. It also displays a dialog box that describes the exception, which in this case is "Input string was not in a correct format."

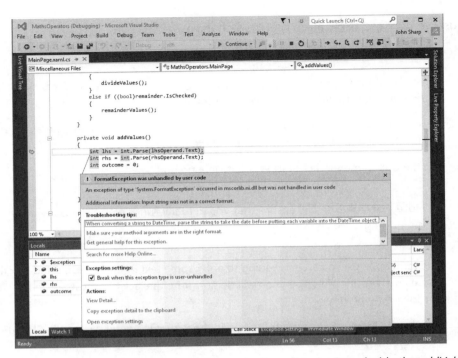

You can see that the exception was thrown by the call to *int.Parse* inside the *addValues* method. The problem is that this method is unable to parse the text "John" into a valid number.

4. In the exception dialog box, click View Detail.

Another dialog box opens in which you can view more information about the exception. If you expand *System.FormatException*, you can see this information:

Tip Some exceptions are the result of other exceptions raised earlier. The exception reported by Visual Studio is just the final exception in this chain, but it is usually the earlier exceptions that highlight the real cause of the problem. You can drill into these earlier exceptions by expanding the *InnerException* property in the View Detail dialog box. Inner exceptions might have further inner exceptions, and you can keep digging down until you find an exception with the *InnerException* property set to *null* (as shown in the previous image). At this point, you have reached the initial exception, and this exception is typically the one that you need to correct.

5. Click OK in the View Detail dialog box, and then, in Visual Studio, on the Debug menu, click Stop Debugging.

6. Display the code for the file MainPage.xaml.cs in the Code and Text Editor window, and locate the *addValues* method.

7. Add a *try* block (including braces) around the statements inside this method, together with a *catch* handler for the *FormatException* exception, as shown in bold here:

```
try
{
    int lhs = int.Parse(lhsOperand.Text);
    int rhs = int.Parse(rhsOperand.Text);
    int outcome = 0;

    outcome = lhs + rhs;
    expression.Text = $"{lhs} + {rhs}";
    result.Text = outcome.ToString();
}
catch (FormatException fEx)
{
    result.Text = fEx.Message;
}
```

If a *FormatException* exception occurs, the *catch* handler displays the text held in the exception's *Message* property in the *result* text box at the bottom of the form.

8. On the Debug menu, click Start Debugging.

9. When the form appears, in the Left Operand box, type **John**, and in the Right Operand box type **2**. Click the + Addition button, and then click Calculate.

The *catch* handler successfully catches the *FormatException*, and the message "Input string was not in a correct format" is written to the Result text box. The application is now a bit more robust.

MathsOperators

024 006

Left Operand   Right Operand

John   2

○ + Addition
○ - Subtraction
○ * Multiplication
○ / Division
○ % Remainder

Calculate

Expression:

Result: Input string was not in a correct format.

10. Replace John with the number **10**. In the Right Operand box, type **Sharp**, and then click Calculate.

   The *try* block surrounds the statements that parse both text boxes, so the same exception handler handles user input errors in both text boxes.

11. In the Right Operand box, replace Sharp with **20**, click the + Addition button, and then click Calculate.

   The application now works as expected and displays the value 30 in the Result box.

12. In the Left Operand box, replace 10 with **John**, click the − Subtraction button, and then click Calculate.

   Visual Studio drops into the debugger and reports a *FormatException* exception again. This time, the error has occurred in the *subtractValues* method, which does not include the necessary *try/catch* processing.

13. On the Debug menu, click Stop Debugging.

Propagating exceptions

Adding a *try/catch* block to the *addValues* method has made that method more robust, but you need to apply the same exception handling to the other methods: *subtractValues*, *multiplyValues*, *divideValues*, and *remainderValues*. The code for each of these exception handlers will likely be very similar, resulting in you writing the same code in each method. Each of these methods is called by the *calculateClick* method when the user clicks the Calculate button. Therefore, to avoid duplication of the exception-handling code, it makes sense to relocate it to the *calculateClick* method. If a *FormatException* occurs in the *subtractValues*, *multiplyValues*, *divideValues*, or *remainderValues* method, it will be propagated back to the *calculateClick* method for handling as described in the section "Unhandled exceptions" earlier in this chapter.

Propagate an exception back to the calling method

1. Display the code for the file MainPage.xaml.cs in the Code and Text Editor window, and locate the *addValues* method.

2. Remove the *try* block and *catch* handler from the *addValues* method and return it to its original state, as shown in the following code:

```
private void addValues()
{
    int leftHandSide = int.Parse(lhsOperand.Text);
    int rightHandSide = int.Parse(rhsOperand.Text);
    int outcome = 0;

    outcome = lhs + rhs;
    expression.Text = lhsOperand.Text + " + " + rhsOperand.Text
    result.Text = outcome.ToString();
}
```

3. Find the *calculateClick* method. Add to this method the *try* block and *catch* handler shown in bold in the following example:

```
private void calculateClick(object sender, RoutedEventArgs e)
{
    try
    {
        if ((bool)addition.IsChecked)
        {
            addValues();
        }
        else if ((bool)subtraction.IsChecked)
        {
            subtractValues();
        }
        else if ((bool)multiplication.IsChecked)
        {
            multiplyValues();
        }
        else if ((bool)division.IsChecked)
        {
            divideValues();
        }
        else if ((bool)remainder.IsChecked)
        {
            remainderValues();
```

```
        }
    }
    catch (FormatException fEx)
    {
        result.Text = fEx.Message;
    }
}
```

4. On the Debug menu, click Start Debugging.

5. When the form appears, in the Left Operand box, type **John**, and in the Right Operand box, type **2**. Click the + Addition button, and then click Calculate.

   As before, the *catch* handler successfully catches the *FormatException*, and the message "Input string was not in a correct format" is written to the Result text box. However, bear in mind that the exception was actually thrown in the *addValues* method, but it was caught by the handler in the *calculateClick* method.

6. Click the − Subtraction button, and then click Calculate.

   This time, the *subtractValues* method causes the exception, but it is propagated back to the *calculateClick* method and handled in the same manner as before.

7. Test the * Multiplication, / Division, and % Remainder buttons, and verify that the *FormatException* exception is caught and handled correctly.

8. Return to Visual Studio and stop debugging.

> **Note** The decision whether to catch unhandled exceptions explicitly in a method depends on the nature of the application you are building. In some cases, it makes sense to catch exceptions as close as possible to the point at which they occur. In other situations, it is more useful to let an exception propagate back to the method that invoked the routine that threw the exception and handle the error there.

Using checked and unchecked integer arithmetic

Chapter 2 discusses how to use binary arithmetic operators such as + and * on primitive data types such as *int* and *double*. It also instructs that the primitive data types have a fixed size. For example, a C# *int* is 32 bits. Because *int* has a fixed size, you know exactly the range of values that it can hold: it is −2147483648 to 2147483647.

> **Tip** If you want to refer to the minimum or maximum value of *int* in code, you can use the *int.MinValue* or *int.MaxValue* property.

The fixed size of the *int* type creates a problem. For example, what happens if you add 1 to an *int* whose value is currently 2147483647? The answer is that it depends on how the application is compiled. By default, the C# compiler generates code that allows the calculation to overflow silently and you get the wrong answer. (In fact, the calculation wraps around to the largest negative integer value, and the result generated is −2147483648.) The reason for this behavior is performance: integer arithmetic is a common operation in almost every program, and adding the overhead of overflow checking to each integer expression could lead to very poor performance. In many cases, the risk is acceptable because you know (or hope!) that your *int* values won't reach their limits. If you don't like this approach, you can turn on overflow checking.

> **Tip** You can turn on and off overflow checking in Visual Studio 2015 by setting the project properties. In Solution Explorer, click *YourProject* (where *YourProject* is the actual name of the project). On the Project menu, click *YourProject* Properties. In the project properties dialog box, click the Build tab. Click the Advanced button in the lower-right corner of the page. In the Advanced Build Settings dialog box, select or clear the Check For Arithmetic Overflow/Underflow check box.

Regardless of how you compile an application, you can use the *checked* and *unchecked* keywords to turn on and off integer arithmetic overflow checking in parts of an application that you think need it. These keywords override the compiler option specified for the project.

Writing checked statements

A checked statement is a block preceded by the *checked* keyword. All integer arithmetic in a checked statement always throws an *OverflowException* if an integer calculation in the block overflows, as shown in this example:

```
int number = int.MaxValue;
checked
{
    int willThrow = number++;
    Console.WriteLine("this won't be reached");
}
```

> **Important** Only integer arithmetic directly inside the *checked* block is subject to overflow checking. For example, if one of the checked statements is a method call, checking does not apply to code that runs in the method that is called.

You can also use the *unchecked* keyword to create an *unchecked* block statement. All integer arithmetic in an *unchecked* block is not checked and never throws an *OverflowException*. For example:

```
int number = int.MaxValue;
unchecked
{
```

```
    int wontThrow = number++;
    Console.WriteLine("this will be reached");
}
```

Writing checked expressions

You can also use the *checked* and *unchecked* keywords to control overflow checking on integer expressions by preceding just the individual parenthesized expression with the *checked* or *unchecked* keyword, as shown in this example:

```
int wontThrow = unchecked(int.MaxValue + 1);
int willThrow = checked(int.MaxValue + 1);
```

The compound operators (such as += and −=) and the increment (++) and decrement (--) operators are arithmetic operators and can be controlled by using the *checked* and *unchecked* keywords. Remember, *x += y* is the same as *x = x + y*

> **Important** You cannot use the *checked* and *unchecked* keywords to control floating-point (noninteger) arithmetic. The *checked* and *unchecked* keywords apply only to integer arithmetic using data types such as *int* and *long*. Floating-point arithmetic never throws *OverflowException*—not even when you divide by 0.0. (Remember from Chapter 2 that the .NET Framework has a special floating-point representation for infinity.)

In the following exercise, you will see how to perform checked arithmetic when using Visual Studio 2015.

Use checked expressions

1. Return to Visual Studio 2015.

2. On the Debug menu, click Start Debugging.

    You will now attempt to multiply two large values.

3. In the Left Operand box, type **9876543**. In the Right Operand box, type **9876543**. Click the * Multiplication button, and then click Calculate.

    The value −1195595903 appears in the Result box on the form. This is a negative value, which cannot possibly be correct. This value is the result of a multiplication operation that silently overflowed the 32-bit limit of the *int* type.

4. Return to Visual Studio and stop debugging.

5. In the Code and Text Editor window displaying MainPage.xaml.cs, locate the *multiplyValues* method, which should look like this:

```
private void multiplyValues()
{
    int lhs = int.Parse(lhsOperand.Text);
    int rhs = int.Parse(rhsOperand.Text);
    int outcome = 0;

    outcome = lhs * rhs;
    expression.Text = $"{lhs} * {rhs}";
    result.Text = outcome.ToString();
}
```

The statement *outcome = lhs * rhs;* contains the multiplication operation that is silently overflowing.

6. Edit this statement so that the calculation value is checked, like this:

```
outcome = checked(lhs * rhs);
```

The multiplication is now checked and will throw an *OverflowException* rather than silently returning the wrong answer.

7. On the Debug menu, click Start Debugging.

8. In the Left Operand box, type **9876543**. In the Right Operand box, type **9876543**. Click the * Multiplication button, and then click Calculate.

Visual Studio drops into the debugger and reports that the multiplication resulted in an *OverflowException* exception. You now need to add a handler to catch this exception and handle it more gracefully than just failing with an error.

9. On the Debug menu, click Stop Debugging.

10. In the Code and Text Editor window displaying the MainPage.xaml.cs file, locate the *calculateClick* method.

11. Add the following *catch* handler (shown in bold) immediately after the existing *FormatException catch* handler in this method:

```
private void calculateClick(object sender, RoutedEventArgs e)
{
    try
    {
        ...
    }
    catch (FormatException fEx)
    {
        result.Text = fEx.Message;
    }
    catch (OverflowException oEx)
    {
        result.Text = oEx.Message;
    }
}
```

The logic of this *catch* handler is the same as that for the *FormatException catch* handler. However, it is still worth keeping these handlers separate instead of simply writing a generic *Exception catch* handler because you might decide to handle these exceptions differently in the future.

12. On the Debug menu, click Start Debugging to build and run the application.

13. In the Left Operand box, type **9876543**. In the Right Operand box, type **9876543**. Click the * Multiplication button, and then click Calculate.

    The second *catch* handler successfully catches the *OverflowException* and displays the message "Arithmetic operation resulted in an overflow" in the Result box.

14. Return to Visual Studio and stop debugging.

Exception handling and the Visual Studio debugger

By default, the Visual Studio debugger only stops an application that is being debugged and reports exceptions that are unhandled. Sometimes it is useful to be able to debug exception handlers themselves, and in this case you need to be able to trace exceptions when they are thrown by the application, before they are caught. You can easily do this. On the Debug menu, click Windows and then click Exception Settings. The Exception Settings pane appears below the Code and Text Editor window:

In the Exception Settings pane, expand Common Language Runtime Exceptions, scroll down, and select System.OverflowException:

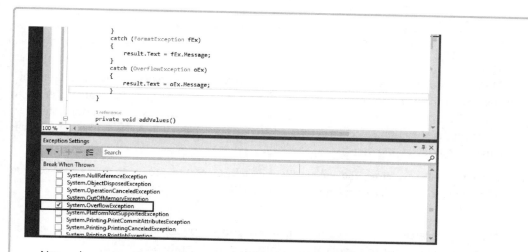

Now, when exceptions such as *OverflowException* occur, Visual Studio will drop into the debugger, and you can use the Step Into button on the Debug toolbar to step into the *catch* handler.

Throwing exceptions

Suppose that you are implementing a method called *monthName* that accepts a single *int* argument and returns the name of the corresponding month. For example, *monthName(1)* returns "January", *monthName(2)* returns "February", and so on. The question is, what should the method return if the integer argument is less than 1 or greater than 12? The best answer is that the method shouldn't return anything at all—it should throw an exception. The .NET Framework class libraries contain lots of exception classes specifically designed for situations such as this. Most of the time, you will find that one of these classes describes your exceptional condition. (If not, you can easily create your own exception class, but you need to know a bit more about the C# language before you can do that.) In this case, the existing .NET Framework *ArgumentOutOfRangeException* class is just right. You can throw an exception by using the *throw* statement, as shown in the following example:

```csharp
public static string monthName(int month)
{
    switch (month)
    {
        case 1 :
            return "January";
        case 2 :
            return "February";
        ...
        case 12 :
            return "December";
```

```
    default :
        throw new ArgumentOutOfRangeException("Bad month");
    }
}
```

The *throw* statement needs an exception object to throw. This object contains the details of the exception, including any error messages. This example uses an expression that creates a new *ArgumentOutOfRangeException* object. The object is initialized with a string that populates its *Message* property by using a constructor. Constructors are covered in detail in Chapter 7, "Creating and managing classes and objects."

In the following exercises, you will modify the MathsOperators project to throw an exception if the user attempts to perform a calculation without specifying an operator.

> **Note** This exercise is a little contrived, as any good application design would provide a default operator, but this application is intended to illustrate a point.

Throw an exception

1. Return to Visual Studio 2015.

2. On the Debug menu, click Start Debugging.

3. In the Left Operand box, type **24**. In the Right Operand box, type **36**, and then click Calculate.

   Nothing appears in the Expression and Result boxes. The fact that you have not selected an operator option is not immediately obvious. It would be useful to write a diagnostic message in the Result box.

4. Return to Visual Studio and stop debugging.

5. In the Code and Text Editor window displaying MainPage.xaml.cs, locate and examine the *calculateClick* method, which should look like this:

```
private int calculateClick(object sender, RoutedEventArgs e)
{
    try
    {
        if ((bool)addition.IsChecked)
        {
            addValues();
        }
        else if ((bool)subtraction.IsChecked)
        {
            subtractValues();
        }
        else if ((bool)multiplication.IsChecked)
        {
            multiplyValues();
        }
```

```
            else if ((bool)division.IsChecked)
            {
                divideValues();
            }
            else if ((bool)remainder.IsChecked)
            {
                remainderValues();
            }
        }
        catch (FormatException fEx)
        {
            result.Text = fEx.Message;
        }
        catch (OverflowException oEx)
        {
            result.Text = oEx.Message;
        }
    }
```

The *addition, subtraction, multiplication, division,* and *remainder* fields are the buttons that appear on the form. Each button has a property called *IsChecked* that indicates whether the user has selected it. The *IsChecked* property is a nullable Boolean that has the value *true* if the button is selected or *false* otherwise. (You learn more about nullable values in Chapter 8, "Understanding values and references.") The cascading *if* statement examines each button in turn to find which one is selected. (The radio buttons are mutually exclusive, so the user can select only one radio button at most.) If none of the buttons is selected, none of the *if* statements will be true and none of the calculation methods is called.

You could try to solve the problem by adding one more *else* statement to the *if-else* cascade to write a message to the *result* text box on the form, but a better solution is to separate the detection and signaling of an error from the catching and handling of that error.

6. Add another *else* statement to the end of the list of *if-else* statements and throw an *InvalidOperationException* as shown in bold in the following:

```
if ((bool)addition.IsChecked)
{
    addValues();
}
...
else if ((bool)remainder.IsChecked)
{
    remainderValues();
}
else
{
    throw new InvalidOperationException("No operator selected");
}
```

7. On the Debug menu, click Start Debugging to build and run the application.

8. In the Left Operand box, type **24**. In the Right Operand box, type **36**, and then click Calculate.

Visual Studio detects that your application has thrown an *InvalidOperationException*, and an exception dialog box opens. Your application has thrown an exception, but the code does not catch it yet.

9. On the Debug menu, click Stop Debugging.

Now that you have written a *throw* statement and verified that it throws an exception, you will write a *catch* handler to handle this exception.

Catch the exception

1. In the Code and Text Editor window displaying MainPage.xaml.cs, add the following *catch* handler shown in bold immediately below the two existing *catch* handlers in the *calculateClick* method:

```
...
catch (FormatException fEx)
{
    result.Text = fEx.Message;
}
catch (OverflowException oEx)
{
    result.Text = oEx.Message;
}
catch (InvalidOperationException ioEx)
{
    result.Text = ioEx.Message;
}
```

This code catches the *InvalidOperationException* that is thrown when no operator button is selected.

2. On the Debug menu, click Start Debugging.

3. In the Left Operand box, type **24**. In the Right Operand box, type **36**, and then click Calculate.

The message "No operator selected" appears in the Result box.

> **Note** If you drop into the Visual Studio debugger, you have probably enabled Visual Studio to catch all common language runtime exceptions as they are thrown. If this happens, on the Debug menu, click Continue. Remember to disable Visual Studio from catching CLR exceptions as they are thrown when you have finished this exercise!

4. Return to Visual Studio and stop debugging.

The application is now a lot more robust. However, several exceptions could still arise that are not caught and will cause the application to fail. For example, if you attempt to divide by 0, an unhandled *DivideByZeroException* will be thrown. (Integer division by 0 does throw an exception, unlike floating-point division by 0.) One way to solve this problem is to write an ever larger number of *catch* handlers inside the *calculateClick* method. Another solution is to add a general *catch* handler that catches *Exception* at the end of the list of *catch* handlers. This will trap all unexpected exceptions that you might have forgotten about or that might be caused as a result of truly unusual circumstances.

> **Note** Using a catchall handler to trap the *Exception* exception is not an excuse to omit catching specific exceptions. The more definite you can be in your exception handling, the easier it will be to maintain your code and spot the causes of any underlying or commonly recurring issues. Only use the *Exception* exception for cases that are really... well, exceptional. For the purposes of the following exercise, the "divide by zero" exception falls into this category. However, having established that this exception is a distinct possibility in a professional application, good practice would be to add a handler for the *DivideByZeroException* exception to the application.

Catch unhandled exceptions

1. In the Code and Text Editor window displaying MainPage.xaml.cs, add the following *catch* handler to the end of the list of existing *catch* handlers in the *calculateClick* method:

```
catch (Exception ex)
{
    result.Text = ex.Message;
}
```

   This *catch* handler will catch all hitherto unhandled exceptions, whatever their specific type.

2. On the Debug menu, click Start Debugging.

   You will now attempt to perform some calculations known to cause exceptions and confirm that they are all handled correctly.

3. In the Left Operand box, type **24**. In the Right Operand box, type **36**, and then click Calculate.

   Confirm that the diagnostic message "No operator selected" still appears in the Result box. This message was generated by the *InvalidOperationException* handler.

4. In the Left Operand box, type **John**, click the + Addition button, and then click Calculate.

   Confirm that the diagnostic message "Input string was not in a correct format" appears in the Result box. This message was generated by the *FormatException* handler.

5. In the Left Operand box, type **24**. In the Right Operand box, type **0**. Click the / Division button, and then click Calculate.

   Confirm that the diagnostic message "Attempted to divide by zero" appears in the Result box. This message was generated by the general *Exception* handler.

6. Experiment with other combinations of values, and verify that exception conditions are handled without causing the application to fail. When you have finished, return to Visual Studio and stop debugging.

Using a *finally* block

It is important to remember that when an exception is thrown, it changes the flow of execution through the program. This means that you can't guarantee that a statement will always run when the previous statement finishes because the previous statement might throw an exception. Remember that in this case, after the *catch* handler has run, the flow of control resumes at the next statement in the block holding this handler and not at the statement immediately following the code that raised the exception.

Look at the example that follows, which is adapted from the code in Chapter 5, "Using compound assignment and iteration statements." It's very easy to assume that the call to *reader.Dispose* will always occur when the *while* loop completes. After all, it's right there in the code.

```
TextReader reader = ...;
...
string line = reader.ReadLine();
while (line != null)
{
    ...
    line = reader.ReadLine();
}
reader.Dispose();
```

Sometimes it's not an issue if one particular statement does not run, but on many occasions it can be a big problem. If the statement releases a resource that was acquired in a previous statement, failing to execute this statement results in the resource being retained. This example is just such a case: when you open a file for reading, this operation acquires a resource (a file handle), and you must ensure that you call *reader.Dispose* to release the resource. If you don't, sooner or later you'll run out of file handles and be unable to open more files. If you find that file handles are too trivial, think of database connections instead.

The way to ensure that a statement is always run, whether or not an exception has been thrown, is to write that statement inside a *finally* block. A *finally* block occurs immediately after a *try* block or immediately after the last *catch* handler after a *try* block. As long as the program enters the *try* block associated with a *finally* block, the *finally* block will always be run, even if an exception occurs. If an exception is thrown and caught locally, the exception handler executes first, followed by the *finally* block. If the exception is not caught locally (that is, the runtime has to search through the list of calling methods to find a handler), the *finally* block runs first. In any case, the *finally* block always executes.

The solution to the *reader.Dispose* problem is as follows:

```
TextReader reader = ...;
...
try
{
    string line = reader.ReadLine();
    while (line != null)
    {
        ...
        line = reader.ReadLine();
    }
}
finally
{
    if (reader != null)
    {
        reader.Dispose();
    }
}
```

Even if an exception occurs while reading the file, the *finally* block ensures that the *reader.Dispose* statement always executes. You'll see another way to handle this situation in Chapter 14, "Using garbage collection and resource management."

Summary

In this chapter, you learned how to catch and handle exceptions by using the *try* and *catch* constructs. You saw how to turn on and off integer overflow checking by using the *checked* and *unchecked* keywords. You learned how to throw an exception if your code detects an exceptional situation, and you saw how to use a *finally* block to ensure that critical code always runs, even if an exception occurs.

- If you want to continue to the next chapter, keep Visual Studio 2015 running and turn to Chapter 7.

- If you want to exit Visual Studio 2015 now, on the File menu, click Exit. If you see a Save dialog box, click Yes and save the project.

Quick reference

To	Do this

Catch a specific exception	Write a *catch* handler that catches the specific exception class. For example:
	
	``
	try
	{
	    ...
	}
	catch (FormatException fEx)
	{
	    ...
	}
	``

Ensure that integer arithmetic is always checked for overflow	Use the *checked* keyword. For example:
	
	``
	int number = Int32.MaxValue;
	checked
	{
	    number++;
	}
	``

Throw an exception	Use a *throw* statement. For example:
	
	``
	throw new FormatException(source);
	``

Catch all exceptions in a single catch handler	Write a *catch* handler that catches *Exception*. For example:
	
	``
	try
	{
	    ...
	}
	catch (Exception ex)
	{
	    ...
	}
	``

Ensure that some code will always run, even if an exception is thrown	Write the code within a *finally* block. For example:
	
	``
	try
	{
	    ...
	}
	finally
	{
	    // always run
	}
	``

Understanding the C# object model

In Part I, you learned how to declare variables, use operators to create values, call methods, and write many of the statements you need when you implement a method. You now know enough to progress to the next stage: combining methods and data into your own functional data structures. The chapters in Part II show you how to do this.

In Part II, you'll learn about classes and structures, the two fundamental types that you use to model the entities and other items that constitute a typical C# application. In particular, you'll see how C# creates objects and value types based on the definitions of classes and structures, and how the common language runtime (CLR) manages the life cycle of these items. You will find out how to create families of classes by using inheritance, and you will learn how to aggregate items by using arrays.

CHAPTER 7

Creating and managing classes and objects

After completing this chapter, you will be able to:

- Define a class containing a related set of methods and data items.

- Control the accessibility of members by using the *public* and *private* keywords.

- Create objects by using the *new* keyword to invoke a constructor.

- Write and call your own constructors.

- Create methods and data that can be shared by all instances of the same class by using the *static* keyword.

- Explain how to create anonymous classes.

The Windows Runtime together with the Microsoft .NET Framework contains thousands of classes. You have used a number of them already, including *Console* and *Exception*. Classes provide a convenient mechanism for modeling the entities manipulated by applications. An entity can represent a specific item, such as a customer, or something more abstract, such as a transaction. Part of the design process for any system focuses on determining the entities that are important to the processes that the system implements and then performing an analysis to see what information these entities need to hold and what operations they should perform. You store the information that a class holds as fields and use methods to implement the operations that a class can perform.

Understanding classification

Class is the root word of the term *classification*. When you design a class, you systematically arrange information and behavior into a meaningful entity. This arranging is an act of classification and is something that everyone does—not just programmers. For example, all cars share common behaviors (they can be steered, stopped, accelerated, and so on) and common attributes (they have a steering wheel, an engine, and so on). People use the word *car* to mean an object that shares these common behaviors and attributes. As long as everyone agrees on what a word means, this system works well, and you can express complex but precise ideas in a concise form. Without classification, it's hard to imagine how people could think or communicate at all.

Given that classification is so deeply ingrained in the way we think and communicate, it makes sense to try to write programs by classifying the different concepts inherent in a problem and its solution and then modeling these classes in a programming language. This is exactly what you can do with object-oriented programming languages, including Microsoft Visual C#.

The purpose of encapsulation

Encapsulation is an important principle when defining classes. The idea is that a program that uses a class should not have to account for how that class actually works internally; the program simply creates an instance of a class and calls the methods of that class. As long as those methods do what they are designed to do, the program does not need to know how they are implemented. For example, when you call the *Console.WriteLine* method, you don't want to be bothered with all the intricate details of how the *Console* class physically arranges for data to be written to the screen. A class might need to maintain all sorts of internal state information to perform its various methods. This additional state information and activity is hidden from the program that is using the class. Therefore, encapsulation is sometimes referred to as *information hiding*. Encapsulation actually has two purposes:

- To combine methods and data within a class; in other words, to support classification

- To control the accessibility of the methods and data; in other words, to control the use of the class

Defining and using a class

In C#, you use the *class* keyword to define a new class. The data and methods of the class occur in the body of the class between a pair of braces. Following is a C# class called *Circle* that contains one method (to calculate the circle's area) and one piece of data (the circle's radius):

```
class Circle
{
    int radius;

    double Area()
    {
        return Math.PI * radius * radius;
    }
}
```

> **Note** The *Math* class contains methods for performing mathematical calculations and fields containing mathematical constants. The *Math.PI* field contains the value 3.14159265358979, which is an approximation of the value of pi.

The body of a class contains ordinary methods (such as *Area*) and fields (such as *radius*). Recall from early on in the book that variables in a class are called *fields*. Chapter 2, "Working with variables, operators, and expressions," shows how to declare variables, and Chapter 3, "Writing methods and applying scope," demonstrates how to write methods, so there's almost no new syntax here.

You can use the *Circle* class in a manner similar to how you have used the other types you have already met. You create a variable specifying *Circle* as its type, and then you initialize the variable with some valid data. Here is an example:

```
Circle c;           // Create a Circle variable
c = new Circle();   // Initialize it
```

A point worth highlighting in this code is the use of the *new* keyword. Previously, when you initialized a variable such as an *int* or a *float*, you simply assigned it a value:

```
int i;
i = 42;
```

You cannot do the same with variables of class types. One reason for this is that C# just doesn't provide the syntax for assigning literal class values to variables. You cannot write a statement such as this:

```
Circle c;
c = 42;
```

After all, what is the *Circle* equivalent of 42? Another reason concerns the way in which memory for variables of class types is allocated and managed by the runtime—this is discussed further in Chapter 8, "Understanding values and references." For now, just accept that the *new* keyword creates a new instance of a class, more commonly called an *object*.

You can, however, directly assign an instance of a class to another variable of the same type, like this:

```
Circle c;
c = new Circle();
Circle d;
d = c;
```

However, this is not as straightforward as it might first appear, for reasons that are described in Chapter 8.

Important Don't confuse the terms *class* and *object*. A class is the definition of a type. An object is an instance of that type created when the program runs. Several different objects can be instances of the same class.

Controlling accessibility

Surprisingly, the *Circle* class is currently of no practical use. By default, when you encapsulate your methods and data within a class, the class forms a boundary to the outside world. Fields (such as *radius*) and methods (such as *Area*) defined in the class can be used by other methods inside the class but not by the outside world; they are private to the class. So, although you can create a *Circle* object in a program, you cannot access its *radius* field or call its *Area* method, which is why the class is not of much use—yet! However, you can modify the definition of a field or method with the *public* and *private* keywords to control whether it is accessible from the outside:

- A method or field is private if it is accessible only from within the class. To declare that a method or field is private, you write the keyword *private* before its declaration. As intimated previously, this is actually the default, but it is good practice to state explicitly that fields and methods are private to avoid any confusion.

- A method or field is public if it is accessible both within and from outside the class. To declare that a method or field is public, you write the keyword *public* before its declaration.

Here is the *Circle* class again. This time, *Area* is declared as a public method and *radius* is declared as a private field:

```
class Circle
{
    private int radius;

    public double Area()
    {
        return Math.PI * radius * radius;
    }
}
```

> **Note** If you are a C++ programmer, be aware that no colon appears after the *public* and *private* keywords. You must repeat the keyword for every field and method declaration.

Although *radius* is declared as a private field and is not accessible from outside the class, *radius* is accessible within the *Circle* class. The *Area* method is inside the *Circle* class, so the body of *Area* has access to *radius*. However, the class is still of limited value because there is no way of initializing the *radius* field. To fix this, you can use a constructor.

> **Tip** Remember that variables declared in a method are not initialized by default. However, the fields in a class are automatically initialized to *0*, *false*, or *null*, depending on their type. Nonetheless, it is still good practice to provide an explicit means of initializing fields.

Naming and accessibility

Many organizations have their own house style that they ask developers to follow when they write code. Part of this style often involves rules for naming identifiers. The purpose of these rules is typically to make the code easier to maintain. The following recommendations are reasonably common and relate to the naming conventions for fields and methods based on the accessibility of class members; however, C# does not enforce these rules:

- Identifiers that are public should start with a capital letter. For example, *Area* starts with *A* (not *a*) because it's public. This system is known as the *PascalCase* naming scheme (because it was first used in the Pascal language).

- Identifiers that are not public (which include local variables) should start with a lowercase letter. For example, *radius* starts with *r* (not *R*) because it's private. This system is known as the *camelCase* naming scheme.

> **Note** Some organizations use the camelCase scheme only for methods and adopt the convention to name private fields starting with an underscore character, such as *_radius*. However, the examples in this book use camelCase naming for private methods and fields.

There's only one exception to this rule: class names should start with a capital letter, and constructors must match the name of their class exactly; therefore, a private constructor must start with a capital letter.

> **Important** Don't declare two public class members whose names differ only in case. If you do, developers using other languages that are not case sensitive (such as Microsoft Visual Basic) might not be able to integrate your class into their solutions.

Working with constructors

When you use the *new* keyword to create an object, the runtime needs to construct that object by using the definition of the class. The runtime must grab a piece of memory from the operating system, fill it with the fields defined by the class, and then invoke a constructor to perform any initialization required.

A *constructor* is a special method that runs automatically when you create an instance of a class. It has the same name as the class, and it can take parameters, but it cannot return a value (not even *void*). Every class must have a constructor. If you don't write one, the compiler automatically generates a default constructor for you. (However, the compiler-generated default constructor doesn't actually do anything.) You can write your own default constructor quite easily. Just add a public method that does not return a value and give it the same name as the class. The following example shows the *Circle* class with a default constructor that initializes the *radius* field to 0:

```
class Circle
{
    private int radius;

    public Circle()  // default constructor
    {
        radius = 0;
    }

    public double Area()
    {
        return Math.PI * radius * radius;
    }
}
```

> **Note** In C# parlance, the *default* constructor is a constructor that does not take any parameters. It does not matter whether the compiler generates it or you write it, it is still the default constructor. You can also write nondefault constructors (constructors that *do* take parameters), as you will see in the upcoming section "Overloading constructors."

In this example, the constructor is marked *public*. If this keyword is omitted, the constructor will be private (just like any other method and field). If the constructor is private, it cannot be used outside the class, which prevents you from being able to create *Circle* objects from methods that are not part of the *Circle* class. You might therefore think that private constructors are not that valuable. They do have their uses, but they are beyond the scope of the current discussion.

Having added a public constructor, you can now use the *Circle* class and exercise its *Area* method. Notice how you use dot notation to invoke the *Area* method on a *Circle* object:

```
Circle c;
c = new Circle();
double areaOfCircle = c.Area();
```

Overloading constructors

You're almost finished, but not quite. You can now declare a *Circle* variable, use it to reference a newly created *Circle* object, and then call its *Area* method. However, there is one last problem. The area of all *Circle* objects will always be 0 because the default constructor sets the radius to 0 and it stays at 0; the *radius* field is private, and there is no easy way of changing its value after it has been initialized. A constructor is just a special kind of method and it—like all methods—can be overloaded. Just as there are several versions of the *Console.WriteLine* method, each of which takes different parameters, so too can you write different versions of a constructor. So, you can add another constructor to the *Circle* class with a parameter that specifies the radius to use, like this:

```
class Circle
{
    private int radius;

    public Circle()  // default constructor
    {
        radius = 0;
    }

    public Circle(int initialRadius) // overloaded constructor
    {
        radius = initialRadius;
    }

    public double Area()
    {
        return Math.PI * radius * radius;
    }
}
```

> **Note** The order of the constructors in a class is immaterial; you can define constructors in the order with which you feel most comfortable.

You can then use this constructor when you create a new *Circle* object, such as in the following:

```
Circle c;
c = new Circle(45);
```

When you build the application, the compiler works out which constructor it should call based on the parameters that you specify to the *new* operator. In this example, you passed an *int*, so the compiler generates code that invokes the constructor that takes an *int* parameter.

You should be aware of an important feature of the C# language: if you write your own constructor for a class, the compiler does not generate a default constructor. Therefore, if you've written your own constructor that accepts one or more parameters and you also want a default constructor, you'll have to write the default constructor yourself.

Partial classes

A class can contain a number of methods, fields, and constructors, as well as other items discussed in later chapters. A highly functional class can become quite large. With C#, you can split the source code for a class into separate files so that you can organize the definition of a large class into smaller pieces that are easier to manage. This feature is used by Visual Studio 2015 for Universal Windows Platform (UWP) apps, where the source code that the developer can edit is maintained in a separate file from the code that is generated by Visual Studio whenever the layout of a form changes.

When you split a class across multiple files, you define the parts of the class by using the *partial* keyword in each file. For example, if the *Circle* class is split between two files called circ1.cs (containing the constructors) and circ2.cs (containing the methods and fields), the contents of circ1.cs look like this:

```
partial class Circle
{
    public Circle()  // default constructor
    {
        this.radius = 0;
    }

    public Circle(int initialRadius) // overloaded constructor
    {
        this.radius = initialRadius;
    }
}
```

The contents of circ2.cs look like this:

```
partial class Circle
{
    private int radius;

    public double Area()
    {
        return Math.PI * this.radius * this.radius;
    }
}
```

When you compile a class that has been split into separate files, you must provide all the files to the compiler.

In the following exercise, you will declare a class that models a point in two-dimensional space. The class will contain two private fields for holding the x- and y-coordinates of a point and will provide constructors for initializing these fields. You will create instances of the class by using the *new* keyword and calling the constructors.

Write constructors and create objects

1. Start Visual Studio 2015 if it is not already running.

2. Open the Classes project, which is located in the \Microsoft Press\VCSBS\Chapter 7\Classes folder in your Documents folder.

3. In Solution Explorer, double-click the file Program.cs to display it in the Code and Text Editor window.

4. In the *Program* class, locate the *Main* method.

The *Main* method calls the *doWork* method, which is wrapped in a *try* block and followed by a *catch* handler. With this *try/catch* block, you can write the code that would typically go inside *Main* in the *doWork* method instead, and be safe in the knowledge that it will catch and handle any exceptions. The *doWork* method currently contains nothing but a *// TODO:* comment.

> **Tip** TODO comments are frequently used by developers as a reminder that they have left a piece of code to revisit. These comments often have a description of the work to be performed, such as *// TODO: Implement the doWork method*. Visual Studio recognizes this form of comment, and you can quickly locate them anywhere in an application by using the Task List window. To display this window, on the View menu, click Task List. The Task List window opens below the Code and Text Editor window by default. All the TODO comments will be listed. You can then double-click any of these comments to go directly to the corresponding code, which will be displayed in the Code and Text Editor window.

5. Display the file Point.cs in the Code and Text Editor window.

This file defines a class called *Point*, which you will use to represent the location of a point in two-dimensional space, defined by a pair of x- and y-coordinates. The *Point* class is currently empty apart from another *// TODO:* comment.

6. Return to the Program.cs file. In the *Program* class, edit the body of the *doWork* method, and replace the *// TODO:* comment with the following statement:

```
Point origin = new Point();
```

This statement creates a new instance of the *Point* class and invokes its default constructor.

7. On the Build menu, click Build Solution.

    The code builds without error because the compiler automatically generates the code for a default constructor for the *Point* class. However, you cannot see the C# code for this constructor because the compiler does not generate any source language statements.

8. Return to the *Point* class in the file Point.cs. Replace the *// TODO:* comment with a public constructor that accepts two *int* arguments, called *x* and *y*, and that calls the *Console.WriteLine* method to display the values of these arguments to the console, as shown in bold type in the following code example:

```
class Point
{
    public Point(int x, int y)
    {
        Console.WriteLine($"x:{x}, y:{y}");
    }
}
```

9. On the Build menu, click Build Solution.

    The compiler now reports an error:

```
There is no argument that corresponds to the required formal parameter 'x' of 'Point.
Point(int, int)'
```

What this rather verbose message means is that the call to the default constructor in the *doWork* method is now invalid because there is no longer a default constructor. You have written your own constructor for the *Point* class, so the compiler does not generate the default constructor. You will now fix this by writing your own default constructor.

10. Edit the *Point* class by adding a public default constructor that calls *Console.WriteLine* to write the string "Default constructor called" to the console, as shown in bold type in the example that follows. The *Point* class should now look like this:

```
class Point
{
    public Point()
    {
        Console.WriteLine("Default constructor called");
    }

    public Point(int x, int y)
    {
        Console.WriteLine($"x:{x}, y:{y}");
    }
}
```

11. On the Build menu, click Build Solution.

The program should now build successfully.

12. In the Program.cs file, edit the body of the *doWork* method. Declare a variable called *bottomRight* of type *Point*, and initialize it to a new *Point* object by using the constructor with two arguments, as shown in bold type in the code that follows. Supply the values 1366 and 768, representing the coordinates at the lower-right corner of the screen based on the resolution 1366 × 768 (a common resolution for many tablet devices). The *doWork* method should now look like this:

```
static void doWork()
{
    Point origin = new Point();
    Point bottomRight = new Point(1366, 768);
}
```

13. On the Debug menu, click Start Without Debugging.

The program builds and runs, displaying the following messages to the console:

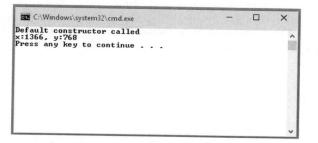

14. Press the Enter key to end the program and return to Visual Studio 2015.

You will now add two *int* fields to the *Point* class to represent the x- and y-coordinates of a point, and you will modify the constructors to initialize these fields.

15. Edit the *Point* class in the Point.cs file by adding two private fields, called *x* and *y*, of type *int*, as shown in bold type in the code that follows. The *Point* class should now look like this:

```
class Point
{
    private int x, y;

    public Point()
    {
        Console.WriteLine("default constructor called");
    }

    public Point(int x, int y)
    {
        Console.WriteLine($"x:{x}, y:{y}");
    }
}
```

You will edit the second *Point* constructor to initialize the *x* and *y* fields to the values of the *x* and *y* parameters. There is a potential trap when you do this. If you are not careful, the constructor will look like this:

```
public Point(int x, int y) // Don't type this!
{
    x = x;
    y = y;
}
```

Although this code will compile, these statements appear to be ambiguous. How does the compiler know in the statement *x = x;* that the first *x* is the field and the second *x* is the parameter? The answer is that it doesn't! A method parameter with the same name as a field hides the field for all statements in the method. All this code actually does is assign the parameters to themselves; it does not modify the fields at all. This is clearly not what you want.

The solution is to use the *this* keyword to qualify which variables are parameters and which are fields. Prefixing a variable with *this* means "the field in this object."

16. Modify the *Point* constructor that takes two parameters by replacing the *Console.WriteLine* statement with the following code shown in bold type:

```
public Point(int x, int y)
{
    this.x = x;
    this.y = y;
}
```

17. Edit the default *Point* constructor to initialize the *x* and *y* fields to –1, as follows in bold type. Note that although there are no parameters to cause confusion, it is still good practice to qualify the field references with *this*:

```
public Point()
{
    this.x = -1;
    this.y = -1;
}
```

18. On the Build menu, click Build Solution. Confirm that the code compiles without errors or warnings. (You can run it, but it does not produce any output.)

Methods that belong to a class and that operate on the data belonging to a particular instance of a class are called *instance methods*. (You will learn about other types of methods later in this chapter.) In the following exercise, you will write an instance method for the *Point* class, called *DistanceTo*, which calculates the distance between two points.

Write and call instance methods

1. In the Classes project in Visual Studio 2015, add the following public instance method called *DistanceTo* to the *Point* class after the constructors. The method accepts a single *Point* argument called *other* and returns a *double*.

   The *DistanceTo* method should look like this:

```
class Point
{
    ...
    public double DistanceTo(Point other)
    {
    }
}
```

   In the following steps, you will add code to the body of the *DistanceTo* instance method to calculate and return the distance between the *Point* object being used to make the call and the *Point* object passed as a parameter. To do this, you must calculate the difference between the x-coordinates and the y-coordinates.

2. In the *DistanceTo* method, declare a local *int* variable called *xDiff* and initialize it with the difference between *this.x* and *other.x*, as shown below in bold type:

```
public double DistanceTo(Point other)
{
    int xDiff = this.x - other.x;
}
```

3. Declare another local *int* variable called *yDiff* and initialize it with the difference between *this.y* and *other.y*, as shown here in bold type:

```
public double DistanceTo(Point other)
{
    int xDiff = this.x - other.x;
    int yDiff = this.y - other.y;
}
```

> **Note** Although the x and y fields are private, other instances of the same class can still access them. It is important to understand that the term *private* operates at the class level and not at the object level; two objects that are instances of the same class can access each other's private data, but objects that are instances of another class cannot.

To calculate the distance, you can use the Pythagorean theorem and calculate the square root of the sum of the square of *xDiff* and the square of *yDiff*. The *System.Math* class provides the *Sqrt* method that you can use to calculate square roots.

4. Declare a variable called *distance* of type *double* and use it to hold the result of the calculation just described.

```
public double DistanceTo(Point other)
{
    int xDiff = this.x - other.x;
    int yDiff = this.y - other.y;
    double distance = Math.Sqrt((xDiff * xDiff) + (yDiff * yDiff));
}
```

5. Add the *return* statement to the end of the *DistanceTo* method and return the value in the *distance* variable:

```
public double DistanceTo(Point other)
{
    int xDiff = this.x - other.x;
    int yDiff = this.y - other.y;
    double distance = Math.Sqrt((xDiff * xDiff) + (yDiff * yDiff));
    return distance;
}
```

You will now test the *DistanceTo* method.

6. Return to the *doWork* method in the *Program* class. After the statements that declare and initialize the *origin* and *bottomRight Point* variables, declare a variable called *distance* of type *double*. Initialize this *double* variable with the result obtained when you call the *DistanceTo* method on the *origin* object, passing the *bottomRight* object to it as an argument.

The *doWork* method should now look like this:

```
static void doWork()
{
    Point origin = new Point();
    Point bottomRight = new Point(1366, 768);
    double distance = origin.DistanceTo(bottomRight);
}
```

> **Note** Microsoft IntelliSense should display the *DistanceTo* method when you type the period character after *origin*.

7. Add to the *doWork* method another statement that writes the value of the *distance* variable to the console by using the *Console.WriteLine* method.

The completed *doWork* method should look like this:

```
static void doWork()
{
    Point origin = new Point();
    Point bottomRight = new Point(1366, 768);
    double distance = origin.DistanceTo(bottomRight);
    Console.WriteLine($"Distance is: {distance}");
}
```

8. On the Debug menu, click Start Without Debugging.

9. Confirm that the value 1568.45465347265 is written to the console window and then press Enter to close the application and return to Visual Studio 2015.

Understanding static methods and data

In the preceding exercise, you used the *Sqrt* method of the *Math* class. Similarly, when looking at the *Circle* class, you read the *PI* field of the *Math* class. If you think about it, the way in which you called the *Sqrt* method or read the *PI* field was slightly odd. You invoked the method or read the field on the class itself, not on an object of type *Math*. It is like trying to write *Point.DistanceTo* rather than *origin.DistanceTo* in the code you added in the preceding exercise. So what's happening, and how does this work?

You will often find that not all methods naturally belong to an instance of a class; they are utility methods inasmuch as they provide a useful function that is independent of any specific class instance. The *WriteLine* method of the *Console* class that has been used extensively throughout this book is a common example. The *Sqrt* method is another example. If *Sqrt* was an instance method of *Math*, you'd have to create a *Math* object on which to call *Sqrt*:

```
Math m = new Math();
double d = m.Sqrt(42.24);
```

This would be cumbersome. The *Math* object would play no part in the calculation of the square root. All the input data that *Sqrt* needs is provided in the parameter list, and the result is passed back to the caller by using the method's return value. Objects are not really needed here, so forcing *Sqrt* into an instance straitjacket is just not a good idea.

> **Note** As well as containing the *Sqrt* method and the *PI* field, the *Math* class contains many other mathematical utility methods, such as *Sin*, *Cos*, *Tan*, and *Log*.

In C#, all methods must be declared within a class. However, if you declare a method or a field as *static*, you can call the method or access the field by using the name of the class. No instance is required. This is how the *Sqrt* method of the *Math* class is declared:

```
class Math
{
    public static double Sqrt(double d)
    {
        ...
    }
    ...
}
```

You can invoke the *Sqrt* method like this:

```
double d = Math.Sqrt(42.24);
```

A static method does not depend on an instance of the class, and it cannot access any instance fields or instance methods defined in the class; it can use only fields and other methods that are marked as *static*.

Creating a shared field

Defining a field as static makes it possible for you to create a single instance of a field that is shared among all objects created from a single class. (Nonstatic fields are local to each instance of an object.) In the following example, the static field *NumCircles* in the *Circle* class is incremented by the *Circle* constructor every time a new *Circle* object is created:

```
class Circle
{
    private int radius;
    public static int NumCircles = 0;

    public Circle()  // default constructor
    {
        radius = 0;
        NumCircles++;
    }

    public Circle(int initialRadius) // overloaded constructor
    {
        radius = initialRadius;
        NumCircles++;
    }
}
```

All *Circle* objects share the same instance of the *NumCircles* field, so the statement *NumCircles++;* increments the same data every time a new instance is created. Notice that you cannot prefix *NumCircles* with the *this* keyword because *NumCircles* does not belong to a specific object.

You can access the *NumCircles* field from outside the class by specifying the *Circle* class rather than a *Circle* object, such as in the following example:

```
Console.WriteLine($"Number of Circle objects: {Circle.NumCircles}");
```

> **Note** Keep in mind that static methods are also called *class methods*. However, static fields aren't usually called *class fields*; they're just called *static fields* (or sometimes *static variables*).

Creating a static field by using the *const* keyword

By prefixing the field with the *const* keyword, you can declare that a field is static but that its value can never change. The keyword *const* is short for *constant*. A *const* field does not use the *static* keyword in its declaration but is nevertheless static. However, for reasons that are beyond the scope of this book, you can declare a field as *const* only when the field is a numeric type (such as *int* or *double*), a string, or an enumeration. (You will learn about enumerations in Chapter 9, "Creating value types with enumerations and structures.") For example, here's how the *Math* class declares *PI* as a *const* field:

```
class Math
{
    ...
    public const double PI = 3.14159265358979;
}
```

Understanding static classes

Another feature of the C# language is the ability to declare a class as *static*. A static class can contain only static members. (All objects that you create by using the class share a single copy of these members.) The purpose of a static class is purely to act as a holder of utility methods and fields. A static class cannot contain any instance data or methods, and it does not make sense to try to create an object from a static class by using the *new* operator. In fact, you can't actually use *new* to create an instance of an object using a static class even if you want to. (The compiler will report an error if you try.) If you need to perform any initialization, a static class can have a default constructor as long as it is also declared as *static*. Any other types of constructor are illegal and will be reported as such by the compiler.

If you were defining your own version of the *Math* class, one containing only static members, it could look like this:

```
public static class Math
{
    public static double Sin(double x) {...}
    public static double Cos(double x) {...}
    public static double Sqrt(double x) {...}
    ...
}
```

> **Note** The real *Math* class is not defined this way because it actually does have some instance methods.

Static *using* statements

Whenever you call a static method or reference a static field, you must specify the class to which the method or field belongs, such as *Math.Sqrt* or *Console.WriteLine*. Static *using* statements enable you to bring a class into scope and omit the class name when accessing static members. They operate in much the same way as ordinary *using* statements that bring namespaces into scope. The following example illustrates how to use them:

```
using static System.Math;
using static System.Console;
...
var root = Sqrt(99.9);
WriteLine($"The square root of 99.9 is {root}");
```

Note the use of the keyword *static* in the *using* statements. The example brings the static methods of the *System.Math* and *System.Console* classes into scope (you have to fully qualify the classes with their namespaces). You can then simply call the *Sqrt* and *WriteLine* methods. The compiler works out to which class each method belongs. However, herein lies a potential maintenance issue. Although you are typing less code, you have to balance this with the additional effort required when someone else has to maintain your code, because it is no longer clear to which class each method belongs. IntelliSense in Visual Studio helps to some extent, but to a developer reading through the code, it can obfuscate matters when the developer is trying to track down the causes of bugs. Use static *using* statements carefully; the preferred style of the author is not to utilize them, although you are free to make your own choice!

In the final exercise in this chapter, you will add a private static field to the *Point* class and initialize the field to 0. You will increment this count in both constructors. Finally, you will write a public static method to return the value of this private static field. With this field, you can find out how many *Point* objects you have created.

Write static members and call static methods

1. In Visual Studio 2015, display the *Point* class in the Code and Text Editor window.

2. Add a private static field called *objectCount* of type *int* to the *Point* class immediately before the constructors. Initialize it to 0 as you declare it, like this:

```
class Point
{
    ...
    private static int objectCount = 0;
    ...
}
```

> **Note** You can write the keywords *private* and *static* in any order when you declare a field such as *objectCount*. However, the preferred order is *private* first, *static* second.

3. Add a statement to both *Point* constructors to increment the *objectCount* field, as shown in bold type in the code example that follows.

The *Point* class should now look like this:

```
class Point
{
    private int x, y;
    private static int objectCount = 0;

    public Point()
    {
        this.x = -1;
        this.y = -1;
        objectCount++;
    }

    public Point(int x, int y)
    {
        this.x = x;
        this.y = y;
        objectCount++;
    }
    public double DistanceTo(Point other)
    {
        int xDiff = this.x - other.x;
        int yDiff = this.y - other.y;
        double distance = Math.Sqrt((xDiff * xDiff) + (yDiff * yDiff));
        return distance;
    }
}
```

Each time an object is created, its constructor is called. As long as you increment the *objectCount* in each constructor (including the default constructor), *objectCount* will hold the number of objects created so far. This strategy works only because *objectCount* is a shared static field. If *objectCount* were an instance field, each object would have its own personal *objectCount* field that would be set to 1.

The question now is this: How can users of the *Point* class find out how many *Point* objects have been created? At the moment, the *objectCount* field is private and not available outside the class. A poor solution would be to make the *objectCount* field publicly accessible. This strategy would break the encapsulation of the class, and you would then have no guarantee that the *objectCount* field's value was correct because anyone could change the value in the field. A much better idea is to provide a public static method that returns the value of the *objectCount* field. This is what you will do now.

4. Add a public static method to the *Point* class called *ObjectCount* that returns an *int* but does not take any parameters. This method should return the value of the *objectCount* field, as shown in bold type here:

```
class Point
{
    ...
    public static int ObjectCount() => objectCount;
}
```

5. Display the *Program* class in the Code and Text Editor window. Add a statement to the *doWork* method to write the value returned from the *ObjectCount* method of the *Point* class to the screen, as shown in bold type in the following code example:

```
static void doWork()
{
    Point origin = new Point();
    Point bottomRight = new Point(1366, 768);
    double distance = origin.distanceTo(bottomRight);
    Console.WriteLine($"Distance is: {distance}");
    Console.WriteLine($"Number of Point objects: {Point.ObjectCount()}");
}
```

The *ObjectCount* method is called by referencing *Point*, the name of the class, and not the name of a *Point* variable (such as *origin* or *bottomRight*). Because two *Point* objects have been created by the time *ObjectCount* is called, the method should return the value 2.

6. On the Debug menu, click Start Without Debugging.

Confirm that the message "Number of Point objects: 2" is written to the console window (after the message displaying the value of the *distance* variable).

7. Press Enter to close the program and return to Visual Studio 2015.

Anonymous classes

An *anonymous class* is a class that does not have a name. This sounds rather strange, but it is actually quite handy in some situations that you will see later in this book, especially when using query expressions. (You learn about query expressions in Chapter 20, "Decoupling application logic and handling events.") For the time being, you'll have to take it on faith that they are useful.

You create an anonymous class simply by using the *new* keyword and a pair of braces defining the fields and values that you want the class to contain, like this:

```
myAnonymousObject = new { Name = "John", Age = 47 };
```

This class contains public fields called *Name* (initialized to the string *"John"*) and *Age* (initialized to the integer *47*). The compiler infers the types of the fields from the types of the data you specify to initialize them.

When you define an anonymous class, the compiler generates its own name for the class, but it won't tell you what it is. Anonymous classes therefore raise a potentially interesting conundrum: if you don't know the name of the class, how can you create an object of the appropriate type and assign an instance of the class to it? In the code example shown earlier, what should the type of the variable *myAnonymousObject* be? The answer is that you don't know—that is the point of anonymous classes! However, this is not a problem if you declare *myAnonymousObject* as an implicitly typed variable by using the *var* keyword, like this:

```
var myAnonymousObject = new { Name = "John", Age = 47 };
```

Remember that the *var* keyword causes the compiler to create a variable of the same type as the expression used to initialize it. In this case, the type of the expression is whatever name the compiler happens to generate for the anonymous class.

You can access the fields in the object by using the familiar dot notation, as demonstrated here:

```
Console.WriteLine($"Name: {myAnonymousObject.Name} Age: {myAnonymousObject.Age}");
```

You can even create other instances of the same anonymous class but with different values, such as in the following:

```
var anotherAnonymousObject = new { Name = "Diana", Age = 46 };
```

The C# compiler uses the names, types, number, and order of the fields to determine whether two instances of an anonymous class have the same type. In this case, the variables *myAnonymousObject* and *anotherAnonymousObject* have the same number of fields, with the same name and type, in the same order, so both variables are instances of the same anonymous class. This means that you can perform assignment statements such as this:

```
anotherAnonymousObject = myAnonymousObject;
```

> **Note** Be warned that this assignment statement might not accomplish what you expect. You'll learn more about assigning object variables in Chapter 8.

There are quite a few restrictions on the contents of an anonymous class. For example, anonymous classes can contain only public fields, the fields must all be initialized, they cannot be static, and you cannot define any methods for them. You will use anonymous classes periodically throughout this book and learn more about them as you do so.

Summary

In this chapter, you saw how to define new classes. You learned that by default the fields and methods of a class are private and inaccessible to code outside the class, but you can use the *public* keyword to expose fields and methods to the outside world. You saw how to use the *new* keyword to create a new instance of a class and how to define constructors that can initialize class instances. Finally, you saw how to implement static fields and methods to provide data and operations that are independent of any specific instance of a class.

- If you want to continue to the next chapter, keep Visual Studio 2015 running and turn to Chapter 8.

- If you want to exit Visual Studio 2015 now, on the File menu, click Exit. If you see a Save dialog box, click Yes and save the project.

Quick reference

To	Do this
Declare a class	Write the keyword *class*, followed by the name of the class, followed by opening and closing braces. The methods and fields of the class are declared between the opening and closing braces. For example: ```class Point\n{\n ...\n}```
Declare a constructor	Write a method whose name is the same as the name of the class and that has no return type (not even *void*). For example: ```class Point\n{\n public Point(int x, int y)\n {\n ...\n }\n}```
Call a constructor	Use the *new* keyword and specify the constructor with an appropriate set of parameters. For example: ```Point origin = new Point(0, 0);```
Declare a static method	Write the keyword *static* before the declaration of the method. For example: ```class Point\n{\n public static int ObjectCount()\n {\n ...\n }\n}```
Call a static method	Write the name of the class, followed by a period, followed by the name of the method. For example: ```int pointsCreatedSoFar = Point.ObjectCount();```

To	Do this
| Declare a static field | Use the keyword *static* before the type of the field. For example:<br><br>```
class Point
{
    ...
    private static int objectCount;
}
``` |
| Declare a *const* field | Write the keyword *const* before the declaration of the field and omit the *static* keyword. For example:<br><br>```
class Math
{
    ...
    public const double PI = ...;
}
``` |
| Access a static field | Write the name of the class, followed by a period, followed by the name of the static field. For example:<br><br>```
double area = Math.PI * radius * radius;
``` |
```

Understanding values and references

After completing this chapter, you will be able to:

- Explain the differences between a value type and a reference type.

- Modify the way in which arguments are passed as method parameters by using the *ref* and *out* keywords.

- Convert a value into a reference by using boxing.

- Convert a reference back to a value by using unboxing and casting.

Chapter 7, "Creating and managing classes and objects," demonstrates how to declare your own classes and how to create objects by using the *new* keyword. That chapter also shows you how to initialize an object by using a constructor. In this chapter, you will learn how the characteristics of the primitive types—such as *int*, *double*, and *char*—differ from the characteristics of class types.

Copying value type variables and classes

Most of the primitive types built into C#, such as *int*, *float*, *double*, and *char* (but not *string*, for reasons that will be covered shortly) are collectively called *value types*. These types have a fixed size, and when you declare a variable as a value type, the compiler generates code that allocates a block of memory big enough to hold a corresponding value. For example, declaring an *int* variable causes the compiler to allocate 4 bytes of memory (32 bits) to hold the integer value. A statement that assigns a value (such as 42) to the *int* causes the value to be copied into this block of memory.

Class types such as *Circle* (described in Chapter 7) are handled differently. When you declare a *Circle* variable, the compiler *does not* generate code that allocates a block of memory big enough to hold a *Circle*; all it does is allot a small piece of memory that can potentially hold the address of (or a reference to) another block of memory containing a *Circle*. (An address specifies the location of an item in memory.) The memory for the actual *Circle* object is allocated only when the *new* keyword is used to create the object. A class is an example of a *reference type*. Reference types hold references to blocks of memory. To write effective C# programs that make full use of the Microsoft .NET Framework, you need to understand the difference between value types and reference types.

Consider a situation in which you declare a variable named *i* as an *int* and assign it the value 42. If you declare another variable called *copyi* as an *int* and then assign *i* to *copyi*, *copyi* will hold the same value as *i* (42). However, even though *copyi* and *i* happen to hold the same value, two blocks of memory contain the value 42: one block for *i* and the other block for *copyi*. If you modify the value of *i*, the value of *copyi* does not change. Let's see this in code:

```
int i = 42;     // declare and initialize i
int copyi = i;  /* copyi contains a copy of the data in i:
                   i and copyi both contain the value 42 */
i++;            /* incrementing i has no effect on copyi;
                   i now contains 43, but copyi still contains 42 */
```

The effect of declaring a variable *c* as a class type, such as *Circle*, is very different. When you declare *c* as a *Circle*, *c* can refer to a *Circle* object; the actual value held by *c* is the address of a *Circle* object in memory. If you declare an additional variable named *refc* (also as a *Circle*) and you assign *c* to *refc*, *refc* will have a copy of the same address as *c*; in other words, there is only one *Circle* object, and both *refc* and *c* now refer to it. Here's the example in code:

```
Circle c = new Circle(42);
Circle refc = c;
```

The following illustration shows both examples. The at sign (@) in the *Circle* objects represents a reference holding an address in memory:

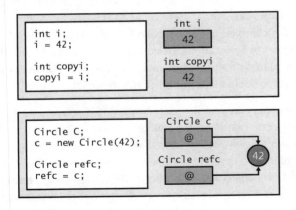

This difference is very important. In particular, it means that the behavior of method parameters depends on whether they are value types or reference types. You'll explore this difference in the next exercise.

Copying reference types and data privacy

If you actually want to copy the contents of a *Circle* object, *c*, into a different *Circle* object, *refc*, instead of just copying the reference, you must make *refc* refer to a new instance of the *Circle* class and then copy the data, field by field, from *c* into *refc*, like this:

```
Circle refc = new Circle();
refc.radius = c.radius;      // Don't try this
```

However, if any members of the *Circle* class are private (like the *radius* field), you will not be able to copy this data. Instead, you can make the data in the private fields accessible by exposing them as properties and then use these properties to read the data from *c* and copy it into *refc*. You will learn how to do this in Chapter 15, "Implementing properties to access fields."

Alternatively, a class could provide a *Clone* method that returns another instance of the same class but populated with the same data. The *Clone* method would have access to the private data in an object and could copy this data directly to another instance of the same class. For example, the *Clone* method for the *Circle* class could be defined as shown here:

```
class Circle
{
    private int radius;
    // Constructors and other methods omitted
    ...
    public Circle Clone()
    {
        // Create a new Circle object
        Circle clone = new Circle();

        // Copy private data from this to clone
        clone.radius = this.radius;

        // Return the new Circle object containing the copied data
        return clone;
    }
}
```

This approach is straightforward if all the private data consists of values, but if one or more fields are themselves reference types (for example, the *Circle* class might be extended to contain a *Point* object from Chapter 7, indicating the position of the *Circle* on a graph), these reference types also need to provide a *Clone* method; otherwise, the *Clone* method of the *Circle* class will simply copy a reference to these fields. This process is known as a *deep copy*. The alternative approach, wherein the *Clone* method simply copies references, is known as a *shallow copy*.

The preceding code example also poses an interesting question: How private is private data? Previously, you saw that the *private* keyword renders a field or method inaccessible from outside a class. However, this does not mean it can be accessed by only a single object. If you create two objects of the same class, they can each access the private data of the other within the code for that class. This sounds curious, but in fact, methods such as *Clone* depend on this feature. The statement *clone.radius = this.radius;* works only because the private *radius* field in the *clone* object is accessible from within the current instance of the *Circle* class. So, private actually means "private to the class" rather than "private to an object." However, don't confuse private with static. If you simply declare a field as *private*, each instance of the class gets its own data. If a field is declared as *static*, each instance of the class shares the same data.

Use value parameters and reference parameters

1. Start Microsoft Visual Studio 2015 if it is not already running.

2. Open the Parameters project, which is located in the \Microsoft Press\VCSBS\Chapter 8\ Parameters folder in your Documents folder.

   The project contains three C# code files: Pass.cs, Program.cs, and WrappedInt.cs.

3. Display the Pass.cs file in the Code and Text Editor window.

   This file defines a class called *Pass* that is currently empty apart from a *// TODO:* comment.

    Tip Remember that you can use the Task List window to locate all TODO comments in a solution.

4. Add a public static method called *Value* to the *Pass* class, replacing the *// TODO:* comment. This method should accept a single *int* parameter (a value type) called *param* and have the return type *void*. The body of the *Value* method should simply assign the value 42 to *param*, as shown in bold type in the following code example:

```
namespace Parameters
{
    class Pass
    {
        public static void Value(int param)
        {
            param = 42;
        }
    }
}
```

5. Display the Program.cs file in the Code and Text Editor window, and then locate the *doWork* method of the *Program* class.

   The *doWork* method is called by the *Main* method when the program starts running. As explained in Chapter 7, the method call is wrapped in a *try* block and followed by a *catch* handler.

6. Add four statements to the *doWork* method to perform the following tasks:

   a. Declare a local *int* variable called *i* and initialize it to 0.

   b. Write the value of *i* to the console by using *Console.WriteLine*.

   c. Call *Pass.Value*, passing *i* as an argument.

   d. Write the value of *i* to the console again.

   With the calls to *Console.WriteLine* before and after the call to *Pass.Value*, you can see whether the call to *Pass.Value* actually modifies the value of *i*. The completed *doWork* method should look exactly like this:

   ```
   static void doWork()
   {
       int i = 0;
       Console.WriteLine(i);
       Pass.Value(i);
       Console.WriteLine(i);
   }
   ```

7. On the Debug menu, click Start Without Debugging to build and run the program.

8. Confirm that the value "0" is written to the console window twice.

   The assignment statement inside the *Pass.Value* method that updates the parameter and sets it to 42 uses a copy of the argument passed in, and the original argument *i* is completely unaffected.

9. Press the Enter key to close the application.

   You will now see what happens when you pass an *int* parameter that is wrapped within a class.

10. Display the WrappedInt.cs file in the Code and Text Editor window. This file contains the *WrappedInt* class, which is empty apart from a *// TODO:* comment.

11. Add a public instance field called *Number* of type *int* to the *WrappedInt* class, as shown in bold type in the following code:

```
namespace Parameters
{
    class WrappedInt
    {
        public int Number;
    }
}
```

12. Display the Pass.cs file in the Code and Text Editor window. Add a public static method called *Reference* to the *Pass* class. This method should accept a single *WrappedInt* parameter called *param* and have the return type *void*. The body of the *Reference* method should assign 42 to *param.Number*, such as shown here:

```
public static void Reference(WrappedInt param)
{
    param.Number = 42;
}
```

13. Display the Program.cs file in the Code and Text Editor window. Comment out the existing code in the *doWork* method and add four more statements to perform the following tasks:

   a. Declare a local *WrappedInt* variable called *wi* and initialize it to a new *WrappedInt* object by calling the default constructor.

   b. Write the value of *wi.Number* to the console.

   c. Call the *Pass.Reference* method, passing *wi* as an argument.

   d. Write the value of *wi.Number* to the console again.

   As before, with the calls to *Console.WriteLine*, you can see whether the call to *Pass.Reference* modifies the value of *wi.Number*. The *doWork* method should now look exactly like this (the new statements are highlighted in bold type):

```
static void doWork()
{
    // int i = 0;
    // Console.WriteLine(i);
    // Pass.Value(i);
    // Console.WriteLine(i);

    WrappedInt wi = new WrappedInt();
    Console.WriteLine(wi.Number);
    Pass.Reference(wi);
    Console.WriteLine(wi.Number);
}
```

14. On the Debug menu, click Start Without Debugging to build and run the application.

This time, the two values displayed in the console window correspond to the value of *wi.Number* before and after the call to the *Pass.Reference* method. You should see that the values 0 and 42 are displayed.

15. Press the Enter key to close the application and return to Visual Studio 2015.

To explain what the previous exercise shows, the value of *wi.Number* is initialized to 0 by the compiler-generated default constructor. The *wi* variable contains a reference to the newly created *WrappedInt* object (which contains an *int*). The *wi* variable is then copied as an argument to the *Pass.Reference* method. Because *WrappedInt* is a class (a reference type), *wi* and *param* both refer to the same *WrappedInt* object. Any changes made to the contents of the object through the *param* variable in the *Pass.Reference* method are visible by using the *wi* variable when the method completes. The following diagram illustrates what happens when a *WrappedInt* object is passed as an argument to the *Pass.Reference* method:

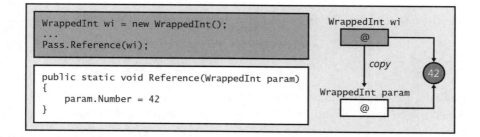

Understanding null values and nullable types

When you declare a variable, it is always a good idea to initialize it. With value types, it is common to see code such as this:

```
int i = 0;
double d = 0.0;
```

Remember that to initialize a reference variable such as a class, you can create a new instance of the class and assign the reference variable to the new object, like this:

```
Circle c = new Circle(42);
```

This is all very well, but what if you don't actually want to create a new object? Perhaps the purpose of the variable is simply to store a reference to an existing object at some later point in your program. In the following code example, the *Circle* variable *copy* is initialized, but later it is assigned a reference to another instance of the *Circle* class:

```
Circle c = new Circle(42);
Circle copy = new Circle(99);   // Some random value, for initializing copy
...
copy = c;                       // copy and c refer to the same object
```

After assigning c to *copy*, what happens to the original *Circle* object with a radius of 99 that you used to initialize *copy*? Nothing refers to it anymore. In this situation, the runtime can reclaim the memory by performing an operation known as *garbage collection*, which you will learn more about in Chapter 14, "Using garbage collection and resource management." The important thing to understand for now is that garbage collection is a potentially time-consuming operation; you should not create objects that are never used because doing so is a waste of time and resources.

You could argue that if a variable is going to be assigned a reference to another object at some point in a program, there is no point to initializing it. But this is poor programming practice, which can lead to problems in your code. For example, you will inevitably find yourself in the situation in which you want to refer a variable to an object only if that variable does not already contain a reference, as shown in the following code example:

```
Circle c = new Circle(42);
Circle copy;                    // Uninitialized !!!
...
if (copy == // only assign to copy if it is uninitialized, but what goes here?)
{
    copy = c;                   // copy and c refer to the same object
    ...
}
```

The purpose of the *if* statement is to test the *copy* variable to see whether it is initialized, but to which value should you compare this variable? The answer is to use a special value called *null*.

In C#, you can assign the *null* value to any reference variable. The *null* value simply means that the variable does not refer to an object in memory. You can use it like this:

```
Circle c = new Circle(42);
Circle copy = null;        // Initialized
...
if (copy == null)
{
    copy = c;                   // copy and c refer to the same object
    ...
}
```

Null-conditional operators

The latest version of C# includes a new operator, the null-conditional operator, that enables you to test for null values more succinctly. To use the null-conditional operator, you append a question mark (?) to the name of your variable.

For example, suppose you attempt to call the *Area* method on a *Circle* object when the *Circle* object has a null value:

```
Circle c = null;
Console.WriteLine($"The area of circle c is {c.Area()}");
```

In this case, the *Circle.Area* method throws a *NullReferenceException*, which makes sense because you cannot calculate the area of a circle that does not exist.

To avoid this exception, you could test whether the *Circle* object is null before you attempt to call the *Circle.Area* method:

```
if (c != null)
{
    Console.WriteLine($"The area of circle c is {c.Area()}");
}
```

In this case, if *c* is null, nothing is written to the command window. Alternatively, you could use the null-conditional operator on the *Circle* object before you attempt to call the *Circle.Area* method:

```
Console.WriteLine($"The area of circle c is {c?.Area()}");
```

The null-conditional operator tells the runtime engine to ignore the current statement if the variable to which you have applied the operator is null. In this case, the command window would display the following text:

```
The area of circle c is
```

Both approaches are valid and might meet your needs in different scenarios. The null-conditional operator can help you keep your code concise, particularly when you deal with complex properties with nested reference types that could all be null valued.

Using nullable types

The *null* value is useful for initializing reference types. Sometimes, you need an equivalent value for value types, but *null* is itself a reference, so you cannot assign it to a value type. The following statement is therefore illegal in C#:

```
int i = null; // illegal
```

However, C# defines a modifier that you can use to declare that a variable is a *nullable* value type. A nullable value type behaves in a similar manner to the original value type, but you can assign the *null* value to it. You use the question mark (?) to indicate that a value type is nullable, like this:

```
int? i = null; // legal
```

You can ascertain whether a nullable variable contains *null* by testing it in the same way as you test a reference type.

```
if (i == null)
    ...
```

You can assign an expression of the appropriate value type directly to a nullable variable. The following examples are all legal:

```
int? i = null;
int j = 99;
i = 100;        // Copy a value type constant to a nullable type
i = j;          // Copy a value type variable to a nullable type
```

You should note that the converse is not true. You cannot assign a nullable variable to an ordinary value type variable. So, given the definitions of variables *i* and *j* from the preceding example, the following statement is not allowed:

```
j = i;       // Illegal
```

This makes sense when you consider that the variable *i* might contain *null*, and *j* is a value type that cannot contain *null*. This also means that you cannot use a nullable variable as a parameter to a method that expects an ordinary value type. If you recall, the *Pass.Value* method from the preceding exercise expects an ordinary *int* parameter, so the following method call will not compile:

```
int? i = 99;
Pass.Value(i);     // Compiler error
```

> **Note** Take care not to confuse nullable types with the null-conditional operator. Nullable types are indicated by appending a question mark to the type name, whereas the null-conditional operator is appended to the variable name.

Understanding the properties of nullable types

A nullable type exposes a pair of properties that you can use to determine whether the type actually has a nonnull value and what this value is. The *HasValue* property indicates whether a nullable type contains a value or is *null*. You can retrieve the value of a nonnull nullable type by reading the *Value* property, like this:

```
int? i = null;
...
if (!i.HasValue)
{
    // If i is null, then assign it the value 99
    i = 99;
}
else
{
    // If i is not null, then display its value
    Console.WriteLine(i.Value);
}
```

Chapter 4, "Using decision statements," instructs that the NOT operator (*!*) negates a Boolean value. This code fragment tests the nullable variable *i*, and if it does not have a value (it is *null*), it assigns it the value 99; otherwise, it displays the value of the variable. In this example, using the *HasValue* property does not provide any benefit over testing for a *null* value directly. Additionally, reading the *Value* property is a long-winded way of reading the contents of the variable. However, these apparent shortcomings are caused by the fact that *int?* is a very simple nullable type. You can create more complex value types and use them to declare nullable variables where the advantages of using the *HasValue* and *Value* properties become more apparent. You will see some examples in Chapter 9, "Creating value types with enumerations and structures."

> **Note** The *Value* property of a nullable type is read-only. You can use this property to read the value of a variable but not to modify it. To update a nullable variable, use an ordinary assignment statement.

Using *ref* and *out* parameters

Ordinarily, when you pass an argument to a method, the corresponding parameter is initialized with a copy of the argument. This is true regardless of whether the parameter is a value type (such as an *int*), a nullable type (such as *int?*), or a reference type (such as a *WrappedInt*). This arrangement means that it's impossible for any change to the parameter to affect the value of the argument passed in. For example, in the following code, the value output to the console is 42, not 43. The *doIncrement* method increments a *copy* of the argument (*arg*) and *not* the original argument, as demonstrated here:

```
static void doIncrement(int param)
{
    param++;
}

static void Main()
{
    int arg = 42;
    doIncrement(arg);
    Console.WriteLine(arg); // writes 42, not 43
}
```

In the preceding exercise, you saw that if the parameter to a method is a reference type, any changes made by using that parameter change the data referenced by the argument passed in. The key point is this: Although the data that was referenced changed, the argument passed in as the parameter did not—it still references the same object. In other words, although it is possible to modify the object that the argument refers to through the parameter, it's not possible to modify the argument itself (for example, to set it to refer to a completely different object). Most of the time, this guarantee is very useful and can help to reduce the number of bugs in a program. Occasionally, however, you might want to write a method that actually needs to modify an argument. C# provides the *ref* and *out* keywords so that you can do this.

Creating *ref* parameters

If you prefix a parameter with the *ref* keyword, the C# compiler generates code that passes a reference to the actual argument rather than a copy of the argument. When using a *ref* parameter, anything you do to the parameter you also do to the original argument because the parameter and the argument both reference the same data. When you pass an argument as a *ref* parameter, you must also prefix the argument with the *ref* keyword. This syntax provides a useful visual cue to the programmer that the argument might change. Here's the preceding example again, this time modified to use the *ref* keyword:

```
static void doIncrement(ref int param) // using ref
{
    param++;
}

static void Main()
{
    int arg = 42;
    doIncrement(ref arg);     // using ref
    Console.WriteLine(arg);   // writes 43
}
```

This time, the *doIncrement* method receives a reference to the original argument rather than a copy, so any changes the method makes by using this reference actually change the original value. That's why the value 43 is displayed on the console.

Remember that C# enforces the rule that you must assign a value to a variable before you can read it. This rule also applies to method arguments; you cannot pass an uninitialized value as an argument to a method even if an argument is defined as a *ref* argument. For example, in the following example, *arg* is not initialized, so this code will not compile. This failure occurs because the statement *param++;* within the *doIncrement* method is really an alias for the statement *arg++;*—and this operation is allowed only if *arg* has a defined value:

```
static void doIncrement(ref int param)
{
    param++;
}

static void Main()
{
    int arg;                     // not initialized
    doIncrement(ref arg);
    Console.WriteLine(arg);
}
```

Creating *out* parameters

The compiler checks whether a *ref* parameter has been assigned a value before calling the method. However, there might be times when you want the method itself to initialize the parameter. You can do this with the *out* keyword.

The *out* keyword is syntactically similar to the *ref* keyword. You can prefix a parameter with the *out* keyword so that the parameter becomes an alias for the argument. As when using *ref*, anything you do to the parameter, you also do to the original argument. When you pass an argument to an *out* parameter, you must also prefix the argument with the *out* keyword.

The keyword *out* is short for *output*. When you pass an *out* parameter to a method, the method *must* assign a value to it before it finishes or returns, as shown in the following example:

```
static void doInitialize(out int param)
{
    param = 42; // Initialize param before finishing
}
```

The following example does not compile because *doInitialize* does not assign a value to *param*:

```
static void doInitialize(out int param)
{
    // Do nothing
}
```

Because an *out* parameter must be assigned a value by the method, you're allowed to call the method without initializing its argument. For example, the following code calls *doInitialize* to initialize the variable *arg*, which is then displayed on the console:

```
static void doInitialize(out int param)
{
    param = 42;
}

static void Main()
{
    int arg;                // not initialized
    doInitialize(out arg);  // legal
    Console.WriteLine(arg); // writes 42
}
```

You will examine *ref* parameters in the next exercise.

Use *ref* parameters

1. Return to the Parameters project in Visual Studio 2015.

2. Display the Pass.cs file in the Code and Text Editor window.

3. Edit the *Value* method to accept its parameter as a *ref* parameter.

   The *Value* method should look like this:

   ```
   class Pass
   {
       public static void Value(ref int param)
       {
   ```

```
        param = 42;
    }
    ...
}
```

4. Display the Program.cs file in the Code and Text Editor window.

5. Uncomment the first four statements. Notice that the third statement of the *doWork* method— *Pass.Value(i);*—indicates an error. The error occurs because the *Value* method now expects a *ref* parameter. Edit this statement so that the *Pass.Value* method call passes its argument as a *ref* parameter.

> **Note** Leave the four statements that create and test the *WrappedInt* object as they are.

The *doWork* method should now look like this:

```
class Program
{
    static void doWork()
    {
        int i = 0;
        Console.WriteLine(i);
        Pass.Value(ref i);
        Console.WriteLine(i);
        ...
    }
}
```

6. On the Debug menu, click Start Without Debugging to build and run the program.

This time, the first two values written to the console window are 0 and 42. This result shows that the call to the *Pass.Value* method has successfully modified the argument *i*.

7. Press the Enter key to close the application and return to Visual Studio 2015.

> **Note** You can use the *ref* and *out* modifiers on reference type parameters as well as on value type parameters. The effect is exactly the same: the parameter becomes an alias for the argument.

How computer memory is organized

Computers use memory to hold programs that are being executed and the data that those programs use. To understand the differences between value and reference types, it is helpful to understand how data is organized in memory.

Operating systems and language runtimes such as that used by C# frequently divide the memory used for holding data into two separate areas, each of which is managed in a distinct manner. These two areas of memory are traditionally called the *stack* and the *heap*. The stack and the heap serve different purposes, which are described here:

■ When you call a method, the memory required for its parameters and its local variables is always acquired from the stack. When the method finishes (because it either returns or throws an exception), the memory acquired for the parameters and local variables is automatically released back to the stack and is available again when another method is called. Method parameters and local variables on the stack have a well-defined life span: they come into existence when the method starts, and they disappear as soon as the method completes.

> **Note** Actually, the same life span applies to variables defined in any block of code enclosed by opening and closing curly braces. In the following code example, the variable *i* is created when the body of the *while* loop starts, but it disappears when the *while* loop finishes and execution continues after the closing brace:
>
> ```
> while (...)
> {
>     int i = …; // i is created on the stack here
>     ...
> }
> // i disappears from the stack here
> ```

■ When you create an object (an instance of a class) by using the *new* keyword, the memory required to build the object is always acquired from the heap. You have seen that the same object can be referenced from several places by using reference variables. When the last reference to an object disappears, the memory used by the object becomes available again (although it might not be reclaimed immediately). Chapter 14 includes a more detailed discussion of how heap memory is reclaimed. Objects created on the heap therefore have a more indeterminate life span; an object is created by using the *new* keyword, but it disappears only sometime after the last reference to the object is removed.

> **Note** All value types are created on the stack. All reference types (objects) are created on the heap (although the reference itself is on the stack). Nullable types are actually reference types, and they are created on the heap.

The names *stack* and *heap* come from the way in which the runtime manages the memory:

■ Stack memory is organized like a stack of boxes piled on top of one another. When a method is called, each parameter is put in a box that is placed on top of the stack. Each local variable is likewise assigned a box, and these are placed on top of the boxes already on the stack. When a method finishes, you can think of the boxes being removed from the stack.

- Heap memory is like a large pile of boxes strewn around a room rather than stacked neatly on top of one another. Each box has a label indicating whether it is in use. When a new object is created, the runtime searches for an empty box and allocates it to the object. The reference to the object is stored in a local variable on the stack. The runtime keeps track of the number of references to each box. (Remember that two variables can refer to the same object.) When the last reference disappears, the runtime marks the box as not in use, and at some point in the future it will empty the box and make it available.

Using the stack and the heap

Now let's examine what happens when a method named *Method* is called:

```
void Method(int param)
{
    Circle c;
    c = new Circle(param);
    ...
}
```

Suppose the argument passed into *param* is the value 42. When the method is called, a block of memory (just enough for an *int*) is allocated from the stack and initialized with the value 42. As execution moves inside the method, another block of memory big enough to hold a reference (a memory address) is also allocated from the stack but left uninitialized. This is for the *Circle* variable, *c*. Next, another piece of memory big enough for a *Circle* object is allocated from the heap. This is what the *new* keyword does. The *Circle* constructor runs to convert this raw heap memory to a *Circle* object. A reference to this *Circle* object is stored in the variable *c*. The following illustration shows the situation:

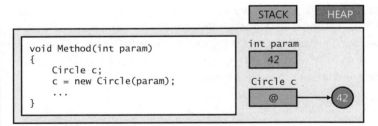

At this point, you should note two things:

- Although the object is stored on the heap, the reference to the object (the variable *c*) is stored on the stack.

- Heap memory is not infinite. If heap memory is exhausted, the *new* operator will throw an *OutOfMemoryException* exception and the object will not be created.

When the method ends, the parameters and local variables go out of scope. The memory acquired for *c* and for *param* is automatically released back to the stack. The runtime notes that the *Circle* object is no longer referenced and at some point in the future will arrange for its memory to be reclaimed by the heap. (See Chapter 14.)

The *System.Object* class

One of the most important reference types in the .NET Framework is the *Object* class in the *System* namespace. To fully appreciate the significance of the *System.Object* class, you need to understand inheritance, which is described in Chapter 12, "Working with inheritance." For the time being, simply accept that all classes are specialized types of *System.Object* and that you can use *System.Object* to create a variable that can refer to any reference type. *System.Object* is such an important class that C# provides the *object* keyword as an alias for *System.Object*. In your code, you can use *object* or you can write *System.Object*—they mean exactly the same thing.

In the following example, the variables *c* and *o* both refer to the same *Circle* object. The fact that the type of *c* is *Circle* and the type of *o* is *object* (the alias for *System.Object*) in effect provides two different views of the same item in memory.

```
Circle c;
c = new Circle(42);
object o;
o = c;
```

The following diagram illustrates how the variables *c* and *o* refer to the same item on the heap.

Boxing

As you have just seen, variables of type *object* can refer to any item of any reference type. However, variables of type *object* can also refer to a value type. For example, the following two statements initialize the variable *i* (of type *int*, a value type) to 42 and then initialize the variable *o* (of type *object*, a reference type) to *i*:

```
int i = 42;
object o = i;
```

The second statement requires a little explanation to appreciate what is actually happening. Remember that *i* is a value type and that it lives on the stack. If the reference inside *o* referred directly to *i*, the reference would refer to the stack. However, all references must refer to objects on the heap; creating references to items on the stack could seriously compromise the robustness of the runtime and create a potential security flaw, so it is not allowed. Therefore, the runtime allocates a piece of memory from the heap, copies the value of integer *i* to this piece of memory, and then refers the object *o* to this copy. This automatic copying of an item from the stack to the heap is called *boxing*. The following diagram shows the result:

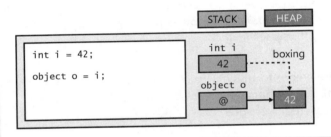

Important If you modify the original value of the variable *i*, the value on the heap referenced through *o* will not change. Likewise, if you modify the value on the heap, the original value of the variable will not change.

Unboxing

Because a variable of type *object* can refer to a boxed copy of a value, it's only reasonable to allow you to get at that boxed value through the variable. You might expect to be able to access the boxed *int* value that a variable *o* refers to by using a simple assignment statement such as this:

```
int i = o;
```

However, if you try this syntax, you'll get a compile-time error. If you think about it, it's pretty sensible that you can't use the *int i = o;* syntax. After all, *o* could be referencing absolutely anything and not just an *int*. Consider what would happen in the following code if this statement were allowed:

```
Circle c = new Circle();
int i = 42;
object o;

o = c;  // o refers to a circle
i = o;  // what is stored in i?
```

To obtain the value of the boxed copy, you must use what is known as a *cast*. This is an operation that checks whether converting an item of one type to another is safe before actually making the copy. You prefix the *object* variable with the name of the type in parentheses, as in this example:

```
int i = 42;
object o = i; // boxes
i = (int)o;    // compiles okay
```

The effect of this cast is subtle. The compiler notices that you've specified the type *int* in the cast. Next, the compiler generates code to check what *o* actually refers to at run time. It could be absolutely anything. Just because your cast says *o* refers to an *int*, that doesn't mean it actually does. If *o* really does refer to a boxed *int* and everything matches, the cast succeeds and the compiler-generated code extracts the value from the boxed *int* and copies it to *i*. (In this example, the boxed value is then stored in *i*.) This is called *unboxing*. The following diagram shows what is happening:

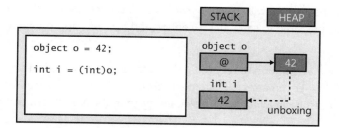

On the other hand, if *o* does not refer to a boxed *int*, there is a type mismatch, causing the cast to fail. The compiler-generated code throws an *InvalidCastException* exception at run time. Here's an example of an unboxing cast that fails:

```
Circle c = new Circle(42);
object o = c;          // doesn't box because Circle is a reference variable
int i = (int)o;        // compiles okay but throws an exception at run time
```

The following diagram illustrates this case:

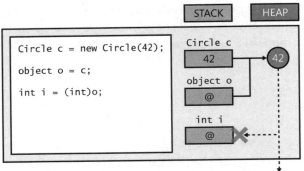

throw InvalidCastException

You will use boxing and unboxing in later exercises. Keep in mind that boxing and unboxing are expensive operations because of the amount of checking required and the need to allocate additional heap memory. Boxing has its uses, but injudicious use can severely impair the performance of a program. You will see an alternative to boxing in Chapter 17, "Introducing generics."

Casting data safely

By using a cast, you can specify that, *in your opinion*, the data referenced by an object has a specific type and that it is safe to reference the object by using that type. The key phrase here is "in your opinion." The C# compiler will not check that this is the case, but the runtime will. If the type of object in memory does not match the cast, the runtime will throw an *InvalidCastException*, as described in the preceding section. You should be prepared to catch this exception and handle it appropriately if it occurs.

However, catching an exception and attempting to recover in the event that the type of an object is not what you expected it to be is a rather cumbersome approach. C# provides two more very useful operators that can help you perform casting in a much more elegant manner: the *is* and *as* operators.

The *is* operator

You can use the *is* operator to verify that the type of an object is what you expect it to be, like this:

```
WrappedInt wi = new WrappedInt();
...
object o = wi;
if (o is WrappedInt)
{
    WrappedInt temp = (WrappedInt)o; // This is safe; o is a WrappedInt
    ...
}
```

The *is* operator takes two operands: a reference to an object on the left, and the name of a type on the right. If the type of the object referenced on the heap has the specified type, *is* evaluates to *true*; otherwise, *is* evaluates to *false*. The preceding code attempts to cast the reference to the *object* variable *o* only if it knows that the cast will succeed.

The *as* operator

The *as* operator fulfills a similar role to *is* but in a slightly truncated manner. You use the *as* operator like this:

```
WrappedInt wi = new WrappedInt();
...
object o = wi;
WrappedInt temp = o as WrappedInt;
if (temp != null)
{
    ...  // Cast was successful
}
```

Like the *is* operator, the *as* operator takes an object and a type as its operands. The runtime attempts to cast the object to the specified type. If the cast is successful, the result is returned and, in this example, is assigned to the *WrappedInt* variable *temp*. If the cast is unsuccessful, the *as* operator evaluates to the *null* value and assigns that to *temp* instead.

There is a little more to the *is* and *as* operators than is described here, and Chapter 12 discusses them in greater detail.

Pointers and unsafe code

This section is purely for your information and is aimed at developers who are familiar with C or C++. If you are new to programming, feel free to skip this section.

If you have already written programs in languages such as C or C++, much of the discussion in this chapter concerning object references might be familiar in that both languages have a construct that provides similar functionality: a pointer.

A *pointer* is a variable that holds the address of, or a reference to, an item in memory (on the heap or on the stack). A special syntax is used to identify a variable as a pointer. For example, the following statement declares the variable *pi* as a pointer to an integer:

```
int *pi;
```

Although the variable *pi* is declared as a pointer, it does not actually point anywhere until you initialize it. For example, to use *pi* to point to the integer variable *i*, you can use the following statements and the address-of operator (&), which returns the address of a variable:

```
int *pi;
int i = 99;
...
pi = &i;
```

You can access and modify the value held in the variable *i* through the pointer variable *pi* like this:

```
*pi = 100;
```

This code updates the value of the variable *i* to 100 because *pi* points to the same memory location as the variable *i*.

One of the main problems that developers learning C and C++ encounter is understanding the syntax used by pointers. The * operator has at least two meanings (in addition to being the arithmetic multiplication operator), and there is often great confusion about when to use & rather than *. The other issue with pointers is that it is easy to point somewhere invalid, or to forget to point somewhere at all, and then try to reference the data pointed to. The result will be either garbage or a program that fails with an error because the operating system detects an attempt to access an illegal address in memory. There is also a whole range of security flaws in many existing systems resulting from the mismanagement of pointers; some environments (not Windows) fail to enforce checks that a pointer does not refer to memory that belongs to another process, opening up the possibility that confidential data could be compromised.

Reference variables were added to C# to avoid all these problems. If you really want to, you can continue to use pointers in C#, but you must mark the code as *unsafe*. The *unsafe* keyword can be used to mark a block of code or an entire method, as shown here:

```
public static void Main(string [] args)
{
    int x = 99, y = 100;
    unsafe
    {
        swap (&x, &y);
    }
    Console.WriteLine($"x is now {x}, y is now {y}");
}

public static unsafe void swap(int *a, int *b)
{
    int temp;
    temp = *a;
    *a = *b;
    *b = temp;
}
```

When you compile programs containing unsafe code, you must specify the Allow Unsafe Code option when building the project. To do this, right-click the project in Solution Explorer and then click Properties. In the Properties window, click the Build tab, select Allow Unsafe Code, and then, on the File menu, click Save All.

Unsafe code also bears on how memory is managed. Objects created in unsafe code are said to be unmanaged. Although situations that require you to access memory in this way are not common, you might encounter some, especially if you are writing code that needs to perform some low-level Windows operations.

You will learn about the implications of using code that accesses unmanaged memory in more detail in Chapter 14.

Summary

In this chapter, you learned about some important differences between value types that hold their value directly on the stack and reference types that refer indirectly to their objects on the heap. You also learned how to use the *ref* and *out* keywords on method parameters to gain access to the arguments. You saw how assigning a value (such as the *int* 42) to a variable of the *System.Object* class creates a boxed copy of the value on the heap and then causes the *System.Object* variable to refer to this boxed copy. You also saw how assigning a variable of a value type (such as an *int*) from a variable of the *System.Object* class copies (or unboxes) the value in the *System.Object* class to the memory used by the *int*.

- If you want to continue to the next chapter, keep Visual Studio 2015 running and turn to Chapter 9.

- If you want to exit Visual Studio 2015 now, on the File menu, click Exit. If you see a Save dialog box, click Yes and save the project.

Quick reference

To	Do this
Copy a value type variable	Simply make the copy. Because the variable is a value type, you will have two copies of the same value. For example: ```\nint i = 42;\nint copyi = i;\n```
Copy a reference type variable	Simply make the copy. Because the variable is a reference type, you will have two references to the same object. For example: ```\nCircle c = new Circle(42);\nCircle refc = c;\n```
Declare a variable that can hold a value type or the *null* value	Declare the variable by using the *?* modifier with the type. For example: ```\nint? i = null;\n```
Pass an argument to a *ref* parameter	Prefix the argument with the *ref* keyword. This makes the parameter an alias for the actual argument rather than a copy of the argument. The method may change the value of the parameter, and this change is made to the actual argument rather than to a local copy. For example: ```\nstatic void Main()\n{\n int arg = 42;\n doWork(ref arg);\n Console.WriteLine(arg);\n}\n```
Pass an argument to an *out* parameter	Prefix the argument with the *out* keyword. This makes the parameter an alias for the actual argument rather than a copy of the argument. The method *must* assign a value to the parameter, and this value is made to the actual argument. For example: ```\nstatic void Main()\n{\n int arg;\n doWork(out arg);\n Console.WriteLine(arg);\n}\n```

To	Do this
| Box a value | Initialize or assign a variable of type *object* with the value. For example:<br><br>```csharp
object o = 42;
``` |
| Unbox a value | Cast the object reference that refers to the boxed value to the type of the value variable. For example:<br><br>```csharp
int i = (int)o;
``` |
| Cast an object safely | Use the *is* operator to test whether the cast is valid. For example:<br><br>```csharp
WrappedInt wi = new WrappedInt();
...
object o = wi;
if (o is WrappedInt)
{
    WrappedInt temp = (WrappedInt)o;
    ...
}
```<br><br>Alternatively, use the *as* operator to perform the cast, and test whether the result is null. For example:<br><br>```csharp
WrappedInt wi = new WrappedInt();
...
object o = wi;
WrappedInt temp = o as WrappedInt;
if (temp != null)
    ...
``` |

Creating value types with enumerations and structures

After completing this chapter, you will be able to:

- Declare an enumeration type.

- Create and use an enumeration type.

- Declare a structure type.

- Create and use a structure type.

- Explain the differences in behavior between a structure and a class.

Chapter 8, "Understanding values and references," covers the two fundamental types that exist in Microsoft Visual C#: *value types* and *reference types*. Recall that a value type variable holds its value directly on the stack, whereas a reference type variable holds a reference to an object on the heap. Chapter 7, "Creating and managing classes and objects," demonstrates how to create your own reference types by defining classes. In this chapter, you'll learn how to create your own value types.

C# supports two kinds of value types: *enumerations* and *structures*. We'll look at each of them in turn.

Working with enumerations

Suppose that you want to represent the seasons of the year in a program. You could use the integers 0, 1, 2, and 3 to represent spring, summer, fall, and winter, respectively. This system would work, but it's not very intuitive. If you used the integer value 0 in code, it wouldn't be obvious that a particular 0 represented spring. It also wouldn't be a very robust solution. For example, if you declare an *int* variable named *season*, there is nothing to stop you from assigning it any legal integer value outside the set 0, 1, 2, or 3. C# offers a better solution. You can create an enumeration (sometimes called an *enum* type) whose values are limited to a set of symbolic names.

Declaring an enumeration

You define an enumeration by using the *enum* keyword, followed by a set of symbols identifying the legal values that the type can have, enclosing them between braces. Here's how to declare an enumeration named *Season* whose literal values are limited to the symbolic names *Spring, Summer, Fall,* and *Winter*:

```
enum Season { Spring, Summer, Fall, Winter }
```

Using an enumeration

After you have declared an enumeration, you can use it in exactly the same way you do any other type. If the name of your enumeration is *Season*, you can create variables of type *Season*, fields of type *Season*, and parameters of type *Season*, as shown in this example:

```
enum Season { Spring, Summer, Fall, Winter }

class Example
{
    public void Method(Season parameter) // method parameter example
    {
        Season localVariable; // local variable example
        ...
    }

    private Season currentSeason; // field example
}
```

Before you can read the value of an enumeration variable, it must be assigned a value. You can assign a value that is defined by the enumeration only to an enumeration variable, as is illustrated here:

```
Season colorful = Season.Fall;
Console.WriteLine(colorful);  // writes out 'Fall'
```

> **Note** As you can with all value types, you can create a nullable version of an enumeration variable by using the *?* modifier. You can then assign the *null* value, as well as the values defined by the enumeration, to the variable:
>
> ```
> Season? colorful = null;
> ```

Notice that you have to write *Season.Fall* rather than just *Fall*. All enumeration literal names are scoped by their enumeration type, which makes it possible for different enumerations to contain literals with the same name.

Also, notice that when you display an enumeration variable by using *Console.WriteLine*, the compiler generates code that writes out the name of the literal whose value matches the value of the variable. If needed, you can explicitly convert an enumeration variable to a string that represents its current value by using the built-in *ToString* method that all enumerations automatically contain, as demonstrated in the following example:

```
string name = colorful.ToString();
Console.WriteLine(name);     // also writes out 'Fall'
```

Many of the standard operators that you can use on integer variables you can also use on enumeration variables (except the bitwise and shift operators, which are covered in Chapter 16, "Using indexers"). For example, you can compare two enumeration variables of the same type for equality by using the equality operator (==), and you can even perform arithmetic on an enumeration variable—although the result might not always be meaningful!

Choosing enumeration literal values

Internally, an enumeration type associates an integer value with each element of the enumeration. By default, the numbering starts at 0 for the first element and goes up in steps of 1. It's possible to retrieve the underlying integer value of an enumeration variable. To do this, you must cast it to its underlying type. The discussion in Chapter 8 on unboxing instructs that casting a type converts the data from one type to another as long as the conversion is valid and meaningful. The following code example writes out the value *2* and not the word *Fall* (remember, in the *Season* enumeration, *Spring* is *0*, *Summer 1*, *Fall 2*, and *Winter 3*):

```
enum Season { Spring, Summer, Fall, Winter }
...
Season colorful = Season.Fall;
Console.WriteLine((int)colorful); // writes out '2'
```

If you prefer, you can associate a specific integer constant (such as 1) with an enumeration literal (such as *Spring*), as in the following example:

```
enum Season { Spring = 1, Summer, Fall, Winter }
```

> **Important** The integer value with which you initialize an enumeration literal must be a compile-time constant value (such as 1).

If you don't explicitly give an enumeration literal a constant integer value, the compiler gives it a value that is one greater than the value of the previous enumeration literal, except for the very first enumeration literal, to which the compiler gives the default value *0*. In the preceding example, the underlying values of *Spring, Summer, Fall*, and *Winter* are now 1, 2, 3, and 4.

You are allowed to give more than one enumeration literal the same underlying value. For example, in the United Kingdom, fall is referred to as autumn. You can cater to both cultures as follows:

```
enum Season { Spring, Summer, Fall, Autumn = Fall, Winter }
```

Choosing an enumeration's underlying type

When you declare an enumeration, the enumeration literals are given values of type *int*. You can also choose to base your enumeration on a different underlying integer type. For example, to declare that the underlying type for *Season* is a *short* rather than an *int*, you can write this:

```
enum Season : short { Spring, Summer, Fall, Winter }
```

The main reason for using *short* is to save memory; an *int* occupies more memory than a *short*, and if you do not need the entire range of values available to an *int*, using a smaller data type can make sense.

You can base an enumeration on any of the eight integer types: *byte, sbyte, short, ushort, int, uint, long*, or *ulong*. The values of all the enumeration literals must fit within the range of the chosen base type. For example, if you base an enumeration on the *byte* data type, you can have a maximum of 256 literals (starting at 0).

Now that you know how to declare an enumeration, the next step is to use it. In the following exercise, you will work with a console application to declare and use an enumeration that represents the months of the year.

Create and use an enumeration

1. Start Microsoft Visual Studio 2015 if it is not already running.

2. Open the StructsAndEnums project, which is located in the \Microsoft Press\VCSBS\Chapter 9\ StructsAndEnums folder in your Documents folder.

3. In the Code and Text Editor window, display the Month.cs file.

   The source file is empty apart from the declaration of a namespace called *StructsAndEnums* and a *// TODO:* comment.

4. Replace the *// TODO:* comment with the enumeration named *Month* within the *StructsAndEnums* namespace, as shown in bold in the code that follows. This enumeration models the months of the year. The 12 enumeration literals for *Month* are *January* through *December*.

   ```
   namespace StructsAndEnums
   {
       enum Month
       {
           January, February, March, April,
           May, June, July, August,
           September, October, November, December
       }
   }
   ```

5. Display the Program.cs file in the Code and Text Editor window.

As in the exercises in previous chapters, the *Main* method calls the *doWork* method and traps any exceptions that occur.

6. In the Code and Text Editor window, add a statement to the *doWork* method to declare a variable named *first* of type *Month* and initialize it to *Month.January*. Add another statement to write the value of the *first* variable to the console.

The *doWork* method should look like this:

```
static void doWork()
{
    Month first = Month.January;
    Console.WriteLine(first);
}
```

 Note When you type the period following *Month*, Microsoft IntelliSense automatically displays all the values in the *Month* enumeration.

7. On the Debug menu, click Start Without Debugging.

Visual Studio 2015 builds and runs the program. Confirm that the word *January* is written to the console.

8. Press Enter to close the program and return to the Visual Studio 2015 programming environment.

9. Add two more statements to the *doWork* method to increment the *first* variable and display its new value to the console, as shown in bold here:

```
static void doWork()
{
    Month first = Month.January;
    Console.WriteLine(first);
    first++;
    Console.WriteLine(first);
}
```

10. On the Debug menu, click Start Without Debugging.

Visual Studio 2015 builds and runs the program. Confirm that the words *January* and *February* are written to the console.

Notice that performing a mathematical operation (such as the increment operation) on an enumeration variable changes the internal integer value of the variable. When the variable is written to the console, the corresponding enumeration value is displayed.

11. Press Enter to close the program and return to the Visual Studio 2015 programming environment.

12. Modify the first statement in the *doWork* method to initialize the *first* variable to *Month.December*, as shown in bold here:

```
static void doWork()
{
    Month first = Month.December;
    Console.WriteLine(first);
    first++;
    Console.WriteLine(first);
}
```

13. On the Debug menu, click Start Without Debugging.

Visual Studio 2015 builds and runs the program. This time, the word *December* is written to the console, followed by the number *12*.

```
C:\Windows\system32\cmd.exe
December
12
Press any key to continue . . .
```

Although you can perform arithmetic on an enumeration, if the results of the operation are outside the range of values defined for the enumeration, all the runtime can do is interpret the value of the variable as the corresponding integer value.

14. Press Enter to close the program and return to the Visual Studio 2015 programming environment.

Working with structures

Chapter 8 illustrated that classes define reference types that are always created on the heap. In some cases, the class can contain so little data that the overhead of managing the heap becomes disproportionate. In these cases, it is better to define the type as a structure. A structure is a value type. Because structures are stored on the stack, as long as the structure is reasonably small, the memory management overhead is often reduced.

Like a class, a structure can have its own fields, methods, and (with one important exception discussed later in this chapter) constructors.

Common structure types

You might not have realized it, but you have already used structures in previous exercises in this book. In C#, the primitive numeric types *int*, *long*, and *float* are aliases for the structures *System.Int32*, *System.Int64*, and *System.Single*, respectively. These structures have fields and methods, and you can actually call methods on variables and literals of these types. For example, all these structures provide a *ToString* method that can convert a numeric value to its string representation. The following statements are all legal in C#:

```
int i = 55;
Console.WriteLine(i.ToString());
Console.WriteLine(55.ToString());
float f = 98.765F;
Console.WriteLine(f.ToString());
Console.WriteLine(98.765F.ToString());
```

You don't see this use of the *ToString* method often because the *Console.WriteLine* method calls it automatically when it is needed. It is more common to use some of the static methods exposed by these structures. For example, in earlier chapters you used the static *int.Parse* method to convert a string to its corresponding integer value. What you are actually doing is invoking the *Parse* method of the *Int32* structure:

```
string s = "42";
int i = int.Parse(s);    // exactly the same as Int32.Parse
```

These structures also include some useful static fields. For example, *Int32.MaxValue* is the maximum value that an *int* can hold, and *Int32.MinValue* is the minimum value that you can store in an *int*.

The following table shows the primitive types in C# and their equivalent types in the Microsoft .NET Framework. Notice that the string and object types are classes (reference types) rather than structures.

Keyword	Type equivalent	Class or structure
bool	System.Boolean	Structure
byte	System.Byte	Structure
decimal	System.Decimal	Structure
double	System.Double	Structure
float	System.Single	Structure
int	System.Int32	Structure
long	System.Int64	Structure
object	System.Object	Class
sbyte	System.SByte	Structure
short	System.Int16	Structure
string	System.String	Class
uint	System.UInt32	Structure
ulong	System.UInt64	Structure
ushort	System.UInt16	Structure

Declaring a structure

To declare your own structure type, you use the *struct* keyword followed by the name of the type and then enclose the body of the structure between opening and closing braces. Syntactically, the process is similar to declaring a class. For example, here is a structure named *Time* that contains three public *int* fields named *hours*, *minutes*, and *seconds*:

```
struct Time
{
    public int hours, minutes, seconds;
}
```

As with classes, making the fields of a structure public is not advisable in most cases; there is no way to control the values held in public fields. For example, anyone could set the value of *minutes* or *seconds* to a value greater than 60. A better idea is to make the fields private and provide your structure with constructors and methods to initialize and manipulate these fields, as shown in this example:

```
struct Time
{
    private int hours, minutes, seconds;
    ...
    public Time(int hh, int mm, int ss)
    {
        this.hours = hh % 24;
        this.minutes = mm % 60;
        this.seconds = ss % 60;
    }

    public int Hours()
    {
        return this.hours;
    }
}
```

> **Note** By default, you cannot use many of the common operators on your own structure types. For example, you cannot use operators such as the equality operator (==) and the inequality operator (!=) on your own structure type variables. However, you can use the built-in *Equals()* method exposed by all structures to compare structure type variables, and you can also explicitly declare and implement operators for your own structure types. The syntax for doing this is covered in Chapter 21, "Querying in-memory data by using query expressions."

When you copy a value type variable, you get two copies of the value. In contrast, when you copy a reference type variable, you get two references to the same object. In summary, use structures for small data values for which it's just as or nearly as efficient to copy the value as it would be to copy an address. Use classes for more complex data that is too big to copy efficiently.

Understanding differences between structures and classes

A structure and a class are syntactically similar, but they have a few important differences. Let's look at some of these variances:

- You can't declare a default constructor (a constructor with no parameters) for a structure. The following example would compile if *Time* were a class, but because *Time* is a structure it does not:

```
struct Time
{
    public Time() { ... } // compile-time error
    ...
}
```

  The reason you can't declare your own default constructor for a structure is that the compiler *always* generates one. In a class, the compiler generates the default constructor only if you don't write a constructor yourself. The compiler-generated default constructor for a structure always sets the fields to *0, false*, or *null*—just as for a class. Therefore, you should ensure that a structure value created by the default constructor behaves logically and makes sense with these default values. This has some ramifications that you will explore in the next exercise.

  You can initialize fields to different values by providing a nondefault constructor. However, when you do this, your nondefault constructor must explicitly initialize all fields in your structure; the default initialization no longer occurs. If you fail to do this, you'll get a compile-time error. For example, although the following example would compile and silently initialize *seconds* to 0 if *Time* were a class, it fails to compile because *Time* is a structure:

```
struct Time
{
    private int hours, minutes, seconds;
    ...
    public Time(int hh, int mm)
    {
        this.hours = hh;
        this.minutes = mm;
    }   // compile-time error: seconds not initialized
}
```

- In a class, you can initialize instance fields at their point of declaration. In a structure, you cannot. The following example would compile if *Time* were a class, but it causes a compile-time error because *Time* is a structure:

```
struct Time
{
    private int hours = 0; // compile-time error
    private int minutes;
    private int seconds;
    ...
}
```

The following table summarizes the main differences between a structure and a class.

Question	Structure	Class
Is this a value type or a reference type?	A structure is a value type.	A class is a reference type.
Do instances live on the stack or the heap?	Structure instances are called *values* and live on the stack.	Class instances are called *objects* and live on the heap.
Can you declare a default constructor?	No	Yes
If you declare your own constructor, will the compiler still generate the default constructor?	Yes	No
If you don't initialize a field in your own constructor, will the compiler automatically initialize it for you?	No	Yes
Are you allowed to initialize instance fields at their point of declaration?	No	Yes

There are other differences between classes and structures concerning inheritance. These differences are covered in Chapter 12, "Working with inheritance."

Declaring structure variables

After you have defined a structure type, you can use it in exactly the same way as you do any other type. For example, if you have defined the *Time* structure, you can create variables, fields, and parameters of type *Time*, as shown in this example:

```
struct Time
{
    private int hours, minutes, seconds;
    ...
}

class Example
{
    private Time currentTime;

    public void Method(Time parameter)
    {
        Time localVariable;
        ...
    }
}
```

Understanding structure initialization

Earlier in this chapter, you saw how you can initialize the fields in a structure by using a constructor. If you call a constructor, the various rules described earlier guarantee that all the fields in the structure will be initialized:

```
Time now = new Time();
```

The following illustration depicts the state of the fields in this structure:

However, because structures are value types, you can also create structure variables without calling a constructor, as shown in the following example:

```
Time now;
```

This time, the variable is created but its fields are left in their uninitialized state. The following illustration depicts the state of the fields in the *now* variable. Any attempt to access the values in these fields will result in a compiler error:

Note that in both cases, the *now* variable is created on the stack.

If you've written your own structure constructor, you can also use that to initialize a structure variable. As explained earlier in this chapter, a structure constructor must always explicitly initialize all its fields. For example:

```
struct Time
{
    private int hours, minutes, seconds;
    ...

    public Time(int hh, int mm)
    {
        hours = hh;
        minutes = mm;
        seconds = 0;
    }
}
```

The following example initializes *now* by calling a user-defined constructor:

```
Time now = new Time(12, 30);
```

The following illustration shows the effect of this example:

It's time to put this knowledge into practice. In the following exercise, you will create and use a structure to represent a date.

Create and use a structure type

1. In the StructsAndEnums project, display the Date.cs file in the Code and Text Editor window.

2. Replace the TODO comment with a structure named *Date* inside the *StructsAndEnums* namespace.

   This structure should contain three private fields: one named *year* of type *int*, one named *month* of type *Month* (using the enumeration you created in the preceding exercise), and one named *day* of type *int*. The *Date* structure should look exactly as follows:

   ```
   struct Date
   {
       private int year;
       private Month month;
       private int day;
   }
   ```

   Consider the default constructor that the compiler will generate for *Date*. This constructor sets the *year* to *0*, the *month* to *0* (the value of January), and the *day* to *0*. The *year* value 0 is not valid (because there was no year 0), and the *day* value 0 is also not valid (because each month starts on day 1). One way to fix this problem is to translate the *year* and *day* values by implementing the *Date* structure so that when the *year* field holds the value *Y*, this value represents the year *Y* + 1900 (or you can pick a different century if you prefer), and when the *day* field holds the value *D*, this value represents the day *D* + 1. The default constructor will then set the three fields to values that represent the date 1 January 1900.

If you could override the default constructor and write your own, this would not be an issue because you could then initialize the year and day fields directly to valid values. You cannot do this, though, so you have to implement the logic in your structure to translate the compiler-generated default values into meaningful values for your problem domain.

However, although you cannot override the default constructor, it is still good practice to define nondefault constructors to allow a user to explicitly initialize the fields in a structure to meaningful nondefault values.

3. Add a public constructor to the *Date* structure. This constructor should take three parameters: an *int* named *ccyy* for the *year*, a *Month* named *mm* for the *month*, and an *int* named *dd* for the *day*. Use these three parameters to initialize the corresponding fields. A *year* field with the value *Y* represents the year *Y* + 1900, so you need to initialize the *year* field to the value *ccyy* − 1900. A *day* field with the value *D* represents the day *D* + 1, so you need to initialize the *day* field to the value *dd* − 1.

The *Date* structure should now look like this (with the constructor shown in bold):

```
struct Date
{
    private int year;
    private Month month;
    private int day;

    public Date(int ccyy, Month mm, int dd)
    {
        this.year = ccyy - 1900;
        this.month = mm;
        this.day = dd - 1;
    }
}
```

4. Add a public method named *ToString* to the *Date* structure after the constructor. This method takes no arguments and returns a string representation of the date. Remember, the value of the *year* field represents *year* + 1900, and the value of the *day* field represents *day* + 1.

> **Note** The *ToString* method is a little different from the methods you have seen so far. Every type, including structures and classes that you define, automatically has a *ToString* method whether or not you want it. Its default behavior is to convert the data in a variable to a string representation of that data. Sometimes the default behavior is meaningful; other times it is less so. For example, the default behavior of the *ToString* method generated for the *Date* structure simply generates the string

"*StructsAndEnums.Date*". To quote Zaphod Beeblebrox in *The Restaurant at the End of the Universe* by Douglas Adams (Pan Macmillan, 1980), this is "shrewd, but dull." You need to define a new version of this method that overrides the default behavior by using the *override* keyword. Overriding methods are discussed in more detail in Chapter 12.

The *ToString* method should look like this:

```
struct Date
{
    ...
    public override string ToString()
    {
        string data = $"{this.month} {this.day + 1} {this.year + 1900}";
        return data;
    }
}
```

In this method, you build a formatted string using the text representations of the values of the *month* field, the expression *this.day + 1*, and the expression *this.year + 1900*. The *ToString* method returns the formatted string as its result.

5. Display the Program.cs file in the Code and Text Editor window.

6. In the *doWork* method, comment out the four existing statements.

7. Add statements to the *doWork* method that declare a local variable named *defaultDate* and initialize it to a *Date* value constructed by using the default *Date* constructor. Add another statement to *doWork* to display the *defaultDate* variable on the console by calling *Console .WriteLine*.

> **Note** The *Console.WriteLine* method automatically calls the *ToString* method of its argument to format the argument as a string.

The *doWork* method should now look like this:

```
static void doWork()
{
    ...
    Date defaultDate = new Date();
    Console.WriteLine(defaultDate);
}
```

> **Note** When you type *new Date(*, IntelliSense automatically detects that two constructors are available for the *Date* type.

8. On the Debug menu, click Start Without Debugging to build and run the program. Verify that the date January 1 1900 is written to the console.

9. Press the Enter key to return to the Visual Studio 2015 programming environment.

10. In the Code and Text Editor window, return to the *doWork* method and add two more statements. In the first statement, declare a local variable named *weddingAnniversary* and initialize it to July 4 2015. (I actually did get married on Independence Day, although it was many years ago.) In the second statement, write the value of *weddingAnniversary* to the console.

The *doWork* method should now look like this:

```
static void doWork()
{
    ...

    Date weddingAnniversary = new Date(2015, Month.July, 4);
    Console.WriteLine(weddingAnniversary);
}
```

11. On the Debug menu, click Start Without Debugging, and then confirm that the date July 4 2015 is written to the console below the previous information.

12. Press Enter to close the program and return to Visual Studio 2015.

Copying structure variables

You're allowed to initialize or assign one structure variable to another structure variable, but only if the structure variable on the right side is completely initialized (that is, if all its fields are populated with valid data rather than undefined values). The following example compiles because *now* is fully initialized. The illustration shows the results of performing such an assignment.

```
Date now = new Date(2012, Month.March, 19);
Date copy = now;
```

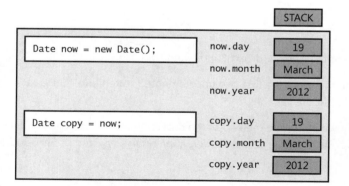

The following example fails to compile because *now* is not initialized:

```
Date now;
Date copy = now; // compile-time error: now has not been assigned
```

When you copy a structure variable, each field on the left side is set directly from the corresponding field on the right side. This copying is done as a fast, single operation that copies the contents of the entire structure, and it never throws an exception. Compare this behavior with the equivalent action if *Time* were a class, in which case both variables (*now* and *copy*) would end up referencing the *same* object on the heap.

> **Note** If you are a C++ programmer, you should note that this copy behavior cannot be customized.

In the final exercise in this chapter, you will contrast the copy behavior of a structure with that of a class.

Compare the behavior of a structure and a class

1. In the StructsAndEnums project, display the Date.cs file in the Code and Text Editor window.

2. Add the following method to the *Date* structure. This method advances the date in the structure by one month. If, after advancing the month, the value of the *month* field has moved beyond December, the code resets the month to January and advances the value of the *year* field by 1.

```
struct Date
{
    ...
    public void AdvanceMonth()
    {
        this.month++;
        if (this.month == Month.December + 1)
        {
            this.month = Month.January;
            this.year++;
        }
    }
}
```

3. Display the Program.cs file in the Code and Text Editor window.

4. In the *doWork* method, comment out the first two uncommented statements that create and display the value of the *defaultDate* variable.

5. Add the following code shown in bold to the end of the *doWork* method. This code creates a copy of the *weddingAnniversary* variable called *weddingAnniversaryCopy* and prints out the value of this new variable.

```
static void doWork()
{
    ...
    Date weddingAnniversaryCopy = weddingAnniversary;
```

```
        Console.WriteLine($"Value of copy is {weddingAnniversaryCopy}");
    }
```

6. Add the following statements shown in bold to the end of the *doWork* method. These statements call the *AdvanceMonth* method of the *weddingAnniversary* variable and then display
the value of the *weddingAnniversary* and *weddingAnniversaryCopy* variables:

```
static void doWork()
{
    ...
    weddingAnniversary.AdvanceMonth();
    Console.WriteLine($"New value of weddingAnniversary is {weddingAnniversary}");
    Console.WriteLine($"Value of copy is still {weddingAnniversaryCopy}");
}
```

7. On the Debug menu, click Start Without Debugging to build and run the application. Verify
that the console window displays the following messages:

```
July 4 2015
Value of copy is July 4 2015
New value of weddingAnniversary is August 4 2015
Value of copy is still July 4 2015
```

The first message displays the initial value of the *weddingAnniversary* variable (July 4 2015).
The second message displays the value of the *weddingAnniversaryCopy* variable. You can see
that it contains the same date held in the *weddingAnniversary* variable (July 4 2015). The third
message displays the value of the *weddingAnniversary* variable after changing the month to
August (August 4 2015). The final statement displays the value of the *weddingAnniversaryCopy*
variable. Notice that it has not changed from its original value of July 4 2015.

If *Date* were a class, creating a copy would reference the same object in memory as the
original instance. Changing the month in the original instance would therefore also change
the date referenced through the copy. You will verify this assertion in the following steps.

8. Press Enter and return to Visual Studio 2015.

9. Display the Date.cs file in the Code and Text Editor window.

10. Change the *Date* structure to a class, as shown in bold in the following code example:

```
class Date
{
    ...
}
```

11. On the Debug menu, click Start Without Debugging to build and run the application again.
Verify that the console window displays the following messages:

```
July 4 2015
Value of copy is July 4 2015
New value of weddingAnniversary is August 4 2015
Value of copy is still August 4 2015
```

The first three messages are the same as before. However, the fourth message shows that the value of the *weddingAnniversaryCopy* variable has changed to August 4 2015.

12. Press Enter and return to Visual Studio 2015.

Structures and compatibility with the Windows Runtime

All C# applications execute by using the common language runtime (CLR) of the .NET Framework. The CLR is responsible for providing a safe and secure environment for your application code in the form of a *virtual machine* (if you have come from a Java background, this concept should be familiar to you). When you compile a C# application, the compiler converts your C# code into a set of instructions using a pseudo-machine code called the Common Intermediate Language (CIL). These are the instructions that are stored in an assembly. When you run a C# application, the CLR takes responsibility for converting the CIL instructions into real machine instructions that the processor on your computer can understand and execute. This whole environment is known as the *managed* execution environment, and C# programs are frequently referred to as *managed code*. You can also write managed code in other languages supported by the .NET Framework, such as Visual Basic and F#.

On Windows 7 and earlier versions, you can additionally write unmanaged applications, also known as *native code*, based on the Win32 APIs, which are the APIs that interface directly with the Windows operating system. (The CLR also converts many of the functions in the .NET Framework into Win32 API calls if you are running a managed application, although this process is totally transparent to your code.) To do this, you can use a language such as C++. The .NET Framework makes it possible for you to integrate managed code into unmanaged applications, and vice versa, through a set of interoperability technologies. Detailing how these technologies work and how you use them is beyond the scope of this book—suffice to say that it was not always straightforward.

Later versions of Windows provide an alternative strategy in the form of the Windows Runtime, or WinRT. WinRT introduces a layer on top of the Win32 API (and other selected native Windows APIs) that provides consistent functionality across different types of hardware, from servers to phones. When you build a Universal Windows Platform (UWP) app, you use the APIs exposed by WinRT rather than Win32. Similarly, the CLR on Windows 10 also uses WinRT; all managed code written by using C# or any other managed language is still executed by the CLR, but at run time the CLR converts your code into WinRT API calls rather than Win32. Between them, the CLR and WinRT are responsible for managing and running your code safely.

A primary purpose of WinRT is to simplify the interoperability between languages so that you can more easily integrate components developed by using different programming languages into a single seamless application. However, this simplicity comes at a cost, and you have to be prepared to make a few compromises based on the different feature sets of the various languages available. In particular, for historical reasons, although C++ supports structures, it does not recognize member functions. In C# terms, a member function is an instance method. So, if you are building C# structures (or structs) that you want to package up in a library to make available to developers programming in C++ (or any other unmanaged language), these structs should not contain any instance methods. The same restriction applies to static methods in structs. If you want to include instance or static methods, you should convert your struct into a class. Additionally, structs cannot contain private fields, and all public fields must be C# primitive types, conforming value types, or strings.

WinRT also imposes some other restrictions on C# classes and structs if you want to make them available to native applications. Chapter 12 provides more information.

Summary

In this chapter, you saw how to create and use enumerations and structures. You learned some of the similarities and differences between a structure and a class, and you saw how to define constructors to initialize the fields in a structure. You also saw how to represent a structure as a string by overriding the *ToString* method.

- If you want to continue to the next chapter, keep Visual Studio 2015 running and turn to Chapter 10, "Using arrays."

- If you want to exit Visual Studio 2015 now, on the File menu, click Exit. If you see a Save dialog box, click Yes and save the project.

Quick reference

To	Do this
Declare an enumeration	Write the keyword *enum*, followed by the name of the type, followed by a pair of braces containing a comma-separated list of the enumeration literal names. For example: `enum Season { Spring, Summer, Fall, Winter }`
Declare an enumeration variable	Write the name of the enumeration on the left followed by the name of the variable, followed by a semicolon. For example: `Season currentSeason;`

To	Do this

Assign an enumeration variable to a value	Write the name of the enumeration literal in combination with the name of the enumeration to which it belongs. For example:
	
	``
	currentSeason = Spring; // error
	currentSeason = Season.Spring; // correct
	``

Declare a structure type	Write the keyword *struct*, followed by the name of the structure type, followed by the body of the structure (the constructors, methods, and fields). For example:
	
	``
	struct Time
	{
	    public Time(int hh, int mm, int ss)
	    { ... }
	    ...
	    private int hours, minutes, seconds;
	}
	``

Declare a structure variable	Write the name of the structure type, followed by the name of the variable, followed by a semicolon. For example: ``` Time now; ```
Initialize a structure variable to a value	Initialize the variable to a structure value created by calling the structure constructor. For example: ``` Time lunch = new Time(12, 30, 0); ```

Using arrays

After completing this chapter, you will be able to:

- Declare array variables.

- Populate an array with a set of data items.

- Access the data items held in an array.

- Iterate through the data items in an array.

You have already seen how to create and use variables of many different types. However, all the examples of variables you have seen so far have one thing in common—they hold information about a single item (an *int*, a *float*, a *Circle*, a *Date*, and so on). What happens if you need to manipulate a set of items? One solution is to create a variable for each item in the set, but this leads to a number of further questions: How many variables do you need? How should you name them? If you need to perform the same operation on each item in the set (such as increment each variable in a set of integers), how would you avoid very repetitive code? Using a variable for separate items assumes that you know, when you write the program, how many items you will need. But how often is this the case? For example, if you are writing an application that reads and processes records from a database, how many records are in the database, and how likely is this number to change?

Arrays provide a mechanism that helps to solve these problems.

Declaring and creating an array

An *array* is an unordered sequence of items. All the items in an array have the same type, unlike the fields in a structure or class, which can have different types. The items in an array live in a contiguous block of memory and are accessed by using an index, unlike fields in a structure or class, which are accessed by name.

Declaring array variables

You declare an array variable by specifying the name of the element type, followed by a pair of square brackets, followed by the variable name. The square brackets signify that the variable is an array. For example, to declare an array of *int* variables named *pins* (for holding a set of personal identification numbers) you can write the following:

```
int[] pins; // Personal Identification Numbers
```

> **Note** If you are a Microsoft Visual Basic programmer, you should observe that square brackets, not parentheses, are used in the declaration. If you're familiar with C and C++, also note that the size of the array is not part of the declaration. Additionally, the square brackets must be placed *before* the variable name.

You are not restricted to using primitive types as array elements. You can also create arrays of structures, enumerations, and classes. For example, you can create an array of *Date* structures like this:

```
Date[] dates;
```

> **Tip** It is often useful to give array variables plural names, such as *places* (where each element is a *Place*), *people* (where each element is a *Person*), or *times* (where each element is a *Time*).

Creating an array instance

Arrays are reference types, regardless of the type of their elements. This means that an array variable *refers* to a contiguous block of memory holding the array elements on the heap, just as a class variable refers to an object on the heap. (For a description of values and references and the differences between the stack and the heap, see Chapter 8, "Understanding values and references.") This rule applies regardless of the type of the data items in the array. Even if the array contains a value type such as *int*, the memory will still be allocated on the heap; this is the one case where value types are not allocated memory on the stack.

Remember that when you declare a class variable, memory is not allocated for the object until you create the instance by using *new*. Arrays follow the same pattern: when you declare an array variable, you do not declare its size and no memory is allocated (other than to hold the reference on the stack). The array is given memory only when the instance is created, and this is also the point at which you specify the size of the array.

To create an array instance, you use the *new* keyword followed by the element type, followed by the size of the array you're creating enclosed between square brackets. Creating an array also initializes its elements by using the now familiar default values (*0*, *null*, or *false*, depending on whether the type is numeric, a reference, or a Boolean, respectively). For example, to create and initialize a new array of four integers for the *pins* variable declared earlier, you write this:

```
pins = new int[4];
```

The following illustration shows what happens when you declare an array, and later when you create an instance of the array:

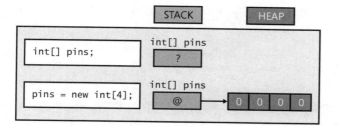

Because the memory for the array instance is allocated dynamically, the size of the array does not have to be a constant; it can be calculated at run time, as shown in this example:

```
int size = int.Parse(Console.ReadLine());
int[] pins = new int[size];
```

You can also create an array whose size is 0. This might sound bizarre, but it's useful for situations in which the size of the array is determined dynamically and could even be 0. An array of size 0 is not a *null* array; it is an array containing zero elements.

Populating and using an array

When you create an array instance, all the elements of the array are initialized to a default value depending on their type. For example, all numeric values default to *0*, objects are initialized to *null*, *DateTime* values are set to the date and time *"01/01/0001 00:00:00"*, and strings are initialized to *null*. You can modify this behavior and initialize the elements of an array to specific values if you prefer. You do this by providing a comma-separated list of values between a pair of braces. For example, to initialize *pins* to an array of four *int* variables whose values are 9, 3, 7, and 2, you write this:

```
int[] pins = new int[4]{ 9, 3, 7, 2 };
```

The values between the braces do not have to be constants; they can be values calculated at run time, as shown in the following example, which populates the *pins* array with four random numbers:

```
Random r = new Random();
int[] pins = new int[4]{ r.Next() % 10, r.Next() % 10,
                         r.Next() % 10, r.Next() % 10 };
```

> **Note** The *System.Random* class is a pseudorandom number generator. The *Next* method returns a nonnegative random integer in the range *0* to *Int32.MaxValue* by default. The *Next* method is overloaded, and other versions enable you to specify the minimum value and maximum value of the range. The default constructor for the *Random* class seeds the random number generator with a time-dependent seed value, which reduces the possibility of the class duplicating a sequence of random numbers. Using an overloaded version of the constructor, you can provide your own seed value. That way, you can generate a repeatable sequence of random numbers for testing purposes.

The number of values between the braces must exactly match the size of the array instance being created:

```
int[] pins = new int[3]{ 9, 3, 7, 2 }; // compile-time error
int[] pins = new int[4]{ 9, 3, 7 };    // compile-time error
int[] pins = new int[4]{ 9, 3, 7, 2 }; // OK
```

When you're initializing an array variable in this way, you can actually omit the *new* expression and the size of the array. In this case, the compiler calculates the size from the number of initializers and generates code to create the array, such as in the following example:

```
int[] pins = { 9, 3, 7, 2 };
```

If you create an array of structures or objects, you can initialize each structure in the array by calling the structure or class constructor, as shown in this example:

```
Time[] schedule = { new Time(12,30), new Time(5,30) };
```

Creating an implicitly typed array

The element type when you declare an array must match the type of elements that you attempt to store in the array. For example, if you declare *pins* to be an array of *int*, as shown in the preceding examples, you cannot store a *double, string, struct*, or anything that is not an *int* in this array. If you specify a list of initializers when declaring an array, you can let the C# compiler infer the actual type of the elements in the array for you, like this:

```
var names = new[]{"John", "Diana", "James", "Francesca"};
```

In this example, the C# compiler determines that the *names* variable is an array of strings. It is worth pointing out a couple of syntactic quirks in this declaration. First, you omit the square brackets from the type; the *names* variable in this example is declared simply as *var*, not *var[]*. Second, you must specify the *new* operator and square brackets before the initializer list.

If you use this syntax, you must ensure that all the initializers have the same type. This next example causes the compile-time error "No best type found for implicitly-typed array":

```
var bad = new[]{"John", "Diana", 99, 100};
```

However, in some cases, the compiler will convert elements to a different type, if doing so makes sense. In the following code, the *numbers* array is an array of *double* because the constants *3.5* and *99.999* are both *double*, and the C# compiler can convert the integer values *1* and *2* to *double* values:

```
var numbers = new[]{1, 2, 3.5, 99.999};
```

Generally, it is best to avoid mixing types, hoping that the compiler will convert them for you.

Implicitly typed arrays are most useful when you are working with anonymous types, as described in Chapter 7, "Creating and managing classes and objects." The following code creates an array of anonymous objects, each containing two fields specifying the name and age of the members of my family:

```
var names = new[] { new { Name = "John", Age = 50 },
                    new { Name = "Diana", Age = 50 },
                    new { Name = "James", Age = 23 },
                    new { Name = "Francesca", Age = 21 } };
```

The fields in the anonymous types must be the same for each element of the array.

Accessing an individual array element

To access an individual array element, you must provide an index indicating which element you require. Array indexes are zero-based; thus, the initial element of an array lives at index 0 and not index 1. An index value of *1* accesses the second element. For example, you can read the contents of element 2 (the third element) of the *pins* array into an *int* variable by using the following code:

```
int myPin;
myPin = pins[2];
```

Similarly, you can change the contents of an array by assigning a value to an indexed element:

```
myPin = 1645;
pins[2] = myPin;
```

All array element access is bounds-checked. If you specify an index that is less than 0 or greater than or equal to the length of the array, the compiler throws an *IndexOutOfRangeException* exception, as in this example:

```
try
{
    int[] pins = { 9, 3, 7, 2 };
    Console.WriteLine(pins[4]); // error, the 4th and last element is at index 3
}
catch (IndexOutOfRangeException ex)
{
    ...
}
```

Iterating through an array

All arrays are actually instances of the *System.Array* class in the Microsoft .NET Framework, and this class defines a number of useful properties and methods. For example, you can query the *Length* property to discover how many elements an array contains and iterate through all the elements of an array by using a *for* statement. The following sample code writes the array element values of the *pins* array to the console:

```
int[] pins = { 9, 3, 7, 2 };
for (int index = 0; index < pins.Length; index++)
{
    int pin = pins[index];
    Console.WriteLine(pin);
}
```

It is common for new programmers to forget that arrays start at element 0 and that the last element is numbered *Length* − 1. C# provides the *foreach* statement, with which you can iterate through the elements of an array without worrying about these issues. For example, here's the preceding *for* statement rewritten as an equivalent *foreach* statement:

```
int[] pins = { 9, 3, 7, 2 };
foreach (int pin in pins)
{
    Console.WriteLine(pin);
}
```

The *foreach* statement declares an iteration variable (in this example, *int pin*) that automatically acquires the value of each element in the array. The type of this variable must match the type of the elements in the array. The *foreach* statement is the preferred way to iterate through an array; it expresses the intention of the code directly, and all of the *for* loop scaffolding drops away. However, in a few cases, you'll find that you have to revert to a *for* statement:

- A *foreach* statement always iterates through the entire array. If you want to iterate through only a known portion of an array (for example, the first half) or bypass certain elements (for example, every third element), it's easier to use a *for* statement.

- A *foreach* statement always iterates from index 0 through index *Length* − 1. If you want to iterate backward or in some other sequence, it's easier to use a *for* statement.

- If the body of the loop needs to know the index of the element rather than just the value of the element, you have to use a *for* statement.

- If you need to modify the elements of the array, you have to use a *for* statement. This is because the iteration variable of the *foreach* statement is a read-only copy of each element of the array.

You can declare the iteration variable as a *var* and let the C# compiler work out the type of the variable from the type of the elements in the array. This is especially useful if you don't actually know the type of the elements in the array, such as when the array contains anonymous objects. The following example demonstrates how you can iterate through the array of family members shown earlier:

```
var names = new[] { new { Name = "John", Age = 50 },
                    new { Name = "Diana", Age = 50 },
                    new { Name = "James", Age = 23 },
```

```
                      new { Name = "Francesca", Age = 21 } };
foreach (var familyMember in names)
{
    Console.WriteLine($"Name: {familyMember.Name}, Age: {familyMember.Age}");
}
```

Passing arrays as parameters and return values for a method

You can define methods that take arrays as parameters or pass them back as return values.

The syntax for passing an array as a parameter is much the same as for declaring an array. For example, the code sample that follows defines a method named *ProcessData* that takes an array of integers as a parameter. The body of the method iterates through the array and performs some unspecified processing on each element:

```
public void ProcessData(int[] data)
{
    foreach (int i in data)
    {
        ...
    }
}
```

It is important to remember that arrays are reference objects, so if you modify the contents of an array passed as a parameter inside a method such as *ProcessData*, the modification is visible through all references to the array, including the original argument passed as the parameter.

To return an array from a method, you specify the type of the array as the return type. In the method, you create and populate the array. The following example prompts the user for the size of an array, followed by the data for each element. The array created by the method is passed back as the return value:

```
public int[] ReadData()
{
    Console.WriteLine("How many elements?");
    string reply = Console.ReadLine();
    int numElements = int.Parse(reply);

    int[] data = new int[numElements];
    for (int i = 0; i < numElements; i++)
    {
        Console.WriteLine($"Enter data for element {i}");
        reply = Console.ReadLine();
        int elementData = int.Parse(reply);
        data[i] = elementData;
    }
    return data;
}
```

You can call the *ReadData* method like this:

```
int[] data = ReadData();
```

Array parameters and the *Main* method

You might have noticed that the *Main* method for an application takes an array of strings as a parameter:

```
static void Main(string[] args)
{
    ...
}
```

Remember that the *Main* method is called when your program starts running; it is the entry point of your application. If you start the application from the command line, you can specify additional command-line arguments. The Windows operating system passes these arguments to the common language runtime (CLR), which in turn passes them as arguments to the *Main* method. This mechanism gives you a simple way to allow a user to provide information when an application starts running instead of prompting the user interactively. This approach is useful if you want to build utilities that can be run from automated scripts.

The following example is taken from a utility application called MyFileUtil that processes files. It expects a set of file names on the command line and calls the *ProcessFile* method (not shown) to handle each file specified:

```
static void Main(string[] args)
{
    foreach (string filename in args)
    {
        ProcessFile(filename);
    }
}
```

The user can run the MyFileUtil application from the command line like this:

```
MyFileUtil C:\Temp\TestData.dat C:\Users\John\Documents\MyDoc.txt
```

Each command-line argument is separated by a space. It is up to the MyFileUtil application to verify that these arguments are valid.

Copying arrays

Arrays are reference types (remember that an array is an instance of the *System.Array* class). An array variable contains a reference to an array instance. This means that when you copy an array variable, you actually end up with two references to the same array instance, as demonstrated in the following example:

```
int[] pins = { 9, 3, 7, 2 };
int[] alias = pins; //  alias and pins refer to the same array instance
```

In this example, if you modify the value at *pins[1]*, the change will also be visible by reading *alias[1]*.

If you want to make a copy of the array instance (the data on the heap) that an array variable refers to, you have to do two things. First, you create a new array instance of the same type and the same length as the array you are copying. Second, you copy the data from the original array element by element to the new array, as in this example:

```
int[] pins = { 9, 3, 7, 2 };
int[] copy = new int[pins.Length];
for (int i = 0; i < pins.Length; i++)
{
    copy[i] = pins[i];
}
```

Note that this code uses the *Length* property of the original array to specify the size of the new array.

Copying an array is actually a common requirement of many applications—so much so that the *System.Array* class provides some useful methods that you can employ to copy an array. For example, the *CopyTo* method copies the contents of one array into another array given a specified starting index. The following example copies all the elements from the *pins* array to the *copy* array starting at element zero:

```
int[] pins = { 9, 3, 7, 2 };
int[] copy = new int[pins.Length];
pins.CopyTo(copy, 0);
```

Another way to copy the values is to use the *System.Array* static method named *Copy*. As with *CopyTo*, you must initialize the target array before calling *Copy*:

```
int[] pins = { 9, 3, 7, 2 };
int[] copy = new int[pins.Length];
Array.Copy(pins, copy, copy.Length);
```

> **Note** Be sure that you specify a valid value for the length parameter of the *Aray.Copy* method. If you provide a negative value, the method throws an *ArgumentOutOfRangeException* exception. If you specify a value that is greater than the number of elements in the source array, the method throws an *ArgumentException* exception.

Yet another alternative is to use the *System.Array* instance method named *Clone*. You can call this method to create an entire array and copy it in one action:

```
int[] pins = { 9, 3, 7, 2 };
int[] copy = (int[])pins.Clone();
```

Using multidimensional arrays

The arrays shown so far have contained a single dimension, and you can think of them as simple lists of values. You can create arrays with more than one dimension. For example, to create a two-dimensional array, you specify an array that requires two integer indexes. The following code creates a two-dimensional array of 24 integers called *items*. If it helps, you can think of the array as a table, with the first dimension specifying a number of rows and the second specifying a number of columns.

```
int[,] items = new int[4, 6];
```

To access an element in the array, you provide two index values to specify the "cell" (the intersection of a row and a column) holding the element. The following code shows some examples using the *items* array:

```
items[2, 3] = 99;              // set the element at cell(2,3) to 99
items[2, 4] = items [2,3];     // copy the element in cell(2, 3) to cell(2, 4)
items[2, 4]++;                 // increment the integer value at cell(2, 4)
```

There is no limit on the number of dimensions that you can specify for an array. The next code example creates and uses an array called *cube* that contains three dimensions. Notice that you must specify three indexes to access each element in the array.

```
int[, ,] cube = new int[5, 5, 5];
cube[1, 2, 1] = 101;
cube[1, 2, 2] = cube[1, 2, 1] * 3;
```

At this point, it is worth offering a word of caution about creating arrays with more than three dimensions. Specifically, arrays can consume a lot of memory. The *cube* array contains 125 elements (5 * 5 * 5). A four-dimensional array for which each dimension has a size of 5 contains 625 elements. If you start to create arrays with three or more dimensions, you can soon run out of memory. Therefore, you should always be prepared to catch and handle *OutOfMemoryException* exceptions when you use multidimensional arrays.

Creating jagged arrays

In C#, ordinary multidimensional arrays are sometimes referred to as *rectangular* arrays. Each dimension has a regular shape. For example, in the following tabular, two-dimensional *items* array, every row has a column containing 40 elements and there are 160 elements in total:

```
int[,] items = new int[4, 40];
```

As mentioned in the previous section, multidimensional arrays can consume a lot of memory. If the application uses only some of the data in each column, allocating memory for unused elements is a waste. In this scenario, you can use a *jagged* array, for which each column has a different length, like this:

```
int[][] items = new int[4][];
int[] columnForRow0 = new int[3];
int[] columnForRow1 = new int[10];
int[] columnForRow2 = new int[40];
int[] columnForRow3 = new int[25];
items[0] = columnForRow0;
items[1] = columnForRow1;
items[2] = columnForRow2;
items[3] = columnForRow3;
...
```

In this example, the application requires only 3 elements in the first column, 10 elements in the second column, 40 elements in the third column, and 25 elements in the final column. This code illustrates an array of arrays—*items*, instead of being a two-dimensional array, has only a single dimension, but the elements in that dimension are themselves arrays. Furthermore, the total size of the *items* array is 78 elements rather than 160; no space is allocated for elements that the application is not going to use.

It is worth highlighting some of the syntax in this example. The following declaration specifies that *items* is an array of arrays of *int*.

```
int[][] items;
```

The following statement initializes *items* to hold four elements, each of which is an array of indeterminate length:

```
items = new int[4][];
```

The arrays *columnForRow0* to *columnForRow3* are all single-dimensional *int* arrays, initialized to hold the required amount of data for each column. Finally, each column array is assigned to the appropriate elements in the *items* array, like this:

```
items[0] = columnForRow0;
```

Recall that arrays are reference objects, so this statement simply adds a reference to *columnForRow0* to the first element in the *items* array; it does not actually copy any data. You can populate data in this column either by assigning a value to an indexed element in *columnForRow0* or by referencing it through the *items* array. The following statements are equivalent:

```
columnForRow0[1] = 99;
items[0][1] = 99;
```

You can extend this idea further if you want to create arrays of arrays of arrays rather than rectangular three-dimensional arrays, and so on.

> **Note** If you have written code using the Java programming language in the past, you should be familiar with this concept. Java does not have multidimensional arrays; instead, you can create arrays of arrays exactly as just described.

In the following exercise, you will use arrays to implement an application that deals playing cards as part of a card game. The application displays a form with four hands of cards dealt at random from a regular (52 cards) pack of playing cards. You will complete the code that deals the cards for each hand.

Use arrays to implement a card game

1. Start Microsoft Visual Studio 2015 if it is not already running.

2. Open the Cards project, which is located in the \Microsoft Press\VCSBS\Chapter 10\Cards folder in your Documents folder.

3. On the Debug menu, click Start Debugging to build and run the application.

   A form appears with the caption Card Game and four text boxes (labeled North, South, East, and West). At the bottom is a command bar with an ellipsis (...). Click the ellipsis to expand the command bar. A button with the caption Deal should appear:

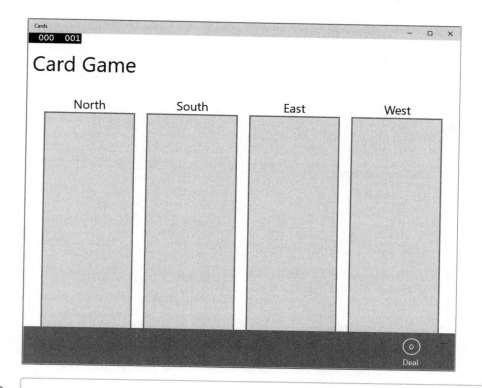

4. Click Deal.

    Nothing happens. You have not yet implemented the code that deals the cards; this is what you will do in this exercise.

5. Return to Visual Studio 2015. On the Debug menu, click Stop Debugging.

6. In Solution Explorer, locate the Value.cs file. Open this file in the Code and Text Editor window.

    This file contains an enumeration called *Value*, which represents the different values that a card can have, in ascending order:

    ```
    enum Value { Two, Three, Four, Five, Six, Seven, Eight, Nine, Ten, Jack, Queen, King, Ace }
    ```

7. Open the Suit.cs file in the Code and Text Editor window.

    This file contains an enumeration called *Suit*, which represents the suits of cards in a regular pack:

```
enum Suit { Clubs, Diamonds, Hearts, Spades }
```

8. Display the PlayingCard.cs file in the Code and Text Editor window.

This file contains the *PlayingCard* class. This class models a single playing card.

```
class PlayingCard
{
    private readonly Suit suit;
    private readonly Value value;

    public PlayingCard(Suit s, Value v)
    {
        this.suit = s;
        this.value = v;
    }

    public override string ToString()
    {
        string result = $"{this.value} of {this.suit}";
        return result;
    }

    public Suit CardSuit()
    {
        return this.suit;
    }

    public Value CardValue()
    {
        return this.value;
    }
}
```

This class has two *readonly* fields that represent the value and suit of the card. The constructor initializes these fields.

> **Note** A *readonly* field is useful for modeling data that should not change after it has been initialized. You can assign a value to a *readonly* field by using an initializer when you declare it or in a constructor, but thereafter you cannot change it.

The class contains a pair of methods named *CardValue* and *CardSuit* that return this information, and it overrides the *ToString* method to return a string representation of the card.

> **Note** The *CardValue* and *CardSuit* methods are actually better implemented as properties, which you learn how to do in Chapter 15.

9. Open the Pack.cs file in the Code and Text Editor window.

This file contains the *Pack* class, which models a pack of playing cards. At the top of the *Pack* class are two *public const int* fields called *NumSuits* and *CardsPerSuit*. These two fields specify the number of suits in a pack of cards and the number of cards in each suit. The private *cardPack* variable is a two-dimensional array of *PlayingCard* objects. You will use the first dimension to specify the suit and the second dimension to specify the value of the card in the suit. The *randomCardSelector* variable is a random number generated based on the *Random* class. You will use the *randomCardSelector* variable to help shuffle the cards before they are dealt to each hand.

```
class Pack
{
    public const int NumSuits = 4;
    public const int CardsPerSuit = 13;
    private PlayingCard[,] cardPack;
    private Random randomCardSelector = new Random();
    ...
}
```

10. Locate the default constructor for the *Pack* class. Currently this constructor is empty apart from a *// TODO:* comment. Delete the comment, and add the following statement shown in bold to instantiate the *cardPack* array with the appropriate values for each dimension:

```
public Pack()
{
    this.cardPack = new PlayingCard[NumSuits, CardsPerSuit];
}
```

11. Add the following code shown in bold to the *Pack* constructor. These statements populate the *cardPack* array with a full, sorted deck of cards.

```
public Pack()
{
    this.cardPack = new PlayingCard[NumSuits, CardsPerSuit];
    for (Suit suit = Suit.Clubs; suit <= Suit.Spades; suit++)
    {
        for (Value value = Value.Two; value <= Value.Ace; value++)
        {
            this.cardPack[(int)suit, (int)value] = new PlayingCard(suit, value);
        }
    }
}
```

The outer *for* loop iterates through the list of values in the *Suit* enumeration, and the inner loop iterates through the values each card can have in each suit. The inner loop creates a new *PlayingCard* object of the specified suit and value and adds it to the appropriate element in the *cardPack* array.

> **Note** You must use one of the integer types as indexes into an array. The *suit* and *value* variables are enumeration variables. However, enumerations are based on the integer types, so it is safe to cast them to *int* as shown in the code.

12. Find the *DealCardFromPack* method in the *Pack* class. The purpose of this method is to pick a random card from the pack, remove the card from the pack to prevent it from being selected again, and then pass it back as the return value from the method.

The first task in this method is to pick a suit at random. Delete the comment and the statement that throws the *NotImplementedException* exception from this method and replace them with the following statement shown in bold:

```
public PlayingCard DealCardFromPack()
{
    Suit suit = (Suit)randomCardSelector.Next(NumSuits);
}
```

This statement uses the *Next* method of the *randomCardSelector* random number generator object to return a random number corresponding to a suit. The parameter to the *Next* method specifies the exclusive upper bound of the range to use; the value selected is between 0 and this value minus 1. Note that the value returned is an *int*, so it has to be cast before you can assign it a *Suit* variable.

There is always the possibility that no cards of the selected suit are left. You need to handle this situation and pick another suit if necessary.

13. After the code that selects a suit at random, add the *while* loop that follows (shown in bold).

This loop calls the *IsSuitEmpty* method to determine whether any cards of the specified suit are left in the pack (you will implement the logic for this method shortly). If not, it picks another suit at random (it might actually pick the same suit again) and checks again. The loop repeats the process until it finds a suit with at least one card left.

```
public PlayingCard DealCardFromPack()
{
    Suit suit = (Suit)randomCardSelector.Next(NumSuits);
    while (this.IsSuitEmpty(suit))
    {
        suit = (Suit)randomCardSelector.Next(NumSuits);
    }
}
```

14. You have now selected at random a suit with at least one card left. The next task is to pick a card at random in this suit. You can use the random number generator to select a card value, but as before, there is no guarantee that the card with the chosen value has not already been dealt. However, you can use the same idiom as before: call the *IsCardAlreadyDealt* method (which you will examine and complete later) to determine whether the card has already been dealt, and if so, pick another card at random and try again, repeating the process until a card is found. To do this, add the following statements shown in bold to the *DealCardFromPack* method, after the existing code:

```
public PlayingCard DealCardFromPack()
{
    ...
```

```
        Value value = (Value)randomCardSelector.Next(CardsPerSuit);
        while (this.IsCardAlreadyDealt(suit, value))
        {
            value = (Value)randomCardSelector.Next(CardsPerSuit);
        }
    }
```

15. You have now selected a random playing card that has not been dealt previously. Add the following code to the end of the *DealCardFromPack* method to return this card and set the corresponding element in the *cardPack* array to *null*:

```
public PlayingCard DealCardFromPack()
{
    ...
    PlayingCard card = this.cardPack[(int)suit, (int)value];
    this.cardPack[(int)suit, (int)value] = null;
    return card;
}
```

16. Locate the *IsSuitEmpty* method. Remember that the purpose of this method is to take a *Suit* parameter and return a Boolean value indicating whether there are any more cards of this suit left in the pack. Delete the comment and the statement that throws the *NotImplementedException* exception from this method, and then add the following code shown in bold:

```
private bool IsSuitEmpty(Suit suit)
{
    bool result = true;
    for (Value value = Value.Two; value <= Value.Ace; value++)
    {
        if (!IsCardAlreadyDealt(suit, value))
        {
            result = false;
            break;
        }
    }

    return result;
}
```

This code iterates through the possible card values and uses the *IsCardAlreadyDealt* method (which you will complete in the next step) to determine whether there is a card left in the *cardPack* array that has the specified suit and value. If the loop finds a card, the value in the *result* variable is set to *false* and the *break* statement causes the loop to terminate. If the loop completes without finding a card, the *result* variable remains set to its initial value of *true*. The value of the *result* variable is passed back as the return value of the method.

17. Find the *IsCardAlreadyDealt* method. The purpose of this method is to determine whether the card with the specified suit and value has already been dealt and removed from the pack. You will see later that when the *DealCardFromPack* method deals a card, it removes the card from the *cardPack* array and sets the corresponding element to *null*. Replace the body of this method with the code shown in bold:

```
private bool IsCardAlreadyDealt(Suit suit, Value value)
    => (this.cardPack[(int)suit, (int)value] == null);
```

This method returns *true* if the element in the *cardPack* array corresponding to the suit and value is *null*, and it returns *false* otherwise.

18. The next step is to add the selected playing card to a hand. Open the Hand.cs file and display it in the Code and Text Editor window. This file contains the *Hand* class, which implements a hand of cards (that is, all cards dealt to one player).

    This file contains a *public const int* field called *HandSize*, which is set to the size of a hand of cards (13). It also contains an array of *PlayingCard* objects, which is initialized by using the *HandSize* constant. The *playingCardCount* field will be used by your code to keep track of how many cards the hand currently contains as it is being populated.

    ```
    class Hand
    {
        public const int HandSize = 13;
        private PlayingCard[] cards = new PlayingCard[HandSize];
        private int playingCardCount = 0;
        ...
    }
    ```

    The *ToString* method generates a string representation of the cards in the hand. It uses a *foreach* loop to iterate through the items in the *cards* array and calls the *ToString* method on each *PlayingCard* object it finds. These strings are concatenated with a newline character in between (the \n character) for formatting purposes.

    ```
    public override string ToString()
    {
        string result = "";
        foreach (PlayingCard card in this.cards)
        {
            result += $"{card.ToString()}\n";
        }

        return result;
    }
    ```

19. Locate the *AddCardToHand* method in the *Hand* class. The purpose of this method is to add the playing card specified as the parameter to the hand. Add the following statements shown in bold to this method:

    ```
    public void AddCardToHand(PlayingCard cardDealt)
    {
        if (this.playingCardCount >= HandSize)
        {
            throw new ArgumentException("Too many cards");
        }
        this.cards[this.playingCardCount] = cardDealt;
        this.playingCardCount++;
    }
    ```

This code first checks to ensure that the hand is not already full. If the hand is full, it throws an *ArgumentException* exception (this should never occur, but it is good practice to be safe). Otherwise, the card is added to the *cards* array at the index specified by the *playingCardCount* variable, and this variable is then incremented.

20. In Solution Explorer, expand the MainPage.xaml node and then open the MainPage.xaml.cs file in the Code and Text Editor window.

    This is the code for the Card Game window. Locate the *dealClick* method. This method runs when the user clicks the Deal button. Currently, it contains an empty *try* block and an exception handler that displays a message if an exception occurs.

21. Add the following statement shown in bold to the *try* block:

```
private void dealClick(object sender, RoutedEventArgs e)
{
    try
    {
        pack = new Pack();
    }
    catch (Exception ex)
    {
        ...
    }
}
```

    This statement simply creates a new pack of cards. You saw earlier that this class contains a two-dimensional array holding the cards in the pack, and the constructor populates this array with the details of each card. You now need to create four hands of cards from this pack.

22. Add the following statements shown in bold to the *try* block:

```
try
{
    pack = new Pack();

    for (int handNum = 0; handNum < NumHands; handNum++)
    {
        hands[handNum] = new Hand();
    }
}
catch (Exception ex)
{
    ...
}
```

    This *for* loop creates four hands from the pack of cards and stores them in an array called *hands*. Each hand is initially empty, so you need to deal the cards from the pack to each hand.

23. Add the following code shown in bold to the *for* loop:

```
try
{
    ...
    for (int handNum = 0; handNum < NumHands; handNum++)
    {
        hands[handNum] = new Hand();
        for (int numCards = 0; numCards < Hand.HandSize; numCards++)
        {
            PlayingCard cardDealt = pack.DealCardFromPack();
            hands[handNum].AddCardToHand(cardDealt);
        }
    }
}
catch (Exception ex)
{
    ...
}
```

The inner *for* loop populates each hand by using the *DealCardFromPack* method to retrieve a card at random from the pack and the *AddCardToHand* method to add this card to a hand.

24. Add the following code shown in bold after the outer *for* loop:

```
try
{
    ...
    for (int handNum = 0; handNum < NumHands; handNum++)
    {
        ...
    }

    north.Text = hands[0].ToString();
    south.Text = hands[1].ToString();
    east.Text = hands[2].ToString();
    west.Text = hands[3].ToString();
}
catch (Exception ex)
{
    ...
}
```

When all the cards have been dealt, this code displays each hand in the text boxes on the form. These text boxes are called *north, south, east,* and *west*. The code uses the *ToString* method of each hand to format the output.

If an exception occurs at any point, the *catch* handler displays a message box with the error message for the exception.

25. On the Debug menu, click Start Debugging. When the Card Game window appears, expand the command bar and click Deal.

The cards in the pack should be dealt at random to each hand, and the cards in each hand should be displayed on the form, as shown in the following image:

Card Game

North	South	East	West
Ace of Spades	Two of Diamonds	Seven of Diamond	Eight of Hearts
Seven of Clubs	Ten of Spades	King of Clubs	Eight of Diamonds
Queen of Spades	Eight of Spades	Jack of Diamonds	Four of Hearts
King of Spades	Six of Clubs	Six of Hearts	Ten of Clubs
Five of Clubs	Nine of Clubs	Four of Spades	Ace of Hearts
Two of Hearts	Seven of Spades	Nine of Spades	King of Diamonds
Ace of Clubs	Nine of Diamonds	Six of Diamonds	Ace of Diamonds
Queen of Clubs	Four of Clubs	King of Hearts	Queen of Diamonc
Eight of Clubs	Three of Clubs	Jack of Hearts	Queen of Hearts
Five of Diamonds	Nine of Hearts	Four of Diamonds	Ten of Diamonds
Three of Diamond:	Three of Spades	Six of Spades	Ten of Hearts
Jack of Spades	Three of Hearts	Five of Spades	Seven of Hearts
Two of Spades	Jack of Clubs	Two of Clubs	Five of Hearts

26. Click Deal again. Verify that a new set of hands is dealt and the cards in each hand change.

27. Return to Visual Studio and stop debugging.

Summary

In this chapter, you learned how to create and use arrays to manipulate sets of data. You saw how to declare and initialize arrays, access data held in arrays, pass arrays as parameters to methods, and return arrays from methods. You also learned how to create multidimensional arrays and how to use arrays of arrays.

- If you want to continue to the next chapter, keep Visual Studio 2015 running and turn to Chapter 11.

- If you want to exit Visual Studio 2015 now, on the File menu, click Exit. If you see a Save dialog box, click Yes and save the project.

Quick reference

To	Do this
Declare an array variable	Write the name of the element type, followed by square brackets, followed by the name of the variable, followed by a semicolon. For example: ```bool[] flags;```
Create an instance of an array	Write the keyword *new*, followed by the name of the element type, followed by the size of the array enclosed in square brackets. For example: ```bool[] flags = new bool[10];```
Initialize the elements of an array to specific values	For an array, write the specific values in a comma-separated list enclosed in braces. For example: ```bool[] flags = { true, false, true, false };```

Find the number of elements in an array	Use the *Length* property. For example:
	
	```bool[] flags = ...;```
	```...```
	```int noOfElements = flags.Length;```

Access a single array element	Write the name of the array variable, followed by the integer index of the element enclosed in square brackets. Remember, array indexing starts at 0, not 1. For example: ```bool initialElement = flags[0];```

Iterate through the elements of an array	Use a *for* statement or a *foreach* statement. For example:
	
	```bool[] flags = { true, false, true, false };```
	```for (int i = 0; i < flags.Length; i++)```
	```{```
	``` Console.WriteLine(flags[i]);```
	```}```
	
	```foreach (bool flag in flags)```
	```{```
	``` Console.WriteLine(flag);```
	```}```

Declare a multidimensional array variable	Write the name of the element type, followed by a set of square brackets with a comma separator indicating the number of dimensions, followed by the name of the variable, followed by a semicolon. For example, use the following to create a two-dimensional array called *table* and initialize it to hold 4 rows of 6 columns:
	
	```int[,] table;```
	```table = new int[4,6];```

Declare a jagged array variable	Declare the variable as an array of child arrays. You can initialize each child array to have a different length. For example, use the following to create a jagged array called *items* and initialize each child array:
	
	```int[][] items;```
	```items = new int[4][];```
	```items[0] = new int[3];```
	```items[1] = new int[10];```
	```items[2] = new int[40];```
	```items[3] = new int[25];```

Understanding parameter arrays

After completing this chapter, you will be able to:

- Write a method that can accept any number of arguments by using the *params* keyword.

- Write a method that can accept any number of arguments of any type by using the *params* keyword in combination with the *object* type.

- Explain the differences between methods that take parameter arrays and methods that take optional parameters.

Parameter arrays are useful if you want to write methods that can take any number of arguments, possibly of different types, as parameters. If you are familiar with object-oriented concepts, you might be grinding your teeth in frustration at the previous sentence. After all, the object-oriented approach to solving this problem is to define overloaded methods. However, overloading is not always the most suitable approach, especially if you need to create a method that can take a truly variable number of parameters, each of which might vary in type whenever the method is invoked. This chapter describes how you can use parameter arrays to address situations such as this.

Overloading—a recap

Overloading is the technical term for declaring two or more methods with the same name in the same scope. Overloading a method is very useful for cases in which you want to perform the same action on arguments of different types. The classic example of overloading in Microsoft Visual C# is the *Console.WriteLine* method. This method is overloaded numerous times so that you can pass any primitive type argument. The following code example illustrates some of the ways in which the *WriteLine* method is defined in the *Console* class:

```
class Console
{
    public static void WriteLine(Int32 value)
    public static void WriteLine(Double value)
    public static void WriteLine(Decimal value)
    public static void WriteLine(Boolean value)
    public static void WriteLine(String value)
    ...
}
```

> **Note** The documentation for the *WriteLine* method uses the structure types defined in the *System* namespace for its parameters rather than the C# aliases for these types. For example, the overload that prints out the value for an *int* actually takes an *Int32* as the parameter. Refer to Chapter 9, "Creating value types with enumerations and structures," for a list of the structure types and their mappings to C# aliases for these types.

As useful as overloading is, it doesn't cover every case. In particular, overloading doesn't easily handle a situation in which the type of parameters doesn't vary but the number of parameters does. For example, what if you want to write many values to the console? Do you have to provide versions of *Console.WriteLine* that can take two parameters of various combinations, other versions that can take three parameters, and so on? That would quickly become tedious. And wouldn't the massive duplication of these overloaded methods worry you? It should. Fortunately, there is a way to write a method that takes a variable number of arguments (a *variadic method*): you can use a parameter array, which is declared by using the *params* keyword.

To understand how *params* arrays solve this problem, it helps to first understand the uses and shortcomings of ordinary arrays.

Using array arguments

Suppose that you want to write a method to determine the minimum value in a set of values passed as parameters. One way is to use an array. For example, to find the smallest of several *int* values, you could write a static method named *Min* with a single parameter representing an array of *int* values:

```
class Util
{
    public static int Min(int[] paramList)
    {
        // Verify that the caller has provided at least one parameter.
        // If not, throw an ArgumentException exception - it is not possible
        // to find the smallest value in an empty list.
        if (paramList == null || paramList.Length == 0)
        {
            throw new ArgumentException("Util.Min: not enough arguments");
        }

        // Set the current minimum value found in the list of parameters to the first item
        int currentMin = paramList[0];

        // Iterate through the list of parameters, searching to see whether any of them
        // are smaller than the value held in currentMin
        foreach (int i in paramList)
        {
            // If the loop finds an item that is smaller than the value held in
            // currentMin, then set currentMin to this value
            if (i < currentMin)
```

```
        {
            currentMin = i;
        }
    }

    // At the end of the loop, currentMin holds the value of the smallest
    // item in the list of parameters, so return this value.
    return currentMin;
    }
}
```

To use the *Min* method to find the minimum of two *int* variables named *first* and *second*, you can write this:

```
int[] array = new int[2];
array[0] = first;
array[1] = second;
int min = Util.Min(array);
```

And to use the *Min* method to find the minimum of three *int* variables (named *first*, *second*, and *third*), you can write this:

```
int[] array = new int[3];
array[0] = first;
array[1] = second;
array[2] = third;
int min = Util.Min(array);
```

You can see that this solution avoids the need for a large number of overloads, but it does so at a price: you have to write additional code to populate the array that you pass in. You can, of course, use an anonymous array if you prefer, like this:

```
int min = Util.Min(new int[] {first, second, third});
```

However, the point is that you still need to create and populate an array, and the syntax can get a little confusing. The solution is to get the compiler to write some of this code for you by using a *params* array as the parameter to the *Min* method.

Declaring a *params* array

Using a *params* array, you can pass a variable number of arguments to a method. You indicate a *params* array by using the *params* keyword as an array parameter modifier when you define the method parameters. For example, here's *Min* again—this time with its array parameter declared as a *params* array:

```
class Util
{
    public static int Min(params int[] paramList)
    {
        // code exactly as before
    }
}
```

The effect of the *params* keyword on the *Min* method is that it allows you to call the method by using any number of integer arguments without worrying about creating an array. For example, to find the minimum of two integer values, you can simply write this:

```
int min = Util.Min(first, second);
```

The compiler translates this call into code similar to this:

```
int[] array = new int[2];
array[0] = first;
array[1] = second;
int min = Util.Min(array);
```

To find the minimum of three integer values, you write the code shown here, which is also converted by the compiler to the corresponding code that uses an array:

```
int min = Util.Min(first, second, third);
```

Both calls to *Min* (one call with two arguments and the other with three arguments) resolve to the same *Min* method with the *params* keyword. And, as you can probably guess, you can call this *Min* method with any number of *int* arguments. The compiler just counts the number of *int* arguments, creates an *int* array of that size, fills the array with the arguments, and then calls the method by passing the single array parameter.

> **Note** If you're a C or C++ programmer, you might recognize *params* as a type-safe equivalent of the *varargs* macros from the header file stdarg.h. Java also has a *varargs* facility that operates in a similar manner to the *params* keyword in C#.

There are several points worth noting about *params* arrays:

- You can't use the *params* keyword with multidimensional arrays. The code in the following example will not compile:

  ```
  // compile-time error
  public static int Min(params int[,] table)
  ...
  ```

- You can't overload a method based solely on the *params* keyword. The *params* keyword does not form part of a method's signature, as shown in this example. Here, the compiler would not be able to distinguish between these methods in code that calls them:

```
// compile-time error: duplicate declaration
public static int Min(int[] paramList)
...
public static int Min(params int[] paramList)
...
```

■ You're not allowed to specify the *ref* or *out* modifier with *params* arrays, as shown in this example:

```
// compile-time errors
public static int Min(ref params int[] paramList)
...
public static int Min(out params int[] paramList)
...
```

■ A *params* array must be the last parameter. (This means that you can have only one *params* array per method.) Consider this example:

```
// compile-time error
public static int Min(params int[] paramList, int i)
...
```

■ A non-*params* method always takes priority over a *params* method. This means that you can still create an overloaded version of a method for the common cases, such as in the following example:

```
public static int Min(int leftHandSide, int rightHandSide)
...
public static int Min(params int[] paramList)
...
```

The first version of the *Min* method is used when it's called using two *int* arguments. The second version is used if any other number of *int* arguments is supplied. This includes the case in which the method is called with no arguments. Adding the non-*params* array method might be a useful optimization technique because the compiler won't have to create and populate so many arrays.

Using *params object[ ]*

A parameter array of type *int* is very useful. With it, you can pass any number of *int* arguments in a method call. However, what if not only the number of arguments varies but also the argument type? C# has a way to solve this problem, too. The technique is based on the facts that *object* is the root of all classes and that the compiler can generate code that converts value types (things that aren't classes) to objects by using boxing, as described in Chapter 8, "Understanding values and references." You can use a parameters array of type *object* to declare a method that accepts any number of *object* arguments, allowing the arguments passed in to be of any type. Look at this example:

```
class Black
{
    public static void Hole(params object[] paramList)
```

```
    ...
}
```

I've called this method *Black.Hole* because no argument can escape from it:

- You can pass the method no arguments at all, in which case the compiler will pass an object array whose length is 0:

```
Black.Hole();
// converted to Black.Hole(new object[0]);
```

- You can call the *Black.Hole* method by passing *null* as the argument. An array is a reference type, so you're allowed to initialize an array with *null*:

```
Black.Hole(null);
```

- You can pass the *Black.Hole* method an actual array. In other words, you can manually create the array normally generated by the compiler:

```
object[] array = new object[2];
array[0] = "forty two";
array[1] = 42;
Black.Hole(array);
```

- You can pass the *Black.Hole* method arguments of different types, and these arguments will automatically be wrapped inside an *object* array:

```
Black.Hole("forty two", 42);
//converted to Black.Hole(new object[]{"forty two", 42});
```

The *Console.WriteLine* method

The *Console* class contains many overloads for the *WriteLine* method. One of these overloads looks like this:

```
public static void WriteLine(string format, params object[] arg);
```

Although string interpolation has very nearly made this version of the *WriteLine* method redundant, this overload was frequently used in previous editions of the C# language. This overload enables the *WriteLine* method to support a format string argument that contains numeric placeholders, each of which can be replaced at run time with a variable of any type that is specified as a list of parameters (placeholder {i} is replaced with the ith variable in the list that follows). Here's an example of a call to this method (the variables *fname* and *lname* are *string*s, *mi* is a *char*, and *age* is an *int*):

```
Console.WriteLine("Forename:{0}, Middle Initial:{1}, Last name:{2}, Age:{3}", fname,
mi, lname, age);
```

The compiler resolves this call into the following:

```
Console.WriteLine("Forename:{0}, Middle Initial:{1}, Last name:{2}, Age:{3}", new
object[4]{fname, mi, lname, age});
```

Using a *params* array

In the following exercise, you will implement and test a static method named *Sum*. The purpose of this method is to calculate the sum of a variable number of *int* arguments passed to it, returning the result as an *int*. You will do this by writing *Sum* to take a *params int[]* parameter. You will implement two checks on the *params* parameter to ensure that the *Sum* method is completely robust. You will then call the *Sum* method with a variety of different arguments to test it.

Write a *params* array method

1. Start Microsoft Visual Studio 2015 if it is not already running.

2. Open the ParamsArray project, which is located in the \Microsoft Press\VCSBS\Chapter 11\ ParamsArray folder in your Documents folder.

   The ParamsArray project contains the *Program* class in the Program.cs file, including the *doWork* method framework that you have seen in previous chapters. You will implement the *Sum* method as a static method of another class called *Util* (short for "utility"), which you will add to the project.

3. In Solution Explorer, right-click the ParamsArray project in the ParamsArray solution, point to Add, and then click Class.

4. In the Add New Item – ParamsArray dialog box, in the middle pane, click the Class template. In the Name box, type **Util.cs**, and then click Add.

   The Util.cs file is created and added to the project. It contains an empty class named *Util* in the *ParamsArray* namespace.

5. Add a public static method named *Sum* to the *Util* class. This method should return an *int* and accept a *params* array of *int* values named *paramList*. It should look like this:

```
public static int Sum(params int[] paramList)
{
}
```

   The first step in implementing the *Sum* method is to check the *paramList* parameter. Apart from containing a valid set of integers, it can also be *null* or it can be an array of zero length. In both of these cases, it is difficult to calculate the sum, so the best option is to throw an *ArgumentException* exception. (You could argue that the sum of the integers in a zero-length array is 0, but you'll treat this situation as an exception in this example.)

6. Add to *Sum* the following code shown in bold. This code throws an *ArgumentException* exception if *paramList* is *null*. The *Sum* method should now look like this:

```
public static int Sum(params int[] paramList)
{
    if (paramList == null)
    {
        throw new ArgumentException("Util.Sum: null parameter list");
```

```
        }
    }
```

7. Add code to the *Sum* method to throw an *ArgumentException* exception if the length of the parameter list *array* is 0, as shown here in bold:

```
public static int Sum(params int[] paramList)
{
    if (paramList == null)
    {
        throw new ArgumentException("Util.Sum: null parameter list");
    }

    if (paramList.Length == 0)
    {
        throw new ArgumentException("Util.Sum: empty parameter list");
    }
}
```

If the array passes these two tests, the next step is to add together all the elements inside the array. You can use a *foreach* statement to do this, and you will need a local variable to hold the running total.

8. Declare an integer variable named *sumTotal* and initialize it to 0, directly following the code from the preceding step.

```
public static int Sum(params int[] paramList)
{
    ...
    if (paramList.Length == 0)
    {
        throw new ArgumentException("Util.Sum: empty parameter list");
    }

    int sumTotal = 0;
}
```

9. Add a *foreach* statement to the *Sum* method to iterate through the *paramList* array. The body of this *foreach* loop should add each element in the array to *sumTotal*. At the end of the method, return the value of *sumTotal* by using a *return* statement, as shown in bold here:

```
public static int Sum(params int[] paramList)
{
    ...
    int sumTotal = 0;
    foreach (int i in paramList)
    {
        sumTotal += i;
    }
    return sumTotal;
}
```

10. On the Build menu, click Build Solution, and then confirm that your solution builds without any errors.

Test the *Util.Sum* method

1. Display the Program.cs file in the Code and Text Editor window.

2. In the Code and Text Editor window, delete the *// TODO:* comment and add the following statement to the *doWork* method:

    ```
    Console.WriteLine(Util.Sum(null));
    ```

3. On the Debug menu, click Start Without Debugging.

    The program builds and runs, writing the following message to the console:

    ```
    Exception: Util.Sum: null parameter list
    ```

    This confirms that the first check in the method works.

4. Press the Enter key to close the program and return to Visual Studio 2015.

5. In the Code and Text Editor window, change the call to *Console.WriteLine* in *doWork* as shown here:

    ```
    Console.WriteLine(Util.Sum());
    ```

    This time, the method is called without any arguments. The compiler translates the empty argument list into an empty array.

6. On the Debug menu, click Start Without Debugging.

    The program builds and runs, writing the following message to the console:

    ```
    Exception: Util.Sum: empty parameter list
    ```

    This confirms that the second check in the method works.

7. Press the Enter key to close the program and return to Visual Studio 2015.

8. Change the call to *Console.WriteLine* in *doWork* as follows:

    ```
    Console.WriteLine(Util.Sum(10, 9, 8, 7, 6, 5, 4, 3, 2, 1));
    ```

9. On the Debug menu, click Start Without Debugging.

    Verify that the program builds, runs, and writes the value *55* to the console.

10. Press Enter to close the application and return to Visual Studio 2015.

Comparing parameter arrays and optional parameters

Chapter 3, "Writing methods and applying scope," illustrates how to define methods that take optional parameters. At first glance, it appears there is a degree of overlap between methods that use parameter arrays and methods that take optional parameters. However, there are fundamental differences between them:

- A method that takes optional parameters still has a fixed parameter list, and you cannot pass an arbitrary list of arguments. The compiler generates code that inserts the default values onto the stack for any missing arguments before the method runs, and the method is not aware of which of the arguments are provided by the caller and which are compiler-generated defaults.

- A method that uses a parameter array effectively has a completely arbitrary list of parameters, and none of them has a default value. Furthermore, the method can determine exactly how many arguments the caller provided.

Generally, you use parameter arrays for methods that can take any number of parameters (including none), whereas you use optional parameters only where it is not convenient to force a caller to provide an argument for every parameter.

There is one final situation worth pondering. If you define a method that takes a parameter list and provide an overload that takes optional parameters, it is not always immediately apparent which version of the method will be called if the argument list in the calling statement matches both method signatures. You will investigate this scenario in the final exercise in this chapter.

Compare a *params* array and optional parameters

1. Return to the ParamsArray solution in Visual Studio 2015 and display the Util.cs file in the Code and Text Editor window.

2. Add the following *Console.WriteLine* statement shown in bold to the start of the *Sum* method in the *Util* class:

```
public static int Sum(params int[] paramList)
{
    Console.WriteLine("Using parameter list");
    ...
}
```

3. Add another implementation of the *Sum* method to the *Util* class. This version should take four optional *int* parameters, each with a default value of 0. In the body of the method, output the message "Using optional parameters" and then calculate and return the sum of the four parameters. The completed method should look like the following code in bold:

```
class Util
{
    ...
    public static int Sum(int param1 = 0, int param2 = 0, int param3 = 0, int param4 = 0)
```

```
        {
            Console.WriteLine("Using optional parameters");
            int sumTotal = param1 + param2 + param3 + param4;
            return sumTotal;
        }
    }
```

4. Display the Program.cs file in the Code and Text Editor window.

5. In the *doWork* method, comment out the existing code and add the following statement:

```
Console.WriteLine(Util.Sum(2, 4, 6, 8));
```

    This statement calls the *Sum* method, passing four *int* parameters. This call matches both overloads of the *Sum* method.

6. On the Debug menu, click Start Without Debugging to build and run the application.

    When the application runs, it displays the following messages:

```
Using optional parameters
20
```

    In this case, the compiler generated code that called the method that takes four optional parameters. This is the version of the method that most closely matches the method call.

7. Press Enter and return to Visual Studio.

8. In the *doWork* method, change the statement that calls the *Sum* method and remove the final argument (8), as shown here:

```
Console.WriteLine(Util.Sum(2, 4, 6));
```

9. On the Debug menu, click Start Without Debugging to build and run the application.

    When the application runs, it displays the following messages:

```
Using optional parameters
12
```

    The compiler still generated code that called the method that takes optional parameters, even though the method signature does not exactly match the call. Given a choice between a method that takes optional parameters and a method that takes a parameter list, the C# compiler will use the method that takes optional parameters.

10. Press Enter and return to Visual Studio.

11. In the *doWork* method, change the statement that calls the *Sum* method again and add two more arguments:

```
Console.WriteLine(Util.Sum(2, 4, 6, 8, 10));
```

12. On the Debug menu, click Start Without Debugging to build and run the application.

When the application runs, it displays the following messages:

```
Using parameter list
30
```

This time, more arguments are provided than the method that takes optional parameters specifies, so the compiler generated code that calls the method that takes a parameter array.

13. Press Enter and return to Visual Studio.

Summary

In this chapter, you learned how to use a *params* array to define a method that can take any number of arguments. You also saw how to use a *params* array of *object* types to create a method that accepts any number of arguments of any type. In addition, you saw how the compiler resolves method calls when it has a choice between calling a method that takes a parameter array and a method that takes optional parameters.

- If you want to continue to the next chapter, keep Visual Studio 2015 running and turn to Chapter 12, "Working with inheritance."

- If you want to exit Visual Studio 2015 now, on the File menu, click Exit. If you see a Save dialog box, click Yes and save the project.

Quick reference

To	Do this
Write a method that accepts any number of arguments of a given type	Write a method whose parameter is a *params* array of the given type. For example, a method that accepts any number of *bool* arguments is declared like this: ```someType Method(params bool[] flags)\n{\n ...\n}```
Write a method that accepts any number of arguments of any type	Write a method whose parameter is a *params* array whose elements are of type *object*. For example: ```someType Method(params object[] paramList)\n{\n ...\n}```

Working with inheritance

After completing this chapter, you will be able to:

- Create a derived class that inherits features from a base class.

- Control method hiding and overriding by using the *new, virtual*, and *override* keywords.

- Limit accessibility within an inheritance hierarchy by using the *protected* keyword.

- Define extension methods as an alternative mechanism to using inheritance.

Inheritance is a key concept in the world of object-oriented programming. You can use inheritance as a tool to avoid repetition when defining different classes that have a number of features in common and are quite clearly related to one another. Perhaps they are different classes of the same type, each with its own distinguishing feature—for example, *managers, manual workers*, and *all employees* of a factory. If you were writing an application to simulate the factory, how would you specify that managers and manual workers have a number of features that are the same but also have features that are different? For example, they all have an employee reference number, but managers have different responsibilities and perform tasks different from those of manual workers.

This is where inheritance proves useful.

What is inheritance?

If you ask several experienced programmers the meaning of the term *inheritance*, you will typically get different and conflicting answers. Part of the confusion stems from the fact that the word inheritance itself has several subtly different meanings. If someone bequeaths something to you in a will, you are said to inherit it. Similarly, we say that you inherit half of your genes from your mother and half of your genes from your father. Both of these uses of the word have very little to do with inheritance in programming.

Inheritance in programming is all about classification—it's a relationship between classes. For example, when you were at school, you probably learned about mammals, and you learned that horses and whales are examples of mammals. Each has every attribute that a mammal does (it breathes air, it suckles its young, it is warm-blooded, and so on), but each also has its own special features (a horse has hooves, but a whale has flippers and a fluke).

How can you model a horse and a whale in a program? One way is to create two distinct classes named *Horse* and *Whale*. Each class can implement the behaviors that are unique to that type of mammal, such as *Trot* (for a horse) or *Swim* (for a whale), in its own way. But how do you handle behaviors that are common to a horse and a whale, such as *Breathe* or *SuckleYoung*? You can add duplicate methods with these names to both classes, but this situation becomes a maintenance nightmare, especially if you also decide to start modeling other types of mammals, such as *Human* and *Aardvark*.

In C#, you can use class inheritance to address these issues. A horse, a whale, a human, and an aardvark are all types of mammals, so you can create a class named *Mammal* that provides the common functionality exhibited by these types. You can then declare that the *Horse, Whale, Human,* and *Aardvark* classes all inherit from *Mammal*. These classes then automatically include the functionality of the *Mammal* class (*Breathe, SuckleYoung,* and so on), but you can also augment each class with the functionality unique to a particular type of mammal—the *Trot* method for the *Horse* class and the *Swim* method for the *Whale* class. If you need to modify the way in which a common method such as *Breathe* works, you need to change it in only one place, the *Mammal* class.

Using inheritance

You declare that a class inherits from another class by using the following syntax:

```
class DerivedClass : BaseClass
{
    ...
}
```

The derived class inherits from the base class, and the methods in the base class become part of the derived class. In C#, a class is allowed to derive from, at most, one base class; a class is *not allowed* to derive from two or more classes. However, unless *DerivedClass* is declared as *sealed*, you can use the same syntax to derive other classes that inherit from *DerivedClass*. (You will learn about sealed classes in Chapter 13, "Creating interfaces and defining abstract classes.")

```
class DerivedSubClass : DerivedClass
{
    ...
}
```

Continuing the example described earlier, you could declare the *Mammal* class as follows. The methods *Breathe* and *SuckleYoung* are common to all mammals.

```
class Mammal
{
    public void Breathe()
    {
        ...
    }
```

```
    public void SuckleYoung()
    {
        ...
    }
    ...
}
```

You could then define classes for each different type of mammal, adding more methods as necessary, such as in the following example:

```
class Horse : Mammal
{
    ...
    public void Trot()
    {
        ...
    }
}

class Whale : Mammal
{
    ...
    public void Swim()
    {
        ...
    }
}
```

> **Note** If you are a C++ programmer, you should notice that you do not and cannot explicitly specify whether the inheritance is public, private, or protected. C# inheritance is always implicitly public. If you're familiar with Java, note the use of the colon and that there is no *extends* keyword.

If you create a *Horse* object in your application, you can call the *Trot*, *Breathe*, and *SuckleYoung* methods:

```
Horse myHorse = new Horse();
myHorse.Trot();
myHorse.Breathe();
myHorse.SuckleYoung();
```

Similarly, you can create a *Whale* object, but this time you can call the *Swim*, *Breathe*, and *SuckleYoung* methods; *Trot* is not available because it is defined only in the *Horse* class.

> **Important** Inheritance applies only to classes, not to structures. You cannot define your own inheritance hierarchy with structures, and you cannot define a structure that derives from a class or another structure.

> All structures actually inherit from an abstract class named *System.ValueType*. (Chapter 13 explores abstract classes.) This is purely an implementation detail of the way in which the Microsoft .NET Framework defines the common behavior for stack-based value types; you are unlikely to make direct use of *ValueType* in your own applications.

The *System.Object* class revisited

The *System.Object* class is the root class of all classes. All classes implicitly derive from *System.Object*. Consequently, the C# compiler silently rewrites the *Mammal* class as the following code (which you can write explicitly if you really want to):

```
class Mammal : System.Object
{
    ...
}
```

Any methods in the *System.Object* class are automatically passed down the chain of inheritance to classes that derive from *Mammal*, such as *Horse* and *Whale*. In practical terms, this means that all classes that you define automatically inherit all the features of the *System.Object* class. This includes methods such as *ToString* (discussed in Chapter 2, "Working with variables, operators, and expressions"), which is used to convert an object to a string, typically for display purposes.

Calling base-class constructors

In addition to the methods that it inherits, a derived class automatically contains all the fields from the base class. These fields usually require initialization when an object is created. You typically perform this kind of initialization in a constructor. Remember that all classes have at least one constructor. (If you don't provide one, the compiler generates a default constructor for you.)

It is good practice for a constructor in a derived class to call the constructor for its base class as part of the initialization, which enables the base-class constructor to perform any additional initialization that it requires. You can specify the *base* keyword to call a base-class constructor when you define a constructor for an inheriting class, as shown in this example:

```
class Mammal // base class
{
    public Mammal(string name)  // constructor for base class
    {
        ...
    }
    ...
}

class Horse : Mammal // derived class
{
    public Horse(string name)
        : base(name) // calls Mammal(name)
```

```
    {
        ...
    }
    ...
}
```

If you don't explicitly call a base-class constructor in a derived-class constructor, the compiler attempts to silently insert a call to the base class's default constructor before executing the code in the derived-class constructor. Taking the earlier example, the compiler rewrites this

```
class Horse : Mammal
{
    public Horse(string name)
    {
        ...
    }
    ...
}
```

as this:

```
class Horse : Mammal
{
    public Horse(string name)
        : base()
    {
        ...
    }
    ...
}
```

This works if *Mammal* has a public default constructor. However, not all classes have a public default constructor (for example, remember that the compiler generates a default constructor only if you don't write any nondefault constructors), in which case forgetting to call the correct base-class constructor results in a compile-time error.

Assigning classes

Previous examples in this book show how to declare a variable by using a class type and how to use the *new* keyword to create an object. There are also examples of how the type-checking rules of C# prevent you from assigning an object of one type to a variable declared as a different type. For example, given the definitions of the *Mammal, Horse,* and *Whale* classes shown here, the code that follows these definitions is illegal:

```
class Mammal
{
    ...
}
class Horse : Mammal
{
    ...
}
```

```
class Whale : Mammal
{
    ...
}
...
Horse myHorse = new Horse(...);
Whale myWhale = myHorse;              // error - different types
```

However, it is possible to refer to an object from a variable of a different type as long as the type used is a class that is higher up the inheritance hierarchy. So the following statements are legal:

```
Horse myHorse = new Horse(...);
Mammal myMammal = myHorse; // legal, Mammal is the base class of Horse
```

If you think about it in logical terms, all *Horses* are *Mammals*, so you can safely assign an object of type *Horse* to a variable of type *Mammal*. The inheritance hierarchy means that you can think of a *Horse* simply as a special type of *Mammal*; it has everything that a *Mammal* has with a few extra bits defined by any methods and fields you added to the *Horse* class. You can also make a *Mammal* variable refer to a *Whale* object. There is one significant limitation, however: When referring to a *Horse* or *Whale* object by using a *Mammal* variable, you can access only methods and fields that are defined by the *Mammal* class. Any additional methods defined by the *Horse* or *Whale* class are not visible through the *Mammal* class.

```
Horse myHorse = new Horse(...);
Mammal myMammal = myHorse;
myMammal.Breathe();        // OK - Breathe is part of the Mammal class
myMammal.Trot();           // error - Trot is not part of the Mammal class
```

> **Note** The preceding discussion explains why you can assign almost anything to an *object* variable. Remember that *object* is an alias for *System.Object*, and all classes inherit from *System.Object*, either directly or indirectly.

Be warned that the converse situation is not true. You cannot unreservedly assign a *Mammal* object to a *Horse* variable:

```
Mammal myMammal = newMammal(...);
Horse myHorse = myMammal;   // error
```

This looks like a strange restriction, but remember that not all *Mammal* objects are *Horses*—some might be *Whales*. You can assign a *Mammal* object to a *Horse* variable as long as you first check that the *Mammal* is really a *Horse*, by using the *as* or *is* operator or by using a cast (Chapter 7, "Creating and managing classes and objects" discusses the *is* and *as* operators and casts). The code example that follows uses the *as* operator to check that *myMammal* refers to a *Horse*, and if it does, the assignment to *myHorseAgain* results in *myHorseAgain* referring to the same *Horse* object. If *myMammal* refers to some other type of *Mammal*, the *as* operator returns *null* instead.

```
Horse myHorse = new Horse(...);
Mammal myMammal = myHorse;               // myMammal refers to a Horse
```

```
...
Horse myHorseAgain = myMammal as Horse;   // OK - myMammal was a Horse
...
Whale myWhale = new Whale(...);
myMammal = myWhale;
...
myHorseAgain = myMammal as Horse;         // returns null - myMammal was a Whale
```

Declaring new methods

One of the hardest tasks in the realm of computer programming is thinking up unique and meaningful names for identifiers. If you are defining a method for a class and that class is part of an inheritance hierarchy, sooner or later you are going to try to reuse a name that is already in use by one of the classes further up the hierarchy. If a base class and a derived class happen to declare two methods that have the same signature, you will receive a warning when you compile the application.

> **Note** The method signature refers to the name of the method and the number and types of its parameters, but not its return type. Two methods that have the same name and that take the same list of parameters have the same signature, even if they return different types.

A method in a derived class masks (or hides) a method in a base class that has the same signature. For example, if you compile the following code, the compiler generates a warning message informing you that *Horse.Talk* hides the inherited method *Mammal.Talk*:

```
class Mammal
{
    ...
    public void Talk() // assume that all mammals can talk
    {
        ...
    }
}

class Horse : Mammal
{
    ...
    public void Talk()  // horses talk in a different way from other mammals!
    {
        ...
    }
}
```

Although your code will compile and run, you should take this warning seriously. If another class derives from *Horse* and calls the *Talk* method, it might be expecting the method implemented in the *Mammal* class to be called. However, the *Talk* method in the *Horse* class hides the *Talk* method in the *Mammal* class, and the *Horse.Talk* method will be called instead. Most of the time, such a coincidence is at best a source of confusion, and you should consider renaming methods to avoid clashes.

However, if you're sure that you want the two methods to have the same signature, thus hiding the *Mammal.Talk* method, you can silence the warning by using the *new* keyword, as follows:

```
class Mammal
{
    ...
    public void Talk()
    {
        ...
    }
}
class Horse : Mammal
{
    ...
    new public void Talk()
    {
        ...
    }
}
```

Using the *new* keyword like this does not change the fact that the two methods are completely unrelated and that hiding still occurs. It just turns the warning off. In effect, the *new* keyword says, "I know what I'm doing, so stop showing me these warnings."

Declaring virtual methods

Sometimes, you do want to hide the way in which a method is implemented in a base class. As an example, consider the *ToString* method in *System.Object*. The purpose of *ToString* is to convert an object to its string representation. Because this method is very useful, it is a member of the *System.Object* class, thereby automatically providing all classes with a *ToString* method. However, how does the version of *ToString* implemented by *System.Object* know how to convert an instance of a derived class to a string? A derived class might contain any number of fields with interesting values that should be part of the string. The answer is that the implementation of *ToString* in *System.Object* is actually a bit simplistic. All it can do is convert an object to a string that contains the name of its type, such as "Mammal" or "Horse." This is not very useful after all. So why provide a method that is so useless? The answer to this second question requires a bit of detailed thought.

Obviously, *ToString* is a fine idea in concept, and all classes should provide a method that can be used to convert objects to strings for display or debugging purposes. It is only the implementation that requires attention. In fact, you are not expected to call the *ToString* method defined by *System.Object*; it is simply a placeholder. Instead, you might find it more useful to provide your own version of the *ToString* method in each class you define, overriding the default implementation in *System.Object*. The version in *System.Object* is there only as a safety net, in case a class does not implement or require its own specific version of the *ToString* method.

A method that is intended to be overridden is called a *virtual* method. You should be clear on the difference between *overriding* a method and *hiding* a method. Overriding a method is a mechanism for providing different implementations of the same method—the methods are all related because they are intended to perform the same task, but in a class-specific manner. Hiding a method is a means of replacing one method with another—the methods are usually unrelated and might perform totally different tasks. Overriding a method is a useful programming concept; hiding a method is often an error.

You can mark a method as a virtual method by using the *virtual* keyword. For example, the *ToString* method in the *System.Object* class is defined like this:

```
namespace System
{
    class Object
    {
        public virtual string ToString()
        {
            ...
        }
        ...
    }
    ...
}
```

> **Note** If you have experience developing in Java, you should note that C# methods are not virtual by default.

Declaring *override* methods

If a base class declares that a method is virtual, a derived class can use the *override* keyword to declare another implementation of that method, as demonstrated here:

```
class Horse : Mammal
{
    ...
    public override string ToString()
    {
        ...
    }
}
```

The new implementation of the method in the derived class can call the original implementation of the method in the base class by using the *base* keyword, like this:

```
public override string ToString()
{
    string temp = base.ToString();
    ...
}
```

There are some important rules you must follow when you declare polymorphic methods (as discussed in the sidebar "Virtual methods and polymorphism") by using the *virtual* and *override* keywords:

- A virtual method cannot be private; it is intended to be exposed to other classes through inheritance. Similarly, override methods cannot be private because a class cannot change the protection level of a method that it inherits. However, override methods can have a special form of privacy known as *protected access*, as you will find out in the next section.

- The signatures of the virtual and override methods must be identical; they must have the same name, number, and types of parameters. In addition, both methods must return the same type.

- You can only override a virtual method. If the base class method is not virtual and you try to override it, you'll get a compile-time error. This is sensible; it should be up to the designer of the base class to decide whether its methods can be overridden.

- If the derived class does not declare the method by using the *override* keyword, it does not override the base class method; it hides the method. In other words, it becomes an implementation of a completely different method that happens to have the same name. As before, this will cause a compile-time warning, which you can silence by using the *new* keyword, as previously described.

- An override method is implicitly virtual and can itself be overridden in a further derived class. However, you are not allowed to explicitly declare that an override method is virtual by using the *virtual* keyword.

Virtual methods and polymorphism

Using virtual methods, you can call different versions of the same method, based on the object type determined dynamically at run time. Consider the following examples of classes that define a variation on the *Mammal* hierarchy described earlier:

```
class Mammal
{
    ...
    public virtual string GetTypeName()
    {
        return "This is a mammal" ;
    }
}

class Horse : Mammal
{
    ...
    public override string GetTypeName()
    {
        return "This is a horse";
    }
}

class Whale : Mammal
{
    ...
```

```
public override string GetTypeName()
    {
        return "This is a whale";
    }
}

class Aardvark : Mammal
{
    ...
}
```

There are two things that you should note: first, the *override* keyword used by the *GetTypeName* method in the *Horse* and *Whale* classes, and second, the fact that the *Aardvark* class does not have a *GetTypeName* method.

Now examine the following block of code:

```
Mammal myMammal;
Horse myHorse = new Horse(...);
Whale myWhale = new Whale(...);
Aardvark myAardvark = new Aardvark(...);

myMammal = myHorse;
Console.WriteLine(myMammal.GetTypeName()); // Horse
myMammal = myWhale;
Console.WriteLine(myMammal.GetTypeName()); // Whale
myMammal = myAardvark;
Console.WriteLine(myMammal.GetTypeName()); // Aardvark
```

What will the three different *Console.WriteLine* statements output? At first glance, you would expect them all to print "This is a mammal" because each statement calls the *GetTypeName* method on the *myMammal* variable, which is a *Mammal*. However, in the first case, you can see that *myMammal* is actually a reference to a *Horse*. (Remember, you are allowed to assign a *Horse* to a *Mammal* variable because the *Horse* class inherits from the *Mammal* class.) Because the *GetTypeName* method is defined as virtual, the runtime works out that it should call the *Horse.GetTypeName* method, so the statement actually prints the message "This is a horse." The same logic applies to the second *Console.WriteLine* statement, which outputs the message "This is a whale." The third statement calls *Console.WriteLine* on an *Aardvark* object. However, the *Aardvark* class does not have a *GetTypeName* method, so the default method in the *Mammal* class is called, returning the string "This is a mammal."

This phenomenon of the same statement invoking a different method depending on its context is called *polymorphism*, which literally means "many forms."

Understanding *protected* access

The *public* and *private* access keywords create two extremes of accessibility: public fields and methods of a class are accessible to everyone, whereas private fields and methods of a class are accessible only to the class itself.

These two extremes are sufficient when you consider classes in isolation. However, as all experienced object-oriented programmers know, isolated classes cannot solve complex problems. Inheritance is a powerful way of connecting classes, and there is clearly a special and close relationship between a derived class and its base class. Frequently, it is useful for a base class to allow derived classes to access some of its members while also hiding these members from classes that are not part of the inheritance hierarchy. In this situation, you can mark members with the *protected* keyword. It works like this:

- If a class A is derived from another class B, it can access the protected class members of class B. In other words, inside the derived class A, a protected member of class B is effectively public.

- If a class A is not derived from another class B, it cannot access any protected members of class B. So, within class A, a protected member of class B is effectively private.

C# gives programmers complete freedom to declare methods and fields as protected. However, most object-oriented programming guidelines recommend that you keep your fields strictly private whenever possible and only relax these restrictions when absolutely necessary. Public fields violate encapsulation because all users of the class have direct, unrestricted access to the fields. Protected fields maintain encapsulation for users of a class, for whom the protected fields are inaccessible. However, protected fields still allow encapsulation to be violated by other classes that inherit from the base class.

> **Note** You can access a protected base class member not only in a derived class but also in classes derived from the derived class.

In the following exercise, you will define a simple class hierarchy for modeling different types of vehicles. You will define a base class named *Vehicle* and derived classes named *Airplane* and *Car*. You will define common methods named *StartEngine* and *StopEngine* in the *Vehicle* class, and you will add some methods to both of the derived classes that are specific to those classes. Finally, you will add a virtual method named *Drive* to the *Vehicle* class and override the default implementation of this method in both of the derived classes.

Create a hierarchy of classes

1. Start Microsoft Visual Studio 2015 if it is not already running.

2. Open the Vehicles project, which is located in the \Microsoft Press\VCSBS\Chapter 12\Vehicles folder in your Documents folder.

   The Vehicles project contains the file Program.cs, which defines the *Program* class with the *Main* and *doWork* methods that you have seen in previous exercises.

3. In Solution Explorer, right-click the Vehicles project, point to Add, and then click Class.

   The Add New Item – Vehicles dialog box opens.

4. In the Add New Item – Vehicles dialog box, verify that the Class template is highlighted. In the Name box, type **Vehicle.cs**, and then click Add.

   The file Vehicle.cs is created and added to the project and appears in the Code and Text Editor window. The file contains the definition of an empty class named *Vehicle*.

5. Add the *StartEngine* and *StopEngine* methods to the *Vehicle* class, as shown next in bold:

```
class Vehicle
{
    public void StartEngine(string noiseToMakeWhenStarting)
    {
        Console.WriteLine($"Starting engine: {noiseToMakeWhenStarting}");
    }

    public void StopEngine(string noiseToMakeWhenStopping)
    {
        Console.WriteLine($"Stopping engine: {noiseToMakeWhenStopping}");
    }
}
```

   All classes that derive from the *Vehicle* class will inherit these methods. The values for the *noiseToMakeWhenStarting* and *noiseToMakeWhenStopping* parameters will be different for each type of vehicle and will help you to identify which vehicle is being started and stopped later.

6. On the Project menu, click Add Class.

   The Add New Item – Vehicles dialog box opens again.

7. In the Name box, type **Airplane.cs**, and then click Add.

   A new file containing a class named *Airplane* is added to the project and appears in the Code and Text Editor window.

8. In the Code and Text Editor window, modify the definition of the *Airplane* class so that it inherits from the *Vehicle* class, as shown in bold here:

```
class Airplane : Vehicle
{
}
```

9. Add the *TakeOff* and *Land* methods to the *Airplane* class, as shown in bold in the following:

```
class Airplane : Vehicle
{
    public void TakeOff()
    {
        Console.WriteLine("Taking off");
    }

    public void Land()
    {
        Console.WriteLine("Landing");
    }
}
```

10. On the Project menu, click Add Class.

    The Add New Item – Vehicles dialog box opens again.

11. In the Name text box, type **Car.cs**, and then click Add.

    A new file containing a class named *Car* is added to the project and appears in the Code and Text Editor window.

12. In the Code and Text Editor window, modify the definition of the *Car* class so that it derives from the *Vehicle* class, as shown here in bold:

```
class Car : Vehicle
{
}
```

13. Add the *Accelerate* and *Brake* methods to the *Car* class, as shown in bold in the following:

```
class Car : Vehicle
{
    public void Accelerate()
    {
        Console.WriteLine("Accelerating");
    }

    public void Brake()
    {
        Console.WriteLine("Braking");
    }
}
```

14. Display the Vehicle.cs file in the Code and Text Editor window.

15. Add the virtual *Drive* method to the *Vehicle* class, as presented here in bold:

```
class Vehicle
{
    ...
    public virtual void Drive()
    {
        Console.WriteLine("Default implementation of the Drive method");
    }
}
```

16. Display the Program.cs file in the Code and Text Editor window.

17. In the *doWork* method, delete the // *TODO:* comment and add code to create an instance of the *Airplane* class and test its methods by simulating a quick journey by airplane, as follows:

```
static void doWork()
{
    Console.WriteLine("Journey by airplane:");
    Airplane myPlane = new Airplane();
    myPlane.StartEngine("Contact");
    myPlane.TakeOff();
```

```
        myPlane.Drive();
        myPlane.Land();
        myPlane.StopEngine("Whirr");
    }
```

18. Add the statements that follow (shown in bold) to the *doWork* method after the code you just wrote. These statements create an instance of the *Car* class and test its methods.

```
static void doWork()
{
    ...
    Console.WriteLine("\nJourney by car:");
    Car myCar = new Car();
    myCar.StartEngine("Brm brm");
    myCar.Accelerate();
    myCar.Drive();
    myCar.Brake();
    myCar.StopEngine("Phut phut");
}
```

19. On the Debug menu, click Start Without Debugging.

    In the console window, verify that the program outputs messages simulating the different stages of performing a journey by airplane and by car, as shown in the following image:

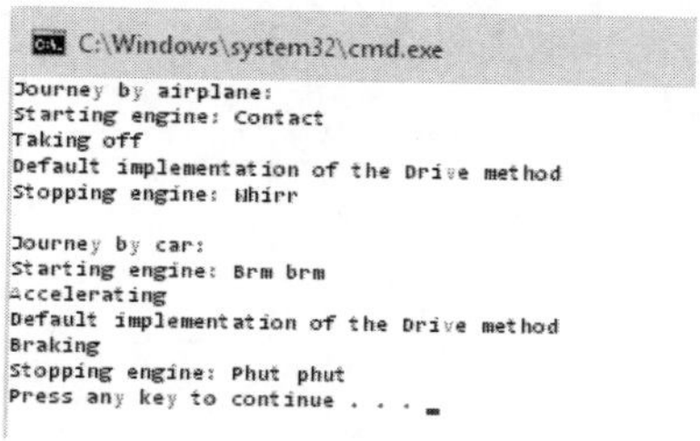

    Notice that both modes of transport invoke the default implementation of the virtual *Drive* method because neither class currently overrides this method.

20. Press Enter to close the application and return to Visual Studio 2015.

21. Display the *Airplane* class in the Code and Text Editor window. Override the *Drive* method in the *Airplane* class, as follows in bold:

```
class Airplane : Vehicle
{
    ...
    public override void Drive()
    {
        Console.WriteLine("Flying");
    }
}
```

> **Note** IntelliSense displays a list of available virtual methods. If you select the *Drive* method from the IntelliSense list, Visual Studio automatically inserts into your code a statement that calls the *base.Drive* method. If this happens, delete the statement, because this exercise does not require it.

22. Display the *Car* class in the Code and Text Editor window. Override the *Drive* method in the *Car* class, as shown in bold in the following:

```
class Car : Vehicle
{
    ...
    public override void Drive()
    {
        Console.WriteLine("Motoring");
    }
}
```

23. On the Debug menu, click Start Without Debugging.

In the console window, notice that the *Airplane* object now displays the message *Flying* when the application calls the *Drive* method, and the *Car* object displays the message *Motoring*:

24. Press Enter to close the application and return to Visual Studio 2015.

25. Display the Program.cs file in the Code and Text Editor window.

26. Add the statements shown here in bold to the end of the *doWork* method:

```
static void doWork()
{
    ...
    Console.WriteLine("\nTesting polymorphism");
    Vehicle v = myCar;
    v.Drive();
    v = myPlane;
    v.Drive();
}
```

This code tests the polymorphism provided by the virtual *Drive* method. The code creates a reference to the *Car* object by using a *Vehicle* variable (which is safe because all *Car* objects are *Vehicle* objects) and then calls the *Drive* method by using this *Vehicle* variable. The final two statements refer the *Vehicle* variable to the *Airplane* object and call what seems to be the same *Drive* method again.

27. On the Debug menu, click Start Without Debugging.

In the console window, verify that the same messages appear as before, followed by this text:

```
Testing polymorphism
Motoring
Flying
```

The *Drive* method is virtual, so the runtime (not the compiler) works out which version of the *Drive* method to call when invoking it through a *Vehicle* variable, based on the real type of the object referenced by this variable. In the first case, the *Vehicle* object refers to a *Car*, so the application calls the *Car.Drive* method. In the second case, the *Vehicle* object refers to an *Airplane*, so the application calls the *Airplane.Drive* method.

28. Press Enter to close the application and return to Visual Studio 2015.

Understanding extension methods

Inheritance is a powerful feature that makes it possible for you to extend the functionality of a class by creating a new class that derives from it. However, sometimes using inheritance is not the most appropriate mechanism for adding new behaviors, especially if you need to quickly extend a type without affecting existing code.

For example, suppose you want to add a new feature to the *int* type, such as a method named *Negate* that returns the negative equivalent value that an integer currently contains. (I know that you could simply use the unary minus operator [−] to perform the same task, but bear with me.) One way to achieve this is to define a new type named *NegInt32* that inherits from *System.Int32* (*int* is an alias for *System.Int32*) and adds the *Negate* method:

```
class NegInt32 : System.Int32  // don't try this!
{
    public int Negate()
    {
        ...
```

```
    }
}
```

The theory is that *NegInt32* will inherit all the functionality associated with the *System.Int32* type in addition to the *Negate* method. There are two reasons why you might not want to follow this approach:

- This method applies only to the *NegInt32* type, and if you want to use it with existing *int* variables in your code, you have to change the definition of every *int* variable to the *NegInt32* type.

- The *System.Int32* type is actually a structure, not a class, and you cannot use inheritance with structures.

This is where extension methods become very useful.

Using an extension method, you can extend an existing type (a class or a structure) with additional static methods. These static methods become immediately available to your code in any statements that reference data of the type being extended.

You define an extension method in a static class and specify the type to which the method applies as the first parameter to the method, along with the *this* keyword. Here's an example showing how you can implement the *Negate* extension method for the *int* type:

```
static class Util
{
    public static int Negate(this int i)
    {
        return -i;
    }
}
```

The syntax looks a little odd, but it is the *this* keyword prefixing the parameter to *Negate* that identifies it as an extension method, and the fact that the parameter that *this* prefixes is an *int* means that you are extending the *int* type.

To use the extension method, bring the *Util* class into scope. (If necessary, add a *using* statement that specifies the namespace to which the *Util* class belongs, or a *using static* statement that specifies the *Util* class directly.) Then you can simply use dot notation (.) to reference the method, like this:

```
int x = 591;
Console.WriteLine($"x.Negate {x.Negate()}");
```

Notice that you do not need to reference the *Util* class anywhere in the statement that calls the *Negate* method. The C# compiler automatically detects all extension methods for a given type from all the static classes that are in scope. You can also invoke the *Util.Negate* method by passing an *int* as the parameter, using the regular syntax you have seen before, although this use obviates the purpose of defining the method as an extension method:

```
int x = 591;
Console.WriteLine($"x.Negate {Util.Negate(x)}");
```

In the following exercise, you will add an extension method to the *int* type. With this extension method, you can convert the value in an *int* variable from base 10 to a representation of that value in a different number base.

Create an extension method

1. In Visual Studio 2015, open the ExtensionMethod project, which is located in the \Microsoft Press\VCSBS\Chapter 12\ExtensionMethod folder in your Documents folder.

2. Display the Util.cs file in the Code and Text Editor window.

   This file contains a static class named *Util* in a namespace named *Extensions*. Remember that you must define extension methods inside a static class. The class is empty apart from the // TODO: comment.

3. Delete the comment and declare a public static method in the *Util* class, named *ConvertToBase*. The method should take two parameters: an *int* parameter named *i*, prefixed with the *this* keyword to indicate that the method is an extension method for the *int* type, and another ordinary *int* parameter named *baseToConvertTo*.

   The method will convert the value in *i* to the base indicated by *baseToConvertTo*. The method should return an *int* containing the converted value.

   The *ConvertToBase* method should look like this:

```
static class Util
{
    public static int ConvertToBase(this int i, int baseToConvertTo)
    {
    }
}
```

4. Add an *if* statement to the *ConvertToBase* method that checks that the value of the *baseToConvertTo* parameter is between 2 and 10.

   The algorithm used by this exercise does not work reliably outside this range of values. Throw an *ArgumentException* exception with a suitable message if the value of *baseToConvertTo* is outside this range.

   The *ConvertToBase* method should look like this:

```
public static int ConvertToBase(this int i, int baseToConvertTo)
{
    if (baseToConvertTo < 2 || baseToConvertTo > 10)
    {
        throw new ArgumentException("Value cannot be converted to base " +
                            baseToConvertTo.ToString());
    }
}
```

5. Add the following statements shown in bold to the *ConvertToBase* method, after the statement that throws the *ArgumentException* exception.

This code implements a well-known algorithm that converts a number from base 10 to a different number base. (Chapter 5, "Using compound assignment and iteration statements," presents a version of this algorithm for converting a decimal number to octal.)

```
public static int ConvertToBase(this int i, int baseToConvertTo)
{
    ...
    int result = 0;
    int iterations = 0;
    do
    {
        int nextDigit = i % baseToConvertTo;
        i /= baseToConvertTo;
        result += nextDigit * (int)Math.Pow(10, iterations);
        iterations++;
    }
    while (i != 0);

    return result;
}
```

6. Display the Program.cs file in the Code and Text Editor window.

7. Add the following *using* directive after the *using System;* directive at the top of the file:

```
using Extensions;
```

This statement brings the namespace containing the *Util* class into scope. The *ConvertToBase* extension method will not be visible in the Program.cs file if you do not perform this task.

8. Add the following statements shown in bold to the *doWork* method of the *Program* class, replacing the *// TODO:* comment:

```
static void doWork()
{
    int x = 591;
    for (int i = 2; i <= 10; i++)
    {
        Console.WriteLine($"{x} in base {i} is {x.ConvertToBase(i)}");

    }
}
```

This code creates an *int* named *x* and sets it to the value *591*. (You can pick any integer value you want.) The code then uses a loop to print out the value 591 in all number bases between 2 and 10. Notice that *ConvertToBase* appears as an extension method in IntelliSense when you type the period (.) after *x* in the *Console.WriteLine* statement.

```
Program.cs* + X  Util.cs*
ExtensionMethod                                    ExtensionMethod.Program                        doWork()
    using System;
    using Extensions;

    namespace ExtensionMethod
    {
        0 references
        class Program
        {
            1 reference
            static void doWork()
            {
                int x = 591;
                for(int i=2;i<=10;i++)
                {
                    Console.WriteLine($"{x} in base {i} is {x.ConvertToBase(i)}");
                }                                    CompareTo
            }                                        ConvertToBase    (extension) int int.ConvertToBase(int baseToConvertTo)
                                                     Equals
            0 references                             GetHashCode
            static void Main()                       GetType
            {                                        GetTypeCode
                try                                  ToString
                {
                    doWork();
                }
                catch (Exception ex)
                {
                    Console.WriteLine("Exception: {0}", ex.Message);
                }
            }
        }
    }
```

9. On the Debug menu, click Start Without Debugging. Confirm that the program displays messages to the console showing the value 591 in the different number bases, like this:

```
C:\Windows\system32\cmd.exe
591 in base 2 is 1001001111
591 in base 3 is 210220
591 in base 4 is 21033
591 in base 5 is 4331
591 in base 6 is 2423
591 in base 7 is 1503
591 in base 8 is 1117
591 in base 9 is 726
591 in base 10 is 591
Press any key to continue . . . _
```

10. Press Enter to close the program and return to Visual Studio 2015.

Summary

In this chapter, you learned how to use inheritance to define a hierarchy of classes, and you should now understand how to override inherited methods and implement virtual methods. You also learned how to add an extension method to an existing type.

- If you want to continue to the next chapter, keep Visual Studio 2015 running and turn to Chapter 13.

- If you want to exit Visual Studio 2015 now, on the File menu, click Exit. If you see a Save dialog box, click Yes and save the project.

Quick reference

To	Do this
| Create a derived class from a base class | Declare the new class name followed by a colon and the name of the base class. For example:<br><br>```csharp
class DerivedClass : BaseClass
{
    ...
}
``` |
| Call a base-class constructor as part of the constructor for an inheriting class | Suffix the definition of the constructor with a call to *base*, before the body of the derived-class constructor, and provide any necessary parameters to the *base* constructor. For example:<br><br>```csharp
class DerivedClass : BaseClass
{
    ...
    public DerivedClass(int x) : base(x)
    {
        ...
    }
    ...
}
``` |
| Declare a virtual method | Use the *virtual* keyword when declaring the method. For example:<br><br>```csharp
class Mammal
{
    public virtual void Breathe()
    {
        ...
    }
    ...
}
``` |
| Implement a method in a derived class that overrides an inherited virtual method | Use the *override* keyword when declaring the method in the derived class. For example:<br><br>```csharp
class Whale : Mammal
{
    public override void Breathe()
    {
        ...
    }
    ...
}
``` |
| Define an extension method for a type | Add a static public method to a static class. The first parameter must be of the type being extended, preceded by the *this* keyword. For example:<br><br>```csharp
static class Util
{
    public static int Negate(this int i)
    {
        return -i;
    }
}
``` |
```

CHAPTER 13

Creating interfaces and defining abstract classes

After completing this chapter, you will be able to:

- Define an interface specifying the signatures and return types of methods.

- Implement an interface in a structure or class.

- Reference a class through an interface.

- Capture common implementation details in an abstract class.

- Implement sealed classes that cannot be used to derive new classes.

Inheriting from a class is a powerful mechanism, but the real power of inheritance comes from inheriting from an interface. An interface does not contain any code or data; it just specifies the methods and properties that a class that inherits from the interface must provide. By using an interface, you can completely separate the names and signatures of the methods of a class from the method's implementation.

Abstract classes are similar to interfaces in many ways, except that abstract classes can contain code and data. However, you can specify certain methods of an abstract class as virtual so that a class that inherits from the abstract class can optionally provide its own implementation of these methods. You frequently use abstract classes with interfaces, and together they provide a key technique with which you can build extensible programming frameworks, as you will discover in this chapter.

Understanding interfaces

Suppose that you want to define a new class in which you can store collections of objects, a bit like you would use an array. However, unlike with an array, you want to provide a method named *RetrieveInOrder* to enable applications to retrieve objects in a sequence that depends on the type of object the collection contains. (With an ordinary array, you can iterate through its contents, and by default you retrieve items according to their index.) For example, if the collection holds alphanumeric objects such as strings, the collection should enable an application to retrieve these strings in sequence according to the collating sequence of the computer, and if the collection holds numeric objects such as integers, the collection should enable the application to retrieve objects in numerical order.

When you define the collection class, you do not want to restrict the types of objects that it can hold (the objects can even be class or structure types), and consequently you don't know how to order these objects. So, how do you provide the collection class with a method that sorts objects whose types you do not know when you actually write the collection class? At first glance, this problem seems similar to the *ToString* problem described in Chapter 12, "Working with inheritance," which could be resolved by declaring a virtual method that subclasses of your collection class can override. However, any similarity is misleading. There is no inheritance relationship between the collection class and the objects that it holds, so a virtual method would not be of much use. If you think for a moment, the problem is that the way in which the objects in the collection should be ordered is dependent on the type of the object in the collection and not on the collection itself. The solution is to require that all the objects provide a method, such as the *CompareTo* method shown in the following example, that the *RetrieveInOrder* method of the collection can call, making it possible for the collection to compare these objects with one another:

```
int CompareTo(object obj)
{
    // return 0 if this instance is equal to obj
    // return < 0 if this instance is less than obj
    // return > 0 if this instance is greater than obj
    ...
}
```

You can define an interface for collectable objects that includes the *CompareTo* method and specify that the collection class can contain only classes that implement this interface. In this way, an interface is similar to a contract. If a class implements an interface, the interface guarantees that the class contains all the methods specified in the interface. This mechanism ensures that you will be able to call the *CompareTo* method on all objects in the collection and sort them.

Using interfaces, you can truly separate the "what" from the "how." An interface gives you only the name, return type, and parameters of the method. Exactly how the method is implemented is not a concern of the interface. The interface describes the functionality that a class should provide but not how this functionality is implemented.

Defining an interface

Defining an interface is syntactically similar to defining a class, except that you use the *interface* keyword instead of the *class* keyword. Within the interface, you declare methods exactly as in a class or a structure, except that you never specify an access modifier (*public*, *private*, or *protected*). Additionally, the methods in an interface have no implementation; they are simply declarations, and all types that implement the interface must provide their own implementations. Consequently, you replace the method body with a semicolon. Here is an example:

```
interface IComparable
{
    int CompareTo(object obj);
}
```

> **Tip** The Microsoft .NET Framework documentation recommends that you preface the name of your interfaces with the capital letter *I*. This convention is the last vestige of Hungarian notation in C#. Incidentally, the *System* namespace already defines the *IComparable* interface as just shown.

An interface cannot contain any data; you cannot add fields (not even private ones) to an interface.

Implementing an interface

To implement an interface, you declare a class or structure that inherits from the interface and that implements *all* the methods specified by the interface. This is not really inheritance as such, although the syntax is the same and some of the semantics that you will see later in this chapter bear many of the hallmarks of inheritance. You should note that unlike class inheritance, a struct can implement an interface.

For example, suppose that you are defining the *Mammal* hierarchy described in Chapter 12, but you need to specify that land-bound mammals provide a method named *NumberOfLegs* that returns as an *int* the number of legs that a mammal has. (Sea-bound mammals do not implement this interface.) You could define the *ILandBound* interface that contains this method as follows:

```
interface ILandBound
{
    int NumberOfLegs();
}
```

You could then implement this interface in the *Horse* class. You inherit from the interface and provide an implementation of every method defined by the interface (in this case, there is just the one method, *NumberOfLegs*).

```
class Horse : ILandBound
{
    ...
    public int NumberOfLegs()
    {
        return 4;
    }
}
```

When you implement an interface, you must ensure that each method matches its corresponding interface method exactly, according to the following rules:

- The method names and return types match exactly.

- Any parameters (including *ref* and *out* keyword modifiers) match exactly.

- All methods implementing an interface must be publicly accessible. However, if you are using an explicit interface implementation, the method should not have an access qualifier.

If there is any difference between the interface definition and its declared implementation, the class will not compile.

> **Tip** The Microsoft Visual Studio integrated development environment (IDE) can help reduce coding errors caused by failing to implement the methods in an interface. The Implement Interface Wizard can generate stubs for each item in an interface that a class implements. You then fill in these stubs with the appropriate code. You will see how to use this wizard in the exercises later in this chapter.

A class can inherit from another class and implement an interface at the same time. In this case, C# does not distinguish between the base class and the interface by using specific keywords as, for example, Java does. Instead, C# uses a positional notation. The base class is always named first, followed by a comma, followed by the interface. The following example defines *Horse* as a class that is a *Mammal* but that additionally implements the *ILandBound* interface:

```
interface ILandBound
{
    ...
}

class Mammal
{
    ...
}

class Horse : Mammal , ILandBound
{
    ...
}
```

> **Note** An interface, InterfaceA, can inherit from another interface, InterfaceB. Technically, this is known as *interface extension* rather than inheritance. In this case, any class or struct that implements InterfaceA must provide implementations of all the methods in InterfaceB and InterfaceA.

Referencing a class through its interface

In the same way that you can reference an object by using a variable defined as a class that is higher up the hierarchy, you can reference an object by using a variable defined as an interface that the object's class implements. Taking the preceding example, you can reference a *Horse* object by using an *ILandBound* variable, as follows:

```
Horse myHorse = new Horse(...);
ILandBound iMyHorse = myHorse; // legal
```

This works because all horses are land-bound mammals, although the converse is not true—you cannot assign an *ILandBound* object to a *Horse* variable without casting it first to verify that it does actually reference a *Horse* object and not some other class that also happens to implement the *ILandBound* interface.

The technique of referencing an object through an interface is useful because you can use it to define methods that can take different types as parameters, as long as the types implement a specified interface. For example, the *FindLandSpeed* method shown here can take any argument that implements the *ILandBound* interface:

```
int FindLandSpeed(ILandBound landBoundMammal)
{
    ...
}
```

You can verify that an object is an instance of a class that implements a specific interface by using the *is* operator, which is demonstrated in Chapter 8, "Understanding values and references." You use the *is* operator to determine whether an object has a specified type, and it works with interfaces as well as with classes and structs. For example, the following block of code checks that the variable *myHorse* actually implements the *ILandBound* interface before attempting to assign it to an *ILandBound* variable:

```
if (myHorse is ILandBound)
{
    ILandBound iLandBoundAnimal = myHorse;
}
```

Note that when referencing an object through an interface, you can invoke only methods that are visible through the interface.

Working with multiple interfaces

A class can have at most one base class, but it is allowed to implement an unlimited number of interfaces. A class must implement all the methods declared by these interfaces.

If a structure or class implements more than one interface, you specify the interfaces as a comma-separated list. If a class also has a base class, the interfaces are listed *after* the base class. For example, suppose that you define another interface named *IGrazable* that contains the *ChewGrass* method for all grazing animals. You can define the *Horse* class like this:

```
class Horse : Mammal, ILandBound, IGrazable
{
    ...
}
```

Explicitly implementing an interface

The examples so far have shown classes that implicitly implement an interface. If you revisit the *ILandBound* interface and the *Horse* class (shown next), you'll see that although the *Horse* class implements from the *ILandBound* interface, nothing in the implementation of the *NumberOfLegs* method in the *Horse* class says that it is part of the *ILandBound* interface:

```
interface ILandBound
{
    int NumberOfLegs();
}

class Horse : ILandBound
{
    ...
    public int NumberOfLegs()
    {
        return 4;
    }
}
```

This might not be an issue in a simple situation, but suppose the *Horse* class implemented multiple interfaces. There is nothing to prevent multiple interfaces from specifying a method with the same name, although they might have different semantics. For example, suppose that you wanted to implement a transportation system based on horse-drawn coaches. A lengthy journey might be broken down into several stages, or "legs." If you wanted to keep track of how many legs each horse had pulled the coach for, you might define the following interface:

```
interface IJourney
{
    int NumberOfLegs();
}
```

Now, if you implement this interface in the *Horse* class, you have an interesting problem:

```
class Horse : ILandBound, IJourney
{
    ...
    public int NumberOfLegs()
    {
        return 4;
    }
}
```

This is legal code, but does the horse have four legs or has it pulled the coach for four legs of the journey? The answer as far as C# is concerned is both of these! By default, C# does not distinguish which interface the method is implementing, so the same method actually implements both interfaces.

To solve this problem and disambiguate which method is part of which interface implementation, you can implement interfaces explicitly. To do this, you specify which interface a method belongs to when you implement it, like this:

```
class Horse : ILandBound, IJourney
{
    ...
    int ILandBound.NumberOfLegs()
    {
        return 4;
    }

    int IJourney.NumberOfLegs()
    {
        return 3;
    }
}
```

Now you can see that the horse has four legs and has pulled the coach for three legs of the journey.

Apart from prefixing the name of the method with the interface name, there is one other subtle difference in this syntax: the methods are not marked public. You cannot specify the protection for methods that are part of an explicit interface implementation. This leads to another interesting phenomenon. If you create a *Horse* variable in code, you cannot actually invoke either of the *NumberOfLegs* methods because they are not visible. As far as the *Horse* class is concerned, they are both private. In fact, this makes sense. If the methods were visible through the *Horse* class, which method would the following code actually invoke, the one for the *ILandBound* interface or the one for the *IJourney* interface?

```
Horse horse = new Horse();
...
// The following statement will not compile
int legs = horse.NumberOfLegs();
```

So, how do you access these methods? The answer is that you reference the *Horse* object through the appropriate interface, like this:

```
Horse horse = new Horse();
...
IJourney journeyHorse = horse;
int legsInJourney = journeyHorse.NumberOfLegs();
ILandBound landBoundHorse = horse;
int legsOnHorse = landBoundHorse.NumberOfLegs();
```

I recommend explicitly implementing interfaces when possible.

Interface restrictions

The essential idea to remember is that an interface never contains any implementation. The following restrictions are natural consequences of this:

- You're not allowed to define any fields in an interface, not even static fields. A field is an implementation detail of a class or structure.

- You're not allowed to define any constructors in an interface. A constructor is also considered to be an implementation detail of a class or structure.

- You're not allowed to define a destructor in an interface. A destructor contains the statements used to destroy an object instance. (Destructors are described in Chapter 14, "Using garbage collection and resource management.")

- You cannot specify an access modifier for any method. All methods in an interface are implicitly public.

- You cannot nest any types (such as enumerations, structures, classes, or interfaces) inside an interface.

- An interface is not allowed to inherit from a structure or a class, although an interface can inherit from another interface. Structures and classes contain implementation; if an interface were allowed to inherit from either, it would be inheriting some implementation.

Defining and using interfaces

In the following exercises, you will define and implement interfaces that constitute part of a simple graphical drawing package. You will define two interfaces, called *IDraw* and *IColor*, and then you will define classes that implement them. Each class will define a shape that can be drawn on a canvas on a form. (A *canvas* is a control that you can use to draw lines, text, and shapes on the screen.)

The *IDraw* interface defines the following methods:

- *SetLocation*   With this method, you can specify the position as x- and y-coordinates of the shape on the canvas.

- *Draw*   This method actually draws the shape on the canvas at the location specified by using the *SetLocation* method.

The *IColor* interface defines the following method:

- *SetColor*   You use this method to specify the color of the shape. When the shape is drawn on the canvas, it will appear in this color.

Define the *IDraw* and *IColor* interfaces

1. Start Microsoft Visual Studio 2015 if it is not already running.

2. Open the Drawing project, which is located in the \Microsoft Press\VCSBS\Chapter 13\Drawing folder in your Documents folder.

   The Drawing project is a graphical application. It contains a form called *DrawingPad*. This form contains a canvas control called *drawingCanvas*. You will use this form and canvas to test your code.

3. In Solution Explorer, click the Drawing project. On the Project menu, click Add New Item.

The Add New Item – Drawing dialog box opens.

4. In the left pane of the Add New Item – Drawing dialog box, click Visual C#, and then click Code. In the middle pane, click the Interface template. In the Name box, type **IDraw.cs**, and then click Add.

   Visual Studio creates the IDraw.cs file and adds it to your project. The IDraw.cs file appears in the Code and Text Editor window, and should look like this:

```
using System;
using System.Collections.Generic;
using System.Linq;
using System.Text;
using System.Threading.Tasks;

namespace Drawing
{
    interface IDraw
    {
    }
}
```

5. In the IDraw.cs file, add the following *using* directive to the list at the top of the file:

```
using Windows.UI.Xaml.Controls;
```

   You will reference the *Canvas* class in this interface. The *Canvas* class is located in the *Windows.UI.Xaml.Controls* namespace for Universal Windows Platform (UWP) apps.

6. Add the methods shown here in bold to the *IDraw* interface:

```
interface IDraw
{
    void SetLocation(int xCoord, int yCoord);
    void Draw(Canvas canvas);
}
```

7. On the Project menu, click Add New Item again.

8. In the Add New Item – Drawing dialog box, in the middle pane, click the Interface template. In the Name box, type **IColor.cs**, and then click Add.

   Visual Studio creates the IColor.cs file and adds it to your project. The IColor.cs file appears in the Code and Text Editor window.

9. In the IColor.cs file, at the top of the file, add the following *using* directive to the list:

```
using Windows.UI;
```

   You will reference the *Color* class in this interface, which is located in the *Windows.UI* namespace for UWP apps.

10. Add the following method shown in bold to the *IColor* interface definition:

```
interface IColor
{
    void SetColor(Color color);
}
```

You have now defined the *IDraw* and *IColor* interfaces. The next step is to create some classes that implement them. In the following exercise, you will create two new shape classes, called *Square* and *Circle*. These classes will implement both interfaces.

Create the *Square* and *Circle* classes, and implement the interfaces

1. On the Project menu, click Add Class.

2. In the Add New Item – Drawing dialog box, in the middle pane, verify that the Class template is selected. In the Name box, type **Square.cs**, and then click Add.

   Visual Studio creates the Square.cs file and displays it in the Code and Text Editor window.

3. At the top of the Square.cs file, add the following *using* directives to the list:

   ```
   using Windows.UI;
   using Windows.UI.Xaml.Media;
   using Windows.UI.Xaml.Shapes;
   using Windows.UI.Xaml.Controls;
   ```

4. Modify the definition of the *Square* class so that it implements the *IDraw* and *IColor* interfaces, as shown here in bold:

   ```
   class Square : IDraw, IColor
   {
   }
   ```

5. Add the following private variables shown in bold to the *Square* class:

   ```
   class Square : IDraw, IColor
   {
       private int sideLength;
       private int locX = 0, locY = 0;
       private Rectangle rect = null;
   }
   ```

   These variables will hold the position and size of the *Square* object on the canvas. The *Rectangle* class is located in the *Windows.UI.Xaml.Shapes* namespace for UWP apps. You will use this class to draw the square.

6. Add the following constructor shown in bold to the *Square* class:

   ```
   class Square : IDraw, IColor
   {
       ...
       public Square(int sideLength)
       {
   ```

```
            this.sideLength = sideLength;
        }
    }
```

This constructor initializes the *sideLength* field and specifies the length of each side of the square.

7. In the definition of the *Square* class, hover over the *IDraw* interface. On the lightbulb context menu that appears, click Implement Interface Explicitly, as shown in the following image:

This feature causes Visual Studio to generate default implementations of the methods in the *IDraw* interface. You can also add the methods to the *Square* class manually if you prefer. The following example shows the code generated by Visual Studio:

```
void IDraw.SetLocation(int xCoord, int yCoord)
{
    throw new NotImplementedException();
}

void IDraw.Draw(Canvas canvas)
{
    throw new NotImplementedException();
}
```

Each of these methods currently throws a *NotImplementedException* exception. You are expected to replace the body of these methods with your own code.

8. In the *IDraw.SetLocation* method, replace the existing code that throws a *NotImplementedException* exception with the following statements shown in bold:

```
void IDraw.SetLocation(int xCoord, int yCoord)
{
    this.locX = xCoord;
    this.locY = yCoord;
}
```

This code stores the values passed in through the parameters in the *locX* and *locY* fields in the *Square* object.

9. Replace the code generated in the *IDraw.Draw* method with the statements shown here in bold:

```
void IDraw.Draw(Canvas canvas)
{
    if (this.rect != null)
    {
        canvas.Children.Remove(this.rect);
    }
    else
    {
        this.rect = new Rectangle();
    }

    this.rect.Height = this.sideLength;
    this.rect.Width = this.sideLength;
    Canvas.SetTop(this.rect, this.locY);
    Canvas.SetLeft(this.rect, this.locX);
    canvas.Children.Add(this.rect);
}
```

This method renders the *Square* object by drawing a *Rectangle* shape on the canvas. (A square is simply a rectangle for which all four sides have the same length.) If the *Rectangle* has been drawn previously (possibly at a different location and with a different color), it is removed from the canvas. The height and width of the *Rectangle* are set by using the value of the *sideLength* field. The position of the *Rectangle* on the canvas is set by using the static *SetTop* and *SetLeft* methods of the *Canvas* class, and then the *Rectangle* is added to the canvas. (This causes it to be displayed.)

10. Add the *SetColor* method from the *IColor* interface to the *Square* class, as shown here:

```
void IColor.SetColor(Color color)
{
    if (this.rect != null)
    {
        SolidColorBrush brush = new SolidColorBrush(color);
        this.rect.Fill = brush;
    }
}
```

This method checks that the *Square* object has actually been displayed. (The *rect* field will be *null* if it has not yet been rendered.) The code sets the *Fill* property of the *rect* field with the specified color by using a *SolidColorBrush* object. (The details of how the *SolidColorBrush* class works are beyond the scope of this discussion.)

11. On the Project menu, click Add Class. In the Add New Item – Drawing dialog box, in the Name box, type **Circle.cs**, and then click Add.

Visual Studio creates the Circle.cs file and displays it in the Code and Text Editor window.

12. At the top of the Circle.cs file, add the following *using* directives to the list:

```
using Windows.UI;
using Windows.UI.Xaml.Media;
using Windows.UI.Xaml.Shapes;
using Windows.UI.Xaml.Controls;
```

13. Modify the definition of the *Circle* class so that it implements the *IDraw* and *IColor* interfaces as shown here in bold:

```
class Circle : IDraw, IColor
{
}
```

14. Add the following private variables shown in bold to the *Circle* class:

```
class Circle : IDraw, IColor
{
    private int diameter;
    private int locX = 0, locY = 0;
    private Ellipse circle = null;
}
```

These variables will hold the position and size of the *Circle* object on the canvas. The *Ellipse* class provides the functionality that you will use to draw the circle.

15. Add the constructor shown here in bold to the *Circle* class:

```
class Circle : IDraw, IColor
{
    ...
    public Circle(int diameter)
    {
        this.diameter = diameter;
    }
}
```

This constructor initializes the *diameter* field.

16. Add the following *SetLocation* method to the *Circle* class:

```
void IDraw.SetLocation(int xCoord, int yCoord)
{
    this.locX = xCoord;
    this.locY = yCoord;
}
```

This method implements part of the *IDraw* interface, and the code is the same as that in the *Square* class.

17. Add the *Draw* method shown here to the *Circle* class:

```
void IDraw.Draw(Canvas canvas)
{
    if (this.circle != null)
```

```
        {
            canvas.Children.Remove(this.circle);
        }
        else
        {
            this.circle = new Ellipse();
        }

        this.circle.Height = this.diameter;
        this.circle.Width = this.diameter;
        Canvas.SetTop(this.circle, this.locY);
        Canvas.SetLeft(this.circle, this.locX);
        canvas.Children.Add(this.circle);
    }
```

This method is also part of the *IDraw* interface. It is similar to the *Draw* method in the *Square* class, except that it renders the *Circle* object by drawing an *Ellipse* shape on the canvas. (A circle is an ellipse for which the width and height are the same.)

18. Add the following *SetColor* method to the *Circle* class:

```
void IColor.SetColor(Color color)
{
    if (this.circle != null)
    {
        SolidColorBrush brush = new SolidColorBrush(color);
        this.circle.Fill = brush;
    }
}
```

This method is part of the *IColor* interface. As before, this method is similar to that of the *Square* class.

You have completed the *Square* and *Circle* classes. You can now use the form to test them.

Test the *Square* and *Circle* classes

1. Display the DrawingPad.xaml file in the Design View window.

2. On the form, click the large shaded area.

   The shaded area of the form is the *Canvas* object, and this action sets the focus to this object.

3. In Properties window, click the Event Handlers button. (This button has an icon that looks like a bolt of lightning.)

4. In the list of events, locate the *Tapped* event, and then double-click in the Tapped text box.

   Visual Studio creates a method called *drawingCanvas_Tapped* for the *DrawingPad* class and displays it in the Code and Text Editor window. This is an event handler that runs when the user taps the canvas with a finger or clicks the left mouse button over the canvas. You can learn more about event handlers in Chapter 20, "Decoupling application logic and handling events."

5. At the top of the DrawingPad.xaml.cs file, add the following *using* directive to the list:

```
using Windows.UI;
```

The Windows.UI namespace contains the definition of the *Colors* class, which you will use when you set the color of a shape as it is drawn.

6. Add the following code shown in bold to the *drawingCanvas_Tapped* method:

```
private void drawingCanvas_Tapped(object sender, TappedRoutedEventArgs e)
{
    Point mouseLocation = e.GetPosition(this.drawingCanvas);
    Square mySquare = new Square(100);

    if (mySquare is IDraw)
    {
        IDraw drawSquare = mySquare;
        drawSquare.SetLocation((int)mouseLocation.X, (int)mouseLocation.Y);
        drawSquare.Draw(drawingCanvas);
    }
}
```

The *TappedRoutedEventArgs* parameter to this method provides useful information about the position of the mouse. In particular, the *GetPosition* method returns a *Point* structure that contains the x- and y-coordinates of the mouse. The code that you have added creates a new *Square* object. It then checks to verify that this object implements the *IDraw* interface (this is good practice and helps to ensure that your code will not fail at run time if you attempt to reference an object through an interface that it does not implement) and creates a reference to the object by using this interface. Remember that when you explicitly implement an interface, the methods defined by the interface are available only by creating a reference to that interface. (The *SetLocation* and *Draw* methods are private to the *Square* class and are available only through the *IDraw* interface.) The code then sets the location of the *Square* to the position of the user's finger or mouse. Note that the x- and y-coordinates in the *Point* structure are actually *double* values, so this code casts them to *ints*. The code then calls the *Draw* method to display the *Square* object.

7. At the end of the *drawingCanvas_Tapped* method, add the following code shown in bold:

```
private void drawingCanvas_Tapped(object sender, TappedRoutedEventArgs e)
{
    ...
    if (mySquare is IColor)
    {
        IColor colorSquare = mySquare;
        colorSquare.SetColor(Colors.BlueViolet);
    }
}
```

This code tests the *Square* class to verify that it implements the *IColor* interface; if it does, the code creates a reference to the *Square* class through this interface and calls the *SetColor* method to set the color of the *Square* object to *Colors.BlueViolet*.

> **Important** You must call *Draw* before you call *SetColor* because the *SetColor* method sets the color of the *Square* only if it has already been rendered. If you invoke *SetColor* before *Draw*, the color will not be set and the *Square* object will not appear.

8. Return to the DrawingPad.xaml file in the Design View window and then click the *Canvas* object.

9. In the list of events, locate the *RightTapped* event, and then double-click the RightTapped text box.

   This event occurs when the user taps, holds, and then releases from the canvas by using his or her finger or clicks the right mouse button on the canvas.

10. Add the following code shown below in bold to the *drawingCanvas_RightTapped* method:

```
private void drawingCanvas_RightTapped(object sender, RightTappedRoutedEventArgs e)
{
    Point mouseLocation = e.GetPosition(this.drawingCanvas);
    Circle myCircle = new Circle(100);

    if (myCircle is IDraw)
    {
        IDraw drawCircle = myCircle;
        drawCircle.SetLocation((int)mouseLocation.X, (int)mouseLocation.Y);
        drawCircle.Draw(drawingCanvas);
    }

    if (myCircle is IColor)
    {
        IColor colorCircle = myCircle;
        colorCircle.SetColor(Colors.HotPink);
    }
}
```

   The logic in this code is similar to the logic in the *drawingCanvas_Tapped* method, except that this code draws and fills a circle rather than a square.

11. On the Debug menu, click Start Debugging to build and run the application.

12. When the Drawing Pad window opens, tap or click anywhere on the canvas displayed in the window. A violet square should appear.

13. Tap, hold, and release, or right-click anywhere on the canvas. A pink circle should appear. You can click the left and right mouse buttons any number of times; each click will draw a square or circle at the mouse position. The following image shows the application running on Windows 10:

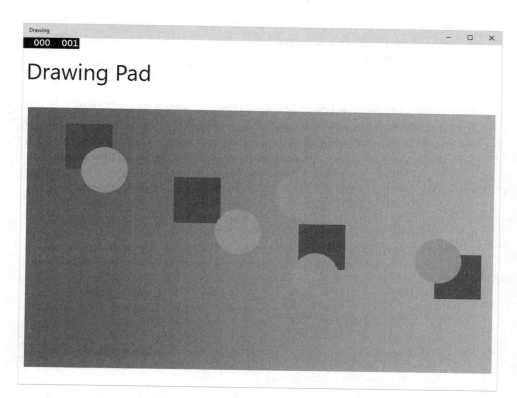

14. Return to Visual Studio and stop debugging.

Abstract classes

You can implement the *ILandBound* and *IGrazable* interfaces discussed before the previous set of exercises in many different classes, depending on how many different types of mammals you want to model in your C# application. In situations such as this, it's quite common for parts of the derived classes to share common implementations. For example, the duplication in the following two classes is obvious:

```
class Horse : Mammal, ILandBound, IGrazable
{
    ...
    void IGrazable.ChewGrass()
    {
        Console.WriteLine("Chewing grass");
        // code for chewing grass
    }
}

class Sheep : Mammal, ILandBound, IGrazable
{
    ...
    void IGrazable.ChewGrass()
```

```
    {
        Console.WriteLine("Chewing grass");
        // same code as horse for chewing grass
    }
}
```

Duplication in code is a warning sign. If possible, you should refactor the code to avoid duplication and reduce any associated maintenance costs. One way to achieve this refactoring is to put the common implementation into a new class created specifically for this purpose. In effect, you can insert a new class into the class hierarchy, as shown by the following code example:

```
class GrazingMammal : Mammal, IGrazable
{
    ...
    void IGrazable.ChewGrass()
    {
        // common code for chewing grass
        Console.WriteLine("Chewing grass");
    }
}

class Horse : GrazingMammal, ILandBound
{
    ...
}

class Sheep : GrazingMammal, ILandBound
{
    ...
}
```

This is a good solution, but there is one thing that is still not quite right: you can actually create instances of the *GrazingMammal* class (and the *Mammal* class, for that matter). This doesn't really make sense. The *GrazingMammal* class exists to provide a common default implementation. Its sole purpose is to be a class from which to inherit. The *GrazingMammal* class is an abstraction of common functionality rather than an entity in its own right.

To declare that creating instances of a class is not allowed, you can declare that the class is abstract by using the *abstract* keyword, such as in the following example:

```
abstract class GrazingMammal : Mammal, IGrazable
{
    ...
}
```

If you now try to instantiate a *GrazingMammal* object, the code will not compile:

```
GrazingMammal myGrazingMammal = new GrazingMammal(...); // illegal
```

Abstract methods

An abstract class can contain abstract methods. An abstract method is similar in principle to a virtual method (covered in Chapter 12), except that it does not contain a method body. A derived class *must* override this method. An abstract method cannot be private. The following example defines the *DigestGrass* method in the *GrazingMammal* class as an abstract method; grazing mammals might use the same code for chewing grass, but they must provide their own implementation of the *DigestGrass* method. An abstract method is useful if it does not make sense to provide a default implementation in the abstract class but you want to ensure that an inheriting class provides its own implementation of that method.

```
abstract class GrazingMammal : Mammal, IGrazable
{
    public abstract void DigestGrass();
    ...
}
```

Sealed classes

Using inheritance is not always easy and requires forethought. If you create an interface or an abstract class, you are knowingly writing something that will be inherited from in the future. The trouble is that predicting the future is a difficult business. With practice and experience, you can develop the skills to craft a flexible, easy-to-use hierarchy of interfaces, abstract classes, and classes, but it takes effort, and you also need a solid understanding of the problem that you are modeling. To put it another way, unless you consciously design a class with the intention of using it as a base class, it's extremely unlikely that it will function well as a base class. With C#, you can use the *sealed* keyword to prevent a class from being used as a base class if you decide that it should not be. For example:

```
sealed class Horse : GrazingMammal, ILandBound
{
    ...
}
```

If any class attempts to use *Horse* as a base class, a compile-time error will be generated. Note that a sealed class cannot declare any virtual methods and that an abstract class cannot be sealed.

Sealed methods

You can also use the *sealed* keyword to declare that an individual method in an unsealed class is sealed. This means that a derived class cannot override this method. You can seal only a method declared with the *override* keyword, and you declare the method as *sealed override*. You can think of the *interface, virtual, override,* and *sealed* keywords as follows:

- An interface introduces the name of a method.

- A virtual method is the first implementation of a method.

- An override method is another implementation of a method.

- A sealed method is the last implementation of a method.

Implementing and using an abstract class

The following exercises use an abstract class to rationalize some of the code that you developed in the previous exercise. The *Square* and *Circle* classes contain a high proportion of duplicate code. It makes sense to factor this code into an abstract class called *DrawingShape* because this will help to ease maintenance of the *Square* and *Circle* classes in the future.

Create the *DrawingShape* abstract class

1. Return to the Drawing project in Visual Studio.

 Note A finished working copy of the previous exercise is available in the Drawing project, which is located in the \Microsoft Press\VCSBS\Chapter 13\Drawing Using Interfaces folder in your Documents folder.

2. In Solution Explorer, click the Drawing project in the Drawing solution. On the Project menu, click Add Class.

   The Add New Item – Drawing dialog box opens.

3. In the Name box, type **DrawingShape.cs**, and then click Add.

   Visual Studio creates the class and displays it in the Code and Text Editor window.

4. In the DrawingShape.cs file, at the list at the top of the file, add the following *using* directives:

```
using Windows.UI;
using Windows.UI.Xaml.Media;
using Windows.UI.Xaml.Shapes;
using Windows.UI.Xaml.Controls;
```

   The purpose of this class is to contain the code common to the *Circle* and *Square* classes. A program should not be able to instantiate a *DrawingShape* object directly.

5. Modify the definition of the *DrawingShape* class to declare it as abstract, as shown here in bold:

```
abstract class DrawingShape
{
}
```

6. Add the following private variables shown in bold to the *DrawingShape* class:

```
abstract class DrawingShape
{
    protected int size;
    protected int locX = 0, locY = 0;
    protected Shape shape = null;
}
```

The *Square* and *Circle* classes both use the *locX* and *locY* fields to specify the location of the object on the canvas, so you can move these fields to the abstract class. Similarly, the *Square* and *Circle* classes both use a field to indicate the size of the object when it was rendered; although it has a different name in each class (*sideLength* and *diameter*), semantically the field performs the same task in both classes. The name *size* is a good abstraction of the purpose of this field.

Internally, the *Square* class uses a *Rectangle* object to render itself on the canvas, and the *Circle* class uses an *Ellipse* object. Both of these classes are part of a hierarchy based on the abstract *Shape* class in the .NET Framework. The *DrawingShape* class uses a *Shape* field to represent both of these types.

7. Add the following constructor to the *DrawingShape* class:

```
abstract class DrawingShape
{
    ...
    public DrawingShape(int size)
    {
        this.size = size;
    }
}
```

This code initializes the *size* field in the *DrawingShape* object.

8. Add the *SetLocation* and *SetColor* methods to the *DrawingShape* class, as shown in bold in the code that follows. These methods provide implementations that are inherited by all classes that derive from the *DrawingShape* class. Notice that they are not marked as *virtual*, and a derived class is not expected to override them. Also, the *DrawingShape* class is not declared as implementing the *IDraw* or *IColor* interfaces (interface implementation is a feature of the *Square* and *Circle* classes and not this abstract class), so these methods are simply declared as public.

```
abstract class DrawingShape
{
    ...
    public void SetLocation(int xCoord, int yCoord)
    {
        this.locX = xCoord;
        this.locY = yCoord;
    }

    public void SetColor(Color color)
    {
        if (this.shape != null)
```

```
        {
            SolidColorBrush brush = new SolidColorBrush(color);
            this.shape.Fill = brush;
        }
    }
}
```

9. Add the *Draw* method to the *DrawingShape* class. Unlike the previous methods, this method is declared as virtual, and any derived classes are expected to override it to extend the functionality. The code in this method verifies that the *shape* field is not null and then draws it on the canvas. The classes that inherit this method must provide their own code to instantiate the *shape* object. (Remember that the *Square* class creates a *Rectangle* object and the *Circle* class creates an *Ellipse* object.)

```
abstract class DrawingShape
{
    ...
    public virtual void Draw(Canvas canvas)
    {
        if (this.shape == null)
        {
            throw new InvalidOperationException("Shape is null");
        }

        this.shape.Height = this.size;
        this.shape.Width = this.size;
        Canvas.SetTop(this.shape, this.locY);
        Canvas.SetLeft(this.shape, this.locX);
        canvas.Children.Add(this.shape);
    }
}
```

You have now completed the *DrawingShape* abstract class. The next steps are to change the *Square* and *Circle* classes so that they inherit from this class and then to remove the duplicated code from the *Square* and *Circle* classes.

Modify the *Square* and *Circle* classes to inherit from the *DrawingShape* class

1. Display the code for the *Square* class in the Code and Text Editor window.

2. Modify the definition of the *Square* class so that it inherits from the *DrawingShape* class in addition to implementing the *IDraw* and *IColor* interfaces.

```
class Square : DrawingShape, IDraw, IColor
{
    ...
}
```

Notice that you must specify the class that the *Square* class inherits from before any interfaces that it implements.

3. In the *Square* class, remove the definitions of the *sideLength, rect, locX,* and *locY* fields. These fields are no longer necessary because they are now provided by the *DrawingShape* class.

4. Replace the existing constructor with the following code, which calls the constructor in the base class:

```
class Square : DrawingShape, IDraw, IColor
{
    public Square(int sideLength)
        : base(sideLength)
    {
    }
    ...
}
```

   Notice that the body of this constructor is empty because the base class constructor performs all the initialization required.

5. Remove the *IDraw.SetLocation* and *IColor.SetColor* methods from the *Square* class. The *DrawingShape* class provides the implementation of these methods.

6. Modify the definition of the *Draw* method. Declare it with *public override* and also remove the reference to the *IDraw* interface. Again, the *DrawingShape* class already provides the base functionality for this method, but you will extend it with specific code required by the *Square* class.

```
public override void Draw(Canvas canvas)
{
    ...
}
```

7. Replace the body of the *Draw* method with the code shown here in bold:

```
public override void Draw(Canvas canvas)
{
    if (this.shape != null)
    {
        canvas.Children.Remove(this.shape);
    }
    else
    {
        this.shape = new Rectangle();
    }

    base.Draw(canvas);
}
```

   These statements instantiate the *shape* field inherited from the *DrawingShape* class as a new instance of the *Rectangle* class if it has not already been instantiated. They then call the *Draw* method in the *DrawingShape* class.

8. Repeat steps 2 through 7 for the *Circle* class, except that the constructor should be called *Circle* with a parameter called *diameter,* and in the *Draw* method you should instantiate the *shape* field as a new *Ellipse* object. The complete code for the *Circle* class should look like this:

```
class Circle : DrawingShape, IDraw, IColor
{
    public Circle(int diameter)
        : base(diameter)
    {
    }

    public override void Draw(Canvas canvas)
    {
        if (this.shape != null)
        {
            canvas.Children.Remove(this.shape);
        }
        else
        {
            this.shape = new Ellipse();
        }

        base.Draw(canvas);
    }
}
```

9. On the Debug menu, click Start Debugging. When the Drawing Pad window opens, verify that *Square* objects appear when you left-click in the window and *Circle* objects appear when you right-click in the window. The application should behave the same as before.

10. Return to Visual Studio and stop debugging.

Compatibility with the Windows Runtime revisited

Chapter 9, "Creating value types with enumerations and structures," describes how the Windows platform from Windows 8 onward implements the Windows Runtime (WinRT) as a layer on top of the native Windows APIs, providing a simplified programming interface for developers building unmanaged applications. (An unmanaged application is an application that does not run by using the .NET Framework; you build them by using a language such as C++ rather than C#). Managed applications use the common language runtime (CLR) to run .NET Framework applications. The .NET Framework provides an extensive set of libraries and features. On Windows 7 and earlier versions, the CLR implements these features by using the native Windows APIs. If you are building desktop or enterprise applications and services on Windows 10, this same feature set is still available (although the .NET Framework itself has been upgraded to version 4.6), and any C# applications that work on Windows 7 should run unchanged on Windows 10.

On Windows 10, UWP apps always run by using WinRT. This means that if you are building UWP apps by using a managed language such as C#, the CLR actually invokes WinRT rather than the native Windows APIs. Microsoft has provided a mapping layer between the CLR and WinRT that can transparently translate requests to create objects and invoke methods that are made to the .NET Framework into the equivalent object requests and method calls in WinRT. For example, when you create a .NET Framework *Int32* value (an *int* in C#), this code is translated to create a value using the equivalent WinRT data type. However, although the CLR and WinRT have a large amount of overlapping functionality, not all the features of the .NET Framework 4.6 have corresponding features in WinRT. Consequently, UWP apps have access to only a reduced subset of the types and methods provided by the .NET Framework 4.6. (IntelliSense in Visual Studio 2015 automatically shows the restricted view of available features when you use C# to build UWP apps, omitting the types and methods not available through WinRT.)

On the other hand, WinRT provides a significant set of features and types that have no direct equivalent in the .NET Framework or that operate in a significantly different way to the corresponding features in the .NET Framework, and so cannot easily be translated. WinRT makes these features available to the CLR through a mapping layer that makes them look like .NET Framework types and methods, and you can invoke them directly from managed code.

So, integration implemented by the CLR and WinRT enables the CLR to transparently use WinRT types, but it also supports interoperability in the reverse direction: you can define types by using managed code and make them available to unmanaged applications as long as these types conform to the expectations of WinRT. Chapter 9 highlights the requirements of structs in this respect (instance and static methods in structs are not available through WinRT, and private fields are unsupported). If you are building classes with the intention that they be consumed by unmanaged applications through WinRT, your classes must follow these rules:

- Any public fields, and the parameters and return values of any public methods, must be WinRT types or .NET Framework types that can be transparently translated by WinRT into WinRT types. Examples of supported .NET Framework types include conforming value types (such as structs and enums) and those corresponding to the C# primitives (*int*, *long*, *float*, *double*, *string*, and so on). Private fields are supported in classes, and they can be of any type available in the .NET Framework; they do not have to conform to WinRT.

- Classes cannot override methods of *System.Object* other than *ToString*, and they cannot declare protected constructors.

- The namespace in which a class is defined must be the same as the name of the assembly implementing the class. Additionally, the namespace name (and therefore the assembly name) must not begin with "Windows".

- You cannot inherit from managed types in unmanaged applications through WinRT. Therefore, all public classes must be sealed. If you need to implement polymorphism, you can create a public interface and implement that interface on the classes that must be polymorphic.

- You can throw any exception type that is included in the subset of the .NET Framework available to UWP apps; you cannot create your own custom exception classes. If your code throws an unhandled exception when called from an unmanaged application, WinRT raises an equivalent exception in the unmanaged code.

WinRT has other requirements concerning features of C# code covered later in this book. These requirements will be highlighted as each feature is described.

Summary

In this chapter, you saw how to define and implement interfaces and abstract classes. The following table summarizes the various valid (yes), and invalid (no) keyword combinations when defining methods for interfaces, classes, and structs.

Keyword	Interface	Abstract class	Class	Sealed class	Structure
abstract	No	Yes	No	No	No
new	Yes[1]	Yes	Yes	Yes	No[2]
override	No	Yes	Yes	Yes	No[3]
private	No	Yes	Yes	Yes	Yes
protected	No	Yes	Yes	Yes	No[4]
public	No	Yes	Yes	Yes	Yes
sealed	No	Yes	Yes	Yes	No
virtual	No	Yes	Yes	No	No

[1] An interface can extend another interface and introduce a new method with the same signature.
[2] Structures do not support inheritance, so they cannot hide methods.
[3] Structures do not support inheritance, so they cannot override methods.
[4] Structures do not support inheritance; a structure is implicitly sealed and cannot be derived from.

If you want to continue to the next chapter, keep Visual Studio 2015 running and turn to Chapter 14.

- If you want to exit Visual Studio 2015 now, on the File menu, click Exit. If you see a Save dialog box, click Yes and save the project.

Quick reference

To	Do this
Declare an interface	Use the *interface* keyword. For example: ```\ninterface IDemo\n{\n string GetName();\n string GetDescription();\n}\n```
Implement an interface	Declare a class by using the same syntax as class inheritance, and then implement all the member functions of the interface. For example: ```\nclass Test : IDemo\n{\n public string IDemo.GetName()\n {\n ...\n }\n\n public string IDemo.GetDescription()\n {\n ...\n }\n}\n```
Create an abstract class that can be used only as a base class, containing abstract methods	Declare the class by using the *abstract* keyword. For each abstract method, declare the method with the *abstract* keyword and without a method body. For example: ```\nabstract class GrazingMammal\n{\n abstract void DigestGrass();\n ...\n}\n```
Create a sealed class that cannot be used as a base class	Declare the class by using the *sealed* keyword. For example: ```\nsealed class Horse\n{\n ...\n}\n```

CHAPTER 14

Using garbage collection and resource management

After completing this chapter, you will be able to:

- Manage system resources by using garbage collection.

- Write code that runs when an object is destroyed.

- Release a resource at a known point in time in an exception-safe manner by writing a *try/finally* statement.

- Release a resource at a known point in time in an exception-safe manner by writing a *using* statement.

- Implement the *IDisposable* interface to support exception-safe disposal in a class.

You have seen in earlier chapters how to create variables and objects, and you should understand how memory is allocated when you create variables and objects. (In case you don't remember, value types are created on the stack, and reference types are allocated memory from the heap.) Computers do not have infinite amounts of memory, so memory must be reclaimed when a variable or an object no longer needs it. Value types are destroyed and their memory reclaimed when they go out of scope. That's the easy bit. How about reference types? You create an object by using the *new* keyword, but how and when is an object destroyed? That's what this chapter is all about.

The life and times of an object

First, let's recap what happens when you create an object.

You create an object by using the *new* operator. The following example creates a new instance of the *Square* class that is discussed in Chapter 13, "Creating interfaces and defining abstract classes"

```
int sizeOfSquare = 99;
Square mySquare = new Square(sizeOfSquare); // Square is a reference type
```

From your point of view, the *new* operation is a single step, but underneath, object creation is really a two-phase process:

1. The *new* operation allocates a chunk of *raw* memory from the heap. You have no control over this phase of an object's creation.

2. The *new* operation converts the chunk of raw memory to an object; it has to initialize the object. You can control this phase by using a constructor.

> **Note** If you are a C++ programmer, you should note that in C#, you cannot overload the *new* operation to control allocation.

After you create an object, you can access its members by using the dot operator (.). For example, the *Square* class includes a method named *Draw* that you can call:

```
mySquare.Draw();
```

> **Note** This code is based on the version of the *Square* class that inherits from the *DrawingShape* abstract class and does not implement the *IDraw* interface explicitly. For more information, refer to Chapter 13.

When the *mySquare* variable goes out of scope, the *Square* object is no longer being actively referenced. The object can then be destroyed, and the memory that it is using can be reclaimed. (This might not happen immediately, however, as you will see later.) Like object creation, object destruction is a two-phase process. The two phases of destruction exactly mirror the two phases of creation:

1. The common language runtime (CLR) must perform some tidying up. You can control this by writing a *destructor*.

2. The CLR must return the memory previously belonging to the object back to the heap; the memory that the object lived in must be deallocated. You have no control over this phase.

The process of destroying an object and returning memory back to the heap is known as *garbage collection*.

> **Note** If you program in C++, keep in mind that C# does not have a delete operator. The CLR controls when an object is destroyed.

Writing destructors

You can use a destructor to perform any tidying up that's required when an object is garbage collected. The CLR will automatically clear up any managed resources that an object uses, so in many of these cases, writing a destructor is unnecessary. However, if a managed resource is large (such as a multidimensional array), it might make sense to make this resource available for immediate disposal by setting any references that the object has to this resource to *null*. Additionally, if an object references an unmanaged resource, either directly or indirectly, a destructor can prove useful.

A destructor is a special method, a little like a constructor, except that the CLR calls it after the reference to an object has disappeared. The syntax for writing a destructor is a tilde (~) followed by the name of the class. For example, here's a simple class that opens a file for reading in its constructor and closes the file in its destructor. (Note that this is simply an example, and I do not recommend that you always follow this pattern for opening and closing files.)

```
class FileProcessor
{
    FileStream file = null;

    public FileProcessor(string fileName)
    {
        this.file = File.OpenRead(fileName); // open file for reading
    }

    ~FileProcessor()
    {
        this.file.Close(); // close file
    }
}
```

There are some very important restrictions that apply to destructors:

- Destructors apply only to reference types; you cannot declare a destructor in a value type, such as a *struct*.

    ```
    struct MyStruct
    {
        ~MyStruct() { ... } // compile-time error
    }
    ```

- You cannot specify an access modifier (such as *public*) for a destructor. You never call the destructor in your own code; part of the CLR called the *garbage collector* does this for you.

    ```
    public ~FileProcessor() { ... } // compile-time error
    ```

- A destructor cannot take any parameters. Again, this is because you never call the destructor yourself.

    ```
    ~FileProcessor(int parameter) { ... } // compile-time error
    ```

Internally, the C# compiler automatically translates a destructor into an override of the *Object.Finalize* method. The compiler converts this destructor

```
class FileProcessor
{
    ~FileProcessor() { // your code goes here }
}
```

into this:

```
class FileProcessor
{
    protected override void Finalize()
    {
        try { // your code goes here }
        finally { base.Finalize(); }
    }
}
```

The compiler-generated *Finalize* method contains the destructor body within a *try* block, followed by a *finally* block that calls the *Finalize* method in the base class. (The *try* and *finally* keywords are described in Chapter 6, "Managing errors and exceptions.") This ensures that a destructor always calls its base-class destructor, even if an exception occurs during your destructor code.

It's important to understand that only the compiler can make this translation. You can't write your own method to override *Finalize*, and you can't call *Finalize* yourself.

Why use the garbage collector?

You can never destroy an object yourself by using C# code. There just isn't any syntax to do it. Instead, the CLR does it for you at a time of its own choosing. In addition, keep in mind that you can also make more than one reference variable refer to the same object. In the following code example, the variables *myFp* and *referenceToMyFp* point to the same *FileProcessor* object:

```
FileProcessor myFp = new FileProcessor();
FileProcessor referenceToMyFp = myFp;
```

How many references can you create to an object? As many as you want! But this lack of restriction has an impact on the lifetime of an object. The CLR has to keep track of all these references. If the variable *myFp* disappears (by going out of scope), other variables (such as *referenceToMyFp*) might still exist, and the resources used by the *FileProcessor* object cannot be reclaimed (the file should not be closed). So the lifetime of an object cannot be tied to a particular reference variable. An object can be destroyed and its memory made available for reuse only when *all* the references to it have disappeared.

You can see that managing object lifetimes is complex, which is why the designers of C# decided to prevent your code from taking on this responsibility. If it were your responsibility to destroy objects, sooner or later one of the following situations would arise:

- You'd forget to destroy the object. This would mean that the object's destructor (if it had one) would not be run, tidying up would not occur, and memory would not be returned back to the heap. You could quite easily run out of memory.

- You'd try to destroy an active object and risk the possibility that one or more variables hold a reference to a destroyed object, which is known as a *dangling reference*. A dangling reference refers either to unused memory or possibly to a completely different object that now happens to occupy the same piece of memory. Either way, the outcome of using a dangling reference would be undefined at best or a security risk at worst. All bets would be off.

- You'd try to destroy the same object more than once. This might or might not be disastrous, depending on the code in the destructor.

These problems are unacceptable in a language like C#, which places robustness and security high on its list of design goals. Instead, the garbage collector destroys objects for you. The garbage collector makes the following guarantees:

- Every object will be destroyed, and its destructor will be run. When a program ends, all outstanding objects will be destroyed.

- Every object will be destroyed exactly once.

- Every object will be destroyed only when it becomes unreachable—that is, when there are no references to the object in the process running your application.

These guarantees are tremendously useful, and they free you, the programmer, from tedious housekeeping chores that are easy to get wrong. They afford you the luxury to concentrate on the logic of the program itself and be more productive.

When does garbage collection occur? This might seem like a strange question. After all, surely garbage collection occurs when an object is no longer needed. Well, it does, but not necessarily immediately. Garbage collection can be an expensive process, so the CLR collects garbage only when it needs to (when available memory is starting to run low or the size of the heap has exceeded the system-defined threshold, for example), and then it collects as much as it can. Performing a few large sweeps of memory is more efficient than performing lots of little dustings.

> **Note** You can invoke the garbage collector in a program by calling the static method *Collect* of the *GC* class located in the *System* namespace. However, except in a few cases, this is not recommended. The *GC.Collect* method starts the garbage collector, but the process runs asynchronously—the *GC.Collect* method does not wait for garbage collection to be complete before it returns, so you still don't know whether your objects have been destroyed. Let the CLR decide when it is best to collect garbage.

One feature of the garbage collector is that you don't know, and should not rely upon, the order in which objects will be destroyed. The final point to understand is arguably the most important: destructors do not run until objects are garbage collected. If you write a destructor, you know it will be executed, but you just don't know when. Consequently, you should never write code that depends on destructors running in a particular sequence or at a specific point in your application.

How does the garbage collector work?

The garbage collector runs in its own thread and can execute only at certain times—typically when your application reaches the end of a method. While it runs, other threads running in your application will temporarily halt because the garbage collector might need to move objects around and update object references, and it cannot do this while objects are in use.

> **Note** A *thread* is a separate path of execution in an application. Windows uses threads to enable an application to perform multiple operations concurrently.

The garbage collector is a complex piece of software that is self-tuning and implements a number of optimizations to try to balance the need to keep memory available with the requirement to maintain the performance of the application. The details of the internal algorithms and structures that the garbage collector uses are beyond the scope of this book (and Microsoft continually refines the way in which the garbage collector performs its work), but at a high level, the steps that the garbage collector takes are as follows:

1. It builds a map of all reachable objects. It does this by repeatedly following reference fields inside objects. The garbage collector builds this map very carefully and ensures that circular references do not cause an infinite recursion. Any object *not* in this map is deemed to be unreachable.

2. It checks whether any of the unreachable objects has a destructor that needs to be run (a process called *finalization*). Any unreachable object that requires finalization is placed in a special queue called the *freachable queue* (pronounced "F-reachable").

3. It deallocates the remaining unreachable objects (those that don't require finalization) by moving the *reachable* objects down the heap, thus defragmenting the heap and freeing memory at its top. When the garbage collector moves a reachable object, it also updates any references to the object.

4. At this point, it allows other threads to resume.

5. It finalizes the unreachable objects that require finalization (now in the *freachable* queue) by running the *Finalize* methods on its own thread.

Recommendations

Writing classes that contain destructors adds complexity to your code and to the garbage collection process and makes your program run more slowly. If your program does not contain any destructors, the garbage collector does not need to place unreachable objects in the *freachable* queue and finalize them. Clearly, not doing something is faster than doing it. Therefore, try to avoid using destructors except when you really need them—use them only to reclaim unmanaged resources. (You can consider a *using* statement instead, as will be described later in this chapter.)

You need to be very careful when you write a destructor. In particular, be aware that if your destructor calls other objects, those other objects might have *already* had their destructor called by the garbage collector. Remember that the order of finalization is not guaranteed. Therefore, ensure that destructors do not depend on one another or overlap one another—don't have two destructors that try to release the same resource, for example.

Resource management

Sometimes it's inadvisable to release a resource in a destructor; some resources are just too valuable to lie around waiting for an arbitrary length of time until the garbage collector actually releases them. Scarce resources such as memory, database connections, or file handles need to be released, and they need to be released as soon as possible. In these situations, your only option is to release the resource yourself. You can achieve this by creating a *disposal method*—a method that explicitly disposes of a resource. If a class has a disposal method, you can call it and control when the resource is released.

> **Note** The term *disposal method* refers to the purpose of the method rather than its name. A disposal method can be named using any valid C# identifier.

Disposal methods

An example of a class that implements a disposal method is the *TextReader* class from the *System.IO* namespace. This class provides a mechanism to read characters from a sequential stream of input. The *TextReader* class contains a virtual method named *Close*, which closes the stream. The *StreamReader* class (which reads characters from a stream, such as an open file) and the *StringReader* class (which reads characters from a string) both derive from *TextReader*, and both override the *Close* method. Here's an example that reads lines of text from a file by using the *StreamReader* class and then displays them on the screen:

```
TextReader reader = new StreamReader(filename);
string line;
while ((line = reader.ReadLine()) != null)
{
    Console.WriteLine(line);
}
reader.Close();
```

The *ReadLine* method reads the next line of text from the stream into a string. The *ReadLine* method returns *null* if there is nothing left in the stream. It's important to call *Close* when you have finished with *reader* to release the file handle and associated resources. However, there is a problem with this example: it's not safe from exceptions. If the call to *ReadLine* or *WriteLine* throws an exception, the call to *Close* will not happen; it will be bypassed. If this happens often enough, you will run out of file handles and be unable to open any more files.

Exception-safe disposal

One way to ensure that a disposal method (such as *Close*) is always called, regardless of whether there is an exception, is to call the disposal method within a *finally* block. Here's the preceding example coded by using this technique:

```
TextReader reader = new StreamReader(filename);
try
{
    string line;
    while ((line = reader.ReadLine()) != null)
    {
        Console.WriteLine(line);
    }
}
finally
{
    reader.Close();
}
```

Using a *finally* block like this works, but it has several drawbacks that make it a less-than-ideal solution:

- It quickly becomes unwieldy if you have to dispose of more than one resource. (You end up with nested *try* and *finally* blocks.)

- In some cases, you might need to modify the code to make it fit this idiom. (For example, you might need to reorder the declaration of the resource reference, remember to initialize the reference to *null*, and remember to check that the reference isn't *null* in the *finally* block.)

- It fails to create an abstraction of the solution. This means that the solution is hard to understand and you must repeat the code everywhere you need this functionality.

- The reference to the resource remains in scope after the *finally* block. This means that you can accidentally try to use the resource after it has been released.

The *using* statement is designed to solve all these problems.

The *using* statement and the *IDisposable* interface

The *using* statement provides a clean mechanism for controlling the lifetimes of resources. You can create an object, and this object will be destroyed when the *using* statement block finishes.

The syntax for a *using* statement is as follows:

```
using ( type variable = initialization )
{
    StatementBlock
}
```

Here is the best way to ensure that your code always calls *Close* on a *TextReader*:

```
using (TextReader reader = new StreamReader(filename))
{
    string line;
    while ((line = reader.ReadLine()) != null)
    {
        Console.WriteLine(line);
    }
}
```

This *using* statement is precisely equivalent to the following transformation:

```
{
    TextReader reader = new StreamReader(filename);
    try
    {
        string line;
        while ((line = reader.ReadLine()) != null)
        {
            Console.WriteLine(line);
        }
    }
    finally
    {
        if (reader != null)
        {
            ((IDisposable)reader).Dispose();
        }
    }
}
```

> **Note** The *using* statement introduces its own block for scoping purposes. This arrangement means that the variable you declare in a *using* statement automatically goes out of scope at the end of the embedded statement and you cannot accidentally attempt to access a disposed resource.

The variable you declare in a *using* statement must be of a type that implements the *IDisposable* interface. The *IDisposable* interface lives in the *System* namespace and contains just one method, named *Dispose*:

```
namespace System
{
    interface IDisposable
    {
        void Dispose();
    }
}
```

The purpose of the *Dispose* method is to free any resources used by an object. It just so happens that the *StreamReader* class implements the *IDisposable* interface, and its *Dispose* method calls *Close* to close the stream. You can employ a *using* statement as a clean, exception-safe, and robust way to ensure that a resource is always released. This approach solves all the problems that existed in the manual *try/finally* solution. You now have a solution that does the following:

- Scales well if you need to dispose of multiple resources.

- Doesn't distort the logic of the program code.

- Abstracts away the problem and avoids repetition.

- Is robust. You can't accidentally reference the variable declared within the *using* statement (in this case, *reader*) after the *using* statement has ended because it's not in scope anymore—you'll get a compile-time error.

Calling the *Dispose* method from a destructor

When writing your own classes, should you write a destructor or implement the *IDisposable* interface so that instances of your class can be managed by a *using* statement? A call to a destructor *will* happen, but you just don't know when. On the other hand, you know exactly when a call to the *Dispose* method happens, but you just can't be sure that it will actually happen because it relies on the programmer who is using your classes to remember to write a *using* statement. However, it is possible to ensure that the *Dispose* method always runs by calling it from the destructor. This acts as a useful backup. You might forget to call the *Dispose* method, but at least you can be sure that it will be called, even if it's only when the program shuts down. You will investigate this feature in detail in the exercises at the end of the chapter, but here's an example of how you might implement the *IDisposable* interface:

```
class Example : IDisposable
{
    private Resource scarce;        // scarce resource to manage and dispose
    private bool disposed = false;  // flag to indicate whether the resource
                                    // has already been disposed

    ...
    ~Example()
    {
        this.Dispose(false);
```

```
    }

    public virtual void Dispose()
    {
        this.Dispose(true);
        GC.SuppressFinalize(this);
    }

    protected virtual void Dispose(bool disposing)
    {
        if (!this.disposed)
        {
            if (disposing)
            {
                // release large, managed resource here
                ...
            }
            // release unmanaged resources here
            ...
            this.disposed = true;
        }
    }

    public void SomeBehavior() // example method
    {
        checkIfDisposed();
        ...
    }

    ...

    private void checkIfDisposed()
    {
        if (this.disposed)
        {
            throw new ObjectDisposedException("Example: object has been disposed of");
        }
    }
}
```

Notice the following features of the *Example* class:

- The class implements the *IDisposable* interface.

- The public *Dispose* method can be called at any time by your application code.

- The public *Dispose* method calls the protected and overloaded version of the *Dispose* method that takes a Boolean parameter, passing the value *true* as the argument. This method actually performs the resource disposal.

- The destructor calls the protected and overloaded version of the *Dispose* method that takes a Boolean parameter, passing the value *false* as the argument. The destructor is called only by the garbage collector when your object is being finalized.

- You can call the protected *Dispose* method safely multiple times. The variable *disposed* indicates whether the method has already been run and is a safety feature to prevent the method from attempting to dispose of the resources multiple times if it is called concurrently. (Your application might call *Dispose*, but before the method completes, your object might be subject to garbage collection and the *Dispose* method run again by the CLR from the destructor.) The resources are released only the first time the method runs.

- The protected *Dispose* method supports disposal of managed resources (such as a large array) and unmanaged resources (such as a file handle). If the disposing parameter is true, this method must have been called from the public *Dispose* method. In this case, the managed resources and unmanaged resources are all released. If the disposing parameter is false, this method must have been called from the destructor, and the garbage collector is finalizing the object. In this case, it is not necessary (or exception-safe) to release the managed resources because they will be, or might already have been, handled by the garbage collector, so only the unmanaged resources are released.

- The public *Dispose* method calls the static *GC.SuppressFinalize* method. This method stops the garbage collector from calling the destructor on this object because the object has already been finalized.

- All the regular methods of the class (such as *SomeBehavior*) check to see whether the object has already been discarded. If it has, they throw an exception.

Implementing exception-safe disposal

In the following set of exercises, you will examine how the *using* statement helps to ensure that resources used by objects in your applications can be released in a timely manner, even if an exception occurs in your application code. Initially, you will implement a simple class that implements a destructor and examine when this destructor is invoked by the garbage collector.

> **Note** The *Calculator* class created in these exercises is intended only to illustrate the essential principles of garbage collection. The class does not actually consume any significant managed or unmanaged resources. You would not normally create a destructor or implement the *IDisposable* interface for such a simple class as this.

Create a simple class that uses a destructor

1. Start Microsoft Visual Studio 2015 if it is not already running.

2. On the File menu, point to New, and then click Project.

   The New Project dialog box opens.

3. In the New Project dialog box, in the left pane under Templates, click Visual C#. In the middle pane, select the Console Application template. In the Name box near the bottom of the dialog box, type **GarbageCollectionDemo**. In the Location field, specify the folder Microsoft Press\ VCSBS\Chapter 14 in your Documents folder, and then click OK.

> **Tip** You can use the Browse button adjacent to the Location field to navigate to the Microsoft Press\VCSBS\Chapter 14 folder instead of typing the path manually.

Visual Studio creates a new console application and displays the Program.cs file in the Code and Text Editor window.

4. On the Project menu, click Add Class.

The Add New Item – GarbageCollectionDemo dialog box opens.

5. In the Add New Item – GarbageCollectionDemo dialog box, ensure that the Class template is selected. In the Name box, type **Calculator.cs**, and then click Add.

The *Calculator* class is created and displayed in the Code and Text Editor window.

6. Add to the *Calculator* class the following public *Divide* method (shown in bold):

```
class Calculator
{
    public int Divide(int first, int second)
    {
        return first / second;
    }
}
```

This is a very straightforward method that divides the first parameter by the second and returns the result. It is provided just to add a bit of functionality that can be called by an application.

7. Above the *Divide* method, add to the start of the *Calculator* class the public constructor shown in bold in the code that follows:

```
class Calculator
{
    public Calculator()
    {
        Console.WriteLine("Calculator being created");
    }
    ...
}
```

The purpose of this constructor is to enable you to verify that a *Calculator* object has been successfully created.

8. Add to the *Calculator* class the destructor shown in bold in the following code, after the constructor:

```
class Calculator
{
    ...
    ~Calculator()
    {
        Console.WriteLine("Calculator being finalized");
    }
    ...
}
```

This destructor simply displays a message so that you can see when the garbage collector runs and finalizes instances of this class. When writing classes for real-world applications, you would not normally output text in a destructor.

9. Display the Program.cs file in the Code and Text Editor window.

10. In the *Program* class, add to the *Main* method the following statements shown in bold:

```
static void Main(string[] args)
{
    Calculator calculator = new Calculator();
    Console.WriteLine($"120 / 15 = {calculator.Divide(120, 15)}");
    Console.WriteLine("Program finishing");
}
```

This code creates a *Calculator* object, calls the *Divide* method of this object (and displays the result), and then outputs a message as the program finishes.

11. On the Debug menu, click Start Without Debugging. Verify that the program displays the following series of messages:

```
Calculator being created
120 / 15 = 8
Program finishing
Calculator being finalized
```

Notice that the finalizer for the *Calculator* object runs only when the application is about to finish, after the *Main* method has completed.

12. In the console window, press the Enter key and return to Visual Studio 2015.

The CLR guarantees that all objects created by your applications will be subject to garbage collection, but you cannot always be sure when this will happen. In the exercise, the program was very short-lived and the *Calculator* object was finalized when the CLR tidied up as the program finished. However, you might also find that this is the case in more substantial applications with classes that consume scarce resources, and unless you take the necessary steps to provide a means of disposal, the objects that your applications create might retain their resources until the application finishes. If the resource is a file, this could prevent other users from being able to access that file; if the resource is a database connection, your application could prevent other users from being able to connect to the same database. Ideally, you want to free resources as soon as you have finished using them rather than wait for the application to terminate.

In the next exercise, you will implement the *IDisposable* interface in the *Calculator* class and enable the program to finalize *Calculator* objects at a time of its choosing.

Implement the *IDisposable* interface

1. Display the Calculator.cs file in the Code and Text Editor window.

2. Modify the definition of the *Calculator* class so that it implements the *IDisposable* interface, as shown here in bold:

```
class Calculator : IDisposable
{
    ...
}
```

3. Add to the end of the *Calculator* class the following method (named *Dispose*). This method is defined by the *IDisposable* interface:

```
class Calculator : IDisposable
{
    ...
    public void Dispose()
    {
        Console.WriteLine("Calculator being disposed");
    }
}
```

You would normally add code to the *Dispose* method that releases the resources held by the object. There are none in this case, and the purpose of the *Console.WriteLine* statement in this method is just to let you see when the *Dispose* method is run. However, you can see that in a real-world application, there would likely be some duplication of code between the destructor and the *Dispose* method. To remove this duplication, you would typically place this code in one place and call it from the other. But because you cannot explicitly invoke a destructor from the *Dispose* method, it makes sense instead to call the *Dispose* method from the destructor and place the logic that releases resources in the *Dispose* method.

4. Modify the destructor so that it calls the *Dispose* method, as shown in bold in the following code. (Leave the statement displaying the message in place in the finalizer so that you can see when it is being run by the garbage collector).

```
~Calculator()
{
    Console.WriteLine("Calculator being finalized");
    this.Dispose();
}
```

When you want to destroy a *Calculator* object in an application, the *Dispose* method does not run automatically; your code must either call it explicitly (with a statement such as *calculator*
.Dispose()) or create the *Calculator* object within a *using* statement. In your program, you will adopt the latter approach.

5. Display the Program.cs file in the Code and Text Editor window. Modify the statements in the *Main* method that create the *Calculator* object and call the *Divide* method, as shown here in bold:

```
static void Main(string[] args)
{
    using (Calculator calculator = new Calculator())
    {
        Console.WriteLine($"120 / 15 = {calculator.Divide(120, 15)}");
    }

    Console.WriteLine("Program finishing");
}
```

6. On the Debug menu, click Start Without Debugging. Verify that the program now displays the following series of messages:

```
Calculator being created
120 / 15 = 8
Calculator being disposed
Program finishing
Calculator being finalized
Calculator being disposed
```

The *using* statement causes the *Dispose* method to run before the statement that displays the "Program finishing" message. However, you can see that the destructor for the *Calculator* object still runs when the application finishes, and it calls the *Dispose* method again. This is clearly a waste of processing.

7. In the console window, press the Enter key and return to Visual Studio 2015.

Disposing of the resources held by an object more than once might or might not be disastrous, but it is definitely not good practice. The recommended approach to resolving this problem is to add a private Boolean field to the class to indicate whether the *Dispose* method has already been invoked, and then examine this field in the *Dispose* method.

Prevent an object from being disposed of more than once

1. Display the Calculator.cs file in the Code and Text Editor window.

2. Add to the *Calculator* class a private Boolean field called *disposed*, and initialize the value of this field to *false*, as shown in bold in the following:

```
class Calculator : IDisposable
{
    private bool disposed = false;
    ...
}
```

The purpose of this field is to track the state of this object and indicate whether the *Dispose* method has been invoked.

3. Modify the code in the *Dispose* method to display the message only if the *disposed* field is false. After displaying the message, set the *disposed* field to true, as demonstrated here in bold:

```
public void Dispose()
{
    if (!this.disposed)
    {
        Console.WriteLine("Calculator being disposed");
    }

    this.disposed = true;
}
```

4. On the Debug menu, click Start Without Debugging. Notice that the program displays the following series of messages:

```
Calculator being created
120 / 15 = 8
Calculator being disposed
Program finishing
Calculator being finalized
```

The *Calculator* object is now discarded only once, but the destructor is still running. Again, this is a waste; there is little point in running a destructor for an object that has already released its resources.

5. In the console window, press the Enter key and return to Visual Studio 2015.

6. In the *Calculator* class, add to the end of the *Dispose* method the following statement shown in bold:

```
public void Dispose()
{
    if (!this.disposed)
    {
        Console.WriteLine("Calculator being disposed");
    }
    this.disposed = true;
    GC.SuppressFinalize(this);
}
```

The *GC* class provides access to the garbage collector, and it implements several static methods with which you can control some of the actions it performs. Using the *SuppressFinalize* method, you can indicate that the garbage collector should not perform finalization on the specified object, and this prevents the destructor from running.

> **Important** The *GC* class exposes a number of methods with which you can configure the garbage collector. However, it is usually better to let the CLR manage the garbage collector itself because you can seriously impair the performance

of your application if you call these methods injudiciously. You should treat the *SuppressFinalize* method with extreme caution because if you fail to dispose of an object, you run the risk of losing data (if you fail to close a file correctly, for example, any data buffered in memory but not yet written to disk could be lost). Call this method only in situations such as that shown in this exercise, when you know that an object has already been discarded.

7. On the Debug menu, click Start Without Debugging. Notice that the program displays the following series of messages:

```
Calculator being created
120 / 15 = 8
Calculator being disposed
Program finishing
```

You can see that the destructor is no longer running because the *Calculator* object has already been disposed of before the program finishes.

8. In the console window, press the Enter key and return to Visual Studio 2015.

Thread safety and the *Dispose* method

The example of using the *disposed* field to prevent an object from being discarded multiple times works well in most cases, but keep in mind that you have no control over when the finalizer runs. In the exercises in this chapter, it has always executed as the program finishes, but this might not always be the case—it can run any time after the last reference to an object has disappeared. So it is possible that the finalizer might actually be invoked by the garbage collector on its own thread while the *Dispose* method is being run, especially if the *Dispose* method has to do a significant amount of work. You could reduce the possibility of resources being released multiple times by moving the statement that sets the *disposed* field to true closer to the start of the *Dispose* method, but in this case you run the risk of not freeing the resources at all if an exception occurs after you have set this variable but before you have released them.

To completely eliminate the chances of two concurrent threads disposing of the same resources in the same object simultaneously, you can write your code in a thread-safe manner by embedding it in a C# *lock* statement, like this:

```csharp
public void Dispose()
{
    lock(this)
    {
        if (!disposed)
        {
            Console.WriteLine("Calculator being disposed");
        }
        this.disposed = true;
        GC.SuppressFinalize(this);
```

```
        }
    }
```

The purpose of the *lock* statement is to prevent the same block of code from being run at the same time on different threads. The argument to the *lock* statement (*this* in the preceding example) should be a reference to an object. The code between the curly braces defines the scope of the *lock* statement. When execution reaches the *lock* statement, if the specified object is currently locked, the thread requesting the lock is blocked and the code is suspended at this point. When the thread that currently holds the lock reaches the closing curly brace of the *lock* statement, the lock is released, enabling the blocked thread to acquire the lock itself and continue. However, by the time this happens, the *disposed* field will have been set to true, so the second thread will not attempt to perform the code in the *if (!disposed)* block.

Using locks in this manner is safe, but it can impair performance. An alternative approach is to use the strategy described earlier in this chapter, whereby only the repeated disposal of managed resources is suppressed. (It is not exception-safe to dispose of managed resources more than once; you will not compromise the security of your computer, but you might affect the logical integrity of your application if you attempt to dispose of a managed object that no longer exists.) This strategy implements overloaded versions of the *Dispose* method; the *using* statement calls *Dispose()*, which in turn runs the statement *Dispose(true)*, while the destructor invokes *Dispose(false)*. Managed resources are freed only if the parameter to the overloaded version of the *Dispose* method is true. For more information, refer back to the example in the section "Calling the dispose method from a destructor."

The purpose of the *using* statement is to ensure that an object is always discarded, even if an exception occurs while it is being used. In the final exercise in this chapter, you will verify that this is the case by generating an exception in the middle of a *using* block.

Verify that an object is disposed of after an exception

1. Display the Program.cs file in the Code and Text Editor window.

2. Modify the statement that calls the *Divide* method of the *Calculator* object as shown in bold:

```
static void Main(string[] args)
{
    using (Calculator calculator = new Calculator())
    {
        Console.WriteLine($"120 / 0 = {calculator.Divide(120, 0)}");
    }
    Console.WriteLine("Program finishing");
}
```

The amended statement attempts to divide 120 by 0.

3. On the Debug menu, click Start Without Debugging.

As you might have anticipated, the application throws an unhandled *DivideByZeroException* exception.

4. In the GarbageCollectionDemo message box, click Cancel. (You need to be quick to do this before the Debug and Close Program buttons appear.)

5. Verify that the message "Calculator being disposed" appears after the unhandled exception in the console window.

> **Note** If you were too slow and the Debug and Close Program buttons already appeared, click Close Program and run the application again without debugging.

6. In the console window, press the Enter key and return to Visual Studio 2015.

Summary

In this chapter, you saw how the garbage collector works and how the .NET Framework uses it to dispose of objects and reclaim memory. You learned how to write a destructor to clean up the resources used by an object when memory is recycled by the garbage collector. You also saw how to use the *using* statement to implement exception-safe disposal of resources and how to implement the *IDisposable* interface to support this form of object disposal.

- If you want to continue to the next chapter, keep Visual Studio 2015 running and turn to Chapter 15, "Implementing properties to access fields."

- If you want to exit Visual Studio 2015 now, on the File menu, click Exit. If you see a Save dialog box, click Yes and save the project.

Quick reference

To	Do this
Write a destructor	Write a method whose name is the same as the name of the class and is prefixed with a tilde (~). The method must not have an access modifier (such as *public*) and cannot have any parameters or return a value. For example: ```class Example` `{` ` ~Example()` ` {` ` ...` ` }` `}```
Call a destructor	You can't call a destructor. Only the garbage collector can call a destructor.
Force garbage collection (not recommended)	Call *GC.Collect*.
Release a resource at a known point in time (but at the risk of resource leaks if an exception interrupts the execution)	Write a disposal method (a method that disposes of a resource) and call it explicitly from the program. For example: ```class TextReader` `{` ` ...` ` public virtual void Close()` ` {` ` ...` ` }` `}` `class Example` `{` ` void Use()` ` {` ` TextReader reader = ...;` ` // use reader` ` reader.Close();` ` }` `}```

To	Do this
| Support exception-safe disposal in a class | Implement the *IDisposable* interface. For example:<br><br>```csharp
class SafeResource : IDisposable
{
    ...
    public void Dispose()
    {
        // Dispose resources here
    }
}
``` |
| Implement exception-safe disposal for an object that implements the *IDisposable* interface | Create the object in a *using* statement. For example:<br><br>```csharp
using (SafeResource resource = new SafeResource())
{
    // Use SafeResource here
    ...
}
``` |

PART III

Defining extensible types with C#

Parts I and II introduced you to the core syntax of the C# language and showed you how to build new types by using structures, enumerations, and classes. You also saw how the common language runtime (CLR) manages the memory used by variables and objects when a program runs, and you should now understand the life cycle of C# objects. The chapters in Part III build on this information, showing you how to use C# to create extensible components—highly functional data types that you can reuse in many applications.

In Part III, you'll learn about more advanced features of C#, such as properties, indexers, generics, and collection classes. You'll see how you can build responsive systems by using events and how you can use delegates to invoke the application logic of one class from another without closely coupling the classes—a powerful technique that enables you to construct highly extensible systems. You will also learn about Language-Integrated Query (LINQ), which enables you to perform complex queries over collections of objects in a clear and natural manner. And you'll see how to overload operators to customize the way in which common C# operators function over your own classes and structures.

CHAPTER 15

Implementing properties to access fields

After completing this chapter, you will be able to:

- Encapsulate logical fields by using properties.

- Control read access to properties by declaring *get* accessors.

- Control write access to properties by declaring *set* accessors.

- Create interfaces that declare properties.

- Implement interfaces containing properties by using structures and classes.

- Generate properties automatically based on field definitions.

- Use properties to initialize objects.

This chapter looks at how to define and use properties to encapsulate fields and data in a class. Previous chapters emphasize that you should make the fields in a class private and provide methods to store values in them and to retrieve their values. This approach ensures safe and controlled access to fields, and you can use it to encapsulate additional logic and rules concerning the values that are permitted. However, the syntax for accessing a field in this way is unnatural. When you want to read or write a variable, you normally use an assignment statement, so calling a method to achieve the same effect on a field (which is, after all, just a variable) feels a little clumsy. Properties are designed to alleviate this awkwardness.

Implementing encapsulation by using methods

First, let's recap the original motivation for using methods to hide fields.

Consider the following structure that represents a position on a computer screen as a pair of coordinates, x and y. Assume that the range of valid values for the x-coordinate lies between 0 and 1280, and the range of valid values for the y-coordinate lies between 0 and 1024.

```
struct ScreenPosition
{
    public int X;
```

```
    public int Y;

    public ScreenPosition(int x, int y)
    {
        this.X = rangeCheckedX(x);
        this.Y = rangeCheckedY(y);
    }

    private static int rangeCheckedX(int x)
    {
        if (x < 0 || x > 1280)
        {
            throw new ArgumentOutOfRangeException("X");
        }
        return x;
    }

    private static int rangeCheckedY(int y)
    {
        if (y < 0 || y > 1024)
        {
            throw new ArgumentOutOfRangeException("Y");
        }
        return y;
    }
}
```

One problem with this structure is that it does not follow the golden rule of encapsulation—that is, it does not keep its data private. Public data is often a bad idea because the class cannot control the values that an application specifies. For example, the *ScreenPosition* constructor checks its parameters to ensure that they are in a specified range, but no such check can be done on the "raw" access to the public fields. Sooner or later (probably sooner), an error or misunderstanding on the part of a developer using this class in an application can cause either *X* or *Y* to stray out of this range:

```
ScreenPosition origin = new ScreenPosition(0, 0);
...
int xpos = origin.X;
origin.Y = -100; // oops
```

The common way to solve this problem is to make the fields private and add an accessor method and a modifier method to respectively read and write the value of each private field. The modifier methods can then check the range for new field values. For example, the code that follows contains an accessor (*GetX*) and a modifier (*SetX*) for the *X* field. Notice that *SetX* checks the parameter passed in.

```
struct ScreenPosition
{
    ...
    public int GetX()
    {
        return this.x;
    }
```

```
        public void SetX(int newX)
        {
            this.x = rangeCheckedX(newX);
        }
        ...
        private static int rangeCheckedX(int x) { ... }
        private static int rangeCheckedY(int y) { ... }
        private int x, y;
}
```

The code now successfully enforces the range constraints, which is good. However, there is a price to pay for this valuable guarantee—*ScreenPosition* no longer has a natural field-like syntax; it uses awkward method-based syntax instead. The example that follows increases the value of *X* by 10. To do so, it has to read the value of *X* by using the *GetX* accessor method and then write the value of *X* by using the *SetX* modifier method.

```
int xpos = origin.GetX();
origin.SetX(xpos + 10);
```

Compare this with the equivalent code if the *X* field were public:

```
origin.X += 10;
```

There is no doubt that, in this case, using public fields is syntactically cleaner, shorter, and easier. Unfortunately, using public fields breaks encapsulation. By using properties, you can combine the best of both worlds (fields and methods) to retain encapsulation while providing a field-like syntax.

What are properties?

A *property* is a cross between a field and a method—it looks like a field but acts like a method. You access a property by using exactly the same syntax that you use to access a field. However, the compiler automatically translates this field-like syntax into calls to accessor methods (sometimes referred to as *property getters* and *property setters*).

The syntax for a property declaration looks like this:

```
AccessModifier Type PropertyName
{
    get
    {
        // read accessor code
    }

    set
    {
        // write accessor code
    }
}
```

A property can contain two blocks of code, starting with the *get* and *set* keywords. The *get* block contains statements that execute when the property is read, and the *set* block contains statements that run upon writing to the property. The type of the property specifies the type of data read and written by the *get* and *set* accessors.

The next code example shows the *ScreenPosition* structure rewritten by using properties. When looking at this code, notice the following:

- Lowercase *_x* and *_y* are private fields.

- Uppercase *X* and *Y* are public properties.

- All *set* accessors are passed the data to be written by using a hidden, built-in parameter named *value*.

```
struct ScreenPosition
{
    private int _x, _y;

    public ScreenPosition(int X, int Y)
    {
        this._x = rangeCheckedX(X);
        this._y = rangeCheckedY(Y);
    }

    public int X
    {
        get { return this._x; }
        set { this._x = rangeCheckedX(value); }
    }

    public int Y
    {
        get { return this._y; }
        set { this._y = rangeCheckedY(value); }
    }

    private static int rangeCheckedX(int x) { ... }
    private static int rangeCheckedY(int y) { ... }
}
```

In this example, a private field directly implements each property, but this is only one way to implement a property. All that is required is for a *get* accessor to return a value of the specified type. Such a value can easily be calculated dynamically rather than being simply retrieved from stored data, in which case there would be no need for a physical field.

> **Note** Although the examples in this chapter show how to define properties for a structure, they are equally applicable to classes; the syntax is the same.

Using properties

When you use a property in an expression, you can use it in a read context (when you are retrieving its value) and in a write context (when you are modifying its value). The following example shows how to read values from the *X* and *Y* properties of the *ScreenPosition* structure:

```
ScreenPosition origin = new ScreenPosition(0, 0);
int xpos = origin.X;    // calls origin.X.get
int ypos = origin.Y;    // calls origin.Y.get
```

Notice that you access properties and fields by using identical syntax. When you use a property in a read context, the compiler automatically translates your field-like code into a call to the *get* accessor of that property. Similarly, if you use a property in a write context, the compiler automatically translates your field-like code into a call to the *set* accessor of that property.

```
origin.X = 40;      // calls origin.X.set, with value set to 40
origin.Y = 100;     // calls origin.Y.Set, with value set to 100
```

The values being assigned are passed in to the *set* accessors by using the *value* variable, as described in the preceding section. The runtime does this automatically.

It's also possible to use a property in a read/write context. In this case, both the *get* accessor and the *set* accessor are used. For example, the compiler automatically translates statements such as the following into calls to the *get* and *set* accessors:

```
origin.X += 10;
```

> **Tip** You can declare static properties in the same way that you can declare static fields and methods. You can access static properties by using the name of the class or structure rather than an instance of the class or structure.

Read-only properties

You can declare a property that contains only a *get* accessor. In this case, you can use the property only in a read context. For example, here's the X property of the *ScreenPosition* structure declared as a read-only property:

```
struct ScreenPosition
{
    private int _x;
    ...
    public int X
    {
        get { return this._x; }
    }
}
```

The X property does not contain a *set* accessor; therefore, any attempt to use X in a write context will fail, as demonstrated in the following example:

```
origin.X = 140; // compile-time error
```

Write-only properties

Similarly, you can declare a property that contains only a *set* accessor. In this case, you can use the property only in a write context. For example, here's the X property of the *ScreenPosition* structure declared as a write-only property:

```
struct ScreenPosition
{
    private int _x;
    ...
    public int X
    {
        set { this._x = rangeCheckedX(value); }
    }
}
```

The *X* property does not contain a *get* accessor; any attempt to use *X* in a read context will fail, as illustrated here:

```
Console.WriteLine(origin.X);      // compile-time error
origin.X = 200;                   // compiles OK
origin.X += 10;                   // compile-time error
```

Note Write-only properties are useful for secure data such as passwords. Ideally, an application that implements security should allow you to set your password but never allow you to read it back. When a user attempts to log on, the user can provide the password. The logon method can compare this password with the stored password and return only an indication of whether they match.

Property accessibility

You can specify the accessibility of a property (using the keywords *public*, *private*, or *protected*) when you declare it. However, it is possible within the property declaration to override the property accessibility for the *get* and *set* accessors. For example, the version of the *ScreenPosition* structure shown in the code that follows defines the *set* accessors of the *X* and *Y* properties as private. (The *get* accessors are public because the properties are public.)

```
struct ScreenPosition
{
    private int _x, _y;
    ...
    public int X
    {
        get { return this._x; }
        private set { this._x = rangeCheckedX(value); }
    }

    public int Y
    {
        get { return this._y; }
        private set { this._y = rangeCheckedY(value); }
    }
    ...
}
```

You must observe some rules when defining accessors that have different accessibility from one another:

- You can change the accessibility of only one of the accessors when you define it. It wouldn't make much sense to define a property as public only to change the accessibility of both accessors to private anyway.

- The modifier must not specify an accessibility that is less restrictive than that of the property. For example, if the property is declared to be private, you cannot specify the read accessor as public. (Instead, you would make the property public and make the write accessor private.)

Understanding the property restrictions

Properties look, act, and feel like fields when you read or write data by using them. However, they are not true fields, and certain restrictions apply to them:

- You can assign a value through a property of a structure or class only after the structure or class has been initialized. The following code example is illegal because the *location* variable has not been initialized (by using *new*):

```
ScreenPosition location;
location.X = 40; // compile-time error, location not assigned
```

> **Note** This might seem trivial, but if *X* were a field rather than a property, the code would be legal. For this reason, you should define structures and classes from the beginning by using properties rather than fields that you later migrate to properties. Code that uses your classes and structures might no longer work after you change fields into properties. You will return to this matter in the section "Generating automatic properties" later in this chapter.

- You can't use a property as a *ref* or an *out* argument to a method (although you can use a writable field as a *ref* or an *out* argument). This makes sense because the property doesn't really point to a memory location; rather, it points to an accessor method, such as in the following example:

```
MyMethod(ref location.X); // compile-time error
```

- A property can contain at most one *get* accessor and one *set* accessor. A property cannot contain other methods, fields, or properties.

- The *get* and *set* accessors cannot take any parameters. The data being assigned is passed to the *set* accessor automatically by using the *value* variable.

- You can't declare properties by using *const*, such as is demonstrated here:

```
const int X { get { ... } set { ... } } // compile-time error
```

Using properties appropriately

Properties are a powerful feature, and used in the correct manner, they can help to make code easier to understand and maintain. However, they are no substitute for careful object-oriented design that focuses on the behavior of objects rather than on the properties of objects. Accessing private fields through regular methods or through properties does not, by itself, make your code well designed. For example, a bank account holds a balance indicating the funds available in the account. You might therefore be tempted to create a *Balance* property on a *BankAccount* class, like this:

```
class BankAccount
{

    private decimal _balance;
    ...
    public decimal Balance
    {
        get { return this._balance; }
        set { this._balance = value; }
    }
}
```

This is a poor design because it fails to represent the functionality required when someone withdraws money from or deposits money into an account. (If you know of a bank that allows you to change the balance of your account directly without physically putting money into the account, please let me know!) When you're programming, try to express the problem you're solving in the solution and don't get lost in a mass of low-level syntax. As the following example illustrates, provide *Deposit* and *Withdraw* methods for the *BankAccount* class rather than a property setter:

```
class BankAccount
{
    private decimal _balance;
    ...
    public decimal Balance { get { return this._balance; } }
    public void Deposit(decimal amount) { ... }
    public bool Withdraw(decimal amount) { ... }
}
```

Declaring interface properties

You encountered interfaces in Chapter 13, "Creating interfaces and defining abstract classes." Interfaces can define properties as well as methods. To do this, you specify the *get* or *set* keyword or both, but you replace the body of the *get* or *set* accessor with a semicolon, as shown here:

```
interface IScreenPosition
{
    int X { get; set; }
    int Y { get; set; }
}
```

Any class or structure that implements this interface must implement the *X* and *Y* properties with *get* and *set* accessor methods.

```
struct ScreenPosition : IScreenPosition
{
    ...
    public int X
    {
        get { ... }
        set { ... }
    }

    public int Y
    {
        get { ... }
        set { ... }
    }
    ...
}
```

If you implement the interface properties in a class, you can declare the property implementations as virtual, which enables derived classes to override the implementations.

```
class ScreenPosition : IScreenPosition
{
    ...
    public virtual int X
    {
        get { ... }
        set { ... }
    }
    public virtual int Y
    {
        get { ... }
        set { ... }
    }
    ...
}
```

> **Note** This example shows a class. Remember that the *virtual* keyword is not valid when creating a struct because structures do not support inheritance.

You can also choose to implement a property by using the explicit interface implementation syntax covered in Chapter 13. An explicit implementation of a property is nonpublic and nonvirtual (and cannot be overridden).

```
struct ScreenPosition : IScreenPosition
{
    ...
    int IScreenPosition.X
    {
        get { ... }
        set { ... }
    }

    int IScreenPosition.Y
    {
        get { ... }
        set { ... }
    }
    ...
}
```

Replacing methods with properties

Chapter 13 teaches you how to create a drawing application with which a user can place circles and squares on a canvas in a window. In the exercises in that chapter, you factor the common functionality for the *Circle* and *Square* classes into an abstract class called *DrawingShape*. The *DrawingShape* class provides the *SetLocation* and *SetColor* methods, which the application uses to specify the position and color of a shape on the screen. In the following exercise, you will modify the *DrawingShape* class to expose the location and color of a shape as properties.

Use properties

1. Start Visual Studio 2015 if it is not already running.

2. Open the Drawing project, which is located in the \Microsoft Press\VCSBS\Chapter 15\ Drawing Using Properties folder in your Documents folder.

3. Display the DrawingShape.cs file in the Code and Text Editor window.

    This file contains the same *DrawingShape* class that is in Chapter 13 except that, following the recommendations described earlier in this chapter, the *size* field has been renamed as *_size*, and the *locX* and *locY* fields have been renamed as *_x* and *_y*.

    ```
    abstract class DrawingShape
    {
        protected int _size;
        protected int _x = 0, _y = 0;
        ...
    }
    ```

4. Open the IDraw.cs file for the Drawing project in the Code and Text Editor window.

    This interface specifies the *SetLocation* method, like this:

```
interface IDraw
{
    void SetLocation(int xCoord, int yCoord);
    ...
}
```

The purpose of this method is to set the _x and _y fields of the *DrawingShape* object to the values passed in. This method can be replaced with a pair of properties.

5. Delete this method and replace it with the definition of a pair of properties named *X* and *Y*, as shown here in bold:

```
interface IDraw
{
    int X { get; set; }
    int Y { get; set; }
    ...
}
```

6. In the *DrawingShape* class, delete the *SetLocation* method and replace it with the following implementations of the *X* and *Y* properties:

```
public int X
{
    get { return this._x; }
    set { this._x = value; }
}

public int Y
{
    get { return this._y; }
    set { this._y = value; }
}
```

7. Display the DrawingPad.xaml.cs file in the Code and Text Editor window and locate the *drawingCanvas_Tapped* method.

This method runs when a user taps the screen or clicks the left mouse button. It draws a square on the screen at the point where the user taps or clicks.

8. Locate the statement that calls the *SetLocation* method to set the position of the square on the screen. It is located in the *if* statement block as highlighted in the following:

```
if (mySquare is IDraw)
{
    IDraw drawSquare = mySquare;
    drawSquare.SetLocation((int)mouseLocation.X, (int)mouseLocation.Y);
    drawSquare.Draw(drawingCanvas);
}
```

9. Replace this statement with code that sets the *X* and *Y* properties of the *Square* object, as shown in bold in the following code:

```
if (mySquare is IDraw)
{
    IDraw drawSquare = mySquare;
    drawSquare.X = (int)mouseLocation.X;
    drawSquare.Y = (int)mouseLocation.Y;
    drawSquare.Draw(drawingCanvas);
}
```

10. Locate the *drawingCanvas_RightTapped* method.

    This method runs when the user taps and holds a finger on the screen or clicks the right mouse button. It draws a circle at the location where the user taps and holds or right-clicks.

11. In this method, replace the statement that calls the *SetLocation* method of the *Circle* object and set the *X* and *Y* properties instead, as shown in bold in the following example:

```
if (myCircle is IDraw)
{
    IDraw drawCircle = myCircle;
    drawCircle.X = (int)mouseLocation.X;
    drawCircle.Y = (int)mouseLocation.Y;
    drawCircle.Draw(drawingCanvas);
}
```

12. Open the IColor.cs file for the Drawing project in the Code and Text Editor window. This interface specifies the *SetColor* method, like this:

```
interface IColor
{
    void SetColor(Color color);
}
```

13. Delete this method and replace it with the definition of a property named *Color*, as presented here:

```
interface IColor
{
    Color Color { set; }
}
```

This is a write-only property, providing a *set* accessor but no *get* accessor. You define the property this way because the color is not actually stored in the *DrawingShape* class and is specified only as each shape is drawn; you cannot actually query a shape to find out which color it is.

 Note It is common practice for a property to share the same name as a type (*Color* in this example).

14. Return to the *DrawingShape* class in the Code and Text Editor window. Replace the *SetColor* method in this class with the *Color* property shown here:

```
    public Color Color
    {
        set
        {
            if (this.shape != null)
            {
                SolidColorBrush brush = new SolidColorBrush(value);
                this.shape.Fill = brush;
            }
        }
    }
```

> **Note** The code for the *set* accessor is almost the same as the original *SetColor* method except that the statement that creates the *SolidColorBrush* object is passed the *value* parameter.

15. Return to the DrawingPad.xaml.cs file in the Code and Text Editor window. In the *drawingCanvas_Tapped* method, modify the statement that sets the color of the *Square* object to match the following code in bold:

```
if (mySquare is IColor)
{
    IColor colorSquare = mySquare;
    colorSquare.Color = Colors.BlueViolet;
}
```

16. Similarly, in the *drawingCanvas_RightTapped* method, modify the·statement that sets the color of the *Circle* object.

```
if (myCircle is IColor)
{
    IColor colorCircle = myCircle;
    colorCircle.Color = Colors.HotPink;
}
```

17. On the Debug menu, click Start Debugging to build and run the project.

18. Verify that the application operates in the same manner as before. If you tap the screen or click the left mouse button on the canvas, the application should draw a square, and if you tap and hold or click the right mouse button, the application should draw a circle. The following image shows the application running:

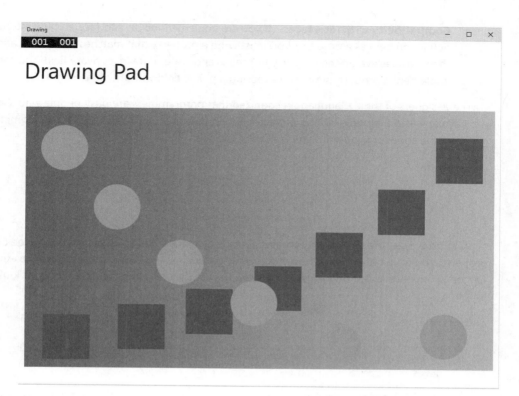

Drawing Pad

19. Return to the Visual Studio 2015 programming environment and stop debugging.

Generating automatic properties

As mentioned earlier in this chapter, the principal purpose of properties is to hide the implementation of fields from the outside world. This is fine if your properties actually perform some useful work, but if the *get* and *set* accessors simply wrap operations that just read or assign a value to a field, you might be questioning the value of this approach. However, there are at least two good reasons why you should define properties rather than expose data as public fields even in these situations:

- **Compatibility with applications**   Fields and properties expose themselves by using different metadata in assemblies. If you develop a class and decide to use public fields, any applications that use this class will reference these items as fields. Although you use the same C# syntax for reading and writing a field that you use when reading and writing a property, the compiled code is actually quite different—the C# compiler just hides the differences from you. If you later decide that you really do need to change these fields to properties (maybe the business requirements have changed and you need to perform additional logic when assigning values), existing applications will not be able to use the updated version of the class without being recompiled. This is awkward if you have deployed the application on a large number of devices throughout an organization. There are ways around this, but it is generally better to avoid getting into this situation in the first place.

- **Compatibility with interfaces**   If you are implementing an interface and the interface defines an item as a property, you must write a property that matches the specification in the interface, even if the property just reads and writes data in a private field. You cannot implement a property simply by exposing a public field with the same name.

The designers of the C# language recognized that programmers are busy people who should not have to waste their time writing more code than they need to. To this end, the C# compiler can generate the code for properties automatically, like this:

```
class Circle
{
    public int Radius{ get; set; }
    ...
}
```

In this example, the *Circle* class contains a property named *Radius*. Apart from the type of this property, you have not specified how this property works—the *get* and *set* accessors are empty. The C# compiler converts this definition to a private field and a default implementation that looks similar to this:

```
class Circle
{
    private int _radius;
    public int Radius{
        get
        {
            return this._radius;
        }
        set
        {
            this._radius = value;
        }
    }
    ...
}
```

So for very little effort you can implement a simple property by using automatically generated code, and if you need to include additional logic later, you can do so without breaking any existing applications.

> **Note** The syntax for defining an automatic property is almost identical to the syntax for defining a property in an interface. The exception is that an automatic property can specify an access modifier such as *private*, *public*, or *protected*.

You can create a read-only automatic property by omitting the empty *set* accessor from your property declaration, like this:

```
class Circle
{
    public DateTime CircleCreatedDate { get; }
```

```
    ...
}
```

This is useful in scenarios where you want to create an immutable property; a property that is set when the object is constructed and cannot subsequently be changed. For example, you might want to set the date on which an object was created or the name of the user who created it, or you might want to generate a unique identifier value for the object. These are values that you typically want to set once and then prevent them from being modified. With this in mind, C# allows you to initialize read-only automatic properties in one of two ways. You can initialize the property from a constructor, like this:

```
class Circle
{
    public Circle()
    {
        CircleCreatedDate = DateTime.Now;
    }


    public DateTime CircleCreatedDate { get; }
    ...
}
```

Alternatively, you can initialize the property as part of the declaration, like this:

```
class Circle
{
    public DateTime CircleCreatedDate { get; } = DateTime.Now;
    ...
}
```

Be aware that if you initialize a property in this way and also set its value in a constructor, the value provided by the constructor will overwrite the value specified by the property initializer; use one approach or the other, but not both!

> **Note** You cannot create write-only automatic properties. If you attempt to create an automatic property without a *get* accessor, you will see a compile-time error.

Initializing objects by using properties

In Chapter 7, you learned how to define constructors to initialize an object. An object can have multiple constructors, and you can define constructors with varying parameters to initialize different elements in an object. For example, you could define a class that models a triangle, like this:

```
public class Triangle
{
    private int side1Length;
    private int side2Length;
```

```
    private int side3Length;

    // default constructor - default values for all sides
    public Triangle()
    {
        this.side1Length = this.side2Length = this.side3Length = 10;
    }

    // specify length for side1Length, default values for the others
    public Triangle(int length1)
    {
        this.side1Length = length1;
        this.side2Length = this.side3Length = 10;
    }

    // specify length for side1Length and side2Length,
    // default value for side3Length
    public Triangle(int length1, int length2)
    {
        this.side1Length = length1;
        this.side2Length = length2;
        this.side3Length = 10;
    }

    // specify length for all sides
    public Triangle(int length1, int length2, int length3)
    {
        this.side1Length = length1;
        this.side2Length = length2;
        this.side3Length = length3;
    }
}
```

Depending on how many fields a class contains and the various combinations you want to enable for initializing the fields, you could end up writing a lot of constructors. There are also potential problems if many of the fields have the same type: you might not be able to write a unique constructor for all combinations of fields. For example, in the preceding *Triangle* class, you could not easily add a constructor that initializes only the *side1Length* and *side3Length* fields because it would not have a unique signature; it would take two *int* parameters, and the constructor that initializes *side1Length* and *side2Length* already has this signature. One possible solution is to define a constructor that takes optional parameters and specify values for the parameters as named arguments when you create a *Triangle* object. However, a better and more transparent solution is to initialize the private fields to a set of default values and expose them as properties, like this:

```
public class Triangle
{
    private int side1Length = 10;
    private int side2Length = 10;
    private int side3Length = 10;

    public int Side1Length
    {
        set { this.side1Length = value; }
    }
```

```
public int Side2Length
{
    set { this.side2Length = value; }
}


public int Side3Length
{
    set { this.side3Length = value; }
}
}
```

When you create an instance of a class, you can initialize it by specifying the names and values for any public properties that have *set* accessors. For example, you can create *Triangle* objects and initialize any combination of the three sides, like this:

```
Triangle tri1 = new Triangle { Side3Length = 15 };
Triangle tri2 = new Triangle { Side1Length = 15, Side3Length = 20 };
Triangle tri3 = new Triangle { Side2Length = 12, Side3Length = 17 };
Triangle tri4 = new Triangle { Side1Length = 9, Side2Length = 12,
                               Side3Length = 15 };
```

This syntax is known as an *object initializer*. When you invoke an object initializer in this way, the C# compiler generates code that calls the default constructor and then calls the *set* accessor of each named property to initialize it with the value specified. You can specify object initializers in combination with nondefault constructors as well. For example, if the *Triangle* class also provided a constructor that took a single string parameter describing the type of triangle, you could invoke this constructor and initialize the other properties, like this:

```
Triangle tri5 = new Triangle("Equilateral triangle") { Side1Length = 3,
                                                        Side2Length = 3,
                                                        Side3Length = 3 };
```

The important point to remember is that the constructor runs first and the properties are set afterward. Understanding this sequencing is important if the constructor sets fields in an object to specific values and the properties that you specify change these values.

You can also use object initializers with automatic properties that are not read-only, as you will see in the next exercise. In this exercise, you will define a class for modeling regular polygons that contains automatic properties for providing access to information about the number of sides the polygon contains and the length of these sides.

Note You cannot initialize automatic read-only properties in this way; you have to use one of the techniques described in the previous section.

Define automatic properties and use object initializers

1. In Visual Studio 2015, open the AutomaticProperties project, which is located in the \Microsoft Press\VCSBS\Chapter 15\AutomaticProperties folder in your Documents folder.

   The AutomaticProperties project contains the Program.cs file, defining the *Program* class with the *Main* and *doWork* methods that you have seen in previous exercises.

2. In Solution Explorer, right-click the AutomaticProperties project, point to Add, and then click Class to open the Add New Item – AutomaticProperties dialog box. In the Name box, type **Polygon.cs**, and then click Add.

   The Polygon.cs file, holding the *Polygon* class, is created and added to the project and appears in the Code and Text Editor window.

3. Add the automatic properties *NumSides* and *SideLength* to the *Polygon* class, as shown here in bold:

   ```
   class Polygon
   {
       public int NumSides { get; set; }
       public double SideLength { get; set; }
   }
   ```

4. Add the following default constructor shown in bold to the *Polygon* class:

   ```
   class Polygon
   {
       ...
       public Polygon()
       {
           this.NumSides = 4;
           this.SideLength = 10.0;
       }
   }
   ```

   This constructor initializes the *NumSides* and *SideLength* fields with default values. In this exercise, the default polygon is a square with sides 10 units long.

5. Display the Program.cs file in the Code and Text Editor window.

6. Add to the *doWork* method the statements shown here in bold, replacing the *// TODO:* comment:

   ```
   static void doWork()
   {
       Polygon square = new Polygon();
       Polygon triangle = new Polygon { NumSides = 3 };
       Polygon pentagon = new Polygon { SideLength = 15.5, NumSides = 5 };
   }
   ```

   These statements create *Polygon* objects. The *square* variable is initialized by using the default constructor. The *triangle* and *pentagon* variables are also initialized by using the default constructor, and then this code changes the value of the properties exposed by the *Polygon* class. In the case of the *triangle* variable, the *NumSides* property is set to *3*, but the *SideLength* property is left at its default value of *10.0*. For the *pentagon* variable, the code changes the values of the *SideLength* and *NumSides* properties.

7. Add to the end of the *doWork* method the following code shown in bold:

```
static void doWork()
{
    ...
    Console.WriteLine($"Square: number of sides is {square.NumSides}, length of each side
is {square.SideLength}");
    Console.WriteLine($"Triangle: number of sides is {triangle.NumSides}, length of each
side is {triangle.SideLength}");
    Console.WriteLine($"Pentagon: number of sides is {pentagon.NumSides}, length of each
side is {pentagon.SideLength}");
}
```

These statements display the values of the *NumSides* and *SideLength* properties for each *Polygon* object.

8. On the Debug menu, click Start Without Debugging.

Verify that the program builds and runs, writing the messages shown here to the console window:

```
C:\Windows\system32\cmd.exe
Square: number of sides is 4, length of each side is 10
Triangle: number of sides is 3, length of each side is 10
Pentagon: number of sides is 5, length of each side is 15.5
Press any key to continue . . .
```

9. Press the Enter key to close the application and return to Visual Studio 2015.

Summary

In this chapter, you saw how to create and use properties to provide controlled access to data in an object. You also saw how to create automatic properties and how to use properties when initializing objects.

- If you want to continue to the next chapter, keep Visual Studio 2015 running and turn to Chapter 16, "Using indexers."

- If you want to exit Visual Studio 2015 now, on the File menu, click Exit. If you see a Save dialog box, click Yes and save the project.

Quick reference

To	Do this
Declare a read/write property for a structure or class	Declare the type of the property, its name, a *get* accessor, and a *set* accessor. For example: ```\nstruct ScreenPosition\n{\n ...\n public int X\n {\n get { ... }\n set { ... }\n }\n ...\n}\n```
Declare a read-only property for a structure or class	Declare a property with only a *get* accessor. For example: ```\nstruct ScreenPosition\n{\n ...\n public int X\n {\n get { ... }\n }\n ...\n}\n```
Declare a write-only property for a structure or class	Declare a property with only a *set* accessor. For example: ```\nstruct ScreenPosition\n{\n ...\n public int X\n {\n set { ... }\n }\n ...\n}\n```
Declare a property in an interface	Declare a property with just the *get* or *set* keyword or both. For example: ```\ninterface IScreenPosition\n{\n int X { get; set; } // no body\n int Y { get; set; } // no body\n}\n```
Implement an interface property in a structure or class	In the class or structure that implements the interface, declare the property and implement the accessors. For example: ```\nstruct ScreenPosition : IScreenPosition\n{\n public int X\n {\n get { ... }\n set { ... }\n }\n\n public int Y\n {\n get { ... }\n set { ... }\n }\n}\n```

To	Do this

Create an automatic property	In the class or structure that contains the property, define the property with empty *get* and *set* accessors. For example:
	
	``csharp
	class Polygon
	{
	    public int NumSides { get; set; }
	}
	``
	
	If the property is read-only, then initialize the property either in the object constructor or as the property is defined. For example:
	
	``csharp
	class Circle
	{
	    public DateTime CircleCreatedDate { get; }
	        = DateTime.Now;
	    ...
	}
	``

Use properties to initialize an object	Specify the properties and their values as a list enclosed in braces when constructing the object. For example:
	
	``csharp
	Triangle tri3 =
	    new Triangle { Side2Length = 12, Side3Length =
	17 };
	``

CHAPTER 16

Using indexers

After completing this chapter, you will be able to:

- Encapsulate logical array-like access to an object by using indexers.

- Control read access to indexers by declaring *get* accessors.

- Control write access to indexers by declaring *set* accessors.

- Create interfaces that declare indexers.

- Implement indexers in structures and classes that inherit from interfaces.

Chapter 15, "Implementing properties to access fields," describes how to implement and use properties as a means of providing controlled access to the fields in a class. Properties are useful for mirroring fields that contain a single value. However, indexers are invaluable if you want to provide access to items that contain multiple values, and to do so by using a natural and familiar syntax.

What is an indexer?

You can think of an *indexer* as a smart array, in much the same way that you can think of a property as a smart field. Whereas a property encapsulates a single value in a class, an indexer encapsulates a set of values. The syntax that you use for an indexer is exactly the same as the syntax that you use for an array.

The best way to understand indexers is to work through an example. First you'll consider a problem and examine a solution that doesn't use indexers. Then you'll work through the same problem and look at a better solution that does use indexers. The problem concerns integers, or more precisely, the *int* type.

An example that doesn't use indexers

You normally use an *int* to hold an integer value. Internally, an *int* stores its value as a sequence of 32 bits, where each bit can be either 0 or 1. Most of the time, you don't care about this internal binary representation; you just use an *int* type as a container that holds an integer value. Sometimes, however, programmers use the *int* type for other purposes—some programs use an *int* as a set of binary flags and manipulate the individual bits within an *int*. If you are an old C hack like I am, what follows should have a very familiar feel.

> **Note** Some older programs used *int* types in an effort to save memory. Such programs typically date from when the size of computer memory was measured in kilobytes rather than the gigabytes available these days, and memory was at an absolute premium. A single *int* holds 32 bits, each of which can be 1 or 0. In some cases, programmers assigned 1 to indicate the value *true* and 0 to indicate *false*, and then employed an *int* as a set of Boolean values.

C# provides a set of operators that you can use to access and manipulate the individual bits in an *int*. These operators are as follows:

- **The NOT (~) operator** This is a unary operator that performs a bitwise complement. For example, if you take the 8-bit value *11001100* (*204* decimal) and apply the ~ operator to it, you obtain the result *00110011* (*51* decimal)—all the 1s in the original value become 0s, and all the 0s become 1s.

> **Note** The examples shown here are purely illustrative and are accurate only to 8 bits. In C#, the *int* type is 32 bits, so if you try any of these examples in a C# application, you will get a 32-bit result that might be different from those shown in this list. For example, in 32 bits, 204 is 00000000000000000000000011001100, so in C#, ~204 is 11111111111111111111111100110011 (which is actually the *int* representation of −205 in C#).

- **The left-shift (<<) operator** This is a binary operator that performs a left shift. The expression *204 << 2* returns the value *48*. (In binary, *204* decimal is *11001100*, and shifting it left by two places yields *00110000*, or 48 decimal.) The far-left bits are discarded, and zeros are introduced from the right. There is a corresponding right-shift operator (>>).

- **The OR (|) operator** This is a binary operator that performs a bitwise OR operation, returning a value containing a 1 in each position in which either of the operands has a 1. For example, the expression *204 | 24* has the value *220* (*204* is *11001100*, *24* is *00011000*, and *220* is *11011100*).

- **The AND (&) operator** This operator performs a bitwise AND operation. AND is similar to the bitwise OR operator, but it returns a value containing a 1 in each position where both of the operands have a 1. So, *204 & 24* is *8* (*204* is *11001100*, *24* is *00011000*, and *8* is *00001000*).

- **The XOR (^) operator** This operator performs a bitwise exclusive OR operation, returning a 1 in each bit where there is a 1 in one operand or the other but not both. (Two 1s yield a 0—this is the "exclusive" part of the operator.) So *204 ^ 24* is *212* (*11001100 ^ 00011000* is *11010100*).

You can use these operators together to determine the values of the individual bits in an *int*. As an example, the following expression uses the left-shift (<<) and bitwise AND (&) operators to determine whether the sixth bit from the right of the *byte* variable named *bits* is set to *0* or to *1*:

```
(bits & (1 << 5)) != 0
```

> **Note** The bitwise operators count the positions of bits from right to left, and the bits are numbered starting at 0. So, bit 0 is the rightmost bit, and the bit at position 5 is the bit six places from the right.

Suppose that the *bits* variable contains the decimal value 42. In binary, this is 00101010. The decimal value 1 is 00000001 in binary, and the expression *1 << 5* has the value 00100000; the sixth bit is 1. In binary, the expression *bits & (1 << 5)* is *00101010 & 00100000*, and the value of this expression is binary 00100000, which is nonzero. If the variable *bits* contains the value *65*, or *01000001* in binary, the value of the expression is *01000001 & 00100000*, which yields the binary result *00000000*, or zero.

This is a fairly complicated example, but it's trivial in comparison to the following expression, which uses the compound assignment operator *&=* to set the bit at position 6 to *0*:

```
bits &= ~(1 << 5)
```

Similarly, if you want to set the bit at position 6 to *1*, you can use the bitwise OR (|) operator. The following complicated expression is based on the compound assignment operator |=:

```
bits |= (1 << 5)
```

The trouble with these examples is that although they work, they are fiendishly difficult to understand. They're complicated, and the solution is a very low-level one: it fails to create an abstraction of the problem that it solves, and it is consequently very difficult to maintain code that performs these kinds of operations.

The same example using indexers

Let's pull back from the preceding low-level solution for a moment and remember what the problem is. You'd like to use an *int* not as an *int* but as an array of bits. Therefore, the best way to solve this problem is to use an *int* as if it were an array of bits; in other words, what you'd like to be able to write in order to access the bit six places from the right in the *bits* variable is an expression such as the following (remember that arrays start with index 0):

```
bits[5]
```

And, to set the bit four places from the right to *true*, you'd like to be able to write this:

```
bits[3] = true
```

Unfortunately, you can't use the square bracket notation on an *int*; it works only on an array or on a type that behaves like an array. So the solution to the problem is to create a new type that acts like, feels like, and is used like an array of *bool* variables but is implemented by using an *int*. You can achieve this feat by defining an indexer. Let's call this new type *IntBits*. *IntBits* will contain an *int* value (initialized in its constructor), but the idea is that you'll use *IntBits* as an array of *bool* variables.

```
struct IntBits
{
    private int bits;

    public IntBits(int initialBitValue)
    {
        bits = initialBitValue;
    }

    // indexer to be written here
}
```

To define the indexer, you use a notation that is a cross between a property and an array. You introduce the indexer with the *this* keyword, specify the type of the value returned by the indexer, and also specify the type of the value to use as the index into the indexer between square brackets. The indexer for the *IntBits* struct uses an integer as its index type and returns a Boolean value. It looks like this:

```
struct IntBits
{
    ...
    public bool this [ int index ]
    {
        get
        {
            return (bits & (1 << index)) != 0;
        }

        set
        {
            if (value)  // turn the bit on if value is true; otherwise, turn it off
                bits |=  (1 << index);
            else
                bits &= ~(1 << index);
```

```
        }
    }
}
```

Notice the following points:

- An indexer is not a method; there are no parentheses containing a parameter, but there are square brackets that specify an index. This index is used to specify which element is being accessed.

- All indexers use the *this* keyword. A class or structure can define at most one indexer (although you can overload it and have several implementations), and it is always named *this*.

- Indexers contain *get* and *set* accessors just like properties. In this example, the *get* and *set* accessors contain the complicated bitwise expressions previously discussed.

- The index specified in the indexer declaration is populated with the index value specified when the indexer is called. The *get* and *set* accessor methods can read this argument to determine which element should be accessed.

> **Note** You should perform a range check on the index value in the indexer to prevent any unexpected exceptions from occurring in your indexer code.

After you have declared the indexer, you can use a variable of type *IntBits* instead of an *int* and apply the square bracket notation, as shown in the next example:

```
int adapted = 126;      // 126 has the binary representation 01111110
IntBits bits = new IntBits(adapted);
bool peek = bits[6];  // retrieve bool at index 6; should be true (1)
bits[0] = true;       // set the bit at index 0 to true (1)
bits[3] = false;      // set the bit at index 3 to false (0)
                      // the value in bits is now 01110111, or 119 in decimal
```

This syntax is certainly much easier to understand. It directly and succinctly captures the essence of the problem.

Understanding indexer accessors

When you read an indexer, the compiler automatically translates your array-like code into a call to the *get* accessor of that indexer. Consider the following example:

```
bool peek = bits[6];
```

This statement is converted to a call to the *get* accessor for *bits*, and the *index* argument is set to 6.

Similarly, if you write to an indexer, the compiler automatically translates your array-like code into a call to the *set* accessor of that indexer, setting the *index* argument to the value enclosed in the square brackets, such as illustrated here:

```
bits[3] = true;
```

This statement is converted to a call to the *set* accessor for *bits* where *index* is *3*. As with ordinary properties, the data you are writing to the indexer (in this case, *true*) is made available inside the *set* accessor by using the *value* keyword. The type of *value* is the same as the type of the indexer itself (in this case, *bool*).

It's also possible to use an indexer in a combined read/write context. In this case, both the *get* and *set* accessors are used. Look at the following statement, which uses the XOR operator (^) to invert the value of the bit at index 6 in the *bits* variable:

```
bits[6] ^= true;
```

This code is automatically translated into the following:

```
bits[6] = bits[6] ^ true;
```

This code works because the indexer declares both a *get* and a *set* accessor.

> **Note** You can declare an indexer that contains only a *get* accessor (a read-only indexer) or only a *set* accessor (a write-only indexer).

Comparing indexers and arrays

When you use an indexer, the syntax is deliberately very array-like. However, there are some important differences between indexers and arrays:

- Indexers can use nonnumeric subscripts, such as a string (as shown in the following example), whereas arrays can use only integer subscripts.

  ```
  public int this [ string name ] { ... } // OK
  ```

- Indexers can be overloaded (just like methods), whereas arrays cannot.

  ```
  public Name this [ PhoneNumber number ] { ... }
  public PhoneNumber this [ Name name ] { ... }
  ```

- Indexers cannot be used as *ref* or *out* parameters, whereas array elements can.

  ```
  IntBits bits;          // bits contains an indexer
  Method(ref bits[1]); // compile-time error
  ```

> ### Properties, arrays, and indexers
>
> It is possible for a property to return an array, but remember that arrays are reference types, so exposing an array as a property creates the possibility of accidentally overwriting a lot of data. Look at the following structure that exposes an array property named *Data*:

```
struct Wrapper
{
    private int[] data;
    ...
    public int[] Data
    {
        get { return this.data; }
        set { this.data = value; }
    }
}
```

Now consider the following code that uses this property:

```
Wrapper wrap = new Wrapper();
...
int[] myData = wrap.Data;
myData[0]++;
myData[1]++;
```

This looks pretty innocuous. However, because arrays are reference types, the variable *myData* refers to the same object as the private *data* variable in the *Wrapper* structure. Any changes you make to elements in *myData* are made to the *data* array; the expression *myData[0]++* has the very same effect as *data[0]++*. If this is not your intention, you should use the *Clone* method in the *get* and *set* accessors of the *Data* property to return a copy of the *data* array, or make a copy of the value being set, as shown in the code that follows. (Chapter 8, "Understanding values and references," discusses the *Clone* method for copying arrays.) Notice that the *Clone* method returns an object, which you must cast to an integer array.

```
struct Wrapper
{
    private int[] data;
    ...
    public int[] Data
    {
        get { return this.data.Clone() as int[]; }
        set { this.data = value.Clone() as int[]; }
    }
}
```

However, this approach can become very messy and expensive in terms of memory use. Indexers provide a natural solution to this problem—don't expose the entire array as a property; just make its individual elements available through an indexer:

```
struct Wrapper
{
    private int[] data;
    ...
    public int this [int i]
    {
        get { return this.data[i]; }
        set { this.data[i] = value; }
    }
}
```

The following code uses the indexer in a similar manner to the property shown earlier:

```
Wrapper wrap = new Wrapper();
...
int[] myData = new int[2];
myData[0] = wrap[0];
myData[1] = wrap[1];
myData[0]++;
myData[1]++;
```

This time, incrementing the values in the *myData* array has no effect on the original array in the *Wrapper* object. If you really want to modify the data in the *Wrapper* object, you must write statements such as this:

```
wrap[0]++;
```

This is much clearer and safer!

Indexers in interfaces

You can declare indexers in an interface. To do this, specify the *get* keyword, the *set* keyword, or both, but replace the body of the *get* or *set* accessor with a semicolon. Any class or structure that implements the interface must implement the *indexer* accessors declared in the interface, as demonstrated here:

```
interface IRawInt
{
    bool this [ int index ] { get; set; }
}

struct RawInt : IRawInt
{
    ...
    public bool this [ int index ]
    {
        get { ... }
        set { ... }
    }
    ...
}
```

If you implement the interface indexer in a class, you can declare the indexer implementations as virtual. This allows further derived classes to override the *get* and *set* accessors, such as in the following:

```
class RawInt : IRawInt
{
    ...
    public virtual bool this [ int index ]
    {
```

```
        get { ... }
        set { ... }
    }
    ...
}
```

You can also choose to implement an indexer by using the explicit interface implementation syntax covered in Chapter 13, "Creating interfaces and defining abstract classes." An explicit implementation of an indexer is nonpublic and nonvirtual (and so cannot be overridden), as shown in this example:

```
struct RawInt : IRawInt
{
    ...
    bool IRawInt.this [ int index ]
    {
        get { ... }
        set { ... }
    }
    ...
}
```

Using indexers in a Windows application

In the following exercise, you will examine a simple phone book application and complete its implementation. You will write two indexers in the *PhoneBook* class: one that accepts a *Name* parameter and returns a *PhoneNumber*, and another that accepts a *PhoneNumber* parameter and returns a *Name*. (The *Name* and *PhoneNumber* structures have already been written.) You will also need to call these indexers from the correct places in the program.

Familiarize yourself with the application

1. Start Microsoft Visual Studio 2015 if it is not already running.

2. Open the Indexers project, which is located in the \Microsoft Press\VCSBS\Chapter 16\Indexers folder in your Documents folder.

   With this graphical application, a user can search for the telephone number for a contact and also find the name of a contact that matches a given telephone number.

3. On the Debug menu, click Start Debugging.

   The project builds and runs. A form appears, displaying two empty text boxes labeled Name and Phone Number. The form initially displays two buttons: one to find a phone number when given a name, and one to find a name when given a phone number. Expanding the command bar at the bottom of the form reveals an additional Add button that will add a name/phone number pair to a list of names and phone numbers held by the application. All buttons (including the Add button in the command bar) currently do nothing. The application looks like this:

Your task is to complete the application so that the buttons work.

4. Return to Visual Studio 2015 and stop debugging.

5. Display the Name.cs file for the Indexers project in the Code and Text Editor window. Examine the *Name* structure. Its purpose is to act as a holder for names.

   The name is provided as a string to the constructor. The name can be retrieved by using the read-only string property named *Text*. (The *Equals* and *GetHashCode* methods are used for comparing *Name*s when searching through an array of *Name* values—you can ignore them for now.)

6. Display the PhoneNumber.cs file in the Code and Text Editor window, and examine the *PhoneNumber* structure. It is similar to the *Name* structure.

7. Display the PhoneBook.cs file in the Code and Text Editor window, and examine the *PhoneBook* class.

   This class contains two private arrays: an array of *Name* values called *names*, and an array of *PhoneNumber* values called *phoneNumbers*. The *PhoneBook* class also contains an *Add* method that adds a phone number and name to the phone book. This method is called when the user clicks the Add button on the form. The *enlargeIfFull* method is called by *Add* to check whether the arrays are full when the user adds another entry. This method creates two new, bigger arrays, copies the contents of the existing arrays to them, and then discards the old arrays.

The *Add* method is deliberately kept simple and does not check whether a name or phone number has already been added to the phone book.

The *PhoneBook* class does not currently provide any functionality with which a user can find a name or telephone number; you will add two indexers to provide this facility in the next exercise.

Write the indexers

1. In the PhoneBook.cs file, delete the comment *// TODO: write 1st indexer here* and replace it with a public read-only indexer for the *PhoneBook* class, as shown in bold in the code that follows. The indexer should return a *Name* and take a *PhoneNumber* item as its index. Leave the body of the *get* accessor blank.

   The indexer should look like this:

   ```
   sealed class PhoneBook
   {
       ...
       public Name this[PhoneNumber number]
       {
           get
           {
           }
       }
       ...
   }
   ```

2. Implement the *get* accessor as shown in bold in the code that follows.

   The purpose of the accessor is to find the name that matches the specified phone number. To do this, you need to call the static *IndexOf* method of the *Array* class. The *IndexOf* method performs a search through an array, returning the index of the first item in the array that matches the specified value. The first argument to *IndexOf* is the array to search through (*phoneNumbers*). The second argument to *IndexOf* is the item for which you are searching. *IndexOf* returns the integer index of the element if it finds it; otherwise, *IndexOf* returns –1. If the indexer finds the phone number, it should return the corresponding name, otherwise, it should return an empty *Name* value. (Note that *Name* is a structure, so the default constructor sets its private *name* field to *null*.)

   ```
   sealed class PhoneBook
   {
       ...
       public Name this [PhoneNumber number]
       {
           get
           {
   ```

```
            int i = Array.IndexOf(this.phoneNumbers, number);
            if (i != -1)
            {
                return this.names[i];
            }
            else
            {
                return new Name();
            }
        }
    }
    ...
}
```

3. Remove the comment *// TODO: write 2nd indexer here* and replace it with a second public read-only indexer for the *PhoneBook* class that returns a *PhoneNumber* and accepts a single *Name* parameter. Implement this indexer in the same way as the first one. (Again, note that *PhoneNumber* is a structure and therefore always has a default constructor.)

The second indexer should look like this:

```
sealed class PhoneBook
{
    ...
    public PhoneNumber this [Name name]
    {
        get
        {
            int i = Array.IndexOf(this.names, name);
            if (i != -1)
            {
                return this.phoneNumbers[i];
            }
            else
            {
                return new PhoneNumber();
            }
        }
    }
    ...
}
```

Notice that these overloaded indexers can coexist because the values that they index are of different types, which means that their signatures are different. If the *Name* and *PhoneNumber* structures were replaced by simple strings (which they wrap), the overloads would have the same signature and the class would not compile.

4. On the Build menu, click Build Solution, correct any syntax errors, and then rebuild the solution if necessary.

1. Display the MainPage.xaml.cs file in the Code and Text Editor window, and then locate the *findByNameClick* method.

This method is called when the Find By Name button is clicked. This method is currently empty. Replace the *// TODO:* comment with the code shown in bold in the example that follows. This code performs these tasks:

a. Reads the value of the *Text* property from the *name* text box on the form. This is a string containing the contact name that the user has typed in.

b. If the string is not empty, the code searches for the phone number corresponding to that name in the *PhoneBook* by using the indexer. (Notice that the *MainPage* class contains a private *PhoneBook* field named *phoneBook*.) It constructs a *Name* object from the string, and passes it as the parameter to the *PhoneBook* indexer.

c. If the *Text* property of the *PhoneNumber* structure returned by the indexer is not *null* or empty, the code writes the value of this property to the *phoneNumber* text box on the form; otherwise, it displays the text "Not Found".

The completed *findByNameClick* method should look like this:

```
private void findByNameClick(object sender, RoutedEventArgs e)
{
    string text = name.Text;
    if (!String.IsNullOrEmpty(text))
    {
        Name personsName = new Name(text);
        PhoneNumber personsPhoneNumber = this.phoneBook[personsName];
        phoneNumber.Text = String.IsNullOrEmpty(personsPhoneNumber.Text) ?
            "Not Found" : personsPhoneNumber.Text;
    }
}
```

Other than the statement that accesses the indexer, there are two further points of interest in this code:

- The static *String* method *IsNullOrEmpty* is used to determine whether a string is empty or contains a *null* value. This is the preferred method for testing whether a string contains a value. It returns *true* if the string contains a null value or it is an empty string; otherwise, it returns *false*.

- The *? :* operator used by the statement that populates the *Text* property of the *phone-Number* text box on the form acts like an inline *if...else* statement for an expression. It is a ternary operator that takes the following three operands: a Boolean expression, an expression to evaluate and return if the Boolean expression is true, and another expression to evaluate and return if the Boolean expression is false. In the preceding code, if the expression *String.IsNullOrEmpty(personsPhoneNumber.Text)* is true, no matching entry was found in the phone book and the text "Not Found" is displayed on the form; otherwise, the value held in the *Text* property of the *personsPhoneNumber* variable is displayed.

The general form of the *?:* operator is as follows:

```
Result = <Boolean Expression> ? <Evaluate if true> : <Evaluate if false>
```

2. Locate the *findByPhoneNumberClick* method in the MainPage.xaml.cs file. It is below the *findByNameClick* method.

The *findByPhoneNumberClick* method is called when the Find By Phone Number button is clicked. This method is currently empty apart from a *// TODO:* comment. You need to implement it as follows (the completed code is shown in bold in the example that follows):

a. Read the value of the *Text* property from the *phoneNumber* box on the form. This is a string containing the phone number that the user has typed.

b. If the string is not empty, use the indexer to search for the name corresponding to that phone number in the *PhoneBook*.

c. Write the *Text* property of the *Name* structure returned by the indexer to the *name* box on the form.

The completed method should look like this:

```
private void findByPhoneNumberClick(object sender, RoutedEventArgs e)
{
    string text = phoneNumber.Text;
    if (!String.IsNullOrEmpty(text))
    {
        PhoneNumber personsPhoneNumber = new PhoneNumber(text);
        Name personsName = this.phoneBook[personsPhoneNumber];
        name.Text = String.IsNullOrEmpty(personsName.Text) ?
            "Not Found" : personsName.Text;
    }
}
```

3. On the Build menu, click Build Solution, and then correct any errors that occur.

Test the application

1. On the Debug menu, click Start Debugging.

2. Type your name and phone number in the appropriate boxes, and then expand the command bar and click Add. (You can expand the command bar by clicking the ellipsis.)

When you click the Add button, the *Add* method stores the information in the phone book and clears the text boxes so that they are ready to perform a search.

3. Repeat step 2 several times with some different names and phone numbers so that the phone book contains a selection of entries. Note that the application performs no checking of the names and telephone numbers that you enter, and you can input the same name and telephone number more than once. For the purposes of this demonstration, to avoid confusion, be sure that you provide different names and telephone numbers.

4. Type a name that you used in step 3 into the Name box, and then click Find By Name.

   The phone number you added for this contact in step 3 is retrieved from the phone book and is displayed in the Phone Number text box.

5. Type a phone number for a different contact in the Phone Number box, and then click Find By Phone Number.

   The contact name is retrieved from the phone book and is displayed in the Name box.

6. Type a name that you did not enter in the phone book into the Name box, and then click Find By Name.

   This time, the Phone Number box displays the message "Not Found".

7. Close the form, and return to Visual Studio 2015.

Summary

In this chapter, you saw how to use indexers to provide array-like access to data in a class. You learned how to create indexers that can take an index and return the corresponding value by using logic defined by the *get* accessor, and you saw how to use the *set* accessor with an index to populate a value in an indexer.

- If you want to continue to the next chapter, keep Visual Studio 2015 running and turn to Chapter 17, "Introducing generics."

- If you want to exit Visual Studio 2015 now, on the File menu, click Exit. If you see a Save dialog box, click Yes and save the project.

Quick reference

To	Do this
| Create an indexer for a class or structure | Declare the type of the indexer, followed by the keyword *this*, and then the indexer arguments in square brackets. The body of the indexer can contain a *get* and/or *set* accessor. For example:<br><br>```csharp
struct RawInt
{
    ...
    public bool this [ int index ]
    {
        get { ... }
        set { ... }
    }
    ...
}
``` |
| Define an indexer in an interface | Define an indexer with the *get* and/or *set* keywords. For example:<br><br>```csharp
interface IRawInt
{
    bool this [ int index ] { get;  set; }
}
``` |
| Implement an interface indexer in a class or structure | In the class or structure that implements the interface, define the indexer and implement the accessors. For example:<br><br>```csharp
struct RawInt : IRawInt
{
    ...
    public bool this [ int index  ]
    {
        get { ... }
        set { ... }
    }
    ...
}
``` |
| Implement an indexer defined by an interface by using explicit interface implementation in a class or structure | In the class or structure that implements the interface, specify the interface but do not specify the indexer accessibility. For example:<br><br>```csharp
struct RawInt : IRawInt
{
    ...
    bool IRawInt.this [ int index  ]
    {
        get { ... }
        set { ... }
    }
    ...
}
``` |

CHAPTER 17

Introducing generics

After completing this chapter, you will be able to:

- Explain the purpose of generics.

- Define a type-safe class by using generics.

- Create instances of a generic class based on types specified as type parameters.

- Implement a generic interface.

- Define a generic method that implements an algorithm independent of the type of data on which it operates.

Chapter 8, "Understanding values and references," shows you how to use the *object* type to refer to an instance of any class. You can use the *object* type to store a value of any type, and you can define parameters by using the *object* type when you need to pass values of any type into a method. A method can also return values of any type by specifying *object* as the return type. Although this practice is very flexible, it puts the onus on the programmer to remember what sort of data is actually being used. This can lead to run-time errors if the programmer makes a mistake. In this chapter, you will learn about generics, a feature that has been designed to help you prevent this kind of mistake.

The problem with the *object* type

To understand generics, it is worth looking in detail at the problem they are designed to solve.

Suppose that you need to model a first-in, first-out structure such as a queue. You could create a class such as the following:

```
class Queue
{
    private const int DEFAULTQUEUESIZE = 100;
    private int[] data;
    private int head = 0, tail = 0;
    private int numElements = 0;

    public Queue()
    {
        this.data = new int[DEFAULTQUEUESIZE];
    }
```

```csharp
    public Queue(int size)
    {
        if (size > 0)
        {
            this.data = new int[size];
        }
        else
        {
            throw new ArgumentOutOfRangeException("size", "Must be greater than zero");
        }
    }

    public void Enqueue(int item)
    {
        if (this.numElements == this.data.Length)
        {
            throw new Exception("Queue full");
        }

        this.data[this.head] = item;
        this.head++;
        this.head %= this.data.Length;
        this.numElements++;
    }

    public int Dequeue()
    {
        if (this.numElements == 0)
        {
            throw new Exception("Queue empty");
        }

        int queueItem = this.data[this.tail];
        this.tail++;
        this.tail %= this.data.Length;
        this.numElements--;
        return queueItem;
    }
}
```

This class uses an array to provide a circular buffer for holding the data. The size of this array is specified by the constructor. An application uses the *Enqueue* method to add an item to the queue and the *Dequeue* method to pull an item off the queue. The private *head* and *tail* fields keep track of where to insert an item into the array and where to retrieve an item from the array. The *numElements* field indicates how many items are in the array. The *Enqueue* and *Dequeue* methods use these fields to determine where to store or retrieve an item and perform some rudimentary error checking. An application can create a *Queue* object and call these methods, as shown in the code example that follows. Notice that the items are dequeued in the same order in which they are enqueued:

```csharp
Queue queue = new Queue(); // Create a new Queue

queue.Enqueue(100);
queue.Enqueue(-25);
queue.Enqueue(33);
```

```
Console.WriteLine($"{queue.Dequeue()}");  // Displays 100
Console.WriteLine($"{queue.Dequeue()}");  // Displays -25
Console.WriteLine($"{queue.Dequeue()}");  // Displays 33
```

Now, the *Queue* class works well for queues of *int*s, but what if you want to create queues of strings, or floats, or even queues of more complex types such as *Circle* (see Chapter 7, "Creating and managing classes and objects"), or *Horse* or *Whale* (see Chapter 12, "Working with inheritance")? The problem is that the way in which the *Queue* class is implemented restricts it to items of type *int*, and if you try to enqueue a *Horse*, you will get a compile-time error.

```
Queue queue = new Queue();
Horse myHorse = new Horse();
queue.Enqueue(myHorse); // Compile-time error: Cannot convert from Horse to int
```

One way around this restriction is to specify that the array in the *Queue* class contains items of type *object*, update the constructors, and modify the *Enqueue* and *Dequeue* methods to take an *object* parameter and return an *object,* such as in the following:

```
class Queue
{
    ...
    private object[] data;
    ...
    public Queue()
    {
        this.data = new object[DEFAULTQUEUESIZE];
    }

    public Queue(int size)
    {
        ...
        this.data = new object[size];
        ...
    }

    public void Enqueue(object item)
    {
        ...
    }

    public object Dequeue()
    {
        ...
        object queueItem = this.data[this.tail];
        ...
        return queueItem;
    }
}
```

Remember that you can use the *object* type to refer to a value or variable of any type. All reference types automatically inherit (either directly or indirectly) from the *System.Object* class in the Microsoft .NET Framework (in C#, *object* is an alias for *System.Object*). Now, because the *Enqueue* and *Dequeue* methods manipulate *objects*, you can operate on queues of *Circles, Horses, Whales,* or any of the other classes that you have seen earlier in this book. However, it is important to notice that you have to cast the value returned by the *Dequeue* method to the appropriate type because the compiler will not perform the conversion from the *object* type automatically.

```
Queue queue = new Queue();
Horse myHorse = new Horse();
queue.Enqueue(myHorse); // Now legal - Horse is an object

...
Horse dequeuedHorse = (Horse)queue.Dequeue(); // Need to cast object back to a Horse
```

If you don't cast the returned value, you will get the compiler error "Cannot implicitly convert type 'object' to 'Horse.'" This requirement to perform an explicit cast degenerates much of the flexibility afforded by the *object* type. Furthermore, it is very easy to write code such as this:

```
Queue queue = new Queue();
Horse myHorse = new Horse();
queue.Enqueue(myHorse);
...
Circle myCircle = (Circle)queue.Dequeue(); // run-time error
```

Although this code will compile, it is not valid and throws a *System.InvalidCastException* exception at run time. The error is caused by trying to store a reference to a *Horse* in a *Circle* variable when it is dequeued, and the two types are not compatible. This error is not spotted until run time because the compiler does not have enough information to perform this check at compile time. The real type of the object being dequeued becomes apparent only when the code runs.

Another disadvantage of using the *object* approach to create generalized classes and methods is that it can consume additional memory and processor time if the runtime needs to convert an *object* to a value type and back again. Consider the following piece of code that manipulates a queue of *int* values:

```
Queue queue = new Queue();
int myInt = 99;
queue.Enqueue(myInt);          // box the int to an object
...
myInt = (int)queue.Dequeue(); // unbox the object to an int
```

The *Queue* data type expects the items it holds to be objects, and *object* is a reference type. Enqueueing a value type, such as an *int*, requires it to be boxed to convert it to a reference type. Similarly, dequeueing into an *int* requires the item to be unboxed to convert it back to a value type. (See the sections "Boxing" and "Unboxing" in Chapter 8 for more details.) Although boxing and unboxing happen transparently, they add performance overhead because they involve dynamic memory allocations. This overhead is small for each item, but it adds up when a program creates queues of large numbers of value types.

The generics solution

C# provides generics to remove the need for casting, improve type safety, reduce the amount of boxing required, and make it easier to create generalized classes and methods. Generic classes and methods accept *type parameters*, which specify the types of objects on which they operate. In C#, you indicate that a class is a generic class by providing a type parameter in angle brackets, like this:

```
class Queue<T>
{
    ...
}
```

The *T* in this example acts as a placeholder for a real type at compile time. When you write code to instantiate a generic *Queue*, you provide the type that should be substituted for *T* (*Circle*, *Horse*, *int*, and so on). When you define the fields and methods in the class, you use this same placeholder to indicate the type of these items, like this:

```
class Queue<T>
{
    ...
    private T[] data; // array is of type 'T' where 'T' is the type parameter
    ...
    public Queue()
    {
        this.data = new T[DEFAULTQUEUESIZE]; // use 'T' as the data type
    }

    public Queue(int size)
    {
        ...
        this.data = new T[size];
        ...
    }

    public void Enqueue(T item)  // use 'T' as the type of the method parameter
    {
        ...
    }

    public T Dequeue() // use 'T' as the type of the return value
    {
        ...
        T queueItem = this.data[this.tail];  // the data in the array is of type 'T'
        ...
        return queueItem;
    }
}
```

The type parameter *T* can be any legal C# identifier, although the lone character *T* is commonly used. It is replaced with the type you specify when you create a *Queue* object. The following examples create a *Queue* of *int*s and a *Queue* of *Horses*:

```
Queue<int> intQueue = new Queue<int>();
Queue<Horse> horseQueue = new Queue<Horse>();
```

Additionally, the compiler now has enough information to perform strict type checking when you build the application. You no longer need to cast data when you call the *Dequeue* method, and the compiler can trap any type mismatch errors early:

```
intQueue.Enqueue(99);
int myInt = intQueue.Dequeue();     // no casting necessary
Horse myHorse = intQueue.Dequeue(); // compiler error: cannot implicitly convert type 'int' to
'Horse'
```

You should be aware that this substitution of *T* for a specified type is not simply a textual replacement mechanism. Instead, the compiler performs a complete semantic substitution so that you can specify any valid type for *T*. Here are more examples:

```
struct Person
{
    ...
}
...
Queue<int> intQueue = new Queue<int>();
Queue<Person> personQueue = new Queue<Person>();
```

The first example creates a queue of integers, whereas the second example creates a queue of *Person* values. The compiler also generates the versions of the *Enqueue* and *Dequeue* methods for each queue. For the *intQueue* queue, these methods look like this:

```
public void Enqueue(int item);
public int Dequeue();
```

For the *personQueue* queue, these methods look like this:

```
public void Enqueue(Person item);
public Person Dequeue();
```

Contrast these definitions with those of the object-based version of the *Queue* class shown in the preceding section. In the methods derived from the generic class, the *item* parameter to *Enqueue* is passed as a value type that does not require boxing. Similarly, the value returned by *Dequeue* is also a value type that does not need to be unboxed. A similar set of methods is generated for the other two queues.

> **Note** The *System.Collections.Generic* namespace in the .NET Framework class library provides an implementation to the *Queue* class that operates in a similar manner to the class just described. This namespace also includes several other collection classes, and they are described in more detail in Chapter 18, "Using collections."

The type parameter does not have to be a simple class or value type. For example, you can create a queue of queues of integers (if you should ever find it necessary), like this:

```
Queue<Queue<int>> queueQueue = new Queue<Queue<int>>();
```

A generic class can have multiple type parameters. For example, the generic *Dictionary* class defined in the *System.Collections.Generic* namespace in the .NET Framework class library expects two type parameters: one type for keys, and another for the values (this class is described in more detail in Chapter 18).

> **Note** You can also define generic structures and interfaces by using the same type-parameter syntax as for generic classes.

Generics vs. generalized classes

It is important to be aware that a generic class that uses type parameters is different from a *generalized* class designed to take parameters that can be cast to different types. For example, the object-based version of the *Queue* class shown earlier is a generalized class. There is a *single* implementation of this class, and its methods take *object* parameters and return *object* types. You can use this class with *ints*, *strings*, and many other types, but in each case you are using instances of the same class and you have to cast the data you are using to and from the *object* type.

Compare this with the *Queue<T>* class. Each time you use this class with a type parameter (such as *Queue<int>* or *Queue<Horse>*), you cause the compiler to generate an entirely new class that happens to have functionality defined by the generic class. This means that *Queue<int>* is a completely different type from *Queue<Horse>*, but they both happen to have the same behavior. You can think of a generic class as one that defines a template that is then used by the compiler to generate new type-specific classes on demand. The type-specific versions of a generic class (*Queue<int>*, *Queue<Horse>*, and so on) are referred to as *constructed types*, and you should treat them as distinctly different types (albeit ones that have a similar set of methods and properties).

Generics and constraints

Occasionally, you will want to ensure that the type parameter used by a generic class identifies a type that provides certain methods. For example, if you are defining a *PrintableCollection* class, you might want to ensure that all objects stored in the class have a *Print* method. You can specify this condition by using a *constraint*.

By using a constraint, you can limit the type parameters of a generic class to those that implement a particular set of interfaces and therefore provide the methods defined by those interfaces. For example, if the *IPrintable* interface defined the *Print* method, you could create the *PrintableCollection* class like this:

```
public class PrintableCollection<T> where T : IPrintable
```

When you build this class with a type parameter, the compiler checks to be sure that the type used for *T* actually implements the *IPrintable* interface; if it doesn't, it stops with a compilation error.

Creating a generic class

The *System.Collections.Generic* namespace in the .NET Framework class library contains a number of generic classes readily available for you. You can also define your own generic classes, which is what you will do in this section. Before you do this, let's cover a bit of background theory.

The theory of binary trees

In the following exercises, you will define and use a class that represents a binary tree.

A *binary tree* is a useful data structure that you can use for a variety of operations, including sorting and searching through data very quickly. Volumes have been written on the minutiae of binary trees, but it is not the purpose of this book to cover this topic in detail. Instead, you'll look at just the pertinent facts. If you are interested in learning more, consult a book such as *The Art of Computer Programming, Volume 3: Sorting and Searching, 2nd Edition* by Donald E. Knuth (Addison-Wesley Professional, 1998). Despite its age, this is the recognized, seminal work on sort and search algorithms.

A binary tree is a recursive (self-referencing) data structure that can be empty or contain three elements: a datum, which is typically referred to as the *node*, and two subtrees, which are themselves binary trees. The two subtrees are conventionally called the *left subtree* and the *right subtree* because they are typically depicted to the left and right of the node, respectively. Each left subtree or right subtree is either empty or contains a node and other subtrees. In theory, the whole structure can continue ad infinitum. The following image shows the structure of a small binary tree.

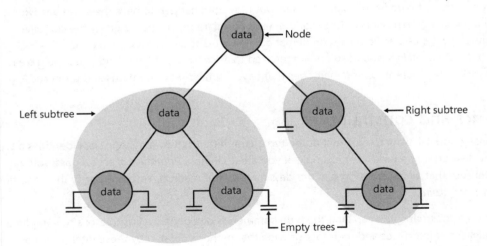

The real power of binary trees becomes evident when you use them for sorting data. If you start with an unordered sequence of objects of the same type, you can construct an ordered binary tree and then walk through the tree to visit each node in an ordered sequence. The algorithm for inserting an item *I* into an ordered binary tree *B* is shown here:

```
If the tree, B, is empty
Then
  Construct a new tree B with the new item I as the node, and empty left and
  right subtrees
Else
  Examine the value of the current node, N, of the tree, B
  If the value of N is greater than that of the new item, I
  Then
    If the left subtree of B is empty
    Then
      Construct a new left subtree of B with the item I as the node, and
      empty left and right subtrees
    Else
      Insert I into the left subtree of B
    End If
  Else
    If the right subtree of B is empty
    Then
      Construct a new right subtree of B with the item I as the node, and
      empty left and right subtrees
    Else
      Insert I into the right subtree of B
    End If
  End If
End If
```

Notice that this algorithm is recursive, calling itself to insert the item into the left or right subtree depending on how the value of the item compares with the current node in the tree.

> **Note** The definition of the expression *greater than* depends on the type of data in the item and node. For numeric data, greater than can be a simple arithmetic comparison, and for text data, it can be a string comparison; however, you must give other forms of data their own means of comparing values. You will learn more about this when you implement a binary tree in the upcoming section "Building a binary tree class by using generics."

If you start with an empty binary tree and an unordered sequence of objects, you can iterate through the unordered sequence, inserting each object into the binary tree by using this algorithm, resulting in an ordered tree. The next image shows the steps in the process for constructing a tree from a set of five integers.

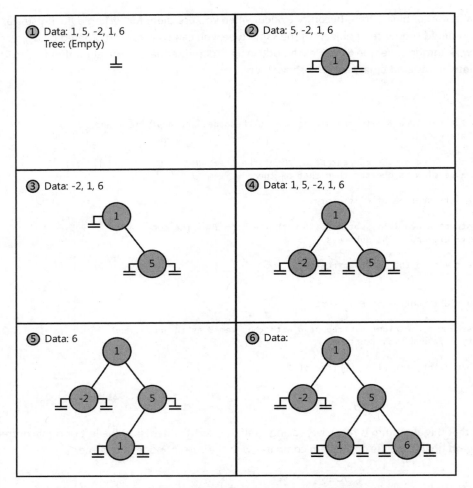

After you have built an ordered binary tree, you can display its contents in sequence by visiting each node in turn and printing the value found. The algorithm for achieving this task is also recursive:

```
If the left subtree is not empty
Then
  Display the contents of the left subtree
End If
Display the value of the node
If the right subtree is not empty
Then
  Display the contents of the right subtree
End If
```

The following image shows the steps in the process for outputting the tree. Notice that the integers are now displayed in ascending order.

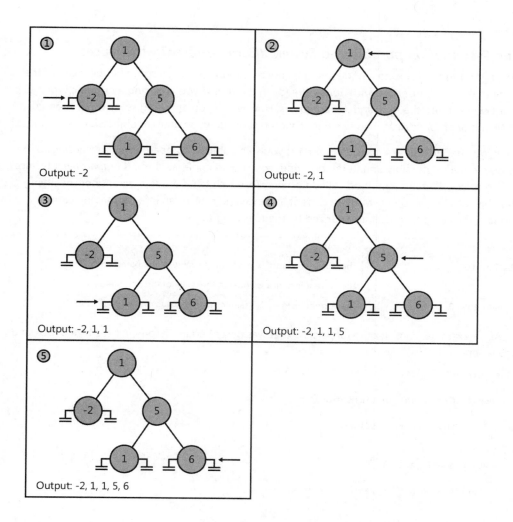

Building a binary tree class by using generics

In the following exercise, you will use generics to define a binary tree class capable of holding almost any type of data. The only restriction is that the data type must provide a means of comparing values between different instances.

The binary tree class is one that you might find useful in many different applications. Therefore, you will implement it as a class library rather than as an application in its own right. You can then use this class elsewhere without having to copy the source code and recompile it. A *class library* is a set of compiled classes (and other types such as structures and delegates) stored in an assembly. An assembly is a file that usually has the .dll suffix. Other projects and applications can make use of the items in a class library by adding a reference to its assembly and then bringing its namespaces into scope by employing *using* directives. You will do this when you test the binary tree class.

The *System.IComparable* and *System.IComparable\<T\>* interfaces

The algorithm for inserting a node into a binary tree requires you to compare the value of the node that you are inserting with nodes already in the tree. If you are using a numeric type, such as *int*, you can use the <, >, and == operators. However, if you are using some other type, such as *Mammal* or *Circle* described in earlier chapters, how do you compare objects?

If you need to create a class that requires you to be able to compare values according to some natural (or possibly unnatural) ordering, you should implement the *IComparable* interface. This interface contains a method called *CompareTo*, which takes a single parameter specifying the object to be compared with the current instance and returns an integer that indicates the result of the comparison, as summarized by the following table.

Value	Meaning
Less than 0	The current instance is less than the value of the parameter.
0	The current instance is equal to the value of the parameter.
Greater than 0	The current instance is greater than the value of the parameter.

As an example, consider the *Circle* class that was described in Chapter 7. Let's take a look at it again here:

```
class Circle
{
    public Circle(int initialRadius)
    {
        radius = initialRadius;
    }

    public double Area()
    {
        return Math.PI * radius * radius;
    }

    private double radius;
}
```

You can make the *Circle* class "comparable" by implementing the *System.IComparable* inter-face and providing the *CompareTo* method. In this example, the *CompareTo* method compares *Circle* objects based on their areas. A circle with a larger area is considered to be greater than a circle with a smaller area.

```
class Circle : System.IComparable
{
    ...
    public int CompareTo(object obj)
    {
        Circle circObj = (Circle)obj; // cast the parameter to its real type
        if (this.Area() == circObj.Area())
            return 0;
```

```
            if (this.Area() > circObj.Area())
                return 1;

            return -1;
        }
    }
```

If you examine the *System.IComparable* interface, you will see that its parameter is defined as an *object*. However, this approach is not type safe. To understand why this is so, consider what happens if you try to pass something that is not a *Circle* to the *CompareTo* method. The *System.IComparable* interface requires the use of a cast to access the *Area* method. If the parameter is not a *Circle* but some other type of object, this cast will fail. However, the *System* namespace also defines the generic *IComparable<T>* interface, which contains the following method:

```
int CompareTo(T other);
```

Notice that this method takes a type parameter (*T*) rather than an *object,* and therefore it is much safer than the nongeneric version of the interface. The following code shows how you can implement this interface in the *Circle* class:

```
class Circle : System.IComparable<Circle>
{
    ...
    public int CompareTo(Circle other)
    {
        if (this.Area() == other.Area())
            return 0;

        if (this.Area() > other.Area())
            return 1;

        return -1;
    }
}
```

The parameter for the *CompareTo* method must match the type specified in the interface, *IComparable<Circle>*. In general, it is preferable to implement the *System.IComparable<T>* interface rather than the *System.IComparable* interface. You can also implement both, just as many of the types in the .NET Framework do.

Create the *Tree<TItem>* class

1. Start Microsoft Visual Studio 2015 if it is not already running.

2. On the File menu, point to New, and then click Project.

3. In the New Project dialog box, in the Templates pane on the left, click Visual C#. In the middle pane, select the Class Library template. In the Name box, type **BinaryTree**. In the Location box, specify \Microsoft Press\VCSBS\Chapter 17 in your Documents folder, and then click OK.

> **Note** Using the Class Library template, you can create assemblies that can be used by multiple applications. To use a class in a class library in an application, you must first copy the assembly containing the compiled code for the class library to your computer (if you did not create it yourself) and then add a reference to this assembly.

4. In Solution Explorer, right-click Class1.cs, click Rename, and then change the name of the file to **Tree.cs**. Allow Visual Studio to change the name of the class as well as the name of the file when you are prompted.

5. In the Code and Text Editor window, change the definition of the *Tree* class to *Tree<TItem>*, as shown in bold in the following code:

```
public class Tree<TItem>
{
}
```

6. In the Code and Text Editor window, modify the definition of the *Tree<TItem>* class to specify that the type parameter *TItem* must denote a type that implements the generic *IComparable<TItem>* interface. The changes are highlighted in bold in the code example that follows.

   The modified definition of the *Tree<TItem>* class should look like this:

```
public class Tree<TItem> where TItem : IComparable<TItem>
{
}
```

7. Add three public, automatic properties to the *Tree<TItem>* class: a *TItem* property called *NodeData* and *Tree<TItem>* properties called *LeftTree* and *RightTree*, as shown in the following code example in bold:

```
public class Tree<TItem> where TItem : IComparable<TItem>
{
    public TItem NodeData { get; set; }
    public Tree<TItem> LeftTree { get; set; }
    public Tree<TItem> RightTree { get; set; }
}
```

8. Add a constructor to the *Tree<TItem>* class that takes a single *TItem* parameter called *nodeValue*. In the constructor, set the *NodeData* property to *nodeValue*, and initialize the *LeftTree* and *RightTree* properties to *null*, as shown in bold in the following code:

```
public class Tree<TItem> where TItem : IComparable<TItem>
{
    ...
    public Tree(TItem nodeValue)
    {
        this.NodeData = nodeValue;
```

```
        this.LeftTree = null;
        this.RightTree = null;
    }
}
```

> **Note** Notice that the name of the constructor does not include the type parameter; it is called *Tree*, not *Tree<TItem>*.

9. Add a public method called *Insert* to the *Tree<TItem>* class as shown in bold in the code that follows. This method inserts a *TItem* value into the tree.

   The method definition should look like this:

```
public class Tree<TItem> where TItem: IComparable<TItem>
{
    ...
    public void Insert(TItem newItem)
    {
    }
}
```

   The *Insert* method implements the recursive algorithm described earlier for creating an ordered binary tree. The constructor creates the initial node of the tree, so the *Insert* method can assume that the tree is not empty. The code that follows is the part of the algorithm that runs after checking whether the tree is empty. It's reproduced here to help you understand the code you will write for the *Insert* method in the following steps:

```
...
Examine the value of the node, N, of the tree, B
If the value of N is greater than that of the new item, I
Then
  If the left subtree of B is empty
  Then
    Construct a new left subtree of B with the item I as the node, and empty
    left and right subtrees
  Else
    Insert I into the left subtree of B
End If
...
```

10. In the *Insert* method, add a statement that declares a local variable of type *TItem*, called *currentNodeValue*. Initialize this variable to the value of the *NodeData* property of the tree, as shown in bold in the following example:

```
public void Insert(TItem newItem)
{
    TItem currentNodeValue = this.NodeData;
}
```

11. Add the *if-else* statement shown in bold in the following code to the *Insert* method after the definition of the *currentNodeValue* variable.

This statement uses the *CompareTo* method of the *IComparable<T>* interface to determine whether the value of the current node is greater than that of the new item:

```
public void Insert(TItem newItem)
{
    TItem currentNodeValue = this.NodeData;
    if (currentNodeValue.CompareTo(newItem) > 0)
    {
        // Insert the new item into the left subtree
    }
    else
    {
        // Insert the new item into the right subtree
    }
}
```

12. In the *if* part of the code, immediately after the comment *// Insert the new item into the left subtree*, add the following statements:

```
if (this.LeftTree == null)
{
    this.LeftTree = new Tree<TItem>(newItem);
}
else
{
    this.LeftTree.Insert(newItem);
}
```

These statements check whether the left subtree is empty. If so, a new tree is created using the new item and it is attached as the left subtree of the current node; otherwise, the new item is inserted into the existing left subtree by calling the *Insert* method recursively.

13. In the *else* part of the outermost *if-else* statement, immediately after the comment *// Insert the new item into the right subtree*, add the equivalent code that inserts the new node into the right subtree:

```
if (this.RightTree == null)
{
    this.RightTree = new Tree<TItem>(newItem);
}
else
{
    this.RightTree.Insert(newItem);
}
```

14. Add another public method called *WalkTree* to the *Tree<TItem>* class after the *Insert* method.

This method walks through the tree, visiting each node in sequence, and generates a string representation of the data that the tree contains. The method definition should look like this:

```
public string WalkTree()
{
}
```

15. Add to the *WalkTree* method the statements shown in bold in the code that follows.

These statements implement the algorithm described earlier for traversing a binary tree. As each node is visited, the node value is returned by the method to the string:

```
public string WalkTree()
{
    string result = "";

    if (this.LeftTree != null)
    {
        result = this.LeftTree.WalkTree();
    }

    result += $" {this.NodeData.ToString()} ";

    if (this.RightTree != null)
    {
        result += this.RightTree.WalkTree();
    }

    return result;
}
```

16. On the Build menu, click Build Solution. The class should compile cleanly, but correct any errors that are reported and rebuild the solution if necessary.

In the next exercise, you will test the *Tree<TItem>* class by creating binary trees of integers and strings.

Test the *Tree<TItem>* class

1. In Solution Explorer, right-click the BinaryTree solution, point to Add, and then click New Project.

> **Note** Be sure that you right-click the BinaryTree *solution* rather than the BinaryTree *project*.

2. Add a new project by using the Console Application template. Give the project the name **BinaryTreeTest**. Set the location to \Microsoft Press\VCSBS\Chapter 17 in your Documents folder, and then click OK.

> **Note** A Visual Studio 2015 solution can contain more than one project. You are using this feature to add a second project to the BinaryTree solution for testing the *Tree<TItem>* class.

3. In Solution Explorer, right-click the BinaryTreeTest project, and then click Set As Startup Project.

   The BinaryTreeTest project is highlighted in Solution Explorer. When you run the application, this is the project that will actually execute.

4. In Solution Explorer, right-click the BinaryTreeTest project, point to Add, and then click Reference.

5. In the left pane of the Reference Manager – BinaryTreeTest dialog box, expand Projects and then click Solution. In the middle pane, select the BinaryTree project (be sure to select the check box and not simply click the assembly), and then click OK.

This step adds the *BinaryTree* assembly to the list of references for the BinaryTreeTest project in Solution Explorer. If you examine the References folder for the BinaryTreeTest project in Solution Explorer, you should see the *BinaryTree* assembly listed at the top. You will now be able to create *Tree<TItem>* objects in the BinaryTreeTest project.

> **Note** If the class library project is not part of the same solution as the project that uses it, you must add a reference to the assembly (the .dll file) and not to the class library project. You can do this by browsing for the assembly in the Reference Manager dialog box. You will use this technique in the final set of exercises in this chapter.

6. In the Code and Text Editor window displaying the *Program* class in the Program.cs file, add the following *using* directive to the list at the top of the class:

```
using BinaryTree;
```

7. Add to the *Main* method the statements shown in bold in the following code:

```
static void Main(string[] args)
{
    Tree<int> tree1 = new Tree<int>(10);
    tree1.Insert(5);
    tree1.Insert(11);
    tree1.Insert(5);
    tree1.Insert(-12);
    tree1.Insert(15);
    tree1.Insert(0);
    tree1.Insert(14);
    tree1.Insert(-8);
    tree1.Insert(10);
    tree1.Insert(8);
    tree1.Insert(8);

    string sortedData = tree1.WalkTree();
    Console.WriteLine($"Sorted data is: {sortedData}");
}
```

These statements create a new binary tree for holding *ints*. The constructor creates an initial node containing the value 10. The *Insert* statements add nodes to the tree, and the *WalkTree* method generates a string representing the contents of the tree, which should appear sorted in ascending order when this string is displayed.

> **Note** Remember that the *int* keyword in C# is just an alias for the *System.Int32* type; whenever you declare an *int* variable, you are actually declaring a *struct* variable of type *System.Int32*. The *System.Int32* type implements the *IComparable* and *IComparable<T>* interfaces, which is why you can create *Tree<int>* objects. Similarly, the *string* keyword is an alias for *System.String*, which also implements *IComparable* and *IComparable<T>*.

8. On the Build menu, click Build Solution, and verify that the solution compiles. Correct any errors if necessary.

9. On the Debug menu, click Start Without Debugging.

Verify that the program runs and displays the values in the following sequence:

–12 –8 0 5 5 8 8 10 10 11 14 15

10. Press the Enter key to return to Visual Studio 2015.

11. Add the following statements shown in bold to the end of the *Main* method in the *Program* class, after the existing code:

```
static void Main(string[] args)
{
    ...
    Tree<string> tree2 = new Tree<string>("Hello");
    tree2.Insert("World");
    tree2.Insert("How");
    tree2.Insert("Are");
    tree2.Insert("You");
    tree2.Insert("Today");
    tree2.Insert("I");
    tree2.Insert("Hope");
    tree2.Insert("You");
    tree2.Insert("Are");
    tree2.Insert("Feeling");
    tree2.Insert("Well");
    tree2.Insert("!");

    sortedData = tree2.WalkTree();
    Console.WriteLine($"Sorted data is: {sortedData}");
}
```

These statements create another binary tree for holding strings, populate it with some test data, and then print the tree. This time the data is sorted alphabetically.

12. On the Build menu, click Build Solution, and verify that the solution compiles. Correct any errors if necessary.

13. On the Debug menu, click Start Without Debugging.

Verify that the program runs and displays the integer values as before, followed by the strings in the following sequence:

! Are Are Feeling Hello Hope How I Today Well World You You

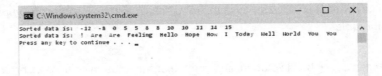

14. Press the Enter key to return to Visual Studio 2015.

Creating a generic method

As well as defining generic classes, you can create generic methods.

With a generic method, you can specify the types of the parameters and the return type by using a type parameter in a manner similar to that used when you define a generic class. In this way, you can define generalized methods that are type safe and avoid the overhead of casting (and boxing, in some cases). Generic methods are frequently used in conjunction with generic classes; you need them for methods that take generic types as parameters or that have a return type that is a generic type.

You define generic methods by using the same type parameter syntax you use when you create generic classes. (You can also specify constraints.) For example, the generic *Swap<T>* method in the code that follows swaps the values in its parameters. Because this functionality is useful regardless of the type of data being swapped, it is helpful to define it as a generic method:

```
static void Swap<T>(ref T first, ref T second)
{
    T temp = first;
    first = second;
    second = temp;
}
```

You invoke the method by specifying the appropriate type for its type parameter. The following examples show how to invoke the *Swap<T>* method to swap over two *ints* and two *strings*:

```
int a = 1, b = 2;
Swap<int>(ref a, ref b);
...
string s1 = "Hello", s2 = "World";
Swap<string>(ref s1, ref s2);
```

> **Note** Just as instantiating a generic class with different type parameters causes the compiler to generate different types, each distinct use of the *Swap<T>* method causes the compiler to generate a different version of the method. *Swap<int>* is not the same method as *Swap<string>*—both methods just happen to have been generated from the same generic template, so they exhibit the same behavior, albeit over different types.

Defining a generic method to build a binary tree

In the previous exercise, you created a generic class for implementing a binary tree. The *Tree<TItem>* class provides the *Insert* method for adding data items to the tree. However, if you want to add a large number of items, repeated calls to the *Insert* method are not very convenient. In the following exercise, you will define a generic method called *InsertIntoTree* that you can use to insert a list of data items into a tree with a single method call. You will test this method by using it to insert a list of characters into a tree of characters.

Write the *InsertIntoTree* method

1. Using Visual Studio 2015, create a new project by using the Console Application template. In the New Project dialog box, name the project **BuildTree**. Set the location to \Microsoft Press\ VCSBS\Chapter 17 in your Documents folder. In the Solution drop-down list, click Create New Solution, and then click OK.

2. On the Project menu, click Add Reference. In the Reference Manager – BuildTree dialog box, click the Browse button (not the Browse tab in the left pane).

3. In the Select The Files To Reference dialog box, browse to the folder \Microsoft Press\VCSBS\ Chapter 17\BinaryTree\BinaryTree\bin\Debug in your Documents folder, click BinaryTree.dll, and then click Add.

4. In the Reference Manager – BuildTree dialog box, verify that the BinaryTree.dll assembly is listed and that the check box for this assembly is selected, and then click OK.

   The *BinaryTree* assembly is added to the list of references shown in Solution Explorer.

5. In the Code and Text Editor window displaying the Program.cs file, add the following *using* directive to the top of the Program.cs file:

   ```
   using BinaryTree;
   ```

   Remember, this namespace contains the *Tree<TItem>* class.

6. After the *Main* method in the *Program* class, add a method named *InsertIntoTree*. This method should be declared as a *static void* method that takes a *Tree<TItem>* parameter and a *params* array of *TItem* elements called *data*. The tree parameter should be passed by reference, for reasons that will be described in a later step.

   The method definition should look like this:

   ```
   static void InsertIntoTree<TItem>(ref Tree<TItem> tree,
       params TItem[] data)
   {
   }
   ```

7. The *TItem* type used for the elements being inserted into the binary tree must implement the *IComparable<TItem>* interface. Modify the definition of the *InsertIntoTree* method and add the *where* clause shown in bold in the following code:

   ```
   static void InsertIntoTree<TItem>(ref Tree<TItem> tree,
       params TItem[] data) where TItem :IComparable<TItem>
   {
   }
   ```

8. Add to the *InsertIntoTree* method the statements shown in bold in the example that follows.

These statements iterate through the *params* list, adding each item to the tree by using the *Insert* method. If the value specified by the tree parameter is *null* initially, a new *Tree<TItem>* is created; this is why the tree parameter is passed by reference.

```
static void InsertIntoTree<TItem>(ref Tree<TItem> tree,
params TItem[] data) where TItem : IComparable<TItem>
{
    foreach (TItem datum in data)
    {
        if (tree == null)
        {
            tree = new Tree<TItem>(datum);
        }
        else
        {
            tree.Insert(datum);
        }
    }
}
```

Test the *InsertIntoTree* method

1. In the *Main* method of the *Program* class, add the following statements shown in bold that create a new *Tree* for holding character data, populate it with some sample data by using the *InsertIntoTree* method, and then display it by using the *WalkTree* method of *Tree*:

```
static void Main(string[] args)
{
    Tree<char> charTree = null;
    InsertIntoTree<char>(ref charTree, 'M', 'X', 'A', 'M', 'Z', 'Z', 'N');
    string sortedData = charTree.WalkTree();
    Console.WriteLine($"Sorted data is: {sortedData}");
}
```

2. On the Build menu, click Build Solution, verify that the solution compiles, and then correct any errors if necessary.

3. On the Debug menu, click Start Without Debugging.

   The program runs and displays the character values in the following order:

   A M M N X Z Z

4. Press the Enter key to return to Visual Studio 2015.

Variance and generic interfaces

Chapter 8 demonstrates that you can use the *object* type to hold a value or reference of any other type. For example, the following code is completely legal:

```
string myString = "Hello";
object myObject = myString;
```

Remember that in inheritance terms, the *String* class is derived from the *Object* class, so all strings are objects.

Now consider the following generic interface and class:

```
interface IWrapper<T>
{
    void SetData(T data);
    T GetData();
}
class Wrapper<T> : IWrapper<T>
{
    private T storedData;

    void IWrapper<T>.SetData(T data)
    {
        this.storedData = data;
    }

    T IWrapper<T>.GetData()
    {
        return this.storedData;
    }
}
```

The *Wrapper<T>* class provides a simple wrapper around a specified type. The *IWrapper* interface defines the *SetData* method that the *Wrapper<T>* class implements to store the data and the *GetData* method that the *Wrapper<T>* class implements to retrieve the data. You can create an instance of this class and use it to wrap a string like this:

```
Wrapper<string> stringWrapper = new Wrapper<string>();
IWrapper<string> storedStringWrapper = stringWrapper;
storedStringWrapper.SetData("Hello");
Console.WriteLine($"Stored value is {storedStringWrapper.GetData()}");
```

The code creates an instance of the *Wrapper<string>* type. It references the object through the *IWrapper<string>* interface to call the *SetData* method. (The *Wrapper<T>* type implements its interfaces explicitly, so you must call the methods through an appropriate interface reference.) The code also calls the *GetData* method through the *IWrapper<string>* interface. If you run this code, it outputs the message "Stored value is Hello".

Take a look at the following line of code:

```
IWrapper<object> storedObjectWrapper = stringWrapper;
```

This statement is similar to the one that creates the *IWrapper<string>* reference in the previous code example, the difference being that the type parameter is *object* rather than *string*. Is this code legal? Remember that all strings are objects (you can assign a *string* value to an *object* reference, as shown earlier), so in theory this statement looks promising. However, if you try it, the statement will fail to compile with the message "Cannot implicitly convert type 'Wrapper<string>' to 'IWrapper<object>'."

You can try an explicit cast such as this:

```
IWrapper<object> storedObjectWrapper = (IWrapper<object>)stringWrapper;
```

This code compiles but will fail at run time with an *InvalidCastException* exception. The problem is that although all strings are objects, the converse is not true. If this statement were allowed, you could write code like this, which ultimately attempts to store a *Circle* object in a *string* field:

```
IWrapper<object> storedObjectWrapper = (IWrapper<object>)stringWrapper;
Circle myCircle = new Circle();
storedObjectWrapper.SetData(myCircle);
```

The *IWrapper<T>* interface is said to be *invariant*. You cannot assign an *IWrapper<A>* object to a reference of type *IWrapper<B>*, even if type *A* is derived from type *B*. By default, C# implements this restriction to ensure the type safety of your code.

Covariant interfaces

Suppose that you defined the *IStoreWrapper<T>* and *IRetrieveWrapper<T>* interfaces, shown in the following example, in place of *IWrapper<T>* and implemented these interfaces in the *Wrapper<T>* class like this:

```
interface IStoreWrapper<T>
{
    void SetData(T data);
}

interface IRetrieveWrapper<T>
{
    T GetData();
}

class Wrapper<T> : IStoreWrapper<T>, IRetrieveWrapper<T>
{
    private T storedData;

    void IStoreWrapper<T>.SetData(T data)
    {
        this.storedData = data;
    }

    T IRetrieveWrapper<T>.GetData()
    {
        return this.storedData;
    }
}
```

Functionally, the *Wrapper<T>* class is the same as before, except that you access the *SetData* and *GetData* methods through different interfaces.

```
Wrapper<string> stringWrapper = new Wrapper<string>();
IStoreWrapper<string> storedStringWrapper = stringWrapper;
storedStringWrapper.SetData("Hello");
IRetrieveWrapper<string> retrievedStringWrapper = stringWrapper;
Console.WriteLine($"Stored value is {retrievedStringWrapper.GetData()}");
```

Thus, is the following code legal?

```
IRetrieveWrapper<object> retrievedObjectWrapper = stringWrapper;
```

The quick answer is no, and it fails to compile with the same error as before. But if you think about it, although the C# compiler has deemed that this statement is not type safe, the reasons for assuming this are no longer valid. The *IRetrieveWrapper<T>* interface only allows you to read the data held in the *Wrapper<T>* object by using the *GetData* method, and it does not provide any way to change the data. In situations such as this where the type parameter occurs only as the return value of the methods in a generic interface, you can inform the compiler that some implicit conversions are legal and that it does not have to enforce strict type safety. You do this by specifying the *out* keyword when you declare the type parameter, like this:

```
interface IRetrieveWrapper<out T>
{
    T GetData();
}
```

This feature is called *covariance*. You can assign an *IRetrieveWrapper<A>* object to an *IRetrieve-Wrapper<B>* reference as long as there is a valid conversion from type *A* to type *B*, or type *A* derives from type *B*. The following code now compiles and runs as expected:

```
// string derives from object, so this is now legal
IRetrieveWrapper<object> retrievedObjectWrapper = stringWrapper;
```

You can specify the *out* qualifier with a type parameter only if the type parameter occurs as the return type of methods. If you use the type parameter to specify the type of any method parameters, the *out* qualifier is illegal and your code will not compile. Also, covariance works only with reference types. This is because value types cannot form inheritance hierarchies. So, the following code will not compile because *int* is a value type:

```
Wrapper<int> intWrapper = new Wrapper<int>();
IStoreWrapper<int> storedIntWrapper = intWrapper; // this is legal
...
// the following statement is not legal - ints are not objects
IRetrieveWrapper<object> retrievedObjectWrapper = intWrapper;
```

Several of the interfaces defined by the .NET Framework exhibit covariance, including the *IEnumerable<T>* interface, which is detailed in Chapter 19, "Enumerating collections."

> **Note** Only interface and delegate types (which are covered in Chapter 18) can be declared as covariant. You do not specify the *out* modifier with generic classes.

Contravariant interfaces

Contravariance follows a similar principle to covariance except that it works in the opposite direction; it enables you to use a generic interface to reference an object of type *B* through a reference to type *A* as long as type *B* derives from type *A*. This sounds complicated, so it is worth looking at an example from the .NET Framework class library.

The *System.Collections.Generic* namespace in the .NET Framework provides an interface called *IComparer*, which looks like this:

```
public interface IComparer<in T>
{
    int Compare(T x, T y);
}
```

A class that implements this interface has to define the *Compare* method, which is used to compare two objects of the type specified by the *T* type parameter. The *Compare* method is expected to return an integer value: zero if the parameters *x* and *y* have the same value, negative if *x* is less than *y*, and positive if *x* is greater than *y*. The following code shows an example that sorts objects according to their hash code. (The *GetHashCode* method is implemented by the *Object* class. It simply returns an integer value that identifies the object. All reference types inherit this method and can override it with their own implementations.)

```
class ObjectComparer : IComparer<Object>
{
    int IComparer<Object>.Compare(Object x, Object y)
    {
        int xHash = x.GetHashCode();
        int yHash = y.GetHashCode();

        if (xHash == yHash)
            return 0;

        if (xHash < yHash)
            return -1;

        return 1;
    }
}
```

You can create an *ObjectComparer* object and call the *Compare* method through the *IComparer<Object>* interface to compare two objects, like this:

```
Object x = ...;
Object y = ...;
ObjectComparer objectComparer = new ObjectComparer();
IComparer<Object> objectComparator = objectComparer;
int result = objectComparator.Compare(x, y);
```

That's the boring bit. What is more interesting is that you can reference this same object through a version of the *IComparer* interface that compares strings, like this:

```
IComparer<String> stringComparator = objectComparer;
```

At first glance, this statement seems to break every rule of type safety that you can imagine. However, if you think about what the *IComparer<T>* interface does, this approach makes sense. The purpose of the *Compare* method is to return a value based on a comparison between the parameters passed in. If you can compare *Objects*, you certainly should be able to compare *Strings*, which are just specialized types of *Objects*. After all, a *String* should be able to do anything that an *Object* can do— that is the purpose of inheritance.

This still sounds a little presumptive, however. How does the C# compiler know that you are not going to perform any type-specific operations in the code for the *Compare* method that might fail if you invoke the method through an interface based on a different type? If you revisit the definition of the *IComparer* interface, you can see the *in* qualifier prior to the type parameter:

```
public interface IComparer<in T>
{
    int Compare(T x, T y);
}
```

The *in* keyword tells the C# compiler that you can either pass the type *T* as the parameter type to methods or pass any type that derives from *T*. You cannot use *T* as the return type from any methods. Essentially, this makes it possible for you to reference an object either through a generic interface based on the object type or through a generic interface based on a type that derives from the object type. Basically, if type *A* exposes some operations, properties, or fields, in that case if type *B* derives from type *A*, it must also expose the same operations (which might behave differently if they have been overridden), properties, and fields. Consequently, it should be safe to substitute an object of type *B* for an object of type *A*.

Covariance and contravariance might seem like fringe topics in the world of generics, but they are useful. For example, the *List<T>* generic collection class (in the *System.Collections.Generic* namespace) uses *IComparer<T>* objects to implement the *Sort* and *BinarySearch* methods. A *List<Object>* object can contain a collection of objects of any type, so the *Sort* and *BinarySearch* methods need to be able to sort objects of any type. Without using contravariance, the *Sort* and *BinarySearch* methods would need to include logic that determines the real types of the items being sorted or searched and then implement a type-specific sort or search mechanism. However, unless you are a mathematician, it can be quite difficult to recall what covariance and contravariance actually do. The way I remember, based on the examples in this section, is as follows:

- **Covariance example**   If the methods in a generic interface can return strings, they can also return objects. (All strings are objects.)

- **Contravariance example**   If the methods in a generic interface can take object parameters, they can take string parameters. (If you can perform an operation by using an object, you can perform the same operation by using a string because all strings are objects.)

> **Note** As with covariance, only interface and delegate types can be declared as contravariant. You do not specify the *in* modifier with generic classes.

Summary

In this chapter, you learned how to use generics to create type-safe classes. You saw how to instantiate a generic type by specifying a type parameter. You also saw how to implement a generic interface and define a generic method. Finally, you learned how to define covariant and contravariant generic interfaces that can operate with a hierarchy of types.

- If you want to continue to the next chapter, keep Visual Studio 2015 running and turn to Chapter 18.

- If you want to exit Visual Studio 2015 now, on the File menu, click Exit. If you see a Save dialog box, click Yes and save the project.

Quick reference

To	Do this
Instantiate an object by using a generic type	Specify the appropriate generic type parameter. For example: `Queue<int> myQueue = new Queue<int>();`

Create a new generic type	Define the class by using a type parameter. For example:
	`public class Tree<TItem>`
	`{`
	`    ...`
	`}`

Restrict the type that can be substituted for the generic type parameter	Specify a constraint by using a *where* clause when defining the class. For example:
	`public class Tree<TItem>`
	`where TItem : IComparable<TItem>`
	`{`
	`    ...`
	`}`

Define a generic method	Define the method by using type parameters. For example:
	`static void InsertIntoTree<TItem>`
	`(Tree<TItem> tree, params TItem[] data)`
	`{`
	`    ...`
	`}`

Invoke a generic method	Provide types for each of the type parameters. For example: `InsertIntoTree<char>(charTree, 'Z', 'X');`

To	Do this
Define a covariant interface	Specify the *out* qualifier for covariant type parameters. Reference the covariant type parameters only as the return types from methods and not as the types for method parameters:

```
interface IRetrieveWrapper<out T>
{
    T GetData();
}
```

Define a contravariant interface	Specify the *in* qualifier for contravariant type parameters. Reference the contravariant type parameters only as the types of method parameters and not as return types:

```
public interface IComparer<in T>
{
    int Compare(T x, T y);
}
```

Using collections

After completing this chapter, you will be able to:

■ Explain the functionality provided in the different collection classes available with the .NET Framework.

■ Create type-safe collections.

■ Populate a collection with a set of data.

■ Manipulate and access the data items held in a collection.

■ Search a list-oriented collection for matching items by using a predicate.

Chapter 10, "Using arrays," introduces arrays for holding sets of data. Arrays are very useful in this respect, but they have their limitations. Arrays provide only limited functionality; for example, it is not easy to increase or reduce the size of an array, and neither is it a simple matter to sort the data held in an array. Also, arrays only really provide a single means of accessing data—by using an integer index. If your application needs to store and retrieve data by using some other mechanism, such as the first-in, first-out queue mechanism described in Chapter 17, "Introducing generics," arrays might not be the most suitable data structure to use. This is where collections can prove useful.

What are collection classes?

The Microsoft .NET Framework provides several classes that collect elements together such that an application can access the elements in specialized ways. These are the collection classes mentioned in Chapter 17, and they live in the *System.Collections.Generic* namespace.

As the namespace implies, these collections are generic types; they all expect you to provide a type parameter indicating the kind of data that your application will be storing in them. Each collection class is optimized for a particular form of data storage and access, and each provides specialized methods that support this functionality. For example, the *Stack<T>* class implements a last-in, first-out model, where you add an item to the top of the stack by using the *Push* method, and you take an item from the top of the stack by using the *Pop* method. The *Pop* method always retrieves the most recently pushed item and removes it from the stack. In contrast, the *Queue<T>* type provides the *Enqueue* and *Dequeue* methods described in Chapter 17. The *Enqueue* method adds an item to the queue, while the *Dequeue* method retrieves items from the queue in the same order, implementing a first-in, first-out model. A variety of other collection classes are also available, and the following table provides a summary of the most commonly used ones.

Collection	Description
List<T>	A list of objects that can be accessed by index, as with an array, but with additional methods with which to search the list and sort the contents of the list.
Queue<T>	A first-in, first-out data structure, with methods to add an item to one end of the queue, remove an item from the other end, and examine an item without removing it.
Stack<T>	A first-in, last-out data structure with methods to push an item onto the top of the stack, pop an item from the top of the stack, and examine the item at the top of the stack without removing it.
LinkedList<T>	A double-ended ordered list, optimized to support insertion and removal at either end. This collection can act like a queue or a stack, but it also supports random access like a list does.
HashSet<T>	An unordered set of values that is optimized for fast retrieval of data. It provides set-oriented methods for determining whether the items it holds are a subset of those in another HashSet<T> object as well as computing the intersection and union of HashSet<T> objects.
Dictionary<TKey, TValue>	A collection of values that can be identified and retrieved by using keys rather than indexes.
SortedList<TKey, TValue>	A sorted list of key/value pairs. The keys must implement the IComparable<T> interface.

The following sections provide a brief overview of these collection classes. Refer to the .NET Framework class library documentation for more details on each class.

> **Note** The .NET Framework class library also provides another set of collection types in the *System.Collections* namespace. These are nongeneric collections, and they were designed before C# supported generic types (generics were added to the version of C# developed for the .NET Framework version 2.0). With one exception, these types all store object references, and you are required to perform the appropriate casts when you store and retrieve items. These classes are included for backward compatibility with existing applications, and it is not recommended that you use them when building new solutions. In fact, these classes are not available if you are building Universal Windows Platform (UWP) apps.
>
> The one class that does not store object references is the *BitArray* class. This class implements a compact array of Boolean values by using an *int*; each bit indicates true (1) or false (0). If this sounds familiar, it should; this is very similar to the *IntBits* struct that you saw in the examples in Chapter 16, "Using indexers." The *BitArray* class is available to UWP apps.
>
> One other important set of collections is available, and these classes are defined in the *System.Collections.Concurrent* namespace. These are thread-safe collection classes that you can use when you're building multithreaded applications. Chapter 24, "Improving response time by performing asynchronous operations," provides more information on these classes.

The *List<T>* collection class

The generic *List<T>* class is the simplest of the collection classes. You can use it much like you use an array—you can reference an existing element in a *List<T>* collection by using ordinary array notation, with square brackets and the index of the element, although you cannot use array notation to add new elements. However, in general, the *List<T>* class provides more flexibility than arrays do and is designed to overcome the following restrictions exhibited by arrays:

- If you want to resize an array, you have to create a new array, copy the elements (leaving out some if the new array is smaller), and then update any references to the original array so that they refer to the new array.

- If you want to remove an element from an array, you have to move all the trailing elements up by one place. Even this doesn't quite work because you end up with two copies of the last element.

- If you want to insert an element into an array, you have to move elements down by one place to make a free slot. However, you lose the last element of the array!

The *List<T>* collection class provides the following features that preclude these limitations:

- You don't need to specify the capacity of a *List<T>* collection when you create it; it can grow and shrink as you add elements. There is an overhead associated with this dynamic behavior, and if necessary you can specify an initial size. However, if you exceed this size, the *List<T>* collection simply grows as necessary.

- You can remove a specified element from a *List<T>* collection by using the *Remove* method. The *List<T>* collection automatically reorders its elements and closes the gap. You can also remove an item at a specified position in a *List<T>* collection by using the *RemoveAt* method.

- You can add an element to the end of a *List<T>* collection by using its *Add* method. You supply the element to be added. The *List<T>* collection resizes itself automatically.

- You can insert an element into the middle of a *List<T>* collection by using the *Insert* method. Again, the *List<T>* collection resizes itself.

- You can easily sort the data in a *List<T>* object by calling the *Sort* method.

> **Note** As with arrays, if you use *foreach* to iterate through a *List<T>* collection, you cannot use the iteration variable to modify the contents of the collection. Additionally, you cannot call the *Remove, Add*, or *Insert* method in a *foreach* loop that iterates through a *List<T>* collection; any attempt to do so results in an *InvalidOperationException* exception.

Here's an example that shows how you can create, manipulate, and iterate through the contents of a *List<int>* collection:

```
using System;
using System.Collections.Generic;
```

```
...
List<int> numbers = new List<int>();

// Fill the List<int> by using the Add method
foreach (int number in new int[12]{10, 9, 8, 7, 7, 6, 5, 10, 4, 3, 2, 1})
{
    numbers.Add(number);
}

// Insert an element in the penultimate position in the list, and move the last item up
// The first parameter is the position; the second parameter is the value being inserted
numbers.Insert(numbers.Count-1, 99);

// Remove the first element whose value is 7 (the 4th element, index 3)
numbers.Remove(7);
// Remove the element that's now the 7th element, index 6 (10)
numbers.RemoveAt(6);

// Iterate the remaining 11 elements using a for statement
Console.WriteLine("Iterating using a for statement:");
for (int i = 0; i < numbers.Count; i++)
{
    int number = numbers[i];  // Note the use of array syntax
    Console.WriteLine(number);
}

// Iterate the same 11 elements using a foreach statement
Console.WriteLine("\nIterating using a foreach statement:");
foreach (int number in numbers)
{
    Console.WriteLine(number);
}
```

Here is the output of this code:

```
Iterating using a for statement:
10
9
8
7
6
5
4
3
2
99
1

Iterating using a foreach statement:
10
9
8
7
6
5
4
```

```
3
2
99
1
```

The *LinkedList<T>* collection class

The *LinkedList<T>* collection class implements a doubly linked list. Each item in the list holds the value for that item together with a reference to the next item in the list (the *Next* property) and the previous item (the *Previous* property). The item at the start of the list has the *Previous* property set to *null*, and the item at the end of the list has the *Next* property set to *null*.

Unlike the *List<T>* class, *LinkedList<T>* does not support array notation for inserting or examining elements. Instead, you can use the *AddFirst* method to insert an element at the start of the list, moving the previous first item up and setting its *Previous* property to refer to the new item. Similarly, you can use the *AddLast* method to insert an element at the end of the list, setting the *Next* property of the previously last item to refer to the new item. You can also use the *AddBefore* and *AddAfter* methods to insert an element before or after a specified item in the list (you have to retrieve the item first).

You can find the first item in a *LinkedList<T>* collection by querying the *First* property, whereas the *Last* property returns a reference to the final item in the list. To iterate through a linked list, you can start at one end and step through the *Next* or *Previous* references until you find an item with a *null* value for this property. Alternatively, you can use a *foreach* statement, which iterates forward through a *LinkedList<T>* object and stops automatically at the end.

You delete an item from a *LinkedList<T>* collection by using the *Remove*, *RemoveFirst*, and *RemoveLast* methods.

The following example shows a *LinkedList<T>* collection in action. Notice how the code that iterates through the list by using a *for* statement steps through the *Next* (or *Previous*) references, stopping only when it reaches a *null* reference, which is the end of the list:

```csharp
using System;
using System.Collections.Generic;
...
LinkedList<int> numbers = new LinkedList<int>();

// Fill the List<int> by using the AddFirst method
foreach (int number in new int[] { 10, 8, 6, 4, 2 })
{
    numbers.AddFirst(number);
}
```

```
// Iterate using a for statement
Console.WriteLine("Iterating using a for statement:");
for (LinkedListNode<int> node = numbers.First; node != null; node = node.Next)
{
    int number = node.Value;
    Console.WriteLine(number);
}

// Iterate using a foreach statement
Console.WriteLine("\nIterating using a foreach statement:");
foreach (int number in numbers)
{
    Console.WriteLine(number);
}

// Iterate backwards
Console.WriteLine("\nIterating list in reverse order:");
for (LinkedListNode<int> node = numbers.Last; node != null; node = node.Previous)
{
    int number = node.Value;
    Console.WriteLine(number);
}
```

Here is the output generated by this code:

```
Iterating using a for statement:
2
4
6
8
10

Iterating using a foreach statement:
2
4
6
8
10

Iterating list in reverse order:
10
8
6
4
2
```

The *Queue<T>* collection class

The *Queue<T>* class implements a first-in, first-out mechanism. An element is inserted into the queue at the back (the *Enqueue* operation) and is removed from the queue at the front (the *Dequeue* operation).

The following code is an example showing a *Queue<int>* collection and its common operations:

```
using System;
using System.Collections.Generic;
...
Queue<int> numbers = new Queue<int>();

// fill the queue
Console.WriteLine("Populating the queue:");
foreach (int number in new int[4]{9, 3, 7, 2})
{
    numbers.Enqueue(number);
    Console.WriteLine($"{number} has joined the queue");
}

// iterate through the queue
Console.WriteLine("\nThe queue contains the following items:");
foreach (int number in numbers)
{
    Console.WriteLine(number);
}

// empty the queue
Console.WriteLine("\nDraining the queue:");
while (numbers.Count > 0)
{
    int number = numbers.Dequeue();
    Console.WriteLine($"{number} has left the queue");
}
```

Here is the output from this code:

```
Populating the queue:
9 has joined the queue
3 has joined the queue
7 has joined the queue
2 has joined the queue

The queue contains the following items:
9
3
7
2

Draining the queue:
9 has left the queue
3 has left the queue
7 has left the queue
2 has left the queue
```

The *Stack<T>* collection class

The *Stack<T>* class implements a last-in, first-out mechanism. An element joins the stack at the top (the push operation) and leaves the stack at the top (the pop operation). To visualize this, think of a stack of dishes: new dishes are added to the top and dishes are removed from the top, making the last dish to be placed on the stack the first one to be removed. (The dish at the bottom is rarely used and will inevitably require washing before you can put any food on it—because it will be covered in grime!) Here's an example—notice the order in which the items are listed by the *foreach* loop:

```csharp
using System;
using System.Collections.Generic;
...
Stack<int> numbers = new Stack<int>();

// fill the stack
Console.WriteLine("Pushing items onto the stack:");
foreach (int number in new int[4]{9, 3, 7, 2})
{
    numbers.Push(number);
    Console.WriteLine($"{number} has been pushed on the stack");
}

// iterate through the stack
Console.WriteLine("\nThe stack now contains:");
foreach (int number in numbers)
{
    Console.WriteLine(number);
}

// empty the stack
Console.WriteLine("\nPopping items from the stack:");
while (numbers.Count > 0)
{
    int number = numbers.Pop();
    Console.WriteLine($"{number} has been popped off the stack");
}
```

Here is the output from this program:

```
Pushing items onto the stack:
9 has been pushed on the stack
3 has been pushed on the stack
7 has been pushed on the stack
2 has been pushed on the stack

The stack now contains:
2
7
3
9

Popping items from the stack:
2 has been popped off the stack
7 has been popped off the stack
3 has been popped off the stack
9 has been popped off the stack
```

The *Dictionary<TKey, TValue>* collection class

The array and *List<T>* types provide a way to map an integer index to an element. You specify an integer index within square brackets (for example, *[4]*), and you get back the element at index 4 (which is actually the fifth element). However, sometimes you might want to implement a mapping in which the type from which you map is not an *int* but some other type, such as *string, double*, or *Time*. In other languages, this is often called an *associative array*. The *Dictionary<TKey, TValue>* class implements this functionality by internally maintaining two arrays, one for the *keys* from which you're mapping and one for the *values* to which you're mapping. When you insert a key/value pair into a *Dictionary<TKey, TValue>* collection, it automatically tracks which key belongs to which value and makes it possible for you to retrieve the value that is associated with a specified key quickly and easily. The design of the *Dictionary<TKey, TValue>* class has some important consequences:

- A *Dictionary<TKey, TValue>* collection cannot contain duplicate keys. If you call the *Add* method to add a key that is already present in the keys array, you'll get an exception. You can, however, use the square brackets notation to add a key/value pair (as shown in the following example) without danger of an exception, even if the key has already been added; any existing value with the same key will be overwritten by the new value. You can test whether a *Dictionary<TKey, TValue>* collection already contains a particular key by using the *ContainsKey* method.

- Internally, a *Dictionary<TKey, TValue>* collection is a sparse data structure that operates most efficiently when it has plenty of memory with which to work. The size of a *Dictionary<TKey, TValue>* collection in memory can grow quite quickly as you insert more elements.

- When you use a *foreach* statement to iterate through a *Dictionary<TKey, TValue>* collection, you get back a *KeyValuePair<TKey, TValue>* item. This is a structure that contains a copy of the key and value elements of an item in the *Dictionary<TKey, TValue>* collection, and you can access each element through the *Key* property and the *Value* property. These elements are read-only; you cannot use them to modify the data in the *Dictionary<TKey, TValue>* collection.

Here is an example that associates the ages of members of my family with their names and then prints the information:

```
using System;
using System.Collections.Generic;
...
Dictionary<string, int> ages = new Dictionary<string, int>();

// fill the Dictionary
ages.Add("John", 51);     // using the Add method
ages.Add("Diana", 50);
ages["James"] = 23;       // using array notation
ages["Francesca"] = 21;
```

```
// iterate using a foreach statement
// the iterator generates a KeyValuePair item
Console.WriteLine("The Dictionary contains:");
foreach (KeyValuePair<string, int> element in ages)
{
    string name = element.Key;
    int age = element.Value;
    Console.WriteLine($"Name: {name}, Age: {age}");
}
```

Here is the output from this program:

```
The Dictionary contains:
Name: John, Age: 51
Name: Diana, Age: 50
Name: James, Age: 23
Name: Francesca, Age: 21
```

> **Note** The *System.Collections.Generic* namespace also includes the *SortedDictionary<TKey, TValue>* collection type. This class maintains the collection in order, sorted by the keys.

The *SortedList<TKey, TValue>* collection class

The *SortedList<TKey, TValue>* class is very similar to the *Dictionary<TKey, TValue>* class in that you can use it to associate keys with values. The primary difference is that the keys array is always sorted. (It is called a *SortedList*, after all.) It takes longer to insert data into a *SortedList<TKey, TValue>* object than a *SortedDictionary<TKey, TValue>* object in most cases, but data retrieval is often quicker (or at least as quick), and the *SortedList<TKey, TValue>* class uses less memory.

When you insert a key/value pair into a *SortedList<TKey, TValue>* collection, the key is inserted into the keys array at the correct index to keep the keys array sorted. The value is then inserted into the values array at the same index. The *SortedList<TKey, TValue>* class automatically ensures that keys and values remain synchronized, even when you add and remove elements. This means that you can insert key/value pairs into a *SortedList<TKey, TValue>* in any sequence; they are always sorted based on the value of the keys.

Like the *Dictionary<TKey, TValue>* class, a *SortedList<TKey, TValue>* collection cannot contain duplicate keys. When you use a *foreach* statement to iterate through a *SortedList<TKey, TValue>*, you receive back a *KeyValuePair<TKey, TValue>* item. However, the *KeyValuePair<TKey, TValue>* items will be returned sorted by the *Key* property.

Here is the same example that associates the ages of members of my family with their names and then prints the information, but this version has been adjusted to use a *SortedList<TKey, TValue>* object rather than a *Dictionary<TKey, TValue>* collection:

```
using System;
using System.Collections.Generic;
...
SortedList<string, int> ages = new SortedList<string, int>();

// fill the SortedList
ages.Add("John", 51);        // using the Add method
ages.Add("Diana", 50);
ages["James"] = 23;          // using array notation
ages["Francesca"] = 21;

// iterate using a foreach statement
// the iterator generates a KeyValuePair item
Console.WriteLine("The SortedList contains:");
foreach (KeyValuePair<string, int> element in ages)
{
    string name = element.Key;
    int age = element.Value;
    Console.WriteLine($"Name: {name}, Age: {age}");
}
```

The output from this program is sorted alphabetically by the names of my family members:

```
The SortedList contains:
Name: Diana, Age: 50
Name: Francesca, Age: 21
Name: James, Age: 23
Name: John, Age: 51
```

The *HashSet<T>* collection class

The *HashSet<T>* class is optimized for performing set operations, such as determining set membership and generating the union and intersection of sets.

You insert items into a *HashSet<T>* collection by using the *Add* method, and you delete items by using the *Remove* method. However, the real power of the *HashSet<T>* class is provided by the *IntersectWith*, *UnionWith*, and *ExceptWith* methods. These methods modify a *HashSet<T>* collection to generate a new set that either intersects with, has a union with, or does not contain the items in a specified *HashSet<T>* collection. These operations are destructive in as much as they overwrite the contents of the original *HashSet<T>* object with the new set of data. You can also determine whether the data in one *HashSet<T>* collection is a superset or subset of another by using the *IsSubsetOf*, *IsSupersetOf*, *IsProperSubsetOf*, and *IsProperSupersetOf* methods. These methods return a Boolean value and are nondestructive.

Internally, a *HashSet<T>* collection is held as a hash table, enabling the fast lookup of items. However, a large *HashSet<T>* collection can require a significant amount of memory in order to operate quickly.

The following example shows how to populate a *HashSet<T>* collection and illustrates the use of the *IntersectWith* method to find data that overlaps two sets:

```csharp
using System;
using System.Collections.Generic;
...
HashSet<string> employees = new HashSet<string>(new string[] {"Fred","Bert","Harry","John"});
HashSet<string> customers = new HashSet<string>(new string[] {"John","Sid","Harry","Diana"});

employees.Add("James");
customers.Add("Francesca");

Console.WriteLine("Employees:");
foreach (string name in employees)
{
    Console.WriteLine(name);
}

Console.WriteLine("\nCustomers:");
foreach (string name in customers)
{
    Console.WriteLine(name);
}

Console.WriteLine("\nCustomers who are also employees:");
customers.IntersectWith(employees);
foreach (string name in customers)
{
    Console.WriteLine(name);
}
```

This code generates the following output:

```
Employees:
Fred
Bert
Harry
John
James

Customers:
John
Sid
Harry
Diana
Francesca

Customers who are also employees:
John
Harry
```

> **Note** The *System.Collections.Generic* namespace also provides the *SortedSet<T>* collection type, which operates in a similar manner to the *HashSet<T>* class. The primary difference, as the name implies, is that the data is maintained in a sorted order. The *SortedSet<T>* and *HashSet<T>* classes are interoperable; you can take the union of a *SortedSet<T>* collection with a *HashSet<T>* collection, for example.

Using collection initializers

The examples in the preceding subsections have shown you how to add individual elements to a collection by using the method most appropriate to that collection (*Add* for a *List<T>* collection, *Enqueue* for a *Queue<T>* collection, *Push* for a *Stack<T>* collection, and so on). You can also initialize *some* collection types when you declare them by using a syntax similar to that supported by arrays. For example, the following statement creates and initializes the *numbers List<int>* object shown earlier, demonstrating an alternative to repeatedly calling the *Add* method:

```
List<int> numbers = new List<int>(){10, 9, 8, 7, 7, 6, 5, 10, 4, 3, 2, 1};
```

Internally, the C# compiler converts this initialization to a series of calls to the *Add* method. Consequently, you can use this syntax only for collections that actually support the *Add* method. (The *Stack<T>* and *Queue<T>* classes do not.)

For more complex collections that take key/value pairs, such as the *Dictionary<TKey, TValue>* class, you can use indexer notation to specify a value for each key, like this:

```
Dictionary<string, int> ages = new Dictionary<string, int>()
    {
        ["John"] = 51,
        ["Diana"] = 50,
        ["James"] = 23,
        ["Francesca"] = 21
    };
```

If you prefer, you can also specify each key/value pair as an anonymous type in the initializer list, like this:

```
Dictionary<string, int> ages = new Dictionary<string, int>()
    {
        {"John", 51},
        {"Diana", 50},
        {"James", 23},
        {"Francesca", 21}
    };
```

In this case, the first item in each pair is the key, and the second is the value. To make your code as readable as possible, I recommend that you use the indexer notation wherever possible when you initialize a dictionary type.

The *Find* methods, predicates, and lambda expressions

Using the dictionary-oriented collections (*Dictionary<TKey, TValue>*, *SortedDictionary<TKey, TValue>*, and *SortedList<TKey, TValue>*), you can quickly find a value by specifying the key to search for, and you can use array notation to access the value, as you have seen in earlier examples. Other collections that support nonkeyed random access, such as the *List<T>* and *LinkedList<T>* classes, do not support array notation but instead provide the *Find* method to locate an item. For these classes, the argument to the *Find* method is a predicate that specifies the search criteria to use. The form of a predicate is a method that examines each item in the collection and returns a Boolean value indicating whether the item matches. In the case of the *Find* method, as soon as the first match is found, the corresponding item is returned. Note that the *List<T>* and *LinkedList<T>* classes also support other methods, such as *FindLast*, which returns the last matching object, and the *List<T>* class additionally provides the *FindAll* method, which returns a *List<T>* collection of all matching objects.

The easiest way to specify the predicate is to use a *lambda expression*. A lambda expression is an expression that returns a method. This sounds rather odd because most expressions that you have encountered so far in C# actually return a value. If you are familiar with functional programming languages such as Haskell, you are probably comfortable with this concept. If you are not, fear not: lambda expressions are not particularly complicated, and after you have become accustomed to a new bit of syntax, you will see that they are very useful.

> **Note** If you are interested in finding out more about functional programming with Haskell, visit the Haskell programming language website at *http://www.haskell.org/haskellwiki/ Haskell*.

Chapter 3, "Writing methods and applying scope," explains that a typical method consists of four elements: a return type, a method name, a list of parameters, and a method body. A lambda expression contains two of these elements: a list of parameters and a method body. Lambda expressions do not define a method name, and the return type (if any) is inferred from the context in which the lambda expression is used. In the case of the *Find* method, the predicate processes each item in the collection in turn; the body of the predicate must examine the item and return true or false depending on whether it matches the search criteria. The example that follows shows the *Find* method (highlighted in bold) on a *List<Person>* collection, where *Person* is a struct. The *Find* method returns the first item in the list that has the *ID* property set to 3:

```
struct Person
{
    public int ID { get; set; }
    public string Name { get; set; }
    public int Age { get; set; }
}
...
// Create and populate the personnel list
List<Person> personnel = new List<Person>()
{
    new Person() { ID = 1, Name = "John", Age = 51 },
    new Person() { ID = 2, Name = "Sid", Age = 28 },
    new Person() { ID = 3, Name = "Fred", Age = 34 },
    new Person() { ID = 4, Name = "Paul", Age = 22 },
};

// Find the member of the list that has an ID of 3
Person match = personnel.Find((Person p) => { return p.ID == 3; });

Console.WriteLine($"ID: {match.ID}\nName: {match.Name}\nAge: {match.Age}");
```

Here is the output generated by this code:

```
ID: 3
Name: Fred
Age: 34
```

In the call to the *Find* method, the argument *(Person p) => { return p.ID == 3; }* is a lambda expression that actually does the work. It has the following syntactic items:

- A list of parameters enclosed in parentheses. As with a regular method, if the method you are defining (as in the preceding example) takes no parameters, you must still provide the parentheses. In the case of the *Find* method, the predicate is provided with each item from the collection in turn, and this item is passed as the parameter to the lambda expression.

- The => operator, which indicates to the C# compiler that this is a lambda expression.

- The body of the method. The example shown here is very simple, containing a single statement that returns a Boolean value indicating whether the item specified in the parameter matches the search criteria. However, a lambda expression can contain multiple statements, and you can format it in whatever way you feel is most readable. Just remember to add a semicolon after each statement, as you would in an ordinary method.

> **Important** You also saw in Chapter 3 how the => operator is used to define expression-bodied methods. Rather confusingly, this is a somewhat overloaded use of the => operator. Although there are some notional similarities, expression-bodied methods and lambda expressions are semantically (and functionally) quite different beasts; you should not confuse them.

Strictly speaking, the body of a lambda expression can be a method body containing multiple statements or be a single expression. If the body of a lambda expression contains only a single expression, you can omit the braces and the semicolon (but you still need a semicolon to complete the entire statement). Additionally, if the expression takes a single parameter, you can omit the parentheses that surround the parameter. Finally, in many cases, you can actually omit the type of the parameters because the compiler can infer this information from the context from which the lambda expression is invoked. A simplified form of the *Find* statement shown previously looks like this (which is much easier to read and understand):

```
Person match = personnel.Find(p => p.ID == 3);
```

The forms of lambda expressions

Lambda expressions are very powerful constructs, and you will encounter them with increasing frequency as you delve deeper into C# programming. The expressions themselves can take a number of subtly different forms. Lambda expressions were originally part of a mathematical notation called the *lambda calculus*, which provides a notation for describing functions. (You can think of a function as a method that returns a value.) Although the C# language has extended the syntax and semantics of the lambda calculus in its implementation of lambda expressions, many of the original principles still apply. Here are some examples showing the different forms of lambda expressions available in C#:

```
x => x * x // A simple expression that returns the square of its parameter
           // The type of parameter x is inferred from the context.

x => { return x * x ; } // Semantically the same as the preceding
                        // expression, but using a C# statement block as
                        // a body rather than a simple expression

(int x) => x / 2 // A simple expression that returns the value of the
                 // parameter divided by 2
                 // The type of parameter x is stated explicitly.

() => folder.StopFolding(0) // Calling a method
                            // The expression takes no parameters.
                            // The expression might or might not
                            // return a value.

(x, y) => { x++; return x / y; } // Multiple parameters; the compiler
                                 // infers the parameter types.
                                 // The parameter x is passed by value, so
                                 // the effect of the ++ operation is
                                 // local to the expression.

(ref int x, int y) => { x++; return x / y; } // Multiple parameters
                                             // with explicit types
                                             // Parameter x is passed by
                                             // reference, so the effect of
                                             // the ++ operation is permanent.
```

To summarize, here are some features of lambda expressions of which you should be aware:

- If a lambda expression takes parameters, you specify them in the parentheses to the left of the => operator. You can omit the types of parameters, and the C# compiler will infer their types from the context of the lambda expression. You can pass parameters by reference (by using the *ref* keyword) if you want the lambda expression to be able to change its values other than locally, but this is not recommended.

- Lambda expressions can return values, but the return type must match that of the corresponding delegate.

- The body of a lambda expression can be a simple expression or a block of C# code made up of multiple statements, method calls, variable definitions, and other code items.

- Variables defined in a lambda expression method go out of scope when the method finishes.

- A lambda expression can access and modify all variables outside the lambda expression that are in scope when the lambda expression is defined. Be very careful with this feature!

Lambda expressions and anonymous methods

Lambda expressions were added to the C# language in version 3.0. C# version 2.0 introduced anonymous methods, which can perform a similar task but are not as flexible. Anonymous methods were added primarily so that you can define delegates without having to create a named method—you simply provide the definition of the method body in place of the method name, like this:

```
this.stopMachinery += delegate { folder.StopFolding(0); };
```

You can also pass an anonymous method as a parameter in place of a delegate, like this:

```
control.Add(delegate { folder.StopFolding(0); } );
```

Notice that whenever you introduce an anonymous method, you must prefix it with the *delegate* keyword. Also, any parameters needed are specified in parentheses following the *delegate* keyword, as illustrated in the following example:

```
control.Add(delegate(int param1, string param2)
    { /* code that uses param1 and param2 */ ... });
```

Lambda expressions provide a more succinct and natural syntax than anonymous methods, and they pervade many of the more advanced aspects of C#, as you will see throughout the subsequent chapters in this book. Generally speaking, you should use lambda expressions rather than anonymous methods in your code.

Comparing arrays and collections

Here's a summary of the important differences between arrays and collections:

- An array instance has a fixed size and cannot grow or shrink. A collection can dynamically resize itself as required.

- An array can have more than one dimension. A collection is linear. However, the items in a collection can be collections themselves, so you can imitate a multidimensional array as a collection of collections.

- You store and retrieve an item in an array by using an index. Not all collections support this notion. For example, to store an item in a *List<T>* collection, you use the *Add* or *Insert* method, and to retrieve an item, you use the *Find* method.

- Many of the collection classes provide a *ToArray* method that creates and populates an array containing the items in the collection. The items are copied to the array and are not removed from the collection. Additionally, these collections provide constructors that can populate a collection directly from an array.

Using collection classes to play cards

In the next exercise, you will convert the card game developed in Chapter 10 to use collections rather than arrays.

Use collections to implement a card game

1. Start Microsoft Visual Studio 2015 if it is not already running.

2. Open the Cards project, which is located in the \Microsoft Press\VCSBS\Chapter 18\Cards folder in your Documents folder.

   This project contains an updated version of the project from Chapter 10 that deals hands of cards by using arrays. The *PlayingCard* class is modified to expose the value and suit of a card as read-only properties.

3. Display the Pack.cs file in the Code and Text Editor window. Add to the top of the file the following *using* directive:

   ```
   using System.Collections.Generic;
   ```

4. In the *Pack* class, change the definition of the *cardPack* two-dimensional array to a *Dictionary<Suit, List<PlayingCard>>* object, as shown here in bold:

   ```
   class Pack
   {
       ...
       private Dictionary<Suit, List<PlayingCard>> cardPack;
       ...
   }
   ```

   The original application used a two-dimensional array for representing a pack of cards. This code replaces the array with a *Dictionary*, where the key specifies the suit and the value is a list of cards in that suit.

5. Locate the *Pack* constructor. Modify the first statement in this constructor to instantiate the *cardPack* variable as a new *Dictionary* collection rather than as an array, as shown here in bold:

   ```
   public Pack()
   {
       this.cardPack = new Dictionary<Suit, List<PlayingCard>>(NumSuits);
       ...
   }
   ```

   Although a *Dictionary* collection will resize itself automatically as items are added, if the collection is unlikely to change in size, you can specify an initial size when you instantiate it. This helps to optimize the memory allocation (although the *Dictionary* collection can still grow if this size is exceeded). In this case, the *Dictionary* collection will contain a collection of four lists (one list for each suit), so it is allocated space for four items (*NumSuits* is a constant with the value 4).

6. In the outer *for* loop, declare a *List<PlayingCard>* collection object called *cardsInSuit* that is big enough to hold the number of cards in each suit (use the *CardsPerSuit* constant), as follows in bold:

```
public Pack()
{
    this.cardPack = new Dictionary<Suit, List<PlayingCard>>(NumSuits);

    for (Suit = Suit.Clubs; suit <= Suit.Spades; suit++)
    {
        List<PlayingCard> cardsInSuit = new List<PlayingCard>(CardsPerSuit);
        for (Value value = Value.Two; value <= Value.Ace; value++)
        {
            ...
        }
    }
}
```

7. Change the code in the inner *for* loop to add new *PlayingCard* objects to this collection rather than to the array, as shown in bold in the following code:

```
for (Suit suit = Suit.Clubs; suit <= Suit.Spades; suit++)
{
    List<PlayingCard> cardsInSuit = new List<PlayingCard>(CardsPerSuit);
    for (Value value = Value.Two; value <= Value.Ace; value++)
    {
        cardsInSuit.Add(new PlayingCard(suit, value));
    }
}
```

8. After the inner *for* loop, add the *List* object to the *cardPack Dictionary* collection, specifying the value of the *suit* variable as the key to this item:

```
for (Suit suit = Suit.Clubs; suit <= Suit.Spades; suit++)
{
    List<PlayingCard> cardsInSuit = new List<PlayingCard>(CardsPerSuit);
    for (Value value = Value.Two; value <= Value.Ace; value++)
    {
        cardsInSuit.Add(new PlayingCard(suit, value));
    }
    this.cardPack.Add(suit, cardsInSuit);
}
```

9. Find the *DealCardFromPack* method.

   This method picks a card at random from the pack, removes the card from the pack, and returns this card. The logic for selecting the card does not require any changes, but the statements at the end of the method that retrieve the card from the array must be updated to use the *Dictionary* collection instead. Additionally, the code that removes the card from the array (it has now been dealt) must be modified; you need to search for the card in the list and then remove it from the list. To locate the card, use the *Find* method and specify a predicate that finds a card with the matching value. The parameter to the predicate should be a *PlayingCard* object (the list contains *PlayingCard* items).

The updated statements occur after the closing brace of the second *while* loop, as shown in bold in the following code:

```
public PlayingCard DealCardFromPack()
{
    Suit suit = (Suit)randomCardSelector.Next(NumSuits);
    while (this.IsSuitEmpty(suit))
    {
        suit = (Suit)randomCardSelector.Next(NumSuits);
    }

    Value value = (Value)randomCardSelector.Next(CardsPerSuit);
    while (this.IsCardAlreadyDealt(suit, value))
    {
        value = (Value)randomCardSelector.Next(CardsPerSuit);
    }

    List<PlayingCard> cardsInSuit = this.cardPack[suit];
    PlayingCard card = cardsInSuit.Find(c => c.CardValue == value);
    cardsInSuit.Remove(card);
    return card;
}
```

10. Locate the *IsCardAlreadyDealt* method.

   This method determines whether a card has already been dealt by checking whether the corresponding element in the array has been set to *null*. You need to modify this method to determine whether a card with the specified value is present in the list for the suit in the *cardPack Dictionary* collection.

   To determine whether an item exists in a *List<T>* collection, you use the *Exists* method. This method is similar to *Find* in as much as it takes a predicate as its argument. The predicate is passed each item from the collection in turn, and it should return true if the item matches some specified criteria, and false otherwise. In this case, the *List<T>* collection holds *PlayingCard* objects, and the criteria for the *Exists* predicate should return true if it is passed a *PlayingCard* item with a suit and value that matches the parameters passed to the *IsCardAlreadyDealt* method.

   Update the method, as shown in the following example in bold:

```
private bool IsCardAlreadyDealt(Suit suit, Value value)
{
    List<PlayingCard> cardsInSuit = this.cardPack[suit];
    return (!cardsInSuit.Exists(c => c.CardSuit == suit && c.CardValue == value));
}
```

11. Display the Hand.cs file in the Code and Text Editor window. Add to the list at the top of the file the following *using* directive:

```
using System.Collections.Generic;
```

12. The *Hand* class currently uses an array called *cards* to hold the playing cards for the hand. Modify the definition of the *cards* variable to be a *List<PlayingCard>* collection, as shown here in bold:

```
class Hand
{
    public const int HandSize = 13;
    private List<PlayingCard> cards = new List<PlayingCard>(HandSize);
    ...
}
```

13. Find the *AddCardToHand* method.

This method currently checks to see whether the hand is full; if it is not, it adds the card provided as the parameter to the *cards* array at the index specified by the *playingCardCount* variable.

Update this method to use the *Add* method of the *List<PlayingCard>* collection instead.

This change also removes the need to explicitly keep track of how many cards the collection holds because you can use the *Count* property of the *cards* collection instead. Therefore, remove the *playingCardCount* variable from the class and modify the *if* statement that checks whether the hand is full to reference the *Count* property of the *cards* collection.

The completed method should look like this, with the changes highlighted in bold:

```
public void AddCardToHand(PlayingCard cardDealt)
{
    if (this.cards.Count >= HandSize)
    {
        throw new ArgumentException("Too many cards");
    }
    this.cards.Add(cardDealt);
}
```

14. On the Debug menu, click Start Debugging to build and run the application.

15. When the Card Game form appears, click Deal.

> **Note** The Deal button is located on the command bar. You may need to expand the command bar to reveal the button.

Verify that the cards are dealt and that the populated hands appear as before. Click Deal again to generate another random set of hands.

The following image shows the application running:

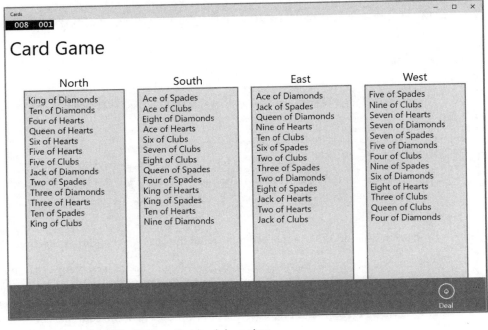

16. Return to Visual Studio 2015 and stop debugging.

Summary

In this chapter, you learned how to use some of the common collection classes to store and access data. In particular, you learned how to use generic collection classes to create type-safe collections. You also learned how to create lambda expressions to search for specific items within collections.

- If you want to continue to the next chapter, keep Visual Studio 2015 running and turn to Chapter 19, "Enumerating collections."

- If you want to exit Visual Studio 2015 now, on the File menu, click Exit. If you see a Save dialog box, click Yes and save the project.

Quick reference

To	Do this
Create a new collection	Use the constructor for the collection class. For example: `List<PlayingCard> cards = new List<PlayingCard>();`

To	Do this
Add an item to a collection	Use the *Add* or *Insert* methods (as appropriate) for lists, hash sets, and dictionary-oriented collections. Use the *Enqueue* method for *Queue<T>* collections. Use the *Push* method for *Stack<T>* collections. For example: ```\nHashSet<string> employees = new HashSet<string>();\nemployees.Add("John");\n...\nLinkedList<int> data = new LinkedList<int>();\ndata.AddFirst(101);\n...\nStack<int> numbers = new Stack<int>();\nnumbers.Push(99);\n```
Remove an item from a collection	Use the *Remove* method for lists, hash sets, and dictionary-oriented collections. Use the *Dequeue* method for *Queue<T>* collections. Use the *Pop* method for *Stack<T>* collections. For example: ```\nHashSet<string> employees = new HashSet<string>();\nemployees.Remove("John");\n...\nLinkedList<int> data = new LinkedList<int>();\ndata.Remove(101);\n...\nStack<int> numbers = new Stack<int>();\n...\nint item = numbers.Pop();\n```
Find the number of elements in a collection	Use the *Count* property. For example: ```\nList<PlayingCard> cards = new List<PlayingCard>();\n...\nint noOfCards = cards.Count;\n```
Locate an item in a collection	For dictionary-oriented collections, use array notation. For lists, use the *Find* methods. For example: ```\nDictionary<string, int> ages =\n new Dictionary<string, int>();\nages.Add("John", 47);\nint johnsAge = ages["John"];\n...\n\nList<Person> personnel = new List<Person>();\nPerson match = personnel.Find(p => p.ID == 3);\n``` Note: The *Stack<T>*, *Queue<T>*, and hash set collection classes do not support searching, although you can test for membership of an item in a hash set by using the *Contains* method.
Iterate through the elements of a collection	Use a *for* statement or a *foreach* statement. For example: ```\nLinkedList<int> numbers = new LinkedList<int>();\n...\nfor (LinkedListNode<int> node = numbers.First;\n node != null; node = node.Next)\n{\n int number = node.Value;\n Console.WriteLine(number);\n}\n...\nforeach (int number in numbers)\n{\n Console.WriteLine(number);\n}\n```

CHAPTER 19

Enumerating collections

After completing this chapter, you will be able to:

- Manually define an enumerator that you can use to iterate over the elements in a collection.

- Implement an enumerator automatically by creating an iterator.

- Provide additional iterators that can step through the elements of a collection in different sequences.

Chapter 10, "Using arrays," and Chapter 18, "Using collections," show how you work with arrays and collection classes for holding sequences or sets of data. Chapter 10 also details the *foreach* statement, which you can use to step through, or iterate over, the elements in a collection. In these chapters, you use the *foreach* statement as a quick and convenient way of accessing the contents of an array or a collection, but now it is time to learn a little more about how this statement actually works. This topic becomes important when you define your own collection classes, and this chapter describes how you can make collections enumerable.

Enumerating the elements in a collection

Chapter 10 presents an example of using the *foreach* statement to list the items in a simple array. The code looks like this:

```
int[] pins = { 9, 3, 7, 2 };
foreach (int pin in pins)
{
   Console.WriteLine(pin);
}
```

The *foreach* construct provides an elegant mechanism that greatly simplifies the code you need to write, but it can be exercised only under certain circumstances—you can use *foreach* only to step through an *enumerable* collection.

But what exactly is an enumerable collection? The quick answer is that it is a collection that implements the *System.Collections.IEnumerable* interface.

The *IEnumerable* interface contains a single method called *GetEnumerator*:

```
IEnumerator GetEnumerator();
```

The *GetEnumerator* method should return an enumerator object that implements the *System.Collections.IEnumerator* interface. The enumerator object is used for stepping through (enumerating) the elements of the collection. The *IEnumerator* interface specifies the following property and methods:

```
object Current { get; }
bool MoveNext();
void Reset();
```

Think of an enumerator as a pointer indicating elements in a list. Initially, the pointer points *before* the first element. You call the *MoveNext* method to move the pointer down to the next (first) item in the list; the *MoveNext* method should return *true* if there actually is another item and *false* if there isn't. You use the *Current* property to access the item currently pointed to, and you use the *Reset* method to return the pointer back to *before* the first item in the list. By using the *GetEnumerator* method of a collection to create an enumerator, repeatedly calling the *MoveNext* method, and using the enumerator to retrieve the value of the *Current* property, you can move forward through the elements of a collection one item at a time. This is exactly what the *foreach* statement does. So, if you want to create your own enumerable collection class, you must implement the *IEnumerable* interface in your collection class and also provide an implementation of the *IEnumerator* interface to be returned by the *GetEnumerator* method of the collection class.

If you are observant, you will have noticed that the *Current* property of the *IEnumerator* interface exhibits non-type-safe behavior in that it returns an *object* rather than a specific type. However, you should be pleased to know that the Microsoft .NET Framework class library also provides the generic *IEnumerator<T>* interface, which has a *Current* property that returns a *T* instead. Likewise, there is also an *IEnumerable<T>* interface containing a *GetEnumerator* method that returns an *Enumerator<T>* object. Both of these interfaces are defined in the *System.Collections.Generic* namespace, and if you are building applications for the .NET Framework version 2.0 or later, you should make use of these generic interfaces rather than the nongeneric versions when you define enumerable collections.

Manually implementing an enumerator

In the following exercise, you will define a class that implements the generic *IEnumerator<T>* interface and create an enumerator for the binary tree class that is demonstrated in Chapter 17, "Introducing generics."

Chapter 17 illustrates how easy it is to traverse a binary tree and display its contents. You would therefore be inclined to think that defining an enumerator that retrieves each element in a binary tree in the same order would be a simple matter. Sadly, you would be mistaken. The main problem is that when defining an enumerator, you need to remember where you are in the structure so that subsequent calls to the *MoveNext* method can update the position appropriately. Recursive algorithms, such as that used when walking a binary tree, do not lend themselves to maintaining state information between method calls in an easily accessible manner. For this reason, you will first preprocess the data in the binary tree into a more amenable data structure (a queue) and actually enumerate this data structure instead. Of course, this deviousness is hidden from the user iterating through the elements of the binary tree!

Create the *TreeEnumerator* class

1. Start Microsoft Visual Studio 2015 if it is not already running.

2. Open the BinaryTree solution, which is located in the \Microsoft Press\VCSBS\Chapter 19\ BinaryTree folder in your Documents folder. This solution contains a working copy of the BinaryTree project you created in Chapter 17. You will add a new class to this project in which to implement the enumerator for the *BinaryTree* class.

3. In Solution Explorer, click the BinaryTree project. On the Project menu, click Add Class to open the Add New Item – BinaryTree dialog box. In the middle pane, select the Class template, type **TreeEnumerator.cs** in the Name box, and then click Add.

   The *TreeEnumerator* class generates an enumerator for a *Tree<TItem>* object. To ensure that the class is type safe, you must provide a type parameter and implement the *IEnumerator<T>* interface. Also, the type parameter must be a valid type for the *Tree<TItem>* object that the class enumerates, so it must be constrained to implement the *IComparable<TItem>* interface (the *BinaryTree* class requires that items in the tree provide a means to be compared for sorting purposes).

4. In the Code and Text Editor window displaying the TreeEnumerator.cs file, modify the definition of the *TreeEnumerator* class to satisfy these requirements, as shown in bold in the following example:

   ```
   class TreeEnumerator<TItem> : IEnumerator<TItem> where TItem : IComparable<TItem>
   {
   }
   ```

5. Add to the *TreeEnumerator<TItem>* class the following three private variables, shown in the following code in bold:

```
class TreeEnumerator<TItem> : IEnumerator<TItem> where TItem : IComparable<TItem>
{
    private Tree<TItem> currentData = null;
    private TItem currentItem = default(TItem);
    private Queue<TItem> enumData = null;
}
```

The *currentData* variable will be used to hold a reference to the tree being enumerated, and the *currentItem* variable will hold the value returned by the *Current* property. You will populate the *enumData* queue with the values extracted from the nodes in the tree, and the *MoveNext* method will return each item from this queue in turn. The *default* keyword is explained in the section "Initializing a variable defined with a type parameter" later in this chapter.

6. Add a constructor that takes a *Tree<TItem>* parameter called *data* to the *TreeEnumerator<TItem>* class. In the body of the constructor, add a statement that initializes the *currentData* variable to *data*:

```
class TreeEnumerator<TItem> : IEnumerator<TItem> where TItem : IComparable<TItem>
{
    ...
    public TreeEnumerator(Tree<TItem> data)
    {
        this.currentData = data;
    }
}
```

7. Add the following private method, called *populate*, to the *TreeEnumerator<TItem>* class, immediately after the constructor:

```
class TreeEnumerator<TItem> : IEnumerator<TItem> where TItem : IComparable<TItem>
{
    ...
    private void populate(Queue<TItem> enumQueue, Tree<TItem> tree)
    {
        if (tree.LeftTree != null)
        {
            populate(enumQueue, tree.LeftTree);
        }

        enumQueue.Enqueue(tree.NodeData);

        if (tree.RightTree != null)
        {
            populate(enumQueue, tree.RightTree);
        }
    }
}
```

This method walks the binary tree, adding the data it contains to the queue. The algorithm used is similar to that used by the *WalkTree* method in the *Tree<TItem>* class, which is described in Chapter 17. The main difference is that rather than appending *NodeData* values to a string, the method stores these values in the queue.

8. Return to the definition of the *TreeEnumerator<TItem>* class. In the class declaration, hover over the text *IEnumerator<TItem>*. On the drop-down context menu that appears (with a lightbulb icon), click Implement Interface Explicitly.

This action generates stubs for the methods in the *IEnumerator<TItem>* interface and the *IEnumerator* interface and adds them to the end of the class. It also generates the *Dispose* method for the *IDisposable* interface.

> **Note** The *IEnumerator<TItem>* interface inherits from the *IEnumerator* and *IDisposable* interfaces, which is why their methods also appear. In fact, the only item that belongs to the *IEnumerator<TItem>* interface is the generic *Current* property. The *MoveNext* and *Reset* methods belong to the nongeneric *IEnumerator* interface. Chapter 14, "Using garbage collection and resource management," describes the *IDisposable* interface.

9. Examine the code that has been generated.

The bodies of the properties and methods contain a default implementation that simply throws a *NotImplementedException* exception. You will replace this code with a real implementation in the following steps.

10. Update the body of the *MoveNext* method with the code shown in bold here:

```
bool IEnumerator.MoveNext()
{
    if (this.enumData == null)
    {
        this.enumData = new Queue<TItem>();
        populate(this.enumData, this.currentData);
    }

    if (this.enumData.Count > 0)
    {
        this.currentItem = this.enumData.Dequeue();
        return true;
    }

    return false;
}
```

The purpose of the *MoveNext* method of an enumerator is actually twofold. The first time it is called, it should initialize the data used by the enumerator and advance to the first piece of data to be returned. (Prior to *MoveNext* being called for the first time, the value returned by the *Current* property is undefined and should result in an exception.) In this case, the initialization process consists of instantiating the queue and then calling the *populate* method to fill the queue with data extracted from the tree.

Subsequent calls to the *MoveNext* method should just move through data items until there are no more left, dequeuing items until the queue is empty, as in this example. It is important to keep in mind that *MoveNext* does not actually return data items—that is the purpose of the *Current* property. All *MoveNext* does is update the internal state in the enumerator (that is, the value of the *currentItem* variable is set to the data item extracted from the queue) for use by the *Current* property, returning *true* if there is a next value and *false* otherwise.

11. Modify the definition of the *get* accessor of the generic *Current* property as follows in bold:

```
TItem IEnumerator<TItem>.Current
{
    get
    {
        if (this.enumData == null)
        {
            throw new InvalidOperationException("Use MoveNext before calling Current");
        }

        return this.currentItem;
    }
}
```

> **⚠ Important** Be sure to add the code to the correct implementation of the *Current* property. Leave the nongeneric version, *System.Collections.IEnumerator.Current*, with its default implementation that throws a *NotImplementedException* exception.

The *Current* property examines the *enumData* variable to ensure that *MoveNext* has been called. (This variable will be *null* prior to the first call to *MoveNext*.) If this is not the case, the property throws an *InvalidOperationException*—this is the conventional mechanism used by .NET Framework applications to indicate that an operation cannot be performed in the current state. If *MoveNext* has been called beforehand, it will have updated the *currentItem* variable, so all the *Current* property needs to do is return the value in this variable.

12. Locate the *IDisposable.Dispose* method. Comment out the *throw new NotImplemented-Exception();* statement as shown in bold in the code that follows. The enumerator does not use any resources that require explicit disposal, so this method does not need to do anything. It must still be present, however. For more information about the *Dispose* method, refer to Chapter 14.

```
void IDisposable.Dispose()
{
    // throw new NotImplementedException();
}
```

13. Build the solution, and correct errors if any are reported.

Initializing a variable defined with a type parameter

You should have noticed that the statement that defines and initializes the *currentItem* variable uses the *default* keyword. The *currentItem* variable is defined by using the type parameter *TItem*. When the program is written and compiled, the actual type that will be substituted for *TItem* might not be known—this issue is resolved only when the code is executed. This makes it difficult to specify how the variable should be initialized. The temptation is to set it to *null*. However, if the type substituted for *TItem* is a value type, this is an illegal assignment. (You cannot set value types to *null*, only reference types.) Similarly, if you set it to *0* with the expectation that the type will be numeric, this will be illegal if the type used is actually a reference type. There are other possibilities as well—*TItem* could be a *boolean*, for example. The *default* keyword solves this problem. The value used to initialize the variable will be determined when the statement is executed. If *TItem* is a reference type, *default(TItem)* returns *null*; if *TItem* is numeric, *default(TItem)* returns *0*; if *TItem* is a *boolean*, *default(TItem)* returns *false*. If *TItem* is a struct, the individual fields in the struct are initialized in the same way. (Reference fields are set to *null*, numeric fields are set to *0*, and *boolean* fields are set to *false*.)

Implementing the *IEnumerable* interface

In the following exercise, you will modify the binary tree class to implement the *IEnumerable<T>* interface. The *GetEnumerator* method will return a *TreeEnumerator<TItem>* object.

Implement the *IEnumerable<TItem>* interface in the *Tree<TItem>* class

1. In Solution Explorer, double-click the file Tree.cs to display the *Tree<TItem>* class in the Code and Text Editor window.

2. Modify the definition of the *Tree<TItem>* class so that it implements the *IEnumerable<TItem>* interface, as shown in bold in the following code:

   ```
   public class Tree<TItem> : IEnumerable<TItem> where TItem : IComparable<TItem>
   ```

   Notice that constraints are always placed at the end of the class definition.

3. Hover over the *IEnumerable<TItem>* interface in the class definition. On the drop-down context menu that appears, click Implement Interface Explicitly.

   This action generates implementations of the *IEnumerable<TItem>.GetEnumerator* and *IEnumerable.GetEnumerator* methods and adds them to the class. The nongeneric *IEnumerable* interface method is implemented because the generic *IEnumerable<TItem>* interface inherits from *IEnumerable*.

4. Locate the generic *IEnumerable<TItem>.GetEnumerator* method near the end of the class. Modify the body of the *GetEnumerator()* method, replacing the existing *throw* statement, as shown in bold in the following example:

```
IEnumerator<TItem> IEnumerable<TItem>.GetEnumerator()
{
    return new TreeEnumerator<TItem>(this);
}
```

The purpose of the *GetEnumerator* method is to construct an enumerator object for iterating through the collection. In this case, all you need to do is build a new *TreeEnumerator<TItem>* object by using the data in the tree.

5. Build the solution. Correct any errors that are reported, and rebuild the solution if necessary.

You will now test the modified *Tree<TItem>* class by using a *foreach* statement to iterate through a binary tree and display its contents.

Test the enumerator

1. In Solution Explorer, right-click the BinaryTree solution, point to Add, and then click New Project. Add a new project by using the Console Application template. Name the project **EnumeratorTest**, set the location to \Microsoft Press\VCSBS\Chapter 19\BinaryTree in your Documents folder, and then click OK.

> **Note** Be sure that you select the Console Application template from the list of Visual C# templates. Sometimes the Add New Project dialog box displays the templates for Visual Basic or C++ by default.

2. Right-click the EnumeratorTest project in Solution Explorer, and then click Set As StartUp Project.

3. On the Project menu, click Add Reference. In the Reference Manager – EnumeratorTest dialog box, in the left pane, expand the Projects node and click Solution. In the middle pane, select the BinaryTree project, and then click OK.

The BinaryTree assembly appears in the list of references for the EnumeratorTest project in Solution Explorer.

4. In the Code and Text Editor window displaying the *Program* class, add the following *using* directive to the list at the top of the file:

```
using BinaryTree;
```

5. Add to the *Main* method the statements shown in bold in the code that follows. These statements create and populate a binary tree of integers:

```
static void Main(string[] args)
{
    Tree<int> tree1 = new Tree<int>(10);
    tree1.Insert(5);
    tree1.Insert(11);
    tree1.Insert(5);
    tree1.Insert(-12);
    tree1.Insert(15);
    tree1.Insert(0);
    tree1.Insert(14);
    tree1.Insert(-8);
    tree1.Insert(10);
}
```

6. Add a *foreach* statement, as follows in bold, that enumerates the contents of the tree and displays the results:

```
static void Main(string[] args)
{
    ...
    foreach (int item in tree1)
    {
        Console.WriteLine(item);
    }
}
```

7. On the Debug menu, click Start Without Debugging.

   The program runs and displays the values in the following sequence:

   −12, −8, 0, 5, 5, 10, 10, 11, 14, 15

8. Press Enter to return to Visual Studio 2015.

Implementing an enumerator by using an iterator

As you can see, the process of making a collection enumerable can become complex and is potentially prone to error. To make life easier, C# provides iterators that can automate much of this process.

An *iterator* is a block of code that yields an ordered sequence of values. An iterator is not actually a member of an enumerable class; rather, it specifies the sequence that an enumerator should use for returning its values. In other words, an iterator is just a description of the enumeration sequence that the C# compiler can use for creating its own enumerator. This concept requires a little thought to understand properly, so consider the following simple example.

A simple iterator

The following *BasicCollection<T>* class illustrates the principles of implementing an iterator. The class uses a *List<T>* object for holding data and provides the *FillList* method for populating this list. Notice also that the *BasicCollection<T>* class implements the *IEnumerable<T>* interface. The *GetEnumerator* method is implemented by using an iterator:

```
using System;
using System.Collections.Generic;
using System.Collections;

class BasicCollection<T> : IEnumerable<T>
{
    private List<T> data = new List<T>();

    public void FillList(params T [] items)
    {
        foreach (var datum in items)
        {
            data.Add(datum);
        }
    }

    IEnumerator<T> IEnumerable<T>.GetEnumerator()
    {
        foreach (var datum in data)
        {
            yield return datum;
        }
    }

    IEnumerator IEnumerable.GetEnumerator()
    {
        // Not implemented in this example
        throw new NotImplementedException();
    }
}
```

The *GetEnumerator* method appears to be straightforward, but it warrants closer examination. The first thing to notice is that it doesn't appear to return an *IEnumerator<T>* type. Instead, it loops through the items in the *data* array, returning each item in turn. The key point is the use of the *yield* keyword. The *yield* keyword indicates the value that should be returned by each iteration. If it helps, you can think of the *yield* statement as calling a temporary halt to the method, passing back a value to the caller. When the caller needs the next value, the *GetEnumerator* method continues at the point at which it left off, looping around and then yielding the next value. Eventually, the data is exhausted, the loop finishes, and the *GetEnumerator* method terminates. At this point, the iteration is complete.

Remember that this is not a normal method in the usual sense. The code in the *GetEnumerator* method defines an *iterator*. The compiler uses this code to generate an implementation of the *IEnumerator<T>* class containing a *Current* method and a *MoveNext* method. This implementation exactly matches the functionality specified by the *GetEnumerator* method. You don't actually get to see this generated code (unless you decompile the assembly containing the compiled code), but that is a small price to pay for the convenience and reduction in code that you need to write. You can invoke the enumerator generated by the iterator in the usual manner, as shown in the following block of code, which displays the words in the first line of the poem "Jabberwocky" by Lewis Carroll:

```
BasicCollection<string> bc = new BasicCollection<string>();
bc.FillList("Twas", "brillig", "and", "the", "slithy", "toves");
foreach (string word in bc)
{
    Console.WriteLine(word);
}
```

This code simply outputs the contents of the *bc* object in this order:

Twas, brillig, and, the, slithy, toves

If you want to provide alternative iteration mechanisms to present the data in a different sequence, you can implement additional properties that implement the *IEnumerable* interface and that use an iterator for returning data. For example, the *Reverse* property of the *BasicCollection<T>* class, shown here, emits the data in the list in reverse order:

```
class BasicCollection<T> : IEnumerable<T>
{
    ...
    public IEnumerable<T> Reverse
    {
        get
        {
            for (int i = data.Count - 1; i >= 0; i--)
            {
                yield return data[i];
            }
        }
    }
}
```

You can invoke this property as follows:

```
BasicCollection<string> bc = new BasicCollection<string>();
bc.FillList("Twas", "brillig", "and", "the", "slithy", "toves");
foreach (string word in bc.Reverse)
{
    Console.WriteLine(word);
}
```

This code outputs the contents of the *bc* object in reverse order:

toves, slithy, the, and, brillig, Twas

Defining an enumerator for the *Tree\<TItem>* class by using an iterator

In the next exercise, you will implement the enumerator for the *Tree\<TItem>* class by using an iterator. Unlike in the preceding set of exercises, which required the data in the tree to be preprocessed into a queue by the *MoveNext* method, here you can define an iterator that traverses the tree by using the more naturally recursive mechanism, similar to the *WalkTree* method discussed in Chapter 17.

Add an enumerator to the *Tree\<TItem>* class

1. Using Visual Studio 2015, open the BinaryTree solution, located in the \Microsoft Press\VCSBS\ Chapter 19\IteratorBinaryTree folder in your Documents folder. This solution contains another copy of the BinaryTree project you created in Chapter 17.

2. Open the file Tree.cs in the Code and Text Editor window. Modify the definition of the *Tree\<TItem>* class so that it implements the *IEnumerable\<TItem>* interface, as shown here in bold:

   ```
   public class Tree<TItem> : IEnumerable<TItem> where TItem : IComparable<TItem>
   {
       ...
   }
   ```

3. Hover over the *IEnumerable\<TItem>* interface in the class definition. On the drop-down context menu that appears, click Implement Interface Explicitly to add the *IEnumerable\<TItem>.GetEnumerator* and *IEnumerable.GetEnumerator* methods to the end of the class.

4. Locate the generic *IEnumerable\<TItem>.GetEnumerator* method. Replace the contents of the *GetEnumerator* method as shown in bold in the following code:

   ```
   IEnumerator<TItem> IEnumerable<TItem>.GetEnumerator()
   {
       if (this.LeftTree != null)
       {
           foreach (TItem item in this.LeftTree)
           {
               yield return item;
           }
       }

       yield return this.NodeData;

       if (this.RightTree != null)
       {
           foreach (TItem item in this.RightTree)
           {
               yield return item;
           }
       }
   }
   ```

It might not be obvious at first glance, but this code follows the same recursive algorithm that you used in Chapter 17 for listing the contents of a binary tree. If *LeftTree* is not empty, the first *foreach* statement implicitly calls the *GetEnumerator* method (which you are currently defining) over it. This process continues until a node is found that has no left subtree. At this point, the value in the *NodeData* property is yielded, and the right subtree is examined in the same way. When the right subtree is exhausted, the process unwinds to the parent node, outputting the parent's *NodeData* property and examining the right subtree of the parent. This course of action continues until the entire tree has been enumerated and all the nodes have been output.

Test the new enumerator

1. In Solution Explorer, right-click the BinaryTree solution, point to Add, and then click Existing Project. In the Add Existing Project dialog box, move to the folder \Microsoft Press\VCSBS\ Chapter 19\BinaryTree\EnumeratorTest, select the EnumeratorTest project file, and then click Open.

   This is the project that you created to test the enumerator you developed manually earlier in this chapter.

2. Right-click the EnumeratorTest project in Solution Explorer, and then click Set As StartUp Project.

3. In Solution Explorer, expand the References folder for the EnumeratorTest project. Right-click the BinaryTree reference and then click Remove.

4. On the Project menu, click Add Reference. In the Reference Manager – EnumeratorTest dialog box, in the left pane, expand the Projects node and click Solution. In the middle pane, select the BinaryTree project, and then click OK.

   Note These two steps ensure that the EnumeratorTest project references the correct version of the *BinaryTree* assembly. It should use the assembly that implements the enumerator by using the iterator rather than the version created in the previous set of exercises in this chapter.

5. Display the Program.cs file for the EnumeratorTest project in the Code and Text Editor window. Review the *Main* method in the Program.cs file. Recall from testing the earlier enumerator that this method instantiates a *Tree<int>* object, fills it with some data, and then uses a *foreach* statement to display its contents.

6. Build the solution, and correct any errors if necessary.

7. On the Debug menu, click Start Without Debugging.

   The program runs and displays the values in the same sequence as before.

–12, –8, 0, 5, 5, 10, 10, 11, 14, 15

8. Press Enter and return to Visual Studio 2015.

Summary

In this chapter, you saw how to implement the *IEnumerable<T>* and *IEnumerator<T>* interfaces with a collection class to enable applications to iterate through the items in the collection. You also saw how to implement an enumerator by using an iterator.

- If you want to continue to the next chapter, keep Visual Studio 2015 running and turn to Chapter 20, "Decoupling application logic and handling events."

- If you want to exit Visual Studio 2015 now, on the File menu, click Exit. If you see a Save dialog box, click Yes and save the project.

Quick reference

To	Do this

Make a collection class enumerable, allowing it to support the *foreach* construct	Implement the *IEnumerable* interface and provide a *GetEnumerator* method that returns an *IEnumerator* object. For example:
	
	``
	public class Tree<TItem> : IEnumerable<TItem>
	{
	    ...
	    IEnumerator<TItem> GetEnumerator()
	    {
	        ...
	    }
	}
	``

Implement an enumerator without using an iterator	Define an enumerator class that implements the *IEnumerator* interface and that provides the *Current* property and the *MoveNext* method (and optionally the *Reset* method). For example:
	
	``
	public class TreeEnumerator<TItem> :
	IEnumerator<TItem>
	{
	    ...
	    TItem Current
	    {
	        get
	        {
	            ...
	        }
	    }
	
	    bool MoveNext()
	    {
	        ...
	    }
	}
	``

Define an enumerator by using an iterator	Implement the enumerator to indicate which items should be returned (using the *yield* statement) and in which order. For example:
	
	``
	IEnumerator<TItem> GetEnumerator()
	{
	    for (...)
	    {
	        yield return ...
	    }
	}
	``

CHAPTER 20

Decoupling application logic and handling events

After completing this chapter, you will be able to:

- Declare a delegate type to create an abstraction of a method signature.

- Create an instance of a delegate to refer to a specific method.

- Call a method through a delegate.

- Define a lambda expression to specify the code to be executed by a delegate.

- Declare an event field.

- Handle an event by using a delegate.

- Raise an event.

Many of the examples and exercises in this book have placed great emphasis on the careful definition of classes and structures to enforce encapsulation. In this way, the implementation of the methods in these types can change without unduly affecting the applications that use them. Sometimes, however, it is not possible or desirable to encapsulate the entire functionality of a type. For example, the logic for a method in a class might depend upon which component or application invokes this method, which might need to perform some application or component-specific processing as part of its operation. However, when you build such a class and implement its methods, you might not know which applications and components are going to use it, and you need to avoid introducing dependencies in your code that might restrict the use of your class. Delegates provide the ideal solution, making it possible for you to fully decouple the application logic in your methods from the applications that invoke them.

Events in C# support a related scenario. Much of the code you have written in the exercises in this book assumes that statements execute sequentially. Although this is the most common case, you will find that it is sometimes necessary to interrupt the current flow of execution to perform another, more important task. When that task is complete, the program can continue where it left off. The classic examples of this style of program are the Universal Windows Platform (UWP) forms that you have been using in the exercises involving graphical applications. A form displays controls such as buttons and text boxes. When you click a button or type text in a text box, you expect the form to respond immediately. The application has to temporarily stop what it is doing and handle your input.

This style of operation applies not only to graphical user interfaces (GUIs), but also to any application where an operation must be performed urgently—shutting down the reactor in a nuclear power plant if it is getting too hot, for example. To handle this kind of processing, the runtime has to provide two things: a means of indicating that something urgent has happened, and a way of specifying the code that should be run when the urgent event happens. Events, in conjunction with delegates, provide the infrastructure with which you can implement systems that follow this approach.

You'll start by looking at delegates.

Understanding delegates

A delegate is a reference to a method. It is a very simple concept with extraordinarily powerful implications. Let me explain.

> **Note** Delegates are so named because they "delegate" processing to the referenced method when they are invoked.

Typically, when you write a statement that invokes a method, you specify the name of the method (and possibly specify the object or structure to which the method belongs). It is clear from your code exactly which method you are running and when you are running it. Look at the following simple example that calls the *performCalculation* method of a *Processor* object (what this method does or how the *Processor* class is defined is immaterial for this discussion):

```
Processor p = new Processor();
p.performCalculation();
```

A *delegate* is an object that refers to a method. You can assign a reference to a method to a delegate in much the same way that you can assign an *int* value to an *int* variable. The next example creates a delegate named *performCalculationDelegate* that references the *performCalculation* method of the *Processor* object. I have deliberately omitted some elements of the statement that declares the delegate because it is more important to understand the concept rather than worry about the syntax (you will see the full syntax shortly).

```
Processor p = new Processor();
delegate ... performCalculationDelegate ...;
performCalculationDelegate = p.performCalculation;
```

Keep in mind that the statement that assigns the method reference to the delegate does not run the method at that point; there are no parentheses after the method name, and you do not specify any parameters (if the method takes them). This is just an assignment statement.

Having stored a reference to the *performCalculation* method of the *Processor* object in the delegate, the application can subsequently invoke the method through the delegate, like this:

```
performCalculationDelegate();
```

This looks like an ordinary method call; if you did not know otherwise, it looks like you might actually be running a method named *performCalculationDelegate*. However, the common language runtime (CLR) knows that this is a delegate, so it retrieves the method that the delegate references and runs that instead. Later on, you can change the method to which a delegate refers, so a statement that calls a delegate might actually run a different method each time it executes. Additionally, a delegate can reference more than one method at a time (think of it as a collection of method references), and when you invoke a delegate all the methods to which it refers will run.

> **Note** If you are familiar with C++, a delegate is similar to a function pointer. However, unlike function pointers, delegates are completely type safe. You can make a delegate refer only to a method that matches the signature of the delegate, and you cannot invoke a delegate that does not refer to a valid method.

Examples of delegates in the .NET Framework class library

The Microsoft .NET Framework class library makes extensive use of delegates for many of its types, two examples of which are in Chapter 18, "Using collections": the *Find* method and the *Exists* method of the *List<T>* class. If you recall, these methods search through a *List<T>* collection, either returning a matching item or testing for the existence of a matching item. When the designers of the *List<T>* class were implementing it, they had absolutely no idea about what should actually constitute a match in your application code, so they let you define that by providing your own code in the form of a predicate. A predicate is really just a delegate that happens to return a Boolean value.

The following code should help to remind you how to use the *Find* method:

```
struct Person
{
    public int ID { get; set; }
    public string Name { get; set; }
    public int Age { get; set; }
}
...
List<Person> personnel = new List<Person>()
{
    new Person() { ID = 1, Name = "John", Age = 47 },
    new Person() { ID = 2, Name = "Sid", Age = 28 },
    new Person() { ID = 3, Name = "Fred", Age = 34 },
    new Person() { ID = 4, Name = "Paul", Age = 22 },
};
...
// Find the member of the list that has an ID of 3
Person match = personnel.Find(p => p.ID == 3);
```

Other examples of methods exposed by the *List<T>* class that use delegates to perform their operations are *Average, Max, Min, Count,* and *Sum*. These methods take a *Func* delegate as the parameter. A *Func* delegate refers to a method that returns a value (a function). In the following examples, the *Average* method is used to calculate the average age of items in the personnel collection (the *Func<T>* delegate simply returns the value in the *Age* field of each item in the collection), the *Max* method is used to determine the item with the highest ID, and the *Count* method calculates how many items have an *Age* between 30 and 39 inclusive.

```
double averageAge = personnel.Average(p => p.Age);
Console.WriteLine($"Average age is {averageAge}");
...
int id = personnel.Max(p => p.ID);
Console.WriteLine($"Person with highest ID is {id}");
...
int thirties = personnel.Count(p => p.Age >= 30 && p.Age <= 39);
Console.WriteLine($"Number of personnel in their thirties is {thirties}");
```

This code generates the following output:

```
Average age is 32.75
Person with highest ID is 4
Number of personnel in their thirties is 1
```

You will meet many examples of these and other delegate types used by the .NET Framework class library throughout the remainder of this book. You can also define your own delegates. The best way to fully understand how and when you might want to do this is to see them in action, so next you'll work through an example.

The *Func<T, …>* and *Action<T, …>* delegate types

The parameter taken by the *Average*, *Max, Count*, and other methods of the *List<T>* class is actually a generic *Func<T, TResult>* delegate; the type parameters refer to the type of the parameter passed to the delegate and the type of the return value. For the *Average*, *Max*, and *Count* methods of the *List<Person>* class shown in the text, the first type parameter *T* is the type of data in the list (the *Person* struct), whereas the *TResult* type parameter is determined by the context in which the delegate is used. In the following example, the type of *TResult* is *int* because the value returned by the *Count* method should be an integer:

```
int thirties = personnel.Count(p => p.Age >= 30 && p.Age <= 39);
```

So, in this example, the type of the delegate expected by the *Count* method is *Func<Person, int>*.

This point might seem somewhat academic because the compiler automatically generates the delegate based on the type of the *List<T>*, but it is worth familiarizing yourself with this idiom as it occurs time and again throughout the .NET Framework class library. In fact, the *System* namespace defines an entire family of *Func* delegate types, from *Func<TResult>* for functions that return a result without taking any parameters, to *Func<T1, T2, T3, T4, …, T16, TResult>* for functions that take 16 parameters. If you find yourself in a situation in which you are creating your own delegate type that matches this pattern, you should consider using an appropriate *Func* delegate type instead. You will meet the *Func* delegate types again in Chapter 21, "Querying in-memory data by using query expressions."

Alongside *Func*, the *System* namespace also defines a series of *Action* delegate types. An *Action* delegate is used to reference a method that performs an action instead of returning a value (a *void* method). Again, a family of *Action* delegate types is available ranging from *Action<T>* (specifying a delegate that takes a single parameter) to *Action<T1, T2, T3, T4, ..., T16>*.

The automated factory scenario

Suppose you are writing the control systems for an automated factory. The factory contains a large number of different machines, each performing distinct tasks in the production of the articles manufactured by the factory—shaping and folding metal sheets, welding sheets together, painting sheets, and so on. Each machine was built and installed by a specialist vendor. The machines are all controlled by computer, and each vendor has provided a set of functions that you can use to control its machine. Your task is to integrate the different systems used by the machines into a single control program. One aspect on which you have decided to concentrate is to provide a means of shutting down all the machines—quickly, if needed!

Each machine has its own unique computer-controlled process (and functions) for shutting down safely, as summarized here:

```
StopFolding();      // Folding and shaping machine
FinishWelding();    // Welding machine
PaintOff();         // Painting machine
```

Implementing the factory control system without using delegates

A simple approach to implementing the shutdown functionality in the control program is as follows:

```
class Controller
{
    // Fields representing the different machines
    private FoldingMachine folder;
    private WeldingMachine welder;
    private PaintingMachine painter;
    ...
    public void ShutDown()
    {
        folder.StopFolding();
        welder.FinishWelding();
        painter.PaintOff();
    }
    ...
}
```

Although this approach works, it is not very extensible or flexible. If the factory buys a new machine, you must modify this code; the *Controller* class and code for managing the machines is tightly coupled.

Implementing the factory by using a delegate

Although the names of each method are different, they all have the same "shape": they take no parameters, and they do not return a value. (You'll consider what happens if this isn't the case later, so bear with me.) The general format of each method, therefore, is this:

```
void methodName();
```

This is where a delegate can be useful. You can use a delegate that matches this shape to refer to any of the machinery shutdown methods. You declare a delegate like this:

```
delegate void stopMachineryDelegate();
```

Note the following points:

- You use the *delegate* keyword.

- You specify the return type (*void* in this example), a name for the delegate (*stopMachinery-Delegate*), and any parameters (there are none in this case).

After you have declared the delegate, you can create an instance and make it refer to a matching method by using the += compound assignment operator. You can do this in the constructor of the controller class like this:

```
class Controller
{
    delegate void stopMachineryDelegate();      // the delegate type
    private stopMachineryDelegate stopMachinery; // an instance of the delegate
    ...
    public Controller()
    {
        this.stopMachinery += folder.StopFolding;
    }
    ...
}
```

It takes a bit of study to get used to this syntax. You *add* the method to the delegate—remember that you are not actually calling the method at this point. The + operator is overloaded to have this new meaning when used with delegates. (You will learn more about operator overloading in Chapter 22, "Operator overloading.") Notice that you simply specify the method name and do not include any parentheses or parameters.

It is safe to use the += operator on an uninitialized delegate. It will be initialized automatically. Alternatively, you can use the *new* keyword to initialize a delegate explicitly with a single specific method, like this:

```
this.stopMachinery = new stopMachineryDelegate(folder.StopFolding);
```

You can call the method by invoking the delegate, like this:

```
public void ShutDown()
{
    this.stopMachinery();
    ...
}
```

You use the same syntax to invoke a delegate as you use to call a method. If the method that the delegate refers to takes any parameters, you should specify them at this time between the parentheses.

> **Note** If you attempt to invoke a delegate that is uninitialized and does not refer to any methods, you will get a *NullReferenceException* exception.

An important advantage of using a delegate is that it can refer to more than one method at the same time. You simply use the += operator to add methods to the delegate, like this:

```
public Controller()
{
    this.stopMachinery += folder.StopFolding;
    this.stopMachinery += welder.FinishWelding;
    this.stopMachinery += painter.PaintOff;
}
```

Invoking *this.stopMachinery()* in the *Shutdown* method of the *Controller* class automatically calls each of the methods in turn. The *Shutdown* method does not need to know how many machines there are or what the method names are.

You can remove a method from a delegate by using the −= compound assignment operator, as demonstrated here:

```
this.stopMachinery -= folder.StopFolding;
```

The current scheme adds the machine methods to the delegate in the *Controller* constructor. To make the *Controller* class totally independent of the various machines, you need to make the *stopMachineryDelegate* type public and supply a means of enabling classes outside *Controller* to add methods to the delegate. You have several options:

- Make the *stopMachinery* delegate variable public:

  ```
  public stopMachineryDelegate stopMachinery;
  ```

- Keep the *stopMachinery* delegate variable private, but create a read/write property to provide access to it:

  ```
  private stopMachineryDelegate stopMachinery;
  ...
  ```

```
public stopMachineryDelegate StopMachinery
{
    get
    {
        return this.stopMachinery;
    }

    set
    {
        this.stopMachinery = value;
    }
}
```

- Provide complete encapsulation by implementing separate *Add* and *Remove* methods. The *Add* method takes a method as a parameter and adds it to the delegate, whereas the *Remove* method removes the specified method from the delegate (notice that you specify a method as a parameter by using a delegate type):

```
public void Add(stopMachineryDelegate stopMethod)
{
    this.stopMachinery += stopMethod;
}

public void Remove(stopMachineryDelegate stopMethod)
{
    this.stopMachinery -= stopMethod;
}
```

An object-oriented purist would probably opt for the *Add/Remove* approach. However, the other approaches are viable alternatives that are frequently used, which is why they are shown here.

Whichever technique you choose, you should remove the code that adds the machine methods to the delegate from the *Controller* constructor. You can then instantiate a *Controller* and objects representing the other machines like this (this example uses the *Add/Remove* approach):

```
Controller control = new Controller();
FoldingMachine folder = new FoldingMachine();
WeldingMachine welder = new WeldingMachine();
PaintingMachine painter = new PaintingMachine();
...
control.Add(folder.StopFolding);
control.Add(welder.FinishWelding);
control.Add(painter.PaintOff);
...
control.ShutDown();
...
```

Declaring and using delegates

In the following exercises, you will complete an application that forms part of a system for a company called Wide World Importers. Wide World Importers imports and sells building materials and tools, and the application that you will be working on gives customers the ability to browse the items that Wide World Importers currently has in stock and place orders for these items. The application contains a form that displays the goods currently available, together with a pane that lists the items that a customer has selected. When the customer wants to place an order, she can click the Checkout button on the form. The order is then processed, and the pane is cleared.

Currently, when the customer places an order, several actions occur:

- Payment is requested from the customer.

- The items in the order are examined, and if any of them are age restricted (such as the power tools), details of the order are audited and tracked.

- A dispatch note is generated for shipping purposes. This dispatch note contains a summary of the order.

The logic for the auditing and shipping processes is independent from the checkout logic, although the order in which these processes occur is immaterial. Furthermore, either of these elements might be amended in the future, and additional processing might be required by the checkout operation as business circumstances or regulatory requirements change in the future. Therefore, it is desirable to decouple the payment and checkout logic from the auditing and shipping processes to make maintenance and upgrades easier. You will start by examining the application to see how it currently fails to fulfill this objective. You will then modify the structure of the application to remove the dependencies between the checkout logic and the auditing and shipping logic.

Examine the Wide World Importers application

1. Start Microsoft Visual Studio 2015 if it is not already running.

2. Open the Delegates project, which is located in the \Microsoft Press\VCSBS\Chapter 20\ Delegates folder in your Documents folder.

3. On the Debug menu, click Start Debugging.

   The project builds and runs. A form appears displaying the items available, together with a panel showing the details of the order (it is empty initially). The app displays the items in a *GridView* control that scrolls horizontally:

Wide World Importers

4. Select one or more items and then click Add to include them in the shopping basket. Be sure that you select at least one age-restricted item.

As you add an item, it appears in the Order Details pane on the right. Notice that if you add the same item more than once, the quantity is incremented for each click. (This version of the application does not implement functionality to remove items from the basket.)

5. In the Order Details pane, click Checkout.

A message appears indicating that the order has been placed. The order is given a unique ID, and this ID is displayed together with the value of the order.

6. Click Close to dismiss the message, and then return to the Visual Studio 2015 environment and stop debugging.

7. In Solution Explorer, expand the Delegates project node, and then open the Package.appxmanifest file.

The package manifest editor appears.

8. In the package manifest editor, click the Packaging tab.

Note the value in the Package Name field. It takes the form of a globally unique identifier (GUID).

9. Using File Explorer, browse to %USERPROFILE%\AppData\Local\Packages\yyy\LocalState, where yyy is an identifier value that begins with the GUID you noted in the previous step. This is the local folder for the Wide World Importers application. You should see two files, one named audit-nnnnnn.xml (where nnnnnn is the ID of the order displayed earlier), and the other dispatch-nnnnnn.txt. The first file was generated by the auditing component of the app, and the second file is the dispatch note generated by the shipping component.

> **Note** If there is no audit-*nnnnnn*.xml file, then you did not select any age-restricted items when you placed the order. In this case, switch back to the application and create a new order that includes one or more of these items.

10. Open the audit-*nnnnnn*.xml file by using Visual Studio. This file contains a list of the age-restricted items in the order together with the order number and date. It should look similar to this:

    Close the file in Visual Studio when you finish examining this list.

11. Open the dispatch-*nnnnnn*.txt file by using Notepad. This file contains a summary of the order, listing the order ID and the value. It should look similar to this:

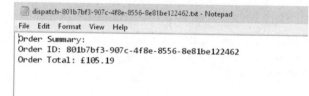

    Close Notepad, return to Visual Studio 2015, and stop debugging.

12. In Visual Studio, notice that the solution consists of the following projects:

    - **Delegates** This project contains the application itself. The MainPage.xaml file defines the user interface, and the application logic is contained in the MainPage.xaml.cs file.

    - **AuditService** This project contains the component that implements the auditing process. It is packaged as a class library and contains a single class named *Auditor*. This class exposes a single public method, *AuditOrder*, that examines an order and generates the audit-*nnnnnn*.xml file if the order contains any age-restricted items.

    - **DeliveryService** This project contains the component that performs the shipping logic, packaged as a class library. The shipping functionality is contained in the *Shipper* class, and it provides a public method named *ShipOrder* that handles the shipping process and also generates the dispatch note.

> **Note** You are welcome to examine the code in the *Auditor* and *Shipper* classes, but it is not necessary to fully understand the inner workings of these components in this application.

- **DataTypes** This project contains the data types used by the other projects. The *Product* class defines the details of the products displayed by the application, and the data for the products is held in the *ProductsDataSource* class. (The application currently uses a small hard-coded set of products. In a production system, this information would be retrieved from a database or web service.) The *Order* and *OrderItem* classes implement the structure of an order; each order contains one or more order items.

13. In the Delegates project, display the MainPage.xaml.cs file in the Code and Text Editor window and examine the private fields and *MainPage* constructor in this file. The important elements look like this:

```
...
private Auditor auditor = null;
private Shipper shipper = null;


public MainPage()
{
    ...
    this.auditor = new Auditor();
    this.shipper = new Shipper();
}
```

The *auditor* and *shipper* fields contain references to instances of the *Auditor* and *Shipper* classes, and the constructor instantiates these objects.

14. Locate the *CheckoutButtonClicked* method. This method runs when the user clicks Checkout to place an order. The first few lines look like this:

```
private void CheckoutButtonClicked(object sender, RoutedEventArgs e)
{
    try
    {
        // Perform the checkout processing
        if (this.requestPayment())
        {
            this.auditor.AuditOrder(this.order);
            this.shipper.ShipOrder(this.order);
        }
        ...
    }
    ...
}
```

This method implements the checkout processing. It requests payment from the customer and then invokes the *AuditOrder* method of the *auditor* object followed by the *ShipOrder* method of the *shipper* object. Any additional business logic required in the future can be added here. The remainder of the code in this method (after the *if* statement) is concerned with managing the user interface: displaying the message box to the user and clearing out the Order Details pane.

> **Note** For simplicity, the *requestPayment* method in this application currently just returns *true* to indicate that payment has been received. In the real world, this method would perform the complete payment processing.

Although the application operates as advertised, the Auditor and Shipper components are tightly integrated into the checkout processing. If these components change, the application will need to be updated. Similarly, if you need to incorporate additional logic into the checkout process, possibly performed by using other components, you will need to amend this part of the application.

In the next exercise, you will see how you can decouple the business processing for the checkout operation from the application. The checkout processing will still need to invoke the Auditor and Shipper components, but it must be extensible enough to allow additional components to be easily incorporated. You will achieve this by creating a component called *CheckoutController*. The *CheckoutController* component will implement the business logic for the checkout process and expose a delegate that enables an application to specify which components and methods should be included within this process. The *CheckoutController* component will invoke these methods by using the delegate.

Create the *CheckoutController* component

1. In Solution Explorer, right-click the Delegates solution, point to Add, and then click New Project.

2. In the Add New Project dialog box, in the left pane, expand Windows, and then click the Universal node. In the middle pane, select the Class Library (Universal Windows) template. In the Name box, type **CheckoutService**, and then click OK.

3. In Solution Explorer, expand the CheckoutService project, right-click the file Class1.cs, and then click Rename. Change the name of the file to **CheckoutController.cs** and then press Enter. Allow Visual Studio to rename all references to Class1 as CheckoutController when prompted.

4. Right-click the References node in the CheckoutService project, and then click Add Reference.

5. In the Reference Manager – CheckoutService dialog box, in the left pane, click Solution. In the middle pane, select the DataTypes project, and then click OK.

   The *CheckoutController* class will use the *Order* class defined in the DataTypes project.

6. In the Code and Text Editor window displaying the CheckoutController.cs file, add the following *using* directive to the list at the top of the file:

```
using DataTypes;
```

7. Add to the *CheckoutController* class a public delegate type called *CheckoutDelegate*, as shown in the following in bold:

```
public class CheckoutController
{
    public delegate void CheckoutDelegate(Order order);
}
```

You can use this delegate type to reference methods that take an *Order* parameter and that do not return a result. This just happens to match the shape of the *AuditOrder* and *ShipOrder* methods of the *Auditor* and *Shipper* classes.

8. Add a public delegate called *CheckoutProcessing* based on this delegate type, like this:

```
public class CheckoutController
{
    public delegate void CheckoutDelegate(Order order);
    public CheckoutDelegate CheckoutProcessing = null;
}
```

9. Display the MainPage.xaml.cs file of the Delegates project in the Code and Text Editor window and locate the *requestPayment* method (it is at the end of the file). Cut this method from the *MainPage* class. Return to the CheckoutController.cs file, and paste the *requestPayment* method into the *CheckoutController* class, as shown in bold in the following:

```
public class CheckoutController
{
    public delegate void CheckoutDelegate(Order order);
    public CheckoutDelegate CheckoutProcessing = null;

    private bool requestPayment()
    {
        // Payment processing goes here

        // Payment logic is not implemented in this example
        // - simply return true to indicate payment has been received
        return true;
    }
}
```

10. Add to the *CheckoutController* class the *StartCheckoutProcessing* method shown here in bold:

```
public class CheckoutController
{
    public delegate void CheckoutDelegate(Order order);
    public CheckoutDelegate CheckoutProcessing = null;

    private bool requestPayment()
    {
        ...
    }
```

```
    public void StartCheckoutProcessing(Order order)
    {
        // Perform the checkout processing
        if (this.requestPayment())
        {
            if (this.CheckoutProcessing != null)
            {
                this.CheckoutProcessing(order);
            }
        }
    }
}
```

This method provides the checkout functionality previously implemented by the *Checkout-ButtonClicked* method of the *MainPage* class. It requests payment and then examines the *CheckoutProcessing* delegate; if this delegate is not *null* (it refers to one or more methods), it invokes the delegate. Any methods referenced by this delegate will run at this point.

11. In Solution Explorer, in the Delegates project, right-click the References node and then click Add Reference.

12. In the Reference Manager – Delegates dialog box, in the left pane, click Solution. In the middle pane, select the CheckoutService project, and then click OK.

13. Return to the MainPage.xaml.cs file of the Delegates project and add the following *using* directive to the list at the top of the file:

```
using CheckoutService;
```

14. Add to the *MainPage* class a private variable named *checkoutController* of type *Checkout-Controller* and initialize it to *null*, as shown in bold in the following:

```
public ... class MainPage : ...
{
    ...
    private Auditor auditor = null;
    private Shipper shipper = null;
    private CheckoutController checkoutController = null;
    ...
}
```

15. Locate the *MainPage* constructor. After the statements that create the *Auditor* and *Shipper* components, instantiate the *CheckoutController* component, as follows in bold:

```
public MainPage()
{
    ...
    this.auditor = new Auditor();
    this.shipper = new Shipper();
    this.checkoutController = new CheckoutController();
}
```

16. After the statement you just entered, add to the constructor the following statements shown in bold:

```
public MainPage()
{
    ...
    this.checkoutController = new CheckoutController();
    this.checkoutController.CheckoutProcessing += this.auditor.AuditOrder;
    this.checkoutController.CheckoutProcessing += this.shipper.ShipOrder;
}
```

This code adds references to the *AuditOrder* and *ShipOrder* methods of the *Auditor* and *Shipper* objects to the *CheckoutProcessing* delegate of the *CheckoutController* object.

17. Find the *CheckoutButtonClicked* method. In the *try* block, replace the code that performs the checkout processing (the *if* statement block) with the statement shown here in bold:

```
private void CheckoutButtonClicked(object sender, RoutedEventArgs e)
{
    try
    {
        // Perform the checkout processing
        this.checkoutController.StartCheckoutProcessing(this.order);

        // Display a summary of the order
        ...
    }
    ...
}
```

You have now decoupled the checkout logic from the components that this checkout processing uses. The business logic in the *MainPage* class specifies which components the *CheckoutController* should use.

Test the application

1. On the Debug menu, click Start Debugging to build and run the application.

2. When the Wide World Importers form appears, select some items (include at least one age-restricted item), and then click Checkout.

3. When the Order Placed message appears, make a note of the order number, and then click Close or OK.

4. Switch to File Explorer and move to the %USERPROFILE%\AppData\Local\Packages*yyy*\ LocalState folder, where *yyy* is an identifier value that begins with the GUID you noted previously. Verify that a new audit-*nnnnnn*.xml file and dispatch-*nnnnnn*.txt file have been created, where *nnnnnn* is the number that identifies the new order. Examine these files and verify that they contain the details of the order.

5. Return to Visual Studio 2015 and stop debugging.

Lambda expressions and delegates

All the examples of adding a method to a delegate that you have seen so far use the method's name. For example, in the automated factory scenario described earlier, you add the *StopFolding* method of the *folder* object to the *stopMachinery* delegate like this:

```
this.stopMachinery += folder.StopFolding;
```

This approach is very useful if there is a convenient method that matches the signature of the delegate. But what if the *StopFolding* method actually had the following signature:

```
void StopFolding(int shutDownTime); // Shut down in the specified number of seconds
```

This signature is now different from that of the *FinishWelding* and *PaintOff* methods, and therefore you cannot use the same delegate to handle all three methods. What do you do?

Creating a method adapter

One way around this problem is to create another method that calls *StopFolding* but that takes no parameters itself, like this:

```
void FinishFolding()
{
    folder.StopFolding(0); // Shut down immediately
}
```

You can then add the *FinishFolding* method to the *stopMachinery* delegate in place of the *StopFolding* method, using the same syntax as before:

```
this.stopMachinery += folder.FinishFolding;
```

When the *stopMachinery* delegate is invoked, it calls *FinishFolding*, which in turn calls the *StopFolding* method, passing in the parameter 0.

> **Note** The *FinishFolding* method is a classic example of an adapter: a method that converts (or adapts) a method to give it a different signature. This pattern is very common and is one of the set of patterns documented in the book *Design Patterns: Elements of Reusable Object-Oriented Software* by Erich Gamma, Richard Helm, Ralph Johnson, and John Vlissides (Addison-Wesley Professional, 1994).

In many cases, adapter methods such as this are small, and it is easy to lose them in a sea of methods, especially in a large class. Furthermore, the method is unlikely to be called except for its use in adapting the *StopFolding* method for use by the delegate. C# provides lambda expressions for situations such as this. Lambda expressions are described in Chapter 18, and there are more examples of them earlier in this chapter. In the factory scenario, you can use the following lambda expression:

```
this.stopMachinery += (() => folder.StopFolding(0));
```

When you invoke the *stopMachinery* delegate, it will run the code defined by the lambda expression, which will, in turn, call the *StopFolding* method with the appropriate parameter.

Enabling notifications by using events

You have now seen how to declare a delegate type, call a delegate, and create delegate instances. However, this is only half the story. Although you can invoke any number of methods indirectly by using delegates, you still have to invoke the delegate explicitly. In many cases, it would be useful to have the delegate run automatically when something significant happens. For example, in the automated factory scenario, it could be vital to be able to invoke the *stopMachinery* delegate and halt the equipment if the system detects that a machine is overheating.

The .NET Framework provides *events*, which you can use to define and trap significant actions and arrange for a delegate to be called to handle the situation. Many classes in the .NET Framework expose events. Most of the controls that you can place on a form in a UWP app, and the *Windows* class itself, use events to run code when, for example, the user clicks a button or types something in a field. You can also declare your own events.

Declaring an event

You declare an event in a class intended to act as an event source. An *event source* is usually a class that monitors its environment and raises an event when something significant happens. In the automated factory, an event source could be a class that monitors the temperature of each machine. The temperature-monitoring class would raise a "machine overheating" event if it detects that a machine has exceeded its thermal radiation boundary (that is, it has become too hot). An event maintains a list of methods to call when it is raised. These methods are sometimes referred to as *subscribers*. These methods should be prepared to handle the "machine overheating" event and take the necessary corrective action: shut down the machines.

You declare an event similarly to how you declare a field. However, because events are intended to be used with delegates, the type of an event must be a delegate, and you must prefix the declaration with the *event* keyword. Use the following syntax to declare an event:

```
event delegateTypeName eventName
```

As an example, here's the *StopMachineryDelegate* delegate from the automated factory. It has been relocated to a class named *TemperatureMonitor*, which provides an interface to the various electronic probes monitoring the temperature of the equipment (this is a more logical place for the event than the *Controller* class):

```
class TemperatureMonitor
{
    public delegate void StopMachineryDelegate();
    ...
}
```

You can define the *MachineOverheating* event, which will invoke the *stopMachineryDelegate*, like this:

```
class TemperatureMonitor
{
    public delegate void StopMachineryDelegate();
    public event StopMachineryDelegate MachineOverheating;
    ...
}
```

The logic (not shown) in the *TemperatureMonitor* class raises the *MachineOverheating* event as necessary. (You will see how to raise an event in an upcoming section.) Also, you add methods to an event (a process known as *subscribing* to the event) rather than add them to the delegate on which the event is based. You will look at this aspect of events next.

Subscribing to an event

Like delegates, events come ready-made with a += operator. You subscribe to an event by using this += operator. In the automated factory, the software controlling each machine can arrange for the shutdown methods to be called when the *MachineOverheating* event is raised like this:

```
class TemperatureMonitor
{
    public delegate void StopMachineryDelegate();
    public event StopMachineryDelegate MachineOverheating;
    ...
}
...
TemperatureMonitor tempMonitor = new TemperatureMonitor();
...
tempMonitor.MachineOverheating += (() => { folder.StopFolding(0); });
tempMonitor.MachineOverheating += welder.FinishWelding;
tempMonitor.MachineOverheating += painter.PaintOff;
```

Notice that the syntax is the same as for adding a method to a delegate. You can even subscribe by using a lambda expression. When the *tempMonitor.MachineOverheating* event runs, it will call all the subscribing methods and shut down the machines.

Unsubscribing from an event

Knowing that you use the += operator to attach a delegate to an event, you can probably guess that you use the −= operator to detach a delegate from an event. Calling the −= operator removes the method from the event's internal delegate collection. This action is often referred to as *unsubscribing* from the event.

Raising an event

You can raise an event by calling it like a method. When you raise an event, all the attached delegates are called in sequence. For example, here's the *TemperatureMonitor* class with a private *Notify* method that raises the *MachineOverheating* event:

```
class TemperatureMonitor
{
    public delegate void StopMachineryDelegate();
    public event StopMachineryDelegate MachineOverheating;
    ...
    private void Notify()
    {
        if (this.MachineOverheating != null)
        {
            this.MachineOverheating();
        }
    }
    ...
}
```

This is a common idiom. The *null* check is necessary because an event field is implicitly null and only becomes nonnull when a method subscribes to it by using the += operator. If you try to raise a null event, you will get a *NullReferenceException* exception. If the delegate defining the event expects any parameters, the appropriate arguments must be provided when you raise the event. You will see some examples of this later.

> **Important** Events have a very useful built-in security feature. A public event (such as *MachineOverheating*) can be raised only by methods in the class that define it (the *TemperatureMonitor* class). Any attempt to raise the event outside the class results in a compiler error.

Understanding user interface events

As mentioned earlier, the .NET Framework classes and controls used for building GUIs employ events extensively. For example, the *Button* class derives from the *ButtonBase* class, inheriting a public event called *Click* of type *RoutedEventHandler*. The *RoutedEventHandler* delegate expects two parameters: a reference to the object that caused the event to be raised, and a *RoutedEventArgs* object that contains additional information about the event:

```
public delegate void RoutedEventHandler(Object sender, RoutedEventArgs e);
```

The *Button* class looks like this:

```
public class ButtonBase: ...
{
    public event RoutedEventHandler Click;
```

```
    ...
}

public class Button: ButtonBase
{
    ...
}
```

The *Button* class automatically raises the *Click* event when you click the button on the screen. This arrangement makes it easy to create a delegate for a chosen method and attach that delegate to the required event. The following example shows the code for a UWP form that contains a button named *okay* and the code to connect the *Click* event of the *okay* button to the *okayClick* method:

```
partial class MainPage :
    global::Windows.UI.Xaml.Controls.Page,
    global::Windows.UI.Xaml.Markup.IComponentConnector,
    global::Windows.UI.Xaml.Markup.IComponentConnector2
{
    ...
    public void Connect(int connectionId, object target)
    {
        switch(connectionId)
        {
            case 1:
            {
                this.okay = (global::Windows.UI.Xaml.Controls.Button)(target);
                ...
                ((global::Windows.UI.Xaml.Controls.Button)this.okay).Click += this.okayClick;
                ...
            }
            break;
        default:
            break;
        }
        this._contentLoaded = true;
    }
    ...
}
```

This code is usually hidden from you. When you use the Design View window in Visual Studio 2015 and set the *Click* property of the *okay* button to *okayClick* in the Extensible Application Markup Language (XAML) description of the form, Visual Studio 2015 generates this code for you. All you have to do is write your application logic in the event-handling method, *okayClick*, in the part of the code to which you do have access, which is the MainPage.xaml.cs file in this case:

```
public sealed partial class MainPage : Page
{
    ...
    private void okayClick(object sender, RoutedEventArgs e)
    {
        // your code to handle the Click event
    }
}
```

The events that the various GUI controls generate always follow the same pattern. The events are of a delegate type whose signature has a *void* return type and two arguments. The first argument is always the sender (the source) of the event, and the second argument is always an *EventArgs* argument (or a class derived from *EventArgs*).

With the *sender* argument, you can reuse a single method for multiple events. The delegated method can examine the *sender* argument and respond accordingly. For example, you can use the same method to subscribe to the *Click* event for two buttons. (You add the same method to two different events.) When the event is raised, the code in the method can examine the *sender* argument to ascertain which button was clicked.

Using events

In the previous exercise, you amended the Wide World Importers application to decouple the auditing and shipping logic from the checkout process. The *CheckoutController* class that you built invokes the auditing and shipping components by using a delegate and has no knowledge about these components or the methods it is running; this is the responsibility of the application that creates the *CheckoutController* object and adds the appropriate references to the delegate. However, it might be useful for a component to be able to alert the application when it has completed its processing and enable the application to perform any necessary tidying up.

This might sound a little strange at first—surely when the application invokes the delegate in the *CheckoutController* object, the methods referenced by this delegate run, and the application only continues with the next statement when these methods have finished. But this is not necessarily the case! Chapter 24, "Improving response time by performing asynchronous operations," demonstrates that methods can run asynchronously, and when you invoke a method, it might not have completed before execution continues with the next statement. This is especially true in UWP apps in which long-running operations are performed on background threads to enable the user interface to remain responsive. In the Wide World Importers application, in the *CheckoutButtonClicked* method, the code that invokes the delegate is followed by a statement that displays a dialog box with a message indicating that the order has been placed:

```
private void CheckoutButtonClicked(object sender, RoutedEventArgs e)
{
    try
    {
        // Perform the checkout processing
        this.checkoutController.StartCheckoutProcessing(this.order);

        // Display a summary of the order
        MessageDialog dlg = new MessageDialog(...);
        dlg.ShowAsync();
        ...
    }
    ...
}
```

In fact, there is no guarantee that the processing performed by the delegated methods has completed by the time the dialog box appears, so the message could actually be misleading. This is where an event is invaluable. The Auditor and Shipper components could both publish an event to which the application subscribes. This event could be raised by the components only when they have completed their processing. When the application receives this event, it can display the message, safe in the knowledge that it is now accurate.

In the following exercise, you will modify the *Auditor* and *Shipper* classes to raise an event that occurs when they have completed their processing. The application will subscribe to the event for each component and display an appropriate message when the event occurs.

Add an event to the *CheckoutController* class

1. Return to Visual Studio 2015 and display the Delegates solution.

2. In the AuditService project, open the Auditor.cs file in the Code and Text Editor window.

3. Add to the *Auditor* class a public delegate called *AuditingCompleteDelegate*. This delegate should specify a method that takes a string parameter called *message* and that returns a *void*. The code in bold in the following example shows the definition of this delegate:

```
class Auditor
{
    public delegate void AuditingCompleteDelegate(string message);
    ...
}
```

4. Add to the *Auditor* class a public event called *AuditProcessingComplete*, after the *Auditing-CompleteDelegate* delegate. This event should be based on the *AuditingCompleteDelegate* delegate as shown in bold in the following code:

```
class Auditor
{
    public delegate void AuditingCompleteDelegate(string message);
    public event AuditingCompleteDelegate AuditProcessingComplete;
    ...
}
```

5. Locate the *AuditOrder* method. This is the method that is run by using the delegate in the *CheckoutController* object. It invokes another private method called *doAuditing* to actually perform the audit operation. The method looks like this:

```
public void AuditOrder(Order order)
{
    this.doAuditing(order);
}
```

6. Scroll down to the *doAuditing* method. The code in this method is enclosed in a *try/catch* block; it uses the XML APIs of the .NET Framework class library to generate

an XML representation of the order being audited and saves it to a file. (The exact details of how this works are beyond the scope of this chapter.)

After the *catch* block, add a *finally* block that raises the *AuditProcessingComplete* event, as shown in the following in bold:

```
private async void doAuditing(Order order)
{
    List<OrderItem> ageRestrictedItems = findAgeRestrictedItems(order);
    if (ageRestrictedItems.Count > 0)
    {
        try
        {
            ...
        }
        catch (Exception ex)
        {
            ...
        }
        finally
        {
            if (this.AuditProcessingComplete != null)
            {
                this.AuditProcessingComplete(
                    $"Audit record written for Order {order.OrderID}");
            }
        }
    }
}
```

7. In the DeliveryService project, open the Shipper.cs file in the Code and Text Editor window.

8. Add a public delegate called *ShippingCompleteDelegate* to the *Shipper* class. This delegate should specify a method that takes a string parameter called *message* and that returns a *void*. The code in bold in the following example shows the definition of this delegate:

```
class Shipper
{
    public delegate void ShippingCompleteDelegate(string message);
    ...
}
```

9. Add to the *Shipper* class a public event called *ShipProcessingComplete* based on the *ShippingCompleteDelegate* delegate as shown in bold in the following code:

```
class Shipper
{
    public delegate void ShippingCompleteDelegate(string message);
    public event ShippingCompleteDelegate ShipProcessingComplete;
    ...
}
```

10. Find the *doShipping* method, which is the method that performs the shipping logic. In the method, after the *catch* block, add a *finally* block that raises the *ShipProcessingComplete* event, as shown here in bold:

```
private async void doShipping(Order order)
{
    try
    {
        ...
    }
    catch (Exception ex)
    {
        ...
    }
    finally
    {
        if (this.ShipProcessingComplete != null)
        {
            this.ShipProcessingComplete(
                $"Dispatch note generated for Order {order.OrderID}");
        }
    }
}
```

11. In the Delegates project, display the layout for the MainPage.xaml file in the Design View window. In the XAML pane, scroll down to the first set of *RowDefinition* items. The XAML code looks like this:

```
<Grid Background="{StaticResource ApplicationPageBackgroundThemeBrush}">
    <Grid Margin="12,0,12,0" Loaded="MainPageLoaded">
        <Grid.RowDefinitions>
            <RowDefinition Height="*"/>
            <RowDefinition Height="2*"/>
            <RowDefinition Height="*"/>
            <RowDefinition Height="10*"/>
            <RowDefinition Height="*"/>
        </Grid.RowDefinitions>
        ...
```

12. Change the *Height* property of the final *RowDefinition* item to *2** as shown in bold in the following code:

```
<Grid.RowDefinitions>
    ...
    <RowDefinition Height="10*"/>
    <RowDefinition Height="2*"/>
</Grid.RowDefinitions>
```

This change in the layout makes available a bit of space at the bottom of the form. You will use this space as an area for displaying the messages received from the Auditor and Shipper components when they raise their events. Chapter 25, "Implementing the user interface for a Universal Windows Platform app," provides more detail on laying out user interfaces by using a *Grid* control.

13. Scroll to the bottom of the XAML pane. Add the following *ScrollViewer* and *TextBlock* elements shown in bold before the penultimate *</Grid>* tag:

```
        ...
      </Grid>
      <ScrollViewer Grid.Row="4" VerticalScrollBarVisibility="Visible">
          <TextBlock x:Name="messageBar" FontSize="18" />
      </ScrollViewer>
    </Grid>
  </Grid>
</Page>
```

This markup adds a *TextBlock* control called *messageBar* to the area at the bottom of the screen. You will use this control to display messages from the *Auditor* and *Shipper* objects.

14. Display the MainPage.xaml.cs file in the Code and Text Editor window. Find the *CheckoutButtonClicked* method and remove the code that displays the summary of the order. The *try* block should look like this after you have deleted the code:

```
private void CheckoutButtonClicked(object sender, RoutedEventArgs e)
{
    try
    {
        // Perform the checkout processing
        this.checkoutController.StartCheckoutProcessing(this.order);

        // Clear out the order details so the user can start again with a new order
        this.order = new Order { Date = DateTime.Now, Items = new List<OrderItem>(),
                                 OrderID = Guid.NewGuid(), TotalValue = 0 };
        this.orderDetails.DataContext = null;
        this.orderValue.Text = $"{order.TotalValue:C}");
        this.listViewHeader.Visibility = Visibility.Collapsed;
        this.checkout.IsEnabled = false;
    }
    catch (Exception ex)
    {
        ...
    }
}
```

15. Add a private method called *displayMessage* to the *MainPage* class. This method should take a string parameter called *message* and should return a *void*. In the body of this method, add a statement that appends the value in the *message* parameter to the *Text* property of the *messageBar TextBlock* control, followed by a newline character, as shown here in bold:

```
private void displayMessage(string message)
{
    this.messageBar.Text += message + "\n";
}
```

This code causes the message to appear in the message area at the bottom of the form.

16. Find the constructor for the *MainPage* class and add the code shown here in bold:

```
public MainPage()
{
    ...
```

```
        this.auditor = new Auditor();
        this.shipper = new Shipper();
        this.checkoutController = new CheckoutController();
        this.checkoutController.CheckoutProcessing += this.auditor.AuditOrder;
        this.checkoutController.CheckoutProcessing += this.shipper.ShipOrder;

        this.auditor.AuditProcessingComplete += this.displayMessage;
        this.shipper.ShipProcessingComplete += this.displayMessage;
}
```

These statements subscribe to the events exposed by the *Auditor* and *Shipper* objects. When the events are raised, the *displayMessage* method runs. Notice that the same method handles both events.

17. On the Debug menu, click Start Debugging to build and run the application.

18. When the Wide World Importers form appears, select some items (include at least one age-restricted item), and then click Checkout.

19. Verify that the "Audit record written" message appears in the *TextBlock* at the bottom of the form, followed by the "Dispatch note generated" message:

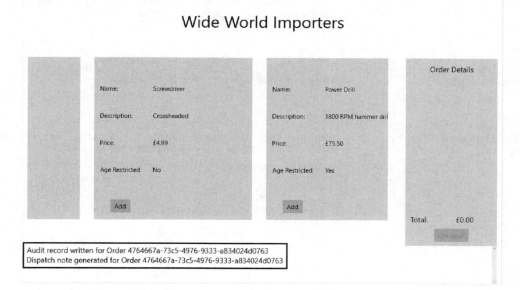

20. Place further orders and note the new messages that appear each time you click Checkout (you might need to scroll down to see them when the message area fills up).

21. When you have finished, return to Visual Studio 2015 and stop debugging.

Summary

In this chapter, you learned how to use delegates to reference methods and invoke those methods. You also saw how to define lambda expressions that can be run by using a delegate. Finally, you learned how to define and use events to trigger execution of a method.

- If you want to continue to the next chapter, keep Visual Studio 2015 running and turn to Chapter 21.

- If you want to exit Visual Studio 2015 now, on the File menu, click Exit. If you see a Save dialog box, click Yes and save the project.

Quick reference

To	Do this
Declare a delegate type	Write the keyword *delegate*, followed by the return type, followed by the name of the delegate type, followed by any parameter types. For example: `delegate void myDelegate();`

Create an instance of a delegate initialized with a single specific method	Use the same syntax you use for a class or structure: write the keyword *new*, followed by the name of the type (the name of the delegate), followed by the argument between parentheses. The argument must be a method whose signature exactly matches the signature of the delegate. For example:
	`delegate void myDelegate();`
	`private void myMethod() { ... }`
	`...`
	`myDelegate del = new myDelegate(this.myMethod);`

Invoke a delegate	Use the same syntax as a method call. For example:
	`myDelegate del;`
	`...`
	`del();`

Declare an event	Write the keyword *event*, followed by the name of the type (the type must be a delegate type), followed by the name of the event. For example:
	
	`class MyClass`
	`{`
	`    public delegate void MyDelegate();`
	`    ...`
	`    public event myDelegate MyEvent;`
	`}`

To	Do this

Subscribe to an event	Create a delegate instance (of the same type as the event), and attach the delegate instance to the event by using the += operator. For example:
	
	``csharp
	class MyEventHandlingClass
	{
	    private MyClass myClass = new MyClass();
	    ...
	    public void Start()
	    {
	        myClass.MyEvent += new myClass.MyDelegate
	            (this.eventHandlingMethod);
	    }
	
	    private void eventHandlingMethod()
	    {
	        ...
	    }
	}
	``
	
	You can also get the compiler to generate the new delegate automatically simply by specifying the subscribing method:
	
	``csharp
	public void Start()
	{
	    myClass.MyEvent += this.eventHandlingMethod;
	}
	``

Unsubscribe from an event	Create a delegate instance (of the same type as the event), and detach the delegate instance from the event by using the −= operator. For example:
	
	``csharp
	class MyEventHandlingClass
	{
	    private MyClass myClass = new MyClass();
	    ...
	    public void Stop()
	    {
	        myClass.MyEvent -= new myClass.MyDelegate
	            (this.eventHandlingMethod);
	    }
	    ...
	}
	``
	
	Or:
	
	``csharp
	public void Stop()
	{
	    myClass.MyEvent -= this.eventHandlingMethod;
	}
	``

Raise an event	Use the same syntax as a method call. You must supply arguments to match the type of the parameters expected by the delegate referenced by the event. Don't forget to check whether the event is null. For example:
	
	``csharp
	class MyClass
	{
	    public event myDelegate MyEvent;
	    ...
	    private void RaiseEvent()
	    {
	        if (this.MyEvent != null)
	        {
	            this.MyEvent();
	        }
	    }
	    ...
	}
	``

CHAPTER 21

Querying in-memory data by using query expressions

After completing this chapter, you will be able to:

- Define Language-Integrated Query (LINQ) queries to examine the contents of enumerable collections.

- Use LINQ extension methods and query operators.

- Explain how LINQ defers evaluation of a query and how you can force immediate execution and cache the results of a LINQ query.

You have now met most of the features of the C# language. However, so far I have glossed over one important aspect of the language that is likely to be used by many applications: the support that C# provides for querying data. You have seen that you can define structures and classes for modeling data and that you can use collections and arrays for temporarily storing data in memory. However, how do you perform common tasks such as searching for items in a collection that match a specific set of criteria? For example, if you have a collection of *Customer* objects, how do you find all customers that are located in London, or how can you find out which town has the most customers who have procured your services? You can write your own code to iterate through a collection and examine the fields in each object, but these types of tasks occur so often that the designers of C# decided to include features in the language to minimize the amount of code you need to write. In this chapter, you will learn how to use these advanced C# language features to query and manipulate data.

What is LINQ?

All but the most trivial of applications need to process data. Historically, most applications provided their own logic for performing these operations. However, this strategy can lead to the code in an application becoming very tightly coupled with the structure of the data that it processes. If the data structures change, you might need to make a significant number of changes to the code that handles the data. The designers of the Microsoft .NET Framework thought long and hard about these issues and decided to make the life of an application developer easier by providing features that abstract the mechanism that an application uses to query data from application code itself. These features are called Language-Integrated Query, or LINQ.

The creators of LINQ took an unabashed look at the way in which relational database management systems such as Microsoft SQL Server separate the language used to query a database from the internal format of the data in the database. Developers accessing a SQL Server database issue Structured Query Language (SQL) statements to the database management system. SQL provides a high-level description of the data that the developer wants to retrieve but does not indicate exactly how the database management system should retrieve this data. These details are controlled by the database management system itself. Consequently, an application that invokes SQL statements does not care how the database management system physically stores or retrieves data. The format used by the database management system can change (for example, if a new version is released) without the application developer needing to modify the SQL statements used by the application.

LINQ provides syntax and semantics very reminiscent of SQL and with many of the same advantages. You can change the underlying structure of the data being queried without needing to change the code that actually performs the queries. You should be aware that although LINQ looks similar to SQL, it is far more flexible and can handle a wider variety of logical data structures. For example, LINQ can handle data organized hierarchically, such as that found in an XML document. However, this chapter concentrates on using LINQ in a relational manner.

Using LINQ in a C# application

Perhaps the easiest way to explain how to use the C# features that support LINQ is to work through some simple examples based on the following sets of customer and address information:

Customer Information

CustomerID	FirstName	LastName	CompanyName
1	Kim	Abercrombie	Alpine Ski House
2	Jeff	Hay	Coho Winery
3	Charlie	Herb	Alpine Ski House
4	Chris	Preston	Trey Research
5	Dave	Barnett	Wingtip Toys
6	Ann	Beebe	Coho Winery
7	John	Kane	Wingtip Toys
8	David	Simpson	Trey Research
9	Greg	Chapman	Wingtip Toys
10	Tim	Litton	Wide World Importers

Address Information

CompanyName	City	Country
Alpine Ski House	Berne	Switzerland
Coho Winery	San Francisco	United States
Trey Research	New York	United States
Wingtip Toys	London	United Kingdom
Wide World Importers	Tetbury	United Kingdom

LINQ requires the data to be stored in a data structure that implements the *IEnumerable* or *IEnumerable<T>* interface, as described in Chapter 19, "Enumerating collections." It does not matter what structure you use (an array, a *HashSet<T>*, a *Queue<T>*, or any of the other collection types, or even one that you define yourself) as long as it is enumerable. However, to keep things straightforward, the examples in this chapter assume that the customer and address information is held in the *customers* and *addresses* arrays shown in the following code example.

> **Note** In a real-world application, you would populate these arrays by reading the data from a file or a database.

```
var customers = new[] {
    new { CustomerID = 1, FirstName = "Kim", LastName = "Abercrombie",
        CompanyName = "Alpine Ski House" },
    new { CustomerID = 2, FirstName = "Jeff", LastName = "Hay",
        CompanyName = "Coho Winery" },
    new { CustomerID = 3, FirstName = "Charlie", LastName = "Herb",
        CompanyName = "Alpine Ski House" },
    new { CustomerID = 4, FirstName = "Chris", LastName = "Preston",
        CompanyName = "Trey Research" },
    new { CustomerID = 5, FirstName = "Dave", LastName = "Barnett",
        CompanyName = "Wingtip Toys" },
    new { CustomerID = 6, FirstName = "Ann", LastName = "Beebe",
        CompanyName = "Coho Winery" },
    new { CustomerID = 7, FirstName = "John", LastName = "Kane",
        CompanyName = "Wingtip Toys" },
    new { CustomerID = 8, FirstName = "David", LastName = "Simpson",
        CompanyName = "Trey Research" },
    new { CustomerID = 9, FirstName = "Greg", LastName = "Chapman",
        CompanyName = "Wingtip Toys" },
    new { CustomerID = 10, FirstName = "Tim", LastName = "Litton",
        CompanyName = "Wide World Importers" }
};
```

```
var addresses = new[] {
    new { CompanyName = "Alpine Ski House", City = "Berne",
        Country = "Switzerland"},
    new { CompanyName = "Coho Winery", City = "San Francisco",
        Country = "United States"},
    new { CompanyName = "Trey Research", City = "New York",
        Country = "United States"},
    new { CompanyName = "Wingtip Toys", City = "London",
        Country = "United Kingdom"},
    new { CompanyName = "Wide World Importers", City = "Tetbury",
        Country = "United Kingdom"}
};
```

> **Note** The sections "Selecting data," "Filtering data," "Ordering, grouping, and aggregating data," and "Joining data" that follow show you the basic capabilities and syntax for querying data by using LINQ methods. The syntax can become a little complex at times, and you will see when you reach the section "Using query operators" that it is not actually necessary to remember how all the syntax works. However, it is useful for you to at least take a look at these sections so that you can fully appreciate how the query operators provided with C# perform their tasks.

Selecting data

Suppose that you want to display a list consisting of the first name of each customer in the *customers* array. You can achieve this task with the following code:

```
IEnumerable<string> customerFirstNames =
    customers.Select(cust => cust.FirstName);

foreach (string name in customerFirstNames)
{
    Console.WriteLine(name);
}
```

Although this block of code is quite short, it does a lot, and it requires a degree of explanation, starting with the use of the *Select* method of the *customers* array.

Using the *Select* method, you can retrieve specific data from the array—in this case, just the value in the *FirstName* field of each item in the array. How does it work? The parameter to the *Select* method is actually another method that takes a row from the *customers* array and returns the selected data from that row. You can define your own custom method to perform this task, but the simplest mechanism is to use a lambda expression to define an anonymous method, as shown in the preceding example. There are three important things that you need to understand at this point:

- The variable *cust* is the parameter passed in to the method. You can think of *cust* as an alias for each row in the *customers* array. The compiler deduces this from the fact that you are calling the *Select* method on the *customers* array. You can use any legal C# identifier in place of *cust*.

- The *Select* method does not actually retrieve the data at this time; it simply returns an enumerable object that will fetch the data identified by the *Select* method when you iterate over it later. We will return to this aspect of LINQ in the section "LINQ and deferred evaluation" later in this chapter.

- The *Select* method is not actually a method of the *Array* type. It is an extension method of the *Enumerable* class. The *Enumerable* class is located in the *System.Linq* namespace and provides a substantial set of static methods for querying objects that implement the generic *IEnumerable<T>* interface.

The preceding example uses the *Select* method of the *customers* array to generate an *IEnumerable<string>* object named *customerFirstNames*. (It is of type *IEnumerable<string>* because the *Select* method returns an enumerable collection of customer first names, which are strings.) The *foreach* statement iterates through this collection of strings, printing out the first name of each customer in the following sequence:

```
Kim
Jeff
Charlie
Chris
Dave
Ann
John
David
Greg
Tim
```

You can now display the first name of each customer. How do you fetch the first and last name of each customer? This task is slightly trickier. If you examine the definition of the *Enumerable.Select* method in the *System.Linq* namespace in the documentation supplied with Microsoft Visual Studio 2015, you will see that it looks like this:

```
public static IEnumerable<TResult> Select<TSource, TResult> (
        this IEnumerable<TSource> source,
        Func<TSource, TResult> selector
)
```

What this actually says is that *Select* is a generic method that takes two type parameters named *TSource* and *TResult* as well as two ordinary parameters named *source* and *selector*. *TSource* is the type of the collection for which you are generating an enumerable set of results (*customer* objects in this example), and *TResult* is the type of the data in the enumerable set of results (*string* objects in this example). Remember that *Select* is an extension method, so the *source* parameter is actually a reference to the type being extended (a generic collection of *customer* objects that implements the *IEnumerable* interface in the example). The *selector* parameter specifies a generic method that identifies the fields to be retrieved. (Remember that *Func* is the name of a generic delegate type in the .NET Framework that you can use for encapsulating a generic method that returns a result.) The method referred to by the *selector* parameter takes a *TSource* (in this case, *customer*) parameter and yields a *TResult* (in this case, *string*) object. The value returned by the *Select* method is an enumerable collection of *TResult* (again *string*) objects.

Note Chapter 12, "Working with inheritance," explains how extension methods work and the role of the first parameter to an extension method.

The important point to understand from the preceding paragraph is that the *Select* method returns an enumerable collection based on a single type. If you want the enumerator to return multiple items of data, such as the first and last name of each customer, you have at least two options:

- You can concatenate the first and last names together into a single string in the *Select* method, like this:

```
IEnumerable<string> customerNames =
    customers.Select(cust => $"{cust.FirstName} {cust.LastName}");
```

- You can define a new type that wraps the first and last names and use the *Select* method to construct instances of this type, like this:

```
class FullName
{
    public string FirstName{ get; set; }
    public string LastName{ get; set; }
}
...
IEnumerable<FullName> customerNames =
    customers.Select(cust => new FullName
    {
        FirstName = cust.FirstName,
        LastName = cust.LastName
    } );
```

The second option is arguably preferable, but if this is the only use that your application makes of the *Names* type, you might prefer to use an anonymous type, as in the following, instead of defining a new type specifically for a single operation:

```
var customerNames =
    customers.Select(cust => new { FirstName = cust.FirstName, LastName = cust.LastName } );
```

Notice the use of the *var* keyword here to define the type of the enumerable collection. The type of objects in the collection is anonymous, so you do not know the specific type for the objects in the collection.

Filtering data

With the *Select* method, you can specify, or *project*, the fields that you want to include in the enumerable collection. However, you might also want to restrict the rows that the enumerable collection contains. For example, suppose you want to list only the names of companies in the *addresses* array that are located in the United States. To do this, you can use the *Where* method, as follows:

```
IEnumerable<string> usCompanies =
    addresses.Where(addr => String.Equals(addr.Country, "United States"))
            .Select(usComp => usComp.CompanyName);

foreach (string name in usCompanies)
{
    Console.WriteLine(name);
}
```

Syntactically, the *Where* method is similar to *Select*. It expects a parameter that defines a method that filters the data according to whatever criteria you specify. This example makes use of another lambda expression. The variable *addr* is an alias for a row in the *addresses* array, and the lambda expression returns all rows where the *Country* field matches the string *"United States"*. The *Where* method returns an enumerable collection of rows containing every field from the original collection. The *Select* method is then applied to these rows to project only the *CompanyName* field from this enumerable collection to return another enumerable collection of *string* objects. (The variable *usComp* is an alias for the type of each row in the enumerable collection returned by the *Where* method.) The type of the result of this complete expression is therefore *IEnumerable<string>*. It is important to understand this sequence of operations—the *Where* method is applied first to filter the rows, followed by the *Select* method to specify the fields. The *foreach* statement that iterates through this collection displays the following companies:

```
Coho Winery
Trey Research
```

Ordering, grouping, and aggregating data

If you are familiar with SQL, you are aware that it makes it possible for you to perform a wide variety of relational operations besides simple projection and filtering. For example, you can specify that you want data to be returned in a specific order, you can group the rows returned according to one or more key fields, and you can calculate summary values based on the rows in each group. LINQ provides the same functionality.

To retrieve data in a particular order, you can use the *OrderBy* method. Like the *Select* and *Where* methods, *OrderBy* expects a method as its argument. This method identifies the expressions that you want to use to sort the data. For example, you can display the name of each company in the *addresses* array in ascending order, like this:

```
IEnumerable<string> companyNames =
    addresses.OrderBy(addr => addr.CompanyName).Select(comp => comp.CompanyName);

foreach (string name in companyNames)
{
    Console.WriteLine(name);
}
```

This block of code displays the companies in the addresses table in alphabetical order.

```
Alpine Ski House
Coho Winery
Trey Research
Wide World Importers
Wingtip Toys
```

If you want to enumerate the data in descending order, you can use the *OrderByDescending* method instead. If you want to order by more than one key value, you can use the *ThenBy* or *ThenByDescending* method after *OrderBy* or *OrderByDescending*.

To group data according to common values in one or more fields, you can use the *GroupBy* method. The following example shows how to group the companies in the *addresses* array by country:

```
var companiesGroupedByCountry =
    addresses.GroupBy(addrs => addrs.Country);

foreach (var companiesPerCountry in companiesGroupedByCountry)
{
    Console.WriteLine(
        $"Country: {companiesPerCountry.Key}\t{companiesPerCountry.Count()} companies");
    foreach (var companies in companiesPerCountry)
    {
        Console.WriteLine($"\t{companies.CompanyName}");
    }
}
```

By now, you should recognize the pattern. The *GroupBy* method expects a method that specifies the fields by which to group the data. However, there are some subtle differences between the *GroupBy* method and the other methods that you have seen so far.

The main point of interest is that you don't need to use the *Select* method to project the fields to the result. The enumerable set returned by *GroupBy* contains all the fields in the original source collection, but the rows are ordered into a set of enumerable collections based on the field identified by the method specified by *GroupBy*. In other words, the result of the *GroupBy* method is an enumerable set of groups, each of which is an enumerable set of rows. In the example just shown, the enumerable set *companiesGroupedByCountry* is a set of countries. The items in this set are themselves enumerable collections containing the companies for each country in turn. The code that displays the companies in each country uses a *foreach* loop to iterate through the *companiesGroupedByCountry* set to yield and display each country in turn, and then it uses a nested *foreach* loop to iterate through the set of companies in each country. Notice in the outer *foreach* loop that you can access the value you are grouping by using the *Key* field of each item, and you can also calculate summary data for each group by using methods such as *Count*, *Max*, *Min*, and many others. The output generated by the example code looks like this:

```
Country: Switzerland    1 companies
        Alpine Ski House
Country: United States  2 companies
        Coho Winery
        Trey Research
Country: United Kingdom 2 companies
        Wingtip Toys
```

You can use many of the summary methods such as *Count, Max,* and *Min* directly over the results of the *Select* method. If you want to know how many companies there are in the *addresses* array, you can use a block of code such as this:

```
int numberOfCompanies = addresses.Select(addr => addr.CompanyName).Count();
Console.WriteLine($"Number of companies: {numberOfCompanies}");
```

Notice that the result of these methods is a single scalar value rather than an enumerable collection. The output from the preceding block of code looks like this:

```
Number of companies: 5
```

I should utter a word of caution at this point. These summary methods do not distinguish between rows in the underlying set that contain duplicate values in the fields you are projecting. This means that, strictly speaking, the preceding example shows you only how many rows in the *addresses* array contain a value in the *CompanyName* field. If you wanted to find out how many different countries are mentioned in this table, you might be tempted to try this:

```
int numberOfCountries = addresses.Select(addr => addr.Country).Count();
Console.WriteLine($"Number of countries: {numberOfCountries}");
```

The output looks like this:

```
Number of countries: 5
```

In fact, the *addresses* array includes only three different countries—it just so happens that United States and United Kingdom both occur twice. You can eliminate duplicates from the calculation by using the *Distinct* method, like this:

```
int numberOfCountries =
    addresses.Select(addr => addr.Country).Distinct().Count();
Console.WriteLine($"Number of countries: {numberOfCountries}");
```

The *Console.WriteLine* statement now outputs the expected result:

```
Number of countries: 3
```

Joining data

Just like SQL, LINQ gives you the ability to join together multiple sets of data over one or more common key fields. The following example shows how to display the first and last names of each customer, together with the name of the country where the customer is located:

```
var companiesAndCustomers = customers
  .Select(c => new { c.FirstName, c.LastName, c.CompanyName })
  .Join(addresses, custs => custs.CompanyName, addrs => addrs.CompanyName,
  (custs, addrs) => new {custs.FirstName, custs.LastName, addrs.Country });

foreach (var row in companiesAndCustomers)
```

```
{
    Console.WriteLine(row);
}
```

The customers' first and last names are available in the *customers* array, but the country for each company that customers work for is stored in the *addresses* array. The common key between the *customers* array and the *addresses* array is the company name. The *Select* method specifies the fields of interest in the *customers* array (*FirstName* and *LastName*), together with the field containing the common key (*CompanyName*). You use the *Join* method to join the data identified by the *Select* method with another enumerable collection. The parameters to the *Join* method are as follows:

- The enumerable collection with which to join

- A method that identifies the common key fields from the data identified by the *Select* method

- A method that identifies the common key fields on which to join the selected data

- A method that specifies the columns you require in the enumerable result set returned by the *Join* method

In this example, the *Join* method joins the enumerable collection containing the *FirstName*, *LastName*, and *CompanyName* fields from the *customers* array with the rows in the *addresses* array. The two sets of data are joined where the value in the *CompanyName* field in the *customers* array matches the value in the *CompanyName* field in the *addresses* array. The result set includes rows containing the *FirstName* and *LastName* fields from the *customers* array with the *Country* field from the *addresses* array. The code that outputs the data from the *companiesAndCustomers* collection displays the following information:

```
{ FirstName = Kim, LastName = Abercrombie, Country = Switzerland }
{ FirstName = Jeff, LastName = Hay, Country = United States }
{ FirstName = Charlie, LastName = Herb, Country = Switzerland }
{ FirstName = Chris, LastName = Preston, Country = United States }
{ FirstName = Dave, LastName = Barnett, Country = United Kingdom }
{ FirstName = Ann, LastName = Beebe, Country = United States }
{ FirstName = John, LastName = Kane, Country = United Kingdom }
{ FirstName = David, LastName = Simpson, Country = United States }
{ FirstName = Greg, LastName = Chapman, Country = United Kingdom }
{ FirstName = Tim, LastName = Litton, Country = United Kingdom }
```

Note Remember that collections in memory are not the same as tables in a relational database, and the data they contain is not subject to the same data integrity constraints. In a relational database, it could be acceptable to assume that every customer has a corresponding company and that each company has its own unique address. Collections do not enforce the same level of data integrity, meaning that you can quite easily have a customer referencing a company that does not exist in the *addresses* array, and you might even have the same company occurring more than once in the *addresses* array. In these situations, the results that you obtain might be accurate but unexpected. Join operations work best when you fully understand the relationships between the data you are joining.

Using query operators

The preceding sections have shown you many of the features available for querying in-memory data by using the extension methods for the *Enumerable* class defined in the *System.Linq* namespace. The syntax makes use of several advanced C# language features, and the resultant code can sometimes be quite hard to understand and maintain. To relieve you of some of this burden, the designers of C# added query operators to the language with which you can employ LINQ features by using a syntax more akin to SQL.

As you saw in the examples shown earlier in this chapter, you can retrieve the first name for each customer like this:

```
IEnumerable<string> customerFirstNames =
    customers.Select(cust => cust.FirstName);
```

You can rephrase this statement by using the *from* and *select* query operators, like this:

```
var customerFirstNames = from cust in customers
                         select cust.FirstName;
```

At compile time, the C# compiler resolves this expression into the corresponding *Select* method. The *from* operator defines an alias for the source collection, and the *select* operator specifies the fields to retrieve by using this alias. The result is an enumerable collection of customer first names. If you are familiar with SQL, notice that the *from* operator occurs before the *select* operator.

Continuing in the same vein, to retrieve the first and last names for each customer, you can use the following statement. (You might want to refer to the earlier example of the same statement based on the *Select* extension method.)

```
var customerNames = from cust in customers
                    select new { cust.FirstName, cust.LastName };
```

You use the *where* operator to filter data. The following example shows how to return the names of the companies based in the United States from the *addresses* array:

```
var usCompanies = from a in addresses
                  where String.Equals(a.Country, "United States")
                  select a.CompanyName;
```

To order data, use the *orderby* operator, like this:

```
var companyNames = from a in addresses
                   orderby a.CompanyName
                   select a.CompanyName;
```

You can group data by using the *group* operator in the following manner:

```
var companiesGroupedByCountry = from a in addresses
                                group a by a.Country;
```

Notice that, as with the earlier example showing how to group data, you do not provide the *select* operator, and you can iterate through the results by using the same code as the earlier example, like this:

```
foreach (var companiesPerCountry in companiesGroupedByCountry)
{
    Console.WriteLine(
        $"Country: {companiesPerCountry.Key}\t{companiesPerCountry.Count()} companies");
    foreach (var companies in companiesPerCountry)
    {
        Console.WriteLine($"\t{companies.CompanyName}");
    }
}
```

You can invoke summary functions such as *Count* over the collection returned by an enumerable collection like this:

```
int numberOfCompanies = (from a in addresses
                         select a.CompanyName).Count();
```

Notice that you wrap the expression in parentheses. If you want to ignore duplicate values, use the *Distinct* method:

```
int numberOfCountries = (from a in addresses
                         select a.Country).Distinct().Count();
```

> **Tip** In many cases, you probably want to count just the number of rows in a collection rather than the number of values in a field across all the rows in the collection. In this case, you can invoke the *Count* method directly over the original collection, like this:
>
> ```
> int numberOfCompanies = addresses.Count();
> ```

You can use the *join* operator to combine two collections across a common key. The following example shows the query returning customers and addresses over the *CompanyName* column in each collection, this time rephrased by using the *join* operator. You use the *on* clause with the *equals* operator to specify how the two collections are related.

> **Note** LINQ currently supports equi-joins (joins based on equality) only. If you are a database developer who is used to SQL, you might be familiar with joins based on other operators, such as > and <, but LINQ does not provide these features.

```
var countriesAndCustomers = from a in addresses
                            join c in customers
                            on a.CompanyName equals c.CompanyName
                            select new { c.FirstName, c.LastName, a.Country };
```

> **Note** In contrast with SQL, the order of the expressions in the *on* clause of a LINQ expression is important. You must place the item you are joining from (referencing the data in the collection in the *from* clause) to the left of the *equals* operator and the item you are joining with (referencing the data in the collection in the *join* clause) to the right.

LINQ provides a large number of other methods for summarizing information and joining, grouping, and searching through data. This section has covered just the most common features. For example, LINQ provides the *Intersect* and *Union* methods, which you can use to perform set-wide operations. It also provides methods such as *Any* and *All* that you can use to determine whether at least one item in a collection or every item in a collection matches a specified predicate. You can partition the values in an enumerable collection by using the *Take* and *Skip* methods. For more information, see the material in the LINQ section of the documentation provided with Visual Studio 2015.

Querying data in *Tree<TItem>* objects

The examples you've seen so far in this chapter have shown how to query the data in an array. You can use exactly the same techniques for any collection class that implements the generic *IEnumerable<T>* interface. In the following exercise, you will define a new class for modeling employees for a company. You will create a *BinaryTree* object containing a collection of *Employee* objects, and then you will use LINQ to query this information. You will initially call the LINQ extension methods directly, but then you will modify your code to use query operators.

Retrieve data from a *BinaryTree* by using the extension methods

1. Start Visual Studio 2015 if it is not already running.

2. Open the QueryBinaryTree solution, which is located in the \Microsoft Press\VCSBS\ Chapter 21\QueryBinaryTree folder in your Documents folder. The project contains the Program.cs file, which defines the *Program* class with the *Main* and *doWork* methods that you have seen in previous exercises.

3. In Solution Explorer, right-click the QueryBinaryTree project, point to Add, and then click Class. In the Add New Item – Query BinaryTree dialog box, type **Employee.cs** in the Name box, and then click Add.

4. Add the automatic properties shown in bold in the following code to the *Employee* class:

```
class Employee
{
    public string FirstName { get; set; }
    public string LastName { get; set; }
    public string Department { get; set; }
    public int Id { get; set; }
}
```

5. Add the *ToString* method shown in bold in the code that follows to the *Employee* class. Types in the .NET Framework use this method when converting the object to a string representation, such as when displaying it by using the *Console.WriteLine* statement.

```
class Employee
{
    ...
    public override string ToString()
    {
        return
            $"Id: {this.Id}, Name: {this.FirstName} {this.LastName}, Dept: {this.
Department}";
    }
}
```

6. Modify the definition of the *Employee* class to implement the *IComparable<Employee>* interface, as shown here:

```
class Employee : IComparable<Employee>
{
}
```

This step is necessary because the *BinaryTree* class specifies that its elements must be "comparable."

7. Hover over the *IComparable<Employee>* interface in the class definition, click the lightbulb icon that appears, and then click Implement Interface Explicitly on the context menu.

This action generates a default implementation of the *CompareTo* method. Remember that the *BinaryTree* class calls this method when it needs to compare elements when inserting them into the tree.

8. Replace the body of the *CompareTo* method with the following code shown in bold. This implementation of the *CompareTo* method compares *Employee* objects based on the value of the *Id* field.

```
int IComparable<Employee>.CompareTo(Employee other)
{
    if (other == null)
    {
        return 1;
    }

    if (this.Id > other.Id)
    {
        return 1;
    }

    if (this.Id < other.Id)
    {
        return -1;
    }
```

```
      return 0;
    }
```

> **Note** For a description of the *IComparable<T>* interface, refer to Chapter 19.

9. In Solution Explorer, right-click the QueryBinaryTree solution, point to Add, and then click Existing Project. In the Add Existing Project dialog box, move to the folder Microsoft Press\ VCSBS\Chapter 21\BinaryTree in your Documents folder, click the BinaryTree project, and then click Open.

   The BinaryTree project contains a copy of the enumerable *BinaryTree* class that you implemented in Chapter 19.

10. In Solution Explorer, right-click the QueryBinaryTree project, point to Add, and then click Reference. In the Reference Manager – QueryBinaryTree dialog box, in the left pane, click Solution. In the middle pane, select the BinaryTree project, and then click OK.

11. Display the Program.cs file for the QueryBinaryTree project in the Code and Text Editor window, and verify that the list of *using* directives at the top of the file includes the following line of code:

```
using System.Linq;
```

12. Add the following *using* directive to the list at the top of the Program.cs file to bring the *BinaryTree* namespace into scope:

```
using BinaryTree;
```

13. In the *doWork* method in the *Program* class, remove the *// TODO:* comment and add the following statements shown in bold to construct and populate an instance of the *BinaryTree* class:

```
static void doWork()
{
  Tree<Employee> empTree = new Tree<Employee>(
    new Employee { Id = 1, FirstName = "Kim", LastName = "Abercrombie", Department = "IT"
});
  empTree.Insert(
    new Employee { Id = 2, FirstName = "Jeff", LastName = "Hay", Department = "Marketing"
});
  empTree.Insert(
    new Employee { Id = 4, FirstName = "Charlie", LastName = "Herb", Department = "IT"
});
  empTree.Insert(
    new Employee { Id = 6, FirstName = "Chris", LastName = "Preston", Department =
"Sales"});
  empTree.Insert(
    new Employee { Id = 3, FirstName = "Dave", LastName = "Barnett", Department = "Sales"
});
  empTree.Insert(
```

```
            new Employee { Id = 5, FirstName = "Tim", LastName = "Litton", Department="Marketing"
    });
    }
```

14. Add the following statements shown in bold to the end of the *doWork* method. This code invokes the *Select* method to list the departments found in the binary tree.

```
static void doWork()
{
    ...
    Console.WriteLine("List of departments");
    var depts = empTree.Select(d => d.Department);

    foreach (var dept in depts)
    {
        Console.WriteLine($"Department: {dept}");
    }
}
```

15. On the Debug menu, click Start Without Debugging.

   The application should output the following list of departments:

```
List of departments
Department: IT
Department: Marketing
Department: Sales
Department: IT
Department: Marketing
Department: Sales
```

   Each department occurs twice because there are two employees in each department. The order of the departments is determined by the *CompareTo* method of the *Employee* class, which uses the *Id* property of each employee to sort the data. The first department is for the employee with the *Id* value 1, the second department is for the employee with the *Id* value 2, and so on.

16. Press Enter to return to Visual Studio 2015.

17. In the *doWork* method in the *Program* class, modify the statement that creates the enumerable collection of departments as shown in bold in the following example:

```
var depts = empTree.Select(d => d.Department).Distinct();
```

   The *Distinct* method removes duplicate rows from the enumerable collection.

18. On the Debug menu, click Start Without Debugging.

   Verify that the application now displays each department only once, like this:

```
List of departments
Department: IT
Department: Marketing
Department: Sales
```

19. Press Enter to return to Visual Studio 2015.

20. Add the following statements shown in bold to the end of the *doWork* method. This block of code uses the *Where* method to filter the employees and return only those in the IT department. The *Select* method returns the entire row rather than projecting specific columns.

```
static void doWork()
{
    ...
    Console.WriteLine("\nEmployees in the IT department");
    var ITEmployees =
        empTree.Where(e => String.Equals(e.Department, "IT"))
        .Select(emp => emp);

    foreach (var emp in ITEmployees)
    {
        Console.WriteLine(emp);
    }
}
```

21. After the code from the preceding step, add the following code shown in bold to the end of the *doWork* method. This code uses the *GroupBy* method to group the employees found in the binary tree by department. The outer *foreach* statement iterates through each group, displaying the name of the department. The inner *foreach* statement displays the names of the employees in each department.

```
static void doWork()
{
    ...
    Console.WriteLine("\nAll employees grouped by department");
    var employeesByDept = empTree.GroupBy(e => e.Department);

    foreach (var dept in employeesByDept)
    {
        Console.WriteLine($"Department: {dept.Key}");
        foreach (var emp in dept)
        {
            Console.WriteLine($"\t{emp.FirstName} {emp.LastName}");
        }
    }
}
```

22. On the Debug menu, click Start Without Debugging. Verify that the output of the application looks like this:

```
List of departments
Department: IT
Department: Marketing
Department: Sales

Employees in the IT department
Id: 1, Name: Kim Abercrombie, Dept: IT
Id: 4, Name: Charlie Herb, Dept: IT
```

```
All employees grouped by department
Department: IT
        Kim Abercrombie
        Charlie Herb
Department: Marketing
        Jeff Hay
        Tim Litton
Department: Sales
        Dave Barnett
        Chris Preston
```

23. Press Enter to return to Visual Studio 2015.

Retrieve data from a *BinaryTree* by using query operators

1. In the *doWork* method, comment out the statement that generates the enumerable collection of departments and replace it with the equivalent statement shown in bold, using the *from* and *select* query operators:

```
// var depts = empTree.Select(d => d.Department).Distinct();
var depts = (from d in empTree
            select d.Department).Distinct();
```

2. Comment out the statement that generates the enumerable collection of employees in the IT department and replace it with the following code shown in bold:

```
// var ITEmployees =
//     empTree.Where(e => String.Equals(e.Department, "IT"))
//     .Select(emp => emp);
var ITEmployees = from e in empTree
                  where String.Equals(e.Department, "IT")
                  select e;
```

3. Comment out the statement that generates the enumerable collection that groups employees by department and replace it with the statement shown in bold in the following code:

```
// var employeesByDept = empTree.GroupBy(e => e.Department);
var employeesByDept = from e in empTree
                      group e by e.Department;
```

4. On the Debug menu, click Start Without Debugging. Verify that the program displays the same results as before.

```
List of departments
Department: IT
Department: Marketing
Department: Sales

Employees in the IT department
Id: 1, Name: Kim Abercrombie, Dept: IT
Id: 4, Name: Charlie Herb, Dept: IT

All employees grouped by department
```

```
Department: IT
        Kim Abercrombie
        Charlie Herb
Department: Marketing
        Jeff Hay
        Tim Litton
Department: Sales
        Dave Barnett
        Chris Preston
```

5. Press Enter to return to Visual Studio 2015.

LINQ and deferred evaluation

When you use LINQ to define an enumerable collection, either by using the LINQ extension methods or by using query operators, you should remember that the application does not actually build the collection at the time that the LINQ extension method is executed; the collection is enumerated only when you iterate over it. This means that the data in the original collection can change in the time between the execution of a LINQ query and when the data that the query identifies is retrieved; you will always fetch the most up-to-date data. For example, the following query (which you saw earlier) defines an enumerable collection of companies in the United States:

```
var usCompanies = from a in addresses
                  where String.Equals(a.Country, "United States")
                  select a.CompanyName;
```

The data in the *addresses* array is not retrieved, and any conditions specified in the *Where* filter are not evaluated, until you iterate through the *usCompanies* collection:

```
foreach (string name in usCompanies)
{
    Console.WriteLine(name);
}
```

If you modify the data in the *addresses* array in the time between defining the *usCompanies* collection and iterating through the collection (for example, if you add a new company based in the United States), you will see this new data. This strategy is referred to as *deferred evaluation*.

You can force the evaluation of a LINQ query when it is defined and generate a static, cached collection. This collection is a copy of the original data and will not change if the data in the collection changes. LINQ provides the *ToList* method to build a static *List* object containing a cached copy of the data. You use it like this:

```
var usCompanies = from a in addresses.ToList()
                  where String.Equals(a.Country, "United States")
                  select a.CompanyName;
```

This time, the list of companies is fixed when you create the query. If you add more United States companies to the *addresses* array, you will not see them when you iterate through the *usCompanies* collection. LINQ also provides the *ToArray* method that stores the cached collection as an array.

In the final exercise in this chapter, you will compare the effects of using deferred evaluation of a LINQ query to generating a cached collection.

Examine the effects of deferred and cached evaluation of a LINQ query

1. Return to Visual Studio 2015, display the QueryBinaryTree project, and then edit the Program.cs file.

2. Comment out the contents of the *doWork* method apart from the statements that construct the *empTree* binary tree, as shown here:

```
static void doWork()
{
  Tree<Employee> empTree = new Tree<Employee>(
    new Employee { Id = 1, FirstName = "Kim", LastName = "Abercrombie", Department = "IT"
});
  empTree.Insert(
    new Employee { Id = 2, FirstName = "Jeff", LastName = "Hay", Department = "Marketing"
});
  empTree.Insert(
    new Employee { Id = 4, FirstName = "Charlie", LastName = "Herb", Department = "IT"
});
  empTree.Insert(
    new Employee { Id = 6, FirstName = "Chris", LastName = "Preston", Department =
"Sales"});
  empTree.Insert(
    new Employee { Id = 3, FirstName = "Dave", LastName = "Barnett", Department = "Sales"
});
  empTree.Insert(
    new Employee { Id = 5, FirstName = "Tim", LastName = "Litton", Department="Marketing"
});

    // comment out the rest of the method
    ...
}
```

> **Tip** You can comment out a block of code by selecting the entire block in the Code and Text Editor window and then clicking the Comment Out The Selected Lines button on the toolbar or pressing Ctrl+K and then pressing C.

3. Add the following statements shown in bold to the *doWork* method, after the code that creates and populates the *empTree* binary tree:

```
static void doWork()
{
    ...
    Console.WriteLine("All employees");
    var allEmployees = from e in empTree
                       select e;
```

```
    foreach (var emp in allEmployees)
    {
        Console.WriteLine(emp);
    }
    ...
}
```

This code generates an enumerable collection of employees named *allEmployees* and then iterates through this collection, displaying the details of each employee.

4. Add the following code immediately after the statements you typed in the preceding step:

```
static void doWork()
{
    ...
    empTree.Insert(new Employee
    {
        Id = 7,
        FirstName = "David",
        LastName = "Simpson",
        Department = "IT"
    });
    Console.WriteLine("\nEmployee added");

    Console.WriteLine("All employees");
    foreach (var emp in allEmployees)
    {
        Console.WriteLine(emp);
    }
    ...
}
```

These statements add a new employee to the *empTree* tree and then iterate through the *allEmployees* collection again.

5. On the Debug menu, click Start Without Debugging. Verify that the output of the application looks like this:

```
All employees
Id: 1, Name: Kim Abercrombie, Dept: IT
Id: 2, Name: Jeff Hay, Dept: Marketing
Id: 3, Name: Dave Barnett, Dept: Sales
Id: 4, Name: Charlie Herb, Dept: IT
Id: 5, Name: Tim Litton, Dept: Marketing
Id: 6, Name: Chris Preston, Dept: Sales

Employee added
All employees
Id: 1, Name: Kim Abercrombie, Dept: IT
Id: 2, Name: Jeff Hay, Dept: Marketing
Id: 3, Name: Dave Barnett, Dept: Sales
Id: 4, Name: Charlie Herb, Dept: IT
Id: 5, Name: Tim Litton, Dept: Marketing
Id: 6, Name: Chris Preston, Dept: Sales
Id: 7, Name: David Simpson, Dept: IT
```

Notice that the second time the application iterates through the *allEmployees* collection, the list displayed includes David Simpson, even though this employee was added only after the *allEmployees* collection was defined.

6. Press Enter to return to Visual Studio 2015.

7. In the *doWork* method, change the statement that generates the *allEmployees* collection to identify and cache the data immediately, as shown here in bold:

```
var allEmployees = from e in empTree.ToList<Employee>()
                   select e;
```

LINQ provides generic and nongeneric versions of the *ToList* and *ToArray* methods. If possible, it is better to use the generic versions of these methods to ensure the type safety of the result. The data returned by the *select* operator is an *Employee* object, and the code shown in this step generates *allEmployees* as a generic *List<Employee>* collection.

8. On the Debug menu, click Start Without Debugging. Verify that the output of the application looks like this:

```
All employees
Id: 1, Name: Kim Abercrombie, Dept: IT
Id: 2, Name: Jeff Hay, Dept: Marketing
Id: 3, Name: Dave Barnett, Dept: Sales
Id: 4, Name: Charlie Herb, Dept: IT
Id: 5, Name: Tim Litton, Dept: Marketing
Id: 6, Name: Chris Preston, Dept: Sales

Employee added
All employees
Id: 1, Name: Kim Abercrombie, Dept: IT
Id: 2, Name: Jeff Hay, Dept: Marketing
Id: 3, Name: Dave Barnett, Dept: Sales
Id: 4, Name: Charlie Herb, Dept: IT
Id: 5, Name: Tim Litton, Dept: Marketing
Id: 6, Name: Chris Preston, Dept: Sales
```

Notice that the second time the application iterates through the *allEmployees* collection, the list displayed does not include David Simpson. In this case, the query is evaluated and the results are cached before David Simpson is added to the *empTree* binary tree.

9. Press Enter to return to Visual Studio 2015.

Summary

In this chapter, you learned how LINQ uses the *IEnumerable<T>* interface and extension methods to provide a mechanism for querying data. You also saw how these features support the query expression syntax in C#.

- If you want to continue to the next chapter, keep Visual Studio 2015 running and turn to Chapter 22, "Operator overloading."

- If you want to exit Visual Studio 2015 now, on the File menu, click Exit. If you see a Save dialog box, click Yes and save the project.

Quick reference

To	Do this

Project specified fields from an enumerable collection	Use the *Select* method and specify a lambda expression that identifies the fields to project. For example:
	
	`var customerFirstNames = customers.Select(cust => cust.FirstName);`
	
	Or use the *from* and *select* query operators. For example:
	
	`var customerFirstNames =`
	`    from cust in customers`
	`    select cust.FirstName;`

Filter rows from an enumerable collection	Use the *Where* method, and specify a lambda expression containing the criteria that rows should match. For example:
	
	`var usCompanies =`
	`    addresses.Where(addr =>`
	`        String.Equals(addr.Country, "United States"))`
	`    .Select(usComp => usComp.CompanyName);`
	
	Or use the *where* query operator. For example:
	
	`var usCompanies =`
	`    from a in addresses`
	`    where String.Equals(a.Country, "United States")`
	`    select a.CompanyName;`

Enumerate data in a specific order	Use the *OrderBy* method and specify a lambda expression identifying the field to use to order rows. For example:
	
	`var companyNames =`
	`    addresses.OrderBy(addr => addr.CompanyName)`
	`    .Select(comp => comp.CompanyName);`
	
	Or, use the *orderby* query operator. For example:
	
	`var companyNames =`
	`    from a in addresses`
	`    orderby a.CompanyName`
	`    select a.CompanyName;`

To	Do this

Group data by the values in a field	Use the *GroupBy* method and specify a lambda expression identifying the field to use to group rows. For example:
	
	```\nvar companiesGroupedByCountry =\n addresses.GroupBy(addrs => addrs.Country);\n```
	
	Or, use the *group by* query operator. For example:
	
	```\nvar companiesGroupedByCountry =\n from a in addresses\n group a by a.Country;\n```

Join data held in two different collections	Use the *Join* method, specifying the collection with which to join, the join criteria, and the fields for the result. For example:
	
	```\nvar countriesAndCustomers =\n customers\n .Select(c => new { c.FirstName, c.LastName,\nc.CompanyName }).\n Join(addresses, custs => custs.CompanyName,\n addrs => addrs.CompanyName,\n (custs, addrs) => new {custs.FirstName,\n custs.LastName, addrs.Country });\n```
	
	Or, use the *join* query operator. For example:
	
	```\nvar countriesAndCustomers =\n from a in addresses\n join c in customers\n on a.CompanyName equals c.CompanyName\n select new { c.FirstName, c.LastName, a.Country\n};\n```

Force immediate generation of the results for a LINQ query	Use the *ToList* or *ToArray* method to generate a list or an array containing the results. For example: ```\nvar allEmployees =\n from e in empTree.ToList<Employee>()\n select e;\n```

CHAPTER 22

Operator overloading

After completing this chapter, you will be able to:

- Implement binary operators for your own types.

- Implement unary operators for your own types.

- Write increment and decrement operators for your own types.

- Understand the need to implement some operators as pairs.

- Implement implicit conversion operators for your own types.

- Implement explicit conversion operators for your own types.

The examples throughout this book make great use of the standard operator symbols (such as + and –) to perform standard operations (such as addition and subtraction) on types (such as *int* and *double*). Many of the built-in types come with their own predefined behaviors for each operator. You can also define how operators should behave for your own structures and classes, which is the subject of this chapter.

Understanding operators

It is worth recapping some of the fundamental aspects of operators before delving into the details of how they work and how you can overload them. The following list summarizes these aspects:

- You use operators to combine operands into expressions. Each operator has its own semantics, dependent on the type with which it works. For example, the + operator means "add" when you use it with numeric types or "concatenate" when you use it with strings.

- Each operator has a *precedence*. For example, the * operator has a higher precedence than the + operator. This means that the expression *a + b * c* is the same as *a + (b * c)*.

- Each operator also has an *associativity* that defines whether the operator evaluates from left to right or from right to left. For example, the = operator is right-associative (it evaluates from right to left), so *a = b = c* is the same as *a = (b = c)*.

- A *unary operator* is an operator that has just one operand. For example, the increment operator (++) is a unary operator.

- A *binary operator* is an operator that has two operands. For example, the multiplication operator (*) is a binary operator.

Operator constraints

This book presents many examples of how with C# you can overload methods when defining your own types. With C#, you can also overload many of the existing operator symbols for your own types, although the syntax is slightly different. When you do this, the operators you implement automatically fall into a well-defined framework with the following rules:

- You cannot change the precedence and associativity of an operator. Precedence and associativity are based on the operator symbol (for example, +) and not on the type (for example, *int*) on which the operator symbol is being used. Hence, the expression *a + b * c* is always the same as *a + (b * c)* regardless of the types of *a*, *b*, and *c*.

- You cannot change the multiplicity (the number of operands) of an operator. For example, * (the symbol for multiplication) is a binary operator. If you declare a * operator for your own type, it must be a binary operator.

- You cannot invent new operator symbols. For example, you can't create an operator symbol such as ** for raising one number to the power of another number. You'd have to define a method to do that.

- You can't change the meaning of operators when they are applied to built-in types. For example, the expression *1 + 2* has a predefined meaning, and you're not allowed to override this meaning. If you could do this, things would be too complicated.

- There are some operator symbols that you can't overload. For example, you can't overload the dot (.) operator, which indicates access to a class member. Again, if you could do this, it would lead to unnecessary complexity.

> **Tip** You can use indexers to simulate *[ ]* as an operator. Similarly, you can use properties to simulate assignment (=) as an operator, and you can use delegates to mimic a function call as an operator.

Overloaded operators

To define your own operator behavior, you must overload a selected operator. You use method-like syntax with a return type and parameters, but the name of the method is the keyword *operator* together with the operator symbol you are declaring. For example, the following code shows a user-defined structure named *Hour* that defines a binary + operator to add together two instances of *Hour*:

```
struct Hour
{
```

```
    public Hour(int initialValue)
    {
        this.value = initialValue;
    }
    public static Hour operator +(Hour lhs, Hour rhs)
    {
        return new Hour(lhs.value + rhs.value);
    }
    ...
    private int value;
}
```

Notice the following:

- The operator is public. All operators *must* be public.

- The operator is static. All operators *must* be static. Operators are never polymorphic and cannot use the *virtual, abstract, override,* or *sealed* modifiers.

- A binary operator (such as the + operator shown in this example) has two explicit arguments, and a unary operator has one explicit argument. (C++ programmers should note that operators never have a hidden *this* parameter.)

> **Tip** When you declare highly stylized functionality (such as operators), it is useful to adopt a naming convention for the parameters. For example, developers often use *lhs* and *rhs* (acronyms for left-hand side and right-hand side, respectively) for binary operators.

When you use the + operator on two expressions of type *Hour*, the C# compiler automatically converts your code to a call to your *operator* + method. The C# compiler transforms this code

```
Hour Example(Hour a, Hour b)
{
    return a + b;
}
```

to this:

```
Hour Example(Hour a, Hour b)
{
    return Hour.operator +(a,b); // pseudocode
}
```

Note, however, that this syntax is pseudocode and not valid C#. You can use a binary operator only in its standard infix notation (with the symbol between the operands).

There is one final rule that you must follow when declaring an operator: at least one of the parameters must always be of the containing type. In the preceding *operator+* example for the *Hour* class, one of the parameters, *a* or *b*, must be an *Hour* object. In this example, both parameters are *Hour* objects. However, there could be times when you want to define additional implementations of *operator+* that add, for example, an integer (a number of hours) to an *Hour* object—the first parameter could be *Hour*, and the second parameter could be the integer. This rule makes it easier for the compiler to know where to look when trying to resolve an operator invocation, and it also ensures that you can't change the meaning of the built-in operators.

Creating symmetric operators

In the preceding section, you saw how to declare a binary + operator to add together two instances of type *Hour*. The *Hour* structure also has a constructor that creates an *Hour* from an *int*. This means that you can add together an *Hour* and an *int*; you just have to first use the *Hour* constructor to convert the *int* to an *Hour*, as in the following example:

```
Hour a = ...;
int b = ...;
Hour sum = a + new Hour(b);
```

This is certainly valid code, but it is not as clear or concise as adding an *Hour* and an *int* directly, like this:

```
Hour a = ...;
int b = ...;
Hour sum = a + b;
```

To make the expression (*a* + *b*) valid, you must specify what it means to add together an *Hour* (*a*, on the left) and an *int* (*b*, on the right). In other words, you must declare a binary + operator whose first parameter is an *Hour* and whose second parameter is an *int*. The following code shows the recommended approach:

```
struct Hour
{
    public Hour(int initialValue)
    {
        this.value = initialValue;
    }
    ...
    public static Hour operator +(Hour lhs, Hour rhs)
    {
        return new Hour(lhs.value + rhs.value);
    }

    public static Hour operator +(Hour lhs, int rhs)
    {
        return lhs + new Hour(rhs);
    }
    ...
    private int value;
}
```

Notice that all the second version of the operator does is construct an *Hour* from its *int* argument and then call the first version. In this way, the real logic behind the operator is held in a single place. The point is that the extra *operator+* simply makes existing functionality easier to use. Also, notice that you should not provide many different versions of this operator, each with a different second parameter type; instead, cater to the common and meaningful cases only, and let the user of the class take any additional steps if an unusual case is required.

This *operator+* declares how to add together an *Hour* as the left operand and an *int* as the right operand. It does not declare how to add together an *int* as the left operand and an *Hour* as the right operand:

```
int a = ...;
Hour b = ...;
Hour sum = a + b; // compile-time error
```

This is counterintuitive. If you can write the expression *a + b*, you expect to also be able to write *b + a*. Therefore, you should provide another overload of *operator+*:

```
struct Hour
{
    public Hour(int initialValue)
    {
        this.value = initialValue;
    }
    ...
    public static Hour operator +(Hour lhs, int rhs)
    {
        return lhs + new Hour(rhs);
    }

    public static Hour operator +(int lhs, Hour rhs)
    {
        return new Hour(lhs) + rhs;
    }
    ...
    private int value;
}
```

Note C++ programmers should notice that you must provide the overload yourself. The compiler won't write the overload for you or silently swap the sequence of the two operands to find a matching operator.

Understanding compound assignment evaluation

A compound assignment operator (such as +=) is always evaluated in terms of its associated simple operator (such as +). In other words, the statement

```
a += b;
```

is automatically evaluated like this:

```
a = a + b;
```

In general, the expression *a @= b* (where @ represents any valid operator) is always evaluated as *a = a @ b*. If you have overloaded the appropriate simple operator, the overloaded version is automatically called when you use its associated compound assignment operator, as is shown in the following example:

```
Hour a = ...;
int b = ...;
a += a; // same as a = a + a
a += b; // same as a = a + b
```

The first compound assignment expression *(a += a)* is valid because *a* is of type *Hour*, and the *Hour* type declares a binary *operator+* whose parameters are both *Hour*. Similarly, the second compound assignment expression *(a += b)* is also valid because *a* is of type *Hour* and *b* is of type *int*. The *Hour* type also declares a binary *operator+* whose first parameter is an *Hour* and whose second parameter is an *int*. Be aware, however, that you cannot write the expression *b += a* because that's the same as *b = b + a*. Although the addition is valid, the assignment is not, because there is no way to assign an *Hour* to the built-in *int* type.

Declaring increment and decrement operators

With C#, you can declare your own version of the increment (++) and decrement (– –) operators. The usual rules apply when declaring these operators: they must be public, they must be static, and they must be unary (they can take only a single parameter). Here is the increment operator for the *Hour* structure:

```
struct Hour
{
    ...
    public static Hour operator ++(Hour arg)
    {
        arg.value++;
        return arg;
    }
    ...
    private int value;
}
```

The increment and decrement operators are unique in that they can be used in prefix and postfix forms. C# cleverly uses the same single operator for both the prefix and postfix versions. The result of a postfix expression is the value of the operand *before* the expression takes place. In other words, the compiler effectively converts the code

```
Hour now = new Hour(9);
Hour postfix = now++;
```

to this:

```
Hour now = new Hour(9);
Hour postfix = now;
now = Hour.operator ++(now); // pseudocode, not valid C#
```

The result of a prefix expression is the return value of the operator, so the C# compiler effectively transforms the code

```
Hour now = new Hour(9);
Hour prefix = ++now;
```

to this:

```
Hour now = new Hour(9);
now = Hour.operator ++(now); // pseudocode, not valid C#
Hour prefix = now;
```

This equivalence means that the return type of the increment and decrement operators must be the same as the parameter type.

Comparing operators in structures and classes

Be aware that the implementation of the increment operator in the *Hour* structure works only because *Hour* is a structure. If you change *Hour* into a class but leave the implementation of its increment operator unchanged, you will find that the postfix translation won't give the correct answer. If you remember that a class is a reference type, and if you revisit the compiler translations explained earlier, you can see in the following example why the operators for the *Hour* class no longer function as expected:

```
Hour now = new Hour(9);
Hour postfix = now;
now = Hour.operator ++(now); // pseudocode, not valid C#
```

If *Hour* is a class, the assignment statement *postfix = now* makes the variable *postfix* refer to the same object as *now*. Updating *now* automatically updates *postfix*! If *Hour* is a structure, the assignment statement makes a copy of *now* in *postfix*, and any changes to *now* leave *postfix* unchanged, which is what you want.

The correct implementation of the increment operator when *Hour* is a class is as follows:

```
class Hour
{
    public Hour(int initialValue)
    {
        this.value = initialValue;
    }
    ...
    public static Hour operator ++(Hour arg)
    {
        return new Hour(arg.value + 1);
    }
    ...
    private int value;
}
```

Notice that *operator* ++ now creates a new object based on the data in the original. The data in the new object is incremented, but the data in the original is left unchanged. Although this works, the compiler translation of the increment operator results in a new object being created each time it is used. This can be expensive in terms of memory use and garbage-collection overhead. Therefore, it is recommended that you limit operator overloads when you define types. This recommendation applies to all operators, not just to the increment operator.

Defining operator pairs

Some operators naturally come in pairs. For example, if you can compare two *Hour* values by using the *!=* operator, you would expect to be able to also compare two *Hour* values by using the *==* operator. The C# compiler enforces this very reasonable expectation by insisting that if you define either *operator* == or *operator* !=, you must define them both. This neither-or-both rule also applies to the < and > operators and the <= and >= operators. The C# compiler does not write any of these operator partners for you. You must write them all explicitly yourself, regardless of how obvious they might seem. Here are the == and != operators for the *Hour* structure:

```
struct Hour
{
    public Hour(int initialValue)
    {
        this.value = initialValue;
    }
    ...
    public static bool operator ==(Hour lhs, Hour rhs)
    {
        return lhs.value == rhs.value;
    }

    public static bool operator !=(Hour lhs, Hour rhs)
    {
        return lhs.value != rhs.value;
    }
    ...
    private int value;
}
```

The return type from these operators does not actually have to be Boolean. However, you should have a very good reason for using some other type, or these operators could become very confusing.

Overriding the equality operators

If you define *operator* == and *operator* != in a class, you should also override the *Equals* and *GetHashCode* methods inherited from *System.Object* (or *System.ValueType* if you are creating a structure). The *Equals* method should exhibit *exactly* the same behavior as *operator* ==. (You should define one in terms of the other.) The *GetHashCode* method is used by other classes in the Microsoft .NET Framework. (When you use an object as a key in a hash table, for example, the *GetHashCode* method is called on the object to help calculate a hash value. For more information, see the .NET Framework reference documentation supplied with Visual Studio 2015.) All this method needs to do is return a distinguishing integer value. Don't return the same integer from the *GetHashCode* method of all your objects, however, because this will nullify the effectiveness of the hashing algorithms.

Implementing operators

In the following exercise, you will develop a class that simulates complex numbers.

A complex number has two elements: a real component and an imaginary component. Typically, a complex number is represented in the form $(x + yi)$, where x is the real component and yi is the imaginary component. The values of x and y are regular integers, and i represents the square root of –1 (hence the reason why yi is imaginary). Despite their rather obscure and theoretical feel, complex numbers have a large number of uses in the fields of electronics, applied mathematics, and physics, and in many aspects of engineering. If you want more information about how and why complex numbers are useful, Wikipedia provides a useful and informative article.

> **Note** The Microsoft .NET Framework version 4.0 and later includes a type called *Complex* in the *System.Numerics* namespace that implements complex numbers, so there is no real need to define your own version of this type anymore. However, it is still instructive to see how to implement some of the common operators for this type.

You will implement complex numbers as a pair of integers that represent the coefficients x and y for the real and imaginary elements. You will also implement the operators necessary for performing simple arithmetic using complex numbers. The following table summarizes how to perform the four primary arithmetic operations on a pair of complex numbers, $(a + bi)$ and $(c + di)$.

Operation	Calculation
$(a + bi) + (c + di)$	$((a + c) + (b + d)i)$
$(a + bi) - (c + di)$	$((a - c) + (b - d)i)$
$(a + bi) * (c + di)$	$((a * c - b * d) + (b * c + a * d)i)$
$(a + bi) / (c + di)$	$(((a * c + b * d) / (c * c + d * d)) + ((b * c - a * d) / (c * c + d * d))i)$

Create the *Complex* class and implement the arithmetic operators

1. Start Visual Studio 2015 if it is not already running.

2. Open the ComplexNumbers project, which is located in the \Microsoft Press\VCSBS\Chapter 22\ComplexNumbers folder in your Documents folder. This is a console application that you will use to build and test your code. The Program.cs file contains the familiar *doWork* method.

3. In Solution Explorer, click the ComplexNumbers project. On the Project menu, click Add Class. In the Add New Item – ComplexNumbers dialog box, in the Name box, type **Complex.cs**, and then click Add.

   Visual Studio creates the *Complex* class and opens the Complex.cs file in the Code and Text Editor window.

4. Add the automatic integer properties *Real* and *Imaginary* to the *Complex* class, as shown by the code in bold that follows.

```
class Complex
{
    public int Real { get; set; }
    public int Imaginary { get; set; }
}
```

These properties will hold the real and imaginary components of a complex number.

5. Add the constructor shown below in bold to the *Complex* class.

```
class Complex
{
    ...
    public Complex (int real, int imaginary)
    {
        this.Real = real;
        this.Imaginary = imaginary;
    }
}
```

This constructor takes two *int* parameters and uses them to populate the *Real* and *Imaginary* properties.

6. Override the *ToString* method as shown next in bold.

```
class Complex
{
    ...
    public override string ToString()
    {
        return $"({this.Real} + {this.Imaginary}i)";
    }
}
```

This method returns a string representing the complex number in the form (x + y*i*).

7. Add the overloaded + operator to the *Complex* class as shown in bold in the code that follows:

```
class Complex
{
    ...
    public static Complex operator +(Complex lhs, Complex rhs)
    {
        return new Complex(lhs.Real + rhs.Real, lhs.Imaginary + rhs.Imaginary);
    }
}
```

This is the binary addition operator. It takes two *Complex* objects and adds them together by performing the calculation shown in the table at the start of the exercise. The operator returns a new *Complex* object containing the results of this calculation.

8. Add the overloaded – operator to the *Complex* class.

```
class Complex
{
    ...
    public static Complex operator -(Complex lhs, Complex rhs)
    {
        return new Complex(lhs.Real - rhs.Real, lhs.Imaginary - rhs.Imaginary);
    }
}
```

This operator follows the same form as the overloaded + operator.

9. Implement the * operator and / operator.

```
class Complex
{
    ...
    public static Complex operator *(Complex lhs, Complex rhs)
    {
        return new Complex(lhs.Real * rhs.Real - lhs.Imaginary * rhs.Imaginary,
            lhs.Imaginary * rhs.Real + lhs.Real * rhs.Imaginary);
    }

    public static Complex operator /(Complex lhs, Complex rhs)
    {
        int realElement = (lhs.Real * rhs.Real + lhs.Imaginary * rhs.Imaginary) /
            (rhs.Real * rhs.Real + rhs.Imaginary * rhs.Imaginary);

        int imaginaryElement = (lhs.Imaginary * rhs.Real - lhs.Real * rhs.Imaginary) /
            (rhs.Real * rhs.Real + rhs.Imaginary * rhs.Imaginary);

        return new Complex(realElement, imaginaryElement);
    }
}
```

These operators follow the same form as the previous two operators, although the calculations are a little more complicated. (The calculation for the / operator has been broken down into two steps to avoid lengthy lines of code.)

10. Display the Program.cs file in the Code and Text Editor window. Add the following statements shown in bold to the *doWork* method of the *Program* class and delete the *// TODO:* comment:

```
static void doWork()
{
    Complex first = new Complex(10, 4);
    Complex second = new Complex(5, 2);

    Console.WriteLine($"first is {first}");
    Console.WriteLine($"second is {second}");

    Complex temp = first + second;
    Console.WriteLine($"Add: result is {temp}");

    temp = first - second;
    Console.WriteLine($"Subtract: result is {temp}");

    temp = first * second;
    Console.WriteLine($"Multiply: result is {temp}");

    temp = first / second;
    Console.WriteLine($"Divide: result is {temp}");
}
```

This code creates two *Complex* objects that represent the complex values (10 + 4*i*) and (5 + 2*i*). The code displays them and then tests each of the operators you have just defined, displaying the results in each case.

11. On the Debug menu, click Start Without Debugging.

   Verify that the application displays the results shown in the following image:

```
C:\Windows\system32\cmd.exe

first is (10 + 4i)
second is (5 + 2i)
Add: result is (15 + 6i)
Subtract: result is (5 + 2i)
Multiply: result is (42 + 40i)
Divide: result is (2 + 0i)
Press any key to continue . . .
```

12. Close the application, and return to the Visual Studio 2015 programming environment.

You have now created a type that models complex numbers and supports basic arithmetic operations. In the next exercise, you will extend the *Complex* class and provide the equality operators, == and !=.

Implement the equality operators

1. In Visual Studio 2015, display the Complex.cs file in the Code and Text Editor window.

2. Add the == and != operators to the *Complex* class as shown in bold in the following example.

```
class Complex
{
    ...
    public static bool operator ==(Complex lhs, Complex rhs)
    {
        return lhs.Equals(rhs);
    }

    public static bool operator !=(Complex lhs, Complex rhs)
    {
        return !(lhs.Equals(rhs));
    }
}
```

Notice that both of these operators make use of the *Equals* method. The *Equals* method compares an instance of a class against another instance specified as an argument. It returns *true* if they have equivalent values and *false* otherwise.

3. On the Build menu, click Rebuild Solution.

   The Error List window displays the following warning messages:

```
'ComplexNumbers.Complex' defines operator == or operator != but does not override
Object.Equals(object o)
'ComplexNumbers.Complex' defines operator == or operator != but does not override
```

```
Object.GetHashCode()
```

If you define the *!=* and *==* operators, you should also override the *Equals* and *GetHashCode* methods inherited from *System.Object*.

> **Note** If the Error List window is not visible, click Error List on the View menu.

4. Override the *Equals* method in the *Complex* class, as shown here in bold:

```
class Complex
{
    ...
    public override bool Equals(Object obj)
    {
        if (obj is Complex)
        {
            Complex compare = (Complex)obj;
            return (this.Real == compare.Real) &&
                (this.Imaginary == compare.Imaginary);
        }
        else
        {
            return false;
        }
    }
}
```

The *Equals* method takes an *Object* as a parameter. This code verifies that the type of the parameter is actually a *Complex* object. If it is, this code compares the values in the *Real* and *Imaginary* properties in the current instance and the parameter passed in. If they are the same, the method returns *true*; otherwise, it returns *false*. If the parameter passed in is not a *Complex* object, the method returns *false*.

> **Important** It is tempting to write the *Equals* method like this:
>
> ```
> public override bool Equals(Object obj)
> {
>     Complex compare = obj as Complex;
>     if (compare != null)
>     {
>         return (this.Real == compare.Real) &&
>                 (this.Imaginary == compare.Imaginary);
>     }
>     else
>     {
>         return false;
>     }
> }
> ```
>
> However, the expression compare *!= null* invokes the *!=* operator of the *Complex* class, which calls the *Equals* method again, resulting in a recursive loop.

5. Override the *GetHashCode* method. This implementation simply calls the method inherited from the *Object* class, but you can provide your own mechanism to generate a hash code for an object if you prefer.

```
Class Complex
{
    ...
    public override int GetHashCode()
    {
        return base.GetHashCode();
    }
}
```

6. On the Build menu, click Rebuild Solution.

   Verify that the solution now builds without reporting any warnings.

7. Display the Program.cs file in the Code and Text Editor window. Add the following code shown in bold to the end of the *doWork* method:

```
static void doWork()
{
    ...
    if (temp == first)
    {
        Console.WriteLine("Comparison: temp == first");
    }
    else
    {
        Console.WriteLine("Comparison: temp != first");
    }

    if (temp == temp)
    {
        Console.WriteLine("Comparison: temp == temp");
    }
    else
    {
        Console.WriteLine("Comparison: temp != temp");
    }
}
```

> **Note** The expression *temp == temp* generates the warning message "Comparison made to same variable; did you mean to compare to something else?" In this case, you can ignore the warning because this comparison is intentional; it is to verify that the == operator is working as expected.

8. On the Debug menu, click Start Without Debugging. Verify that the final two messages displayed are these:

```
Comparison: temp != first
Comparison: temp == temp
```

CHAPTER 22   Operator overloading   **507**

9. Close the application, and return to Visual Studio 2015.

Understanding conversion operators

Sometimes, you need to convert an expression of one type to another. For example, the following method is declared with a single *double* parameter:

```
class Example
{
    public static void MyDoubleMethod(double parameter)
    {
        ...
    }
}
```

You might reasonably expect that only values of type *double* could be used as arguments when your code calls *MyDoubleMethod*, but this is not so. The C# compiler also allows *MyDoubleMethod* to be called with an argument of some other type, but only if the value of the argument can be converted to a *double*. For example, if you provide an *int* argument, the compiler generates code that converts the value of the argument to a *double* when the method is called.

Providing built-in conversions

The built-in types have some built-in conversions. For example, as mentioned previously, an *int* can be implicitly converted to a *double*. An implicit conversion requires no special syntax and never throws an exception.

```
Example.MyDoubleMethod(42); // implicit int-to-double conversion
```

An implicit conversion is sometimes called a *widening conversion* because the result is *wider* than the original value—it contains at least as much information as the original value, and nothing is lost. In the case of *int* and *double*, the range of *double* is greater than that of *int*, and all *int* values have an equivalent *double* value. However, the converse is not true, and a *double* value cannot be implicitly converted to an *int*:

```
class Example
{
    public static void MyIntMethod(int parameter)
    {
        ...
    }
}
...
Example.MyIntMethod(42.0); // compile-time error
```

When you convert a *double* to an *int*, you run the risk of losing information, so the conversion will not be performed automatically. (Consider what would happen if the argument to *MyIntMethod* were 42.5. How should this be converted?) A *double* can be converted to an *int*, but the conversion requires an explicit notation (a cast):

```
Example.MyIntMethod((int)42.0);
```

An explicit conversion is sometimes called a *narrowing conversion* because the result is *narrower* than the original value (that is, it can contain less information) and can throw an *OverflowException* exception if the resulting value is out of the range of the target type. In C#, you can create conversion operators for your own user-defined types to control whether it is sensible to convert values to other types, and you can also specify whether these conversions are implicit or explicit.

Implementing user-defined conversion operators

The syntax for declaring a user-defined conversion operator has some similarities to that for declaring an overloaded operator, but it also has some important differences. Here's a conversion operator that allows an *Hour* object to be implicitly converted to an *int*:

```
struct Hour
{
    ...
    public static implicit operator int (Hour from)
    {
        return from.value;
    }

    private int value;
}
```

A conversion operator must be *public* and it must also be *static*. The type from which you are converting is declared as the parameter (in this case, *Hour*), and the type to which you are converting is declared as the type name after the keyword *operator* (in this case, *int*). There is no return type specified before the keyword *operator*.

When declaring your own conversion operators, you must specify whether they are implicit conversion operators or explicit conversion operators. You do this by using the *implicit* and *explicit* keywords. The *Hour* to *int* conversion operator shown in the preceding example is implicit, meaning that the C# compiler can use it without requiring a cast.

```
class Example
{
    public static void MyOtherMethod(int parameter) { ... }
    public static void Main()
    {
        Hour lunch = new Hour(12);
        Example.MyOtherMethod(lunch); // implicit Hour to int conversion
    }
}
```

If the conversion operator had been declared with *explicit*, the preceding example would not have compiled because an explicit conversion operator requires a cast.

```
Example.MyOtherMethod((int)lunch); // explicit Hour to int conversion
```

When should you declare a conversion operator as explicit or implicit? If a conversion is always safe, does not run the risk of losing information, and cannot throw an exception, it can be defined as an *implicit* conversion. Otherwise, it should be declared as an *explicit* conversion. Converting from an *Hour* to an *int* is always safe—every *Hour* has a corresponding *int* value—so it makes sense for it to be implicit. An operator that converts a *string* to an *Hour* should be explicit because not all strings represent valid *Hours*. (The string "7" is fine, but how would you convert the string "Hello, World" to an *Hour*?)

Creating symmetric operators, revisited

Conversion operators provide you with an alternative way to resolve the problem of providing symmetric operators. For example, instead of providing three versions of *operator+* (*Hour + Hour*, *Hour + int*, and *int + Hour*) for the *Hour* structure, as shown earlier, you can provide a single version of *operator+* (that takes two *Hour* parameters) and an implicit *int* to *Hour* conversion, like this:

```
struct Hour
{
    public Hour(int initialValue)
    {
        this.value = initialValue;
    }

    public static Hour operator +(Hour lhs, Hour rhs)
    {
        return new Hour(lhs.value + rhs.value);
    }

    public static implicit operator Hour (int from)
    {
        return new Hour (from);
    }
    ...
    private int value;
}
```

If you add an *Hour* to an *int* (in either order), the C# compiler automatically converts the *int* to an *Hour* and then calls *operator+* with two *Hour* arguments, as demonstrated here:

```
void Example(Hour a, int b)
{
    Hour eg1 = a + b; // b converted to an Hour
    Hour eg2 = b + a; // b converted to an Hour
}
```

Writing conversion operators

In the final exercise of this chapter, you will add conversion operators to the *Complex* class. You will start by writing a pair of conversion operators that convert between the *int* type and the *Complex* type. Converting an *int* to a *Complex* object is always a safe process and never loses information (because an *int* is really just a complex number without an imaginary element). You will implement this as an implicit conversion operator. However, the converse is not true—to convert a *Complex* object into an *int*, you have to discard the imaginary element. Thus, you will implement this conversion operator as explicit.

Implement the conversion operators

1. Return to Visual Studio 2015 and display the Complex.cs file in the Code and Text Editor window. Add the constructor shown in bold in the code that follows to the *Complex* class, immediately after the existing constructor and before the *ToString* method. This new constructor takes a single *int* parameter, which it uses to initialize the *Real* property. The *Imaginary* property is set to *0*.

   ```
   class Complex
   {
       ...
       public Complex(int real)
       {
           this.Real = real;
           this.Imaginary = 0;
       }
       ...
   }
   ```

2. Add the following implicit conversion operator to the *Complex* class.

   ```
   class Complex
   {
       ...
       public static implicit operator Complex(int from)
       {
           return new Complex(from);
       }
       ...
   }
   ```

   This operator converts from an *int* to a *Complex* object by returning a new instance of the *Complex* class built using the constructor you created in the previous step.

3. Add the following explicit conversion operator shown in bold to the *Complex* class.

```
class Complex
{
    ...
    public static explicit operator int(Complex from)
    {
        return from.Real;
    }
    ...
}
```

This operator takes a *Complex* object and returns the value of the *Real* property. This conversion discards the imaginary element of the complex number.

4. Display the Program.cs file in the Code and Text Editor window. Add the following code shown in bold to the end of the *doWork* method:

```
static void doWork()
{
    ...
    Console.WriteLine($"Current value of temp is {temp}");

    if (temp == 2)
    {
        Console.WriteLine("Comparison after conversion: temp == 2");
    }
    else
    {
        Console.WriteLine("Comparison after conversion: temp != 2");
    }

    temp += 2;
    Console.WriteLine($"Value after adding 2: temp = {temp}");
}
```

These statements test the implicit operator that converts an *int* to a *Complex* object. The *if* statement compares a *Complex* object to an *int*. The compiler generates code that converts the *int* into a *Complex* object first and then invokes the == operator of the *Complex* class. The statement that adds 2 to the *temp* variable converts the *int* value 2 into a *Complex* object and then uses the + operator of the *Complex* class.

5. Add the following statements to end of the *doWork* method:

```
static void doWork()
{
    ...
    int tempInt = temp;
    Console.WriteLine($"Int value after conversion: tempInt == {tempInt}");
}
```

The first statement attempts to assign a *Complex* object to an *int* variable.

6. On the Build menu, click Rebuild Solution.

   The solution fails to build, and the compiler reports the following error in the Error List window:

   ```
   Cannot implicitly convert type 'ComplexNumbers.Complex' to 'int'. An explicit
   conversion exists (are you missing a cast?)
   ```

   The operator that converts from a *Complex* object to an *int* is an explicit conversion operator, so you must specify a cast.

7. Modify the statement that attempts to store a *Complex* value in an *int* variable to use a cast, like this:

   ```
   int tempInt = (int)temp;
   ```

8. On the Debug menu, click Start Without Debugging. Verify that the solution now builds and that the final four messages displayed look like this:

   ```
   Current value of temp is (2 + 0i)
   Comparison after conversion: temp == 2
   Value after adding 2: temp = (4 + 0i)
   Int value after conversion: tempInt == 4
   ```

9. Close the application, and return to Visual Studio 2015.

Summary

In this chapter, you learned how to overload operators and provide functionality specific to a class or structure. You implemented a number of common arithmetic operators, and you also created operators with which you can compare instances of a class. Finally, you learned how to create implicit and explicit conversion operators.

- If you want to continue to the next chapter, keep Visual Studio 2015 running and turn to Chapter 23, "Improving throughput by using tasks."

- If you want to exit Visual Studio 2015 now, on the File menu, click Exit. If you see a Save dialog box, click Yes and save the project.

Quick reference

To	Do this

Implement an operator	Write the keywords *public* and *static*, followed by the return type, followed by the *operator* keyword, followed by the operator symbol being declared, followed by the appropriate parameters between parentheses. Implement the logic for the operator in the body of the method. For example:
	
	<pre>class Complex
	{
	    ...
	    public static bool operator==(Complex lhs,
	                                 Complex rhs)
	    {
	        ... // Implement logic for == operator
	    }
	    ...
	}</pre>

Define a conversion operator	Write the keywords *public* and *static*, followed by the keyword *implicit* or *explicit*, followed by the *operator* keyword, followed by the type being converted to, followed by the type being converted from as a single parameter between parentheses. For example:
	
	<pre>class Complex
	{
	    ...
	    public static implicit operator Complex(
	                                    int from)
	    {
	        ... // code to convert from an int
	    }
	    ...
	}</pre>

Building Universal Windows Platform applications with C#

So far, you have gained a thorough grounding in the syntax and semantics of the C# language. It's now time to examine how you can use this knowledge to take advantage of the features that Windows 10 provides for building applications that run unchanged on devices ranging from a desktop PC to a smartphone. You can build applications that run in different environments by using the Universal Windows Platform (UWP) application framework. UWP applications can detect and adapt to the hardware on which they execute. They can receive input through a touch-sensitive screen or by using voice commands, and a UWP app can be designed to be aware of the location and orientation of the device on which it is running. Capabilities in Windows 10 also enable you to build cloud-connected applications that are not tied to a specific computer but can follow users when they sign in on another device. In short, Windows 10 provides a platform for developing highly mobile, highly graphical, highly connected universal applications.

Part IV introduces you to the requirements of building UWP applications. You will see examples of the asynchronous model of programming developed as part of the .NET Framework. You will also learn how to integrate voice activation into your application and how to build a UWP application that connects to the cloud to retrieve and present complex information in a natural and easily navigable style.

CHAPTER 23

Improving throughput by using tasks

After completing the chapter, you will be able to:

- Describe the benefits of implementing parallel operations in an application.

- Use the *Task* class to create and run parallel operations in an application.

- Use the *Parallel* class to parallelize some common programming constructs.

- Cancel long-running tasks and handle exceptions raised by parallel operations.

In the bulk of the preceding chapters in this book, you've learned how to use C# to write programs that run in a single-threaded manner. By *single-threaded*, I mean that at any one point in time, a program has been executing a single instruction. This might not always be the most efficient approach for an application to take. If you have the appropriate processing resources available, some applications might run more quickly if you divide them into parallel paths of execution that can run concurrently. This chapter is concerned with improving throughput in your applications by maximizing the use of available processing power. Specifically, in this chapter you will learn how to use *Task* objects to apply effective multitasking to computationally intensive applications.

Why perform multitasking by using parallel processing?

There are two primary reasons why you might want to perform multitasking in an application:

- **To improve responsiveness** A long-running operation may involve tasks that do not require processor time. Common examples include I/O bound operations such as reading from or writing to a local disk or sending and receiving data across a network. In both of these cases, it does not make sense to have a program burn CPU cycles waiting for the operation to complete when the program could be doing something more useful instead (such as responding to user input). Most users of mobile devices take this form of responsiveness for granted and don't expect their tablet to simply halt while it is sending and receiving email, for example. Chapter 24, "Improving response time by performing asynchronous operations," discusses these features in more detail.

- **To improve scalability**   If an operation is CPU bound, you can improve scalability by making efficient use of the processing resources available and using these resources to reduce the time required to execute the operation. A developer can determine which operations include tasks that can be performed in parallel and arrange for these elements to be run concurrently. As more computing resources are added, more instances of these tasks can be run in parallel. Until relatively recently, this model was suitable only for scientific and engineering systems that either had multiple CPUs or were able to spread the processing across different computers networked together. However, most modern computing devices now contain powerful CPUs that are capable of supporting true multitasking, and many operating systems provide primitives that enable you to parallelize tasks quite easily.

The rise of the multicore processor

At the turn of the century, the cost of a decent personal computer was in the range of $800 to $1,500. Today, a decent personal computer still costs about the same, even after 15 years of price inflation. The specification of a typical computer these days is likely to include a processor running at a speed of between 2 GHz and 3 GHz, over 1,000 GB of hard disk storage, 4–8 GB of RAM, high-speed and high-resolution graphics, fast network interfaces, and a rewritable DVD drive. Fifteen years ago, the processor speed for a typical machine was between 500 MHz and 1 GHz, 80 GB was a large hard disk, Windows ran quite happily with 256 MB or less of RAM, and rewritable CD drives cost well over $100. (Rewritable DVD drives were rare and extremely expensive.) This is the joy of technological progress: ever faster and more powerful hardware at cheaper and cheaper prices.

This is not a new trend. In 1965, Gordon E. Moore, cofounder of Intel, wrote a paper titled "Cramming More Components onto Integrated Circuits," which discussed how the increasing miniaturization of components enabled more transistors to be embedded on a silicon chip, and how the falling costs of production as the technology became more accessible would lead economics to dictate squeezing as many as 65,000 components onto a single chip by 1975. Moore's observations lead to the dictum frequently referred to as Moore's Law, which basically states that the number of transistors that can be placed inexpensively on an integrated circuit will increase exponentially, doubling approximately every two years. (Actually, Gordon Moore was initially more optimistic than this, postulating that the volume of transistors was likely to double every year, but he later modified his calculations.) The ability to pack transistors together led to the ability to pass data between them more quickly. This meant we could expect to see chip manufacturers produce faster and more powerful microprocessors at an almost unrelenting pace, enabling software developers to write ever more complicated software that would run more quickly.

Moore's Law concerning the miniaturization of electronic components still holds, even half a century later. However, physics has started to intervene. A limit occurs when it is not possible to transmit signals between transistors on a single chip any faster, no matter how small or densely packed they are. To a software developer, the most noticeable result of this limitation is that processors have stopped getting faster. Ten years ago, a fast processor ran at 3 GHz. Today, a fast processor still runs at 3 GHz.

The limit to the speed at which processors can transmit data between components has caused chip companies to look at alternative mechanisms for increasing the amount of work a processor can do. The result is that most modern processors now have two or more *processor cores*. Effectively, chip manufacturers have put multiple processors on the same chip and added the necessary logic to enable them to communicate and coordinate with one another. Quad-core (four cores) and eight-core processors are now common. Chips with 16, 32, and 64 cores are available, and the price of dual-core and quad-core processors is now sufficiently low that they are an expected element in laptops, tablets, and smart cellphones. So, although processors have stopped speeding up, you can now expect to get more of them on a single chip.

What does this mean to a developer writing C# applications?

In the days before multicore processors, you could speed up a single-threaded application simply by running it on a faster processor. With multicore processors, this is no longer the case. A single-threaded application will run at the same speed on a single-core, dual-core, or quad-core processor that all have the same clock frequency. The difference is that on a dual-core processor, as far as your application is concerned, one of the processor cores will be sitting around idle, and on a quad-core processor, three of the cores will be simply ticking away, waiting for work. To make the best use of multicore processors, you need to write your applications to take advantage of multitasking.

Implementing multitasking by using the Microsoft .NET Framework

Multitasking is the ability to do more than one thing at the same time. It is one of those concepts that is easy to describe but until recently has been difficult to implement.

In the optimal scenario, an application running on a multicore processor performs as many concurrent tasks as there are processor cores available, keeping each of the cores busy. However, you need to consider many issues to implement concurrency, including the following:

- How can you divide an application into a set of concurrent operations?

- How can you arrange for a set of operations to execute concurrently, on multiple processors?

- How can you ensure that you attempt to perform only as many concurrent operations as there are processors available?

- If an operation is blocked (such as while waiting for I/O to complete), how can you detect this and arrange for the processor to run a different operation rather than sit idle?

- How can you determine when one or more concurrent operations have completed?

To an application developer, the first question is a matter of application design. The remaining questions depend on the programmatic infrastructure. Microsoft provides the *Task* class and a collection of associated types in the *System.Threading.Tasks* namespace to help address these issues.

Tasks, threads, and the *ThreadPool*

The *Task* class is an abstraction of a concurrent operation. You create a *Task* object to run a block of code. You can instantiate multiple *Task* objects and start them running in parallel if sufficient processors or processor cores are available.

> **Note** From now on, I will use the term *processor* to refer to either a single-core processor or a single processor core on a multicore processor.

Internally, the Windows Runtime (WinRT) implements tasks and schedules them for execution by using *Thread* objects and the *ThreadPool* class. Multithreading and thread pools have been available with the .NET Framework since version 1.0, and if you are building traditional desktop applications, you can use the *Thread* class in the *System.Threading* namespace directly in your code. However, the *Thread* class is not available for Universal Windows Platform (UWP) apps; instead, you use the *Task* class.

The *Task* class provides a powerful abstraction for threading with which you can easily distinguish between the degree of parallelization in an application (the tasks) and the units of parallelization (the threads). On a single-processor computer, these items are usually the same. However, on a computer with multiple processors or with a multicore processor, they are different. If you design a program based directly on threads, you will find that your application might not scale very well; the program will use the number of threads you explicitly create, and the operating system will schedule only that number of threads. This can lead to overloading and poor response time if the number of threads greatly exceeds the number of available processors, or to inefficiency and poor throughput if the number of threads is less than the number of processors.

WinRT optimizes the number of threads required to implement a set of concurrent tasks and schedules them efficiently according to the number of available processors. It implements a queuing mechanism to distribute the workload across a set of threads allocated to a thread pool (implemented by using a *ThreadPool* object). When a program creates a *Task* object, the task is added to a global queue. When a thread becomes available, the task is removed from the global queue and is executed by that thread. The *ThreadPool* class implements a number of optimizations and uses a work-stealing algorithm to ensure that threads are scheduled efficiently.

> **Note** The *ThreadPool* class was available in previous editions of the .NET Framework, but it was enhanced significantly in .NET Framework 4.0 to support *Task*s.

You should note that the number of threads created to handle your tasks is not necessarily the same as the number of processors. Depending on the nature of the workload, one or more processors might be busy performing high-priority work for other applications and services. Consequently, the optimal number of threads for your application might be less than the number of processors in the machine. Alternatively, one or more threads in an application might be waiting for long-running memory access, I/O, or network operation to complete, leaving the corresponding processors free. In this case, the optimal number of threads might be more than the number of available processors. WinRT follows an iterative strategy, known as a *hill-climbing* algorithm, to dynamically determine the ideal number of threads for the current workload.

The important point is that all you have to do in your code is divide, or partition, your application into tasks that can be run in parallel. WinRT takes responsibility for creating the appropriate number of threads based on the processor architecture and workload of your computer, associating your tasks with these threads and arranging for them to be run efficiently. It does not matter if you partition your work into too many tasks because WinRT will attempt to run only as many concurrent threads as is practical; in fact, you are encouraged to *overpartition* your work because this will help ensure that your application scales if you move it to a computer that has more processors available.

Creating, running, and controlling tasks

You can create *Task* objects by using the *Task* constructor. The *Task* constructor is overloaded, but all versions expect you to provide an *Action* delegate as a parameter. Chapter 20, "Decoupling application logic and handling events," illustrates that an *Action* delegate references a method that does not return a value. A *Task* object invokes this delegate when it is scheduled to run. The following example creates a *Task* object that uses a delegate to run the method called *doWork*:

```
Task task = new Task(doWork);
...
private void doWork()
{
    // The task runs this code when it is started
    ...
}
```

> **Tip** The default *Action* type references a method that takes no parameters. Other overloads of the *Task* constructor take an *Action<object>* parameter representing a delegate that refers to a method that takes a single *object* parameter. With these overloads, you can pass data into the method run by the task. The following code shows an example:
>
> ```
> Action<object> action;
> action = doWorkWithObject;
> object parameterData = ...;
> Task task = new Task(action, parameterData);
> ...
> private void doWorkWithObject(object o)
> {
>     ...
> }
> ```

After you create a *Task* object, you can set it running by using the *Start* method, like this:

```
Task task = new Task(...);
task.Start();
```

The *Start* method is overloaded, and you can optionally specify a *TaskCreationOptions* object to provide hints about how to schedule and run the task.

> **More info** For more information about the *TaskCreationOptions* enumeration, consult the documentation describing the .NET Framework class library that is provided with Visual Studio.

Creating and running a task is a very common process, and the *Task* class provides the static *Run* method with which you can combine these operations. The *Run* method takes an *Action* delegate specifying the operation to perform (like the *Task* constructor), but starts the task running immediately. It returns a reference to the *Task* object. You can use it like this:

```
Task task = Task.Run(() => doWork());
```

When the method run by the task completes, the task finishes, and the thread used to run the task can be recycled to execute another task.

When a task completes, you can arrange for another task to be scheduled immediately by creating a *continuation*. To do this, call the *ContinueWith* method of a *Task* object. When the action performed by the *Task* object completes, the scheduler automatically creates a new *Task* object to run the action specified by the *ContinueWith* method. The method specified by the continuation expects a *Task* parameter, and the scheduler passes into the method a reference to the task that completed. The value returned by *ContinueWith* is a reference to the new *Task* object. The following code example creates a *Task* object that runs the *doWork* method and specifies a continuation that runs the *doMoreWork* method in a new task when the first task completes:

```
Task task = new Task(doWork);
task.Start();
Task newTask = task.ContinueWith(doMoreWork);
...
private void doWork()
{
    // The task runs this code when it is started
    ...
}
...
private void doMoreWork(Task task)
{
    // The continuation runs this code when doWork completes
    ...
}
```

The *ContinueWith* method is heavily overloaded, and you can provide a number of parameters that specify additional items, including a *TaskContinuationOptions* value. The *TaskContinuation-Options* type is an enumeration that contains a superset of the values in the *TaskCreationOptions* enumeration. The additional values available include the following:

- **NotOnCanceled and OnlyOnCanceled**   The *NotOnCanceled* option specifies that the continuation should run only if the previous action completes and is not canceled, and the *OnlyOnCanceled* option specifies that the continuation should run only if the previous action is canceled. The section "Canceling tasks and handling exceptions" later in this chapter describes how to cancel a task.

- **NotOnFaulted and OnlyOnFaulted**   The *NotOnFaulted* option indicates that the continuation should run only if the previous action completes and does not throw an unhandled exception. The *OnlyOnFaulted* option causes the continuation to run only if the previous action throws an unhandled exception. The section "Canceling tasks and handling exceptions" provides more information on how to manage exceptions in a task.

- **NotOnRanToCompletion and OnlyOnRanToCompletion**   The *NotOnRanToCompletion* option specifies that the continuation should run only if the previous action does not complete successfully; it must either be canceled or throw an exception. *OnlyOnRanToCompletion* causes the continuation to run only if the previous action completes successfully.

The following code example shows how to add a continuation to a task that runs only if the initial action does not throw an unhandled exception:

```
Task task = new Task(doWork);
task.ContinueWith(doMoreWork, TaskContinuationOptions.NotOnFaulted);
task.Start();
```

A common requirement of applications that invoke operations in parallel is to synchronize tasks. The *Task* class provides the *Wait* method, which implements a simple task coordination mechanism. Using this method, you can suspend execution of the current thread until the specified task completes, like this:

```
Task task2 = ...
task2.Start();
...
task2.Wait(); // Wait at this point until task2 completes
```

You can wait for a set of tasks by using the static *WaitAll* and *WaitAny* methods of the *Task* class. Both methods take a *params* array containing a set of *Task* objects. The *WaitAll* method waits until all specified tasks have completed, and *WaitAny* stops until at least one of the specified tasks has finished. You use them like this:

```
Task.WaitAll(task, task2); // Wait for both task and task2 to complete
Task.WaitAny(task, task2); // Wait for either task or task2 to complete
```

Using the *Task* class to implement parallelism

In the next exercise, you will use the *Task* class to parallelize processor-intensive code in an application, and you will see how this parallelization reduces the time taken for the application to run by spreading the computations across multiple processor cores.

The application, called GraphDemo, consists of a page that uses an *Image* control to display a graph. The application plots the points for the graph by performing a complex calculation.

> **Note** The exercises in this chapter are intended to be run on a computer with a multicore processor. If you have only a single-core CPU, you will not observe the same effects. Also, you should not start any additional programs or services between exercises because these might affect the results that you see.

Examine and run the GraphDemo single-threaded application

1. Start Microsoft Visual Studio 2015 if it is not already running.

2. Open the GraphDemo solution, which is located in the \Microsoft Press\VCSBS\Chapter 23\ GraphDemo folder in your Documents folder. This is a Universal Windows Platform app.

3. In Solution Explorer, in the GraphDemo project, double-click the file MainPage.xaml to display the form in the Design View window.

   Apart from the *Grid* control defining the layout, the form contains the following important controls:

   - An *Image* control called *graphImage*. This image control displays the graph rendered by the application.

   - A *Button* control called *plotButton*. The user clicks this button to generate the data for the graph and display it in the *graphImage* control.

   > **Note** In the interest of keeping the operation of the application in this exercise simple, it displays the button on the page. In a production UWP app, buttons such as this should be located on a command bar.

   - A *TextBlock* control called *duration*. The application displays the time taken to generate and render the data for the graph in this label.

4. In Solution Explorer, expand the MainPage.xaml file and then double-click MainPage.xaml.cs to display the code for the form in the Code and Text Editor window.

The form uses a *WriteableBitmap* object (defined in the *Windows.UI.Xaml.Media.Imaging* namespace) called *graphBitmap* to render the graph. The variables *pixelWidth* and *pixelHeight* specify the horizontal and vertical resolution, respectively, for the *WriteableBitmap* object:

```
public partial class MainPage : Window
{
    // Reduce pixelWidth and pixelHeight if there is insufficient space available
    private int pixelWidth = 15000;
    private int pixelHeight = 10000;

    private WriteableBitmap graphBitmap = null;
    ...
}
```

> **Note** This application has been developed and tested on a desktop computer with 8 GB of memory. If your computer has less memory than this available, you might need to reduce the values in the *pixelWidth* and *pixelHeight* variables; otherwise, the application might generate *OutOfMemoryException* exceptions. Similarly, if you have much more memory available, you might want to increase the values of these variables to see the full effects of this exercise.

5. Examine the last three lines of the *MainPage* constructor, which look like this:

```
public MainPage()
{
    ...
    int dataSize = bytesPerPixel * pixelWidth * pixelHeight;
    data = new byte[dataSize];

    graphBitmap = new WriteableBitmap(pixelWidth, pixelHeight);
}
```

The first two lines instantiate a byte array that will hold the data for the graph. The size of this array depends on the resolution of the *WriteableBitmap* object, determined by the *pixelWidth* and *pixelHeight* fields. Additionally, this size has to be scaled by the amount of memory required to render each pixel; the *WriteableBitmap* class uses 4 bytes for each pixel, which specify the relative red, green, and blue intensity of each pixel and the alpha blending value of the pixel. (The alpha blending value determines the transparency and brightness of the pixel.)

The final statement creates the *WriteableBitmap* object with the specified resolution.

6. Examine the code for the *plotButton_Click* method:

```
private void plotButton_Click(object sender, RoutedEventArgs e)
{
    Random rand = new Random();
    redValue = (byte)rand.Next(0xFF);
    greenValue = (byte)rand.Next(0xFF);
    blueValue = (byte)rand.Next(0xFF);
```

```
Stopwatch watch = Stopwatch.StartNew();
generateGraphData(data);

duration.Text = $"Duration (ms): {watch.ElapsedMilliseconds}";

Stream pixelStream = graphBitmap.PixelBuffer.AsStream();
pixelStream.Seek(0, SeekOrigin.Begin);
pixelStream.Write(data, 0, data.Length);
graphBitmap.Invalidate();
graphImage.Source = graphBitmap;
}
```

This method runs when the user clicks the *plotButton* button.

You will click this button several times later in the exercise, which will let you see that a new version of the graph has been drawn each time this method generates a random set of values for the red, green, and blue intensity of the points that are plotted. (The graph will be a different color each time you click this button.)

The *watch* variable is a *System.Diagnostics.Stopwatch* object. The *StopWatch* type is useful for timing operations. The static *StartNew* method of the *StopWatch* type creates a new instance of a *StopWatch* object and starts it running. You can query the running time of a *StopWatch* object by examining the *ElapsedMilliseconds* property.

The *generateGraphData* method populates the *data* array with the data for the graph to be displayed by the *WriteableBitmap* object. You will examine this method in the next step.

When the *generateGraphData* method has completed, the elapsed time (in milliseconds) appears in the duration *TextBox* control.

The final block of code takes the information held in the data array and copies it to the *WriteableBitmap* object for rendering. The simplest technique is to create an in-memory stream that can be used to populate the *PixelBuffer* property of the *WriteableBitmap* object. You can then use the *Write* method of this stream to copy the contents of the data array into this buffer. The *Invalidate* method of the *WriteableBitmap* class requests that the operating system redraws the bitmap by using the information held in the buffer. The *Source* property of an *Image* control specifies the data that the *Image* control should display. The final statement sets the *Source* property to the *WriteableBitmap* object.

7. Examine the code for the *generateGraphData* method, shown here:

```
private void generateGraphData(byte[] data)
{
    int a = pixelWidth / 2;
    int b = a * a;
    int c = pixelHeight / 2;

    for (int x = 0; x < a; x ++)
    {
        int s = x * x;
        double p = Math.Sqrt(b - s);
        for (double i = -p; i < p; i += 3)
```

```
        {
            double r = Math.Sqrt(s + i * i) / a;
            double q = (r - 1) * Math.Sin(24 * r);
            double y = i / 3 + (q * c);
            plotXY(data, (int)(-x + (pixelWidth / 2)), (int)(y + (pixelHeight / 2)));
            plotXY(data, (int)(x + (pixelWidth / 2)), (int)(y + (pixelHeight / 2)));
        }
    }
}
```

This method performs a series of calculations to plot the points for a rather complex graph. (The actual calculation is unimportant—it just generates a graph that looks attractive.) As it calculates each point, it calls the *plotXY* method to set the appropriate bytes in the *data* array that correspond to these points. The points for the graph are reflected around the x-axis, so the *plotXY* method is called twice for each calculation: once for the positive value of the x-coordinate, and once for the negative value.

8. Examine the *plotXY* method:

```
private void plotXY(byte[] data, int x, int y)
{
    int pixelIndex = (x + y * pixelWidth) * bytesPerPixel;
    data[pixelIndex] = blueValue;
    data[pixelIndex + 1] = greenValue;
    data[pixelIndex + 2] = redValue;
    data[pixelIndex + 3] = 0xBF;
}
```

This method sets the appropriate bytes in the *data* array that corresponds to x- and y-coordinates passed in as parameters. Each point plotted corresponds to a pixel, and each pixel consists of 4 bytes, as described earlier. Any pixels left unset are displayed as black. The value 0xBF for the alpha blend byte indicates that the corresponding pixel should be displayed with a moderate intensity; if you decrease this value, the pixel will become fainter, while setting the value to 0xFF (the maximum value for a byte) will display the pixel at its brightest intensity.

9. On the Debug menu, click Start Debugging to build and run the application.

10. When the Graph Demo window appears, click Plot Graph, and then wait.

Please be patient. The application takes several seconds to generate and display the graph, and the application is unresponsive while this occurs. (Chapter 24 explains why this is, and also instructs you how to avoid this behavior.) The following image shows the graph. Note the value in the Duration (ms) label in the following figure. In this case, the application took 4,907 milliseconds (ms) to plot the graph. Note that this duration does not include the time to actually render the graph, which might be another few seconds.

> **Note** The application was run on a computer with 8 GB of memory and a quad-core processor running at 2.40 GHz. Your times might vary if you are using a slower

or faster processor with a different number of cores, or a computer with a greater or lesser amount of memory.

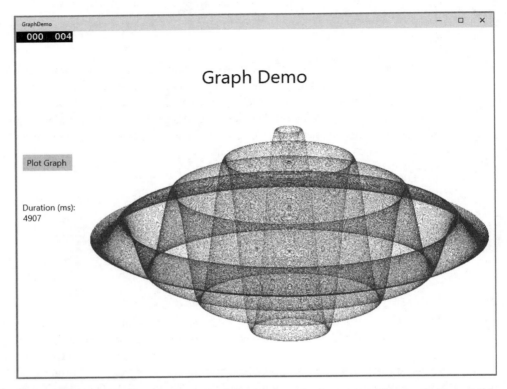

11. Click Plot Graph again, and take note of the time required to redraw the graph. Repeat this action several times to obtain an average value.

Note You might find that occasionally the graph takes an extended time to appear (more than 30 seconds). This tends to occur if you are running close to the memory capacity of your computer and Windows has to page data between memory and disk. If you encounter this phenomenon, discard this time and do not include it when calculating your average.

12. Leave the application running and right-click an empty area of the taskbar. On the shortcut menu that appears, click Task Manager.

13. In the Task Manager window, click the Performance tab and display the CPU utilization. If the Performance tab is not visible, click More Details. Right-click the CPU Utilization graph, point to Change Graph To, and then click Overall Utilization. This action causes Task Manager to display the utilization of all the processor cores running on your computer in a single graph. The following image shows the Performance tab of Task Manager configured in this way:

14. Return to the Graph Demo application and adjust the size and position of the application window and the Task Manager window so that both are visible.

15. Wait for the CPU utilization to level off, and then, in the Graph Demo window, click Plot Graph.

16. Wait for the CPU utilization to level off again, and then click Plot Graph again.

17. Repeat step 16 several times, waiting for the CPU utilization to level off between clicks.

18. In the Task Manager window, observe the CPU utilization. Your results will vary, but on a dual-core processor, the CPU utilization will probably be somewhere around 50–55 percent while the graph was being generated. On a quad-core machine, the CPU utilization will likely be somewhere between 25 and 30 percent, as shown in the image that follows. Note that other factors, such as the type of graphics card in your computer, can also impact the performance:

19. Return to Visual Studio 2015 and stop debugging.

You now have a baseline for the time the application takes to perform its calculations. However, it is clear from the CPU usage displayed by Task Manager that the application is not making full use of the processing resources available. On a dual-core machine, it is using just over half of the CPU power, and on a quad-core machine, it is employing a little more than a quarter of the CPU. This phenomenon occurs because the application is single-threaded, and in a Windows application, a single thread can provide work only to a single core on a multicore processor. To spread the load over all the available cores, you need to divide the application into tasks and arrange for each task to be executed by a separate thread, each running on a different core. This is what you will do next.

Using Performance Explorer to identity CPU bottlenecks

The GraphDemo application was specifically designed to create a CPU bottleneck at a known point (in the *generateGraphData* method). In the real world you might be aware that something is causing your application to run slowly and become unresponsive, but you might not know where the offending code is located. This is where the Visual Studio Performance Explorer and Profiler can prove invaluable.

The Profiler can sample the run-time state of the application periodically and capture information about which statement was running at the time. The more frequently a particular line of code is executed and the longer this line takes to run, the more frequently this statement will be observed. The Profiler uses this data to generate a run-time profile of the application and produce a report that details the hotspots in your code. These hotspots can be useful in identifying areas on which you should focus your optimizations. The following optional steps walk you through this process.

> **Note** Performance Explorer and the Profiler are not available in Visual Studio 2015 Community Edition.

1. In Visual Studio, on the Debug menu, point to Profiler, point to Performance Explorer, and then click New Performance Session. The Performance Explorer window should appear in Visual Studio:

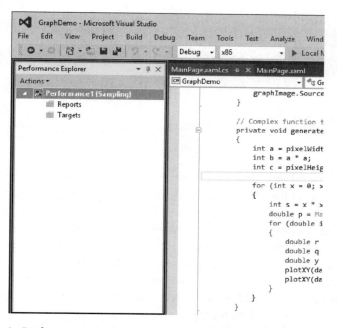

2. In Performance Explorer, right-click Targets and then click Add Target Project. The GraphDemo application will be added as a target.

3. In the Performance Explorer menu bar, click Actions, and then click Start Profiling. The GraphDemo application starts running.

4. Click Plot Graph and wait for the graph to be generated. Repeat this process several times, and then close the GraphDemo application.

5. Return to Visual Studio and wait while the Profiler analyzes the sampling data collected and generates a report that should look similar to this:

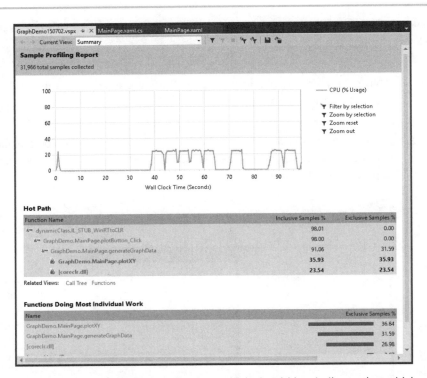

This report shows the CPU utilization (which should be similar to that which you observed using Task Manager earlier, with peaks whenever you clicked Plot Graph), and the Hot Path for the application. This path identifies the sequence through the application that consumed the most processing. In this case, the application spent 98 percent of the time in the *plotButton_Click* method, 91.06 percent of the time was spent executing the *generateGraphData* method, and 35.93 percent of the time was spent in the *plotXY* method. A considerable amount of time (23.54 percent) was also consumed by the runtime (coreclr.dll).

Note that you can zoom in on particular areas of the CPU utilization graph (click and drag using the mouse), and filter the report to cover only the zoomed-in part of the sampled data.

6. In the Hot Path part of the report, click the *GraphDemo.MainPage.generateGraphData* method. The Report window displays the details of the method, together with the proportion of the CPU time spent executing the most expensive statements:

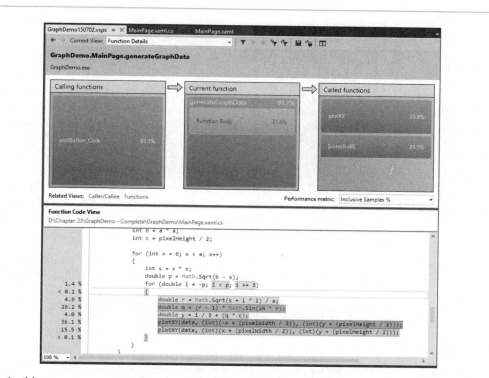

In this case, you can see that the code in the *for* loop should be the primary target for any optimization effort.

Modify the GraphDemo application to use *Task* objects

1. Return to Visual Studio 2015, and display the MainPage.xaml.cs file in the Code and Text Editor window, if it is not already open.

2. Examine the *generateGraphData* method.

   The purpose of this method is to populate the items in the *data* array. It iterates through the array by using the outer *for* loop based on the *x* loop control variable, highlighted in bold here:

```
private void generateGraphData(byte[] data)
{
    int a = pixelWidth / 2;
    int b = a * a;
    int c = pixelHeight / 2;
```

```
for (int x = 0; x < a; x ++)
{
    int s = x * x;
    double p = Math.Sqrt(b - s);
    for (double i = -p; i < p; i += 3)
    {
        double r = Math.Sqrt(s + i * i) / a;
        double q = (r - 1) * Math.Sin(24 * r);
        double y = i / 3 + (q * c);
        plotXY(data, (int)(-x + (pixelWidth / 2)), (int)(y + (pixelHeight / 2)));
        plotXY(data, (int)(x + (pixelWidth / 2)), (int)(y + (pixelHeight / 2)));
    }
}
}
```

The calculation performed by one iteration of this loop is independent of the calculations performed by the other iterations. Therefore, it makes sense to partition the work performed by this loop and run different iterations on a separate processor.

3. Modify the definition of the *generateGraphData* method to take two additional *int* parameters, called *partitionStart* and *partitionEnd*, as shown in bold in the following example:

```
private void generateGraphData(byte[] data, int partitionStart, int partitionEnd)
{
    ...
}
```

4. In the *generateGraphData* method, change the outer *for* loop to iterate between the values of *partitionStart* and *partitionEnd*, as shown here in bold:

```
private void generateGraphData(byte[] data, int partitionStart, int partitionEnd)
{
    ...
    for (int x = partitionStart; x < partitionEnd; x++)
    {
        ...
    }
}
```

5. In the Code and Text Editor window, add the following *using* directive to the list at the top of the MainPage.xaml.cs file:

```
using System.Threading.Tasks;
```

6. In the *plotButton_Click* method, comment out the statement that calls the *generateGraphData* method and add the statement shown in bold in the following code that creates a *Task* object and starts it running:

```
...
Stopwatch watch = Stopwatch.StartNew();
// generateGraphData(data);
Task first = Task.Run(() => generateGraphData(data, 0, pixelWidth / 4));
...
```

The task runs the code specified by the lambda expression. The values for the *partitionStart* and *partitionEnd* parameters indicate that the *Task* object calculates the data for the first half of the graph. (The data for the complete graph consists of points plotted for the values between 0 and *pixelWidth / 2*.)

7. Add another statement that creates and runs a second *Task* object on another thread, as shown in the following bold-highlighted code:

```
...
Task first = Task.Run(() => generateGraphData(data, 0, pixelWidth / 4));
Task second = Task.Run(() => generateGraphData(data, pixelWidth / 4, pixelWidth / 2));
...
```

This *Task* object invokes the *generateGraphData* method and calculates the data for the values between *pixelWidth / 4* and *pixelWidth / 2*.

8. Add the following statement shown in bold that waits for both *Task* objects to complete their work before continuing:

```
Task second = Task.Run(() => generateGraphData(data, pixelWidth / 4, pixelWidth / 2));
Task.WaitAll(first, second);
...
```

9. On the Debug menu, click Start Debugging to build and run the application. Adjust the display to ensure that you can see the Task Manager window displaying the CPU utilization.

10. In the Graph Demo window, click Plot Graph. In the Task Manager window, wait for the CPU utilization to level off.

11. Repeat step 10 several more times, waiting for the CPU utilization to level off between clicks. Make a note of the duration recorded each time you click the button, and then calculate the average.

You should see that the application runs significantly quicker than it did previously. On my computer, the typical time dropped to 2,858 milliseconds—a reduction in time of approximately 40 percent.

In most cases, the time required to perform the calculations will be cut by nearly half, but the application still has some single-threaded elements, such as the logic that actually displays the graph after the data has been generated. This is why the overall time is still more than half the time taken by the previous version of the application.

12. Switch to the Task Manager window.

You should see that the application uses more cores of the CPU. On my quad-core machine, the CPU usage peaked at approximately 50 percent each time I clicked Plot Graph. This happens because the two tasks were each run on separate cores, but the remaining two cores were left unoccupied. If you have a dual-core machine, you will likely see processor utilization briefly approach 100 percent each time the graph is generated.

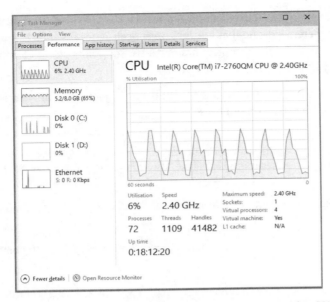

If you have a quad-core computer, you can increase the CPU utilization and reduce the time further by adding two more *Task* objects and dividing the work into four chunks in the *plotButton_Click* method, as shown here in bold:

```
...
Task first = Task.Run(() => generateGraphData(data, 0, pixelWidth / 8));
Task second = Task.Run(() => generateGraphData(data, pixelWidth / 8,
pixelWidth / 4));
Task third = Task.Run(() => generateGraphData(data, pixelWidth / 4,
pixelWidth * 3 / 8));
Task fourth = Task.Run(() => generateGraphData(data, pixelWidth * 3 / 8,
pixelWidth / 2));
Task.WaitAll(first, second, third, fourth);
...
```

If you have only a dual-core processor, you can still try this modification, and you should notice a small beneficial effect on the time. This is primarily because of the way in which the algorithms used by the CLR optimize the way in which the threads for each task are scheduled.

Abstracting tasks by using the *Parallel* class

By using the *Task* class, you have complete control over the number of tasks your application creates. However, you had to modify the design of the application to accommodate the use of *Task* objects. You also had to add code to synchronize operations; the application can render the graph only when all the tasks have completed. In a complex application, the synchronization of tasks can become a nontrivial process that is easily prone to mistakes.

With the *Parallel* class, you can parallelize some common programming constructs without having to redesign an application. Internally, the *Parallel* class creates its own set of *Task* objects, and it synchronizes these tasks automatically when they have completed. The *Parallel* class is located in the

System.Threading.Tasks namespace and provides a small set of static methods that you can use to indicate that code should be run in parallel if possible. These methods are as follows:

- **Parallel.For**   You can use this method in place of a C# *for* statement. It defines a loop in which iterations can run in parallel by using tasks. This method is heavily overloaded, but the general principle is the same for each: you specify a start value, an end value, and a reference to a method that takes an integer parameter. The method is executed for every value between the start value and one below the end value specified, and the parameter is populated with an integer that specifies the current value. For example, consider the following simple *for* loop that performs each iteration in sequence:

```
for (int x = 0; x < 100; x++)
{
    // Perform loop processing
}
```

Depending on the processing performed by the body of the loop, you might be able to replace this loop with a *Parallel.For* construct that can perform iterations in parallel, like this:

```
Parallel.For(0, 100, performLoopProcessing);
...
private void performLoopProcessing(int x)
{
    // Perform loop processing
}
```

Using the overloads of the *Parallel.For* method, you can provide local data that is private to each thread, specify various options for creating the tasks run by the *For* method, and create a *ParallelLoopState* object that can be used to pass state information to other concurrent iterations of the loop. (Using a *ParallelLoopState* object is described later in this chapter.)

- **Parallel.ForEach<T>**   You can use this method in place of a C# *foreach* statement. Like the *For* method, *ForEach* defines a loop in which iterations can run in parallel. You specify a collection that implements the *IEnumerable<T>* generic interface and a reference to a method that takes a single parameter of type *T*. The method is executed for each item in the collection, and the item is passed as the parameter to the method. Overloads are available with which you can provide private local thread data and specify options for creating the tasks run by the *ForEach* method.

- **Parallel.Invoke**   You can use this method to execute a set of parameterless method calls as parallel tasks. You specify a list of delegated method calls (or lambda expressions) that take no parameters and do not return values. Each method call can be run on a separate thread, in any order. For example, the following code makes a series of method calls:

```
doWork();
doMoreWork();
doYetMoreWork();
```

You can replace these statements with the following code, which invokes these methods by using a series of tasks:

```
Parallel.Invoke(
    doWork,
    doMoreWork,
    doYetMoreWork
);
```

You should bear in mind that the *Parallel* class determines the actual degree of parallelism appropriate for the environment and workload of the computer. For example, if you use *Parallel.For* to implement a loop that performs 1,000 iterations, the *Parallel* class does not necessarily create 1,000 concurrent tasks (unless you have an exceptionally powerful processor with 1,000 cores). Instead, the *Parallel* class creates what it considers to be the optimal number of tasks that balances the available resources against the requirement to keep the processors occupied. A single task might perform multiple iterations, and the tasks coordinate with each other to determine which iterations each task will perform. An important consequence of this is that you cannot guarantee the order in which the iterations are executed, so you must ensure that there are no dependencies between iterations; otherwise, you might encounter unexpected results, as you will see later in this chapter.

In the next exercise, you will return to the original version of the GraphDemo application and use the *Parallel* class to perform operations concurrently.

Use the *Parallel* class to parallelize operations in the GraphDemo application

1. Using Visual Studio 2015, open the GraphDemo solution, which is located in the \Microsoft Press\VCSBS\Chapter 23\Parallel GraphDemo folder in your Documents folder.

   This is a copy of the original GraphDemo application. It does not use tasks yet.

2. In Solution Explorer, in the GraphDemo project, expand the MainPage.xaml node, and then double-click MainPage.xaml.cs to display the code for the form in the Code and Text Editor window.

3. Add the following *using* directive to the list at the top of the file:

   ```
   using System.Threading.Tasks;
   ```

4. Locate the *generateGraphData* method. It looks like this:

   ```
   private void generateGraphData(byte[] data)
   {
       int a = pixelWidth / 2;
       int b = a * a;
       int c = pixelHeight / 2;

       for (int x = 0; x < a; x++)
       {
           int s = x * x;
           double p = Math.Sqrt(b - s);
           for (double i = -p; i < p; i += 3)
           {
               double r = Math.Sqrt(s + i * i) / a;
               double q = (r - 1) * Math.Sin(24 * r);
   ```

```
            double y = i / 3 + (q * c);
            plotXY(data, (int)(-x + (pixelWidth / 2)), (int)(y + (pixelHeight / 2)));
            plotXY(data, (int)(x + (pixelWidth / 2)), (int)(y + (pixelHeight / 2)));
        }
    }
}
```

The outer *for* loop that iterates through values of the integer variable *x* is a prime candidate for parallelization. You might also consider the inner loop based on the variable *i*, but this loop takes more effort to parallelize because of the type of *i*. (The methods in the *Parallel* class expect the control variable to be an integer.) Additionally, if you have nested loops such as those that occur in this code, it is good practice to parallelize the outer loops first and then test to see whether the performance of the application is sufficient. If it is not, work your way through nested loops and parallelize them working from outer to inner loops, testing the performance after modifying each one. You will find that in many cases parallelizing outer loops has the most impact on performance, whereas the effects of modifying inner loops becomes more marginal.

5. Cut the code in the body of the *for* loop, and create a new private *void* method called *calculateData* with this code. The *calculateData* method should take an *int* parameter called *x* and a byte array called *data*. Also, move the statements that declare the local variables *a, b,* and *c* from the *generateGraphData* method to the start of the *calculateData* method. The following code shows the *generateGraphData* method with this code removed and the *calculateData* method (do not try to compile this code yet):

```
private void generateGraphData(byte[] data)
{
    for (int x = 0; x < a; x++)
    {
    }
}

private void calculateData(int x, byte[] data)
{
    int a = pixelWidth / 2;
    int b = a * a;
    int c = pixelHeight / 2;

    int s = x * x;
    double p = Math.Sqrt(b - s);
    for (double i = -p; i < p; i += 3)
    {
        double r = Math.Sqrt(s + i * i) / a;
        double q = (r - 1) * Math.Sin(24 * r);
        double y = i / 3 + (q * c);
        plotXY(data, (int)(-x + (pixelWidth / 2)), (int)(y + (pixelHeight / 2)));
        plotXY(data, (int)(x + (pixelWidth / 2)), (int)(y + (pixelHeight / 2)));
    }
}
```

6. In the *generateGraphData* method, replace the *for* loop with the following statement that calls the static *Parallel.For* method:

```
private void generateGraphData(byte[] data)
{
    Parallel.For(0, pixelWidth / 2, x => calculateData(x, data));
}
```

This code is the parallel equivalent of the original *for* loop. It iterates through the values from 0 to *pixelWidth / 2 – 1* inclusive. Each invocation runs by using a task, and each task might run more than one iteration. The *Parallel.For* method finishes only when all the tasks it has created complete their work. Remember that the *Parallel.For* method expects the final parameter to be a method that takes a single integer parameter. It calls this method passing the current loop index as the parameter. In this example, the *calculateData* method does not match the required signature because it takes two parameters: an integer and a byte array. For this reason, the code uses a lambda expression that acts as an adapter that calls the *calculateData* method with the appropriate arguments.

7. On the Debug menu, click Start Debugging to build and run the application.

8. In the Graph Demo window, click Plot Graph. When the graph appears in the Graph Demo window, record the time taken to generate the graph. Repeat this action several times to get an average value.

   You should notice that the application runs as least as quickly as the previous version that used *Task* objects (and possibly faster, depending on the number of CPUs you have available). If you examine Task Manager, you should notice that the CPU usage peaks closer to 100 percent regardless of whether you have a dual-core or quad-core computer.

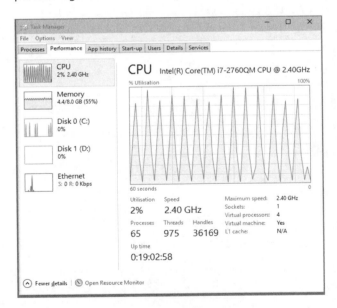

9. Return to Visual Studio and stop debugging.

When not to use the *Parallel* class

You should be aware that despite appearances and the best efforts of the .NET Framework development team at Microsoft, the *Parallel* class is not magic—you cannot use it without due consideration and just expect your applications to suddenly run significantly faster and produce the same results. The purpose of the *Parallel* class is to parallelize CPU-bound, independent areas of your code.

If you are not running CPU-bound code, parallelizing it might not improve performance. In this case, the overhead of creating a task, running this task on a separate thread, and waiting for the task to complete is likely to be greater than the cost of running this method directly. The additional overhead might account for only a few milliseconds each time a method is called, but you should bear in mind the number of times that a method runs. If the method call is located in a nested loop and is executed thousands of times, all of these small overhead costs will add up. The general rule is to use *Parallel.Invoke* only when it is worthwhile. You should reserve *Parallel.Invoke* for operations that are computationally intensive; otherwise, the overhead of creating and managing tasks can actually slow down an application.

The other key consideration for using the *Parallel* class is that parallel operations should be independent. For example, if you attempt to use *Parallel.For* to parallelize a loop in which iterations have a dependency on each other, the results will be unpredictable.

To see what I mean, look at the following code (you can find this example in the ParallelLoop solution, which is located in the \Microsoft Press\VCSBS\Chapter 23\ParallelLoop folder in your Documents folder):

```csharp
using System;
using System.Threading;
using System.Threading.Tasks;

namespace ParallelLoop
{
    class Program
    {
        private static int accumulator = 0;

        static void Main(string[] args)
        {
            for (int i = 0; i < 100; i++)
            {
                AddToAccumulator(i);
            }
            Console.WriteLine($"Accumulator is {accumulator}");
        }

        private static void AddToAccumulator(int data)
        {
            if ((accumulator % 2) == 0)
            {
                accumulator += data;
            }
            else
            {
```

```
            accumulator -= data;
        }
    }
}
```

This program iterates through the values from 0 to 99 and calls the *AddToAccumulator* method with each value in turn. The *AddToAccumulator* method examines the current value of the *accumulator* variable and, if it is even, adds the value of the parameter to the *accumulator* variable; otherwise, it subtracts the value of the parameter. At the end of the program, the result is displayed. If you run this program, the value output should be −100.

To increase the degree of parallelism in this simple application, you might be tempted to replace the *for* loop in the *Main* method with *Parallel.For*, like this:

```
static void Main(string[] args)
{
    Parallel.For (0, 100, AddToAccumulator);
    Console.WriteLine($"Accumulator is {accumulator}");
}
```

However, there is no guarantee that the tasks created to run the various invocations of the *AddToAccumulator* method will execute in any specific sequence. (The code is also not thread-safe because multiple threads running the tasks might attempt to modify the *accumulator* variable concurrently.) The value calculated by the *AddToAccumulator* method depends on the sequence being maintained, so the result of this modification is that the application might now generate different values each time it runs. In this simple case, you might not actually see any difference in the value calculated because the *AddToAccumulator* method runs very quickly and the .NET Framework might elect to run each invocation sequentially by using the same thread. However, if you make the following change (shown in bold) to the *AddToAccumulator* method, you will get different results:

```
private static void AddToAccumulator(int data)
{
    if ((accumulator % 2) == 0)
    {
        accumulator += data;
        Thread.Sleep(10); // wait for 10 milliseconds
    }
    else
    {
        accumulator -= data;
    }
}
```

The *Thread.Sleep* method simply causes the current thread to wait for the specified period of time. This modification simulates the thread, performing additional processing, and affects the way in which the *Parallel* class schedules the tasks, which now run on different threads, resulting in a different sequence.

The general rule is to use *Parallel.For* and *Parallel.ForEach* only if you can guarantee that each iteration of the loop is independent, and test your code thoroughly. A similar consideration applies to *Parallel.Invoke*: use this construct to make method calls only if they are independent and the application does not depend on them being run in a particular sequence.

Canceling tasks and handling exceptions

A common requirement of applications that perform long-running operations is the ability to stop those operations if necessary. However, you should not simply abort a task, as this could leave the data in your application in an indeterminate state. Instead, the *Task* class implements a cooperative cancellation strategy. Cooperative cancellation enables a task to select a convenient point at which to stop processing and also enables it to undo any work it has performed prior to cancellation if necessary.

The mechanics of cooperative cancellation

Cooperative cancellation is based on the notion of a *cancellation token*. A cancellation token is a structure that represents a request to cancel one or more tasks. The method that a task runs should include a *System.Threading.CancellationToken* parameter. An application that wants to cancel the task sets the Boolean *IsCancellationRequested* property of this parameter to *true*. The method running in the task can query this property at various points during its processing. If this property is set to *true* at any point, it knows that the application has requested that the task be canceled. Also, the method knows what work it has done so far, so it can undo any changes if necessary and then finish. Alternatively, the method can simply ignore the request and continue running.

> **Tip** You should examine the cancellation token in a task frequently, but not so frequently that you adversely impact the performance of the task. If possible, you should aim to check for cancellation at least every 10 milliseconds, but no more frequently than every millisecond.

An application obtains a *CancellationToken* by creating a *System.Threading.CancellationToken-Source* object and querying the *Token* property of this object. The application can then pass this *CancellationToken* object as a parameter to any methods started by tasks that the application creates and runs. If the application needs to cancel the tasks, it calls the *Cancel* method of the *Cancellation-TokenSource* object. This method sets the *IsCancellationRequested* property of the *CancellationToken* passed to all the tasks.

The code example that follows shows how to create a cancellation token and use it to cancel a task. The *initiateTasks* method instantiates the *cancellationTokenSource* variable and obtains a reference to the *CancellationToken* object available through this variable. The code then creates and runs a task that executes the *doWork* method. Later on, the code calls the *Cancel* method of the cancellation token source, which sets the cancellation token. The *doWork* method queries the *IsCancellation-Requested* property of the cancellation token. If the property is set, the method terminates; otherwise, it continues running.

```csharp
public class MyApplication
{
    ...
    // Method that creates and manages a task
    private void initiateTasks()
    {
        // Create the cancellation token source and obtain a cancellation token
        CancellationTokenSource cancellationTokenSource = new CancellationTokenSource();
        CancellationToken cancellationToken = cancellationTokenSource.Token;
        // Create a task and start it running the doWork method
        Task myTask = Task.Run(() => doWork(cancellationToken));
        ...
        if (...)
        {
            // Cancel the task
            cancellationTokenSource.Cancel();
        }
        ...
    }

    // Method run by the task
    private void doWork(CancellationToken token)
    {
        ...
        // If the application has set the cancellation token, finish processing
        if (token.IsCancellationRequested)
        {
            // Tidy up and finish
            ...
            return;
        }
        // If the task has not been canceled, continue running as normal
        ...
    }
}
```

In addition to providing a high degree of control over the cancellation processing, this approach is scalable across any number of tasks; you can start multiple tasks and pass the same *CancellationToken* object to each of them. If you call *Cancel* on the *CancellationTokenSource* object, each task will check whether the *IsCancellationRequested* property has been set and proceed accordingly.

You can also register a callback method (in the form of an *Action* delegate) with the cancellation token by using the *Register* method. When an application invokes the *Cancel* method of the corresponding *CancellationTokenSource* object, this callback runs. However, you cannot guarantee when this method executes; it might be before or after the tasks have performed their own cancellation processing, or even during that process.

```csharp
...
cancellationToken,Register(doAdditionalWork);
...
private void doAdditionalWork()
{
    // Perform additional cancellation processing
}
```

In the next exercise, you will add cancellation functionality to the GraphDemo application.

Add cancellation functionality to the GraphDemo application

1. Using Visual Studio 2015, open the GraphDemo solution, which is located in the \Microsoft Press\VCSBS\Chapter 23\GraphDemo With Cancellation folder in your Documents folder.

   This is a completed copy of the GraphDemo application from the earlier exercise that uses tasks to improve processing throughput. The user interface also includes a button named *cancelButton* that the user can use to stop the tasks that calculate the data for the graph.

2. In Solution Explorer, in the GraphDemo project, double-click MainPage.xaml to display the form in the Design View window. Note the Cancel button that appears in the left pane of the form.

3. Open the MainPage.xaml.cs file in the Code and Text Editor window. Locate the *cancelButton_Click* method.

   This method runs when the user clicks Cancel. It is currently empty.

4. Add the following *using* directive to the list at the top of the file:

   ```
   using System.Threading;
   ```

   The types used by cooperative cancellation reside in this namespace.

5. Add a *CancellationTokenSource* field called *tokenSource* to the *MainPage* class, and initialize it to *null*, as shown in the following code in bold:

   ```
   public sealed partial class MainPage : Page
   {
       ...
       private byte redValue, greenValue, blueValue;
       private CancellationTokenSource tokenSource = null;
       ...
   }
   ```

6. Find the *generateGraphData* method and add a *CancellationToken* parameter called *token* to the method definition, as shown here in bold:

   ```
   private void generateGraphData(byte[] data, int partitionStart, int partitionEnd,
   CancellationToken token)
   {
       ...
   }
   ```

7. In the *generateGraphData* method, at the start of the inner *for* loop, add the following code shown in bold to check whether cancellation has been requested. If so, return from the method; otherwise, continue calculating values and plotting the graph.

```
private void generateGraphData(byte[] data, int partitionStart, int partitionEnd,
CancellationToken token)
{
    int a = pixelWidth / 2;
    int b = a * a;
    int c = pixelHeight / 2;

    for (int x = partitionStart; x < partitionEnd; x ++)
    {
        int s = x * x;
        double p = Math.Sqrt(b - s);
        for (double i = -p; i < p; i += 3)
        {
            if (token.IsCancellationRequested)
            {
                return;
            }

            double r = Math.Sqrt(s + i * i) / a;
            double q = (r - 1) * Math.Sin(24 * r);
            double y = i / 3 + (q * c);
            plotXY(data, (int)(-x + (pixelWidth / 2)), (int)(y + (pixelHeight / 2)));
            plotXY(data, (int)(x + (pixelWidth / 2)), (int)(y + (pixelHeight / 2)));
        }
    }
}
```

8. In the *plotButton_Click* method, add the following statements shown in bold that instantiate the *tokenSource* variable and retrieve the *CancellationToken* object into a variable called *token*:

```
private void plotButton_Click(object sender, RoutedEventArgs e)
{
    Random rand = new Random();
    redValue = (byte)rand.Next(0xFF);
    greenValue = (byte)rand.Next(0xFF);
    blueValue = (byte)rand.Next(0xFF);

    tokenSource = new CancellationTokenSource();
    CancellationToken token = tokenSource.Token;
    ...
}
```

9. Modify the statements that create and run the two tasks, and pass the *token* variable as the final parameter to the *generateGraphData* method:

```
...
Task first = Task.Run(() => generateGraphData(data, 0, pixelWidth / 4,
token));
Task second = Task.Run(() => generateGraphData(data, pixelWidth / 4,
pixelWidth / 2, token));
...
```

10. Edit the definition of the *plotButton_Click* method and add the *async* modifier as shown in bold here:

```
private async void plotButton_Click(object sender, RoutedEventArgs e)
{
    ...
}
```

11. In the body of the *plotButton_Click* method, comment out the *Task.WaitAll* statement that waits for the tasks to complete and replace it with the following statements in bold that use the *await* operator instead.

```
...
// Task.WaitAll(first, second);
await first;
await second;

duration.Text = string.Format(...);
...
```

The changes in these two steps are necessary because of the single-threaded nature of the Windows user interface. Under normal circumstances, when an event handler for a user interface component such as a button starts running, event handlers for other user interface components are blocked until the first event handler completes (even if the event handler is using tasks). In this example, using the *Task.WaitAll* method to wait for the tasks to complete would render the Cancel button useless because the event handler for the Cancel button will not run until the handler for the Plot Graph button completes, in which case there is no point in attempting to cancel the operation. In fact, as mentioned earlier, when you click the Plot Graph button, the user interface is completely unresponsive until the graph appears and the *plotButton_Click* method finishes.

The *await* operator is designed to handle situations such as this. You can use this operator only inside a method marked as *async*. Its purpose is to release the current thread and wait for a task to complete in the background. When that task finishes, control returns to the method, which continues with the next statement. In this example, the two *await* statements simply allow each of the tasks to complete in the background. After the second task has finished, the method continues, displaying the time taken for these tasks to complete in the duration *TextBlock*. Note that it is not an error to await for a task that has already completed; the *await* operator will simply return immediately and pass control to the following statement.

 More info Chapter 24 discusses the *async* modifier and the *await* operator in detail.

12. Find the *cancelButton_Click* method. Add to this method the code shown here in bold:

```
private void cancelButton_Click(object sender, RoutedEventArgs e)
{
    if (tokenSource != null)
    {
        tokenSource.Cancel();
    }
}
```

This code checks that the *tokenSource* variable has been instantiated. If it has, the code invokes the *Cancel* method on this variable.

13. On the Debug menu, click Start Debugging to build and run the application.

14. In the GraphDemo window, click Plot Graph, and verify that the graph appears as it did before. However, you should notice that it takes slightly longer to generate the graph than before. This is because of the additional check performed by the *generateGraphData* method.

15. Click Plot Graph again, and then quickly click Cancel.

If you are quick and click Cancel before the data for the graph is generated, this action causes the methods being run by the tasks to return. The data is not complete, so the graph appears with "holes," as shown in the following figure. (The previous graph should still be visible where these holes occur, and the size of the holes depends on how quickly you clicked Cancel.)

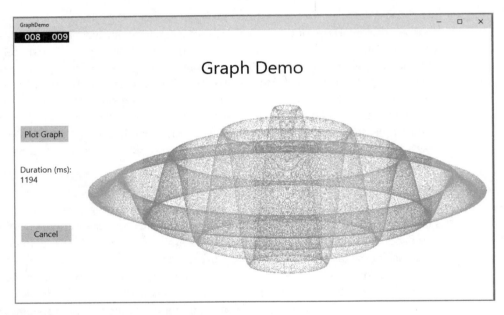

16. Return to Visual Studio and stop debugging.

You can determine whether a task completed or was canceled by examining the *Status* property of the *Task* object. The *Status* property contains a value from the *System.Threading.Tasks.TaskStatus* enumeration. The following list describes some of the status values that you might commonly encounter (there are others):

- **Created** This is the initial state of a task. It has been created but has not yet been scheduled to run.

- **WaitingToRun** The task has been scheduled but has not yet started to run.

- **Running** The task is currently being executed by a thread.

- **RanToCompletion**   The task completed successfully without any unhandled exceptions.

- **Canceled**   The task was canceled before it could start running, or it acknowledged cancellation and completed without throwing an exception.

- **Faulted**   The task terminated because of an exception.

In the next exercise, you will attempt to report the status of each task so that you can see when they have completed or have been canceled.

Canceling a *Parallel For* or *ForEach* loop

The *Parallel.For* and *Parallel.ForEach* methods don't provide you with direct access to the *Task* objects that have been created. Indeed, you don't even know how many tasks are running—the .NET Framework uses its own heuristics to work out the optimal number to use based on the resources available and the current workload of the computer.

If you want to stop the *Parallel.For* or *Parallel.ForEach* method early, you must use a *ParallelLoopState* object. The method you specify as the body of the loop must include an additional *ParallelLoopState* parameter. The *Parallel* class creates a *ParallelLoopState* object and passes it as this parameter into the method. The *Parallel* class uses this object to hold information about each method invocation. The method can call the *Stop* method of this object to indicate that the *Parallel* class should not attempt to perform any iterations beyond those that have already started and finished. The example that follows shows the *Parallel.For* method calling the *doLoopWork* method for each iteration. The *doLoopWork* method examines the iteration variable; if it is greater than 600, the method calls the *Stop* method of the *ParallelLoopState* parameter. This causes the *Parallel.For* method to stop running further iterations of the loop. (Iterations currently running might continue to completion.)

> **Note**   Remember that the iterations in a *Parallel.For* loop are not run in a specific sequence. Consequently, canceling the loop when the iteration variable has the value 600 does not guarantee that the previous 599 iterations have already run. Likewise, some iterations with values greater than 600 might already have completed.

```
Parallel.For(0, 1000, doLoopWork);
...
private void doLoopWork(int i, ParallelLoopState p)
{
    ...
    if (i > 600)
    {
        p.Stop();
    }
}
```

Display the status of each task

1. In Visual Studio, display the MainPage.xaml file in the Design View window. In the XAML pane, add the following markup to the definition of the MainPage form before the penultimate *</Grid>* tag, as shown in the following in bold:

```
        <Image x:Name="graphImage" Grid.Column="1" Stretch="Fill" />
    </Grid>
    <TextBlock x:Name="messages" Grid.Row="4" FontSize="18"
HorizontalAlignment="Left"/>
    </Grid>
</Page>
```

This markup adds a *TextBlock* control named *messages* to the bottom of the form.

2. Display the MainPage.xaml.cs file in the Code and Text Editor window and find the *plotButton_Click* method.

3. Add to this method the code in bold that follows. These statements generate a string that contains the status of each task after it has finished running and then display this string in the *messages TextBlock* control at the bottom of the form.

```
private async void plotButton_Click(object sender, RoutedEventArgs e)
{
    ...
    await first;
    await second;

    duration.Text = $"Duration (ms): {watch.ElapsedMilliseconds}";

    string message = $"Status of tasks is {first.Status}, {second.Status}";
    messages.Text = message;
    ...
}
```

4. On the Debug menu, click Start Debugging.

5. In the GraphDemo window, click Plot Graph but do not click Cancel. Verify that the message displayed reports that the status of the tasks is *RanToCompletion* (two times).

6. In the GraphDemo window, click Plot Graph again, and then quickly click Cancel.

Surprisingly, the message that appears still reports the status of each task as *RanToCompletion*, even though the graph appears with holes.

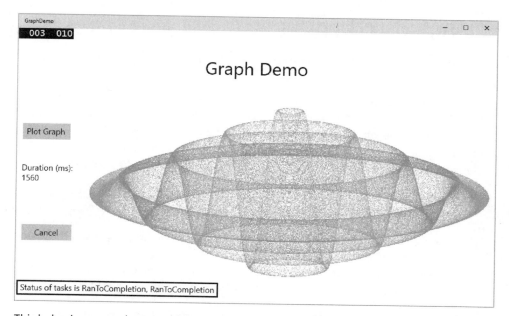

This behavior occurs because although you sent a cancellation request to each task by using the cancellation token, the methods they were running simply returned. The .NET Framework runtime does not know whether the tasks were actually canceled or whether they were allowed to run to completion, and it simply ignored the cancellation requests.

7. Return to Visual Studio and stop debugging.

So, how do you indicate that a task has been canceled rather than allowed to run to completion? The answer lies in the *CancellationToken* object passed as a parameter to the method that the task is running. The *CancellationToken* class provides a method called *ThrowIfCancellationRequested*. This method tests the *IsCancellationRequested* property of a cancellation token; if it is *true*, the method throws an *OperationCanceledException* exception and aborts the method that the task is running.

The application that started the thread should be prepared to catch and handle this exception, but this leads to another question. If a task terminates by throwing an exception, it actually reverts to the *Faulted* state. This is true even if the exception is an *OperationCanceledException* exception. A task enters the *Canceled* state only if it is canceled without throwing an exception. So, how does a task throw an *OperationCanceledException* without it being treated as an exception?

This time, the answer lies in the task itself. For a task to recognize that an *OperationCanceled-Exception* exception is the result of canceling the task in a controlled manner and not just an exception caused by other circumstances, it has to know that the operation has actually been canceled. It can do this only if it can examine the cancellation token. You passed this token as a parameter to the method run by the task, but the task does not actually check any of these parameters. Instead, you specify the cancellation token when you create and run the task. The code that follows shows an example based on the GraphDemo application. Notice how the *token* parameter is passed to the *generateGraphData* method (as before) but also as a separate parameter to the *Run* method.

```
tokenSource = new CancellationTokenSource();
CancellationToken token = tokenSource.Token;
...
Task first = Task.Run(() => generateGraphData(data, 0, pixelWidth / 4, token),
token);
```

Now, when the method being run by the task throws an *OperationCanceledException* exception, the infrastructure behind the task examines the *CancellationToken*. If it indicates that the task has been canceled, the infrastructure sets the status of the task to *Canceled*. If you are using the *await* operator to wait for the tasks to complete, you also need to be prepared to catch and handle the *OperationCanceledException* exception. This is what you will do in the next exercise.

Acknowledge cancellation, and handle the *OperationCanceledException* exception

1. In Visual Studio, return to the Code and Text Editor window displaying the MainPage.xaml.cs file. In the *plotButton_Click* method, modify the statements that create and run the tasks and specify the *CancellationToken* object as the second parameter to the *Run* method (and also as a parameter to the *generateGraphData* method), as shown in bold in the following code:

```
private async void plotButton_Click(object sender, RoutedEventArgs e)
{
    ...
    tokenSource = new CancellationTokenSource();
    CancellationToken token = tokenSource.Token;

    ...
    Task first = Task.Run(() => generateGraphData(data, 0, pixelWidth / 4,
token), token);
    Task second = Task.Run(() => generateGraphData(data, pixelWidth / 4,
pixelWidth / 2, token), token);
    ...
}
```

2. Add a *try* block around the statements that create and run the tasks, wait for them to complete, and display the elapsed time. Add a *catch* block that handles the *Operation-CanceledException* exception. In this exception handler, display the reason for the exception reported in the *Message* property of the exception object in the *duration TextBlock* control. The following code shown in bold highlights the changes you should make:

```
private async void plotButton_Click(object sender, RoutedEventArgs e)
{
    ...
    try
    {
        await first;
        await second;

        duration.Text = $"Duration (ms): {watch.ElapsedMilliseconds}";
    }
    catch (OperationCanceledException oce)
    {
```

```
            duration.Text = oce.Message;
        }

        string message = $"Status of tasks is {first.Status, {second.Status}";
        ...
    }
```

3. In the *generateGraphData* method, comment out the *if* statement that examines the *IsCancellationRequested* property of the *CancellationToken* object and add a statement that calls the *ThrowIfCancellationRequested* method, as shown here in bold:

```
private void generateGraphData(byte[] data, int partitionStart, int partitionEnd,
CancellationToken token)
{
    ...
    for (int x = partitionStart; x < partitionEnd; x++);
    {
        ...
        for (double i = -p; i < p; i += 3)
        {
            //if (token.IsCancellationRequested)
            //{
            //    return;
            //}
            token.ThrowIfCancellationRequested();
            ...
        }
    }
    ...
}
```

4. On the Debug menu, point to Windows, and then click Exception Settings. In the Exception Settings window, clear the check box for Common Language Runtime Exceptions. Right-click Common Language Runtime Exceptions, and then ensure that Continue When Unhandled In User Code is enabled.

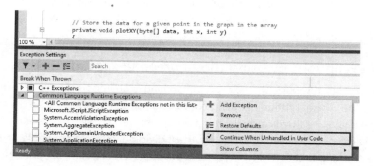

This configuration is necessary to prevent the Visual Studio debugger from intercepting the *OperationCanceledException* exception that you will generate when you run the application in debug mode.

5. On the Debug menu, click Start Debugging.

6. In the Graph Demo window, click Plot Graph, wait for the graph to appear, and verify that the status of both tasks is reported as *RanToCompletion* and the graph is generated.

7. Click Plot Graph again, and then quickly click Cancel.

   If you are quick, the status of one or both tasks should be reported as *Canceled*, the *duration TextBox* control should display the text "The operation was canceled," and the graph should be displayed with holes. If you were not quick enough, repeat this step to try again.

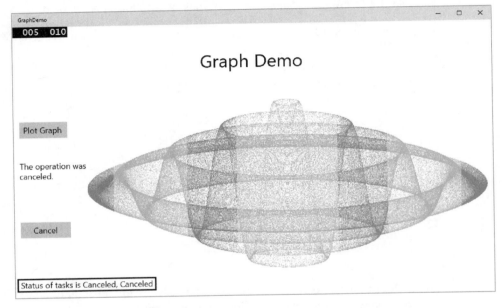

8. Return to Visual Studio and stop debugging.

9. On the Debug menu, point to Windows, and then click Exception Settings. In the Exception Settings window toolbar, click the Restore The List To The Default Settings button, and then click OK.

Handling task exceptions by using the *AggregateException* class

You have seen throughout this book that exception handling is an important element in any commercial application. The exception handling constructs you have met so far are straight-forward to use, and if you use them carefully, it is a simple matter to trap an exception and determine which piece of code raised it. When you start dividing work into multiple concurrent tasks, though, tracking and handling exceptions becomes a more complex problem. The previous exercise showed how you can catch the *OperationCanceledException* exception that is thrown when you cancel a task. However, there are plenty of other exceptions that might also occur, and different tasks might each generate their own exceptions. Therefore, you need a way to catch and handle multiple exceptions that might be thrown concurrently.

If you are using one of the *Task* wait methods to wait for multiple tasks to complete (using the instance *Wait* method or the static *Task.WaitAll* and *Task.WaitAny* methods), any exceptions thrown by the methods that these tasks are running are gathered together into a single exception referred to as an *AggregateException* exception. An *AggregateException* exception acts as a wrapper for a collection of exceptions. Each of the exceptions in the collection might be thrown by different tasks. In your application, you can catch the *AggregateException* exception and then iterate through this collection and perform any necessary processing. To help you, the *AggregateException* class provides the *Handle* method. The *Handle* method takes a *Func<Exception, bool>* delegate, which references a method that takes an *Exception* object as its parameter and returns a Boolean value. When you call *Handle*, the referenced method runs for each exception in the collection in the *AggregateException* object. The referenced method can examine the exception and take the appropriate action. If the referenced method handles the exception, it should return *true*. If not, it should return *false*. When the *Handle* method completes, any unhandled exceptions are bundled together into a new *AggregateException* exception, and this exception is thrown. A subsequent outer exception handler can then catch this exception and process it.

The code fragment that follows shows an example of a method that can be registered with an *AggregateException* exception handler. This method simply displays the message "Division by zero occurred" if it detects a *DivideByZeroException* exception, or the message "Array index out of bounds" if an *IndexOutOfRangeException* exception occurs. Any other exceptions are left unhandled.

```
private bool handleException(Exception e)
{
    if (e is DivideByZeroException)
    {
        displayErrorMessage("Division by zero occurred");
        return true;
    }

    if (e is IndexOutOfRangeException)
    {
        displayErrorMessage("Array index out of bounds");
        return true;
    }
    return false;
}
```

When you use one of the *Task* wait methods, you can catch the *AggregateException* exception and register the *handleException* method, like this:

```
try
{
    Task first = Task.Run(...);
    Task second = Task.Run(...);
    Task.WaitAll(first, second);
}
```

```
catch (AggregateException ae)
{
    ae.Handle(handleException);
}
```

If any of the tasks generate a *DivideByZeroException* exception or an *IndexOutOfRange-Exception* exception, the *handleException* method will display an appropriate message and acknowledge the exception as handled. Any other exceptions are classified as unhandled and will propagate out from the *AggregateException* exception handler in the customary manner.

There is one additional complication of which you should be aware. When you cancel a task, you have seen that the CLR throws an *OperationCanceledException* exception, and this is the exception that is reported if you are using the *await* operator to wait for the task. However, if you are using one of the *Task* wait methods, this exception is transformed into a *TaskCanceled-Exception* exception, and this is the type of exception that you should be prepared to handle in the *AggregateException* exception handler.

Using continuations with canceled and faulted tasks

If you need to perform additional work when a task is canceled or raises an unhandled exception, remember that you can use the *ContinueWith* method with the appropriate *TaskContinuationOptions* value. For example, the following code creates a task that runs the method *doWork*. If the task is canceled, the *ContinueWith* method specifies that another task should be created and run the method *doCancellationWork*. This method can perform some simple logging or tidying up. If the task is not canceled, the continuation does not run.

```
Task task = new Task(doWork);
task.ContinueWith(doCancellationWork, TaskContinuationOptions.OnlyOnCanceled);
task.Start();
...
private void doWork()
{
    // The task runs this code when it is started
    ...
}
...
private void doCancellationWork(Task task)
{
    // The task runs this code when doWork completes
    ...
}
```

Similarly, you can specify the value *TaskContinuationOptions.OnlyOnFaulted* to specify a continuation that runs if the original method run by the task raises an unhandled exception.

Summary

In this chapter, you learned why it is important to write applications that can scale across multiple processors and processor cores. You saw how to use the Task class to run operations in parallel and how to synchronize concurrent operations and wait for them to complete. You learned how to use the *Parallel* class to parallelize some common programming constructs, and you also saw when it is inappropriate to parallelize code. You used tasks and threads together in a graphical user interface to improve responsiveness and throughput, and you saw how to cancel tasks in a clean and controlled manner.

- If you want to continue to the next chapter, keep Visual Studio 2015 running and turn to Chapter 24.

- If you want to exit Visual Studio 2015 now, on the File menu, click Exit. If you see a Save dialog box, click Yes and save the project.

Quick reference

To	Do this

Create a task and run it	Use the static *Run* method of the *Task* class to create and run the task in a single step:
	
	```Task task = Task.Run(() => doWork());```
	```...```
	```private void doWork()```
	```{```
	``` // The task runs this code when it is started```
	``` ...```
	```}```
	
	Or, create a new *Task* object that references a method to run and call the *Start* method:
	
	```Task task = new Task(doWork);```
	```task.Start();```

Wait for a task to finish	Call the *Wait* method of the *Task* object:
	
	```Task task = ...;```
	```...```
	```task.Wait();```
	
	Or, use the *await* operator (only in an async method):
	
	```await task;```

Wait for several tasks to finish	Call the static *WaitAll* method of the *Task* class, and specify the tasks to wait for:
	
	```Task task1 = ...;```
	```Task task2 = ...;```
	```Task task3 = ...;```
	```Task task4 = ...;```
	```...```
	```Task.WaitAll(task1, task2, task3, task4);```

To	Do this
Specify a method to run in a new task when a task has completed	Call the *ContinueWith* method of the task and specify the method as a continuation: ```\nTask task = new Task(doWork);\ntask.ContinueWith(doMoreWork,\n TaskContinuationOptions.NotOnFaulted);\n```

Perform loop iterations and statement sequences by using parallel tasks	Use the *Parallel.For* and *Parallel.ForEach* methods to perform loop iterations by using tasks:
	
	```\nParallel.For(0, 100, performLoopProcessing);\n...\nprivate void performLoopProcessing(int x)\n{\n // Perform loop processing\n}\n```
	
	Use the *Parallel.Invoke* method to perform concurrent method calls by using separate tasks:
	
	```\nParallel.Invoke(\n doWork,\n doMoreWork,\n doYetMoreWork\n);\n```

Handle exceptions raised by one or more tasks	Catch the *AggregateException* exception. Use the *Handle* method to specify a method that can handle each exception in the *AggregateException* object. If the exception-handling method handles the exception, return true; otherwise, return false: ```\ntry\n{\n Task task = Task.Run(...);\n task.Wait();\n ...\n}\ncatch (AggregateException ae)\n{\n ae.Handle(handleException);\n}\n...\nprivate bool handleException(Exception e)\n{\n if (e is TaskCanceledException)\n {\n ...\n return true;\n }\n else\n {\n return false;\n }\n}\n```
Enable cancellation in a task	Implement cooperative cancellation by creating a *CancellationTokenSource* object and using a *CancellationToken* parameter in the method run by the task. In the task method, call the *ThrowIfCancellationRequested* method of the *CancellationToken* parameter to throw an *OperationCanceledException* exception and terminate the task: ```\nprivate void generateGraphData(..., CancellationToken\ntoken)\n{\n ...\n token.ThrowIfCancellationRequested();\n ...\n}\n```

CHAPTER 24

Improving response time by performing asynchronous operations

After completing this chapter, you will be able to:

- Define and use asynchronous methods to improve the interactive response time of applications that perform long-running and I/O-bound operations.

- Explain how to reduce the time taken to perform complex LINQ queries by using parallelization.

- Use the concurrent collection classes to safely share data between parallel tasks.

Chapter 23, "Improving throughput by using tasks," demonstrates how to use the *Task* class to perform operations in parallel and improve throughput in compute-bound applications. However, while maximizing the processing power available to an application can make it run more quickly, responsiveness is also important. Remember that the Windows user interface operates by using a single thread of execution, but users expect an application to respond when they click a button on a form, even if the application is currently performing a large and complex calculation. Additionally, some tasks might take a considerable time to run even if they are not compute-bound (an I/O-bound task waiting to receive information across the network from a remote website, for example), and blocking user interaction while waiting for an event that might take an indeterminate time to happen is clearly not good design practice. The solution to both of these problems is the same: perform the task asynchronously and leave the user interface thread free to handle user interactions.

Issues with response time are not limited to user interfaces. For example, Chapter 21, "Querying in-memory data by using query expressions," shows how you can access data held in memory in a declarative manner by using Language-Integrated Query (LINQ). A typical LINQ query generates an enumerable result set, and you can iterate serially through this set to retrieve the data. If the data source used to generate the result set is large, running a LINQ query can take a long time. Many database management systems faced with the issue of optimizing queries address this issue by using algorithms that break down the process of identifying the data for a query into a series of tasks, and they then run these tasks in parallel, combining the results when the tasks have completed to gener-ate the complete result set. The designers of the Microsoft .NET Framework decided to provide LINQ with a similar facility, and the result is Parallel LINQ, or PLINQ. You will study PLINQ in the second part of this chapter.

Asynchronicity and scalability

Asynchronicity is a powerful concept that you need to understand if you are building large-scale solutions such as enterprise web applications and services. A web server typically has limited resources with which to handle requests from a potentially very large audience, each member of which expects his or her requests to be handled quickly. In many cases, a user request can invoke a series of operations that individually can take significant time (perhaps as much as a second or two). Consider an ecommerce system in which a user is querying the product catalog or placing an order, for example. Both of these operations typically involve reading and writing data held in a database that might be managed by a database server remote from the web server. Many web servers can support only a limited number of concurrent connections, and if the thread associated with a connection is waiting for an I/O operation to complete, that connection is effectively blocked. If the thread creates a separate task to handle the I/O asynchronously, then the thread can be released and the connection recycled for another user. This approach is far more scalable than implementing such operations synchronously.

For an example and a detailed explanation of why performing synchronous I/O is bad in this situation, read about the Synchronous I/O anti-pattern in the public Microsoft Patterns & Practices Git repository, at *https://github.com/mspnp/performance-optimization/tree/master/SynchronousIO*.

Implementing asynchronous methods

An *asynchronous* method is one that does not block the current thread on which it starts to run. When an application invokes an asynchronous method, an implied contract expects the method to return control to the calling environment quite quickly and to perform its work on a separate thread. The definition of *quite* is not a mathematically defined quantity, but the expectation is that if an asynchronous method performs an operation that might cause a noticeable delay to the caller, it should do so by using a background thread, enabling the caller to continue running on the current thread. This process sounds complicated, and indeed in earlier versions of the .NET Framework it was. However, C# now provides the *async* method modifier and the *await* operator, which abstract much of this complexity to the compiler, meaning that (most of the time) you no longer have to concern yourself with the intricacies of multithreading.

Defining asynchronous methods: The problem

You have already seen how you can implement concurrent operations by using *Task* objects. To quickly recap, when you initiate a task by using the *Start* or *Run* method of the *Task* type, the common language runtime (CLR) uses its own scheduling algorithm to allocate the task to a thread and set this thread running at a time convenient to the operating system, when sufficient resources are available. This approach frees your code from the requirement to recognize and manage the workload of your computer. If you need to perform another operation when a specific task completes, you have the following choices:

- You can manually wait for the task to finish by using one of the *Wait* methods exposed by the *Task* type. You can then initiate the new operation, possibly by defining another task.

- You can define a continuation. A continuation simply specifies an operation to be performed when a given task completes. The .NET Framework automatically executes the continuation operation as a task that it schedules when the original task finishes. The continuation reuses the same thread as the original task.

However, even though the *Task* type provides a convenient generalization of an operation, you still often have to write potentially awkward code to solve some of the common problems that developers encounter when using a background thread. For example, suppose that you define the following method, which performs a series of long-running operations that must run in a serial manner and then displays a message in a *TextBox* control on the screen:

```
private void slowMethod()
{
    doFirstLongRunningOperation();
    doSecondLongRunningOperation();
    doThirdLongRunningOperation();
    message.Text = "Processing Completed";
}

private void doFirstLongRunningOperation()
{
    ...
}

private void doSecondLongRunningOperation()
{
    ...
}

private void doThirdLongRunningOperation()
{
    ...
}
```

If you invoke *slowMethod* from a piece of user interface code (such as the *Click* event handler for a button control), the user interface will become unresponsive until this method completes. You can make the *slowMethod* method more responsive by using a *Task* object to run the *doFirstLongRunningOperation* method and define continuations for the same *Task* that run the *doSecondLongRunningOperation* and *doThirdLongRunningOperation* methods in turn, like this:

```
private void slowMethod()
{
    Task task = new Task(doFirstLongRunningOperation);
    task.ContinueWith(doSecondLongRunningOperation);
```

```
    task.ContinueWith(doThirdLongRunningOperation);
    task.Start();
    message.Text = "Processing Completed"; // When does this message appear?
}

private void doFirstLongRunningOperation()
{
    ...
}

private void doSecondLongRunningOperation(Task t)
{
    ...
}

private void doThirdLongRunningOperation(Task t)
{
    ...
}
```

Although this refactoring seems fairly simple, there are points that you should note. Specifically, the signatures of the *doSecondLongRunningOperation* and *doThirdLongRunningOperation* methods have changed to accommodate the requirements of continuations (the *Task* object that instigated the continuation is passed as a parameter to a continuation method). More important, you need to ask yourself, "When is the message displayed in the *TextBox* control?" The issue with this second point is that although the *Start* method initiates a *Task*, it does not wait for it to complete, so the message appears while the processing is being performed rather than when it has finished.

This is a somewhat trivial example, but the general principle is important, and there are at least two solutions. The first is to wait for the *Task* to complete before displaying the message, like this:

```
private void slowMethod()
{
    Task task = new Task(doFirstLongRunningOperation);
    task.ContinueWith(doSecondLongRunningOperation);
    task.ContinueWith(doThirdLongRunningOperation);
    task.Start();
    task.Wait();
    message.Text = "Processing Completed";
}
```

However, the call to the *Wait* method now blocks the thread executing the *slowMethod* method and obviates the purpose of using a *Task* in the first place.

> **Important** Generally speaking, you should *never* call the *Wait* method directly in the user interface thread.

A better solution is to define a continuation that displays the message and arrange for it to run only when the *doThirdLongRunningOperation* method finishes, in which case you can remove the call to the *Wait* method. You might be tempted to implement this continuation as a delegate as shown in bold in the following code (remember that a continuation is passed a *Task* object as an argument; that is the purpose of the *t* parameter to the delegate):

```
private void slowMethod()
{
    Task task = new Task(doFirstLongRunningOperation);
    task.ContinueWith(doSecondLongRunningOperation);
    task.ContinueWith(doThirdLongRunningOperation);
    task.ContinueWith((t) => message.Text = "Processing Complete");
    task.Start();
}
```

Unfortunately, this approach exposes another problem. If you try to run this code in Debug mode, you will find that the final continuation generates a *System.Exception* exception with the rather obscure message, "The application called an interface that was marshaled for a different thread." The issue here is that only the user interface thread can manipulate user interface controls, and now you are attempting to write to a *TextBox* control from a different thread—the thread being used to run the *Task*. You can resolve this problem by using the *Dispatcher* object. The *Dispatcher* object is a component of the user interface infrastructure, and you can send it requests to perform work on the user interface thread by calling its *RunAsync* method. This method takes an *Action* delegate that specifies the code to run. The details of the *Dispatcher* object and the *RunAsync* method are beyond the scope of this book, but the following example shows how you might use them to display the message required by the *slowMethod* method from a continuation:

```
private void slowMethod()
{
    Task task = new Task(doFirstLongRunningOperation);
    task.ContinueWith(doSecondLongRunningOperation);
    task.ContinueWith(doThirdLongRunningOperation);
    task.ContinueWith((t) => this.Dispatcher.RunAsync(
        CoreDispatcherPriority.Normal,
        () => message.Text = "Processing Complete"));
    task.Start();
}
```

This works, but it is messy and difficult to maintain. You now have a delegate (the continuation) specifying another delegate (the code to be run by *RunAsync*).

> **More info** You can find more information about the *Dispatcher* object and the *RunAsync* method on the Microsoft website at *https://msdn.microsoft.com/library/windows.ui.core .coredispatcher.runasync*.

Defining asynchronous methods: The solution

The purpose of the *async* and *await* keywords in C# is to enable you to define and call methods that can run asynchronously. This means that you don't have to concern yourself with specifying continuations or scheduling code to run on *Dispatcher* objects to ensure that data is manipulated on the correct thread. Very simply:

- The *async* modifier indicates that a method contains functionality that can be run asynchronously.

- The *await* operator specifies the points at which this asynchronous functionality should be performed.

The following code example shows the *slowMethod* method implemented as an asynchronous method with the *async* modifier and *await* operators:

```
private async void slowMethod()
{
    await doFirstLongRunningOperation();
    await doSecondLongRunningOperation();
    await doThirdLongRunningOperation();
    message.Text = "Processing Complete";
}
```

This method now looks remarkably similar to the original version, and that is the power of *async* and *await*. In fact, this magic is nothing more than an exercise in reworking your code by the C# compiler. When the C# compiler encounters the *await* operator in an *async* method, it effectively reformats the operand that follows this operator as a task that runs on the same thread as the *async* method. The remainder of the code is converted into a continuation that runs when the task completes, again running on the same thread. Now, because the thread that was running the *async* method was the thread running the user interface, it has direct access to the controls in the window, which means it can update them directly without routing them through the *Dispatcher* object.

Although this approach looks quite simple at first glance, be sure to keep in mind the following points and avoid some possible misconceptions:

- The *async* modifier does not signify that a method runs asynchronously on a separate thread. All it does is specify that the code in the method can be divided into one or more continuations. When these continuations run, they execute on the same thread as the original method call.

- The *await* operator specifies a point at which the C# compiler can split the code into a continuation. The *await* operator itself expects its operand to be an *awaitable* object. An awaitable object is a type that provides the *GetAwaiter* method, which returns an object that in turn provides methods for running code and waiting for it to complete. The C# compiler converts your code into statements that use these methods to create an appropriate continuation.

In the current implementation of the *await* operator, the awaitable object it expects you to specify as the operand is a *Task*. This means that you must make some modifications to the *doFirstLong-RunningOperation*, *doSecondLongRunningOperation*, and *doThirdLongRunningOperation* methods. Specifically, each method must now create and run a *Task* to perform its work and return a reference to this *Task*. The following example shows an amended version of the *doFirstLongRunningOperation* method:

```
private Task doFirstLongRunningOperation()
{
    Task t = Task.Run(() => { /* original code for this method goes here */ });
    return t;
}
```

It is also worth considering whether there are opportunities to break the work done by the *doFirstLongRunningOperation* method into a series of parallel operations. If so, you can divide the work into a set of *Task*s, as described in Chapter 23. However, which of these *Task* objects should you return as the result of the method?

```
private Task doFirstLongRunningOperation()
{
    Task first = Task.Run(() => { /* code for first operation */ });
    Task second = Task.Run(() => { /* code for second operation */ });
    return ...; // Do you return first or second?
}
```

If the method returns *first*, the *await* operator in the *slowMethod* will wait only for that *Task* to complete and not for *second*. Similar logic applies if the method returns *second*. The solution is to define the *doFirstLongRunningOperation* method with *async* and await each of the *Task*s, as shown here:

```
private async Task doFirstLongRunningOperation()
{
    Task first = Task.Run(() => { /* code for first operation */ });
    Task second = Task.Run(() => { /* code for second operation */ });
    await first;
    await second;
}
```

Remember that when the compiler encounters the *await* operator, it generates code that waits for the item specified by the argument to complete, together with a continuation that runs the statements that follow. You can think of the value returned by the *async* method as a reference to the *Task* that runs this continuation (this description is not completely accurate, but it is a good enough model for the purposes of this chapter). So, the *doFirstLongRunningOperation* method creates and starts the tasks *first* and *second* running in parallel, the compiler reformats the *await* statements into code that waits for *first* to complete followed by a continuation that waits for *second* to finish, and the *async* modifier causes the compiler to return a reference to this continuation. Notice that because the compiler now determines the return value of the method, you no longer specify a return value yourself (in fact, if you try to return a value in this case, your code will not compile).

> **Note** If you don't include an *await* statement in an *async* method, the method is simply a reference to a *Task* that performs the code in the body of the method. As a result, when you invoke the method, it does not actually run asynchronously. In this case, the compiler will warn you with the message, "This *async* method lacks await operators and will run synchronously."

> **Tip** You can use the *async* modifier to prefix a delegate, making it possible to create delegates that incorporate asynchronous processing by using the *await* operator.

In the following exercise, you will work with the GraphDemo application from Chapter 23 and modify it to generate the data for the graph by using an asynchronous method.

Modify the GraphDemo application to use an asynchronous method

1. Using Microsoft Visual Studio 2015, open the GraphDemo solution, which is located in the \Microsoft Press\VCSBS\Chapter 24\GraphDemo folder in your Documents folder.

2. In Solution Explorer, expand the MainPage.xaml node and open the MainPage.xaml.cs file in the Code and Text Editor window.

3. In the *MainPage* class, locate the *plotButton_Click* method.

    The code in this method looks like this:

    ```
    private void plotButton_Click(object sender, RoutedEventArgs e)
    {
        Random rand = new Random();
        redValue = (byte)rand.Next(0xFF);
        greenValue = (byte)rand.Next(0xFF);
        blueValue = (byte)rand.Next(0xFF);

        tokenSource = new CancellationTokenSource();
        CancellationToken token = tokenSource.Token;

        Stopwatch watch = Stopwatch.StartNew();

        try
        {
            generateGraphData(data, 0, pixelWidth / 2, token);
            duration.Text = $"Duration (ms): {watch.ElapsedMilliseconds}";
        }
    ```

```
catch (OperationCanceledException oce)
{
    duration.Text = oce.Message;
}

Stream pixelStream = graphBitmap.PixelBuffer.AsStream();
pixelStream.Seek(0, SeekOrigin.Begin);
pixelStream.Write(data, 0, data.Length);
graphBitmap.Invalidate();
graphImage.Source = graphBitmap;
}
```

This is a simplified version of the application from the previous chapter. It invokes the *generateGraphData* method directly from the user interface thread and does not use *Task* objects to generate the data for the graph in parallel.

> **Note** If you reduced the size of the *pixelWidth* and *pixelHeight* fields in the exercises in Chapter 23 to save memory, do so again in this version before proceeding with the next step.

4. On the Debug menu, click Start Debugging.

5. In the GraphDemo window, click Plot Graph. While the data is being generated, try to click Cancel.

   Notice that the user interface is completely unresponsive as the graph is being generated and displayed. This is because the *plotButton_Click* method performs all its work synchronously, including the generation of the data for the graph.

6. Return to Visual Studio and stop debugging.

7. In the Code and Text Editor window displaying the *MainPage* class, above the *generateGraph-Data* method, add a new private method called *generateGraphDataAsync*.

   This method should take the same list of parameters as the *generateGraphData* method, but it should return a *Task* object rather than a *void*. The method should also be marked with *async*, and it should look like this:

```
private async Task generateGraphDataAsync(byte[] data,
    int partitionStart, int partitionEnd,
    CancellationToken token)
{
}
```

> **Note** It is recommended practice to name asynchronous methods with the *Async* suffix.

8. In the *generateGraphDataAsync* method, add the statements shown here in bold.

```
private async Task generateGraphDataAsync(byte[] data, int partitionStart, int
partitionEnd, CancellationToken token)
{
    Task task = Task.Run(() => generateGraphData(data, partitionStart, partitionEnd,
token));
    await task;
}
```

This code creates a *Task* object that runs the *generateGraphData* method and uses the *await* operator to wait for the *Task* to complete. The task generated by the compiler as a result of the *await* operator is the value returned from the method.

9. Return to the *plotButton_Click* method and change the definition of this method to include the *async* modifier, as shown in bold in the following code:

```
private async void plotButton_Click(object sender, RoutedEventArgs e)
{
    ...
}
```

10. In the *try* block in the *plotButton_Click* method, modify the statement that generates the data for the graph to call the *generateGraphDataAsync* method asynchronously, as shown here in bold:

```
try
{
    await generateGraphDataAsync(data, 0, pixelWidth / 2, token);
    duration.Text = $"Duration (ms): {watch.ElapsedMilliseconds}");
}
...
```

11. On the Debug menu, point to Windows, and then click Exception Settings. In the Exception Settings window, clear the check box for Common Language Runtime Exceptions. Right-click Common Language Runtime Exceptions, and then be sure that Continue When Unhandled In User Code is enabled.

12. On the Debug menu, click Start Debugging.

13. In the GraphDemo window, click Plot Graph and verify that the application generates the graph correctly.

14. Click Plot Graph, and then, while the data is being generated, click Cancel.

This time, the user interface should be responsive. Only part of the graph should be generated, and the *duration TextBlock* should display the message "The operation was cancelled."

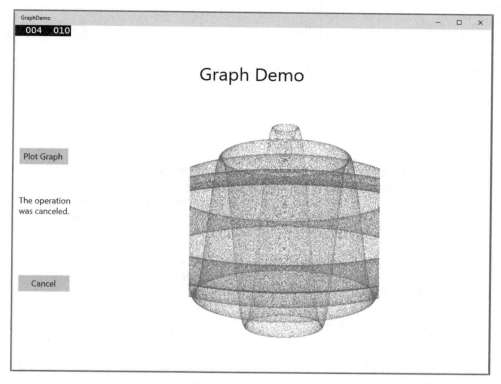

15. Return to Visual Studio and stop debugging.

Defining asynchronous methods that return values

So far, all the examples you have seen use a *Task* object to perform a piece of work that does not return a value. However, you also use tasks to run methods that calculate a result. To do this, you use the generic *Task<TResult>* class, where the type parameter, *TResult*, specifies the type of the result.

You create and start a *Task<TResult>* object in a similar way as for an ordinary *Task*. The primary difference is that the code you execute should return a value. For example, the method named *calculateValue* shown in the code example that follows generates an integer result. To invoke this method by using a task, you create and run a *Task<int>* object. You obtain the value returned by the method by querying the *Result* property of the *Task<int>* object. If the task has not finished running the method and the result is not yet available, the *Result* property blocks the caller. This means that you don't have to perform any synchronization yourself, and you know that when the *Result* property returns a value, the task has completed its work.

```
Task<int> calculateValueTask = Task.Run(() => calculateValue(...));
...
int calculatedData = calculateValueTask.Result; // Block until calculateValueTask completes
...
private int calculateValue(...)
{
    int someValue;
    // Perform calculation and populate someValue
    ...
    return someValue;
}
```

The generic *Task<TResult>* type is also the basis of the mechanism for defining asynchronous methods that return values. In previous examples, you saw that you implement asynchronous *void* methods by returning a *Task*. If an asynchronous method actually generates a result, it should return a *Task<TResult>*, as shown in the following example, which creates an asynchronous version of the *calculateValue* method:

```
private async Task<int> calculateValueAsync(...)
{
    // Invoke calculateValue using a Task
    Task<int> generateResultTask = Task.Run(() => calculateValue(...));
    await generateResultTask;
    return generateResultTask.Result;
}
```

This method looks slightly confusing inasmuch as the return type is specified as *Task<int>*, but the *return* statement actually returns an *int*. Remember that when you define an *async* method, the compiler performs some refactoring of your code, and it essentially returns a reference to *Task* that runs the continuation for the statement *return generateResultTask.Result;*. The type of the expression returned by this continuation is *int*, so the return type of the method is *Task<int>*.

To invoke an asynchronous method that returns a value, use the *await* operator, like this:

```
int result = await calculateValueAsync(...);
```

The *await* operator extracts the value from the *Task* returned by the *calculateValueAsync* method, and in this case assigns it to the *result* variable.

Asynchronous method gotchas

The *async* and *await* operators have been known to cause confusion amongst programmers. It is important to understand that:

- Marking a method as *async* does not mean that it runs asynchronously. It means that the method can contain statements that may run asynchronously.

- The *await* operator indicates that a method should be run by a separate task, and the calling code is suspended until the method call completes. The thread used by the calling code is released and can be reused. This is important if the thread is the user interface thread, as it enables the user interface to remain responsive.

- The *await* operator is not the same as using the *Wait* method of a task. The *Wait* method always blocks the current thread and does not allow it to be reused until the task completes.

- By default, the code that resumes execution after an *await* operator attempts to obtain the original thread that was used to invoke the asynchronous method call. If this thread is busy, the code will be blocked. You can use the *ConfigureAwait(false)* method to specify that the code can be resumed on any available thread and reduce the chances of blocking. This is especially useful for web applications and services that may need to handle many thousands of concurrent requests.

- You shouldn't use *ConfigureAwait(false)* if the code that runs after an *await* operator must execute on the original thread. In the example discussed earlier, adding *ConfigureAwait(false)* to each awaited operation will result in the likelihood that the continuations the compiler generates will run on separate threads. This includes the continuation that attempts to set the *Text* property for *message*, causing the exception "The application called an interface that was marshaled for a different thread" again.

```
private async void slowMethod()
{
    await doFirstLongRunningOperation().ConfigureAwait(false);
    await doSecondLongRunningOperation().ConfigureAwait(false);
    await doThirdLongRunningOperation().ConfigureAwait(false);
    message.Text = "Processing Complete";
}
```

- Careless use of asynchronous methods that return results and that run on the user interface thread can generate deadlocks, causing the application to freeze. Consider the following example:

```
private async void myMethod()
{
    var data = generateResult();
    ...
    message.Text = $"result: {data.Result}";
}

private async Task<string> generateResult()
{
    string result;
    ...
    result = ...
    return result;
}
```

In this code, the *generateResult* method returns a string value. However, the *myMethod* method does not actually start the task that runs the *generateResult* method until it attempts to access the *data.Result* property; *data* is a reference to the task, and if the *Result* property is not available because the task has not been run, then accessing this property will block the current thread until the *generateResult* method completes. Furthermore, the task used to run the *generateResult* method attempts to resume the thread on which it was invoked when the method completes (the user interface thread), but this thread is now blocked. The result is that the *myMethod* method cannot finish until the *generateResult* method completes, and the *generateResult* method cannot finish until the *myMethod* method completes.

The solution to this problem is to await the task that runs the *generateResult* method. You can do this as follows:

```
private async void myMethod()
{
    var data = generateResult();
    ...
    message.Text = $"result: {await data}";
}
```

Asynchronous methods and the Windows Runtime APIs

The designers of Windows 8 and later versions wanted to ensure that applications were as responsive as possible, so they made the decision when they implemented WinRT that any operation that might take more than 50 milliseconds to perform should be available only through an asynchronous API. You might have noticed one or two instances of this approach already in this book. For example, to display a message to a user, you can use a *MessageDialog* object. However, when you display this message, you must use the *ShowAsync* method, like this:

```
using Windows.UI.Popups;
...
MessageDialog dlg = new MessageDialog("Message to user");
await dlg.ShowAsync();
```

The *MessageDialog* object displays the message and waits for the user to click the Close button that appears as part of this dialog box. Any form of user interaction might take an indeterminate length of time (the user might have gone for lunch before clicking Close), and it is often important not to block the application or prevent it from performing other operations (such as responding to events) while the dialog box is displayed. The *MessageDialog* class does not provide a synchronous version of the *ShowAsync* method, but if you need to display a dialog box synchronously, you can simply call *dlg.ShowAsync()* without the *await* operator.

Another common example of asynchronous processing concerns the *FileOpenPicker* class, which you saw in Chapter 5, "Using compound assignment and iteration statements." The *FileOpenPicker* class displays a list of files from which the user can select. As with the *MessageDialog* class, the user might take a considerable time browsing and selecting files, so this operation should not block the application. The following example shows how to use the *FileOpenPicker* class to display the files in the user's Documents folder and wait while the user selects a single file from this list:

```
using Windows.Storage;
using Windows.Storage.Pickers;
...
FileOpenPicker fp = new FileOpenPicker();
fp.SuggestedStartLocation = PickerLocationId.DocumentsLibrary;
fp.ViewMode = PickerViewMode.List;
```

```
fp.FileTypeFilter.Add("*");
StorageFile file = await fp.PickSingleFileAsync();
```

The key statement is the line that calls the *PickSingleFileAsync* method. This is the method that displays the list of files and allows the user to navigate around the file system and select a file. (The *FileOpenPicker* class also provides the *PickMultipleFilesAsync* method by which a user can select more than one file.) The value returned by this method is *Task<StorageFile>*, and the *await* operator extracts the *StorageFile* object from this result. The *StorageFile* class provides an abstraction of a file held on hard disk, and by using this class, you can open a file and read from it or write to it.

> **Note** Strictly speaking, the *PickSingleFileAsync* method returns an object of type *IAsyncOperation<StorageFile>*. WinRT uses its own abstraction of asynchronous operations and maps .NET Framework *Task* objects to this abstraction; the *Task* class implements the *IAsyncOperation* interface. If you are programming in C#, your code is not affected by this transformation, and you can simply use *Task* objects without concerning yourself with how they get mapped to WinRT asynchronous operations.

File input/output (I/O) is another source of potentially slow operations, and the *StorageFile* class implements a raft of asynchronous methods by which these operations can be performed without impacting the responsiveness of an application. For example, in Chapter 5, after the user selects a file using a *FileOpenPicker* object, the code then opens this file for reading, asynchronously:

```
StorageFile file = await fp.PickSingleFileAsync();
...
var fileStream = await file.OpenAsync(FileAccessMode.Read);
```

One final example that is directly applicable to the exercises you have seen in this and the previous chapter concerns writing to a stream. You might have noticed that although the time reported to generate the data for the graph is a few seconds, it can take up to twice that amount of time before the graph actually appears. This happens because of the way the data is written to the bitmap. The bitmap renders data held in a buffer as part of the *WriteableBitmap* object, and the *AsStream* extension method provides a *Stream* interface to this buffer. The data is written to the buffer via this stream by using the *Write* method, like this:

```
...
Stream pixelStream = graphBitmap.PixelBuffer.AsStream();
pixelStream.Seek(0, SeekOrigin.Begin);
pixelStream.Write(data, 0, data.Length);
...
```

Unless you have reduced the value of the *pixelWidth* and *pixelHeight* fields to save memory, the volume of data written to the buffer is just over 570 MB (15,000 * 10,000 * 4 bytes), so this *Write* operation can take a few seconds. To improve response time, you can perform this operation asynchronously by using the *WriteAsync* method:

```
await pixelStream.WriteAsync(data, 0, data.Length);
```

In summary, when you build applications for Windows, you should seek to exploit asynchronicity wherever possible.

The *IAsyncResult* design pattern in earlier versions of the .NET Framework

Asynchronicity has long been recognized as a key element in building responsive applications with the .NET Framework, and the concept predates the introduction of the *Task* class in the .NET Framework version 4.0. Microsoft introduced the *IAsyncResult* design pattern based on the *AsyncCallback* delegate type to handle these situations. The exact details of how this pattern works are not appropriate in this book, but from a programmer's perspective the implementation of this pattern meant that many types in the .NET Framework class library exposed long-running operations in two ways: in a synchronous form consisting of a single method, and in an asynchronous form that used a pair of methods, named *BeginOperationName* and *EndOperationName*, where *OperationName* specified the operation being performed. For example, the *MemoryStream* class in the *System.IO* namespace provides the *Write* method to write data synchronously to a stream in memory, but it also provides the *BeginWrite* and *EndWrite* methods to perform the same operation asynchronously. The *BeginWrite* method initiates the write operation that is performed on a new thread. The *BeginWrite* method expects the programmer to provide a reference to a callback method that runs when the write operation completes; this reference is in the form of an *AsyncCallback* delegate. In this method, the programmer should implement any appropriate tidying up and call the *EndWrite* method to signify that the operation has completed. The following code example shows this pattern in action:

```
...
Byte[] buffer = ...; // populated with data to write to the MemoryStream
MemoryStream ms = new MemoryStream();
AsyncCallback callback = new AsyncCallback(handleWriteCompleted);
ms.BeginWrite(buffer, 0, buffer.Length, callback, ms);
...

private void handleWriteCompleted(IAsyncResult ar)
{
    MemoryStream ms = ar.AsyncState as MemoryStream;
    ... // Perform any appropriate tidying up
    ms.EndWrite(ar);
}
```

The parameter to the callback method (*handleWriteCompleted*) is an *IAsyncResult* object that contains information about the status of the asynchronous operation and any other state information. You can pass user-defined information to the callback in this parameter; the final argument supplied to the *BeginOperationName* method is packaged into this parameter. In this example, the callback is passed a reference to the *MemoryStream*.

Although this sequence works, it is a messy paradigm that obscures the operation you are performing. The code for the operation is split into two methods, and it is easy to lose the mental connection between these methods if you have to maintain this code. If you are using *Task* objects, you can simplify this model by calling the static *FromAsync* method of the *TaskFactory* class. This method takes the *BeginOperationName* and *EndOperationName* methods and wraps them into code that is performed by using a *Task*. There is no need to create an *AsyncCallback* delegate because this is generated behind the scenes by the *FromAsync* method. So you can perform the same operation shown in the previous example like this:

```
...
Byte[] buffer = ...;
MemoryStream s = new MemoryStream();
Task t = Task<int>.Factory.FromAsync(s.Beginwrite, s.EndWrite, buffer, 0,
                               buffer.Length, null);
t.Start();
await t;
...
```

This technique is useful if you need to access asynchronous functionality exposed by types developed in earlier versions of the .NET Framework.

Using PLINQ to parallelize declarative data access

Data access is another area for which response time is important, especially if you are building applications that have to search through lengthy data structures. In earlier chapters, you saw how powerful LINQ is for retrieving data from an enumerable data structure, but the examples shown were inherently single-threaded. PLINQ provides a set of extensions to LINQ that is based on *Task*s and that can help you boost performance and parallelize some query operations.

PLINQ works by dividing a data set into partitions and then using tasks to retrieve the data that matches the criteria specified by the query for each partition in parallel. When the tasks have completed, the results retrieved for each partition are combined into a single enumerable result set. PLINQ is ideal for scenarios that involve data sets with large numbers of elements, or if the criteria specified for matching data involve complex, computationally expensive operations.

An important aim of PLINQ is to be as nonintrusive as possible. To convert a LINQ query into a PLINQ query you use the *AsParallel* extension method. The *AsParallel* method returns a *ParallelQuery* object that acts in a similar manner to the original enumerable object, except that it provides parallel implementations of many of the LINQ operators, such as *join* and *where*. These implementations of the LINQ operators are based on tasks and use various algorithms to try to run parts of your LINQ query in parallel wherever possible. However, as ever in the world of parallel computing, the *AsParallel* method is not magic. You cannot guarantee that your code will speed up; it all depends on the nature of your LINQ queries and whether the tasks they are performing lend themselves to parallelization.

To understand how PLINQ works and the situations in which it is useful, it helps to see some examples. The exercises in the following sections demonstrate a pair of simple scenarios.

Using PLINQ to improve performance while iterating through a collection

The first scenario is simple. Consider a LINQ query that iterates through a collection and retrieves elements from the collection based on a processor-intensive calculation. This form of query can benefit from parallel execution as long as the calculations are independent. The elements in the collection can be divided into a number of partitions; the exact number depends on the current load of the computer and the number of CPUs available. The elements in each partition can be processed by a separate thread. When all the partitions have been processed, the results can be merged. Any collection that supports access to elements through an index, such as an array or a collection that implements the *IList<T>* interface, can be managed in this way.

Parallelize a LINQ query over a simple collection

1. Using Visual Studio 2015, open the PLINQ solution, which is located in the \Microsoft Press\ VCSBS\Chapter 24\PLINQ folder in your Documents folder.

2. In Solution Explorer, double-click Program.cs in the PLINQ project to display the file in the Code and Text Editor window.

   This is a console application. The skeleton structure of the application has been created for you. The *Program* class contains methods named *Test1* and *Test2* that illustrate a pair of common scenarios. The *Main* method calls each of these test methods in turn.

   Both test methods have the same general structure: they create a LINQ query (you will add the code to do this later in this set of exercises), run it, and display the time taken. The code for each of these methods is almost completely separate from the statements that actually create and run the queries.

3. Examine the *Test1* method.

   This method creates a large array of integers and populates it with a set of random numbers between 0 and 200. The random number generator is seeded, so you should get the same results every time you run the application.

4. Immediately after the first *TO DO* comment in this method, add the LINQ query shown here in bold:

   ```
   // TO DO: Create a LINQ query that retrieves all numbers that are greater than 100
   var over100 = from n in numbers
                 where TestIfTrue(n > 100)
                 select n;
   ```

   This LINQ query retrieves all the items in the *numbers* array that have a value greater than 100. The test *n > 100* is not by itself computationally intensive enough to show the benefits of parallelizing this query, so the code calls a method named *TestIfTrue*, which slows it down a little by performing a *SpinWait* operation. The *SpinWait* method causes the processor to continually execute a loop of special "no operation" instructions for a short period of time, keeping the processor busy but not actually doing any work. (This is known as *spinning*.) The *TestIfTrue* method looks like this:

```
public static bool TestIfTrue(bool expr)
{
    Thread.SpinWait(1000);
    return expr;
}
```

5. After the second *TO DO* comment in the *Test1* method, add the following code shown in bold:

```
// TO DO: Run the LINQ query, and save the results in a List<int> object
List<int> numbersOver100 = new List<int>(over100);
```

Remember that LINQ queries use deferred execution, so they do not run until you retrieve the results from them. This statement creates a *List<int>* object and populates it with the results of running the *over100* query.

6. After the third *TO DO* comment in the *Test1* method, add the following statement shown in bold:

```
// TO DO: Display the results
Console.WriteLine($"There are {numbersOver100.Count} numbers over 100");
```

7. On the Debug menu, click Start Without Debugging. Note the time that running *Test 1* takes and the number of items in the array that are greater than 100.

8. Run the application several times, and take an average for the time. Verify that the number of items greater than 100 is the same each time (the application uses the same random number seed each time it runs to ensure the repeatability of the tests). Return to Visual Studio when you have finished.

9. The logic that selects each item returned by the LINQ query is independent of the selection logic for all the other items, so this query is an ideal candidate for partitioning. Modify the statement that defines the LINQ query, and specify the *AsParallel* extension method to the *numbers* array, as shown here in bold:

```
var over100 = from n in numbers.AsParallel()
              where TestIfTrue(n > 100)
              select n;
```

> **Note** If the selection logic or calculations require access to shared data, you must synchronize the tasks that run in parallel; otherwise, the results might be unpredictable. However, synchronization can impose an overhead and might negate the benefits of parallelizing the query.

10. On the Debug menu, click Start Without Debugging. Verify that the number of items reported by *Test1* is the same as before but that the time taken to perform the test has decreased

significantly. Run the test several times, and take an average of the duration required for the test.

If you are running on a dual-core processor (or a twin-processor computer), you should see the time reduced by 40 to 45 percent. If you have more processor cores, the decrease should be even more dramatic (on my quad-core machine, the processing time dropped from 10.3 seconds to 2.8).

11. Close the application, and return to Visual Studio.

The preceding exercise shows the performance improvement you can attain by making a small change to a LINQ query. However, keep in mind that you will see results such as this only if the calculations performed by the query take some time. I cheated a little by spinning the processor. Without this overhead, the parallel version of the query is actually slower than the serial version. In the next exercise, you will see a LINQ query that joins two arrays in memory. This time, the exercise uses more realistic data volumes, so there is no need to slow down the query artificially.

Parallelize a LINQ query that joins two collections

1. In Solution Explorer, open the Data.cs file in the Code and Text Editor window and locate the *CustomersInMemory* class.

This class contains a public string array called *Customers*. Each *string* in the *Customers* array holds the data for a single customer, with the fields separated by commas; this format is typical of data that an application might read in from a text file that uses comma-separated fields. The first field contains the customer ID, the second field contains the name of the company that the customer represents, and the remaining fields hold the address, city, country or region, and postal code.

2. Find the *OrdersInMemory* class.

This class is similar to the *CustomersInMemory* class except that it contains a string array called *Orders*. The first field in each string is the order number, the second field is the customer ID, and the third field is the date that the order was placed.

3. Find the *OrderInfo* class. This class contains four fields: the customer ID, company name, order ID, and order date for an order. You will use a LINQ query to populate a collection of *OrderInfo* objects from the data in the *Customers* and *Orders* arrays.

4. Display the Program.cs file in the Code and Text Editor window and locate the *Test2* method in the *Program* class.

In this method, you will create a LINQ query that joins the *Customers* and *Orders* arrays by using the customer ID to return a list of customers and the orders that each customer has placed. The query will store each row of the result in an *OrderInfo* object.

5. In the *try* block in this method, after the first *TO DO* comment, add the code shown next in bold:

```
// TO DO: Create a LINQ query that retrieves customers and orders from arrays
// Store each row returned in an OrderInfo object
var orderInfoQuery = from c in CustomersInMemory.Customers
                     join o in OrdersInMemory.Orders
                     on c.Split(',')[0] equals o.Split(',')[1]
                     select new OrderInfo
                     {
                         CustomerID = c.Split(',')[0],
                         CompanyName = c.Split(',')[1],
                         OrderID = Convert.ToInt32(o.Split(',')[0]),
                         OrderDate = Convert.ToDateTime(o.Split(',')[2],
                             new CultureInfo("en-US"))
                     };
```

This statement defines the LINQ query. Notice that it uses the *Split* method of the *String* class to split each string into an array of strings. The strings are split on the comma character. (The commas are stripped out.) One complication is that the dates in the array are held in United States English format, so the code that converts them into *DateTime* objects in the *OrderInfo* object specifies the United States English formatter. If you use the default formatter for your locale, the dates might not parse correctly. All in all, this query performs a significant amount of work to generate the data for each item.

6. In the *Test2* method, after the second *TO DO* statement, add the following code shown in bold:

    ```
    // TO DO: Run the LINQ query, and save the results in a List<OrderInfo> object
    List<OrderInfo> orderInfo = new List<OrderInfo>(orderInfoQuery);
    ```

    This statement runs the query and populates the *orderInfo* collection.

7. After the third *TO DO* statement, add the statement shown here in bold:

    ```
    // TO DO: Display the results
    Console.WriteLine($"There are {orderInfo.Count} orders");
    ```

8. In the *Main* method, comment out the statement that calls the *Test1* method and uncomment the statement that calls the *Test2* method, as shown in the following code in bold:

    ```
    static void Main(string[] args)
    {
        // Test1();
        Test2();
    }
    ```

9. On the Debug menu, click Start Without Debugging.

10. Verify that *Test2* retrieves 830 orders, and note the duration of the test. Run the application several times to obtain an average duration, and then return to Visual Studio.

11. In the *Test2* method, modify the LINQ query and add the *AsParallel* extension method to the *Customers* and *Orders* arrays, as shown here in bold:

    ```
    var orderInfoQuery = from c in CustomersInMemory.Customers.AsParallel()
    ```

```
join o in OrdersInMemory.Orders.AsParallel()
on c.Split(',')[0] equals o.Split(',')[1]
select new OrderInfo
{
    CustomerID = c.Split(',')[0],
    CompanyName = c.Split(',')[1],
    OrderID = Convert.ToInt32(o.Split(',')[0]),
    OrderDate = Convert.ToDateTime(o.Split(',')[2],
        New CultureInfo("en-US"))
};
```

> **!**
>
> **Warning** When you join two data sources in this way, they must both be *IEnumerable* objects or *ParallelQuery* objects. This means that if you specify the *AsParallel* method for one source, you should also specify *AsParallel* for the other. If you fail to do this, your code will not run—it will stop with an error.

12. Run the application several times. Notice that the time taken for *Test2* should be significantly less than it was previously. PLINQ can make use of multiple threads to optimize join operations by fetching the data for each part of the join in parallel.

13. Close the application and return to Visual Studio.

These two simple exercises have shown you the power of the *AsParallel* extension method and PLINQ. Note that PLINQ is an evolving technology, and the internal implementation is very likely to change over time. Additionally, the volumes of data and the amount of processing you perform in a query also have a bearing on the effectiveness of using PLINQ. Therefore, you should not regard these exercises as defining fixed rules that you should always follow. Rather, they illustrate the point that you should carefully measure and assess the likely performance or other benefits of using PLINQ with your own data, in your own environment.

Canceling a PLINQ query

Unlike with ordinary LINQ queries, you can cancel a PLINQ query. To do this, you specify a *CancellationToken* object from a *CancellationTokenSource* and use the *WithCancellation* extension method of the *ParallelQuery*.

```
CancellationToken tok = ...;
...
var orderInfoQuery =
    from c in CustomersInMemory.Customers.AsParallel().WithCancellation(tok)
    join o in OrdersInMemory.Orders.AsParallel()
    on ...
```

You specify *WithCancellation* only once in a query. Cancellation applies to all sources in the query. If the *CancellationTokenSource* object used to generate the *CancellationToken* is canceled, the query stops with an *OperationCanceledException* exception.

Synchronizing concurrent access to data

PLINQ is not always the most appropriate technology to use for an application. If you create your own tasks manually, you need to ensure that these tasks coordinate their activities correctly. The .NET Framework class library provides methods with which you can wait for tasks to complete, and you can use these methods to coordinate tasks at a very coarse level. But consider what happens if two tasks attempt to access and modify the same data. If both tasks run at the same time, their overlapping operations might corrupt the data. This situation can lead to bugs that are difficult to correct, primarily because of their unpredictability.

The *Task* class provides a powerful framework with which you can design and build applications that take advantage of multiple CPU cores to perform tasks in parallel. However, you need to be careful when building solutions that perform concurrent operations, especially if those operations share access to data. You have little control over how parallel operations are scheduled, or even the degree of parallelism that the operating system might provide to an application constructed by using tasks. These decisions are left as run-time considerations and depend on the workload and hardware capabilities of the computer running your application. This level of abstraction was a deliberate design decision on the part of the Microsoft development team, and it removes the need for you to understand the low-level threading and scheduling details when you build applications that require concurrent tasks. But this abstraction comes at a cost. Although it all appears to work magically, you must make some effort to understand how your code runs; otherwise, you can end up with applications that exhibit unpredictable (and erroneous) behavior, as shown in the following example (this sample is available in the ParallelTest project in the folder containing the code for Chapter 24):

```
using System;
using System.Threading;

class Program
{
    private const int NUMELEMENTS = 10;

    static void Main(string[] args)
    {
        SerialTest();
    }

    static void SerialTest()
    {
        int[] data = new int[NUMELEMENTS];
        int j = 0;

        for (int i = 0; i < NUMELEMENTS; i++)
        {
            j = i;
            doAdditionalProcessing();
            data[i] = j;
            doMoreAdditionalProcessing();
        }

        for (int i = 0; i < NUMELEMENTS; i++)
```

```
    {
        Console.WriteLine($"Element {i} has value {data[i]}");
    }
}

static void doAdditionalProcessing()
{
    Thread.Sleep(10);
}

static void doMoreAdditionalProcessing()
{
    Thread.Sleep(10);
}
}
```

The *SerialTest* method populates an integer array with a set of values (in a rather long-winded way) and then iterates through this list, printing the index of each item in the array together with the value of the corresponding item. The *doAdditionalProcessing* and *doMoreAdditionalProcessing* methods simply simulate the performance of long-running operations as part of the processing that might cause the runtime to yield control of the processor. The output of the program method is shown here:

```
Element 0 has value 0
Element 1 has value 1
Element 2 has value 2
Element 3 has value 3
Element 4 has value 4
Element 5 has value 5
Element 6 has value 6
Element 7 has value 7
Element 8 has value 8
Element 9 has value 9
```

Now consider the *ParallelTest* method, shown next. This method is the same as the *SerialTest* method except that it uses the *Parallel.For* construct to populate the *data* array by running concurrent tasks. The code in the lambda expression run by each task is identical to that in the initial *for* loop in the *SerialTest* method.

```
using System.Threading.Tasks;
...

static void ParallelTest()
{
    int[] data = new int[NUMELEMENTS];
    int j = 0;

    Parallel.For  (0, NUMELEMENTS, (i) =>
    {
        j = i;
        doAdditionalProcessing();
        data[i] = j;
        doMoreAdditionalProcessing();
    });
```

```
        for (int i = 0; i < NUMELEMENTS; i++)
        {
            Console.WriteLine($"Element {i} has value {data[i]}");
        }
    }
```

The intention is for the *ParallelTest* method to perform the same operation as the *SerialTest* method, except by using concurrent tasks and (with good luck) running a little faster as a result. The problem is that it might not always work as expected. Some sample output generated by the *ParallelTest* method is shown here:

```
Element 0 has value 1
Element 1 has value 1
Element 2 has value 4
Element 3 has value 8
Element 4 has value 4
Element 5 has value 1
Element 6 has value 4
Element 7 has value 8
Element 8 has value 8
Element 9 has value 9
```

The values assigned to each item in the *data* array are not always the same as the values generated by using the *SerialTest* method. Additionally, further runs of the *ParallelTest* method can produce different sets of results.

If you examine the logic in the *Parallel.For* construct, you should see where the problem lies. The lambda expression contains the following statements:

```
j = i;
doAdditionalProcessing();
data[i] = j;
doMoreAdditionalProcessing();
```

The code looks innocuous enough. It copies the current value of the variable *i* (the index variable identifying which iteration of the loop is running) into the variable *j*, and later on it stores the value of *j* in the element of the data array indexed by *i*. If *i* contains 5, *j* is assigned the value 5, and later on the value of *j* is stored in *data[5]*. But between assigning the value to *j* and then reading it back, the code does more work; it calls the *doAdditionalProcessing* method. If this method takes a long time to execute, the runtime might suspend the thread and schedule another task. A concurrent task running another iteration of the *Parallel.For* construct might run and assign a new value to *j*. Consequently, when the original task resumes, the value of *j* it assigns to *data[5]* is not the value it stored, and the result is data corruption. More troublesome is that sometimes this code might run as expected and produce the correct results, and at other times it might not; it all depends on how busy the computer is and when the various tasks are scheduled. Consequently, these types of bugs can lie dormant during testing and then suddenly manifest in a production environment.

The variable *j* is shared by all the concurrent tasks. If a task stores a value in *j* and later reads it back, it has to ensure that no other task has modified *j* in the meantime. This requires synchronizing access to the variable across all concurrent tasks that can access it. One way in which you can achieve synchronized access is to lock data.

Locking data

The C# language provides locking semantics through the *lock* keyword, which you can use to guarantee exclusive access to resources. You use the *lock* keyword like this:

```
object myLockObject = new object();
...
lock (myLockObject)
{
    // Code that requires exclusive access to a shared resource
    ...
}
```

The *lock* statement attempts to obtain a mutual-exclusion lock over the specified object (you can actually use any reference type, not just *object*), and it blocks if this same object is currently locked by another thread. When the thread obtains the lock, the code in the block following the *lock* statement runs. At the end of this block, the lock is released. If another thread is blocked waiting for the lock, it can then grab the lock and continue its processing.

Synchronization primitives for coordinating tasks

The *lock* keyword is fine for many simple scenarios, but in some situations you might have more complex requirements. The *System.Threading* namespace includes a number of additional synchronization primitives that you can use to address these situations. These synchronization primitives are classes designed for use with tasks; they expose locking mechanisms that restrict access to a resource while a task holds the lock. They support a variety of locking techniques that you can use to implement different styles of concurrent access, ranging from simple exclusive locks (where a single task has sole access to a resource), to semaphores (where multiple tasks can access a resource simultaneously but in a controlled manner), to reader/writer locks that enable different tasks to share read-only access to a resource while guaranteeing exclusive access to a thread that needs to modify the resource.

The following list summarizes some of these primitives. For more information and examples, consult the documentation provided with Visual Studio 2015.

> **Note** The .NET Framework has included a respectable set of synchronization primitives since its initial release. The following list describes only the more recent primitives included in the *System.Threading* namespace. There is some overlap between the new primitives and those provided previously. Where overlapping functionality exists, you should use the more recent alternatives because they have been designed and optimized for computers with multiple CPUs.

Detailed discussion of the theory of all the possible synchronization mechanisms available for building multithreaded applications is beyond the scope of this book. For more information about the general theory of multiple threads and synchronization, see the topic "Synchronizing Data for Multithreading" in the documentation provided with Visual Studio 2015.

- **ManualResetEventSlim** The *ManualResetEventSlim* class provides functionality by which one or more tasks can wait for an event.

  A *ManualResetEventSlim* object can be in one of two states: *signaled* (true) and *unsignaled* (false). A task creates a *ManualResetEventSlim* object and specifies its initial state. Other tasks can wait for the *ManualResetEventSlim* object to be signaled by calling the *Wait* method. If the *ManualResetEventSlim* object is in the *unsignaled* state, the *Wait* method blocks the tasks. Another task can change the state of the *ManualResetEventSlim* object to *signaled* by calling the *Set* method. This action releases all tasks waiting on the *ManualResetEventSlim* object, which can then resume running. The *Reset* method changes the state of a *ManualResetEventSlim* object back to *unsignaled*.

- **SemaphoreSlim** You can use the *SemaphoreSlim* class to control access to a pool of resources.

  A *SemaphoreSlim* object has an initial value (a nonnegative integer) and an optional maximum value. Typically, the initial value of a *SemaphoreSlim* object is the number of resources in the pool. Tasks accessing the resources in the pool first call the *Wait* method. This method attempts to decrement the value of the *SemaphoreSlim* object, and if the result is nonzero, the thread is allowed to continue and can take a resource from the pool. When it has finished, the task should call the *Release* method on the *SemaphoreSlim* object. This action increments the value of the *Semaphore*.

  If a task calls the *Wait* method and the result of decrementing the value of the *SemaphoreSlim* object would result in a negative value, the task waits until another task calls *Release*.

  The *SemaphoreSlim* class also provides the *CurrentCount* property, which you can use to determine whether a *Wait* operation is likely to succeed immediately or will result in blocking.

- **CountdownEvent** You can think of the *CountdownEvent* class as a cross between the inverse of a semaphore and a manual reset event.

  When a task creates a *CountdownEvent* object, it specifies an initial value (a nonnegative integer). One or more tasks can call the *Wait* method of the *CountdownEvent* object, and if its value is nonzero, the tasks are blocked. *Wait* does not decrement the value of the *CountdownEvent* object; instead, other tasks can call the *Signal* method to reduce the value. When the value of the *CountdownEvent* object reaches zero, all blocked tasks are signaled and can resume running.

  A task can set the value of a *CountdownEvent* object back to the value specified in its constructor by using the *Reset* method, and a task can increase this value by calling the

AddCount method. You can determine whether a call to *Wait* is likely to block by examining the *CurrentCount* property.

- **ReaderWriterLockSlim** The *ReaderWriterLockSlim* class is an advanced synchronization primitive that supports a single writer and multiple readers. The idea is that modifying (writing to) a resource requires exclusive access, but reading a resource does not; multiple readers can access the same resource at the same time, but not at the same time as a writer.

  A task that wants to read a resource calls the *EnterReadLock* method of a *ReaderWriterLockSlim* object. This action grabs a read lock on the object. When the task has finished with the resource, it calls the *ExitReadLock* method, which releases the read lock. Multiple tasks can read the same resource at the same time, and each task obtains its own read lock.

  When a task modifies the resource, it can call the *EnterWriteLock* method of the same *ReaderWriterLockSlim* object to obtain a write lock. If one or more tasks currently have a read lock for this object, the *EnterWriteLock* method blocks until they are all released. After a task has a write lock, it can then modify the resource and call the *ExitWriteLock* method to release the lock.

  A *ReaderWriterLockSlim* object has only a single write lock. If another task attempts to obtain the write lock, it is blocked until the first task releases this write lock.

  To ensure that writing tasks are not blocked indefinitely, as soon as a task requests the write lock, all subsequent calls to *EnterReadLock* made by other tasks are blocked until the write lock has been obtained and released.

- **Barrier** With the *Barrier* class, you can temporarily halt the execution of a set of tasks at a particular point in an application and continue only when all tasks have reached this point. It is useful for synchronizing tasks that need to perform a series of concurrent operations in step with one another.

  When a task creates a *Barrier* object, it specifies the number of tasks in the set that will be synchronized. You can think of this value as a task counter maintained internally inside the *Barrier* class. This value can be amended later by calling the *AddParticipant* or *RemoveParticipant* method. When a task reaches a synchronization point, it calls the *SignalAndWait* method of the *Barrier* object, which decrements the thread counter inside the *Barrier* object. If this counter is greater than zero, the task is blocked. Only when the counter reaches zero are all the tasks waiting on the *Barrier* object released, and only then can they continue running.

  The *Barrier* class provides the *ParticipantCount* property, which specifies the number of tasks that it synchronizes, and the *ParticipantsRemaining* property, which indicates how many tasks need to call *SignalAndWait* before the barrier is raised and blocked tasks can continue running.

  You can also specify a delegate in the *Barrier* constructor. This delegate can refer to a method that runs when all the tasks have arrived at the barrier. The *Barrier* object is passed in as a parameter to this method. The barrier is not raised and the tasks are not released until this method completes.

Canceling synchronization

The *ManualResetEventSlim, SemaphoreSlim, CountdownEvent*, and *Barrier* classes all support cancellation by following the cancellation model described in Chapter 23. The wait operations for each of these classes can take an optional *CancellationToken* parameter, retrieved from a *CancellationTokenSource* object. If you call the *Cancel* method of the *CancellationTokenSource* object, each wait operation referencing a *CancellationToken* generated from this source is aborted with an *OperationCanceledException* exception (possibly wrapped in an *AggregateException* exception, depending on the context of the wait operation).

The following code shows how to invoke the *Wait* method of a *SemaphoreSlim* object and specify a cancellation token. If the wait operation is canceled, the *OperationCanceledException* catch handler runs.

```
CancellationTokenSource cancellationTokenSource = new CancellationTokenSource();
CancellationToken cancellationToken = cancellationTokenSource.Token;
...
// Semaphore that protects a pool of 3 resources
SemaphoreSlim semaphoreSlim = new SemaphoreSlim(3);
...
// Wait on the semaphore, and catch the OperationCanceledException if
// another thread calls Cancel on cancellationTokenSource
try
{
    semaphoreSlim.Wait(cancellationToken);
}
catch (OperationCanceledException e)
{
    ...
}
```

The concurrent collection classes

A common requirement of many multithreaded applications is to store and retrieve data in a collection. The standard collection classes provided with the .NET Framework are not thread safe by default, although you can use the synchronization primitives described in the previous section to wrap code that adds, queries, and removes elements in a collection. However, this process is potentially prone to error and not very scalable, so the .NET Framework class library includes a small set of thread-safe collection classes and interfaces in the *System.Collections.Concurrent* namespace that are designed specifically for use with tasks. The following list briefly summarizes the key types in this namespace:

- **ConcurrentBag<T>**   This is a general-purpose class for holding an unordered collection of items. It includes methods to insert (*Add*), remove (*TryTake*), and examine (*TryPeek*) items in the collection. These methods are thread safe. The collection is also enumerable, so you can iterate over its contents by using a *foreach* statement.

- **ConcurrentDictionary<TKey, TValue>**   This class implements a thread-safe version of the generic *Dictionary<TKey, TValue>* collection class described in Chapter 18, "Using collections."

It provides the methods *TryAdd, ContainsKey, TryGetValue, TryRemove,* and *TryUpdate*, which you can use to add, query, remove, and modify items in the dictionary.

- **ConcurrentQueue<T>** This class provides a thread-safe version of the generic *Queue<T>* class described in Chapter 18. It includes the methods *Enqueue, TryDequeue,* and *TryPeek*, which you can use to add, remove, and query items in the queue.

- **ConcurrentStack<T>** This is a thread-safe implementation of the generic *Stack<T>* class, also described in Chapter 18. It provides methods such as *Push, TryPop,* and *TryPeek*, which you can use to push, pop, and query items on the stack.

> **Note** Adding thread safety to the methods in a collection class imposes additional run-time overhead, so these classes are not as fast as the regular collection classes. You need to keep this fact in mind when deciding whether to parallelize a set of operations that requires access to a shared collection.

Using a concurrent collection and a lock to implement thread-safe data access

In the following set of exercises, you will implement an application that calculates pi by using a geometric approximation. Initially, you will perform the calculation in a single-threaded manner, and then you will change the code to perform the calculation by using parallel tasks. In the process, you will uncover some data synchronization issues that you need to address and that you will solve by using a concurrent collection class and a lock to ensure that the tasks coordinate their activities correctly.

The algorithm that you will implement calculates pi based on some simple mathematics and statistical sampling. If you draw a circle of radius *r* and draw a square with sides that touch the circle, the sides of the square are *2 * r* in length, as shown in the following image:

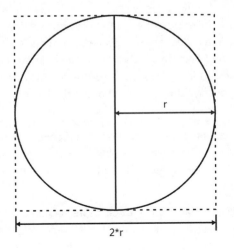

You can calculate the area of the square, S, like this

$S = (2 * r) * (2 * r)$

or

$S = 4 * r * r$

The area of the circle, C, is calculated as follows:

$C = pi * r * r$

Rearranging these formulas, you can see that

$r * r = C / pi$

and

$r * r = S / 4$

Combining these equations, you get:

$S / 4 = C / pi$

And therefore:

$pi = 4 * C / S$

The trick is to determine the value of the ratio of the area of the circle, C, with respect to the area of the square, S. This is where the statistical sampling comes in. You can generate a set of random points that lie within the square and count how many of these points also fall within the circle. If you generate a sufficiently large and random sample, the ratio of points that lie within the circle to the points that lie within the square (and also in the circle) approximates the ratio of the areas of the two shapes, C / S. All you have to do is count them.

How do you determine whether a point lies within the circle? To help visualize the solution, draw the square on a piece of graph paper with the center of the square at the origin, point (0,0). You can then generate pairs of values, or coordinates, that lie within the range (-r, -r) to (+r, +r). You can determine whether any set of coordinates (x, y) lie within the circle by applying the Pythagorean theorem to determine the distance d of these coordinates from the origin. You can calculate d as the square root of $((x * x) + (y * y))$. If d is less than or equal to r, the radius of the circle, the coordinates (x, y) specify a point within the circle, as shown in the following diagram:

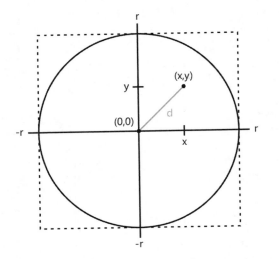

You can simplify matters further by generating coordinates that lie only in the upper-right quadrant of the graph so that you only have to generate pairs of random numbers between 0 and *r*. This is the approach you will take in the exercises.

> **Note** The exercises in this chapter are intended to be run on a computer with a multicore processor. If you have only a single-core CPU, you will not observe the same effects. Also, you should not start any additional programs or services between exercises, because these might affect the results you see.

Calculate pi by using a single thread

1. Start Visual Studio 2015 if it is not already running.

2. Open the CalculatePI solution, which is located in the \Microsoft Press\VCSBS\Chapter 24\ CalculatePI folder in your Documents folder.

3. In Solution Explorer, in the CalculatePI project, double-click Program.cs to display the file in the Code and Text Editor window.

   This is a console application. The skeleton structure of the application has already been created for you.

4. Scroll to the bottom of the file and examine the *Main* method. It looks like this:

```
static void Main(string[] args)
{
    double pi = SerialPI();
    Console.WriteLine($"Geometric approximation of PI calculated serially: {pi}");

    Console.WriteLine();
```

```
    // pi = ParallelPI();
    // Console.WriteLine($"Geometric approximation of PI calculated in parallel: {pi}");
}
```

This code calls the *SerialPI* method, which calculates pi by using the geometric algorithm described before this exercise. The value is returned as a *double* and displayed. The code that is currently commented out calls the *ParallelPI* method, which performs the same calculation but by using concurrent tasks. The result displayed should be the same as that returned by the *SerialPI* method.

5. Examine the *SerialPI* method.

```
static double SerialPI()
{
    List<double> pointsList = new List<double>();
    Random random = new Random(SEED);
    int numPointsInCircle = 0;
    Stopwatch timer = new Stopwatch();
    timer.Start();

    try
    {
        // TO DO:  Implement the geometric approximation of PI
        return 0;
    }
    finally
    {
        long milliseconds = timer.ElapsedMilliseconds;
        Console.WriteLine($"SerialPI complete: Duration: {milliseconds} ms",);
        Console.WriteLine(
            $"Points in pointsList: {pointsList.Count}. Points within circle:
{numPointsInCircle}");
    }
}
```

This method generates a large set of coordinates and calculates the distances of each set of coordinates from the origin. The size of the set is specified by the constant *NUMPOINTS* at the top of the *Program* class. The bigger this value is, the greater the set of coordinates and the more accurate the value of pi calculated by this method. If your computer has sufficient memory, you can increase the value of *NUMPOINTS*. Similarly, if you find that the application throws *OutOfMemoryException* exceptions when you run it, you can reduce this value.

You store the distance of each point from the origin in the *pointsList List<double>* collection. The data for the coordinates is generated by using the *random* variable. This is a *Random* object, seeded with a constant to generate the same set of random numbers each time you run the program. (This helps you determine that it is running correctly.) You can change the *SEED* constant at the top of the *Program* class if you want to seed the random number generator with a different value.

You use the *numPointsInCircle* variable to count the number of points in the *pointsList* collection that lie within the bounds of the circle. The radius of the circle is specified by the *RADIUS* constant at the top of the *Program* class.

To help you compare performance between this method and the *ParallelPI* method, the code creates a *Stopwatch* variable called *timer* and starts it running. The *finally* block determines how long the calculation took and displays the result. For reasons that will be described later, the *finally* block also displays the number of items in the *pointsList* collection and the number of points that it found that lie within the circle.

You will add the code that actually performs the calculation to the *try* block in the next few steps.

6. In the *try* block, delete the comment and remove the *return* statement. (This statement was provided only to ensure that the code compiles.) Add to the *try* block the *for* block and statements shown in bold in the following code:

```
try
{
    for (int points = 0; points < NUMPOINTS; points++)
    {
        int xCoord = random.Next(RADIUS);
        int yCoord = random.Next(RADIUS);
        double distanceFromOrigin = Math.Sqrt(xCoord * xCoord + yCoord * yCoord);
        pointsList.Add(distanceFromOrigin);
        doAdditionalProcessing();
    }
}
```

This block of code generates a pair of coordinate values that lie in the range 0 to *RADIUS*, and it stores them in the *xCoord* and *yCoord* variables. The code then employs Pythagoras's theorem to calculate the distance of these coordinates from the origin and adds the result to the *pointsList* collection.

> **Note** Although there is a little bit of computational work performed by this block of code, in a real-world scientific application you are likely to include far more complex calculations that will keep the processor occupied for longer. To simulate this situation, this block of code calls another method, *doAdditionalProcessing*. All this method does is occupy a number of CPU cycles as shown in the following code sample. I opted to follow this approach to better demonstrate the data synchronization requirements of multiple tasks rather than have you write an application that performs a highly complex calculation such as a fast Fourier transform (FFT) to keep the CPU busy:
>
> ```
> private static void doAdditionalProcessing()
> {
>     Thread.SpinWait(SPINWAITS);
> }
> ```
>
> *SPINWAITS* is another constant defined at the top of the *Program* class.

7. In the *SerialPI* method, in the *try* block, after the *for* block, add the *foreach* statement shown in bold in the following example.

```
try
{
    for (int points = 0; points < NUMPOINTS; points++)
    {
        ...
    }

    foreach (double datum in pointsList)
    {
        if (datum <= RADIUS)
        {
            numPointsInCircle++;
        }
    }
}
```

This code iterates through the *pointsList* collection and examines each value in turn. If the value is less than or equal to the radius of the circle, it increments the *numPointsInCircle* variable. At the end of this loop, *numPointsInCircle* should contain the total number of coordinates that were found to lie within the bounds of the circle.

8. After the *foreach* statement, add to the *try* block the following statements shown in bold:

```
try
{
    for (int points = 0; points < NUMPOINTS; points++)
    {
        ...
    }

    foreach (double datum in pointsList)
    {
        ...
    }

    double pi = 4.0 * numPointsInCircle / NUMPOINTS;
    return pi;
}
```

The first statement calculates pi based on the ratio of the number of points that lie within the circle to the total number of points, using the formula described earlier. The value is returned as the result of the method.

9. On the Debug menu, click Start Without Debugging.

The program runs and displays its approximation of pi, as shown in the following image. (It took just over 46 seconds on my computer, so be prepared to wait for a little while.) The time taken to calculate the result also appears.

```
C:\Windows\system32\cmd.exe

SerialPI complete: Duration: 48567 ms
Points in pointsList: 10000000. Points within circle: 7853722
Geometric approximation of PI calculated serially: 3.1414888

Press any key to continue . . .
```

> **Note** Apart from the timing, your results should be the same unless you have
> changed the *NUMPOINTS*, *RADIUS*, or *SEED* constants.

10. Close the console window, and return to Visual Studio.

In the *SerialPI* method, the code in the *for* loop that generates the points and calculates their
distance from the origin is an obvious area that can be parallelized. This is what you will do in the
next exercise.

Calculate pi by using parallel tasks

1. In Solution Explorer, double-click Program.cs to display the file in the Code and Text Editor
window if it is not already open.

2. Locate the *ParallelPI* method. It contains the same code as the initial version of the *SerialPI*
method before you added the code to the *try* block to calculate pi.

3. In the *try* block, delete the comment and remove the *return* statement. Add the *Parallel.For*
statement shown here in bold to the *try* block:

```
try
{
    Parallel.For (0, NUMPOINTS, (x) =>
    {
        int xCoord = random.Next(RADIUS);
        int yCoord = random.Next(RADIUS);
        double distanceFromOrigin = Math.Sqrt(xCoord * xCoord + yCoord * yCoord);
        pointsList.Add(distanceFromOrigin);
        doAdditionalProcessing();
    });
}
```

This construct is the parallel analog of the code in the *for* loop in the *SerialPI* method.
The body of the original *for* loop is wrapped in a lambda expression. Remember that each
iteration of the loop is performed by using a task, and tasks can run in parallel. The degree
of parallelism depends on the number of processor cores and other resources available on
your computer.

4. Add the following code shown in bold to the *try* block, after the *Parallel.For* statement. This
code is the same as the corresponding statements in the *SerialPI* method.

```
    try
    {
        Parallel.For (...
        {
            ...
        });

        foreach (double datum in pointsList)
        {
            if (datum <= RADIUS)
            {
                numPointsInCircle++;
            }
        }

        double pi = 4.0 * numPointsInCircle / NUMPOINTS;
        return pi;
    }
```

5. In the *Main* method near the end of the Program.cs file, uncomment the code that calls the *ParallelPI* method and the *Console.WriteLine* statement that displays the results.

6. On the Debug menu, click Start Without Debugging.

    The program runs. The following image shows the typical output (your timings might be different; I was using a quad-core processor):

    The value calculated by the *SerialPI* method should be exactly as before, but the result of the *ParallelPI* method actually looks a little suspect. The random number generator is seeded with the same value as that used by the *SerialPI* method, so it should produce the same sequence of random numbers with the same result and the same number of points within the circle. Another curious point is that the *pointsList* collection in the *ParallelPI* method seems to contain fewer points than the same collection in the *SerialPI* method.

    Note If the *pointsList* collection actually contains the expected number of items, run the application again. You should find that it contains fewer items than expected in most (but not necessarily all) runs.

7. Close the console window, and return to Visual Studio.

What went wrong with the parallel calculation? A good place to start is the number of items in the *pointsList* collection. This collection is a generic *List<double>* object. However, this type is not thread safe. The code in the *Parallel.For* statement calls the *Add* method to append a value to the collection, but remember that this code is being executed by tasks running as concurrent threads. Consequently, given the number of items being added to the collection, it is highly probable that some of the calls to *Add* will interfere with one another and cause some corruption. A solution is to use one of the collections from the *System.Collections.Concurrent* namespace because these collections are thread safe. The generic *ConcurrentBag<T>* class in this namespace is probably the most suitable collection to use for this example.

Use a thread-safe collection

1. In Solution Explorer, double-click Program.cs to display the file in the Code and Text Editor window if it is not already open.

2. Add the following *using* directive to the list at the top of the file:

   ```
   using System.Collections.Concurrent;
   ```

3. Locate the *ParallelPI* method. At the start of this method, replace the statement that instantiates the *List<double>* collection with code that creates a *ConcurrentBag<double>* collection, as shown in bold in the following code example:

   ```
   static double ParallelPI()
   {
       ConcurrentBag<double> pointsList = new ConcurrentBag<double>();
       Random random = ...;
       ...
   }
   ```

   Notice that you cannot specify a default capacity for this class, so the constructor does not take a parameter.

   You do not need to change any other code in this method; you add an item to a *ConcurrentBag<T>* collection by using the *Add* method, which is the same mechanism that you use to add an item to a *List<T>* collection.

4. On the Debug menu, click Start Without Debugging.

   The program runs and displays its approximation of pi by using the *SerialPI* and *ParallelPI* methods. The following image shows the typical output.

   ```
   C:\Windows\system32\cmd.exe
   SerialPI complete: Duration: 50004 ms
   Points in pointsList: 10000000. Points within circle: 7853722
   Geometric approximation of PI calculated serially: 3.1414888

   ParallelPI complete: Duration: 15129 ms
   Points in pointsList: 10000000. Points within circle: 9965637
   Geometric approximation of PI calculated in parallel: 3.9862548
   Press any key to continue . . . _
   ```

This time, the *pointsList* collection in the *ParallelPI* method contains the correct number of points, but the number of points within the circle still appears to be very high; it should be the same as that reported by the *SerialPI* method.

You should also note that the time taken by the *ParallelPI* method has increased compared with the previous exercise. This is because the methods in the *ConcurrentBag<T>* class have to lock and unlock data to guarantee thread safety, and this process adds to the overhead of calling these methods. Keep this point in mind when you're considering whether it is appropriate to parallelize an operation.

5. Close the console window, and return to Visual Studio.

You currently have the correct number of points in the *pointsList* collection, but the value recorded for each of these points is now questionable. The code in the *Parallel.For* construct calls the *Next* method of a *Random* object, but like the methods in the generic *List<T>* class, this method is not thread safe. Sadly, there is no concurrent version of the *Random* class, so you must resort to using an alternative technique to serialize calls to the *Next* method. Because each invocation is relatively brief, it makes sense to use a simple lock to guard calls to this method.

Use a lock to serialize method calls

1. In Solution Explorer, double-click Program.cs to display the file in the Code and Text Editor window if it is not already open.

2. Locate the *ParallelPI* method. Modify the code in the lambda expression in the *Parallel.For* statement to protect the calls to *random.Next* by using a *lock* statement. Specify the *pointsList* collection as the subject of the lock, as shown here in bold:

```
static double ParallelPI()
{
    ...
    Parallel.For(0, NUMPOINTS, (x) =>
    {
        int xCoord;
        int yCoord;

        lock(pointsList)
        {
            xCoord = random.Next(RADIUS);
            yCoord = random.Next(RADIUS);
        }

        double distanceFromOrigin = Math.Sqrt(xCoord * xCoord + yCoord * yCoord);
        pointsList.Add(distanceFromOrigin);
        doAdditionalProcessing();
    });

    ...
}
```

Notice that the *xCoord* and *yCoord* variables are declared outside the *lock* statement. You do this because the *lock* statement defines its own scope, and any variables defined within the block specifying the scope of the *lock* statement disappear when the construct exits.

3. On the Debug menu, click Start Without Debugging.

   This time, the values of pi calculated by the *SerialPI* and *ParallelPI* methods are the same. The only difference is that the *ParallelPI* method runs more quickly.

```
C:\Windows\system32\cmd.exe
SerialPI complete: Duration: 51366 ms
Points in pointsList: 10000000. Points within circle: 7853722
Geometric approximation of PI calculated serially: 3.1414888

ParallelPI complete: Duration: 15736 ms
Points in pointsList: 10000000. Points within circle: 7853722
Geometric approximation of PI calculated in parallel: 3.1414888
Press any key to continue . . . _
```

4. Close the console window, and return to Visual Studio.

Summary

In this chapter, you saw how to define asynchronous methods by using the *async* modifier and the *await* operator. Asynchronous methods are based on tasks, and the *await* operator specifies the points at which a task can be used to perform asynchronous processing.

You also learned a little about PLINQ and how you can use the *AsParallel* extension method to parallelize some LINQ queries. However, PLINQ is a big subject in its own right, and this chapter has only shown you how to get started. For more information, see the topic "Parallel LINQ (PLINQ)" in the documentation provided with Visual Studio.

This chapter also showed you how to synchronize data access in concurrent tasks by using the synchronization primitives provided for use with tasks. You saw how to use the concurrent collection classes to maintain collections of data in a thread-safe manner.

- If you want to continue to the next chapter, keep Visual Studio 2015 running and turn to Chapter 25, "Implementing the user interface for a Universal Windows Platform app."

- If you want to exit Visual Studio 2015 now, on the File menu, click Exit. If you see a Save dialog box, click Yes and save the project.

Quick reference

To	Do this
Implement an asynchronous method	Define the method with the *async* modifier and change the type of the method to return a *Task* (or a *void*). In the body of the method, use the *await* operator to specify points at which asynchronous processing can be performed. For example: ```\nprivate async Task<int> calculateValueAsync(...)\n{\n // Invoke calculateValue using a Task\n Task<int> generateResultTask =\n Task.Run(() => calculateValue(...));\n await generateResultTask;\n return generateResultTask.Result;\n}\n```
Parallelize a LINQ query	Specify the *AsParallel* extension method with the data source in the query. For example: ```\nvar over100 = from n in numbers.AsParallel()\n where ...\n select n;\n```
Enable cancellation in a PLINQ query	Use the *WithCancellation* method of the *ParallelQuery* class in the PLINQ query and specify a cancellation token. For example: ```\nCancellationToken tok = ...;\n...\nvar orderInfoQuery = from c in\n CustomersInMemory.Customers.AsParallel().\n WithCancellation(tok)\n join o in OrdersInMemory.Orders.AsParallel()\n on ...\n```
Synchronize one or more tasks to implement thread-safe exclusive access to shared data	Use the *lock* statement to guarantee exclusive access to the data. For example: ```\nobject myLockObject = new object();\n...\nlock (myLockObject)\n{\n // Code that requires exclusive access to a\nshared resource\n ...\n}\n```
Synchronize threads and make them wait for an event	Use a *ManualResetEventSlim* object to synchronize an indeterminate number of threads. Use a *CountdownEvent* object to wait for an event to be signaled a specified number of times. Use a *Barrier* object to coordinate a specified number of threads and synchronize them at a particular point in an operation.
Synchronize access to a shared pool of resources	Use a *SemaphoreSlim* object. Specify the number of items in the pool in the constructor. Call the *Wait* method prior to accessing a resource in the shared pool. Call the *Release* method when you have finished with the resource. For example: ```\nSemaphoreSlim semaphore = new SemaphoreSlim(3);\n...\nsemaphore.Wait();\n// Access a resource from the pool\n...\nsemaphore.Release();\n```

To	Do this
Provide exclusive write access to a resource but shared read access	Use a *ReaderWriterLockSlim* object. Prior to reading the shared resource, call the *EnterReadLock* method. Call the *ExitReadLock* method when you have finished. Before writing to the shared resource, call the *EnterWriteLock* method. Call the *ExitWriteLock* method when you have completed the write operation. For example: ```csharp\nReaderWriterLockSlim readerWriterLock = new\nReaderWriterLockSlim();\n\nTask readerTask = Task.Factory.StartNew(() =>\n {\n readerWriterLock.EnterReadLock();\n // Read shared resource\n readerWriterLock.ExitReadLock();\n });\n\nTask writerTask = Task.Factory.StartNew(() =>\n {\n readerWriterLock.EnterWriteLock();\n // Write to shared resource\n readerWriterLock.ExitWriteLock();\n });\n```
Cancel a blocking wait operation	Create a cancellation token from a *CancellationTokenSource* object, and specify this token as a parameter to the wait operation. To cancel the wait operation, call the *Cancel* method of the *CancellationTokenSource* object. For example: ```csharp\nCancellationTokenSource cancellationTokenSource = new\nCancellationTokenSource();\nCancellationToken cancellationToken =\ncancellationTokenSource.Token;\n...\n// Semaphore that protects a pool of 3 resources\nSemaphoreSlim semaphoreSlim = new SemaphoreSlim(3);\n...\n// Wait on the semaphore, and throw an\nOperationCanceledException if\n// another thread calls Cancel on\ncancellationTokenSource\nsemaphore.Wait(cancellationToken);\n```

CHAPTER 25

Implementing the user interface for a Universal Windows Platform app

After completing the chapter, you will be able to:

- Describe the features of a typical Universal Windows Platform app.

- Implement a scalable user interface for a Universal Windows Platform app that can adapt to different form factors and device orientations.

- Create and apply styles to a Universal Windows Platform app.

Recent versions of Windows have introduced a platform for building and running highly interactive applications with continuously connected, touch-driven user interfaces and support for embedded device sensors. An updated application security and life-cycle model changed the way that users and applications work together. This platform is called the Windows Runtime (WinRT), and I have referred to it occasionally throughout this book. You can use Visual Studio to build WinRT applications that can adapt themselves to a variety of device form factors, ranging from handheld tablets to desktop PCs with large, high-resolution screens. Using Windows 8 and Visual Studio 2013, you could also publish these applications in the Windows Store as Windows Store apps.

Separately, you could use the Windows Phone SDK 8.0 (integrated into Visual Studio) to design and implement applications that run on Windows Phone 8 devices. These applications share many similarities with their tablet and desktop-oriented siblings, but they operate in a more restricted environment, typically with fewer resources and a requirement to support a different user interface layout. Consequently, Windows Phone 8 applications use a different version of the WinRT, called the Windows Phone Runtime, and you can market Windows Phone 8 applications as Windows Phone Store apps. You could create a class library with which to share application and business logic between a Windows tablet/desktop application and a Windows Phone 8 application by using the Portable Class Library template in Visual Studio, but Windows Store apps and Windows Phone Store apps are distinct beasts with differences in the features that they can make available.

Subsequently, Microsoft sought to converge these platforms and reduce the number of differences. This strategy has culminated in Windows 10 with Universal Windows Platform apps. A Universal Windows Platform app uses an amended version of WinRT called the Universal Windows Platform

(UWP). Using the UWP, you can build applications that will run on the widest range of Windows 10 devices without the need to maintain separate code bases. In addition to many phones, tablets, and desktop computers, UWP is also available on Xbox.

> **Note** The UWP defines a core set of features and functionality. The UWP divides devices into device families: the desktop device family, the mobile device family, the Xbox device family, and so on. Each device family defines the set of APIs and devices on which those APIs are implemented. Additionally, the Universal device family defines a core set of features and functionality that is available across all device families. The libraries available for each device family include conditional methods that enable an app to test on which device family it is currently running.

The purpose of this chapter is to provide a brief description of the concepts that underpin the UWP and to help you get started using Visual Studio 2015 to build apps that operate in this environment. In this chapter, you will learn about some of the features and tools included with Visual Studio 2015 for building UWP apps, and you will construct an app that conforms to the Windows 10 look and feel. You will concentrate on learning how to implement a user interface (UI) that scales and adapts to different device resolutions and form factors, and how to apply styling to give the app a distinctive look and feel. Subsequent chapters will focus on the functionality and other features of the app.

> **Note** There is not enough space in a book such as this to provide a comprehensive treatise on building UWP apps. Rather, these final chapters concentrate on the basic principles of building an interactive app that uses the Windows 10 UI. For detailed information on writing UWP apps, visit the "Guide to Universal Windows Platform (UWP) apps" page on the Microsoft website at *https://msdn.microsoft.com/library/dn894631.aspx*.

Features of a Universal Windows Platform app

Many modern handheld and tablet devices make it possible for users to interact with apps by using touch. You should design your UWP apps based on this style of user experience (UX). Windows 10 includes an extensive collection of touch-based controls that also work with a mouse and keyboard. You don't need to separate the touch and mouse features in your apps; simply design your apps for touch, and users can still operate them by using the mouse and keyboard if they prefer or when they are using a device that does not support touch interaction.

The way in which the graphical user interface (GUI) responds to gestures to provide feedback to the user can greatly enhance the professional feel of your apps. The UWP app templates included with Visual Studio 2015 include an animation library that you can use in your apps to standardize this feedback and blend in seamlessly with the operating system and software that Microsoft provides.

Note The term *gesture* refers to the manual touch-oriented operations that a user can perform. For example, a user can tap an item with a finger, and this gesture typically responds in the same way that you would expect a mouse click to behave. However, gestures can be far more expressive than the simple operations that can be captured by using a mouse. For example, the rotate gesture involves the user placing two fingers on the screen and tracing the arc of a circle with them; in a typical Windows 10 app, this gesture should cause the UI to rotate the selected object in the direction indicated by the movement of the user's fingers. Other gestures include pinching to zoom in on an item to display more detail, pressing and holding to reveal more information about an item (similar to right-clicking the mouse click), and sliding to select an item and drag it across the screen.

The UWP is intended to run on a wide range of devices with varying screen sizes and resolutions. Therefore, when you implement a UWP app, you need to construct your software so that it adapts to the environment in which it is running, scaling automatically to the screen size and orientation of the device. This approach opens your software to an increasingly broad market. Additionally, many modern devices can also detect their orientation and the speed at which the user changes this orientation through the use of built-in sensors and accelerometers. UWP apps can adapt their layout as the user tilts or rotates a device, making it possible for the user to work in a mode that is most comfortable for that individual. You should also understand that mobility is a key requirement for many modern apps, and with UWP apps, users can roam and their data can migrate through the cloud to whatever device they happen to be running your app on at a particular moment.

The lifetime of a UWP app is somewhat different from that of a traditional desktop app. You should design apps that can run on devices such as smartphones to suspend execution when the user switches focus to another app and then to resume running when the focus returns. This approach can help to conserve resources and battery life on a constrained device. Windows might actually decide to close a suspended app if it determines that it needs to release system resources such as memory. When the app next runs, it should be able to resume where it left off. This means that you need to be prepared to manage app state information in your code, save it to hard disk, and restore it at the appropriate juncture.

Note You can find more information about how to manage the life cycle of a UWP app at the page "Guidelines for app suspend and resume" on the Microsoft website at *https://msdn.microsoft.com/library/windows/apps/hh465088.aspx*.

When you build a new UWP app, you can package it by using the tools provided with Visual Studio 2015 and upload it to the Windows Store. Other users can then connect to the Store, download your app, and install it. You can charge a fee for your apps, or you can make them available at no cost. This distribution and deployment mechanism depends on your apps being trustworthy and conforming to security policies specified by Microsoft. When you upload an app to the Windows Store, it undergoes a number of checks to verify that it does not contain malicious code and that it conforms to the security requirements of a UWP app. These security constraints dictate how your app accesses resources on the computer on which it is installed. For example, by default a UWP app cannot write directly to the file system or listen for incoming requests from the network (two of the behaviors commonly exhibited by viruses and other malware). However, if your app needs to perform restricted operations, you can specify them as capabilities in the app's manifest data held in the Package.appxmanifest file. This information is recorded in the metadata of your app and signals Microsoft to perform additional tests to verify the way in which your app uses these features.

The Package.appxmanifest file is an XML document, but you can edit it in Visual Studio by using the Manifest Designer. The following image shows an example. Here, the Capabilities tab is being used to specify the restricted operations that the application can perform.

In this example, the application declares that it needs to:

- Receive incoming data from the Internet but cannot act as a server and has no local network access.

- Read and write files held in the user's Documents folder.

- Access GPS information that provides information about the location of the device.

- Access the video feed of a built-in camera or external webcam.

The user is made aware of these requirements, and in all cases the user can disable the settings after installing the app; the application must detect when this has occurred and be prepared to fall back to an alternative solution or disable the functionality that requires these features.

Note You can find more information about the capabilities that UWP apps support on the "App capability declarations" page on the Microsoft website at *http://msdn.microsoft.com/library/windows/apps/hh464936.aspx*.

Enough theory—let's get started building a UWP app.

Using the Blank App template to build a Universal Windows Platform app

The simplest way to build a UWP app is to use the UWP app templates included with Visual Studio 2015 on Windows 10. Many of the GUI-based applications implemented in earlier chapters have made use of the Blank App template, and this is a good place to start.

In the following exercises, you will design the user interface for a simple app for a fictitious company called Adventure Works. This company manufactures and supplies bicycles and associated paraphernalia. The app will enable a user to enter and modify the details of Adventure Works's customers.

Create the Adventure Works Customers app

1. Start Visual Studio 2015 if it is not already running.

2. On the File menu, point to New, and then click Project.

3. In the New Project dialog box, in the left pane, expand Templates, expand Visual C#, expand Windows, and then click Universal.

4. In the middle pane, click the Blank App (Windows Universal) icon.

5. In the Name field, type **Customers**.

6. In the Location field, type **\Microsoft Press\VCSBS\Chapter 25** in your Documents folder.

7. Click OK.

   The new app is created, and the App.xaml.cs file is displayed in the Code and Text Editor window. You can ignore this file for the time being.

8. In Solution Explorer, double-click MainPage.xaml.

   The Design View window appears and displays a blank page. You can drag controls from the Toolbox to add the various controls required by the app, as demonstrated in Chapter 1, "Welcome to C#." However, for the purposes of this exercise, it is more instructive to concentrate on the XAML markup that defines the layout for the form. If you examine this markup, it should look like this:

```
<Page
    x:Class="Customers.MainPage"
    xmlns="http://schemas.microsoft.com/winfx/2006/xaml/presentation"
    xmlns:x="http://schemas.microsoft.com/winfx/2006/xaml"
    xmlns:local="using:Customers"
    xmlns:d="http://schemas.microsoft.com/expression/blend/2008"
    xmlns:mc="http://schemas.openxmlformats.org/markup-compatibility/2006"
    mc:Ignorable="d">

    <Grid Background="{ThemeResource ApplicationPageBackgroundThemeBrush}">

    </Grid>
</Page>
```

The form starts with the XAML *<Page>* tag and finishes with a closing *</Page>* tag. Everything between these tags defines the content of the page.

The attributes of the *<Page>* tag contain a number of declarations of the form *xmlns:id = "..."*. These are XAML namespace declarations, and they operate in a similar manner to C# *using* directives inasmuch as they bring items into scope. Many of the controls and other items that you can add to a page are defined in these XAML namespaces, and you can ignore most of these declarations. However, there is one rather curious-looking declaration to which you should pay attention:

```
xmlns:local="using:Customers"
```

This declaration brings the items in the C# *Customers* namespace into scope. You can reference classes and other types in this namespace in your XAML code by prefixing them with *local*. The *Customers* namespace is the namespace generated for the code in your app.

9. In Solution Explorer, expand MainPage.xaml, and then double-click MainPage.xaml.cs to display it in the Code and Text Editor window.

10. Remember from the exercises earlier in this book that this is the C# file that contains the app logic and event handlers for the form. It looks like this (the *using* directives at the top of the file have been omitted to save space):

```
// The Blank Page item template is documented at  http://go.microsoft.com/fwlink/?LinkId
=402352&clcid=0x409

namespace Customers
{
    /// <summary>
    /// An empty page that can be used on its own or navigated to within a Frame.
    /// </summary>
    public sealed partial class MainPage : Page
    {
        public MainPage()
        {
            this.InitializeComponent();
        }
    }
}
```

This file defines the types in the *Customers* namespace. The page is implemented by a class called *MainPage*, and it inherits from the *Page* class. The *Page* class implements the default functionality of a XAML page for a UWP app, so all you have to do is write the code that defines the logic specific to your app in the *MainPage* class.

11. Return to the MainPage.xaml file in the Design View window. If you look at the XAML markup for the page, you should notice that the *<Page>* tag includes the following attribute:

```
x:Class="Customers.MainPage"
```

This attribute connects the XAML markup that defines the layout of the page to the *MainPage* class that provides the logic behind the page.

That's the basic plumbing of a simple UWP app. Of course, what makes a graphical app valuable is the way in which it presents information to a user. This is not always as simple as it sounds. Designing an attractive and easy-to-use graphical interface requires specialist skills that not all developers have (I know, because I lack them myself). However, many graphic artists who do have these skills are not programmers, so although they might be able to design a wonderful user interface, they might not be able to implement the logic required to make it useful. Fortunately, Visual Studio 2015 makes it possible for you to separate the user interface design from the business logic so that a graphic artist and a developer can cooperate to build a really cool-looking app that also works well. All a developer has to do is concentrate on the basic layout of the app and let a graphic artist provide the styling.

Implementing a scalable user interface

The key to laying out the user interface for a UWP app is to understand how to make it scale and adapt to the different form factors available for the devices on which users might run the app. In the following exercises, you will investigate how to achieve this scaling.

Lay out the page for the Customers app

1. In the toolbar at the top of the Design View window, notice the drop-down list box that enables you to select the resolution and form factor of the design surface and a pair of buttons that enable you to select the orientation (portrait or landscape) for devices that support rotations (tablets and phones do; desktops don't). The intent is that you can use these options to quickly see how a user interface will appear on different devices.

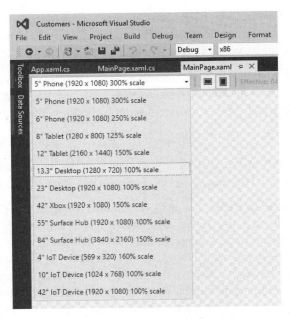

The default layout is for a smartphone with a 5-inch screen in the portrait orientation. In the drop-down list box, select 13.3" Desktop (1280 x 720) 100% scale. Note that this form factor defaults to the landscape orientation.

2. Review the XAML markup for the MainPage page.

The page contains a single *Grid* control:

```
<Grid Background="{ThemeResource ApplicationPageBackgroundThemeBrush}">

</Grid>
```

 Note Don't worry about the way in which the *Background* property is specified for the *Grid* control. This is an example of using a style, and you will learn about using styles later in this chapter.

Understanding how the *Grid* control works is fundamental to building scalable and flexible user interfaces. The *Page* element can contain only a single item, and if you want, you can replace the *Grid* control with a *Button*, as shown in the example that follows:

Note Don't type the following code. It is shown for illustrative purposes only.

```
<Page
   ...
   <Button Content="Click Me"/>
</Page>
```

However, the resulting app is probably not very useful—a form that contains a button and that displays nothing else is unlikely to win an award as the world's greatest app. If you attempt to add a second control, such as a *TextBox*, to the page, your code will not compile and the errors shown in the following image will occur:

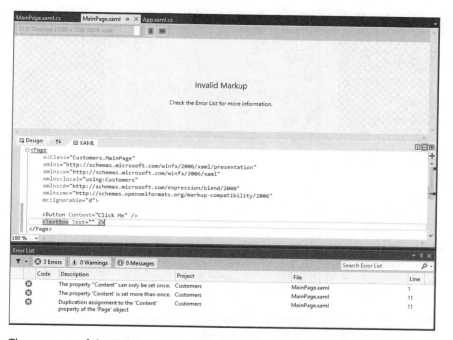

The purpose of the *Grid* control is to facilitate adding multiple items to a page. The *Grid* control is an example of a container control; it can contain a number of other controls, and you can specify the position of these other controls within the grid. Other container controls are also available. For example, the *StackPanel* control automatically places the controls it contains in a vertical arrangement, with each control positioned directly below its immediate predecessor.

In this app, you will use a *Grid* to hold the controls necessary for a user to be able to enter and view data for a customer.

3. Add a *TextBlock* control to the page, either by dragging it from the Toolbox or by typing the text **<TextBlock />** directly into the XAML pane, on the blank line after the opening *<Grid>* tag, like this:

```
<Grid Background="{ThemeResource ApplicationPageBackgroundThemeBrush}">
    <TextBlock />
</Grid>
```

> **Tip** if the Toolbox does not appear, click Toolbox on the View menu, and it should be displayed in the toolbar to the left. Also, note that you can type the code for a

control directly into the XAML window for a page; you do not have to drag controls from the Toolbox.

4. This *TextBlock* provides the title for the page. Set the properties of the *TextBlock* control by using the values in the following table:

Property	Value
HorizontalAlignment	Left
Margin	400,90,0,0
TextWrapping	Wrap
Text	Adventure Works Customers
VerticalAlignment	Top
FontSize	50

You can set these properties by using the Properties window or by typing the equivalent XAML markup into the XAML window, as shown here in bold:

```
<TextBlock HorizontalAlignment="Left" Margin="400,90,0,0" TextWrapping="Wrap"
Text="Adventure Works Customers" VerticalAlignment="Top" FontSize="50"/>
```

The resulting text should appear in the Design View window, like this:

Notice that when you drag a control from the Toolbox to a form, connectors appear that specify the distance of two of the sides of the control from the edge of the container control in which it is placed. In the preceding example, these connectors for the *TextBlock* control are labeled with the values 400 (from the left edge of the grid) and 90 (from the top edge of the grid). At run time, if the *Grid* control is resized, the *TextBlock* will move to retain these distances, which in this case might cause the distance of the *TextBlock* in pixels from the right and bottom edges of the *Grid* to change. You can specify the edge or edges to which a control is anchored by setting the *HorizontalAlignment* and *VerticalAlignment* properties. The *Margin* property specifies the distance from the anchored edges. Again, in this example, the *HorizontalAlignment* property of the *TextBlock* is set to *Left* and the *VerticalAlignment* property is set to *Top*, which is why the control is anchored to the left and top edges of the grid. The *Margin* property contains four values that specify the distance of the left, top, right, and bottom sides (in that order) of the control from the corresponding edge of the container. If one side of a control is not anchored to an edge of the container, you can set the corresponding value in the *Margin* property to *0*.

5. Add four more *TextBlock* controls to the page. These *TextBlock* controls are labels that help the user identify the data that is displayed on the page. Use the values in the following table to set the properties of these controls:

Control	Property	Value
First *Label*	HorizontalAlignment	Left
	Margin	330,190,0,0
	TextWrapping	Wrap
	Text	ID
	VerticalAlignment	Top
	FontSize	20
Second *Label*	HorizontalAlignment	Left
	Margin	460,190,0,0
	TextWrapping	Wrap
	Text	Title
	VerticalAlignment	Top
	FontSize	20
Third *Label*	HorizontalAlignment	Left
	Margin	620,190,0,0
	TextWrapping	Wrap
	Text	First Name
	VerticalAlignment	Top
	FontSize	20
Fourth *Label*	HorizontalAlignment	Left
	Margin	975,190,0,0
	TextWrapping	Wrap
	Text	Last Name
	VerticalAlignment	Top
	FontSize	20

As before, you can either drag the controls from the Toolbox and use the Properties window to set their properties, or you can type the following XAML markup into the XAML pane, after the existing *TextBlock* control and before the closing *</Grid>* tag:

```
<TextBlock HorizontalAlignment="Left" Margin="330,190,0,0" TextWrapping="Wrap"
Text="ID" VerticalAlignment="Top" FontSize="20"/>
<TextBlock HorizontalAlignment="Left" Margin="460,190,0,0" TextWrapping="Wrap"
Text="Title" VerticalAlignment="Top" FontSize="20"/>
<TextBlock HorizontalAlignment="Left" Margin="620,190,0,0" TextWrapping="Wrap"
Text="First Name" VerticalAlignment="Top" FontSize="20"/>
<TextBlock HorizontalAlignment="Left" Margin="975,190,0,0" TextWrapping="Wrap"
Text="Last Name" VerticalAlignment="Top" FontSize="20"/>
```

6. Below the *TextBlock* controls, add three *TextBox* controls that display the text ID, First Name, and Last Name. Use the following table to set the values of these controls. Notice that the *Text* property should be set to the empty string (""). Also notice that the *id TextBox* control is marked as read-only. This is because customer IDs will be generated automatically in the code that you add later:

Control	Property	Value
First *TextBox*	x:Name	id
	HorizontalAlignment	Left
	Margin	300,240,0,0
	TextWrapping	Wrap
	Text	
	VerticalAlignment	Top
	FontSize	20
	IsReadOnly	True
Second *TextBox*	x:Name	firstName
	HorizontalAlignment	Left
	Margin	550,240,0,0
	TextWrapping	Wrap
	Text	
	VerticalAlignment	Top
	FontSize	20
Third *TextBox*	x:Name	lastName
	HorizontalAlignment	Left
	Margin	875,240,0,0
	TextWrapping	Wrap
	Text	
	VerticalAlignment	Top
	FontSize	20

The following code shows the equivalent XAML markup for these controls:

```
<TextBox x:Name="id" HorizontalAlignment="Left" Margin="300,240,0,0" TextWrapping="Wrap"
Text="" VerticalAlignment="Top" FontSize="20" IsReadOnly="True"/>
<TextBox x:Name="firstName" HorizontalAlignment="Left" Margin="550,240,0,0"
TextWrapping="Wrap" Text="" VerticalAlignment="Top" Width="300" FontSize="20"/>
<TextBox x:Name="lastName" HorizontalAlignment="Left" Margin="875,240,0,0"
TextWrapping="Wrap" Text="" VerticalAlignment="Top" Width="300" FontSize="20"/>
```

The *Name* property is not required for a control, but it is useful if you want to refer to the control in the C# code for the app. Notice that the *Name* property is prefixed with *x:*. This is a reference to the XML namespace *http://schemas.microsoft.com/winfx/2006/xaml* specified in the *Page* attributes at the top of the XAML markup. This namespace defines the *Name* property for all controls.

> **Note** It is not necessary to understand why the *Name* property is defined this way, but for more information, you can read the article "x:Name Directive" at *http://msdn.microsoft.com/library/ms752290.aspx*.

The *Width* property specifies the width of the control, and the *TextWrapping* property indicates what happens if the user attempts to enter information into the control that exceeds its width. In this case, all the *TextBox* controls will wrap the text onto another line of the same width (the control will expand vertically). The alternative value, *NoWrap*, causes the text to scroll horizontally as the user enters it.

7. Add a *ComboBox* control to the form, placing it below the *Title TextBlock* control, between the *id* and *firstName TextBox* controls. Set the properties of this control as follows:

Property	Value
x:Name	title
HorizontalAlignment	Left
Margin	420,240,0,0
VerticalAlignment	Top
Width	100
FontSize	20

The equivalent XAML markup for this control is as follows:

```
<ComboBox x:Name="title" HorizontalAlignment="Left" Margin="420,240,0,0"
VerticalAlignment="Top" Width="100" FontSize="20"/>
```

You use a *ComboBox* control to display a list of values from which the user can select.

8. In the Design View window, click the ComboBox control. In the Properties window, expand the Common property category if it is not already expanded. Then, click the ellipsis button that appears alongside the Items property.

The Object Collection Editor window opens.

9. In the list toward the lower left of the window, select ComboBoxItem, and then click Add. In the right pane displaying the properties for the item, expand the Common section if it is not already expanded, and then type **Mr** in the Content property.

10. Click OK.

The Object Collection Editor closes. If you examine the XAML markup for the *title ComboBox*, it should now look like this:

```
<ComboBox x:Name="title" HorizontalAlignment="Left" Margin="420,240,0,0"
  VerticalAlignment="Top" Width="100" FontSize="20"/>
    <ComboBoxItem Content="Mr"/>
</ComboBox>
```

There are two things to notice here. The first is that the *ComboBox* markup has been split into an opening *<ComboBox>* tag and a closing *</ComboBox>* tag. The second is that between these tags, Visual Studio has added a *ComboBoxItem* element with the *Content* property set to *Mr*. This item will be displayed in a drop-down list when the app runs.

11. Add the values *Mrs*, *Ms*, and *Miss* to the *title ComboBox*. You can use the Object Collection Editor or type the XAML markup by hand. The resulting markup should look like this:

```
<ComboBox x:Name="title" HorizontalAlignment="Left" Margin="420,240,0,0"
    VerticalAlignment="Top" Width="75" FontSize="20">
    <ComboBoxItem Content="Mr"/>
    <ComboBoxItem Content="Mrs"/>
    <ComboBoxItem Content="Ms"/>
    <ComboBoxItem Content="Miss"/>
</ComboBox>
```

> **Note** A *ComboBox* control can display simple elements such as a set of *ComboBoxItem* controls that display text, but it can also contain more complex elements such as buttons, check boxes, and radio buttons. If you are adding simple *ComboBoxItem* controls, it is probably easier to type the XAML markup by hand, but if you are adding more complex controls, the Object Collection Editor can prove very useful. However, you should avoid trying to be too clever in a combo box; the best apps are those that provide the most intuitive UIs, and embedding complex controls in a combo box can be confusing to a user.

12. Add two more *TextBox* controls and two more *TextBlock* controls to the form. With the *TextBox* controls, the user will be able to enter an email address and telephone number for the customer, and the *TextBlock* controls provide the labels for the text boxes. Use the values in the following table to set the properties of the controls.

Control	Property	Value
First *TextBlock*	HorizontalAlignment	Left
	Margin	300,390,0,0
	TextWrapping	Wrap
	Text	Email
	VerticalAlignment	Top
	FontSize	20
First *TextBox*	x:Name	email
	HorizontalAlignment	Left
	Margin	450,390,0,0
	TextWrapping	Wrap
	Text	Leave Empty
	VerticalAlignment	Top
	Width	400
	FontSize	20

Control	Property	Value
Second *TextBlock*	*HorizontalAlignment*	*Left*
	Margin	*300,540,0,0*
	TextWrapping	*Wrap*
	Text	*Phone*
	VerticalAlignment	*Top*
	FontSize	*20*
Second *TextBox*	*x:Name*	*phone*
	HorizontalAlignment	*Left*
	Margin	*450,540,0,0*
	TextWrapping	*Wrap*
	Text	*Leave Empty*
	VerticalAlignment	*Top*
	Width	*200*
	FontSize	*20*

The XAML markup for these controls should look like this:

```
<TextBlock HorizontalAlignment="Left" Margin="300,390,0,0" TextWrapping="Wrap"
Text="Email" VerticalAlignment="Top" FontSize="20"/>
<TextBox x:Name="email" HorizontalAlignment="Left" Margin="450,390,0,0"
TextWrapping="Wrap" Text="" VerticalAlignment="Top" Width="400" FontSize="20"/>
<TextBlock HorizontalAlignment="Left" Margin="300,540,0,0" TextWrapping="Wrap"
Text="Phone" VerticalAlignment="Top" FontSize="20"/>
<TextBox x:Name="phone" HorizontalAlignment="Left" Margin="450,540,0,0"
TextWrapping="Wrap" Text="" VerticalAlignment="Top" Width="200" FontSize="20"/>
```

The completed form in the Design View window should look like this:

13. On the Debug menu, click Start Debugging to build and run the app.

The app starts and displays the form. You can enter data into the form and select a title from the combo box, but you cannot do much else yet. However, a much bigger problem is that the form looks awful. The right side of the display has been cut off, much of the text has wrapped around, and the Last Name text box has been truncated:

14. Click and drag the right side of the window to expand the display so that the text and controls are displayed as they appeared in the Design View window in Visual Studio. This is the optimal size of the form as it was designed.

15. Resize the window displaying the Customer app to its minimum width. This time, much of the form disappears. Some of the *TextBlock* content wraps, but the form is clearly not usable in this view.

16. Return to Visual Studio, and on the Debug menu, click Stop Debugging.

That was a salutary lesson in being careful about how you lay out an app. Although the app looked fine when it ran in a window that was the same size as the Design View, as soon as you resized the window to a narrower view, it became less useful (or even completely useless). Additionally, the app assumes that the user will be viewing the screen on a device in the landscape orientation. If you temporarily switch the Design View window to the 12" Tablet form factor and click the Portrait orientation button, you can see what the form would look like if the user ran the app on a tablet that supports different orientations and rotated the device to switch to portrait mode. (Don't forget to switch back to the 13.3" Desktop form factor afterward.)

The issue is that the layout technique shown so far does not scale and adapt to different form factors and orientations. Fortunately, you can use the properties of the *Grid* control and another feature called the Visual State Manager to solve these problems.

Using the Simulator to test a Universal Windows Platform app

Even if you don't have a tablet computer, you can still test your UWP apps and see how they behave on a mobile device by using the Simulator provided with Visual Studio 2015. The Simulator mimics a tablet device, providing you with the ability to emulate user gestures such as pinching and swiping objects, as well as rotating and changing the resolution of the device.

To run an app in the Simulator, open the Debug Target drop-down list box on the Visual Studio toolbar. By default, the debug target is set to Local Machine, which causes the app to run full-screen on your computer, but you can select Simulator from this list, which starts the Simulator when you debug the app. Note that you can also set the debug target to a different computer if you need to perform remote debugging (you will be prompted for the network address of the remote computer when you select this option). The following image shows the Debug Target list:

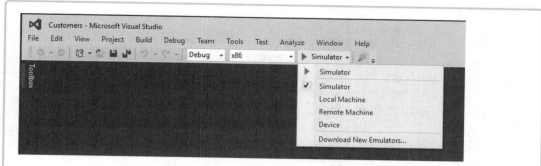

After you have selected the Simulator, when you run the app from the Debug menu in Visual Studio, the Simulator starts and displays your app. The toolbar down the right side of the Simulator window contains a selection of tools with which you can emulate user gestures by using the mouse. You can even simulate the location of the user if the app requires information about the geographic position of the device. However, for testing the layout of an app, the most important tools are Rotate Clockwise, Rotate Counterclockwise, and Change Resolution. The following image shows the Customers app running in the Simulator. The app has been maximized to occupy the full screen. The labels describe the function of each of the buttons for the Simulator.

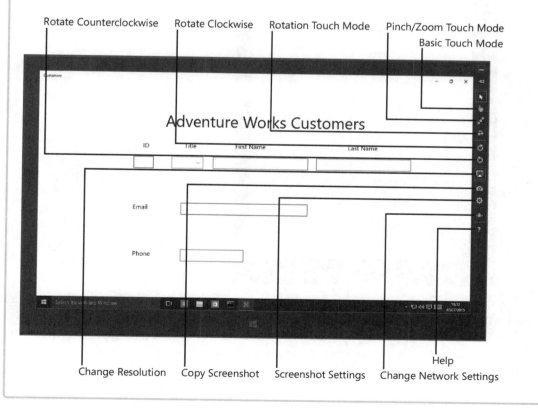

The following image shows the same app after the user has clicked the Rotate Clockwise button, which causes the app to run in the portrait orientation:

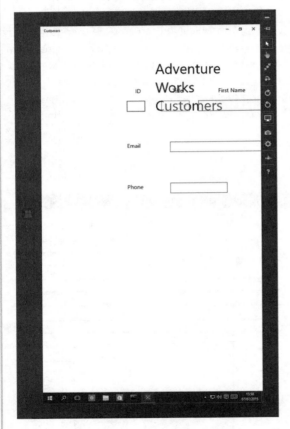

You can also try to see how the app behaves if you change the resolution of the Simulator. The following image shows the Customers app running when the Simulator is set to a high resolution device (2560 × 1440, the typical resolution of a 27-inch monitor). You can see that the display for the app is squeezed into the upper-left corner of the screen:

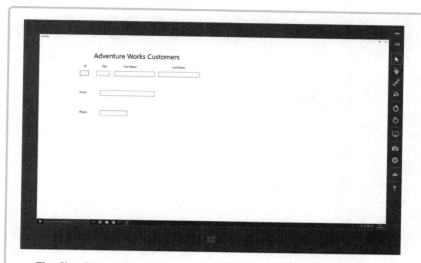

The Simulator behaves exactly like a Windows 10 computer (it is, in fact, a remote-desktop connection to your own computer). To stop the Simulator, click the Windows button (in the Simulator, not on your desktop), click Power, and then click Disconnect.

You should notice that Visual Studio also supports emulators for specific mobile devices. Some may be listed in the Simulator drop-down list box, but you can download new emulators as they become available by selecting Download New Emulators.

Implementing a tabular layout by using a *Grid* control

You can use the *Grid* control to implement a tabular layout. A *Grid* contains rows and columns, and you can specify in which rows and columns other controls should be placed. The beauty of the *Grid* control is that you can specify the sizes of the rows and columns that it contains as relative values; as the grid shrinks or grows to adapt itself to the different form factors and orientations to which users might switch, the rows and columns can shrink and grow in proportion to the grid. The intersection of a row and a column in a grid defines a cell, and if you position controls in cells, they will move as the rows and columns shrink and grow. Therefore, the key to implementing a scalable UI is to break it down into a collection of cells and place related elements in the same cell. A cell can contain another grid, giving you the ability to fine-tune the exact positioning of each element.

If you consider the Customers app, you can see that the UI breaks down into two main areas: a heading containing the title and the body containing the customers' details. Allowing for some spacing between these areas and a margin at the bottom of the form, you can assign relative sizes to each of these areas, as shown in the following diagram:

The diagram shows only rough approximations, but the row for the heading is twice as high as the row for the spacer below it. The row for the body is ten times as high as the spacer, and the bottom margin is twice the height of the spacer.

To hold the elements in each area, you can define a grid with four rows and place the appropriate items in each row. However, the body of the form can be described by another, more complex grid, as shown in the following diagram:

Again, the height of each row is specified in relative terms, as is the width of each column. Also, you can clearly see that the *TextBox* elements for Email and Phone do not quite fit this grid pattern. If you were being pedantic, you might choose to define further grids inside the body of the form to make these items fit. However, you should keep in mind the purpose of this grid, which is to define the relative positioning and spacing of elements. Therefore, it is acceptable for an element to extend beyond the boundaries of a cell in the grid arrangement.

In the next exercise, you will modify the layout of the Customers app to use this grid format to position the controls.

Modify the layout to scale to different form factors and orientations

1. In the XAML pane for the Customers app, add another *Grid* inside the existing *Grid* element. Give this new *Grid* a margin of 10 pixels from the left and right edges of the parent *Grid* and 20 pixels from the top and bottom, as shown in bold in the following code:

```
<Grid Background="{ThemeResource ApplicationPageBackgroundThemeBrush}">
    <Grid Margin="10,20,10,20">
    </Grid>
    <TextBlock HorizontalAlignment="Left" TextWrapping="Wrap"
Text="Adventure Works Customers" ... />
    ...
</Grid>
```

You could define the rows and columns as part of the existing *Grid*, but to maintain a consistent look and feel with other UWP apps, you should leave some blank space to the left and at the top of a page.

2. Add to the new *Grid* element the following *<Grid.RowDefinitions>* section shown in bold.

```
<Grid Margin="10,20,10,20">
    <Grid.RowDefinitions>
        <RowDefinition Height="2*"/>
        <RowDefinition Height="*"/>
        <RowDefinition Height="10*"/>
        <RowDefinition Height="2*"/>
    </Grid.RowDefinitions>
</Grid>
```

The *<Grid.RowDefinitions>* section defines the rows for the grid. In this example, you have defined four rows. You can specify the size of a row as an absolute value specified in pixels, or you can use the * operator to indicate that the sizes are relative and that Windows should calculate the row sizes itself when the app runs, depending on the form factor and resolution of the screen. The values used in this example correspond to the relative row sizes for the header, body, spacer, and bottom margin of the Customers form shown in the earlier diagram.

3. Move the *TextBlock* control that contains the text "Adventure Works Customers" into the *Grid*, directly after the closing *</Grid.RowDefinitions>* tag.

4. Add a *Grid.Row* attribute to the *TextBlock* control and set the value to *0*.

This indicates that the *TextBlock* should be positioned within the first row of the *Grid*. (*Grid* controls number rows and columns starting at zero.)

> **Note** The *Grid.Row* attribute is an example of an attached property. An *attached property* is a property that a control receives from the container control in which it is placed. Outside a grid, a *TextBlock* does not have a *Row* property (it would be meaningless), but when positioned within a grid, the *Row* property is attached to the *TextBlock*, and the *TextBlock* control can assign it a value. The *Grid* control then uses this value to determine where to display the *TextBlock* control. Attached properties are easy to spot because they have the form *ContainerType.PropertyName*.

5. Remove the *Margin* property, and set the *HorizontalAlignment* and *VerticalAlignment* properties to *Center*.

   This will cause the *TextBlock* to appear centered in the row.

   The XAML markup for the *Grid* and *TextBlock* controls should look like this (the changes to the *TextBlock* are highlighted in bold):

```
<Grid Margin="10,20,10,20">
    <Grid.RowDefinitions>
        <RowDefinition Height="2*"/>
        <RowDefinition Height="*"/>
        <RowDefinition Height="10*"/>
        <RowDefinition Height="2*"/>
    </Grid.RowDefinitions>
    <TextBlock Grid.Row="0" HorizontalAlignment="Center" TextWrapping="Wrap"
Text="Adventure Works Customers" VerticalAlignment="Center" FontSize="50"/>
    ...
</Grid>
```

6. After the *TextBlock* control, add another nested *Grid* control. This *Grid* will be used to lay out the controls in the body of the form and should appear in the third row of the outer *Grid* (the row of size *10**), so set the *Grid.Row* property to *2*, as shown in bold in the following code:

```
<Grid Margin="10,20,10,20">
    <Grid.RowDefinitions>
        <RowDefinition Height="2*"/>
        <RowDefinition Height="*"/>
        <RowDefinition Height="10*"/>
        <RowDefinition Height="2*"/>
    </Grid.RowDefinitions>
    <TextBlock Grid.Row="0" HorizontalAlignment="Center" .../>
    <Grid Grid.Row="2">
    </Grid>
    ...
</Grid>
```

7. Add the following *<Grid.RowDefinitions>* and *<Grid.ColumnDefinitions>* sections to the new *Grid* control:

```
<Grid Grid.Row="2">
    <Grid.RowDefinitions>
```

```
            <RowDefinition Height="*"/>
            <RowDefinition Height="*"/>
            <RowDefinition Height="2*"/>
            <RowDefinition Height="*"/>
            <RowDefinition Height="2*"/>
            <RowDefinition Height="*"/>
            <RowDefinition Height="4*"/>
        </Grid.RowDefinitions>
        <Grid.ColumnDefinitions>
            <ColumnDefinition Width="*"/>
            <ColumnDefinition Width="*"/>
            <ColumnDefinition Width="20"/>
            <ColumnDefinition Width="*"/>
            <ColumnDefinition Width="20"/>
            <ColumnDefinition Width="2*"/>
            <ColumnDefinition Width="20"/>
            <ColumnDefinition Width="2*"/>
            <ColumnDefinition Width="*"/>
        </Grid.ColumnDefinitions>
    </Grid>
```

These row and column definitions specify the height and width of each of the rows and columns shown earlier in the diagram that depicted the structure of the body of the form. There is a small space of 20 pixels between each of the columns that will hold controls.

8. Move the *TextBlock* controls that display the ID, Title, Last Name, and First Name labels inside the nested *Grid* control, immediately after the closing *<Grid.ColumnDefinitions>* tag.

9. Set the *Grid.Row* property for each *TextBlock* control to *0* (these labels will appear in the first row of the grid). Set the *Grid.Column* property for the ID label to *1*, the *Grid.Column* property for the Title label to *3*, the *Grid.Column* property for the First Name label to *5*, and the *Grid. Column* property for the Last Name label to *7*.

10. Remove the *Margin* property from each of the *TextBlock* controls, and set the *Horizontal-Alignment* and *VerticalAlignment* properties to *Center*. The XAML markup for these controls should look like this (the changes are highlighted in bold):

```
<Grid Grid.Row="2">
    <Grid.RowDefinitions>

    ...
    </Grid.RowDefinitions>
    <Grid.ColumnDefinitions>

    ...
    </Grid.ColumnDefinitions>
    <TextBlock Grid.Row="0" Grid.Column="1" HorizontalAlignment="Center"
TextWrapping="Wrap" Text="ID" VerticalAlignment="Center" FontSize="20"/>
    <TextBlock Grid.Row="0" Grid.Column="3" HorizontalAlignment="Center"
TextWrapping="Wrap" Text="Title" VerticalAlignment="Center" FontSize="20"/>
    <TextBlock Grid.Row="0" Grid.Column="5" HorizontalAlignment="Center"
TextWrapping="Wrap" Text="First Name" VerticalAlignment="Center" FontSize="20"/>
    <TextBlock Grid.Row="0" Grid.Column="7" HorizontalAlignment="Center"
TextWrapping="Wrap" Text="Last Name" VerticalAlignment="Center" FontSize="20"/>
</Grid>
```

11. Move the *id, firstName,* and *lastName TextBox* controls and the *title ComboBox* control inside the nested *Grid* control, immediately after the *Last Name TextBlock* control.

Place these controls in row 1 of the *Grid* control. Put the *id* control in column 1, the *title* control in column 3, the *firstName* control in column 5, and the *lastName* control in column 7.

Remove the *Margin* of each of these controls, and set the *VerticalAlignment* property to *Center.* Remove the *Width* property, and set the *HorizontalAlignment* property to *Stretch.* This causes the control to occupy the entire cell when it is displayed, and the control shrinks or grows as the size of the cell changes.

The completed XAML markup for these controls should look like this, with changes highlighted in bold:

```
<Grid Grid.Row="2">
    <Grid.RowDefinitions>
        ...
    </Grid.RowDefinitions>
    <Grid.ColumnDefinitions>
        ...
    </Grid.ColumnDefinitions>
    ...
    <TextBlock Grid.Row="0" Grid.Column="7" ... Text="Last Name" .../>
    <TextBox Grid.Row="1" Grid.Column="1" x:Name="id" HorizontalAlignment="Stretch"
TextWrapping="Wrap" Text="" VerticalAlignment="Center" FontSize="20" IsReadOnly="True"/>
    <TextBox Grid.Row="1" Grid.Column="5" x:Name="firstName" HorizontalAlignment="Stretch"
TextWrapping="Wrap" Text="" VerticalAlignment="Center" FontSize="20"/>
    <TextBox Grid.Row="1" Grid.Column="7" x:Name="lastName" HorizontalAlignment="Stretch"
TextWrapping="Wrap" Text="" VerticalAlignment="Center" FontSize="20"/>
    <ComboBox Grid.Row="1" Grid.Column="3" x:Name="title" HorizontalAlignment="Stretch"
    VerticalAlignment="Center" FontSize="20">
        <ComboBoxItem Content="Mr"/>
        <ComboBoxItem Content="Mrs"/>
        <ComboBoxItem Content="Ms"/>
        <ComboBoxItem Content="Miss"/>
    </ComboBox>
</Grid>
```

12. Move the *TextBlock* control for the Email label and the *email TextBox* control to the nested *Grid* control, immediately after the closing tag of the *title ComboBox* control.

Place these controls in row 3 of the *Grid* control. Put the Email label in column 1 and the *email TextBox* control in column 3. Additionally, set the *Grid.ColumnSpan* property for the *email TextBox* control to 5; this way, the column can spread to the value specified by its *Width* property across five columns, as shown in the earlier diagram.

Set the *HorizontalAlignment* property of the Email label control to *Center,* but leave the *HorizontalAlignment* property of the *email TextBox* set to *Left*; this control should remain left-justified against the first column that it spans rather than being centered across them all.

Set the *VerticalAlignment* property of the Email label and the *email TextBox* control to *Center.*

Remove the *Margin* property for both of these controls.

The following XAML markup shows the completed definitions of these controls:

```
<Grid Grid.Row="2">
    <Grid.RowDefinitions>
        ...
    </Grid.RowDefinitions>
    <Grid.ColumnDefinitions>
        ...
    </Grid.ColumnDefinitions>
    ...
    <ComboBox Grid.Row="1" Grid.Column="3" x:Name="title" ...>
        ...
    </ComboBox>
    <TextBlock Grid.Row="3" Grid.Column="1" HorizontalAlignment="Center"
TextWrapping="Wrap" Text="Email" VerticalAlignment="Center" FontSize="20"/>
    <TextBox Grid.Row="3" Grid.Column="3" Grid.ColumnSpan="5" x:Name="email"
HorizontalAlignment="Left" TextWrapping="Wrap" Text="" VerticalAlignment="Center"
Width="400" FontSize="20"/>
</Grid>
```

13. Move the *TextBlock* control for the Phone label and *phone TextBox* control to the nested *Grid* control, immediately after the *email TextBox* control.

    Place these controls in row 5 of the *Grid* control. Put the Phone label in column 1 and the *phone TextBox* control in column 3. Set the *Grid.ColumnSpan* property for the *phone TextBox* control to 3.

    Set the *HorizontalAlignment* property of the Phone label control to *Center*, and leave the *HorizontalAlignment* property of the *phone TextBox* set to *Left*.

    Set the *VerticalAlignment* property of both controls to *Center*, and remove the Margin property.

    The following XAML markup shows the completed definitions of these controls:

```
<Grid Grid.Row="2">
    <Grid.RowDefinitions>
        ...
    </Grid.RowDefinitions>
    <Grid.ColumnDefinitions>
        ...
    </Grid.ColumnDefinitions>
    ....
    <TextBox ... x:Name="email" .../>
    <TextBlock Grid.Row="5" Grid.Column="1" HorizontalAlignment="Center"
TextWrapping="Wrap" Text="Phone" VerticalAlignment="Center" FontSize="20"/>
    <TextBox Grid.Row="5" Grid.Column="3" Grid.ColumnSpan="3" x:Name="phone"
HorizontalAlignment="Left" TextWrapping="Wrap" Text="" VerticalAlignment="Center"
Width="200" FontSize="20"/>
</Grid>
```

14. On the Visual Studio toolbar, in the Debug Target list, select Simulator.

You will run the app in the Simulator so that you can see how the layout adapts in different resolutions and form factors.

15. On the Debug menu, click Start Debugging.

The Simulator starts and the Customers app runs. Maximize the app so that it occupies the entire screen in the Simulator. Click Change Resolution, and then configure the Simulator to display the app using a screen resolution of 1366 × 768. Also, ensure that the Simulator is displayed in landscape orientation (click Rotate Clockwise if it is running in portrait orientation). Verify that the controls are evenly spaced in this orientation.

16. Click the Rotate Clockwise button to rotate the Simulator to portrait orientation.

The Customers app should adjust the layout of the user interface, and the controls should still be evenly spaced and usable:

17. Click Rotate Counterclockwise to put the Simulator back to landscape orientation, and then click Change Resolution and switch the resolution of the Simulator to 2560 × 1400.

    Notice that the controls remain evenly spaced on the form, although the labels might be quite difficult to read unless you actually have a 27-inch screen.

18. Click Change Resolution again and switch the resolution to 1024 × 768.

    Again, notice how the spacing and size of the controls are adjusted to maintain the even balance of the user interface:

19. Click Change Resolution again and switch the resolution back to 1366 × 768.

20. In the Simulator, double-click the top edge of the form to restore the view as a window, and then drag and resize the window so that the form is displayed in the left half of the screen. Reduce the width of the window to its minimum. This is how the app might appear on a device such as a smartphone.

    All the controls remain visible, but the text for the Phone label and the title wrap, making them difficult to read, and the controls are not particularly easy to use anymore:

21. In the Simulator, click the Start button, click Settings, click Power, and then click Disconnect.

The Simulator closes and you return to Visual Studio.

22. On the Visual Studio toolbar, in the Debug Target drop-down list box, select Local Machine.

Adapting the layout by using the Visual State Manager

The user interface for the Customers app scales for different resolutions and form factors, but it still does not work well if you reduce the width of the view, and it probably would not look too good on a smartphone, which has an even narrower width. If you think about it, the solution to the problem in these cases is not so much a matter of scaling the controls as actually laying them out in a different way. For example, it would make better sense if the Customers form looked like this in a narrow view:

You can achieve this effect in several ways:

- You can create several versions of the MainPage.xaml file, one for each device family. Each of these XAML files can be linked to the same code-behind (MainPage.xaml.cs) so that they all run the same code. For example, to create a XAML file for a smartphone, add a folder named DeviceFamily-Mobile (this name is important) to the project and then add a new XAML view named MainPage.xaml to the folder by using the Add New Item menu command. Lay out the controls on this page folder as they should be displayed on a smartphone. The XAML view will be linked automatically to the existing MainPage.xaml.cs file. At run time, the UWP will select the appropriate view based on the type of device on which the app is running.

- You can use the Visual State Manager to modify the layout of the page at run time. All UWP apps implement a Visual State Manager that tracks the visual state of an app. It can detect when the height and width of the window changes, and you can add XAML markup that positions controls depending on the size of the window. This markup can move controls around or display and hide controls.

- You can use the Visual State Manager to switch between views based on the height and width of the window. This approach is a hybrid combination of the first two options described here, but it is the least messy (you don't have lots of tricky XAML code calculating the best position for each control) and is also the most flexible (it will work if the window is narrowed on the same device).

You'll follow the third of these approaches in the next exercises. The first step is to define a layout for the customers' data that should appear in a narrow view.

Define a layout for the narrow view

1. In the XAML pane for the Customers app, add the *x:Name* and *Visibility* properties shown below in bold to the *Grid* control:

```
<Grid Background="{ThemeResource ApplicationPageBackgroundThemeBrush}">
    <Grid x:Name="customersTabularView" Margin="10,20,10,20" Visibility="Collapsed">
        ...
    </Grid>
</Grid>
```

This *Grid* control will hold the default view of the form. You will reference this *Grid* control in other XAML markup later in this set of exercises, hence the requirement to give it a name. The *Visibility* property specifies whether the control is displayed (*Visible*) or hidden (*Collapsed*). The default value is *Visible*, but for the time being you will hide this *Grid* while you define another for displaying the data in a columnar format.

2. After the closing *</Grid>* tag for the *customersTabularView* Grid control, add another *Grid* control. Set the *x:Name* property to *customersColumnarView*, set the *Margin* property to *10,20,10,20*, and set the *Visibility* property to *Visible*.

> **Tip** You can expand and contract elements in the XAML pane of the Design View window and make the structure easier to read by clicking the + and – signs that appear down the left edge of the XAML markup.

```
<Grid Background="{ThemeResource ApplicationPageBackgroundThemeBrush}">
    <Grid x:Name="customersTabularView" Margin="10,20,10,20" Visibility="Collapsed">
        ...
    </Grid>
    <Grid x:Name="customersColumnarView" Margin="10,20,10,20" Visibility="Visible">
    </Grid>
</Grid>
```

This *Grid* control will hold the "narrow" view of the form. The fields in this grid will be layed out in a columnar manner as described earlier.

3. In the *customersColumnarView* Grid control, add the following row definitions:

```
<Grid x:Name="customersColumnarView" Margin="10,20,10,20" Visibility="Visible">
    <Grid.RowDefinitions>
        <RowDefinition Height="*"/>
        <RowDefinition Height="10*"/>
    </Grid.RowDefinitions>
</Grid>
```

You will use the top row to display the title and the second, much larger row to display the controls in which users enter data.

4. Immediately after the row definitions, add the *TextBlock* control shown below in bold. This control displays a truncated title, Customers, in the first row of the *Grid* control. Set *FontSize* to 30.

```
<Grid x:Name="customersColumnarView" Margin="10,20,10,20" Visibility="Visible">
    <Grid.RowDefinitions>
        ...
    </Grid.RowDefinitions>
    <TextBlock Grid.Row="0" HorizontalAlignment="Center" TextWrapping="Wrap"
Text="Customers" VerticalAlignment="Center" FontSize="30"/>
</Grid>
```

5. Add another *Grid* control to row 1 of the *customersColumnarView Grid* control, directly after the *TextBlock* control that contains the Customers title. This *Grid* control will display the labels and data-entry controls in two columns, so add the row and columns definitions shown in bold in the following code example to this *Grid*.

```
<TextBlock Grid.Row="0" ... />
<Grid Grid.Row="1">
    <Grid.ColumnDefinitions>
        <ColumnDefinition/>
        <ColumnDefinition/>
    </Grid.ColumnDefinitions>
    <Grid.RowDefinitions>
        <RowDefinition/>
        <RowDefinition/>
        <RowDefinition/>
        <RowDefinition/>
        <RowDefinition/>
        <RowDefinition/>
    </Grid.RowDefinitions>
</Grid>
```

Notice that if all the rows or columns in a set have the same height or width, you do not need to specify their size.

6. Copy the XAML markup for the ID, Title, First Name, and Last Name *TextBlock* controls from the *customersTabularView Grid* control to the new *Grid* control, immediately after the row definitions that you just added. Put the ID control in row 0, the Title control in row 1, the First Name control in row 2, and the Last Name control in row 3. Place all controls in column 0.

```
<Grid.RowDefinitions>
    ...
</Grid.RowDefinitions>
<TextBlock Grid.Row="0" Grid.Column="0" HorizontalAlignment="Center"
TextWrapping="Wrap" Text="ID" VerticalAlignment="Center" FontSize="20"/>
<TextBlock Grid.Row="1" Grid.Column="0" HorizontalAlignment="Center"
TextWrapping="Wrap" Text="Title" VerticalAlignment="Center" FontSize="20"/>
<TextBlock Grid.Row="2" Grid.Column="0" HorizontalAlignment="Center"
TextWrapping="Wrap" Text="First Name" VerticalAlignment="Center" FontSize="20"/>
```

```
<TextBlock Grid.Row="3" Grid.Column="0" HorizontalAlignment="Center"
TextWrapping="Wrap" Text="Last Name" VerticalAlignment="Center" FontSize="20"/>
```

7. Copy the XAML markup for the *id*, *title*, *firstName*, and *lastName TextBox* and *ComboBox* controls from the *customersTabularView Grid* control to the new *Grid* control, immediately after the *TextBox* controls. Put the *id* control in row 0, the *title* control in row 1, the *firstName* control in row 2, and the *lastName* control in row 3. Place all four controls in column 1. Also, change the names of the controls by prefixing them with the letter *c* (for column). This final change is necessary to avoid clashing with the names of the existing controls in the *customersTabularView Grid* control.

```
<TextBlock Grid.Row="3" Grid.Column="0" HorizontalAlignment="Center"
TextWrapping="Wrap" Text="Last Name" .../>
<TextBox Grid.Row="0" Grid.Column="1" x:Name="cId" HorizontalAlignment="Stretch"
TextWrapping="Wrap" Text="" VerticalAlignment="Center" FontSize="20" IsReadOnly="True"/>
<TextBox Grid.Row="2" Grid.Column="1" x:Name="cFirstName" HorizontalAlignment="Stretch"
TextWrapping="Wrap" Text="" VerticalAlignment="Center" FontSize="20"/>
<TextBox Grid.Row="3" Grid.Column="1" x:Name="cLastName" HorizontalAlignment="Stretch"
TextWrapping="Wrap" Text="" VerticalAlignment="Center" FontSize="20"/>
<ComboBox Grid.Row="1" Grid.Column="1" x:Name="cTitle" HorizontalAlignment="Stretch"
VerticalAlignment="Center" FontSize="20">
        <ComboBoxItem Content="Mr"/>
        <ComboBoxItem Content="Mrs"/>
        <ComboBoxItem Content="Ms"/>
        <ComboBoxItem Content="Miss"/>
</ComboBox>
```

8. Copy the *TextBlock* and *TextBox* controls for the email address and telephone number from the *customersTabularView Grid* control to the new *Grid* control, placing them after the *cTitle ComboBox* control. Place the *TextBlock* controls in column 0, in rows 4 and 5, and the *TextBox* controls in column 1, in rows 4 and 5. Change the name of the *email TextBox* control to *cEmail* and the name of the *phone TextBox* control to *cPhone*. Remove the *Width* properties of the *cEmail* and *cPhone* controls, and set their *HorizontalAlignment* properties to *Stretch*.

```
<ComboBox ...>
    ...
</ComboBox>
<TextBlock Grid.Row="4" Grid.Column="0" HorizontalAlignment="Center" TextWrapping="Wrap"
Text="Email" VerticalAlignment="Center" FontSize="20"/>
<TextBox Grid.Row="4" Grid.Column="1" x:Name="cEmail" HorizontalAlignment="Stretch"
TextWrapping="Wrap" Text="" VerticalAlignment="Center" FontSize="20"/>
<TextBlock Grid.Row="5" Grid.Column="0" HorizontalAlignment="Center" TextWrapping="Wrap"
Text="Phone" VerticalAlignment="Center" FontSize="20"/>
<TextBox Grid.Row="5" Grid.Column="1" x:Name="cPhone" HorizontalAlignment="Stretch"
TextWrapping="Wrap" Text="" VerticalAlignment="Center" FontSize="20"/>
```

The Design View window should display the columnar layout like this:

9. Return to the XAML markup for the *customersTabularView Grid* control and set the *Visibility* property to *Visible*.

```
<Grid x:Name="customersTabularView" Margin="10,20,10,20" Visibility="Visible">
```

10. In the XAML markup for the *customersColumnarView Grid* control, set the *Visibility* property to *Collapsed*.

```
<Grid x:Name="customersColumnarView" Margin="10,20,10,20" Visibility="Collapsed">
```

The Design View window should display the original tabular layout of the Customers form. This is the default view that will be used by the app.

You have now defined the layout that will appear in the narrow view. You might be concerned that in essence all you have done is duplicated many of the controls and laid them out in a different manner. If you run the form and switch between views, how will data in one view transfer to the other? For example, if you enter the details for a customer when the app is running full screen, and then you switch to the narrow view, the newly displayed controls will not contain the same data that you just entered. UWP apps address this problem by using *data binding*. This is a technique by which you can associate the same piece of data to multiple controls, and as the data changes, all controls display the updated information. You will see how this works in Chapter 26. For the time being, you need to consider only how to use the Visual State Manager to switch between layouts when the view changes.

You can use triggers that alert the Visual State Manager when some aspect (such as the height or width) of the display changes. You can define the visual state transitions performed by these triggers in the XAML markup of your app. This is what you will do in the next exercise.

Use the Visual State Manager to modify the layout

1. In the XAML pane for the Customers app, after the closing *</Grid>* tag for the *customers-ColumnarView Grid* control, add the following markup:

```
<Grid x:Name="customersColumnarView" Margin="10,20,10,20" Visibility="Visible">
    ...
</Grid>
<VisualStateManager.VisualStateGroups>
    <VisualStateGroup>
        <VisualState x:Name="TabularLayout">
        </VisualState>
    </VisualStateGroup>
</VisualStateManager.VisualStateGroups>
```

You define the visual state transitions by implementing one or more visual state groups. Each visual state group specifies the transitions that should occur when the Visual State Manager switches to this state. Each state should be given a meaningful name to help you identify its purpose.

2. Add the following visual state trigger shown in bold to the visual state group:

```
<VisualStateManager.VisualStateGroups>
    <VisualStateGroup>
        <VisualState x:Name="TabularLayout">
            <VisualState.StateTriggers>
                <AdaptiveTrigger MinWindowWidth="660"/>
            </VisualState.StateTriggers>
        </VisualState>
    </VisualStateGroup>
</VisualStateManager.VisualStateGroups>
```

This trigger will fire whenever the width of the window drops below 660 pixels. This is the width at which the controls and labels on the Customers form start to wrap and become difficult to use.

3. After the trigger definition, add the following code shown in bold to the XAML markup:

```
<VisualStateManager.VisualStateGroups>
    <VisualStateGroup>
        <VisualState x:Name="TabularLayout">
            <VisualState.StateTriggers>
                <AdaptiveTrigger MinWindowWidth="660"/>
            </VisualState.StateTriggers>
            <VisualState.Setters>
                <Setter Target="customersTabularView.Visibility" Value="Visible"/>
                <Setter Target="customersColumnarView.Visibility" Value="Collapsed"/>
            </VisualState.Setters>
        </VisualState>
    </VisualStateGroup>
</VisualStateManager.VisualStateGroups>
```

This code specifies the actions that occur when the trigger is fired. In this example, the actions are defined by using *Setter* elements. A *Setter* element specifies a property to set and the value to which the property should be set. For this view, the *Setter* commands change the values of specified properties; the *customersTabularView Grid* control is made visible and the *customersColumnarView Grid* control is collapsed (made invisible).

4. After the *TabularLayout* visual state definition, add the following markup shown in bold, which defines the equivalent functionality for the narrow view:

```
<VisualStateManager.VisualStateGroups>
    <VisualStateGroup>
        <VisualState x:Name="TabularLayout">
            ...
        </VisualState>
        <VisualState x:Name="ColumnarLayout">
            <VisualState.StateTriggers>
                <AdaptiveTrigger MinWindowWidth="0"/>
            </VisualState.StateTriggers>
            <VisualState.Setters>
                <Setter Target="customersTabularView.Visibility" Value="Collapsed"/>
                <Setter Target="customersColumnarView.Visibility" Value="Visible"/>
            </VisualState.Setters>
        </VisualState>
    </VisualStateGroup>
</VisualStateManager.VisualStateGroups>
```

This transition will occur when the window width drops below 660 pixels. The app switches to the ColumnarLayout state; the *customersTabularView Grid* control is collapsed and the *customersColumnarView Grid* control is made visible.

5. On the Debug menu, click Start Debugging.

The app starts and displays the Customer form full screen. The data is displayed using the tabular layout.

> **Note** If you are using a display with a resolution of less than 1366 × 768, start the app running in the Simulator as described earlier. Configure the Simulator with a resolution of 1366 × 768.

6. Resize the Customer app window to display the form in a narrow view. When the window width drops below 660 pixels, the display switches to the columnar layout.

7. Resize the Customer app window to make it wider than 660 pixels (or maximize it to full screen).

The Customer form reverts to the tabular layout.

8. Return to Visual Studio and stop debugging.

Applying styles to a UI

Now that you have the mechanics of the basic layout of the app resolved, the next step is to apply some styling to make the UI look more attractive. The controls in a UWP app have a varied range of properties that you can use to change features such as the font, color, size, and other attributes of an element. You can set these properties individually for each control, but this approach can become cumbersome and repetitive if you need to apply the same styling to a number of controls. Also, the best apps apply a consistent styling across the UI, and it is difficult to maintain consistency if you have to repeatedly set the same properties and values as you add or change controls. The more times you have to do the same thing, the greater the chances are that you will get it wrong at least once!

With UWP apps, you can define reusable styles. You can implement them as app-wide resources by creating a resource dictionary, and then they are available to all controls in all pages in an app. You can also define local resources that apply to only a single page in the XAML markup for that page. In the following exercise, you will define some simple styles for the Customers app and apply these styles to the controls on the Customers form.

Define styles for the Customers form

1. In Solution Explorer, right-click the Customers project, point to Add, and then click New Item.

2. In the Add New Item – Customers dialog box, click Resource Dictionary. In the Name box, type **AppStyles.xaml**, and then click Add.

   The AppStyles.xaml file appears in the Code and Text Editor window. A resource dictionary is a XAML file that contains resources that the app can use. The AppStyles.xaml file looks like this:

   ```
   <ResourceDictionary
       xmlns="http://schemas.microsoft.com/winfx/2006/xaml/presentation"
       xmlns:x="http://schemas.microsoft.com/winfx/2006/xaml"
       xmlns:local="using:Customers">

   </ResourceDictionary>
   ```

   Styles are one example of a resource, but you can also add other items. In fact, the first resource that you will add is not actually a style but an *ImageBrush* that will be used to paint the background of the outermost *Grid* control on the Customers form.

3. In Solution Explorer, right-click the Customers project, point to Add, and then click New Folder. Change the name of the new folder to **Images**.

4. Right-click the Images folder, point to Add, and then click Existing Item.

5. In the Add Existing Item – Customers dialog box, browse to the \Microsoft Press\VCSBS\ Chapter 25\Resources folder in your Documents folder, click wood.jpg, and then click Add.

   The wood.jpg file is added to the Images folder in the Customers project. This file contains an image of a tasteful wooden background that you will use for the Customers form.

6. In the Code and Text Editor window displaying the AppStyles.xaml file, add the following XAML markup shown in bold:

```
<ResourceDictionary
    xmlns="http://schemas.microsoft.com/winfx/2006/xaml/presentation"
    xmlns:x="http://schemas.microsoft.com/winfx/2006/xaml"
    xmlns:local="using:Customers">

    <ImageBrush x:Key="WoodBrush" ImageSource="Images/wood.jpg"/>
</ResourceDictionary>
```

This markup creates an *ImageBrush* resource called *WoodBrush* that is based on the wood.jpg file. You can use this image brush to set the background of a control, and it will display the image in the wood.jpg file.

7. Underneath the *ImageBrush* resource, add the following style shown in bold to the AppStyles.xaml file:

```
<ResourceDictionary
    ...>

    <ImageBrush x:Key="WoodBrush" ImageSource="Images/wood.jpg"/>
    <Style x:Key="GridStyle" TargetType="Grid">
        <Setter Property="Background" Value="{StaticResource WoodBrush}"/>
    </Style>
</ResourceDictionary>
```

This markup shows how to define a style. A *Style* element should have a name (a key that enables it to be referenced elsewhere in the app), and it should specify the type of control to which the style can be applied. You are going to use this style with the *Grid* control.

The body of a style consists of one or more *Setter* elements. In this example, the *Background* property is set to the *WoodBrush ImageBrush* resource. The syntax is a little curious, though. In a value, you can either reference one of the appropriate system-defined values for the property (such as *"Red"* if you want to set the background to a solid red color) or specify a resource that you have defined elsewhere. To reference a resource defined elsewhere, you use the *StaticResource* keyword and then place the entire expression in curly braces.

8. Before you can use this style, you must update the global resource dictionary for the app in the App.xaml file by adding a reference to the AppStyles.xaml file. In Solution Explorer, double-click App.xaml to display it in the Code and Text Editor window. The App.xaml file looks like this:

```
<Application
    x:Class="Customers.App"
    xmlns="http://schemas.microsoft.com/winfx/2006/xaml/presentation"
    xmlns:x="http://schemas.microsoft.com/winfx/2006/xaml"
    xmlns:local="using:Customers"
    RequestedTheme="Light">

</Application>
```

Currently, the App.xaml file defines only the app object and brings a few namespaces into scope; the global resource dictionary is empty.

9. Add to the App.xaml file the code shown here in bold:

```
<Application
    x:Class="Customers.App"
    xmlns="http://schemas.microsoft.com/winfx/2006/xaml/presentation"
    xmlns:x="http://schemas.microsoft.com/winfx/2006/xaml"
    xmlns:local="using:Customers"
    RequestedTheme="Light">
    <Application.Resources>
        <ResourceDictionary>
            <ResourceDictionary.MergedDictionaries>
                <ResourceDictionary Source="AppStyles.xaml"/>
            </ResourceDictionary.MergedDictionaries>
        </ResourceDictionary>
    </Application.Resources>
</Application>
```

This markup adds the resources defined in the AppStyles.xaml file to the list of resources available in the global resource dictionary. These resources are now available for use throughout the app.

10. Switch to the MainPage.xaml file displaying the UI for the Customers form. In the XAML pane, find the outermost *Grid* control:

```
<Grid Background="{ThemeResource ApplicationPageBackgroundThemeBrush}">
```

In the XAML markup for this control, replace the *Background* property with a *Style* property that references the *GridStyle* style, as shown in bold in the following code:

```
<Grid Style="{StaticResource GridStyle}">
```

The background of the *Grid* control in the Design View window should switch and display a wooden panel, like this:

Note Ideally, you should ensure that any background image that you apply to a page or control maintains its aesthetics as the device form factor and orientation change. An image that looks cool on a 30-inch monitor might appear distorted and squashed on a Windows phone. It might be necessary to provide alternative backgrounds for different views and orientations and use the Visual State Manager to modify the *Background* property of a control to switch between them as the visual state changes.

11. Return to AppStyles.xaml in the Code and Text Editor window and add the following *FontStyle* style after the *GridStyle* style:

```xaml
<Style x:Key="GridStyle" TargetType="Grid">
    ...
</Style>
<Style x:Key="FontStyle" TargetType="TextBlock">
    <Setter Property="FontFamily" Value="Segoe Print"/>
</Style>
```

This style applies to *TextBlock* elements and changes the font to Segoe Print. This font resembles a handwriting style.

At this stage, it would be possible to reference the *FontStyle* style in every *TextBlock* control that required this font, but this approach would not provide any advantage over simply setting the *FontFamily* directly in the markup for each control. The real power of styles occurs when you combine multiple properties, as you will see in the next few steps.

Add the *HeaderStyle* style shown here to the AppStyles.xaml file: <Style x:Key="FontStyle" TargetType="TextBlock">

```
<Style x:Key="FontStyle" TargetType="TextBlock">
    ...
</Style>
<Style x:Key="HeaderStyle" TargetType="TextBlock" BasedOn="{StaticResource FontStyle}">
    <Setter Property="HorizontalAlignment" Value="Center"/>
    <Setter Property="TextWrapping" Value="Wrap"/>
    <Setter Property="VerticalAlignment" Value="Center"/>
    <Setter Property="Foreground" Value="SteelBlue"/>
</Style>
```

This is a composite style that sets the *HorizontalAlignment*, *TextWrapping*, *VerticalAlignment*, and *Foreground* properties of a *TextBlock*. Additionally, the *HeaderStyle* style references the *FontStyle* style by using the *BasedOn* property. The *BasedOn* property provides a simple form of inheritance for styles.

You will use this style to format the labels that appear at the top of the *customersTabularView* and *customersColumnarView* controls. However, these headings have different font sizes (the heading for the tabular layout is bigger than that of the columnar layout), so you will create two more styles that extend the *HeaderStyle* style.

12. Add the following styles to the AppStyles.xaml file:

```
<Style x:Key="HeaderStyle" TargetType="TextBlock" BasedOn="{StaticResource FontStyle}">
    ...
</Style>
<Style x:Key="TabularHeaderStyle" TargetType="TextBlock"
BasedOn="{StaticResource HeaderStyle}">
    <Setter Property="FontSize" Value="40"/>
</Style>

<Style x:Key="ColumnarHeaderStyle" TargetType="TextBlock"
BasedOn="{StaticResource HeaderStyle}">
    <Setter Property="FontSize" Value="30"/>
</Style>
```

Note that the font sizes for these styles are slightly smaller than the font sizes currently used by the headings in the *Grid* controls. This is because the Segoe Print font is bigger than the default font.

13. Switch back to the MainPage.xaml file and find the XAML markup for the *TextBlock* control for the Adventure Works Customers label in the *customersTabularView Grid* control:

```
<TextBlock Grid.Row="0" HorizontalAlignment="Center" TextWrapping="Wrap"
```

```
Text="Adventure Works Customers" VerticalAlignment="Center" FontSize="50"/>
```

14. Change the properties of this control to reference the *TabularHeaderStyle* style, as shown in bold in the following code:

```
<TextBlock Grid.Row="0" Style="{StaticResource TabularHeaderStyle}"
Text="Adventure Works Customers"/>
```

The heading displayed in the Design View window should change color, size, and font and look like this:

15. Find the XAML markup for the *TextBlock* control for the Customers label in the *customers-ColumnarView Grid* control:

```
<TextBlock Grid.Row="0" HorizontalAlignment="Center" TextWrapping="Wrap"
Text="Customers" VerticalAlignment="Center" FontSize="30"/>
```

Modify the markup of this control to reference the *ColumnarHeaderStyle* style, as shown here in bold:

```
<TextBlock Grid.Row="0" Style="{StaticResource ColumnarHeaderStyle}"
Text="Customers"/>
```

Be aware that you won't see this change in the Design View window because the *customers-ColumnarView Grid* control is collapsed by default. However, you will see the effects of this change when you run the app later in this exercise.

16. Return to the AppStyles.xaml file in the Code and Text Editor window. Modify the *HeaderStyle* style with the additional property *Setter* elements shown in bold in the following example:

```
<Style x:Key="HeaderStyle" TargetType="TextBlock" BasedOn="{StaticResource FontStyle}">
    <Setter Property="HorizontalAlignment" Value="Center"/>
    <Setter Property="TextWrapping" Value="Wrap"/>
    <Setter Property="VerticalAlignment" Value="Center"/>
    <Setter Property="Foreground" Value="SteelBlue"/>
    <Setter Property="RenderTransformOrigin" Value="0.5,0.5"/>
    <Setter Property="RenderTransform">
        <Setter.Value>
            <CompositeTransform Rotation="-5"/>
        </Setter.Value>
    </Setter>
</Style>
```

These elements rotate the text displayed in the header about its midpoint by an angle of 5 degrees by using a transformation.

> **Note** This example shows a simple transformation. Using the *RenderTransform* property, you can perform a variety of other transformations to an item, and you can combine multiple transformations. For example, you can translate (move) an item on the x- and y-axes, skew the item (make it lean), and scale an element.
>
> You should also notice that the value of the *RenderTransform* property is itself another property/value pair (the property is *Rotation*, and the value is −5). In cases such as this, you specify the value by using the *<Setter.Value>* tag.

17. Switch to the MainPage.xaml file. In the Design View window, the title should now be displayed at a jaunty angle:

18. In the AppStyles.xaml file, add the following style:

```
<Style x:Key="LabelStyle" TargetType="TextBlock" BasedOn="{StaticResource FontStyle}">
    <Setter Property="FontSize" Value="30"/>
    <Setter Property="HorizontalAlignment" Value="Center"/>
    <Setter Property="TextWrapping" Value="Wrap"/>
    <Setter Property="VerticalAlignment" Value="Center"/>
    <Setter Property="Foreground" Value="AntiqueWhite"/>
</Style>
```

You will apply this style to the *TextBlock* elements that provide the labels for the various *TextBox* and *ComboBox* controls that the user employs to enter customer information. The style references the same font style as the headings but sets the other properties to values more appropriate for the labels.

19. Go back to the MainPage.xaml file. In the XAML pane, modify the markup for the *TextBlock* controls for each of the labels in the *customersTabularView* and *customersColumnarView Grid* controls. Remove the *HorizontalAlignment*, *TextWrapping*, *VerticalAlignment*, and *FontSize* properties, and reference the *LabelStyle* style, as shown here in bold:

```
<Grid x:Name="customersTabularView" Margin="10,20,10,20" Visibility="Visible">
    ...
    <Grid Grid.Row="2">
        ...
        <TextBlock Grid.Row="0" Grid.Column="1" Style="{StaticResource LabelStyle}"
Text="ID"/>
        <TextBlock Grid.Row="0" Grid.Column="3" Style="{StaticResource LabelStyle}"
Text="Title"/>
        <TextBlock Grid.Row="0" Grid.Column="5" Style="{StaticResource LabelStyle}"
Text="First Name"/>
        <TextBlock Grid.Row="0" Grid.Column="7" Style="{StaticResource LabelStyle}"
Text="Last Name"/>
        ...
        <TextBlock Grid.Row="3" Grid.Column="1" Style="{StaticResource LabelStyle}"
Text="Email"/>
        ...
        <TextBlock Grid.Row="5" Grid.Column="1" Style="{StaticResource LabelStyle}"
Text="Phone"/>
        ...
    </Grid>
</Grid>
<Grid x:Name="customersColumnarView" Margin="10,20,10,20" Visibility="Collapsed">
    ...
    <Grid Grid.Row="1">
        ...
        <TextBlock Grid.Row="0" Grid.Column="0" Style="{StaticResource LabelStyle}"
Text="ID"/>
        <TextBlock Grid.Row="1" Grid.Column="0" Style="{StaticResource LabelStyle}"
Text="Title"/>
        <TextBlock Grid.Row="2" Grid.Column="0" Style="{StaticResource LabelStyle}"
Text="First Name"/>
        <TextBlock Grid.Row="3" Grid.Column="0" Style="{StaticResource LabelStyle}"
Text="Last Name"/>
        ...
        <TextBlock Grid.Row="4" Grid.Column="0" Style="{StaticResource LabelStyle}"
Text="Email"/>
        ...
        <TextBlock Grid.Row="5" Grid.Column="0" Style="{StaticResource LabelStyle}"
Text="Phone"/>
        ...
    </Grid>
</Grid>
```

The labels on the form should change to the Segoe Print font and be displayed in white, in a font size of 30 points:

20. On the Debug menu, click Start Debugging to build and run the app.

> 📝 **Note** Use the Simulator if you are running on a display with a resolution less than 1366 × 768.

The Customers form should appear and be styled in the same way that it appears in the Design View window in Visual Studio. Notice that if you enter any text into the various fields on the form, they use the default font and styling for the *TextBox* controls.

> 📝 **Note** Although the Segoe Print font is good for labels and titles, it is not recommended as a font for data-entry fields because some of the characters can be difficult to distinguish from one another. For example, the lowercase letter *l* is very similar to the digit 1, and the uppercase letter *O* is almost indistinguishable from the digit 0. For this reason, it makes sense to stick with the default font for the *TextBox* controls.

21. Resize the window to make it narrower and verify that the styling has been applied to the controls in the *customersColumnarView* grid. The form should look like this:

22. Return to Visual Studio and stop debugging.

For completeness, the following image shows the Customers app running on the Windows Phone 10 Emulator:

You can see that by using styles, you can easily implement a number of really cool effects. In addition, careful use of styles makes your code much more maintainable than it would be if you set properties on individual controls. For example, if you want to switch the font used by the labels and headings in the Customers app, you need to make only a single change to the *FontStyle* style. In general, you should use styles wherever possible; besides assisting maintainability, the use of styles helps to keep the XAML markup for your forms clean and uncluttered, and the XAML for a form needs to specify only the controls and layout rather than how the controls should appear on the form. You can also use Microsoft Blend for Visual Studio 2015 to define complex styles that you can integrate into an app. Professional graphics artists can use Blend to develop custom styles and provide these styles in the form of XAML markup to developers building apps. All the developer has to do is add the appropriate *Style* tags to the user interface elements to reference the corresponding styles.

Summary

In this chapter, you learned how to use the *Grid* control to implement a user interface that can scale to different device form factors and orientations. You also learned how to use the Visual State Manager to adapt the layout of controls when the user changes the size of the window displaying the app. Finally, you learned how to create custom styles and apply them to the controls on a form. Now that you have defined the user interface, the next challenge is to add functionality to the app, enabling the user to display and update data, which is what you will do in the final chapters.

- If you want to continue to the next chapter, keep Visual Studio 2015 running and turn to Chapter 26.

- If you want to exit Visual Studio 2015 now, on the File menu, click Exit. If you see a Save dialog box, click Yes and save the project.

Quick reference

To	Do this
Create a new UWP app	Use one of the UWP templates in Visual Studio 2015, such as the Blank App template.
Implement a user interface that scales to different device form factors and orientations	Use a *Grid* control. Divide the *Grid* control into rows and columns, and place controls in these rows and columns rather than specifying an absolute location relative to the edges of the *Grid*.
Implement a user interface that can adapt to different display widths	Create different layouts for each view that display the controls in an appropriate manner. Use the Visual State Manager to select the layout to display when the visual state changes.

Create custom styles	Add a resource dictionary to the app. Define styles in this dictionary by using the *<Style>* element, and specify the properties that each style changes. For example:
	
	`<Style x:Key="GridStyle" TargetType="Grid">`
	`    <Setter Property="Background" Value="{StaticResource WoodBrush}"/>`
	`</Style>`

Apply a custom style to a control	Set the *Style* property of the control and reference the style by name. For example: `<Grid Style="{StaticResource GridStyle}">`

CHAPTER 26

Displaying and searching for data in a Universal Windows Platform app

After completing the chapter, you will be able to:

- Explain how to use the Model-View-ViewModel pattern to implement the logic for a Universal Windows Platform app.

- Use data binding to display and modify data in a view.

- Create a ViewModel with which a view can interact with a model.

- Integrate a Universal Windows Platform app with Cortana to provide voice-activated search capabilities.

Chapter 25, "Implementing the user interface for a Universal Windows Platform app," demonstrates how to design a user interface (UI) that can adapt to the different device form factors, orientations, and views that a customer running your app might use. The sample app developed in that chapter is a simple one designed for displaying and editing details about customers.

In this chapter, you will see how to display data in the UI and learn about the features in Windows 10 with which you can search for data in an app. In performing these tasks, you will also learn about the way in which you can structure a UWP app. This chapter covers a lot of ground. In particular, you will look at how to use data binding to connect the UI to the data that it displays and how to create a ViewModel in order to separate the user interface logic from the data model and business logic for an app. You will also see how to integrate a UWP app with Cortana to enable a user to perform voice-activated searches.

Implementing the Model-View-ViewModel pattern

A well-structured graphical app separates the design of the user interface from the data that the application uses and the business logic that comprises the functionality of the app. This separation helps to remove the dependencies between the various components, enabling different presentations of the data without needing to change the business logic or the underlying data model. This approach also clears the way for different elements to be designed and implemented by individuals who have the appropriate specialist skills. For example, a graphic artist can focus attention on designing an appealing and intuitive UI, a database specialist can concentrate on implementing an optimized set of data structures for storing and accessing the data, and a C# developer can direct her efforts toward implementing the business logic for the app. This is a common goal that has been the aim of many development approaches, not just for UWP apps, and over the past few years many techniques have been devised to help structure an app in this way.

Arguably, the most popular approach is to follow the Model-View-ViewModel (MVVM) design pattern. In this design pattern, the model provides the data used by the app, and the view represents the way in which the data is displayed in the UI. The ViewModel contains the logic that connects the two, taking the user input and converting it into commands that perform business operations on the model, and also taking the data from the model and formatting it in the manner expected by the view. The following diagram shows a simplified relationship between the elements of the MVVM pattern. Note that an app might provide multiple views of the same data. In a UWP app, for example, you might implement different view states, which can present information by using different screen layouts. One job of the ViewModel is to ensure that the data from the same model can be displayed and manipulated by many different views. In a UWP app, the view can utilize data binding to connect to the data presented by the ViewModel. Additionally, the view can request that the ViewModel update data in the model or perform business tasks by invoking commands implemented by the ViewModel.

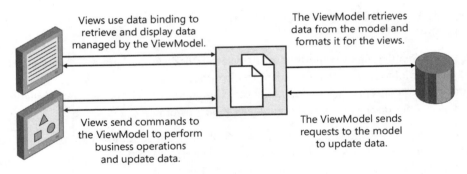

Displaying data by using data binding

Before you get started implementing a ViewModel for the Customers app, it helps to understand a little more about data binding and how you can apply this technique to display data in a UI. Using data binding, you can link a property of a control to a property of an object; if the value of the specified property of the object changes, the property in the control that is linked to the object also changes. In addition, data binding can be bidirectional: if the value of a property in a control that uses data binding changes, the modification is propagated to the object to which the control is linked. The following exercise provides a quick introduction to how data binding is used to display data. It is based on the Customers app from Chapter 25.

Use data binding to display Customer information

1. Start Visual Studio 2015 if it is not already running.

2. Open the Customers project, which is located in the \Microsoft Press\VCSBS\Chapter 26\ Data Binding folder in your Documents folder. This is a version of the Customers app that was developed in Chapter 25, but the layout of the UI has been modified slightly—the controls are displayed on a blue background, which makes them stand out more easily.

> **Note** The blue background was created by using a *Rectangle* control that spans the same rows and columns as the *TextBlock* and *TextBox* controls that display the headings and data. The rectangle is filled by using a *LinearGradientBrush* that gradually changes the color of the rectangle from a medium blue at the top to a very dark blue at the bottom. The XAML markup for the *Rectangle* control that is displayed in *customersTabularView Grid* control views looks like this (the XAML markup for the *customersColumnarView Grid* control includes a similar *Rectangle* control, spanning the rows and columns used by that layout):

```
<Rectangle Grid.Row="0" Grid.RowSpan="6" Grid.Column="1" Grid.ColumnSpan="7" ...>
    <Rectangle.Fill>
        <LinearGradientBrush EndPoint="0.5,1" StartPoint="0.5,0">
            <GradientStop Color="#FF0E3895"/>
            <GradientStop Color="#FF141415" Offset="0.929"/>
        </LinearGradientBrush>
    </Rectangle.Fill>
</Rectangle>
```

3. In Solution Explorer, right-click the Customers project, point to Add, and then click Class.

4. In the Add New Items – Customers dialog box, ensure that the Class template is selected. In the Name box, type **Customer.cs**, and then click Add.

    You will use this class to implement the *Customer* data type and then implement data binding to display the details of *Customer* objects in the UI.

5. In the Code and Text Editor window displaying the Customer.cs file, make the *Customer* class public and add the following private fields and properties shown in bold:

```
public class Customer
{
    public int _customerID;
    public int CustomerID
    {
        get { return this._customerID; }
        set { this._customerID = value; }
    }

    public string _title;
    public string Title
```

```
    {
        get { return this._title; }
        set { this._title = value; }
    }

    public string _firstName;
    public string FirstName
    {
        get { return this._firstName; }
        set { this._firstName = value; }
    }

    public string _lastName;
    public string LastName
    {
        get { return this._lastName; }
        set { this._lastName = value; }
    }

    public string _emailAddress;
    public string EmailAddress
    {
        get { return this._emailAddress; }
        set { this._emailAddress = value; }
    }

    public string _phone;
    public string Phone
    {
        get { return this._phone; }
        set { this._phone = value; }
    }
}
```

You might be wondering why these properties are not implemented as automatic properties, given that all they do is get and set the value in a private field. You will add additional code to these properties in a later exercise.

6. In Solution Explorer, in the Customers project, double-click the MainPage.xaml file to display the user interface for the application in the Design View window.

7. In the XAML pane, locate the markup for the *id TextBox* control. Modify the XAML markup that sets the *Text* property for this control as shown here in bold:

```
<TextBox Grid.Row="1" Grid.Column="1" x:Name="id" ...
    Text="{Binding CustomerID}" .../>
```

The syntax *Text="{Binding Path}"* specifies that the value of the *Text* property will be provided by the value of the *Path* expression at run time. In this case, *Path* is set to *CustomerID*, so the value held in the *CustomerID* expression will be displayed by this control. However, you need to provide a bit more information to indicate that *CustomerID* is actually a property of a *Customer* object. To do this, you set the *DataContext* property of the control, which you will do shortly.

8. Add the following binding expressions for each of the other text controls on the form. Apply data binding to the *TextBox* controls in the *customersTabularView* and *customers-ColumnarView Grid* controls, as shown in bold in the following code. (The *ComboBox* controls require slightly different handling, which you will address in the section "Using data binding with a *ComboBox* control" later in this chapter.)

```
<Grid x:Name="customersTabularView" ...>
    ...
    <TextBox Grid.Row="1" Grid.Column="1" x:Name="id" ...
Text="{Binding CustomerID}" .../>
    ...
    <TextBox Grid.Row="1" Grid.Column="5" x:Name="firstName" ...
Text="{Binding FirstName}" .../>
    <TextBox Grid.Row="1" Grid.Column="7" x:Name="lastName" ...
Text="{Binding LastName}" .../>
    ...
    <TextBox Grid.Row="3" Grid.Column="3" Grid.ColumnSpan="3"
x:Name="email" ... Text="{Binding EmailAddress}" .../>
    ...
    <TextBox Grid.Row="5" Grid.Column="3" Grid.ColumnSpan="3"
x:Name="phone" ... Text="{Binding Phone}" .../>
</Grid>
<Grid x:Name="customersColumnarView" Margin="10,20,10,20"
Visibility="Collapsed">
    ...
    <TextBox Grid.Row="0" Grid.Column="1" x:Name="cId" ...
Text="{Binding CustomerID}" .../>
    ...
    <TextBox Grid.Row="2" Grid.Column="1" x:Name="cFirstName" ...
Text="{Binding FirstName}" .../>
    <TextBox Grid.Row="3" Grid.Column="1" x:Name="cLastName" ...
Text="{Binding LastName}" .../>
    ...
    <TextBox Grid.Row="4" Grid.Column="1" x:Name="cEmail" ...
Text="{Binding EmailAddress}" .../>
    ...
    <TextBox Grid.Row="5" Grid.Column="1" x:Name="cPhone" ...
Text="{Binding Phone}" .../>
</Grid>
```

Notice how the same binding expression can be used with more than one control. For example, the expression *{Binding CustomerID}* is referenced by the *id* and *cId TextBox* controls, which causes both controls to display the same data.

9. In Solution Explorer, expand the MainPage.xaml file, and then double-click the MainPage.xaml.cs file to display the code for the MainPage.xaml form in the Code and Text Editor window. Add the statement shown below in bold to the *MainPage* constructor.

```
public MainPage()
{
    this.InitializeComponent();

    Customer customer = new Customer
    {
```

```
        CustomerID = 1,
        Title = "Mr",
        FirstName = "John",
        LastName = "Sharp",
        EmailAddress = "john@contoso.com",
        Phone = "111-1111"
    };
}
```

This code creates a new instance of the *Customer* class and populates it with some sample data.

10. After the code that creates the new *Customer* object, add the following statement shown in bold:

```
Customer customer = new Customer
{
    ...
};

this.DataContext = customer;
```

This statement specifies the object to which controls on the MainPage form should bind. In each of the controls, the XAML markup *Text="{Binding Path}"* will be resolved against this object. For example, the *id TextBox* and *cId TextBox* controls both specify *Text="{Binding CustomerID}"*, so they will display the value found in the *CustomerID* property of the *Customer* object to which the form is bound.

> **Note** In this example, you have set the *DataContext* property of the form, so the same data binding automatically applies to all the controls on the form. You can also set the *DataContext* property for individual controls if you need to bind specific controls to different objects.

11. On the Debug menu, click Start Debugging to build and run the app.

Verify that the form occupies the full screen and displays the details for the customer John Sharp, as shown in the following image:

12. Resize the app window to display it in the narrow view. Verify that it displays the same data, as illustrated here:

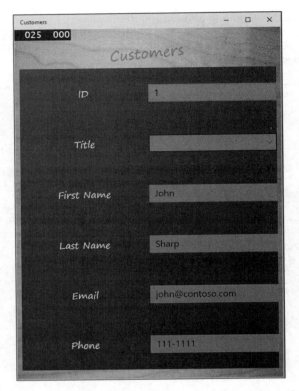

The controls displayed in the narrow view are bound to the same data as the controls displayed in the full-screen view.

13. In the narrow view, change the email address to **john@treyresearch.com**.

14. Expand the app window to switch to the wide view.

   Notice that the email address displayed in this view has not changed.

15. Return to Visual Studio and stop debugging.

16. In Visual Studio, display the code for the *Customer* class in the Code and Text Editor window and set a breakpoint in the *set* property accessor for the *EmailAddress* property.

17. On the Debug menu, click Start Debugging to build and run the application again.

18. When the debugger reaches the breakpoint for the first time, press F5 to continue running the app.

19. When the UI for the Customers app appears, resize the application window to display the narrow view and change the email address to **john@treyresearch.com**.

20. Expand the app window back to the wide view.

Notice that the debugger does not reach the breakpoint in the *set* accessor for the *Email-Address* property; the updated value is not written back to the *Customer* object when the email *TextBox* loses the focus.

21. Return to Visual Studio and stop debugging.

22. Remove the breakpoint in the *set* accessor of the *EmailAddress* property in the *Customer* class.

Modifying data by using data binding

In the previous exercise, you saw how easily data in an object can be displayed by using data binding. However, data binding is a one-way operation by default, and any changes you make to the displayed data are not copied back to the data source. In the exercise, you saw this when you changed the email address displayed in the narrow view; when you switched back to the wide view, the data had not changed. You can implement bidirectional data binding by modifying the *Mode* parameter of the *Binding* specification in the XAML markup for a control. The *Mode* parameter indicates whether data binding is one-way or two-way. This is what you will do next.

Implement *TwoWay* data binding to modify customer information

1. Display the MainPage.xaml file in the Design View window and modify the XAML markup for each of the *TextBox* controls as shown in bold in the following code:

```
<Grid x:Name="customersTabularView" ...>
    ...
    <TextBox Grid.Row="1" Grid.Column="1" x:Name="id" ...
Text="{Binding CustomerID, Mode=TwoWay}" .../>
    ...
    <TextBox Grid.Row="1" Grid.Column="5" x:Name="firstName" ...
Text="{Binding FirstName, Mode=TwoWay}" .../>
    <TextBox Grid.Row="1" Grid.Column="7" x:Name="lastName" ...
Text="{Binding LastName, Mode=TwoWay}" .../>
    ...
    <TextBox Grid.Row="3" Grid.Column="3" Grid.ColumnSpan="3"
x:Name="email" ... Text="{Binding EmailAddress, Mode=TwoWay}" .../>
    ...
    <TextBox Grid.Row="5" Grid.Column="3" Grid.ColumnSpan="3"
x:Name="phone" ... Text="{Binding Phone, Mode=TwoWay}" ..."/>
</Grid>
<Grid x:Name="customersColumnarView" Margin="10,20,10,20" ...>
    ...
    <TextBox Grid.Row="0" Grid.Column="1" x:Name="cId" ...
Text="{Binding CustomerID, Mode=TwoWay}" .../>
    ...
    <TextBox Grid.Row="2" Grid.Column="1" x:Name="cFirstName" ...
Text="{Binding FirstName, Mode=TwoWay}" .../>
    <TextBox Grid.Row="3" Grid.Column="1" x:Name="cLastName" ...
Text="{Binding LastName, Mode=TwoWay}" .../>
    ...
    <TextBox Grid.Row="4" Grid.Column="1" x:Name="cEmail" ...
```

```
Text="{Binding EmailAddress, Mode=TwoWay}" .../>
    ...
    <TextBox Grid.Row="5" Grid.Column="1" x:Name="cPhone" ...
Text="{Binding Phone, Mode=TwoWay}" .../>
</Grid>
```

The *Mode* parameter to the *Binding* specification indicates whether data binding is one-way (the default) or two-way. Setting *Mode* to *TwoWay* causes any changes made by the user to be passed back to the object to which a control is bound.

2. On the Debug menu, click Start Debugging to build and run the app again.

3. With the app in the wide view, change the email address to **john@treyresearch.com**, and then resize the window to display the app in the narrow view.

    Notice that despite the change in the data binding to *TwoWay* mode, the email address displayed in the narrow view has not been updated—it is still john@contoso.com.

4. Return to Visual Studio and stop debugging.

Clearly, something is not working correctly! The problem now is not that the data has not been updated but rather that the view is not displaying the latest version of the data. (If you reinstate the breakpoint in the *set* accessor for the *EmailAddress* property of the *Customer* class and run the app in the debugger, you will see the debugger reach the breakpoint whenever you change the value of the email address and move the focus away from the *TextBox* control.) Despite appearances, the data-binding process is not magic, and a data binding does not know when the data to which it is bound has been changed. The object needs to inform the data binding of any modifications by sending a *PropertyChanged* event to the UI. This event is part of an interface named *INotifyPropertyChanged*, and all objects that support two-way data binding should implement this interface. You will implement this interface in the next exercise.

Implement the *INotifyPropertyChanged* interface in the *Customer* class

1. In Visual Studio, display the Customer.cs file in the Code and Text Editor window.

2. Add the following *using* directive to the list at the top of the file:

    ```
    using System.ComponentModel;
    ```

    The *INotifyPropertyChanged* interface is defined in this namespace.

3. Modify the definition of the *Customer* class to specify that it implements the *INotify-PropertyChanged* interface, as shown here in bold:

    ```
    class Customer : INotifyPropertyChanged
    ```

4. After the *Phone* property in the *Customer* class, add the *PropertyChanged* event shown in bold in the following code:

```
class Customer : INotifyPropertyChanged
{
    ...
    public string _phone;
    public string Phone {
        get { return this._phone; }
        set { this._phone = value; }
    }

    public event PropertyChangedEventHandler PropertyChanged;
}
```

This event is the only item that the *INotifyPropertyChanged* interface defines. All objects that implement this interface must provide this event, and they should raise this event whenever they want to notify the outside world of a change to a property value.

5. Add the *OnPropertyChanged* method shown below in bold to the *Customer* class, after the *PropertyChanged* event:

```
class Customer : INotifyPropertyChanged
{
    ...
    public event PropertyChangedEventHandler PropertyChanged;

    protected virtual void OnPropertyChanged(string propertyName)
    {
        if (PropertyChanged != null)
        {
            PropertyChanged(this,
                new PropertyChangedEventArgs(propertyName));
        }
    }
}
```

The *OnPropertyChanged* method raises the *PropertyChanged* event. The *PropertyChanged-EventArgs* parameter to the *PropertyChanged* event should specify the name of the property that has changed. This value is passed in as a parameter to the *OnPropertyChanged* method.

6. Modify the property *set* accessors for each of the properties in the *Customer* class to call the *OnPropertyChanged* method whenever the value that they contain is modified, as shown in bold here:

```
class Customer : INotifyPropertyChanged
{
    public int _customerID;
    public int CustomerID
    {
        get { return this._customerID; }
        set
        {
            this._customerID = value;
            this.OnPropertyChanged(nameof(CustomerID));
        }
    }
}
```

```csharp
public string _title;
public string Title
{
    get { return this._title; }
    set
    {
        this._title = value;
        this.OnPropertyChanged(nameof(Title));
    }
}

public string _firstName;
public string FirstName
{
    get { return this._firstName; }
    set
    {
        this._firstName = value;
        this.OnPropertyChanged(nameof(FirstName));
    }
}

public string _lastName;
public string LastName
{
    get { return this._lastName; }
    set
    {
        this._lastName = value;
        this.OnPropertyChanged(nameof(LastName));
    }
}

public string _emailAddress;
public string EmailAddress
{
    get { return this._emailAddress; }
    set
    {
        this._emailAddress = value;
        this.OnPropertyChanged(nameof(EmailAddress));
    }
}

public string _phone;
public string Phone
{
    get { return this._phone; }
    set
    {
        this._phone = value;
        this.OnPropertyChanged(nameof(Phone));
    }
}
...
}
```

> ### The *nameof* operator
>
> The *nameof* operator demonstrated in the *Customer* class is a little-used but highly useful feature of C# in code such as this. It returns the name of the variable passed in as its parameter as a string. Without using the *nameof* operator, you would have had to use hard-coded string values. For example:
>
> ```
> public int CustomerID
> {
>     get { return this._customerID; }
>     set
>     {
>         this._customerID = value;
>         this.OnPropertyChanged("CustomerID");
>     }
> }
> ```
>
> Although using the string values requires less typing, consider what would happen if you needed to change the name of the property at some point in the future. Using the string approach, you would need to modify the string value as well. If you didn't, the code would still compile and run, but any changes made to the property value at run time would not be notified, leading to difficult-to-find bugs. Using the *nameof* operator, if you change the name of the property but forget to change the argument to *nameof*, the code will not compile, alerting you immediately to an error that should be quick and easy to fix.

7. On the Debug menu, click Start Debugging to build and run the app again.

8. When the Customers form appears, change the email address to **john@treyresearch.com**, and change the phone number to **222-2222**.

9. Resize the window to display the app in the narrow view and verify that the email address and phone number have changed.

10. Change the first name to **James**, expand the window to display the wide view, and verify that the first name has changed.

11. Return to Visual Studio and stop debugging.

Using data binding with a *ComboBox* control

Using data binding with a control such as a *TextBox* or *TextBlock* is a relatively straightforward matter. On the other hand, *ComboBox* controls require a little more attention. The issue is that a *ComboBox* control actually displays two things: a list of values in the drop-down list from which the user can select an item and the value of the currently selected item. If you implement data binding to display a list of items in the drop-down list of a *ComboBox* control, the value that the user selects must be a member of this list. In the Customers app, you can configure data binding for the selected value in the *title ComboBox* control by setting the *SelectedValue* property, like this:

```
<ComboBox ... x:Name="title" ... SelectedValue="{Binding Title}" ... />
```

However, remember that the list of values for the drop-down list is hard-coded into the XAML markup, like this:

```
<ComboBox ... x:Name="title" ... >
    <ComboBoxItem Content="Mr"/>
    <ComboBoxItem Content="Mrs"/>
    <ComboBoxItem Content="Ms"/>
    <ComboBoxItem Content="Miss"/>
</ComboBox>
```

This markup is not applied until the control has been created, so the value specified by the data binding is not found in the list because the list does not yet exist when the data binding is constructed. The result is that the value is not displayed. You can try this if you like—configure the binding for the *SelectedValue* property as just shown and run the app. The *title ComboBox* will be empty when it is initially displayed, despite the fact that the customer has the title of Mr.

There are several solutions to this problem, but the simplest is to create a data source that contains the list of valid values and then specify that the *ComboBox* control should use this list as its set of values for the drop-down. Also, you need to do this before the data binding for the *ComboBox* is applied.

Implement data binding for the *title ComboBox* controls

1. In Visual Studio, display the MainPage.xaml.cs file in the Code and Text Editor window.

2. Add the following code shown in bold to the *MainPage* constructor:

```
public MainPage()
{
    this.InitializeComponent();

    List<string> titles = new List<string>
    {
        "Mr", "Mrs", "Ms", "Miss"
    };

    this.title.ItemsSource = titles;
    this.cTitle.ItemsSource = titles;

    Customer customer = new Customer
    {
        ...
    };

    this.DataContext = customer;
}
```

This code creates a list of strings containing the valid titles that customers can have. The code then sets the *ItemsSource* property of both *title ComboBox* controls to reference this list (remember that each view has a *ComboBox* control).

The placement of this code is important. It must run before the statement that sets the *DataContext* property of the *MainPage* form because this statement is when the data binding to the controls on the form occurs.

3. Display the MainPage.xaml file in the Design View window.

4. Modify the XAML markup for the *title* and *cTitle ComboBox* controls, as shown here in bold:

```xml
<Grid x:Name="customersTabularView" ...>
    ...
    <ComboBox Grid.Row="1" Grid.Column="3" x:Name="title" ...
SelectedValue="{Binding Title, Mode=TwoWay}">
    </ComboBox>
    ...
</Grid>
<Grid x:Name="customersColumnarView" ...>
    ...
    <ComboBox Grid.Row="1" Grid.Column="1" x:Name="cTitle" ...
SelectedValue="{Binding Title, Mode=TwoWay}">
    </ComboBox>
    ...
</Grid>
```

Notice that the list of *ComboBoxItem* elements for each control has been removed and that the *SelectedValue* property is configured to use data binding with the *Title* field in the *Customer* object.

5. On the Debug menu, click Start Debugging to build and run the application.

6. Verify that the value of the customer's title is displayed correctly (it should be Mr). Click the drop-down arrow for the *ComboBox* control and verify that it contains the values *Mr*, *Mrs*, *Ms*, and *Miss*.

7. Resize the window to display the app in the narrow view and perform the same checks. Note that you can change the title, and when you switch back to the wide view, the new title is displayed.

8. Return to Visual Studio and stop debugging.

Creating a ViewModel

You have now seen how to configure data binding to connect a data source to the controls in a user interface, but the data source that you have been using is very simple, consisting of a single customer. In the real world, the data source is likely to be much more complex, comprising collections of different types of objects. Remember that in MVVM terms, the data source is often provided by the model, and the UI (the view) communicates with the model only indirectly through a ViewModel object. The rationale behind this approach is that the model and the views that display the data provided by the model should be independent; you should not have to change the model if the user interface is modified, nor should you be required to adjust the UI if the underlying model changes.

The ViewModel provides the connection between the view and the model, and it also implements the business logic for the app. Again, this business logic should be independent of the view and the model. The ViewModel exposes the business logic to the view by implementing a collection of commands. The UI can trigger these commands based on the way in which the user navigates through the app. In the following exercise, you will extend the Customers app by implementing a model that contains a list of *Customer* objects and creating a ViewModel that provides commands with which a user can move between customers in the view.

Create a ViewModel for managing customer information

1. Open the Customers project, which is located in the \Microsoft Press\VCSBS\Chapter 26\ ViewModel folder in your Documents folder. This project contains a completed version of the Customers app from the previous set of exercises; if you prefer, you can continue to use your own version of the project.

2. In Solution Explorer, right-click the Customers project, point to Add, and then click Class.

3. In the Add New Items – Customers dialog box, in the Name box, type **ViewModel.cs**, and then click Add.

   This class provides a basic ViewModel that contains a collection of *Customer* objects. The user interface will bind to the data exposed by this ViewModel.

4. In the Code and Text Editor window displaying the ViewModel.cs file, mark the class as public and add the code shown in bold in the following example to the *ViewModel* class:

```
public class ViewModel
{
    private List<Customer> customers;

    public ViewModel()
    {
        this.customers = new List<Customer>
        {
            new Customer
            {
                CustomerID = 1,
                Title = "Mr",
                FirstName="John",
                LastName="Sharp",
                EmailAddress="john@contoso.com",
                Phone="111-1111"
            },
            new Customer
            {
```

```
                    CustomerID = 2,
                    Title = "Mrs",
                    FirstName="Diana",
                    LastName="Sharp",
                    EmailAddress="diana@contoso.com",
                    Phone="111-1112"
                },
                new Customer
                {
                    CustomerID = 3,
                    Title = "Ms",
                    FirstName="Francesca",
                    LastName="Sharp",
                    EmailAddress="frankie@contoso.com",
                    Phone="111-1113"
                }
            };
        }
    }
```

The *ViewModel* class uses a *List<Customer>* object as its model, and the constructor populates this list with some sample data. Strictly speaking, this data should be held in a separate *Model* class, but for the purposes of this exercise we will make do with this sample data.

5. Add the private variable *currentCustomer* shown in bold in the following code to the *ViewModel* class, and initialize this variable to zero in the constructor:

```
class ViewModel
{
    private List<Customer> customers;
    private int currentCustomer;

    public ViewModel()
    {
        this.currentCustomer = 0;
        this.customers = new List<Customer>
        {
            ...
        }
    }
}
```

The *ViewModel* class will use this variable to track which *Customer* object the view is currently displaying.

6. Add the *Current* property shown below in bold to the *ViewModel* class, after the constructor:

```
class ViewModel
{
    ...

    public ViewModel()
    {
        ...
    }
```

```
        public Customer Current
        {
            get { return this.customers.Count > 0 ? this.customers[currentCustomer] : null; }
        }
}
```

The *Current* property provides access to the current *Customer* object in the model. If there are no customers, it returns a null object.

> **Note** It is good practice to provide controlled access to a data model; only the ViewModel should be able to modify the model. However, this restriction does not prevent the view from being able to update the data presented by the ViewModel—it just cannot switch the model and make it refer to a different data source.

7. Open the MainPage.xaml.cs file in the Code and Text Editor window.

8. In the *MainPage* constructor, remove the code that creates the *Customer* object and replace it with a statement that creates an instance of the *ViewModel* class. Change the statement that sets the *DataContext* property of the *MainPage* object to reference the new *ViewModel* object, as shown here in bold:

```
public MainPage()
{
    ...
    this.cTitle.ItemsSource = titles;

    ViewModel viewModel = new ViewModel();
    this.DataContext = viewModel;
}
```

9. Open the MainPage.xaml file in the Design View window.

10. In the XAML pane, modify the data bindings for the *TextBox* and *ComboBox* controls to reference properties through the *Current* object presented by the ViewModel, as shown in bold in the following code:

```
<Grid x:Name="customersTabularView" ...>
    ...
    <TextBox Grid.Row="1" Grid.Column="1" x:Name="id" ...
Text="{Binding Current.CustomerID, Mode=TwoWay}" .../>
    <TextBox Grid.Row="1" Grid.Column="5" x:Name="firstName" ...
Text="{Binding Current.FirstName, Mode=TwoWay }" .../>
    <TextBox Grid.Row="1" Grid.Column="7" x:Name="lastName" ...
Text="{Binding Current.LastName, Mode=TwoWay }" .../>
    <ComboBox Grid.Row="1" Grid.Column="3" x:Name="title" ...
SelectedValue="{Binding Current.Title, Mode=TwoWay}">
    </ComboBox>
    ...
    <TextBox Grid.Row="3" Grid.Column="3" ... x:Name="email" ...
Text="{Binding Current.EmailAddress, Mode=TwoWay }" .../>
```

```
...
    <TextBox Grid.Row="5" Grid.Column="3" ... x:Name="phone" ...
Text="{Binding Current.Phone, Mode=TwoWay }" .../>
</Grid>
<Grid x:Name="customersColumnarView" Margin="20,10,20,110" ...>
    ...
    <TextBox Grid.Row="0" Grid.Column="1" x:Name="cId" ...
Text="{Binding Current.CustomerID, Mode=TwoWay }" .../>
    <TextBox Grid.Row="2" Grid.Column="1" x:Name="cFirstName" ...
Text="{Binding Current.FirstName, Mode=TwoWay }" .../>
    <TextBox Grid.Row="3" Grid.Column="1" x:Name="cLastName" ...
Text="{Binding Current.LastName, Mode=TwoWay }" .../>
    <ComboBox Grid.Row="1" Grid.Column="1" x:Name="cTitle" ...
SelectedValue="{Binding Current.Title, Mode=TwoWay}">
    </ComboBox>
    ...
    <TextBox Grid.Row="4" Grid.Column="1" x:Name="cEmail" ...
Text="{Binding Current.EmailAddress, Mode=TwoWay }" .../>
    ...
    <TextBox Grid.Row="5" Grid.Column="1" x:Name="cPhone" ...
Text="{Binding Current.Phone, Mode=TwoWay }" .../>
</Grid>
```

11. On the Debug menu, click Start Debugging to build and run the app.

12. Verify that the app displays the details of John Sharp (the first customer in the customers list). Change the details of the customer and switch between views to prove that the data binding is still functioning correctly.

13. Return to Visual Studio and stop debugging.

The ViewModel provides access to customer information through the *Current* property, but currently it does not supply any way to navigate between customers. You can implement methods that increment and decrement the *currentCustomer* variable so that the *Current* property retrieves different customers, but you should do so in a manner that does not tie the view to the ViewModel. The most commonly accepted technique is to use the Command pattern. In this pattern, the View-Model exposes methods in the form of commands that the view can invoke. The trick is to avoid explicitly referencing these methods by name in the code for the view. To do this, XAML makes it possible for you to declaratively bind commands to the actions triggered by controls in the UI, as you will see in the exercises in the next section.

Adding commands to a ViewModel

The XAML markup that binds the action of a control to a command requires that commands exposed by a ViewModel implement the *ICommand* interface. This interface defines the following items:

- **CanExecute** This method returns a Boolean value indicating whether the command can run. Using this method, a ViewModel can enable or disable a command depending on the context. For example, a command that fetches the next customer from a list should be able to run only if there is a next customer to fetch; if there are no more customers, the command should be disabled.

- **Execute** This method runs when the command is invoked.

- **CanExecuteChanged** This event is triggered when the state of the ViewModel changes. Under these circumstances, commands that could previously run might now be disabled and vice versa. For example, if the UI invokes a command that fetches the next customer from a list, if that customer is the last customer, then subsequent calls to *CanExecute* should return *false*. In these circumstances, the *CanExecuteChanged* event should fire to indicate that the command has been disabled.

In the next exercise, you will create a generic class that implements the *ICommand* interface.

Implement the *Command* class

1. In Visual Studio, right-click the Customers project, point to Add, and then click Class.

2. In the Add New Item – Customers dialog box, select the Class template. In the Name box, type **Command.cs**, and then click Add.

3. In the Code and Text Editor window displaying the Command.cs file, add the following *using* directive to the list at the top of the file:

```
using System.Windows.Input;
```

The *ICommand* interface is defined in this namespace.

4. Make the *Command* class public and specify that it implements the *ICommand* interface, as follows in bold:

```
public class Command : ICommand
{
}
```

5. Add the following private fields to the *Command* class:

```
public class Command : ICommand
{
    private Action methodToExecute = null;
    private Func<bool> methodToDetectCanExecute = null;
}
```

The *Action* and *Func* types are briefly described in Chapter 20, "Decoupling application logic and handling events." The *Action* type is a delegate that you can use to reference a method that takes no parameters and does not return a value, and the *Func<T>* type is also a delegate that can reference a method that takes no parameters but returns a value of the type specified by the type parameter *T*. In this class, you will use the *methodToExecute* field to reference the code that the *Command* object will run when it is invoked by the view. The *methodToDetect-CanExecute* field will be used to reference the method that detects whether the command can run (it may be disabled for some reason, depending on the state of the app or the data).

6. Add a constructor to the *Command* class. This constructor should take two parameters: an *Action* object and a *Func<T>* object. Assign these parameters to the *methodToExecute* and *methodToDetectCanExecute* fields, as shown here in bold:

```
public Command : ICommand
{
    ...
    public Command(Action methodToExecute, Func<bool> methodToDetectCanExecute)
    {
        this.methodToExecute = methodToExecute;
        this.methodToDetectCanExecute = methodToDetectCanExecute;
    }
}
```

The ViewModel will create an instance of this class for each command. The ViewModel will supply the method to run the command and the method to detect whether the command should be enabled when it calls the constructor.

7. Implement the *Execute* and *CanExecute* methods of the *Command* class by using the methods referenced by the *methodToExecute* and *methodToDetectCanExecute* fields, as follows:

```
public Command : ICommand
{
    ...
    public Command(Action methodToExecute,
        Func<bool> methodToDetectCanExecute)
    {
        ...
    }

    public void Execute(object parameter)
    {
        this.methodToExecute();
    }

    public bool CanExecute(object parameter)
    {
        if (this.methodToDetectCanExecute == null)
        {
            return true;
        }
        else
        {
            return this.methodToDetectCanExecute();
        }
    }
}
```

Notice that if the ViewModel provides a *null* reference for the *methodToDetectCanExecute* parameter of the constructor, the default action is to assume that the command can run, and the *CanExecute* method returns *true*.

8. Add the public *CanExecuteChanged* event to the *Command* class:

```
public Command : ICommand
{
    ...
    public bool CanExecute(object parameter)
    {
        ...
    }

    public event EventHandler CanExecuteChanged;
}
```

When you bind a command to a control, the control automatically subscribes to this event. This event should be raised by the *Command* object if the state of the ViewModel is updated and the value returned by the *CanExecute* method changes. The simplest strategy is to use a timer to raise the *CanExecuteChanged* event once a second or so. The control can then invoke *CanExecute* to determine whether the command can still be executed and take steps to enable or disable itself depending on the result.

9. Add the *using* directive shown next to the list at the top of the file:

```
using Windows.UI.Xaml;
```

10. Add the following field shown in bold to the *Command* class above the constructor:

```
public class Command : ICommand
{
    ...
    private Func<bool> methodToDetectCanExecute = null;
    private DispatcherTimer canExecuteChangedEventTimer = null;

    public Command(Action methodToExecute,
        Func<bool> methodToDetectCanExecute)
    {
        ...
    }
}
```

The *DispatcherTimer* class, defined in the *Windows.UI.Xaml* namespace, implements a timer that can raise an event at specified intervals. You will use the *canExecuteChangedEventTimer* field to trigger the *CanExecuteChanged* event at one-second intervals.

11. Add the *canExecuteChangedEventTimer_Tick* method shown in bold in the following code to the end of the *Command* class:

```
public class Command : ICommand
{
    ...
    public event EventHandler CanExecuteChanged;

    void canExecuteChangedEventTimer_Tick(object sender, object e)
    {
        if (this.CanExecuteChanged != null)
        {
            this.CanExecuteChanged(this, EventArgs.Empty);
```

```
            }
        }
    }
```

This method simply raises the *CanExecuteChanged* event if at least one control is bound to the command. Strictly speaking, this method should also check whether the state of the object has changed before raising the event. However, you will set the timer interval to a lengthy period (in processing terms) to minimize any inefficiencies in not checking for a change in state.

12. In the *Command* constructor, add the following statements shown in bold.

```
public class Command : ICommand
{
    ...
    public Command(Action methodToExecute, Func<bool> methodToDetectCanExecute)
    {
        this.methodToExecute = methodToExecute;
        this.methodToDetectCanExecute = methodToDetectCanExecute;

        this.canExecuteChangedEventTimer = new DispatcherTimer();
        this.canExecuteChangedEventTimer.Tick +=
            canExecuteChangedEventTimer_Tick;
        this.canExecuteChangedEventTimer.Interval = new TimeSpan(0, 0, 1);
        this.canExecuteChangedEventTimer.Start();
    }
    ...
}
```

This code initiates the *DispatcherTimer* object and sets the interval for timer events to one second before it starts the timer running.

13. On the Build menu, click Build Solution and ensure that your app builds without errors.

You can now use the *Command* class to add commands to the *ViewModel* class. In the next exercise, you will define commands to enable a user to move between customers in the view.

Add *NextCustomer* and *PreviousCustomer* commands to the *ViewModel* class

1. In Visual Studio, open the ViewModel.cs file in the Code and Text Editor window.

2. Add the following *using* directive to the top of the file and modify the definition of the *ViewModel* class to implement the *INotifyPropertyChanged* interface.

```
...
using System.ComponentModel;

namespace Customers
{
    public class ViewModel : INotifyPropertyChanged
    {
        ...
    }
}
```

3. Add the *PropertyChanged* event and *OnPropertyChanged* method to the end of the
   ViewModel class. This is the same code that you included in the *Customer* class.

```
public class ViewModel : INotifyPropertyChanged
{
    ...
    public event PropertyChangedEventHandler PropertyChanged;

    protected virtual void OnPropertyChanged(string propertyName)
    {
        if (PropertyChanged != null)
        {
            PropertyChanged(this,
                new PropertyChangedEventArgs(propertyName));
        }
    }
}
```

Remember that the view references data through the *Current* property in the data-binding
expressions for the various controls that it contains. When the *ViewModel* class moves to a
different customer, it must raise the *PropertyChanged* event to notify the view that the data
to be displayed has changed.

4. Add the following fields and properties to the *ViewModel* class immediately after the
   constructor:

```
public class ViewModel : INotifyPropertyChanged
{
    ...
    public ViewModel()
    {
        ...
    }

    private bool _isAtStart;
    public bool IsAtStart
    {
        get { return this._isAtStart; }
        set
        {
            this._isAtStart = value;
            this.OnPropertyChanged(nameof(IsAtStart));
        }
    }

    private bool _isAtEnd;
    public bool IsAtEnd
    {
        get { return this._isAtEnd; }
        set
        {
            this._isAtEnd = value;
            this.OnPropertyChanged(nameof(IsAtEnd));
        }
    }
}
```

```
    ...
}
```

You will use these two properties to track the state of the ViewModel. The *IsAtStart* property will be set to *true* when the *currentCustomer* field in the ViewModel is positioned at the start of the customers collection, and the *IsAtEnd* property will be set to *true* when the ViewModel is positioned at the end of the customers collection.

5. Modify the constructor to set the *IsAtStart* and *IsAtEnd* properties, as shown here in bold.:

```
public ViewModel()
{
    this.currentCustomer = 0;
    this.IsAtStart = true;
    this.IsAtEnd = false;

    this.customers = new List<Customer>
    ...
}
```

6. After the *Current* property, add the *Next* and *Previous* private methods shown in bold to the *ViewModel* class:

```
public class ViewModel : INotifyPropertyChanged
{
    ...
    public Customer Current
    {
        ...
    }

    private void Next()
    {
        if (this.customers.Count - 1 > this.currentCustomer)
        {
            this.currentCustomer++;
            this.OnPropertyChanged(nameof(Current));
            this.IsAtStart = false;
            this.IsAtEnd =
              (this.customers.Count - 1 == this.currentCustomer);
        }
    }

    private void Previous()
    {
        if (this.currentCustomer > 0)
        {
            this.currentCustomer--;
            this.OnPropertyChanged(nameof(Current));
            this.IsAtEnd = false;
            this.IsAtStart = (this.currentCustomer == 0);
        }
    }
    ...
}
```

These methods update the *currentCustomer* variable to refer to the next (or previous) customer in the customers list. Notice that these methods maintain the values for the *IsAtStart* and *IsAtEnd* properties and indicate that the current customer has changed by raising the *PropertyChanged* event for the *Current* property. These methods are private because they should not be accessible from outside the *ViewModel* class. External classes will run these methods by using commands, which you will add in the following steps.

7. Add the *NextCustomer* and *PreviousCustomer* automatic properties to the *ViewModel* class, as shown here in bold:

```
public class ViewModel : INotifyPropertyChanged
{
    private List<Customer> customers;
    private int currentCustomer;
    public Command NextCustomer { get; private set; }
    public Command PreviousCustomer { get; private set; }
    ...
}
```

The view will bind to these *Command* objects so that the user can navigate between customers.

8. In the *ViewModel* constructor, set the *NextCustomer* and *PreviousCustomer* properties to refer to new *Command* objects, as follows:

```
public ViewModel()
{
    this.currentCustomer = 0;
    this.IsAtStart = true;
    this.IsAtEnd = false;
    this.NextCustomer = new Command(this.Next, () =>
        { return this.customers.Count > 1 && !this.IsAtEnd; });
    this.PreviousCustomer = new Command(this.Previous, () =>
        { return this.customers.Count > 0 && !this.IsAtStart; });
    ...
}
```

The *NextCustomer Command* specifies the *Next* method as the operation to perform when the *Execute* method is invoked. The lambda expression *() => { return this.customers.Count > 1 && !this.IsAtEnd; }* is specified as the function to call when the *CanExecute method* runs.

This expression returns *true* as long as the customers list contains more than one customer and the ViewModel is not positioned on the final customer in this list. The *PreviousCustomer Command* follows the same pattern: it invokes the *Previous* method to retrieve the previous customer from the list, and the *CanExecute* method references the expression *() => { return this.customers.Count > 0 && !this.IsAtStart; }*, which returns *true* as long as the customers list contains at least one customer and the ViewModel is not positioned on the first customer in this list.

9. On the Build menu, click Build Solution and verify that your app still builds without errors.

Now that you have added the *NextCustomer* and *PreviousCustomer* commands to the ViewModel, you can bind these commands to buttons in the view. When the user clicks a button, the appropriate command will run.

Microsoft publishes guidelines for adding buttons to views in UWP apps, and the general recommendation is that buttons that invoke commands should be placed on a command bar. UWP apps provide two command bars: one appears at the top of the form and the other at the bottom. Buttons that navigate through an app or data are commonly placed on the top command bar, and this is the approach that you will adopt in the next exercise.

> **Note** You can find the Microsoft guidelines for implementing command bars at *http://msdn.microsoft.com/library/windows/apps/hh465302.aspx*.

Add Next and Previous buttons to the Customers form

1. Open the MainPage.xaml file in the Design View window.

2. Scroll to the bottom of the XAML pane and add the following markup shown in bold, immediately above the closing *</Page>* tag:

```
...
<Page.TopAppBar>
    <CommandBar>
        <AppBarButton x:Name="previousCustomer" Icon="Previous"
Label="Previous" Command="{Binding Path=PreviousCustomer}"/>
        <AppBarButton x:Name="nextCustomer" Icon="Next"
Label="Next" Command="{Binding Path=NextCustomer}"/>
    </CommandBar>
</Page.TopAppBar>
</Page>
```

There are several points to notice in this fragment of XAML markup:

- By default, the command bar appears at the top of the screen and displays icons for the buttons that it contains. The label for each button is displayed only when the user clicks the More (...) button that appears on the right side of the command bar. However, if you are designing an application that could be used in multiple cultures, you should not use hard-coded values for labels but instead store the text for these labels in a culture-specific resources file and bind the *Label* property dynamically when the application runs. For more information, visit the page "Quickstart: Translating UI resources (XAML)" on the Microsoft website at *https://msdn.microsoft.com/library/windows/apps/xaml/hh965329.aspx*.

- The *CommandBar* control can contain only a limited set of controls (controls that implement the *ICommandBarElement* interface). This set includes the AppBarButton, AppBarToggleButton, and AppBarSeparator controls. These controls are specifically designed to operate within a *CommandBar*. If you attempt to add a control such as a button to a command bar, you will receive the error message "The specified value cannot be assigned to the collection."

- The UWP app templates include a variety of stock icons (such as for Previous and Next, shown in the sample code above), that you can display on an *AppBarButton* control. You can browse the full set of available stock icons by using the Properties window. In the Icon section, click Symbol Icon. The available stock icons appear in the list box that is displayed. You can also define your own icons and bitmaps.

- Each button has a *Command* property, which is the property that you can bind to an object that implements the *ICommand* interface. In this application, you have bound the buttons to the *PreviousCustomer* and *NextCustomer* commands in the *ViewModel* class. When the user clicks either of these buttons at run time, the corresponding command will run.

3. On the Debug menu, click Start Debugging.

The Customers form should appear and display the details for John Sharp. The command bar should be displayed at the top of the form and contain the Next and Previous buttons, as shown in the following image:

Notice that the Previous button is not available. This is because the *IsAtStart* property of the ViewModel is *true*, and the *CanExecute* method of the *Command* object referenced by the Previous button indicates that the command cannot run.

4. Click the ellipsis button on the command bar. The labels for the buttons should appear. These labels will be displayed until you click one of the buttons on the command bar.

5. On the command bar, click Next.

The details for customer 2, Diana Sharp, should appear, and after a short delay (of up to one second), the Previous button should become available. The *IsAtStart* property is no longer *true*, so the *CanExecute* method of the command returns *true*. However, the button is not notified of this change in state until the timer object in the command expires and triggers the *CanExecuteChanged* event, which might take up to a second to occur.

Note If you require a more instantaneous reaction to the change in state of commands, you can arrange for the timer in the *Command* class to expire more frequently. However, avoid reducing the time by too much because raising the *CanExecuteChanged* event too frequently can impact the performance of the UI.

6. On the command bar, click Next again.

7. The details for customer 3, Francesca Sharp, should appear, and after a short delay of up to one second, the Next button should no longer be available. This time, the *IsAtEnd* property of the ViewModel is *true*, so the *CanExecute* method of the *Command* object for the Next button returns *false* and the command is disabled.

8. Resize the window to display the app in the narrow view and verify that the app continues to function correctly. The Next and Previous buttons should step forward and backward through the list of customers.

9. Return to Visual Studio and stop debugging.

Searching for data using Cortana

A key feature of Windows 10 apps is the ability to integrate with the voice-activated digital assistant, also known as Cortana. Using Cortana, you can activate applications and pass them commands. A common requirement is to use Cortana to initiate a search request and have an application respond with the results of that request. The app can send the results back to Cortana for display (known as *background activation*), or the app itself can display the results (known as *foreground activation*). In this section, you will extend the Customers app to enable a user to search for specific customers by name. You can expand this example to cover other attributes or possibly combine search elements into more complex queries.

> **Note** The exercises in this section assume that you have enabled Cortana. To do this, click the Search button on the Windows taskbar. In the toolbar on the left side of the window, click Settings (the cog icon). In the Settings menu, slide the Cortana switch from Off to On.
>

Cortana also requires that you have signed in to your computer by using a Microsoft account, and will prompt you to connect if necessary. This step is required because speech recognition is handled by an external service running in the cloud rather than on your local device.

Adding voice activation to an app is a three-stage process:

1. Create a voice-command definition (VCD) file that describes the commands to which your app can respond. This is an XML file that you deploy as part of your application.

2. Register the voice commands with Cortana. You typically do this when the app starts running. You must run the app at least once before Cortana will recognize it. Thereafter, if Cortana associates a particular command with your app, it will launch your app automatically. To avoid cluttering up its vocabulary, Cortana will "forget" commands associated with an app if the app is not activated for a couple of weeks, and the commands have to be registered again to be recognized. Therefore, it is common practice to register voice commands every time the app starts running—to reset the "forget" counter and give the app another couple of weeks of grace.

3. Handle voice activation in your app. Your app is passed information from Cortana about the command that causes the app to be activated. It is the responsibility of your code to parse this command, extract any arguments, and perform the appropriate operations. This is the most complicated part of implementing voice integration.

The following exercises walk through this process using the Customers app.

Create the voice-command definition (VCD) file for the Customers app

1. In Visual Studio, open the Customers project in the \Microsoft Press\VCSBS\Chapter 26\ Cortana folder in your Documents folder.

   This version of the Customers app has the same ViewModel that you created in the previous exercise, but the data source contains details for many more customers. The customer information is still held in a *List<Customer>* object, but this object is now created by the *DataSource* class in the DataSource.cs file. The *ViewModel* class references this list instead of creating the small collection of three customers used in the previous exercise.

2. In Solution Explorer, right-click the Customers project, point to Add, and then click New Item.

3. In the Add New Item – Customers dialog box, in the left pane, click Visual C#. In the middle pane, scroll down and select the XML File template. In the Name box, type **CustomerVoiceCommands.xml**, and then click Add, as shown in the following image:

Visual Studio generates a default XML file and opens it in the Code and Text Editor window.

4. Add the following markup shown in bold to the XML file.

```xml
<?xml version="1.0" encoding="utf-8"?>
<VoiceCommands xmlns="http://schemas.microsoft.com/voicecommands/1.2">
  <CommandSet xml:lang="en-us" Name="CustomersCommands">
    <CommandPrefix>Customers</CommandPrefix>
    <Example>Show details of John Sharp</Example>
  </CommandSet>
</VoiceCommands>
```

Voice commands are defined in a command set. Each command set has a command prefix (specified by the *CommandPrefix* element), which can be used by Cortana to identify the application at run time. The command prefix does not have to be the same as the name of the application. For example, if your application name is lengthy or contains numeric characters, Cortana might have difficulty recognizing it, so you can use the command prefix to provide a shorter and more pronounceable alias. The *Example* element contains a phrase that shows how a user can invoke the command. Cortana displays this example in response to inquiries such as "What can I say?" or "Help."

> **Note** The command prefix should reflect the purpose of the application and should not conflict with other well-known applications or services. For example, if you specify a command prefix of "Facebook," your application is unlikely to pass verification testing if it is submitted to the Windows Store.

5. If you are not located in the United States, change the *xml:lang* attribute of the *CommandSet* element to reflect your locale. For example, if you are in the United Kingdom, specify *xml:lang="en-gb"*.

   This is important. If the language specified does not match your locale, Cortana will not recognize your voice commands at run time. The rationale behind this is that you should specify a separate *CommandSet* element for each locale in which your application will run. This enables you to provide alternative commands for different languages. Cortana uses the locale of the machine on which the app is running to determine which command set to use.

6. Add the *Command* and *PhraseTopic* elements shown in bold to the *CommandSet* element in the XML file:

```
<?xml version="1.0" encoding="utf-8"?>
<VoiceCommands xmlns="http://schemas.microsoft.com/voicecommands/1.2">
  <CommandSet xml:lang="en-us" Name="CustomersCommands">
    <CommandPrefix>Customers</CommandPrefix>
    <Example>Show details of John Sharp</Example>

    <Command Name="showDetailsOf">
      <Example>show details of John Sharp</Example>
      <ListenFor RequireAppName="BeforeOrAfterPhrase">
        show details of {customer}
      </ListenFor>
      <ListenFor RequireAppName="BeforeOrAfterPhrase">
        show details for {customer}
      </ListenFor>
      <ListenFor RequireAppName="BeforeOrAfterPhrase">
        search for {customer}
      </ListenFor>
      <Feedback>Looking for {customer}</Feedback>
      <Navigate/>
    </Command>
    <PhraseTopic Label="customer" Scenario="Search">
        <Subject>Person Names</Subject>
    </PhraseTopic>

  </CommandSet>
</VoiceCommands>
```

You can add one or more commands to a command set, each of which can invoke a different operation in your application. Each command has a unique identifier (the *Name* attribute). This identifier is passed to the application that Cortana invokes so that the application can determine which command the user spoke and thereby determine which operation to perform.

The text in the *Example* element is displayed by Cortana if the user selects your app in response to the query "What can I say?"; Cortana will display the sample phrase for each of the commands that your app understands.

The *ListenFor* element is used by Cortana to recognize the requests that should invoke this app. You can specify multiple *ListenFor* phrases to provide flexibility to the user. In this case, the user can speak three variations of the same phrase to invoke the command. A phrase spoken by the user should include either the name of the app or the prefix specified in the *CommandSet* element. In this example, the name (or prefix) can be specified at the beginning or end of the spoken phrase (the *RequireAppName* attribute is set to *BeforeOrAfterPhrase*)— for example, "Customers, show details of John Sharp" or "Search for John Sharp in Customers". The text *{customer}* in the *ListenFor* phrase is a placeholder that is governed by the *PhraseTopic* element (described shortly).

The *Feedback* element is spoken by Cortana when it recognizes a request. The customer specified by the user is substituted into the *{customer}* placeholder.

The *Navigate* element indicates that Cortana will start the app in the foreground. You can optionally specify which page should be displayed (if the app contains multiple pages) as the *Target* attribute of this element. The Customers app contains only a single page, so the *Target* attribute is not specified. If the app is intended to run in the background and pass data back for Cortana to display, you specify a *VoiceCommandService* element instead of *Navigate*. For more information, visit the page "Launch a background app with voice commands" in Cortana online at *https://msdn.microsoft.com/library/dn974228.aspx*.

The *PhraseTopic* element is used to define a placeholder in spoken phrases. The *Label* attribute specifies with which placeholder the element is associated. At run time, Cortana substitutes the word or words spoken at this point in the phrase into the phrase topic. The *Scenario* attribute and the *Subject* elements are optional and provide hints to Cortana about how to interpret these words. In this example, the words are being used as search arguments and constitute human names. You can specify other scenarios such as *Short Message* or *Natural Language*, in which case Cortana may attempt to parse these words in a different manner. You can also specify alternative subjects such as addresses, phone number, or city and state.

7. On the File menu, click Save CustomerVoiceCommands.xml, and then close the file.

8. In Solution Explorer, select the CustomerVoiceCommands.xml file. In the Properties window, change the Copy To Output Directory property to Copy If Newer.

    This action causes the XML file to be copied to the application folder if it changes and be deployed with the app.

The next step is to register the voice commands with Cortana when the app runs. You can do this in the code for the *OnLaunched* method in the App.xaml.cs file. The *OnLaunched* method occurs every time a *Launched* event occurs when the application starts running. When the application shuts down, you can save information about the application state (which customer the user was viewing, for example), and you can use this event to restore the state of the application (by displaying the same customer) when the application starts up again. You can also use this event to perform operations that should occur every time the application runs.

Register voice commands with Cortana

1. In Solution Explorer, expand App.xaml and then double-click App.xaml.cs to display the file in the Code and Text Editor window.

2. Add the following *using* directives to the list at the top of the file.

```
using Windows.Storage;
using Windows.ApplicationModel.VoiceCommands;
using System.Diagnostics;
```

3. Find the *OnLaunched* method and enable asynchronous operations by adding the *async* modifier:

```
protected async override void OnLaunched(LaunchActivatedEventArgs e)
{
    ...
}
```

4. Add the code shown below in bold to the end of the *OnLaunched* method:

```
protected async override void OnLaunched(LaunchActivatedEventArgs e)
{
    ...
    // Ensure the current window is active
    Window.Current.Activate();

    try
    {
        var storageFile = await Package.Current.
            InstalledLocation.GetFileAsync(@"CustomerVoiceCommands.xml");
        await VoiceCommandDefinitionManager.
            InstallCommandDefinitionsFromStorageFileAsync(storageFile);
    }
    catch (Exception ex)
    {
        Debug.WriteLine(
            $"Installing Voice Commands Failed: {ex.ToString()}");
    }
}
```

The first statement retrieves the XML file that contains the voice-command definitions from the application folder. This file is then passed to the *VoiceCommandDefinitionManager* manager. This class provides the interface to the operating system for registering and querying voice-command definitions. The static *InstallCommandDefinitionsFromStorageFileAsync* method registers voice commands found in the specified storage file. If an exception occurs during this process, the exception is logged, but the application is allowed to continue running (it just won't respond to voice commands).

The final step is to have your app respond when Cortana recognizes a voice command intended for the app. In this case, you can capture the *Activated* event by using the *OnActivated* method of the

App class. This method is passed a parameter of type *IActivatedEventArgs*, which contains information describing data passed to the app, including the details of any voice-activation commands.

Handle voice activation in the Customers app

1. In the Code and Text Editor window, add the *OnActivated* event method shown here to the end of the *App* class:

    ```
    protected override void OnActivated(IActivatedEventArgs args)
    {
        base.OnActivated(args);
    }
    ```

    This statement invokes the overridden *OnActivated* method to perform any default activation processing required before handling voice activation.

2. Add the following *if* statement block shown in bold to the *OnActivated* method:

    ```
    protected override void OnActivated(IActivatedEventArgs args)
    {
        base.OnActivated(args);

        if (args.Kind == ActivationKind.VoiceCommand)
        {
            var commandArgs = args as VoiceCommandActivatedEventArgs;
            var speechRecognitionResult = commandArgs.Result;
            var commandName = speechRecognitionResult.RulePath.First();
        }
    }
    ```

    This block determines whether the app has been activated by Cortana as the result of a voice command. If so, the *args* parameter contains a *VoiceCommandActivatedEventArgs* object. The *Result* property contains a *speechRecognitionResult* object that contains information about the command. The *RulePath* list in this object contains the elements of the phrase that triggered activation, and the first item in this list contains the name of the command recognized by Cortana. In the Customers application, the only command defined in the CustomerSearch-Commands.xml file is the *showDetailsOf* command.

3. Add the following code shown in bold to the *OnActivated* method:

    ```
    if (args.Kind == ActivationKind.VoiceCommand)
    {
        ...
        var commandName = speechRecognitionResult.RulePath.First();
        string customerName = "";

        switch (commandName)
        {
            case "showDetailsOf":
                customerName = speechRecognitionResult.SemanticInterpretation.
                    Properties["customer"].FirstOrDefault();
    ```

```
                break;

        default:
            break;
    }
}
```

The *switch* statement verifies that the voice command is the *showDetailsOf* command. If you add more voice commands, you should extend this *switch* statement. If the voice data contains some other unknown command, it is ignored.

The *SemanticInterpretation* property of the *speechRecognitionResult* object contains information about the properties of the phrase recognized by Cortana. Commands for the Customers app include the *{customer}* placeholder, and this code retrieves the text value for this placeholder as spoken by the user and interpreted by Cortana.

4. Add the following code to the end of the *OnActivated* method, after the *switch* statement:

```
protected override void OnActivated(IActivatedEventArgs args)
{
    ...
    if (args.Kind == ActivationKind.VoiceCommand)
    {
        ...
        switch (commandName)
        {
            ...
        }

        Frame rootFrame = Window.Current.Content as Frame;
        if (rootFrame == null)
        {
            rootFrame = new Frame();
            rootFrame.NavigationFailed += OnNavigationFailed;
            Window.Current.Content = rootFrame;
        }

        rootFrame.Navigate(typeof(MainPage), customerName);
        Window.Current.Activate();
    }
}
```

The first block here is boilerplate code that ensures that an application window is open to display a page. The second block displays the *MainPage* page in this window. The *Navigate* method of the *Frame* object causes *MainPage* to become the active page. The second parameter is passed as an object that can be used by the page to provide context information about what to display. In this code, the parameter is a string containing the customer name.

5. Open the ViewModel.cs file in the Code and Text Editor window and find the *ViewModel* constructor. The code in this constructor has been refactored slightly, and the statements that initialize the view state have been moved to a separate method named *_initializeState*, as shown here:

```
public ViewModel()
{
    _initializeState();
    this.customers = DataSource.Customers;
}

private void _initializeState()
{
    this.currentCustomer = 0;
    this.IsAtStart = true;
    this.IsAtEnd = false;
    this.NextCustomer = new Command(this.Next, () =>
        { return this.customers.Count > 1 && !this.IsAtEnd; });
    this.PreviousCustomer = new Command(this.Previous, () =>
        { return this.customers.Count > 0 && !this.IsAtStart; });
}
```

6. Add another constructor to the *ViewModel* class. This constructor should take a string containing a customer name and filter the records in the data source by using this name, as follows:

```
public ViewModel(string customerName)
{
    _initializeState();

    string[] names = customerName.Split(new[] {' '}, 2,
        StringSplitOptions.RemoveEmptyEntries);

    this.customers =
        (from c in DataSource.Customers
         where string.Compare(c.FirstName.ToUpper(), names[0].ToUpper()) == 0 &&
         (names.Length > 1 ?
             string.Compare(c.LastName.ToUpper(), names[1].ToUpper()) == 0 : true)
         select c).ToList();
}
```

A customer's name can contain two parts: a first name and a last name. The *Split* method of the *String* class can break a string into substrings based on a list of separator characters. In this case, the *Split* method divides the customer name into a maximum of two pieces if the user provides a first name and a last name separated by one or more space characters. The results are stored in the *names* array. The LINQ query uses this data to find all customers where the first name matches the first item in the *names* array and the last name matches the second item in the *names* array. If the user specifies a single name, the *names* array will contain only one item, and the LINQ query matches only against the first name. To remove any case sensitivity, all string comparisons are performed against the upper case versions of the strings. The resulting list of matching customers is assigned to the customers list in the view model.

7. Return to the MainPage.xaml.cs file in the Code and Text Editor window.

8. Add the *OnNavigatedTo* method shown here to the end of the *MainPage* class, after the constructor:

```
public sealed partial class MainPage : Page
{
```

```
public MainPage()
{
    ...
}

protected override void OnNavigatedTo(NavigationEventArgs e)
{
    string customerName = e.Parameter as string;

    if (!string.IsNullOrEmpty(customerName))
    {
        ViewModel viewModel = new ViewModel(customerName);
        this.DataContext = viewModel;
    }
}
}
```

The *OnNavigatedTo* method runs when the application displays (navigates to) this page by using the *Navigate* method. Any arguments provided appear in the *Parameter* property of the *NavigationEventArgs* parameter. This code attempts to convert the data in the *Parameter* property to a string, and if it is successful, it passes this string as the customer name to the *ViewModel* constructor. The resulting *ViewModel* (which should contain only customers that match this name) is then set as the data context for the page.

9. On the Build menu, click Build Solution and verify that the solution compiles successfully.

As a final bit of polish, the next exercise adds a set of icons that Windows 10 and Cortana can use to represent the app visually. These icons are more colorful than the stock gray-and-white cross images provided by the Blank App template.

Add icons to the Customers app

1. In Solution Explorer, right-click the Assets folder, point to Add, and then click Existing Item.

2. In the Add Existing Item – Customers dialog box, move to the \Microsoft Press\VCSBS\ Chapter 26\Resources folder in your Documents folder, select the three AdventureWorks logo files in this folder, and then click Add.

3. In Solution Explorer, double-click the Package.appxmanifest file to display it in the Manifest Designer window.

4. Click the Visual Assets tab. Then, in the left pane, click All Image Assets.

5. Scroll down to the Square 150x150 logo section. Click the ellipsis button directly below the Scale 100 image, browse to the Assets folder, click AdventureWorksLogo150x150.png, and then click Open. The image for this asset should be displayed in the box.

6. Following the same process as in step 5, set the Scale 100 image for the Square 44x44 logo to AdventureWorksLogo44x44.png in the Assets folder, and change the value of the Scale

100 image for the splash screen to the AdventureWorksLogo620x300.png, also in the Assets folder.

7. On the Debug menu, click Start Without Debugging to build and run the application. Verify that the splash screen appears momentarily when the app starts running, and then the details of the customer named Orlando Gee are displayed. You should be able to move back and forth through the list of customers as before. By running the app, you have also registered the voice commands that Cortana can use to invoke the app.

8. Close the app.

You can now test voice activation for the Customers app.

Test the search capability

1. Activate Cortana, and then speak the following query or type it in the search box:

   Customers show details for Brian Johnson

   > **Note** Cortana should respond in the same way regardless of whether you speak a command or type it.

   Cortana should recognize that this command should be directed to the Customers app.

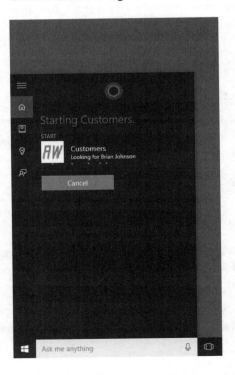

Cortana will then launch the Customers app and display the details for Brian Johnson. Notice that the Previous and Next buttons in the command bar are not available because there is only one matching customer.

2. Return to Cortana, and then speak the following query or type it in the search box:

Search for John in Customers

This time the app finds all customers who have the first name John. More than one match is returned, and you can use the Previous and Next buttons in the command bar to move between the results.

3. Experiment with other searches. Notice that you can use the forms "Search for ...," "Show details for ...," and "Show details of ..." with the app name specified at the start of the command or at the end (prefixed by "in"). Notice that if you type a query with a different form, Cortana will not understand it and will instead perform a Bing search.

4. When you have finished, return to Visual Studio.

Providing a vocal response to voice commands

In addition to sending voice commands to an app, you can make an app respond vocally. To do this, UWP apps make use of the speech synthesis features provided by Windows 10. Implementing this functionality is actually reasonably straightforward, but there is one caveat: an app should respond vocally only if it is spoken to. If the user types a phrase instead of uttering it, the app should remain silent. Fortunately, you can detect whether a command is spoken or typed by examining the *commandMode* property returned by performing the semantic interpretation of the command, as follows:

```
SpeechRecognitionResult speechRecognitionResult = ...;
string commandMode = speechRecognitionResult.SemanticInterpretation.
    Properties["commandMode"].FirstOrDefault();
```

The value of the *commandMode* property is a string that will contain either "text" or "voice" depending on how the user entered the command. In the following exercise, you will use this string to determine whether the app should respond vocally or remain silent.

Add a voice response to search requests

1. In Visual Studio, open the App.xaml.cs file and display it in the Code and Text Editor window.

2. In the *OnActivated* method, add the following statement shown in bold:

```
protected override void OnActivated(IActivatedEventArgs args)
{
    ...
    if (args.Kind == ActivationKind.VoiceCommand)
    {
        var commandArgs = args as VoiceCommandActivatedEventArgs;
        var speechRecognitionResult = commandArgs.Result;
        var commandName = speechRecognitionResult.RulePath.First();
        string commandMode = speechRecognitionResult.SemanticInterpretation.
            Properties["commandMode"].FirstOrDefault();
        string customerName = "";
        ...
    }
}
```

3. At the end of the method, change the statement that calls the *Navigate* method so that it passes in a *NavigationArgs* object as the second parameter. This object wraps the customer name and the command mode.

```
protected override void OnActivated(IActivatedEventArgs args)
{
    ...
    if (args.Kind == ActivationKind.VoiceCommand)
    {
        ...
        switch (commandName)
```

```
            {
                ...
            }

            ...
        rootFrame.Navigate(typeof(MainPage),
            new NavigationArgs(customerName, commandMode));
        Window.Current.Activate();
    }
}
```

Visual Studio will report that the *NavigationArgs* type cannot be found. This happens because the *NavigationArgs* type does not exist yet; you need to create it.

4. Right-click the reference to the *NavigationArgs* object in the code, and then click Quick Actions. In the Quick Actions popup, click Generate Class For NavigationArgs In Customers (In New File), as shown here:

This action creates a new file, called NavigationArgs.cs, that contains a class with private fields named *commandMode* and *customerName*, together with a public constructor that populates these fields. You must modify this class to make the fields accessible to the outside world. The best way to achieve this is to convert the fields into read-only properties.

5. In Solution Explorer, double-click the NavigationArgs.cs file to display it in the Code and Text Editor window.

6. Modify the *commandMode* and *customerName* fields to make them read-only fields that can be accessed by other types in the application, as shown in bold in the following code:

```
internal class NavigationArgs
```

```
    {
        internal string commandMode { get; }
        internal string customerName { get; }

        public NavigationArgs(string customerName, string commandMode)
        {
            this.customerName = customerName;
            this.commandMode = commandMode;
        }
    }
}
```

7. Return to MainPage.xaml.cs in the Code and Text Editor window and locate the *OnNavigatedTo* method. Modify this method as follows:

```
protected override async void OnNavigatedTo(NavigationEventArgs e)
{
    NavigationArgs args = e.Parameter as NavigationArgs;
    if (args != null)
    {
        string customerName = args.customerName;
        ViewModel viewModel = new ViewModel(customerName);
        this.DataContext = viewModel;
        if (args.commandMode == "voice")
        {
            if (viewModel.Current != null)
            {
                await Say($"Here are the details for {customerName}");
            }
            else
            {
                await Say($"{customerName} was not found");
            }
        }
    }
}
```

Note that the *Say* method has not been implemented yet. You will create this method shortly.

8. Add the following *using* directives to the list at the top of the file:

```
using Windows.Media.SpeechSynthesis;
using System.Threading.Tasks;
```

9. Add the *Say* method shown here to the end of the *MainPage* class:

```
private async Task Say(string message)
{
    MediaElement mediaElement = new MediaElement();
    var synth = new SpeechSynthesizer();
    SpeechSynthesisStream stream =
        await synth.SynthesizeTextToStreamAsync(message);

    mediaElement.SetSource(stream, stream.ContentType);
    mediaElement.Play();
}
```

The *SpeechSynthesizer* class in the *Windows.Media.SpeechSynthesis* namespace can generate a media stream containing speech synthesized from text. This stream is then passed to a *MediaElement* object, which plays it.

10. On the Debug menu, click Start Without Debugging to build and run the application.

11. Activate Cortana, and then speak the following query:

    Customers show details for Brian Johnson

    Cortana should respond by displaying the details for Brian Johnson in the Customers app and saying "Here are the details for Brian Johnson."

12. Type the following query into the Cortana search box:

    Customers show details for John

    Verify that this time the application remains mute after displaying the list of customers with the first name John.

13. Experiment by performing other queries by typing and with your voice. Close the app when you are finished.

Summary

In this chapter, you learned how to display data on a form by using data binding. You saw how to set the data context for a form and how to create a data source that supports data binding by implementing the *INotifyPropertyChanged* interface. You also learned how to use the Model-View-ViewModel pattern to create a UWP app, and you saw how to create a ViewModel with which a view can interact with a data source by using commands. Finally, you learned how to integrate an app with Cortana to provide voice-activated search functionality.

Quick reference

To	Do this
Bind the property of a control to the property of an object	Use a data-binding expression in the XAML markup of the control. For example: `<TextBox ...  Text="{Binding FirstName}" .../>`
Enable an object to notify a binding of a change in a data value	Implement the *INotifyPropertyChanged* interface in the class that defines the object and raise the *PropertyChanged* event each time a property value changes. For example: ```class Customer : INotifyPropertyChanged
{
  ...
  public event PropertyChangedEventHandler
    PropertyChanged;

  protected virtual void OnPropertyChanged(
    string propertyName)
  {
    if (PropertyChanged != null)
    {
      PropertyChanged(this,
        new PropertyChangedEventArgs(propertyName));
    }
  }
}``` |
Enable a control that uses data binding to update the value of the property to which it is bound	Configure the data binding as two-way. For example: `<TextBox ... Text="{Binding FirstName, Mode=TwoWay}" .../>`

Separate the business logic that runs when a user clicks a *Button* control from the user interface that contains the *Button* control	Use a ViewModel that provides commands implemented with the *ICommand* interface, and bind the *Button* control to one of these commands. For example:
	
	`<Button x:Name="nextCustomer" ...`
	`  Command="{Binding Path=NextCustomer}"/>`

Support searching in a UWP app by using Cortana	Add a voice-command definition (VCD) file to the application that specifies the commands to be recognized, and then register these commands when the application starts running by using the static *InstallCommandDefinitionsFromStorageFileAsync* method of the *VoiceCommandDefinitionManager* class. At run time, capture the *Activated* event. If the *ActivationKind* value of the *IActivatedEventArgs* parameter to this event indicates a voice command, then parse the speech recognition data in the *Result* property of this parameter to determine the action to take.

CHAPTER 27

Accessing a remote database from a Universal Windows Platform app

After completing the chapter, you will be able to:

- Use the Entity Framework to create an entity model that can retrieve and modify information held in a database.

- Create a Representational State Transfer (REST) web service that provides remote access to a database through an entity model.

- Fetch data from a remote database by using a REST web service.

- Insert, update, and delete data in a remote database by using a REST web service.

Chapter 26, "Displaying and searching for data in a Universal Windows Platform app," shows how to implement the Model-View-ViewModel (MVVM) pattern. It also explains how to separate the business logic of an app from the user interface (UI) by using a *ViewModel* class that provides access to the data in the model and implements commands that the UI can use to invoke the logic of the app. Chapter 26 also illustrates how to use data binding to display the data presented by the ViewModel and how the UI can update this data. This all results in a fully functional Universal Windows Platform (UWP) app.

In this chapter, you will turn your attention to the model aspect of the MVVM pattern. In particular, you will see how to implement a model that a UWP app can use to retrieve and update data in a remote database.

> **Note** Microsoft Azure provides Mobile Services that you can use to build RESTful web services that provide access to a back-end database, together with a Windows app that can access these services from Windows devices. However, at the time of writing, this offering can generate apps only for Windows 8.1, although support for Windows 10 is likely to be available soon (if it is not available by the time you read this book.) Even so, it is still useful to understand how to build such a system by hand. For more information about Mobile Services for building mobile apps, see "Create a Windows app" at *https://azure.microsoft .com/documentation/articles/app-service-mobile-dotnet-backend-windows-store-dotnet- get-started-preview/.*

Retrieving data from a database

So far, the data you have used has been confined to a simple collection embedded in the ViewModel of the app. In the real world, the data displayed and maintained by an app is more likely to be stored in a data source such as a relational database.

UWP apps cannot directly access a relational database by using technologies provided by Microsoft (although some third-party database solutions are available). This might sound like a severe restriction, but there are sensible reasons for this limitation. Primarily, it eliminates dependencies that a UWP app might have on external resources, making the app a standalone item that can be easily packaged and downloaded from the Windows Store without requiring users to install and configure a database-management system on their computer. Additionally, many Windows 10 devices are resource constrained and don't have the memory or disk space available to run a local database-management system. However, many business apps will still have a requirement to access a database, and to address this scenario, you can use a *web service*.

Web services can implement a variety of functions, but one common scenario is to provide an interface with which an app can connect to a remote data source to retrieve and update data. A web service can be located almost anywhere, from the computer on which the app is running to a web server hosted on a computer on a different continent. As long as you can connect to the web service, you can use it to provide access to the repository of your information. Microsoft Visual Studio provides templates and tools with which you can build a web service very quickly and easily. The simplest strategy is to base the web service on an entity model generated by using the Entity Framework, as shown in the following diagram:

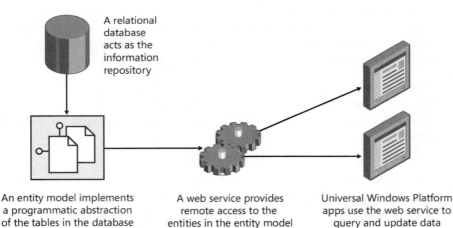

A relational database acts as the information repository

An entity model implements a programmatic abstraction of the tables in the database

A web service provides remote access to the entities in the entity model

Universal Windows Platform apps use the web service to query and update data

The Entity Framework is a powerful technology with which you can connect to a relational database. It can reduce the amount of code that most developers need to write to add data access capabilities to an app. This is where you will start, but first you need to set up the AdventureWorks database, which contains the details of Adventure Works customers.

Note There is not sufficient space in this book to go into great detail on how to use the Entity Framework, and the exercises in this section walk you through only the most essential steps to get started. If you want more information, look at "Entity Framework" on the Microsoft website at *http://msdn.microsoft.com/data/aa937723*.

To make the scenario more realistic, the exercises in this chapter show you how to create the database in the cloud by using Microsoft Azure SQL Database and how to deploy the web service to Azure. This architecture is common to many commercial apps, including ecommerce applications, mobile banking services, and even video streaming systems.

Note The exercises require that you have an Azure account and subscription. If you don't already have an Azure account, you can sign up for a free trial account at *https://azure.microsoft.com/pricing/free-trial/*. Additionally, Azure requires that you have a valid Microsoft account with which it can associate your Azure account. You can sign up for a Microsoft account at *https://signup.live.com/*.

Create an Azure SQL Database server and install the AdventureWorks sample database

1. Using a web browser, connect to the Azure portal at *https://portal.azure.com*. Sign in using your Microsoft account.

2. In the toolbar on the left of the portal, click New.

3. On the Create page, click Data + Storage, and then click SQL Database.

4. In the SQL Database pane, perform the following tasks:

   a. In the Name box, type **AdventureWorks**.

   b. Click Server, and then click Create A New Server. In the New Server pane, type a unique name for your server. (Use your company name or even your own name—I used **csharpstepbystep**. If the name you enter has been used by someone else, you will be alerted, in which case enter another name.) Enter a name and password for the administrator login (make a note of these items—I used JohnSharp, but I am not going to tell you my password), select the location closest to you, and then click OK.

   c. Click Select Source, and then click Sample. Verify that AdventureWorksLT [V12] is selected.

   d. Click Pricing Tier. In the Choose Your Pricing Tier pane, click Basic and then click Select. (This is the cheapest option if you are paying for the database yourself, and it will suffice for the exercises in this chapter. If you are building a large-scale commercial app, you will probably need to use a Premium pricing tier, which provides much more space and higher performance but at a higher cost.) The following image shows these settings.

> **Important** Do not select any pricing tier other than Basic unless you want to receive a potentially significant bill at the end of the month. For information about SQL Database pricing, see *https://azure.microsoft.com/en-us/pricing/ details/sql-database/*.

e. Click Create, and wait while the database server and database are created. You can monitor progress by clicking Notifications in the toolbar at the left of the portal.

5. In the toolbar on the left of the portal, click Browse All.

6. On the Browse page, in the All Resources pane, click your database server (not the Adventure-Works database).

7. In the toolbar above the Database Server pane, click Settings.

8. In the Settings pane, click Firewall, as shown in the following screen shot.

9. On the toolbar for the Firewall Settings pane, click Add Client IP.

10. Click Save. Verify that the message "Successfully updated server firewall rules" appears, and then click OK.

> **Note** These steps are important. Without them you will not be able to connect to the database from applications running on your computer. You can also create firewalls that span a range of IP addresses if you need to open access to a set of computers.

11. Close the Firewall Settings pane, close the Settings pane, and then close the database server pane.

The sample AdventureWorks database contains a table named Customer in the SalesLT schema. This table includes the columns containing the data presented by the Customers UWP app and also several others. Using the Entity Framework, you can choose to ignore columns that are not relevant, but you will not be able to create new customers if any of the columns you ignore do not allow nulls and do not have default values. In the Customer table, this restriction applies to the Name-Style, PasswordHash, and PasswordSalt columns (used for encrypting users' passwords). To avoid complications and to enable you to focus on the functionality of the app itself, in the next exercise you will remove these columns from the Customer table.

Remove unneeded columns from the AdventureWorks database

1. In the Azure portal, in the All Resources pane, click the AdventureWorks database.

2. In the toolbar above the AdventureWorks SQL Database pane, click Open In Visual Studio.

3. In the Open In Visual Studio pane, click Open In Visual Studio.

4. If the Did You Mean To Switch Applications? message appears, click Yes.

Visual Studio will start up and prompt you to connect to the database.

5. If the Connect To Server dialog box appears, enter the administrator password that you specified earlier, and then click Connect.

Visual Studio connects to the database, which appears in the SQL Server Object Explorer pane on the left side of the Visual Studio IDE.

6. In the SQL Server Object Explorer pane, expand the AdventureWorks database, expand Tables, expand SalesLT.Customer, and then expand Columns.

The columns in the table are listed. The three columns that are not used by the application and that disallow null values must be removed (otherwise the application will not be able to create new customers).

7. Click the NameStyle column, press the Ctrl key, and then click the PasswordHash and PasswordSalt columns. Right-click the PasswordSalt column, and then click Delete.

8. Visual Studio analyzes these columns. In the Preview Database Updates dialog box, it displays a list of warnings and other issues that could occur if the columns are removed.

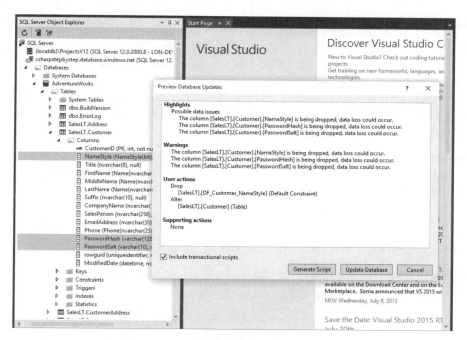

9. In the Preview Database Updates dialog box, click Update Database.

10. Close the SQL Server Object Explorer pane, but leave Visual Studio 2015 open.

Creating an entity model

Now that you have created the AdventureWorks database in the cloud, you can use the Entity Framework to create an entity model that an app can use to query and update information in this database. If you have worked with databases in the past, you might be familiar with technologies such as ADO.NET, which provides a library of classes that you can use to connect to a database and run SQL commands. ADO.NET is useful, but it requires that you have a decent understanding of SQL, and if you are not careful, it can force you into structuring your code around the logic necessary to perform SQL commands instead of focusing on the business operations of your app. The Entity Framework provides a level of abstraction that reduces the dependencies that your apps have on SQL.

Essentially, the Entity Framework implements a mapping layer between a relational database and your app; it generates an entity model that consists of collections of objects that your app can use just as it would any other collection. A collection typically corresponds to a table in the database, and each row in a table corresponds to an item in the collection. You perform queries by iterating through the items in a collection, usually with Language-Integrated Query (LINQ). Behind the scenes, the entity model converts your queries into SQL SELECT commands that fetch the data. You can modify the data in the collection, and then you can arrange for the entity model to generate and perform the appropriate SQL INSERT, UPDATE, and DELETE commands to perform the equivalent operations in the database. In short, the Entity Framework is an excellent vehicle for connecting to a database and retrieving and managing data without requiring you to embed SQL commands in your code.

In the following exercise, you will create a very simple entity model for the Customer table in the AdventureWorks database. You will follow what is known as the *database-first* approach to entity modeling. In this approach, the Entity Framework generates classes based on the definitions of tables in the database. The Entity Framework also provides a *code-first* approach; that strategy can generate a set of tables in a database based on classes that you have implemented in your app.

> **Note** If you want more information about the code-first approach to creating an entity model, see "Code First to an Existing Database" on the Microsoft website at *http://msdn.microsoft.com/data/jj200620*.

Create the AdventureWorks entity model

1. In Visual Studio, open the Customers project, located in the \Microsoft Press\VCSBS\ Chapter 27\Web Service folder in your Documents folder.

   This project contains a modified version of the Customers app from Chapter 26. The ViewModel implements additional commands, which let a user navigate to the first or last customer in the customers collection, and the command bar contains First and Last buttons that invoke these commands. Additionally, the Cortana search functionality has been removed to enable you to focus on the tasks at hand. (You are more than welcome to add this feature back if you want a voice-activated version of the app.)

2. In Solution Explorer, right-click the Customers solution (not the Customers project), point to Add, and then click New Project.

3. In the Add New Project dialog box, in the left pane, click the Web node. In the middle pane, click the ASP.NET Web Application template. Verify that the version specified in the drop-down list box above the middle pane is set to .NET Framework 4.6 (and change it if necessary). In the Name box, type **AdventureWorksService**, and then click OK.

4. In the New ASP.NET Project – AdventureWorksService dialog box, under Select A Template, click Web API in the ASP.NET 4.6 Templates section, and then click Change Authentication.

5. In the Change Authentication dialog box, select No Authentication, and then click OK to return to the New ASP.NET Project dialog box.

> **Note** The ASP.NET Web API template can generate code to handle user logins, but Azure provides its own scalable identity and access-management system that is preferable to embedding security handling into your own code if you are deploying the service to the cloud. Azure security is outside the scope of this book, but for more information, see "Azure Active Directory" at *http://azure.microsoft.com/services/active-directory/*, and "Azure Multi-Factor Authentication" at *http://azure.microsoft.com/services/multi-factor-authentication/*.

6. In the New ASP.NET Project dialog box, be sure that the Host In The Cloud check box is clear (you will test the Web API locally first and then deploy to the cloud), and then click OK.

As mentioned at the start of this section, you cannot access a relational database directly from a UWP app, including when you use the Entity Framework. Instead, you have created a web app (this is not a UWP app), and you will host the entity model that you create in this app. The Web API template provides wizards and tools with which you can quickly implement a web service, which is what you will do in the next exercise. This web service will provide remote access to the entity model for the Customers UWP app.

7. In Solution Explorer, right-click the Customers solution, and then click Set StartUp Projects.

8. In the Solution 'Customers' Property Pages dialog box, click Multiple Startup Projects. Set the action for the AdventureWorksService project to Start Without Debugging, set the action for the Customers project to Start, and then click OK.

9. This configuration ensures that the AdventureWorksService web app runs whenever you start the project from the Debug menu. In Solution Explorer, right-click the AdventureWorksService project, and then click Properties.

10. On the properties page, click the Web tab in the left column.

11. On the Web page, click "Don't open a page. Wait for a request from an external application."

   Normally, when you run a web app from Visual Studio, the web browser (Microsoft Edge) opens and attempts to display the home page for the app. But the AdventureWorksService app does not have a home page; the purpose of this app is to host the web service to which client apps can connect and retrieve data from the AdventureWorks database.

12. In the Project Url box, change the address of the web app to **http://localhost:50000/**, and then click Create Virtual Directory. In the Microsoft Visual Studio message box that appears, verify that the virtual directory was created successfully, and then click OK.

   By default, the ASP.NET project template creates a web app that is hosted with IIS Express, and it selects a random port for the URL. This configuration sets the port to 50000 so that the subsequent steps in the exercises in this chapter can be described more easily.

13. On the File menu, click Save All, and then close the Properties page.

14. In Solution Explorer, in the AdventureWorksService project, right-click the Models folder, point to Add, and then click New Item.

15. In the Add New Item – AdventureWorksService dialog box, in the left column, click the Data node. In the middle pane, click the ADO.NET Entity Data Model template. In the Name box, type **AdventureWorksModel**, and then click Add.

   The Entity Data Model Wizard starts. You can use this wizard to generate an entity model from an existing database.

16. On the Choose Model Contents page of the wizard, click EF Designer From Database, and then click Next.

17. On the Choose Your Data Connection page, click New Connection.

18. If the Choose Data Source dialog box appears, select Microsoft SQL Server in the Data Source box, and then click OK.

Note The Choose Data Source dialog box appears only if you have not previously used the Data Connection wizard and selected a data source.

19. In the Connection Properties dialog box, in the Server Name box, type the following: **tcp:\<servername\>.database.windows.net,1433,** where *\<servername\>* is the unique name of the Azure SQL Database server that you created in the previous exercise. Click Use SQL Server Authentication and enter the name and password that you specified for the administrator login in the previous exercise. In the Select Or Enter A Database Name box, type **AdventureWorks**, and then click OK.

This action creates a connection to the AdventureWorks database running in the cloud.

20. On the Choose Your Data Connection page, click No, Exclude Sensitive Data From The Connection String. I Will Set It In My Application Code. Verify that Save Connection Settings In Web.Config As is selected, and then confirm that the name of the connection string is AdventureWorksEntities. Click Next.

21. On the Choose Your Version page, select Entity Framework 6.x, and then click Next.

22. On the Choose Your Database Objects And Settings page, expand Tables, expand SalesLT, and then select Customer. Verify that the Pluralize Or Singularize Generated Object Names check box is selected. (The other two options on this page will also be selected by default.) Observe that the Entity Framework generates the classes for the entity model in the *AdventureWorksModel* namespace, and then click Finish.

The Entity Data Model Wizard generates an entity model for the Customer table and displays a graphical representation in the Entity Model editor on the screen, like this:

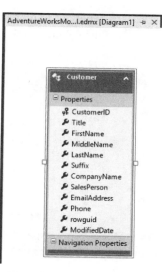

If the following Security Warning message box appears, select the Do Not Show This Message Again check box, and then click OK. This security warning appears because the Entity Framework uses a technology known as T4 templates to generate the code for your entity model, and it has downloaded these templates from the web by using NuGet. The Entity Framework templates have been verified by Microsoft and are safe to use.

Security Warning ? ×

Running this text template can potentially harm your computer. Do not run it if you obtained it from an untrusted source.

Click OK to run the template.
Click Cancel to stop the process.

☐ Do not show this message again

OK   Cancel

23. In the Entity Model editor, right-click the MiddleName column and then click Delete From Model. Using the same process, delete the Suffix, CompanyName, and SalesPerson columns from the entity model.

The Customers app does not use these columns, and there is no need to retrieve them from the database. They allow null values, so they can safely be left as part of the database table. However, you should not remove the rowguid and ModifiedDate columns. These columns are used by the database to identify rows in the Customer table and track changes to these rows in a multiuser environment. If you remove these columns, you will not be able to save data back to the database correctly.

24. On the Build menu, click Build Solution.

25. In Solution Explorer, in the AdventureWorksService project, expand the Models folder, expand AdventureWorksModel.edmx, expand AdventureWorksModel.tt, and then double-click Customer.cs.

This file contains the class that the Entity Data Model Wizard generates to represent a customer. This class contains automatic properties for each of the columns in the Customer table that you have included in the entity model:

```
public partial class Customer
{
    public int CustomerID { get; set; }
    public string Title { get; set; }
    public string FirstName { get; set; }
    public string LastName { get; set; }
    public string EmailAddress { get; set; }
    public string Phone { get; set; }
    public System.Guid rowguid { get; set; }
    public System.DateTime ModifiedDate { get; set; }
}
```

26. In Solution Explorer, under the entry for AdventureWorksModel.edmx, expand Adventure-WorksModel.Context.tt, and then double-click AdventureWorksModel.Context.cs.

This file contains the definition of a class called *AdventureWorksEntities*. (It has the same name as you used when you generated the connection to the database in the Entity Data Model Wizard.)

```
public partial class AdventureWorksEntities : DbContext
{
    public AdventureWorksEntities()
        : base("name=AdventureWorksEntities")
    {
    }

    protected override void OnModelCreating(DbModelBuilder modelBuilder)
    {
        throw new UnintentionalCodeFirstException();
    }

    public DbSet<Customer> Customers { get; set; }
}
```

The *AdventureWorksEntities* class is descended from the *DbContext* class, and this class provides the functionality that an app uses to connect to the database. The default constructor passes a parameter to the base-class constructor that specifies the name of the connection string to use to connect to the database. If you look in the web.config file, you will find this string in the *<ConnectionStrings>* section. It contains the parameters (among other things) that you specified when you ran the Entity Data Model Wizard. However, this string does not contain the password information required to authenticate the connection because you elected to provide this data at run time. You will handle this in the following steps.

You can ignore the *OnModelCreating* method in the *AdventureWorksEntities* class. The only other item is the *Customers* collection. This collection has the type *DbSet<Customer>*. The *DbSet* generic type provides methods with which you can add, insert, delete, and query objects in a database. It works in conjunction with the *DbContext* class to generate the appropriate SQL SELECT commands necessary to fetch customer information from the database and populate the collection. It is also used to create the SQL INSERT, UPDATE, and DELETE commands that run if *Customer* objects are added, modified, or removed from the collection. A *DbSet* collection is frequently referred to as an *entity set*.

27. In Solution Explorer, right-click the Models folder, click Add, and then click Class.

28. In the Add New Item – AdventureWorksService dialog box, ensure that the Class template is selected. In the Name box, type **AdventureWorksEntities**, and then click Add.

   A new class named *AdventureWorksEntities* is added to the project and is displayed in the Code and Text Editor window. This class currently conflicts with the existing class of the same name generated by the Entity Framework, but you will use this class to augment the Entity Framework code by converting it to a partial class. A partial class is a class in which the code is split across one or more source files. This approach is useful for tools such as the Entity Framework because it enables you to add your own code without the risk of having it accidentally overwritten if the Entity Framework code is regenerated at some point in the future.

29. In the Code and Text editor window, modify the definition of the *AdventureWorksEntities* class to make it partial, as shown in bold in the following.

```
public partial class AdventureWorksEntities
{
}
```

30. In the *AdventureWorksEntities* class, add a constructor that takes a string parameter named *password*. The constructor should invoke the base-class constructor with the name of the connection string previously written to the web.config file by the Entity Data Model Wizard (specified on the Choose Data Connection page).

```
public partial class AdventureWorksEntities
{
    public AdventureWorksEntities(string password)
        : base("name=AdventureWorksEntities")
    {
    }
}
```

31. Add the code shown below in bold to the constructor. This code modifies the connection string used by the Entity Framework to include the password. The Customers app will call this constructor and provide the password at run time.

```
public partial class AdventureWorksEntities
{
    public AdventureWorksEntities(string password)
        : base("name=AdventureWorksEntities")
    {
        this.Database.Connection.ConnectionString += $";Password={password}";
    }
}
```

Creating and using a REST web service

You have created an entity model that provides operations to retrieve and maintain customer information. The next step is to implement a web service so that a UWP app can access the entity model.

With Visual Studio 2015, you can create a web service in an ASP.NET web app based directly on an entity model generated by the Entity Framework. The web service uses the entity model to retrieve data from a database and update the database. You create a web service by using the Add Scaffold wizard. This wizard can generate a web service that implements the REST model, which uses a navigational scheme to represent business objects and services over a network and the HTTP protocol to transmit requests to access these objects and services. A client app that accesses a resource submits a request in the form of a URL, which the web service parses and processes. For example, Adventure Works might publish customer information, exposing the details of each customer as a single resource, by using a scheme similar to this:

```
http://Adventure-Works.com/DataService/Customers/1
```

Accessing this URL causes the web service to retrieve the data for customer 1. This data can be returned in a number of formats, but for portability the most common formats include XML and JavaScript Object Notation (JSON). A typical JSON response generated by a REST web service request issuing the previous query looks like this:

```
{
"CustomerID":1,
"Title":"Mr",
"FirstName":"Orlando",
"LastName":"Gee",
"EmailAddress":"orlando0@adventure-works.com",
"Phone":"245-555-0173"
}
```

The REST model relies on the app that accesses the data to send the appropriate HTTP verb as part of the request to access the data. For example, the simple request shown previously should send an HTTP GET request to the web service. HTTP supports other verbs as well, such as POST, PUT, and DELETE, which you can use to create, modify, and remove resources, respectively. Writing the code to generate the appropriate HTTP requests and parsing the responses returned by a REST web service all sounds quite complicated. Fortunately, the Add Scaffold wizard can generate most of this code for you.

In the following exercise, you will create a simple REST web service for the AdventureWorks entity model. This web service will make it possible for a client app to query and maintain customer information.

Create the AdventureWorks web service

1. In Visual Studio, in the AdventureWorksService project, right-click the Controllers folder, point to Add, and then click New Scaffolded Item.

2. In the Add Scaffold wizard, in the middle pane, click the Web API 2 Controller With Actions, Using Entity Framework template, and then click Add.

3. In the Add Controller dialog box, in the Model Class drop-down list, select Customer (AdventureWorksService.Models). In the Data Context Class drop-down list, select Adventure-WorksEntities (AdventureWorksService.Models). Select the Use Async Controller Actions check box. Verify that the Controller name is set to CustomersController, and then click Add.

In a web service created by using the ASP.NET Web API template, all incoming web requests are handled by one or more controller classes, and each controller class exposes methods that map to the different types of REST requests for each of the resources that the controller exposes. For example, the CustomersController looks like this:

```
public class CustomersController : ApiController
{
    private AdventureWorksEntities db = new AdventureWorksEntities();

    // GET: api/Customers
```

```csharp
    public IQueryable<Customer> GetCustomers()
    {
        return db.Customers;
    }

    // GET: api/Customers/5
    [ResponseType(typeof(Customer))]
    public async Task<IHttpActionResult> GetCustomer(int id)
    {
        Customer customer = await db.Customers.FindAsync(id);
        if (customer == null)
        {
            return NotFound();
        }

        return Ok(customer);
    }

    // PUT: api/Customers/5
    [ResponseType(typeof(void))]
    public async Task<IHttpActionResult> PutCustomer(int id, Customer customer)
    {
        if (!ModelState.IsValid)
        {
            return BadRequest(ModelState);
        }

        if (id != customer.CustomerID)
        {
            return BadRequest();
        }

        db.Entry(customer).State = EntityState.Modified;

        try
        {
            await db.SaveChangesAsync();
        }
        catch (DbUpdateConcurrencyException)
        {
            if (!CustomerExists(id))
            {
                return NotFound();
            }
            else
            {
                throw;
            }
        }

        return StatusCode(HttpStatusCode.NoContent);
    }

    // POST: api/Customers
    [ResponseType(typeof(Customer))]
    public async Task<IHttpActionResult> PostCustomer(Customer customer)
    {
```

```
        . . .
    }

    // DELETE: api/Customers/5
    [ResponseType(typeof(Customer))]
    public async Task<IHttpActionResult> DeleteCustomer(int id)
    {
        . . .
    }

    . . .
}
```

The *GetCustomers* method handles requests to retrieve all customers, and it satisfies this request by simply returning the entire *Customers* collection from the Entity Framework data model that you created previously. Behind the scenes, the Entity Framework fetches all the customers from the database and uses this information to populate the *Customers* collection. This method is invoked if an app sends an HTTP GET request to the *api/Customers* URL in this web service.

The *GetCustomer* method (not to be confused with *GetCustomers*) takes an integer parameter. This parameter specifies the CustomerID of a specific customer, and the method uses the Entity Framework to find the details of this customer before returning it. *GetCustomer* runs when an app sends an HTTP GET request to the *api/Customers/*n URL, where *n* is the ID of the customer to retrieve.

The *PutCustomer* method runs when an app sends an HTTP PUT request to the web service. The request specifies a customer ID and the details of a customer, and the code in this method uses the Entity Framework to update the specified customer with the details. The *PostCustomer* method responds to HTTP POST requests and takes the details of a customer as its parameter. This method adds a new customer with these details to the database (the details are not shown in the preceding code sample). Finally, the *DeleteCustomer* method handles HTTP DELETE requests and removes the customer with the specified customer ID.

> **Note** The code generated by the Web API template optimistically assumes that it will always be able to connect to the database. In the world of distributed systems, where the database and web service are located on separate servers, this might not always be the case. Networks are prone to transient errors and timeouts; a connection attempt might fail because of a temporary glitch and succeed if it is retried a short time later. Reporting a temporary glitch to a client as an error can be frustrating to the user. If possible, it might be better to silently retry the failing operation as long as the number of retries is not excessive (you don't want the web service to freeze if the database is really unavailable.) For detailed information on this strategy, see "Cloud Service Fundamentals Data Access Layer—Transient Fault Handling" at *http://social.technet.microsoft.com/wiki/contents/articles/18665.cloud-service-fundamentals-data-access-layer-transient-fault-handling.aspx*.

The ASP.NET Web API template automatically generates code that directs requests to the appropriate method in the controller classes, and you can add more controller classes if you need to manage other resources, such as products or orders.

> **Note** For detailed information on implementing REST web services by using the ASP.NET Web API template, see "Web API" at *http://www.asp.net/web-api*.

You can also create controller classes manually by using the same pattern as that shown by the *CustomersController* class—you do not have to fetch and store data in a database by using the Entity Framework. The ASP.Net Web API template contains an example controller in the ValuesController.cs file that you can copy and augment with your own code.

4. In the *CustomersController* class, modify the statement that creates the *AdventureWorks-Entities* context object to use the constructor that takes a password as its parameter. As the argument to the constructor, provide the administrator password that you specified when you created the database. (In the following code sample, replace the string *YourPassword* with your own password.)

```
public class CustomersController : ApiController
{
    private AdventureWorksEntities db = new AdventureWorksEntities("YourPassword");

    // GET: api/Customers
    public IQueryable<Customer> GetCustomers()
    {
        return db.Customers;
    }
    ...
}
```

> **Note** In the real world, you could prompt the user running the Customers app for this information (or enable the application to save the password locally on the user's device as part of the configuration data for the app). The Customers app would then pass this information to the web service.

5. In the Controllers folder, right-click the ValuesController.cs file, and then click Delete. In the Message box, click OK to confirm that you want to delete this file.

You will not be using the example *ValuesController* class in this exercise.

Note Do not delete the *HomeController* class. This controller acts as the entry point to the web app hosting the web service.

6. In Solution Explorer, right-click the AdventureWorksService project, click View, and then click View In Browser (Microsoft Edge).

   If the web service is configured correctly, your web browser should start and display the following page:

   ![Screenshot of the ASP.NET Home Page displayed in Microsoft Edge at localhost:50000, with the Application name, Home, and API navigation links, the ASP.NET banner reading "ASP.NET is a free web framework for building great Web sites and Web applications using HTML, CSS, and JavaScript." with a Learn more button, and three columns titled Getting started, Get more libraries, and Web Hosting, each with descriptive text and a Learn more button. Footer reads © 2015 - My ASP.NET Application.]

7. On the title bar, click API.

   Another page appears, summarizing the REST requests that an app can send to the web service:

8. In the address bar, type **http://localhost:50000/api/Customers/1**, and then press Enter.

This request is directed to the overloaded *GetCustomer* method in the *CustomersController* class, and the value 1 is passed as the parameter to this method. Note that the Web API uses routes that start with the path "api" after the address of the server.

The *GetCustomer* method retrieves the details of customer 1 from the database and returns them as a JSON-formatted object, which is displayed in the browser. The data looks like this (the value for *ModifiedDate* might differ from that shown here):

```
{"CustomerID":1,"Title":"Mr","FirstName":"Orlando","LastName":"Gee","EmailAddress":
"orlando0@adventure-works.com","Phone":"245-555-0173","rowguid":
"3f5ae95e-b87d-4aed-95b4-c3797afcb74f","ModifiedDate":"2001-08-01T00:00:00"}
```

9. Close the web browser and return to Visual Studio.

You can now deploy the web service to Azure rather than run it locally. You can do this by using the Publish Web wizard available with Visual Studio 2015 to create a web app in the cloud and upload the web service to this app.

Deploy the web service to the cloud

1. In Solution Explorer, right-click the AdventureWorksService project and then click Publish. The Publish Web wizard starts.

2. Under Select A Publish Target, click Microsoft Azure Web Apps.

3. In the Select Existing Web App dialog box, select your Azure account. If the Add An Account option appears instead of a list of accounts, click this option, and then click Add An Account. In the Sign In To Visual Studio dialog box, sign in using your Microsoft account details.

4. In the Select Existing Web App dialog box, click New.

5. In the Create Web App On Microsoft Azure dialog box, provide a unique name for the web app and specify the region closest to you for hosting the app. Do not specify a database server (the Entity Framework code in your web service takes care of connecting to the database). In the App Service Plan box, click Create New App Service Plan and give it a name of your choice. Similarly, in the Resource group box, click Create New Resource Group and give it a name. When you have entered all the data, click Create.

Create Web App on Microsoft Azure ✕

Create a Web App on Microsoft Azure

Microsoft account ⌄

Web App name: CSharpStepByStep ✓
.azurewebsites.net

Subscription: ⌄

App Service plan: Create new App Service plan ⌄
CSharpStepByStepPlan

Resource group: Create new resource group ⌄
CSharpStepByStepGroup

Region: North Europe ⌄

Database server: No database ⌄

If you have removed your spending limit or you are using Pay As You Go, there may be monetary impact if you provision additional resources. legal terms
Learn more

Create   Cancel

6. On the Connection page of the Publish Web wizard, accept the default values, click Validate Connection to verify that the web app for hosting the web service has been successfully created, and then click Next.

7. On the Settings page, accept the default values and then click Next.

8. On the Preview page, click Publish.

The web service should be uploaded. The browser should open and display the home page for the site, as you saw earlier when you ran the service locally.

9. Close the web browser and return to Visual Studio.

The next phase of this journey is to connect to the web service from the Customers UWP app and then use the web service to fetch some data. The .NET Framework provides the *HttpClient* class, which an app can use to formulate and send HTTP REST requests to a web service, and the *HttpResponse-Message* class, which an app can use to process the result from the web service. These classes abstract the details of the HTTP protocol away from your app code. As such, you can focus on the business logic that displays and manipulates the objects published through the web service. You will use these classes in the following exercise. You will also use the JSON parser implemented by the Json.NET package. You will have to add this package to the Customers project.

> **Important** This exercise retrieves the data for every customer. This is useful as a prototype to prove the concept of retrieving data via a web service located in the cloud, but in the real world you should be more selective. If the database contained a large volume of data,

this approach could be very wasteful in terms of network bandwidth and the memory requirements of the app running on the user's device. A better approach is to use paging, whereby customer data is fetched in blocks (maybe of 20 customers at a time). The web service would need to be updated to support this approach, and the ViewModel in the Customers app would need to manage fetching blocks of customers transparently. This is left as an exercise for the reader ☺.

Fetch data from the AdventureWorks web service

1. In Solution Explorer, in the Customers project, right-click the DataSource.cs file and then click Delete. In the message box, click OK to confirm that you want to delete the file.

   This file contained the sample data used by the Customers app. You are going to modify the *ViewModel* class to fetch this data from the web service, so this file is no longer required.

2. Right-click the Customers project, and then click Manage NuGet Packages.

   Note If you are prompted for a password to connect to SQL Server, close the dialog box. The password information is already provided by the web service.

3. In the NuGet Package Manager: Customers window, make sure that the Filter drop-down list box is set to All, and then type **Json.NET** in the search box.

4. In the pane displaying the search results, select the Newtonsoft.Json package. In the right pane, set the Action to Install, and then click Install.

5. In the Preview window, click OK.

6. Wait for the package to be installed, and then close the NuGet Package Manager: Customers window.

7. In Solution Explorer, double-click ViewModel.cs to display the file in the Code and Text Editor window.

8. Add the following *using* directives to the list at the top of the file:

```
using System.Net.Http;
using System.Net.Http.Headers;
using Newtonsoft.Json;
```

9. In the *ViewModel* class, add the following variables shown in bold before the *ViewModel* constructor. Replace *<webappname>* with the name of the web app that you created to host the web service in the previous exercise.

```
public class ViewModel : INotifyPropertyChanged
{
```

```
...
    private const string ServerUrl = "http://<webappname>.azurewebsites.net/";
    private HttpClient client = null;

    public ViewModel()
    {
        ...
    }
    ...
}
```

The *ServerUrl* variable contains the base address of the web service. You will use the *client* variable to connect to the web service.

10. In the *ViewModel* constructor, initialize the *customers* list to null and add the following statements in bold to configure the *client* variable:

```
public ViewModel()
{
    ...
    this.customers = null;
    this.client = new HttpClient();
    this.client.BaseAddress = new Uri(ServerUrl);
    this.client.DefaultRequestHeaders.Accept.
        Add(new MediaTypeWithQualityHeaderValue("application/json"));
}
```

The *customers* list contains the customers displayed by the app; it was previously populated with the data in the DataSource.cs file that you removed.

The *client* variable is initialized with the address of the web server to which it will send requests. A REST web service can receive requests and send responses in a variety of formats, but the Customers app will use JSON. The final statement in the preceding code configures the *client* variable to submit requests in this format.

11. In Solution Explorer, double-click the Customer.cs file in the root folder of the Customers project to display it in the Code and Text Editor window.

12. Immediately after the *Phone* property, add the following public properties shown in bold to the *Customer* class:

```
public class Customer : INotifyPropertyChanged
{
    ...
    public string Phone
    {
        ...
    }

    public System.Guid rowguid { get; set; }
    public System.DateTime ModifiedDate { get; set; }

    ...
}
```

The web service retrieves these fields from the database, and the Customers app must be prepared to handle them; otherwise, they will be lost if the user decides to modify the details of a customer. (You will add this capability to the Customers app later in this chapter.)

13. Return to the *ViewModel* class. After the constructor, add the public *GetDataAsync* method shown here:

```
public async Task GetDataAsync()
{
    try
    {
        var response = await this.client.GetAsync("api/customers");
        if (response.IsSuccessStatusCode)
        {
            var customerData =
                await response.Content.ReadAsStringAsync();
            this.customers =
                JsonConvert.DeserializeObject<List<Customer>>(customerData);
            this.currentCustomer = 0;
            this.OnPropertyChanged(nameof(Current));
            this.IsAtStart = true;
            this.IsAtEnd = (this.customers.Count == 0);
        }
        else
        {
            // TODO: Handle GET failure
        }
    }
    catch (Exception e)
    {
        // TODO: Handle exceptions
    }
}
```

This method is asynchronous; it uses the *GetAsync* method of the *HttpClient* object to invoke the *api/customers* operation in the web service. This operation fetches the details of the customers from the AdventureWorks database. The *GetAsync* method is itself asynchronous, and returns an *HttpResponseMessage* object wrapped in a *Task*. The *HttpResponseMessage* object contains a status code that indicates whether a request is successful, and if it is, the app uses the *ReadAsStringAsync* method of the *Content* property of the *HttpResponse-Message* object to actually retrieve the data returned by the web service. This data consists of a JSON-formatted string containing the details of every customer, so it is converted into a list of *Customer* objects and assigned to the *customers* collection by using the static *DeserializeObject* method of the *JsonConvert* class (which is part of the Json.NET package). The *currentCustomer* property of the ViewModel is then set to point to the first customer in this collection, and the *IsAtStart* and *IsAtEnd* properties are initialized to indicate the state of the ViewModel.

Notice that currently the *GetDataAsync* method does not handle any exceptions or failures other than to consume them silently. You will see a technique for reporting exceptions in a UWP app later in this chapter.

14. Modify the *get* accessor for the *Current* property, as shown in the following:

```
public Customer Current
{
    get
    {
        if (this.customers != null)
        {
            return this.customers[currentCustomer];
        }
        else
        {
            return null;
        }
    }
}
```

The *GetDataAsync* method is asynchronous, so it is possible that the *customers* collection might not be populated when the controls on the MainPage form attempt to bind to a customer. In this situation, this modification prevents the data bindings from generating a *null* reference exception when they access the customers collection.

15. In the *ViewModel* constructor, update the conditions that enable each of the commands to run, as shown in bold in the following code:

```
public ViewModel()
{
    ...
    this.NextCustomer = new Command(this.Next,
        () => { return this.customers != null &&
                this.customers.Count > 1 && !this.IsAtEnd; });
    this.PreviousCustomer = new Command(this.Previous,
        () => { return this.customers != null &&
                this.customers.Count > 0 && !this.IsAtStart; });
    this.FirstCustomer = new Command(this.First,
        () => { return this.customers != null &&
                this.customers.Count > 0 && !this.IsAtStart; });
    this.LastCustomer = new Command(this.Last,
        () => { return this.customers != null &&
                this.customers.Count > 1 && !this.IsAtEnd; });
}
```

These changes ensure that the buttons on the command bar are not enabled until there is some data to display.

16. In Solution Explorer, expand MainPage.xaml and double-click MainPage.xaml.cs to open it in the Code and Text Editor window.

17. Add the following statement shown in bold to the *MainPage* constructor:

```
public MainPage()
{
    ...
    ViewModel viewModel = new ViewModel();
    viewModel.GetDataAsync();
    this.DataContext = viewModel;
}
```

This statement populates the ViewModel.

18. On the Debug menu, click Start Debugging to build and run the app.

The form will initially appear empty while the *GetDataAsync* method runs, but after a few seconds, the details of the first customer, Orlando Gee, should be displayed:

19. Use the navigation buttons in the command bar to move through the list of customers to verify that the form works as expected.

20. Return to Visual Studio and stop debugging.

As a final flourish in this section, it would be helpful to let users know, when the form is initially displayed, that although the form appears to be empty, the app is actually in the process of fetching the data. In a UWP app, you can use a *ProgressRing* control to provide this feedback. This control should be displayed when the ViewModel is busy communicating with the web service but be inactive otherwise.

Add a busy indicator to the Customers form

1. Open the ViewModel.cs file in the Code and Text Editor window. After the *GetDataAsync* method, add the private *_isBusy* field and public *IsBusy* property to the *ViewModel* class, as shown here:

```
private bool _isBusy;
public bool IsBusy
{
    get { return this._isBusy; }
    set
    {
```

```
        this._isBusy = value;
        this.OnPropertyChanged(nameof(IsBusy));
    }
}
```

2. In the *GetDataAsync* method, add the following statements shown in bold:

```
public async Task GetDataAsync()
{
    try
    {
        this.IsBusy = true;
        var response = await this.client.GetAsync("api/customers");
        ...
    }
    catch (Exception e)
    {
        // TODO: Handle exceptions
    }
    finally
    {
        this.IsBusy = false;
    }
}
```

The *GetData* method sets the *IsBusy* property to *true* prior to running the query to fetch the customer information. The *finally* block ensures that the *IsBusy* property is set back to *false* even if an exception occurs.

3. Open the MainPage.xaml file in the Design View window.

4. In the XAML pane, add the *ProgressRing* control shown in bold in the following code as the first item in the top-level *Grid* control:

```
<Grid Style="{StaticResource GridStyle}">
    <ProgressRing HorizontalAlignment="Center"
VerticalAlignment="Center" Foreground="AntiqueWhite"
Height="100" Width="100" IsActive="{Binding IsBusy}"
Canvas.ZIndex="1"/>
    <Grid x:Name="customersTabularView" Margin="40,104,0,0" ...>
    ...
```

Setting the *Canvas.ZIndex* property to *"1"* ensures that the *ProgressRing* appears in front of the other controls displayed by the *Grid* control.

5. On the Debug menu, click Start Debugging to build and run the app.

Notice that when the app starts, the progress ring briefly appears before the first customer is displayed. If you find that the first customer appears too quickly, you can introduce a small delay in the *GetDataAsync* method just to satisfy yourself that the progress ring is working. Add the following statement, which pauses the method for five seconds:

```
public async Task GetDataAsync()
{
```

```
try
{
    this.IsBusy = true;
    await Task.Delay(5000);
    var response = await this.client.GetAsync(...);
    ...
}
...
}
```

Be sure to remove this statement after you finish testing the progress ring.

6. Return to Visual Studio and stop debugging.

Inserting, updating, and deleting data through a REST web service

Apart from giving users the ability to query and display data, many apps have the requirement to let users insert, update, and delete information. The ASP.NET Web API implements a model that supports these operations through the use of HTTP PUT, POST, and DELETE requests. Conventionally, a PUT request modifies an existing resource in a web service, and a POST request creates a new instance of a resource. A DELETE request removes a resource. The code generated by the Add Scaffold wizard in the ASP.NET Web API template follows these conventions.

> ## Idempotency in REST web services
>
> In a REST web service, PUT requests should be idempotent, which means that if you perform the same update repeatedly, the result should always be the same. In the case of the AdventureWorksService example, if you modify a customer and set the telephone number to "888-888-8888," it does not matter how many times you perform this operation because the effect is identical. This might seem obvious, but you should design a REST web service with this requirement in mind. With this design approach, a web service can be robust in the face of concurrent requests, or even in the event of network failures (if a client app loses the connection to the web service, it can simply attempt to reconnect and perform the same request again without being concerned whether the previous request was successful). Therefore, you should think of a REST web service as a means for storing and retrieving data, and you should not attempt to implement business-specific operations.
>
> For example, if you were building a banking system, you might be tempted to provide a *CreditAccount* method that adds an amount to the balance in a customer's account and expose this method as a PUT operation. However, each time you invoke this operation, the result is an incremental credit to the account. Therefore, it becomes necessary to track whether calls to the operation are successful. Your app cannot invoke this operation repeatedly if it thinks an earlier call failed or timed out because the result could be multiple, duplicated credits to the same account.

For more information about managing data consistency in cloud applications, see "Data Consistency Primer" at *https://msdn.microsoft.com/library/dn589800.aspx*.

In the next exercise, you will extend the Customers app and add features with which users can add new customers and modify the details of existing customers. The app will construct the appropriate REST requests and send them to the AdventureWorksService web service. You will not provide any functionality to delete customers. This restriction ensures that you have a record of all customers that have done business with the Adventure Works organization, which might be required for auditing purposes. Additionally, even if a customer has not been active for a long time, there is a chance that the customer might place an order at some point in the future.

> **Note** It is becoming increasingly commonplace for business applications never to delete data but simply to perform an update that marks the data as "removed" in some way and prevents it from being displayed. This is primarily because of the requirements to keep complete data records, often to meet regulatory requirements.

Implement add and edit functionality in the *ViewModel* class

1. Return to Visual Studio.

2. In the Customers project, delete the ViewModel.cs file to remove it from the project. Allow Visual Studio to delete this file permanently.

3. Right-click the Customers project, point to Add, and then click Existing Item. Select the ViewModel.cs file, which is located in the \Microsoft Press\VCSBS\Chapter 27 folder in your Documents folder, and then click Add.

    The code in the ViewModel.cs file is getting rather lengthy, so it has been reorganized into regions to make it easier to manage. The *ViewModel* class has also been extended with the following Boolean properties that indicate the mode in which the ViewModel is operating: Browsing, Adding, or Editing. These properties are defined in the region named Properties For Managing The Edit Mode:

    -   **IsBrowsing** This property indicates whether the ViewModel is in Browsing mode. When the ViewModel is in Browsing mode, the *FirstCustomer, LastCustomer, PreviousCustomer*, and *NextCustomer* commands are enabled and a view can invoke these commands to browse data.

    -   **IsAdding** This property indicates whether the ViewModel is in Adding mode. In this mode, the *FirstCustomer, LastCustomer, PreviousCustomer*, and *NextCustomer* commands are disabled. You will define an *AddCustomer* command, a *SaveChanges* command, and a *DiscardChanges* command that will be enabled in this mode.

- **IsEditing**   This property indicates whether the ViewModel is in Editing mode. As in Adding mode, in this mode, the *FirstCustomer*, *LastCustomer*, *PreviousCustomer*, and *NextCustomer* commands are disabled. You will define an *EditCustomer* command that will be enabled in this mode. The *SaveChanges* command and *DiscardChanges* command will also be enabled, but the *AddCustomer* command will be disabled. The *EditCustomer* command will be disabled in Adding mode.

- **IsAddingOrEditing**   This property indicates whether the ViewModel is in Adding or Editing mode. You will use this property in the methods that you define in this exercise.

- **CanBrowse**   This property returns *true* if the ViewModel is in Browsing mode and there is an open connection to the web service. The code in the constructor that creates the *FirstCustomer*, *LastCustomer*, *PreviousCustomer*, and *NextCustomer* commands has been updated to use this property to determine whether these commands should be enabled or disabled, as follows:

```
public ViewModel()
{
    ...
    this.NextCustomer = new Command(this.Next,
        () => { return this.CanBrowse &&
                this.customers != null && !this.IsAtEnd; });
    this.PreviousCustomer = new Command(this.Previous,
        () => { return this.CanBrowse &&
                this.customers != null && !this.IsAtStart; });
    this.FirstCustomer = new Command(this.First,
        () => { return this.CanBrowse &&
                this.customers != null && !this.IsAtStart; });
    this.LastCustomer = new Command(this.Last,
        () => { return this.CanBrowse &&
            this.customers != null && !this.IsAtEnd; });
}
```

- **CanSaveOrDiscardChanges**   This property returns *true* if the ViewModel is in Adding or Editing mode and has an open connection to the web service.

The Methods For Fetching And Updating Data region contains the following methods:

- **GetDataAsync**   This is the same method that you created earlier in this chapter. It connects to the web service and retrieves the details of every customer.

- **ValidateCustomer**   This method takes a *Customer* object and examines the *FirstName* and *LastName* properties to ensure that they are not empty. It also inspects the *EmailAddress* and *Phone* properties to verify that they contain information that is in a valid format. The method returns *true* if the data is valid and *false* otherwise. You will use this method when you create the *SaveChanges* command later in this exercise.

> **Note** The code that validates the *EmailAddress* and *Phone* properties performs regular expression matching by using the *Regex* class defined in the *System.Text.RegularExpressions* namespace. To use this class, you define a regular expression in a *Regex* object that specifies the pattern that the data should match, and then you invoke the *IsMatch* method of the *Regex* object with the data that you need to validate. For more information about regular expressions and the *Regex* class, see "The Regular Expression Object Model" on the Microsoft website at *http://msdn.microsoft.com/library/30wbz966*.

- **CopyCustomer** The purpose of this method is to create a shallow copy of a *Customer* object. You will use it when you create the *EditCustomer* command to make a copy of the original data of a customer before it is changed. If the user decides to discard the changes, the original data can simply be copied back from the copy made by this method.

4. In Solution Explorer, expand the Customers project and double-click the ViewModel.cs file to open it in the Code and Text Editor window.

5. The definition of the *ServerUrl* string variable near the top of the ViewModel class looks like this:

```
private const string ServerUrl = "http://<webappname>.azurewebsites.net/";
```

Change this string and replace the text *<webappname>* with the name of the web service that you created in earlier in this chapter.

6. In the ViewModel.cs file, find the Methods For Fetching And Updating Data region (expand this region if necessary). In this region, above the *ValidateCustomer* method, create the *Add* method shown here:

```
// Create a new (empty) customer
// and put the form into Adding mode
private void Add()
{
    Customer newCustomer = new Customer { CustomerID = 0 };
    this.customers.Insert(currentCustomer, newCustomer);
    this.IsAdding = true;
    this.OnPropertyChanged(nameof(Current));
}
```

This method creates a new *Customer* object. It is empty apart from the *CustomerID* property, which is temporarily set to *0* for display purposes. The real value for this property is generated when the customer is saved to the database, as described earlier. The customer is added to the customers list (the view uses data binding to display the data in this list), the ViewModel is placed in Adding mode, and the *PropertyChanged* event is raised to indicate that the *Current* customer has changed.

7. Add the following *Command* variable shown in bold to the list at the start of the *ViewModel* class:

```
public class ViewModel : INotifyPropertyChanged
{
    ...
    public Command LastCustomer { get; private set; }
    public Command AddCustomer { get; private set; }
    ...
}
```

8. In the *ViewModel* constructor, instantiate the *AddCustomer* command as shown here in bold:

```
public ViewModel()
{
    ...
    this.LastCustomer = new Command(this.Last, ...);
    this.AddCustomer = new Command(this.Add,
        () => { return this.CanBrowse; });
    ...
}
```

This code references the *Add* method that you just created. The command is enabled if the ViewModel has a connection to the web service and is in Browsing mode (the *AddCustomer* command will not be enabled if the ViewModel is already in Adding mode).

9. After the *Add* method in the Methods For Fetching And Updating Data region, create a private *Customer* variable called *oldCustomer* and define another method called *Edit*:

```
// Edit the current customer
// - save the existing details of the customer
//   and put the form into Editing mode
private Customer oldCustomer;

private void Edit ()
{
    this.oldCustomer = new Customer();
    this.CopyCustomer(this.Current, this.oldCustomer);
    this.IsEditing = true;
}
```

This method copies the details of the *Current* customer to the *oldCustomer* variable and puts the ViewModel into Editing mode. In this mode, the user can change the details of the current customer. If the user subsequently decides to discard these changes, the original data can be copied back from the *oldCustomer* variable.

10. Add the following *Command* variable shown in bold to the list at the start of the *ViewModel* class:

```
public class ViewModel : INotifyPropertyChanged
{
    ...
    public Command AddCustomer { get; private set; }
```

```
        public Command EditCustomer { get; private set; }
        ...
    }
```

11. In the *ViewModel* constructor, instantiate the *EditCustomer* command as shown in bold in the following code:

```
public ViewModel()
{
    ...
    this.AddCustomer = new Command(this.Add, ...);
    this.EditCustomer = new Command(this.Edit,
        () => { return this.CanBrowse; });
    ...
}
```

This code is similar to the statement for the *AddCustomer* command, except that it references the *Edit* method.

12. After the *Edit* method in the Methods For Fetching And Updating Data region, add a method named *Discard* to the *ViewModel* class, as shown here:

```
// Discard changes made while in Adding or Editing mode
// and return the form to Browsing mode
private void Discard ()
{
    // If the user was adding a new customer, then remove it
    if (this.IsAdding)
    {
        this.customers.Remove(this.Current);
        this.OnPropertyChanged(nameof(Current));
    }

    // If the user was editing an existing customer,
    // then restore the saved details
    if (this.IsEditing)
    {
        this.CopyCustomer(this.oldCustomer, this.Current);
    }

    this.IsBrowsing = true;
}
```

The purpose of this method is to enable the user to discard any changes made when the ViewModel is in Adding or Editing mode. If the ViewModel is in Adding mode, the current customer is removed from the list (this is the new customer created by the *Add* method), and the *PropertyChanged* event is raised to indicate that the current customer in the customers list has changed. If the ViewModel is in Editing mode, the original details in the *oldCustomer* variable are copied back to the currently displayed customer. Finally, the ViewModel is returned to Browsing mode.

13. Add the *DiscardChanges Command* variable to the list at the start of the *ViewModel* class, and update the constructor to instantiate this command, as shown here in bold:

```
public class ViewModel : INotifyPropertyChanged
{
    ...
    public Command EditCustomer { get; private set; }
    public Command DiscardChanges { get; private set; }
    ...
    public ViewModel()
    {
        ...
        this.EditCustomer = new Command(this.Edit, ...);
        this.DiscardChanges = new Command(this.Discard,
            () => { return this.CanSaveOrDiscardChanges; });
    }
    ...
}
```

Notice that the *DiscardChanges* command is enabled only if the *CanSaveOrDiscardChanges* property is *true*, the ViewModel has a connection to the web service, and the ViewModel is in Adding or Editing mode.

14. In the Methods For Fetching And Updating Data region, after the *Discard* method, add one more method, named *SaveAsync*, as shown in the code that follows. This method should be marked with the *async* modifier.

```
// Save the new or updated customer back to the web service
// and return the form to Browsing mode
private async void SaveAsync()
{
    // Validate the details of the Customer
    if (this.ValidateCustomer(this.Current))
    {
        // Only continue if the customer details are valid
        this.IsBusy = true;
        try
        {
            // Convert the current customer into HTTP request format with a JSON payload
            var serializedData = JsonConvert.SerializeObject(this.Current);
            StringContent content =
                new StringContent(serializedData, Encoding.UTF8, "text/json");

            // If the user is adding a new customer,
            // send an HTTP POST request to the web service with the details
            if (this.IsAdding)
            {
                var response =
                    await client.PostAsync("api/customers", content);
                if (response.IsSuccessStatusCode)
                {
                    // TODO: Display the details of the new customer
                }
                // TODO: Handle POST failure
            }
            // The user must be editing an existing customer,
            // so send the details by using a PUT request
            else
```

```
        {
            string path = $"api/customers/{this.Current.CustomerID}";

            var response = await client.PutAsync(path, content);
            if (response.IsSuccessStatusCode)
            {
                this.IsEditing = false;
                this.IsBrowsing = true;
            }
            // TODO: Handle PUT failure
        }
    }
    catch (Exception e)
    {
        // TODO: Handle exceptions
    }
    finally
    {
        this.IsBusy = false;
    }
}
}
```

This method is not yet complete. The code you just entered verifies that the customer details are valid. If they are, the details can be saved, and then the *IsBusy* property of the ViewModel is set to *true* to indicate that the save operation can take some time while the information is sent over the network to the web service. (Remember that the *IsActive* property of the *ProgressRing* control on the Customers form is bound to this property, and the progress ring will be displayed while the data is being saved.)

The code in the *try* block determines whether the user is adding a new customer or editing the details of an existing customer. If the user is adding a new customer, the code uses the *PostAsync* method of the *HttpClient* object to send a POST message to the web service. Keep in mind that the POST request is sent to the *PostCustomer* method in the *CustomersController* class in the web service, and this method expects a *Customer* object as its parameter. The details are transmitted in JSON format.

If the user is editing an existing customer, the app calls the *PutAsync* method of the *HttpClient* object. This method generates a PUT request that is passed to the *PutCustomer* method in the *CustomersController* class in the web service. The *PutCustomer* method updates the details of the customer in the database and expects the customer ID and customer details as parameters. Again, this data is transmitted to the web service in JSON format.

When the data has been sent, the *IsBusy* property is set to *false*, which causes the *ProgressRing* control to disappear from the display.

15. In the *SaveAsync* method, replace the comment *// TODO: Display the details of the new customer* with the following code shown in bold:

```
if (response.IsSuccessStatusCode)
{
    // Get the ID of the newly created customer and display it
```

```
            Uri customerUri = response.Headers.Location;
            var newCust = await this.client.GetAsync(customerUri);
            if (newCust.IsSuccessStatusCode)
            {
                var customerData = await newCust.Content.ReadAsStringAsync();
                this.CopyCustomer(
                    JsonConvert.DeserializeObject<Customer>(customerData), this.Current);
                this.OnPropertyChanged(nameof(Current));
                this.IsAdding = false;
                this.IsBrowsing = true;
            }
            else
            {
                // TODO: Handle GET failure
            }
        }
```

The *CustomerID* column in the Customer table in the AdventureWorks database contains
automatically generated values. The user does not provide a value for this data when a
customer is created; rather, the database itself generates the value when a customer is
added to the database. In this way, the database can ensure that each customer has a unique
customer ID. Therefore, after you have sent the POST request to the web service, you must
send a GET request to obtain the customer ID. Fortunately, the *HttpResponseMessage* object
passed back by the web service as the result of the POST request contains a URL that an app
can use to query the new data. This URL is available in the *Headers.Location* property of the
response, and it will have the form *api/Customers/n,* where *n* is the ID of the customer. The
code that you have just added sends a GET request to this URL by using the *GetAsync*
method of the *HttpClient* object; it reads the data back for the new customer by using the
ReadAsStringAsync method of the response. The code then updates the details of the
customer held in the customers collection with this data.

> **Note** It might look like this code is performing an unnecessary round-trip to the
> web service to fetch the customer ID, which is available in the *Headers.Location*
> property of the response message from the POST request. However, this step
> verifies that the data has been saved correctly, and there might well be other fields
> that are transformed by the web service when the data is saved, so this process
> ensures that the app displays the data as it appears in the database.

16. Add the *SaveChanges Command* variable shown here to the list at the start of the *ViewModel*
    class, and update the constructor to instantiate this command, as shown in the following:

```
public class ViewModel : INotifyPropertyChanged
{
    ...
    public Command DiscardChanges { get; private set; }
    public Command SaveChanges { get; private set; }
    ...
    public ViewModel()
    {
```

```
...
this.DiscardChanges = new Command(this.Discard, ...);
this.SaveChanges = new Command(this.SaveAsync,
    () => { return this.CanSaveOrDiscardChanges; });
...

    }
    ...
}
```

17. On the Build menu, click Build Solution and verify that your app compiles without any errors.

The web service needs to be updated to support the edit functionality. Specifically, if you are adding or editing a customer, you should set the *ModifiedDate* property of the customer to reflect the date on which the change was made. Additionally, if you are creating a new customer, you must populate the *rowguid* property of the *Customer* object with a new GUID before you can save it. (This is a mandatory column in the Customer table; other apps inside the Adventure Works organization use this column to track information about customers.)

> **Note** GUID stands for *globally unique identifier*. A GUID is a string, generated by Windows, that is almost guaranteed to be unique (there is a very small possibility that Windows might generate a nonunique GUID, but the possibility is so infinitesimally small that it can be discounted). GUIDs are frequently used by databases as key values used to identify individual rows, as in the case of the Customer table in the AdventureWorks database.

Update the web service to support add and edit functionality

1. In Solution Explorer, in the AdventureWorksService project, expand the Controllers folder and open the CustomersController.cs file to display it in the Code and Text Editor window.

2. In the *PostCustomer* method, before the statements that save the new customer in the database, add the following code shown in bold.

```
// POST api/Customers
[ResponseType(typeof(Customer))]
public async Task<IHttpActionResult> PostCustomer(Customer customer)
{
    if (!ModelState.IsValid)
    {
        ...
    }

    customer.ModifiedDate = DateTime.Now;
    customer.rowguid = Guid.NewGuid();
    db.Customers.Add(customer);
    await db.SaveChangesAsync();
    ...
}
```

3. In the *PutCustomer* method, update the *ModifiedDate* property of the customer before the statement that indicates that the customer has been modified, as shown here in bold:

```
// PUT api/Customers/5
[ResponseType(typeof(void))]
public async Task<IHttpActionResult> PutCustomer(int id, Customer customer)
{
    ...
    customer.ModifiedDate = DateTime.Now;
    db.Entry(customer).State = EntityState.Modified;
    ...
}
```

4. Deploy the web service to the cloud by following the procedure described earlier in this chapter in the exercise "Deploy the web service to the cloud," but upload the web service to the existing web app in the cloud rather than to a new one.

Reporting errors and updating the UI

You have added the commands by which a user can retrieve, add, edit, and save customer information. However, if something goes wrong and an error occurs, the user is not going to know what has happened because the *ViewModel* class does not include any error-reporting capabilities. One way to add such a feature is to capture the exception messages that occur and expose them as a property of the *ViewModel* class. A view can use data binding to connect to this property and display the error messages.

Add error reporting to the *ViewModel* class

1. Return to the Customers project and display the ViewModel.cs file in the Code and Text Editor window.

2. Find (and expand if necessary) the region named Properties For "Busy" And Error Message Handling.

3. After the *IsBusy* property, add the private *_lastError* string variable and public *LastError* string property shown here:

```
private string _lastError = null;
public string LastError
{
    get { return this._lastError; }
    private set
    {
        this._lastError = value;
        this.OnPropertyChanged(nameof(LastError));
    }
}
```

4. In the Methods For Fetching And Updating Data region, find the *GetDataAsync* method. This method contains the following exception handler:

```
catch (Exception e)
{
    // TODO: Handle exceptions
}
```

5. Replace the *// TODO: Handle exceptions* comment with the following code shown in bold:

```
catch (Exception e)
{
    this.LastError = e.Message;
}
```

6. In the *else* block immediately preceding the exception handler, replace the *// TODO: Handle GET failure* comment with the following code shown in bold:

```
else
{
    this.LastError = response.ReasonPhrase;
}
```

The *ReasonPhrase* property of the *HttpResponseMessage* object contains a string indicating the reason for the failure reported by the web service.

7. At the end of the *if* block, immediately preceding the *else* block, add the following statement shown in bold:

```
if
{
    ...
    this.IsAtEnd = (this.customers.Count == 0);
    this.LastError = String.Empty;
}
else
{
    this.LastError = response.ReasonPhrase;
}
```

This statement removes any error messages from the *LastError* property.

8. Find the *ValidateCustomer* method, and add the following statement shown in bold immediately before the *return* statement:

```
private bool ValidateCustomer(Customer customer)
{
    ...
    this.LastError = validationErrors;
    return !hasErrors;
}
```

The *ValidateCustomer* method populates the *validationErrors* variable with information about any properties in the *Customer* object that contain invalid data. The statement that you have just added copies this information to the *LastError* property.

9. Find the *SaveAsync* method. In this method, add the following code shown in bold to catch any errors and HTTP web service failures:

```csharp
private async void SaveAsync()
{
    // Validate the details of the Customer
    if (this.ValidateCustomer(this.Current))
    {
        ...
        try
        {
            ...
            // If the user is adding a new customer,
            // send an HTTP POST request to the web service with the details
            if (this.IsAdding)
            {
                ...
                if (response.IsSuccessStatusCode)
                {
                    ...
                    if (newCust.IsSuccessStatusCode)
                    {
                        ...
                        this.IsBrowsing = true;
                        this.LastError = String.Empty;
                    }
                    else
                    {
                        // TODO: Handle GET failure
                        this.LastError = response.ReasonPhrase;
                    }
                }
                // TODO: Handle POST failure
                else
                {
                    this.LastError = response.ReasonPhrase;
                }
            }
            // The user must be editing an existing customer,
            // so send the details by using a PUT request
            else
            {
                ...
                if (response.IsSuccessStatusCode)
                {
                    this.IsEditing = false;
                    this.IsBrowsing = true;
                    this.LastError = String.Empty;
                }
                // TODO: Handle PUT failure
                else
                {
                    this.LastError = response.ReasonPhrase;
                }
            }
        }
    }
}
```

```
            catch (Exception e)
            {
                // TODO: Handle exceptions
                this.LastError = e.Message;
            }
            finally
            {
                this.IsBusy = false;
            }
        }
    }
```

10. Find the *Discard* method, and then add the statement shown here in bold to the end of it:

```
private void Discard()
{
    ...
    this.LastError = String.Empty;
}
```

11. On the Build menu, click Build Solution and verify that the app builds without any errors.

The ViewModel is now complete. The final stage is to incorporate the new commands, state information, and error-reporting features into the view provided by the Customers form.

Integrate add and edit functionality into the Customers form

1. Open the MainPage.xaml file in the Design View window.

   The XAML markup for the *MainPage* form has already been modified, and the following *TextBlock* controls have been added to the *Grid* controls that display the data:

```
<Page
    x:Class="Customers.MainPage"
    ...>

    <Grid Style="{StaticResource GridStyle}">
        ...
        <Grid x:Name="customersTabularView" ...>
            ...
            <Grid Grid.Row="2">
                ...
                <TextBlock Grid.Row="6" Grid.Column="1"
Grid.ColumnSpan="7" Style="{StaticResource ErrorMessageStyle}"/>
            </Grid>
        </Grid>
        <Grid x:Name="customersColumnarView" Margin="20,10,20,110" ...>
            ...
            <Grid Grid.Row="1">
                ...
                <TextBlock Grid.Row="6" Grid.Column="0"
Grid.ColumnSpan="2" Style="{StaticResource ErrorMessageStyle}"/>
            </Grid>
        </Grid>
```

```
    ...
    </Grid>
    ...
</Page>
```

The *ErrorMessageStyle* referenced by these *TextBlock* controls is defined in the AppStyles.xaml file.

2. Set the *Text* property of both *TextBlock* controls to bind to the *LastError* property of the ViewModel, as shown here in bold:

```
...
<TextBlock Grid.Row="6" Grid.Column="1" Grid.ColumnSpan="7"
Style="{StaticResource ErrorMessageStyle}" Text="{Binding LastError}"/>
...
<TextBlock Grid.Row="6" Grid.Column="0" Grid.ColumnSpan="2"
Style="{StaticResource ErrorMessageStyle}" Text="{Binding LastError}"/>
```

3. The *TextBox* and *ComboBox* controls that display customer data on the form should allow the user to modify this data only if the ViewModel is in Adding or Editing mode; otherwise, they should be disabled. Add the *IsEnabled* property to each of these controls and bind it to the *IsAddingOrEditing* property of the ViewModel as follows:

```
...
<TextBox Grid.Row="1" Grid.Column="1" x:Name="id"
IsEnabled="{Binding IsAddingOrEditing}" .../>
<TextBox Grid.Row="1" Grid.Column="5" x:Name="firstName"
IsEnabled="{Binding IsAddingOrEditing}" .../>
<TextBox Grid.Row="1" Grid.Column="7" x:Name="lastName"
IsEnabled="{Binding IsAddingOrEditing}" .../>
<ComboBox Grid.Row="1" Grid.Column="3" x:Name="title"
IsEnabled="{Binding IsAddingOrEditing}" .../>
...
<TextBox Grid.Row="3" Grid.Column="3" ... x:Name="email"
IsEnabled="{Binding IsAddingOrEditing}" .../>
...
<TextBox Grid.Row="5" Grid.Column="3" ... x:Name="phone"
IsEnabled="{Binding IsAddingOrEditing}" .../>
...
...
<TextBox Grid.Row="0" Grid.Column="1" x:Name="cId" />
IsEnabled="{Binding IsAddingOrEditing}" .../>
<TextBox Grid.Row="2" Grid.Column="1" x:Name="cFirstName"
IsEnabled="{Binding IsAddingOrEditing}" .../>
<TextBox Grid.Row="3" Grid.Column="1" x:Name="cLastName"
IsEnabled="{Binding IsAddingOrEditing}" .../>
<ComboBox Grid.Row="1" Grid.Column="1" x:Name="cTitle"
IsEnabled="{Binding IsAddingOrEditing}" .../>
...
<TextBox Grid.Row="4" Grid.Column="1" x:Name="cEmail"
IsEnabled="{Binding IsAddingOrEditing}" .../>
...
<TextBox Grid.Row="5" Grid.Column="1" x:Name="cPhone"
IsEnabled="{Binding IsAddingOrEditing}" .../>
```

4. Add a command bar to the bottom of the page, immediately after the top command bar, using the *<Page.BottomAppBar>* element. This command bar should contain buttons for the *AddCustomer*, *EditCustomer*, *SaveChanges*, and *DiscardChanges* commands, as follows:

```
<Page ...>
    ...
    <Page.TopAppBar >
        ...
    </Page.TopAppBar>
    <Page.BottomAppBar>
        <CommandBar>
            <AppBarButton x:Name="addCustomer" Icon="Add"
Label="New Customer" Command="{Binding Path=AddCustomer}"/>
            <AppBarButton x:Name="editCustomer" Icon="Edit"
Label="Edit Customer" Command="{Binding Path=EditCustomer}"/>
            <AppBarButton x:Name="saveChanges" Icon="Save"
Label="Save Changes" Command="{Binding Path=SaveChanges}"/>
            <AppBarButton x:Name="discardChanges" Icon="Undo"
Label="Undo Changes" Command="{Binding Path=DiscardChanges}"/>
        </CommandBar>
    </Page.BottomAppBar>
</Page>
```

Note that the icons referenced by the buttons are the standard images provided with the Blank App template.

Test the Customers app

1. On the Debug menu, click Start Debugging to build and run the app.

When the Customers form appears, notice that the *TextBox* and *ComboBox* controls are disabled because the view is in Browsing mode.

2. Right-click the form, and verify that both the upper and lower command bars appear.

You can use the First, Next, Previous, and Last buttons in the upper command bar as before (remember that the First and Previous buttons will not be enabled until you move away from the first customer). In the lower command bar, the Add and Edit buttons should be enabled, but the Save button and the Discard button should be disabled because the *AddCustomer* and *EditCustomer* commands are enabled when the ViewModel is in Browsing mode, and the *SaveChanges* and *DiscardChanges* commands are enabled only when the ViewModel is in Adding or Editing mode.

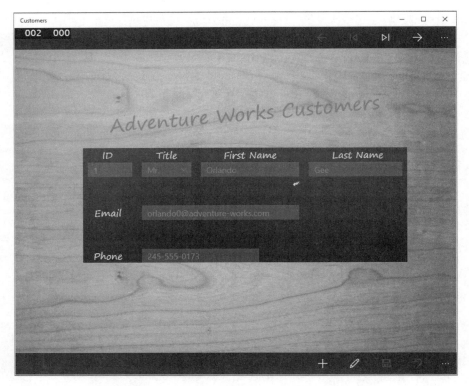

3. In the bottom command bar, click the Edit Customer button.

4. The buttons in the top command bar become disabled because the ViewModel is now in Editing mode. Additionally, the Add and Edit buttons are also disabled, but the Save and Discard buttons should now be enabled. Furthermore, the data entry fields on the form should now be enabled, and the user can modify the details of the customer.

5. Modify the details of the customer: blank out the first name, type **Test** for the email address, type **Test 2** for the phone number, and then click Save.

These changes violate the validation rules implemented by the *ValidateCustomer* method. The *ValidateCustomer* method populates the *LastError* property of the ViewModel with validation messages, which are displayed on the form in the *TextBlock* that binds to the *LastError* property:

6. Click Discard, and verify that the original data is reinstated on the form. The validation messages disappear, and the ViewModel reverts to Browsing mode.

7. Click Add. The fields on the form should be cleared (apart from the ID field, which displays the value 0). Enter the details for a new customer. Be sure to provide a first name and last name, a valid email address of the form *name@organization.com*, and a numeric phone number (you can also include parentheses, hyphens, and spaces).

8. Click Save. If the data is valid (there are no validation errors), your data should be saved to the database. You should see the ID generated for the new customer in the ID field, and the ViewModel should switch back to Browsing mode.

9. Experiment with the app by adding and editing more customers. Notice that you can resize the view to display the columnar layout, and the form should still work.

10. When you finish, return to Visual Studio and stop debugging.

Summary

In this chapter, you learned how to use the Entity Framework to create an entity model that you can use to connect to a SQL Server database. The database can be running locally or in the cloud. You also saw how to create a REST web service that a UWP app can use to query and update data in the database through the entity model, and you learned how to integrate code that calls the web service into a ViewModel.

You have now completed all the exercises in this book. I hope you are thoroughly conversant with the C# language and understand how to use Visual Studio 2015 to build professional apps for Windows 10. However, this is not the end of the story. You have cleared the first hurdle, but the best C# programmers learn from continued experience, and you can gain this experience only by building C# apps. As you do so, you will discover new ways to use the C# language and many features in Visual Studio 2015 that I have not had space to cover in this book. Also, remember that C# is an evolving language. Back in 2001, when I wrote the first edition of this book, C# introduced the syntax and semantics necessary to build apps that made use of Microsoft .NET Framework 1.0. Some enhancements were added to Visual Studio and .NET Framework 1.1 in 2003, and then in 2005, C# 2.0 emerged with support for generics and .NET Framework 2.0. C# 3.0 added numerous features, such as anonymous types, lambda expressions, and, most significantly, LINQ. C# 4.0 extended the language further with support for named arguments, optional parameters, contravariant and covariant interfaces, and integration with dynamic languages. C# 5.0 added full support for asynchronous processing through the *async* keyword and the *await* operator. C# 6.0 has provided further tweaks to the language, such as expression-bodied methods, string interpolation, the *nameof* operator, exception filters, and many others.

In parallel with the evolution of the C# programming language, the Windows operating system has changed considerably since the first edition of this book. Arguably, the changes instigated by Windows 8 onward have been the most radical in this period, and developers familiar with earlier editions of Windows now have exciting new challenges to build apps for the modern, touch-centric, mobile platform that Windows 10 provides. Visual Studio 2015 and C# will undoubtedly be instrumental in assisting you to address these challenges.

What will the next version of C# and Visual Studio bring? Watch this space!

Quick reference

To	Do this
Create an entity model by using the Entity Framework	Add a new item to your project by using the ADO.NET Entity Data Model template. Use the Entity Data Model Wizard to connect to the database containing the tables that you want to model and select the tables that your app requires. In the data model, remove any columns that are not used by your app (as long as they have default values), if your app is inserting new items into the database).
Create a REST web service that provides remote access to a database through an entity model	Create an ASP.NET project using the Web API template. Run the Add Scaffold wizard and select Web API 5 Controller With Read/Write Actions, Using Entity Framework. Specify the name of the appropriate entity class from the entity model as the model class, and the data context class for the entity model as the data context class.

To	Do this
| Consume a REST web service in a UWP app | Add the ASP.NET Web client libraries to the project and use an *HttpClient* object to connect to the database. Set the *BaseAddress* property of the *HttpClient* object to reference the address of the web service. For example:<br><br>```csharp
string ServerUrl = "http://localhost:50000/";
HttpClient client = new HttpClient();
client.BaseAddress = new Uri(ServerUrl);
``` |
| Retrieve data from a REST web service in a UWP app | Call the *GetAsync* method of the *HttpClient* object and specify the URI of the resource to access. If the *GetAsync* method is successful, fetch the data by using the *ReadAsStringAsync* method of the *HttpResponseMessage* object returned by the *GetAsync* method. For example:<br><br>```csharp
HttpClient client = ...;
var response = await
    client.GetAsync("api/customers");
if (response.IsSuccessStatusCode)
{
    var customerData = await
        response.Content.
        ReadAsStringAsync();
    ...
}
else
{

    // GET failed
}
``` |
| Add a new data item to a REST web service from a UWP app | Use the *PostAsync* method of the *HttpClient* object and specify the new item to create and the URI of the collection to hold this item as parameters. Examine the status of the *HttpResponseMessage* object returned by *PostAsync* to verify that the POST operation succeeded. For example:<br><br>```csharp
HttpClient client = ...;
StringContent newCustomer = ...;
var response = await client.PostAsync(
    "api/customers", newCustomer);
if (!response.IsSuccessStatusCode)
{
    // POST failed
}
``` |
| Update an existing item in a REST web service from a UWP app | Use the *PutAsync* method of the *HttpClient* object and specify the item to update and the URL of this item as parameters. Examine the status of the *HttpResponseMessage* object returned by *PutAsync* to verify that the PUT operation succeeded. For example:<br><br>```csharp
HttpClient client = ...;
StringContent updatedCustomer = ...;
string path =
    $"api/customers/{updatedCustomer.CustomerID}";
var response = await client.PutAsync(
    path, updatedCustomer);
if (!response.IsSuccessStatusCode)
{
    // PUT failed
}
``` |

Index

H

handheld devices. *See* Universal Windows Platform (UWP) apps
Handle method, 555, 558
handleException method, 555–556
HashSet<T> class, 400, 409–410
Haskell, 412
HasValue property, 186–187
HeaderStyle style, 642–643
heap, 191–193
    allocating memory from, 306
    array elements, 222
    boxing and unboxing requirements, 196
    deallocating memory, 306. *See also* garbage collection
    freachable queue, 310
    object references, 194
Helm, Richard, 455
hidden code, 27
hill-climbing algorithm, 521
HorizontalAlignment property, 21
HTTP PUT, POST, and DELETE requests, 728
HttpClient class, 720, 748
HttpResponseMessage class, 720
HttpResponseMessage objects, 736, 748
Hungarian notation, 36

I

IActivatedEventArgs type, 686
IAsyncResult design pattern, 574–575
ICommand interface, 669–670
    implementing, 670–673
ICommandBarElement interface, 679
IComparable interface, 279, 380–381, 482
IComparable<T> interface, 381
IComparer interface, 395–396
IComparer<T> objects, 396
icons
    IntelliSense, 11
    in UWP apps, 678, 689–690
idempotency, 728
identifiers, 34–35
    keywords, 34–35
    naming, 157
    overloading, 68
    scope, 66

syntax, 34
IDisposable interface, 314, 326, 427
    implementing, 314–316, 319–320
IEnumerable interface, 424–431
    implementing, 429–431, 437
    for LINQ, 471
IEnumerable<T> interface, 424
    covariance, 394
    for LINQ, 471
IEnumerable<TItem> interface, 434–436
IEnumerable objects, 582
IEnumerable.GetEnumerator method, 429–430, 434–436
IEnumerable<TItem>.GetEnumerator method, 429–430, 434–436
IEnumerator interface, 424
IEnumerator<T> interface, 424–429
if statements, 91–99, 105. *See also* Boolean expressions
    cascading, 94–99
    grouping statements, 93
    rewriting as switch statements, 99
    writing, 94–99
if-else statements, 383–384
Image controls, 524, 526
ImageBrush resource, 639
immutable properties, 345
Implement Interface Explicitly command, 287, 427, 429, 482
Implement Interface Wizard, 280
implicit keyword, 509, 514
implicitly typed arrays, 224–225
implicitly typed variables, 56–57
in qualifier, 396
increment (++) operator, 54–55, 499
indexers, 353–368
    as [ ], 494
    accessing array elements, 359–360
    accessor methods, 357–358, 363–364, 368
    vs. arrays, 358–360
    calling, 365–366
    creating, 368
    defined, 353
    explicit implementations, 361, 368
    in interfaces, 360–361, 368
    notation, 411
    overloading, 363–364
    range checks on index values, 357
    read/write context, 358

U

W

About the author

 **John Sharp** is a principal technologist for CM Group Ltd, a software development and consultancy company in the United Kingdom. He is well versed as a software consultant, developer, author, and trainer, with nearly 30 years of experience, ranging from Pascal programming on CP/M and C/Oracle application development on various flavors of UNIX to the design of C# and JavaScript distributed applications and development on Windows 10 and Microsoft Azure. He is an expert on building applications with the Microsoft .NET Framework and is also the author of *Windows Communication Foundation 4 Step By Step* (Microsoft Press).

Visit us today at

microsoftpressstore.com

- **Hundreds of titles available** – Books, eBooks, and online resources from industry experts

- **Free U.S. shipping**

- **eBooks in multiple formats** – Read on your computer, tablet, mobile device, or e-reader

- **Print & eBook Best Value Packs**

- **eBook Deal of the Week** – Save up to 60% on featured titles

- **Newsletter and special offers** – Be the first to hear about new releases, specials, and more

- **Register your book** – Get additional benefits

Wait, there's more...

Find more great content and resources in the
Microsoft Press Guided Tours app.

The Microsoft Press Guided Tours app provides insightful tours by Microsoft Press authors of new and evolving Microsoft technologies.

- Share text, code, illustrations, videos, and links with peers and friends
- Create and manage highlights and notes
- View resources and download code samples
- Tag resources as favorites or to read later
- Watch explanatory videos
- Copy complete code listings and scripts

Free ebooks

From technical overviews to drilldowns on special topics, get *free* ebooks from Microsoft Press at:

www.microsoftvirtualacademy.com/ebooks

Download your free ebooks in PDF, EPUB, and/or Mobi for Kindle formats.

Look for other great resources at Microsoft Virtual Academy, where you can learn new skills and help advance your career with free Microsoft training delivered by experts.

Microsoft Press

Now that you've read the book...

Tell us what you think!

Was it useful?
Did it teach you what you wanted to learn?
Was there room for improvement?

Let us know at http://aka.ms/tellpress

Your feedback goes directly to the staff at Microsoft Press,
and we read every one of your responses. Thanks in advance!

 Microsoft